Why do you need this new edition?

PEARSON

After talking with students and teachers about what they found most useful in the first edition—and about what they wanted in a second edition—we offer you a new **compose ▪ design ▪ advocate**. This new edition helps you:

See the same research develop into a paper, an oral report with slides, and a photo essay. Along the way, you'll see an annotated bibliography as well as statements of purpose and design plans for each text. These new sample texts are in chapters 4–7.

Learn how to be an ethical researcher. We've revised chapter 4, on research, to help you better develop practices for working with and respecting the ideas and words of others.

Observe other students analyze and compose. Throughout the book are new and updated compositions—written and visual—by students like you.

Learn how a rhetorical approach helps you analyze and design written, visual, and oral texts. We've revised chapters 1–7 to emphasize how the same composing approach works across multiple media—and we've added a new chapter (chapter 9) on rhetorical analysis.

Read and analyze new texts. All through the book—alongside the texts teachers and students told us they liked best in the first edition—are new readings and visual texts. We've used these texts in our own classes and know that most students enjoy them—and find them intriguing openings to thinking and writing.

Know what teachers all around the country want you to learn. Pages 10–13 now present learning outcomes developed by experienced college writing teachers; these outcomes are sought by teachers all across the country and we show how this book helps you achieve these outcomes.

Find and explore what you need more easily. We've streamlined the book's design to support your learning.

THE CONCEPTUAL SHAPE OF THIS BOOK

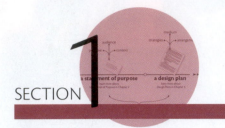

SECTION **1**

SECTION **2**

SECTION **3**

designing compositions rhetorically

Learn a process for making specific and detailed choices about any communication you compose. Learn how statements of purpose and design plans support you in developing confident communication and building the relations you want with others.

researching to support composing

All composing requires research, which can involve digging into books and articles or observing or interviewing others. Strengthen your research abilities by watching one student research a topic and develop the research into a written paper, an oral presentation with a supporting slide show, and a photo essay; chapters on written, oral, and visual texts offer strategies specific to those particular kinds of texts. Learn, also, how to use research to support advocacy.

analyzing the arguments of others

We use the examples of this section—posters, photographs, opinion pieces, essays, comics— to demonstrate analysis of different kinds of communication. Analyze these readings to learn more about strategies and approaches for making your own communication stronger— and for deciding whether you want to be persuaded by a text.

Your own productions

This book's resources for analysis and composition are arranged to help you develop your own texts that do the work you want them to do.

compose · design · advocate

a rhetoric for integrating written, oral, and visual communication

Anne Frances Wysocki ▪ Dennis A. Lynch

PEARSON

Boston   Columbus   Indianapolis   New York   San Francisco   Upper Saddle River
Amsterdam   Cape Town   Dubai   London   Madrid   Milan   Munich   Paris   Montreal   Toronto
Delhi   Mexico City   São Paulo   Sydney   Hong Kong   Seoul   Singapore   Taipei   Tokyo

Senior Vice President, Publisher: Joe Opiela
Senior Sponsoring Editor: Katharine Glynn
Assistant Editor: Rebecca Gilpin
Senior Marketing Manager: Sandra McGuire
Senior Supplements Editor: Donna Campion
Executive Digital Producer: Stefanie Snajder
Digital Project Manager: Janell Lantana
Digital Editor: Sara Gordus
Production/Project Manager: Eric Jorgensen

Text Design: Anne Frances Wysocki
Project Coordination, and Electronic Page Makeup:
    Cenveo Publisher Services
Cover Design Manager: Wendy Fredericks
Cover Designer: Anne Frances Wysocki
Cover Photo: Anne Frances Wysocki
Senior Manufacturing Buyer: Roy L. Pickering Jr.
Printer/Binder & Cover Printer: Courier Kendallville

Credits and acknowledgments borrowed from other sources and reproduced, with permission, in this textbook appear on the appropriate page within text [or on pages 497–498].

Library of Congress Cataloging-in-Publication Data

Wysocki, Anne Frances
  Compose design advocate : a rhetoric for integrating written, visual, and oral communication / Anne Frances Wysocki, Dennis A. Lynch.
    p. cm.
  ISBN-13: 978-0-205-69306-1
  ISBN-10: 0-205-69306-7
1. Rhetoric. 2. Written communication. 3. Oral communication. 4. Visual communication. I. Lynch, Dennis A. II. Title.
  P301.W97 2013
  808--dc23
                                                                        2012018580

10 9 8 7 6 5 4 3 2 1—CRK—15 14 13 12

http://www.pearsonhighered.com

ISBN 10: 0-205-69306-7
ISBN 13: 978-0-205-69306-1

PURPOSES OF THIS BOOK

This book presents an approach to communication intended to help you determine the most effective strategies, arrangements, and media to use in different contexts.

By giving you a systematic approach for analyzing situations in which you must produce different kinds of documents and presentations, and by giving you concepts and vocabulary that will help you make thoughtful choices in presenting visual, oral, and written communication, we hope to help you gain more confidence and fluency in communication.

In addition, because we see communication as being about building relationships among people, and because we see thoughtful and careful communication as being central to active and engaged citizenship, we present our approach to communication with a focus on civic advocacy. We hope to support you in gaining a thoughtful and strong presence in the organizations and practices that help shape the country and communities we share and nurture together.

BRIEF CONTENTS

DETAILED CONTENTS

■ **ASSIGNMENTS**

■ **SAMPLE STUDENT WORK**

■ **READINGS**

■ **ASSIGNMENTS**

■ **SAMPLE STUDENT WORK**

■ **READINGS**

viii

CHAPTER 4

RESEARCHING FOR ARGUMENT AND ADVOCACY   97

ix

■   **ASSIGNMENTS**

■   **SAMPLE STUDENT WORK**

■   **READINGS**

■   **ASSIGNMENTS**

■   **SAMPLE STUDENT WORK**

■   **READINGS**

■ **ASSIGNMENTS**

■ **SAMPLE STUDENT WORK**

■ **READINGS**

■ **ASSIGNMENTS**

■ **SAMPLE STUDENT WORK**

■ **READINGS**

xii

■ **ASSIGNMENTS**

■ **SAMPLE STUDENT WORK**

■ **READINGS**

xiv

🟦 **ASSIGNMENTS**

🟥 **SAMPLE STUDENT WORK**

🟨 **READINGS**

NEW to this edition

WPA Learning Outcomes

On pages 10–13, we discuss the Outcomes and approaches you might take to integrate them into a class; we show how the Outcomes correlate with sections of this textbook.

Enhanced rhetorical focus

In response to feedback from teachers and students, we have enhanced still further the rhetorical focus of this book. A new chapter—chapter 9, "Doing rhetorical analysis of others' texts"—supplements the introductions to rhetoric and to a rhetorical approach to composing, and the examples of rhetorical analysis, that fill the other chapters.

More student sample texts

We have more than doubled the number of sample student texts; the blue box to the right lists all the sample student texts.

Research develops into a paper, an oral report, and a photo esaay

In chapters 4 through 8, as part of the expansion of sample student writing, you can see how one student carries out research (including developing an annotated bibliography) and then uses that research to develop a draft and a final revision of a written research paper, an oral report with supporting slides, and an argumentative photo essay.

New readings and visual samples

Chapters 8–14 contain many new readings and visual examples in addition to the first edition's texts that teachers and students told us were keepers.

Rhetorical multimodal composition

Chapters 5–7 have been streamlined to demonstrate a consistent application of the rhetorical composition process of chapters 1–3 to written, oral, and visual texts.

Strengthened approaches to plagiarism and ethics

Pages 116–123 in chapter 4 (on research) help students engage with and cite their sources; pages 126–130 help students evaluate sources for relevance and credibility. This builds on the discussions of a composer's responsibilties in chapters 2 and 3.

Streamlined look

The book has a whole new, streamlined look to make it even easier for you to find and explore what you need.

"Reading and Responding Rhetorically"

Student writing rhetorically analyzes:

- a website, p. 323

- movie posters, p. 324

- a photographic essay, p. 358

- editorials, p. 384 and p. 390

- two opinion pieces for comparison, p. 398

- an essay, p. 417

Students developing texts

- In chapters 2–3, we show Renee working through the rhetorical process for composing as she develops a letter for the dean.

In chapters 4–8, we show Ajay carrying out the following work:

- In chapter 4, Ajay determines a topic and carries out his research on that topic, ending in an annotated bibliography.

- In chapter 5, Ajay develops a statement of purpose, a design plan, a first draft, and a revised draft of a research paper, based on the work shown in chapter 4.

- In chapter 6, Ajay develops a statement of purpose and a design plan that result in an oral research report with supporting slides.

- In chapter 7, Ajay develops a statement of purpose and a design plan that result in a photographic essay.

ACKNOWLEDGMENTS

The names of those who helped us become teachers of rhetoric and composition make a long list, and it is a list that gives us much pleasure in memories. We are forced to put the names in some order because this is writing, but we hope that those whose names follow here know our gratitude for their generosity, spirit, and example: Arthur Quinn, Marilyn Cooper, Stephen Jukuri, Alice Gillam, Chuck Schuster, Dani Goldstein, Casey Gerhart, Jennifer Kontny, Kristi Prins, Adam Andrews, Paige Conley, Terry Theumling, Diana George, Nancy Grimm, Dickie Selfe, Cindy Selfe, Jeff Walker, Kathy Yancey, Doug Hesse, Chris Anson, Linda Brodkey, Richard Miller, John Schilb, John Trimber, Mary Hocks, Sharon Hillis, Bruce Beiderwell, Randy Woodland, Jeanne Gunner, Jennifer Bradley, Sonja Maasik, John Gage, Joe Harris, Martha Diepenbrock, Bruce Saito, Amy Sedivy, Ann Savage, Hubert Dreyfus, and Czeslaw Milosz.

This book had its seeds in a course we developed with others at Michigan Technological University. Those in the Rhetoric and Technical Communication graduate program at MTU whose commitment to teaching were invaluable in how this book took shape include Julia Jasken, Cyndi Weber, Patti Sotirin, Randy Freisinger, Kristin Arola, Matt Hill, and Karen Springsteen. We wish to thank Julia Jasken, in particular, for the dedication she showed to classrooms and programs that thoughtfully engage students.

In both its first and second editions, this book required more time than any of us imagined. For their intelligence about how people learn but also for their humored patience and many cheering phone calls, we thank Lynn Huddon, Michael Greer, and Katharine Glynn. Everyone who helped with the production on this book showed considerable grace and generosity given how this book was not produced following the, um, usual process.

Finally, this book would not be what it is without the thoughtful, helpful, and encouraging feedback of its many reviewers. We give them heartfelt thanks for the valuable time they have given us.

Thank you, second edition reviewers:

James C. Bower, Walla Walla Community College

Angela Buchanan, University of Colorado at Boulder

Lisa Bickmore, Salt Lake Community College

Elyse Demaray, Iowa State University

S. Morgan Gresham, University of South Florida St. Petersburg

Kimberly R. LeVelle, Iowa State University

Berwyn Moore, Gannon University

Jason A. Pierce, Mars Hill College

Erica L. Scott, Slippery Rock University

Cayenne Sullivan, DePaul University

Continued thanks to the first edition reviewers:

Danielle Nicole DeVoss, Michigan State University

Stephanie L. Dowdle, Salt Lake Community College

Carolyn Handa, Southern Illinois University, Edwardsville

H. Brooke Hessler, Oklahoma City University

Karla Saari Kitalong, University of Central Florida

Marshall Kitchens, Oakland University

Rita Malenczyk, Eastern Connecticut State University

Randall McClure, Minnesota State University

Deborah L. Church Miller, University of Georgia

Martin Mundell, Washington State University

Donna Niday, Iowa State University

Bridget Ruetenik, Penn State University

David R. Russell, Iowa State University

Robert Schwegler, University of Rhode Island

Kirk Swenson, Paradise Valley Community College

Pamela Takayoshi, Kent State University

Summer Smith Taylor, Clemson University (whom we miss deeply)

Deborah Coxwell Teague, Florida State University

Steven T. Varela, University of Texas at El Paso

Cynthia Walker, Faulkner University

Patricia Webb, Arizona State University

introduction

Take a few minutes to write about each of these words:

composing

designing

advocating

What do you think when you hear these words? What experiences or pictures come to mind? What do you think you are getting into with this book that has *compose design advocate* as its title—and what would be the best possible outcome for you from using this book?

In the next few pages, we explain how we use these terms, why we titled the book as we did, and what we hope you will learn from working through the chapters that follow.

People compose music, they compose salads, and they compose themselves. If someone describes you as "composed," it is generally a compliment: It means you are calm and collected and at ease, well put together. "To compose," that is, is to make or form by combining pieces into a whole.

COMPOSING

Composing to think, composing to communicate

Since the late 1800s there has been academic interest in teaching writing. Those who study the discipline of composition are interested in how people write and in using what they learn to help others write more easily, confidently, and self-awarely.

Compositionists have observed that people sometimes write for themselves, in order to make sense of what they experience and see around them. This is using writing to think, to work out the implications of ideas, and to make new connections among thoughts, feelings, beliefs, memories, and what we have heard, seen, felt, and tried to understand. This is writing that appears in journals or on scraps of paper. It is not usually meant for others to read, and often others will have trouble understanding it because the writer used names of people or places without explanation or used a kind of personal shorthand for referring to events and thoughts.

People also write to communicate. Writing to communicate might start with the writer doing some personal scribbling to work out ideas, but for other people to be able to read this writing it has to be modified: It has to be shaped so that others can follow its logical structure; names and places have to be explained; transitions have to be written so that readers can see the connections between ideas—and some parts of the writing may need to be expanded and others deleted so that readers can understand what the writer wants to emphasize.

College composition classes are often about helping people make the transition from writing to think to writing to communicate. In composition classes people learn to observe their own writing practices so that they understand why they sometimes have trouble writing and how they can change what they are doing in order to strengthen their writing. They learn to get clearer about what they want to say and do by reading, thinking, writing, and talking with others. And they learn how to work through multiple drafts of writing: They put their ideas into an initial arrangement on the page, get feedback from others, and then rearrange their ideas in response to the feedback, all in order to make the writing more readable for others.

Composing socially

Compositionists also observe that writing is always social: It always connects people in particular times and places—and so writing is itself connected to and shaped by its time and place—and so writing can't simply be picked up and understood by just anyone in any other place or time.

Consider, for example, how archaeologists work to decipher texts they find in dusty tombs or caves. This deciphering is not simply about figuring out what of our words corresponds to which shapes on papyrus or rock; people who decipher texts can make sense of a text only if they also can figure out who wrote it, when, for whom, and for what purpose. That is, the decipherers can learn to read such a text only if they learn something about the lives of the people who produced the text; they must think about the text as woven into a web of social practices.

When we say writing is social we mean that it comes out of and fits back into this web of practices—always with the possibility that the web itself is changed as a result of the writing process. As critical thinking and as communication, writing shapes people's ideas about what is possible and about what we ought to do and be as individuals and as groups, together and alone.

Composition and rhetoric

The discipline of composition has always been closely tied to the practices of *rhetoric*, an approach to speaking that first developed in ancient Greece. Over centuries, rhetoricians in Greece, Rome, the Mediterranean area and Europe, and the United States have developed systematic processes for speakers and, eventually, writers to compose texts; these processes ask composers to think about the particular times and places in which particular people—audiences—will encounter the spoken or written text being produced. These processes also help composers consider what textual strategies and arrangements will best help the composers persuade audiences to consider matters in the way the composer hopes.

In this book, we consider composition through a rhetorical lens.

Composing and this book

Words matter to us. We are all too aware, from spats we have had with others and from times we have wanted to disappear because our talk hurt someone else, of the power of words. We have seen political speeches that motivate audiences to action and we have listened to the carefully crafted arguments that shape jury trials. We have giggled and felt unsettled over love letters and have worked hard to write letters that will let our parents know how much we appreciate what they have put up with and taught us. We have been knocked into silence by hearing strangers respond enthusiastically and thoughtfully to articles we've written. We've gotten much pleasure from words.

The traditions of composition and rhetoric have helped us—and many others—approach writing and speaking situations systematically and thoughtfully. These traditions have helped us write with an awareness of the responsibilities of our words and of the power we have to shape situations around us when we shape our words to fit them. These traditions have helped us, also, to take pleasure and satisfaction from shaping our words to please or move others.

Through this book, we hope to help you become a stronger communicator through drawing on what the disciplines of composition and rhetoric bring to communication.

DESIGNING

Just as words matter to us, so do the other objects we can make to communicate. We've been moved to sweet tears by photographic collages made by friends as gifts when we were moving away, and we've been moved to make angry but informative posters in response to factory working conditions in our state.

Such texts are easier to make now than in earlier times. In the last decades, changes in technologies—especially digital technologies—have made it easier for people to produce documents that are more visually active than was possible when the printing press and the typewriter were the technologies for producing documents. When you used a typewriter, you could use only the typeface that was built into the typewriter, in its one size; you could change the color of the type by changing the typewriter ribbon, but you certainly couldn't (and probably didn't even think about) producing curvy lines of words. With a computer, you can have wavy lines of type, in multiple colors and sizes, and you can produce pages with photographs or drawings. If you are producing pages for the computer screen, you can use animation, sound, or video and you can make your pages interactive, so that things happen when others move the mouse.

Composition and design

Because of changes in communication technologies, compositionists have over the last years been broadening their notion of composition. They've been broadening their thinking about words to include thinking about photographs, typography, and color, and about how pages and screens on which alphabetic characters are mixed with drawings (for example) make sense to others. Because compositionists are thinking of these matters, they are seeing the usefulness of design practices.

Compositionists are often drawn first to graphic design, because this is a field that mixes words (which have been given careful typographic treatment in terms of typeface, size, weight, color, and so on) with photographs or drawings. But in addition to graphic design there is industrial design, product design, interior design, information design, clothing design, experience design, and interface design; people design theater sets and costumes as well as wheelchairs and doorknobs and bridges and buildings and cities and neighborhoods.

Two concerns link all these different categories of design, as the different areas of design have developed since the early part of the twentieth century: Designers are concerned with how people use things, and they are concerned that what they design is engaging and that it improves people's lives.

Design, therefore, is similar to composition and rhetoric in several ways: All are concerned with audiences and with how audiences respond to what we make…

…but design also differs from composition and rhetoric:

■ Design is a physically material process. Composition and rhetoric have been historically most concerned with words, and hence with what people long thought you could do only with words: communicate abstract ideas. People who write usually don't think about the paper they use or the shapes and colors of the words they make; shape and color just aren't considered to contribute to what a writer communicates.

Designers, on the other hand, consider how others will see, hold, and use what they make, or (in the case of architects) how people will move inside and out of what they make. Designers think about how the size of what they make will relate to the sizes of people's bodies, and about how people with different abilities and ages will be able to use what they make; they think about whether the materials they use are cost-effective or save energy. Designers work to ensure that every part of what they make contributes to the overall purpose of their products.

■ Design has a stronger tradition of creativity than composition and rhetoric. Since its beginnings centuries ago, rhetoric has had as one of its parts the process of "invention," in which a speaker or writer considers multiple strategies for approaching an audience in order to figure out which strategy is most effective—but this process often gets lost in how writing is taught. Design processes, on the other hand, include time for designers to brainstorm, generate, mull over, and have fun with multiple approaches to a design problem. Often designers don't know what they'll be producing, exactly: They'll know the purpose of what they need to make, and they'll know the audience and context— but they'll spend time thinking about the different kinds of objects, using different media, they could make and how they can approach the process in order to develop what will engage users and be highly functional. Designers have developed myriad approaches to enhancing and engaging their creative faculties.

■ Design has a stronger tradition of testing its productions. Although compositionists encourage writers to go through multiple drafts of a piece of writing and to get feedback from others in order to make the piece as effective as possible, the focus is often on how well an audience can read the writing or on the clarity of the arguments; writers often wait until a piece is pretty much worked out before they give it to others for feedback. In design fields, people making things will often show their preliminary sketches to others and get feedback while a product is still a concept; designers will often, at every step of their development process, watch people use what they make to see if it works. There is even an approach called "Participatory Design": Starting with the conceptual work of developing a product or process, designers make sure the intended users take part in discussions about how the product will be used, and why.

DESIGNING, continued

- Finally, because of the emphases design puts on materiality, creativity, and testing, designers tend to think hard about how what they make will function in the world, shaping and changing the lives of others.

If you have read this far and thought that what we've written about composition and design shows the two approaches to communication to be not all that different, you are right: The differences between design and composition (we believe) tend to be not so much hard differences as they are differences in levels of abstraction.

Writers, like designers, think carefully about how their inventions will function in the world, changing and shaping the lives of others, and they work to be creative; they watch to see how others respond to what they make—but writers rarely think in concrete, day-to-day imaginings about their audiences and how their audiences will use what they make. They rarely think about what they make as being useful and as needing to fit into people's day-to-day lives, in the way that can openers and drills are and do.

Designing and this book

We bring together composition and design—the practices of industry and interface and product and information and graphic design as well as of architecture—because we think:

- Design's emphasis on the material conditions of production and consumption can help communicators think in new, stimulating, and usefully concrete ways about how what they make fits into and can affect people's day-to-day lives and futures.

- Design's approaches to the visual and physical aspects of texts can help writers move from being fluid with words to being fluid with words, typefaces, colors, photographs, charts, drawings, animations, sizes and shapes of papers and screens, and environments.

- Design's approaches to creativity—in terms of both technique and media—can help writers expand from thinking about text-on-paper as their only possible product. Design's approaches can help writers think about different media for developing a multitude of possible responses to the contexts in which they are working and the audiences for whom they are composing; this helps writers, finally, design what is most effective and fitting and what can shape the best futures.

Concrete examples of design

Buildings

Called "Soe Ker Tie Hias" ("Butterfly House"), these small structures in Thailand each house six children; the children are orphans, refugees from conflict in Burma. The houses are made out of sustainable local materials and were designed—in collaboration with local people—by a Norwegian non-profit organization composed mostly of architecture students. While small, each house has common space for all and private space for each child; swings for playing hang from the roofs (which are shaped for shade and ventilation and to collect rainwater).

To learn and see more:

http://www.tyintegnestue.no/

Graphic design

According to their website, Adbusters is "a global network of culture jammers and creatives working to change the way information flows, the way corporations wield power, and the way meaning is produced in our society." The organization creates texts of all kinds—and modifies and so changes the meanings of existing texts like ads (this is "culture jamming")—to encourage people to rethink how their lives are shaped by consumption and the companies that support consumption. The flag above, used on the cover of *Adbusters* magazine, replaces the stars of the U.S. flag with logos for large corporations. What are the effects on us, they ask, when corporations take over aspects of government that we once could symbolize with the stars that belong to us all and that ask us to think toward a shared future?

To learn and see more:

http://www.adbusters.org/

Toilets

U.S. citizens visiting Japan are often surprised to find toilets like the one above in Japanese bathrooms. The toilets save considerable water because users wash their hands in the clean water that enters a toilet to fill the tank after a flush; using such a sink can cut bathroom water use by more than half.

Seeing such a sink and toilet can surprise us into realizing how we judge water uses: Even though the water for washing is clean, we have to fight our sense that the water is dirty because it is entering the toilet. As with the flag, design can confront us with our unconscious assumptions and help us consider which are worth holding.

To learn and see more, the following link goes to a U.S. company that makes such toilets:

http://sinkpositive.com

ADVOCATING

If to "advocate" is "to speak or write in favor of," then every communication is advocacy.

Every communication—written, spoken, printed—argues for an attitude or position on something. The position can be about simply whether to stay home tonight or go out, or it can be about how the U.S. tax system distributes money to individuals. And because every communication implies a position, it implies an action about the position: again, that could be the action of staying home or of going out, or of joining with others to push for changes in the U.S. tax system.

The two-headed arrow below suggests how we might think about the differing possibilities of advocacy, and of how every utterance and related act asks us to place ourselves in relation to those for whom we advocate.

Because you cannot avoid being an advocate, where do you wish to place your utterances and actions on the spectrum below?

Why advocate?

Composition and design both emphasize that any communication you make—writing, a webpage, a house—comes out of and fits back into (for better or worse) the society around it. Any communication, that is, draws on patterns and arrangements that already exist (imagine people trying to make sense out of a paper written in a language you made up). Any communication also modifies and reshapes those patterns and arrangements for the context and audience at hand, and then is read by people whose thinking or behaviors will be affected.

The observations above reinforce what we wrote in the column to the left, that each and every communication advocates a view or position on the world.

Obviously, as implied by our two-headed arrow, some communications do this more directly and self-awarely than others, and the composers of some communications work to cause direct, explicit, and large changes as a result of what they do.

$\longleftrightarrow$

Advocacy for...

- one's self

- those immediately around one

- something happening right here, right now

Advocacy for...

- others

- those whom one does not know

- something happening at a distance or in the future

If you ask to borrow money for a movie from a friend, and your friend agrees, you have for better or worse changed your relationship and so made a dent in the world. Perhaps the change is slight, but it *is* a change—and so think of the words you spoke not just as having meaning but as *having done something*.

Put otherwise, if you start thinking of your communication as doing something, then you can start thinking about how much you can and are willing to do. You can decide that your worldly efforts—everyday actions and life-plans—fall along the spectrum between staking a quick claim in the heat of a momentary discussion and deciding that a cause is worth your time and attention.

If you think about your communications as doing something instead of as words or pages that just exist, then you can begin to appreciate the power you have to build the relationships with and between others that you think should shape our world. You can design our futures.

And thus, you can begin to think about how you can build and shape and participate productively within the families, communities, civic and public service organizations, and political structures that are your life.

It is because of the possibilities of understanding communication as advocacy in the ways we've described that we've written this book.

Advocating and this book

When we consider oral, written, and visual communication in this book, we always treat composing and designing as actions that DO something in and to the world.

The word "advocate" might sound to you like "activist"—and you might not see yourself as an activist. That's fine. What is important is that you recognize the power you have as a result of the communications you compose and design—a power that exists simply because of what communication is—and that you take responsibility for the effects of your communication.

Time—the time you are in, the time you have, and the time that stretches out before you—defines who you are, what you want to do, what you are doing, and what you plan to do. And all of this will shift over time, of course. Sometimes you will be busy with what seem like mundane but necessary matters, and sometimes you will stop and decide that now it is time to fight the good fight.

We hope that by working through this book, you strengthen your abilities to communicate to achieve what matters to you in the world. We hope you strengthen your insights about the effects different communication strategies, arrangements, and media have on others.

WHAT WILL YOU LEARN, IN DETAIL?
The WPA Learning Outcomes

We've composed this book to help you become a stronger communicator. Because communication can occur in many different media—videos, webpages, brochures, essays, speeches, quick conversations, even buildings—we offer you an approach to communicating that helps you move comfortably among media. We want you to make smart decisions about the purpose-building strategies of different media so you can produce engaging and strong communication.

To help you achieve that, in this book we take a rhetorical approach—as we explain more in chapter 1.

To achieve those ends, we have also designed this book around learning outcomes from the **Council of Writing Program Administrators** (**WPA**), a group focused on improving writing instruction in the United States.

We list the outcomes on the following pages; read each as though it begins, "With the help of this book I will better learn to…" If you want to focus on a particular outcome, find it and then go to the pages listed next to the outcome. In addition, as you work through the chapters, use this chart to help you articulate—and test—what it is you have learned.

How to use the learning outcomes

Because the outcomes are an attempt to describe the abilities one needs to successfully compose texts, you can use them in multiple ways:

❑ Read the outcomes to understand what your class will be about. Imagine, too, how these outcomes will shape what you do in class.

❑ Check off the outcomes you think you know well; the unchecked outcomes then show you where you can focus your energies. Or choose outcomes that seem particularly important to you for focusing your attention over the term.

❑ When you are having trouble starting a project, or are stuck in the middle, choose one or two outcomes and discuss—with yourself or someone else—how the outcomes ask you to think about your project.

❑ Choose outcomes and evaluate finished work according to how well it meets the outcomes.

❑ When you have finished a project, reflect on what outcomes the work meets—and which it could meet better. What more do you need to learn?

Rhetorical Knowledge

As we describe more in chapter 1, rhetoric is about understanding how the audiences, purposes, and contexts of texts entwine—for when you compose your own texts as well as when you analyze the texts of others.

Focus on a purpose: As a composer of texts, do you understand how to articulate a purpose for your text and then to start shaping your text around that purpose? Do you also understand that your purpose might shift as you develop your text?

Chapters 1, 2, and 3 each include pages on general approaches to purpose; chapters 5, 6, and 7 have pages on purposes specific to written, oral, and visual texts.

Respond to the needs of different audiences: As a composer of texts, do you understand how to describe those for whom you compose and then how to shape texts for them?

Chapters 1, 2, and 3 include pages about audiences in general; chapters 5, 6, and 7 have pages on audiences for written, oral, and visual texts.

Respond appropriately to different kinds of rhetorical situations: As a composer of texts, can you describe the contexts in which your audience(s) receive the texts you compose for them, and how those contexts shape audiences' responses?

Chapters 1, 2, and 3 each include pages on general approaches to rhetorical context; chapters 5, 6, and 7 have pages on contexts specific to written, oral, and visual texts.

Use conventions of format and structure appropriate to the rhetorical situation: As you compose, do you understand how and why to choose and use the formats and structures your audiences expect, given the contexts in which they receive your texts?

Chapters 1 and 3 discuss arrangement as a strategy for composing your own texts. Each chapter in section 3 offers examples of texts whose arrangements fit—or work against—conventional expectations.

Adopt appropriate voice, tone, and level of formality: As you compose, do you understand how and why to choose and use a voice, tone, and level of formality your audiences expect, given the contexts in which they receive your texts?

Pages 155–161 in chapter 5, on writing, discuss these matters—but any of this book's sections on ethos will help you think about how you compose yourself in a text (see chapters 1–3, 4–7, and 12).

Understand how genres shape reading and writing: As you compose, can you draw on knowledge of how genres are composed of texts that share characteristics (format, style of writing, and so on), and of how audiences expect texts that fit into a genre to follow the genre's conventions? Can you describe the different kinds of communication work that differing genres do?

Each chapter in section 3 of this book considers a particular kind of text—posters, documentary photography, opinion pieces, essays, and comics—in terms of the work and genres of the text.

Write in several genres: Can you choose among and compose within different genres to create texts responsive to different audiences in differing contexts?

The "Thinking through Production" pages at the end of each chapter include exercises and activities to help you compose in, compare, and reflect upon the work of differing genres.

Critical Thinking, Reading, and Writing

What parts of this book focus on these abilities and approaches?

To think—or to write or read—critically takes you beyond summary and beyond merely looking for support for an idea you have. Instead, critical work asks you to consider the reach and limitations of ideas, including ideas that might seem in tension or conflict. What can you learn from putting ideas in dialogue with each other?

Use writing and reading for inquiry, learning, thinking, and communicating: Composing is not only for communicating; do you know how to approach composing when you need to learn or when you need to communicate?

Section 2's opening pages—92–96—describe differences between composing-to-learn and composing-to-communicate and how to use those differences to compose. Chapter 4—on research—offers an inquiry-based process. The overall rhetorical approach of this book, reflected in the "To Analyze" activities, asks you to question the work of composing. Section 3 offers texts—and approaches—for analysis.

Understand a writing assignment as a series of tasks, including finding, evaluating, analyzing, and synthesizing appropriate primary and secondary sources: By being able to differentiate the tasks that go into composing a text, are you able to help yourself understand what you need to do at any point in your composing process?

Chapters 1–3 offer approaches to developing ideas and strategies for composing; chapters 4–8 offer examples of finding, evaluating, analyzing, and synthesizing sources.

Integrate your ideas with those of others: For any text you compose, can you articulate what matters to you, what matters to others, and how your ideas and concerns entwine with others'?

The students' texts we show being developed in chapters 4–7 show how other students find and work with others' ideas.

Understand relationships among language, knowledge, and power: As you compose, do you understand how your choices both result from but also help shape what you can know and how you relate with others?

Each chapter of this book discusses how, in composing any text, we compose relations with others: our audiences as well as those with whose ideas we are in dialogue.

Knowledge of Conventions

When you hear "convention," do not think "rule." Instead, think about how and why we—in the differing groups to which we belong—come to expect texts to have the shapes they do. Also think about how and why sometimes breaking conventions is necessary.

Learn common formats for different kinds of texts: Are you able to recognize differing formats? Can you say when, how, and why to use different formats?

Chapters 1 and 3 discuss arrangement as a strategy for composing your own texts. Each chapter in section 3 offers examples of texts whose arrangements fit—or work against—conventional expectations.

Develop knowledge of genre conventions ranging from structure and paragraphing to tone and mechanics: Are you able to collect texts that fit into any particular genre and analyze how they do their work? Can you then use your analysis to shape your own texts?

In section 3, as we discuss differing kinds of texts and how they function, we aim at helping you develop abilities to identify and use features connected to audience expectations.

Practice appropriate means of documenting your work: Do you know why to document the sources you use, and how to cite and document them?

Pages 118–123 in chapter 4 discuss documentation; pages 167, 181, and 231 show documentation in use.

Control such surface features as syntax, grammar, punctuation, and spelling: Do you understand that people use differing syntax (word order), grammar, punctuation, and spelling depending on their audiences and contexts (compare text messaging to writing an academic paper, for example)? Do you know how to check that your own syntax, grammar, punctuation, and spelling are appropriate for your audiences and contexts? Do you know what resources you can use to help you with this work?

Chapter 5 specifically addresses these issues as strategies of writing. Pages 171–175 offer specific information on revising, editing, and proofreading.

Processes

What parts of this book focus on these abilities and approaches?

The pleasure of having a finished composition can encourage us to focus only on being finished. Finishing, however, takes time and so takes process. What processes most help us? How can understanding our own processes help us find more pleasure and ease—as well as pleasurable challenge—in the development of texts?

Be aware that it usually takes multiple drafts to create and complete a successful text: Do you understand that successful compositions rarely come full-blown and all-at-once out of our heads? Can you you make composing easier for yourself by recognizing when your ideas are not yet fully explained or shaped for audiences?

Chapter 5 provides a sample of one student's first and final drafts of a paper—but those drafts have their origins in work initially shown in chapter 4, and other versions of the work are shown in chapters 6 and 7.

Develop flexible strategies for generating, revising, editing, and proofreading: Can you relax into understanding that different texts—with their differing audiences and contexts—will often need you to find different approaches for composing?

Chapters 4–7 show one student's approaches to generating and revising. Pages 171–175 offer specific information on revising, editing, and proofreading.

Understand writing as an open process that permits you to use later invention and rethinking to revise your work: Are you willing to recognize that often you need to change directions in composing, finding new ideas and approaches?

In chapter 5, you can watch one student rework his ideas while composing a paper—and then see those ideas differently developed in an oral presentation (chapter 6) and a photo essay (chapter 7).

Understand the collaborative and social aspects of writing processes: Communicating always takes place socially and so requires collaboration—explicit or no—both for production and consumption.

Throughout this book we emphasize the need to learn about and work with the audiences for whom you compose. The "To Analyze" activities often ask you to collaborate and engage with others.

Learn to critique their own and others' works: Can you develop feedback that will be helpful for others and for yourself?

We discuss how to give and receive feedback on pages 168–171.

Balance the advantages of relying on others with the responsibility of doing your part: Do you understand when to turn to others for help and when to trust your own thinking?

Many reflection activities of the "To Analyze" and "Thinking through Production" pages aim at helping you consider this balance.

Use a variety of technologies to address a range of audiences: Do you have approaches for thinking about, deciding among, and appropriately using differing technologies and media for composing?

Chapters 1 and 3—in discussing medium and other strategies—help you learn to think about these choices; chapters 5, 6, and 7 focus on these matters for written, oral, and visual texts. Section 3—in its considerations of different kinds of texts—will help you think in more detail about relations between audiences and technologies.

Composing in Electronic Environments

How we have designed electronic environments—such as computers, cellphones, and the Internet—shapes the sense of speed and distance in our communications with others, and so shapes how we think of those others and the appropriate sorts of texts to compose and offer. How does all this differ from when we use paper to communicate with others?

Understand and exploit the differences in the rhetorical strategies and in the affordances available for both print and electronic composing processes and texts: Can you describe the differing expectations audiences have for texts composed for paper or screen? Can you describe when and why you would design a text for print instead of for a digital screen, and vice versa?

Throughout the book we show examples of texts designed for print and texts designed for screens; with each example, we ask you to consider the strategies appropriate for the medium.

THINKING THROUGH PRODUCTION

■ Your abilities as a communicator

What do you consider your strengths as a communicator? Do you speak well with others? Are you known as the family listener? Do all your friends want you to make flyers for their concerts or webpages because you're good with visual arrangement? Are you comfortable with writing? Are you funny? Do you like to think at length about current issues? Are you happiest or most focused when you are composing song lyrics?

List, on a piece of paper, anything at all that gives you pleasure or satisfaction when you communicate, in any medium, in any context.

Then list areas where you see you could be stronger in your communicative abilities. Again, think across media and contexts and audiences, and list ways you could be a more confident communicator. On what would you like to focus as you move through the chapters of this book?

Keep your lists with you and add to them as you work through this book and as you build different kinds of communication with others. If you want to be a communicator whose ideas stay with and move others, it is important to know the strengths on which you can draw as well as the aspects you can make stronger.

■ What makes good communication?

In a small group with two or three others, come up with as many criteria as you can for what characterizes "a good communicator."

Consolidate your list with everyone else in class, on a blackboard or large piece of paper.

As a group, categorize the different criteria. *Do these criteria only work for specifically oral, written, or visual communication—or a combination? For example, "grammatically correct" might fit into both written and oral communication, while "attentive to audience" would probably fit into all three. Because our schooling has tended to emphasize written communication, you might want to attribute a characteristic just to written communication, but consider, for example, "clarity": This might seem to be appropriate for just written—or perhaps written and oral—communication, but can a photograph or a page layout have clarity? Does clear writing matter if the layout of a page confuses a viewer?*

Finally, use your criteria to build a checklist for effective communication. Keep hold of your checklist as you move through this book. Use the checklist to help as you produce your own communications—and see if there are more criteria you want to add or shift around the categories.

■ How have you been shaped as a communicator?

Produce a text that shows how you have been shaped as a communicator. Make something that you can show to others, using any mix of photographs, drawings, alphabetic text, or any other material that will help others see what influenced you in becoming the communicator you are.

Think about how you characterize yourself as a talker or writer or listener or photographer or artist or musician or software developer . . . Then think about growing up, being in school, working, your personal life. In all that you have experienced, what situations or events have had the most effect in making you the communicator you are?

Once you have built your text, show it to others. First, show it without talking, and have the others tell you what they understand about what you have made, and why; listen to how they are making sense out of what you made, and how they are linking the pieces of your text to try to make a whole. Then explain your process to the others, why you chose to show what you did (and how you showed it), and what effect you hoped the text would have on others.

In a short writing, reflect on what you learned about how and why others interpreted your composition.

designing

compositions

rhetorically

15

WHAT IS RHETORIC?

Rhetoric is a method for understanding how communication works. Rhetoric grew out of the particular cultural and historical situations of the then city-state Athens in what is now Greece, as democratic forms of government were being shaped and as male land-owning citizens were expected—and wanted—to take part in the public conversations that decided how the city was run. Because so much depended on the conversations people had, especially on speeches that citizens made to assemblies in order to argue what they thought should happen in the city, some men started trying to think systematically about how speeches worked.

Those who thought, talked, and wrote about the workings of speeches thought about how speech makers achieved their ends. That is, why did audiences trust some speech makers but not others? How did speech makers persuade their audiences to take up certain decisions or actions? What characteristics of their audiences did speech makers keep in mind as they were working out the arrangements of their speeches? How did speech makers use emotion to move audiences?

This attention to the relations among speech maker, audience, and text shapes what we do in this book: We are interested in persuasion, in how you—as you make a text—think about your audience and the kinds of effects you hope to achieve with them.

Our rhetorical approach has differences from the original Greek approach: We apply our approach to any situation in which you need to address an audience, not just to speech making, and we are working at a time when audiences and situations are more diverse than they were in the city-state of Athens. Nonetheless, our approach holds on to the core of rhetoric: We ask you to consider how you, as a text's maker, establish relations with an audience through how you shape and deliver your text.

As you will read over the next pages, a rhetorical approach offers you an organized approach for producing texts—as well as for analyzing the texts of others. By asking you to think about those for whom you compose a text and for what purposes, rhetoric helps you compose texts of all different kinds: print, visual, oral, or any mix.

a rhetorical process for designing compositions

CHAPTER 1

A year ago, Dennis (one of the composers of this book) had a conversation with someone who had been in a class with him a few years before; we'll call the man "Walter." What Walter described to Dennis was a fairly funny (and also fairly embarrassing) communication failure—the kind of failure we've all experienced at one time or another. We'd all also probably like to forget such failures—but, even though we can be made uncomfortable by admitting our failures, in reflecting on them we can learn how to communicate better in future situations.

And so on the next few pages we start our book with Walter's story (after a little necessary background information) because, in reflecting on it later with Dennis, Walter figured out what had gone wrong and what he could have done differently.

In Walter's reflection are the seeds of the process we lay out in this book, a process that we think can help you be a better communicator—whether you have a speech to give, a website to make, or a research paper to write.

THE BACKGROUND TO OUR STORY

At the university where we used to teach, students can take part in the "Enterprise Program." The Enterprise Program solicits tasks or problems from business, government, or local community groups and then forms a team of students (with a faculty adviser) whose job it is to perform the task or solve the problem. Some of the teams work on design competitions, such as "Fast Car" or "Fast Truck," in which they use their engineering knowledge to develop highly efficient (and fast) vehicles. What all the teams have in common is that they must work together on a large project, learn how to organize and plan the steps of such a project, develop a timeframe for completion, make a business plan for expenses, and prepare a project logo, letterhead, and marketing plan. Throughout the project they must communicate with each other, with suppliers, with the sponsoring organization or national competition organizations, with the rest of the campus, and with their advisers.

One day Dennis (who was Director of the Writing Programs on our campus and hence often called upon to help out all across campus when people wanted to learn about writing) met with a room full of people involved with the Enterprise Program (students, team leaders, advisers, and administrators of the program) to discuss how they could better learn to compose all the memos, plans, reports, and other documents they needed to produce. After the meeting, Walter came up to Dennis and told him the following story.

WALTER'S STORY

You were always telling us that communication affects how people get along . . . I've got a story that'll make you laugh. I'm the team leader for the Fast Car project, and a few weeks ago we met—all guys, so far—and decided we needed more (or at least some!) women on the project. So we set up a meeting with the campus group Society of Women Engineers to pitch our project to them and get some to join us. But it bombed.

We all showed up at the meeting and began talking about Fast Car and how much fun it is, and then one of the women asked, "Why do you want women to join?" And we said, "Well, there are lots of things you can help out with: We need people to take minutes at meetings and write memos to the adviser, secretarial-type stuff, and you might enjoy that."

Well, the reaction was icy. We tried to explain we did not mean that is all they could do, but it was too late. Did we blow it! No one joined. So we are back to square one! I guess we need to work on our communication skills, hey? Ha!

As you read about what we learned from talking with Walter, keep in mind a communication situation of your own that you wish had gone differently.

Ask yourself the same questions Walter should have asked, to see what you could have done differently.

WHAT WE LEARNED: SEEING THE PIECES

After Walter told his story, Dennis talked with him and another member of the Fast Car team who had been at the unsuccessful meeting. It was a good conversation, and they were glad they talked with Dennis because until he began asking them what went wrong, they thought they understood but then realized they didn't completely—at least not completely enough to prevent doing something similar again.

They knew they shouldn't have said the thing about needing secretaries. But they hadn't thought much beyond that.

Here is what Dennis, Walter, and Walter's friend came up with together as they talked:

1

Their biggest overall problem was lack of specific **PURPOSE**: They hadn't given themselves time to think through carefully what they were doing and why.

They had thought that what they were doing was a no-brainer. After all, they knew their general purpose: They wanted women in their group. They knew that they therefore needed to communicate with women about joining their group, and so they set up a meeting with the Society of Women Engineers (SWE) so they could describe their project.

They didn't think they needed a more detailed and specific statement of purpose to guide them in the meeting; it never occurred to them to make a plan for how to proceed in the meeting.

They should have asked: **Why are we communicating? What are the purposes we are after here?**

2

They hadn't thought at all about their **AUDIENCE**, women who are interested in a meeting about a Fast Car project. Because they hadn't thought about what might motivate women to want to work on such a project, they hadn't anticipated that someone might ask, "Why do you want women on your team?" If they had thought about—and talked to—women who were studying to be engineers, and learned about their passions to design, build, and fix engines and computers and other equipment, Walter's group might have had a better sense of how to describe their project to this audience in order to interest them.

Instead, because they hadn't done this work, they ended up responding as though they thought women would be useful only as secretaries—which isn't what they really thought. But those were the first words out of their mouths, to their embarrassment.

Once they said these things it was too late. The women from SWE were hurt, offended, and angry that their fellow students saw them through such limited and limiting categories.

They should have asked: **Who are the people we want to reach with our communication—our audience—so we can understand how to communicate with them?**

3

They hadn't thought about the larger **CONTEXT** of their meeting with their audience.

First, if they had learned what it's like to be a woman in a career dominated by men, or to be on a campus (like ours was) where men outnumber women 3 to 1, they would have had an even better sense of how most effectively to address their audience in the particular place and time of the meeting they called.

Second, they had called the meeting, so it was their responsibility to run the meeting and to anticipate as much as possible what might go on.

They should have asked: **How will the place and time—the contexts—of our communication affect its outcome?**

4

Because they hadn't thought about their purpose, audience, or the context of their communicative situation, they hadn't thought about what kinds of communication **STRATEGIES** would help them appeal effectively to the members of SWE.

If they had learned that women in engineering often feel that many men do not think women capable of doing engineering work (which is, after all, the message the Fast Car group sent when they said that the women could help with the secretarial work of the project), the group might have realized that they could show their seriousness and respect for the women by acknowledging how women are often treated in engineering.

They should have asked: **What are the strategies that will help us achieve our ends?**

5

They hadn't thought about the **MEDIUM** of communication they were using.

They were making an oral presentation, and so they should have considered what audiences often expect from such presentations. It's not unusual for someone giving an oral presentation to have supporting visual information: the Fast Car group could have brought slides of their work, which would have given their audience a concrete sense of the work they could do on the project.

Most importantly for the Fast Car group, however, is that audiences for oral presentations very frequently expect to ask questions and discuss the presentation with the presenters. Had the group thought about this, they could have discussed the kinds of questions they might be asked—and they might have then been prepared to thoughtfully and respectfully respond to the question of why they wanted women in their group.

They should have asked: **What do audiences tend to expect about the medium we're using? Are we using the best possible medium?**

6

They hadn't thought about the **ARRANGEMENT** of their communication strategies in order to build the most persuasive presentation.

Imagine, for example, the kind of reception SWE would have given the Fast Car group if the group had started their presentation by acknowledging the problems women engineers face on our campus and in the larger world. (They would probably also have to acknowledge that others might think they wanted more women involved just because they wanted more dates—and they could laugh about this and say, "Well, that might be a small part of it." Their honesty and humor would deflect some of the criticism they should've known would be lying in wait for them.) They could have then argued that the Fast Car project was a way for the women, by being involved, to demonstrate how competent they were in areas traditionally thought to be male.

They should have asked: **How will our audience respond to the order in which we present our arguments? Is there a better order than the one we have for achieving what we want?**

7

Finally, Walter and his group didn't **TEST** their communication beforehand.

They went into the meeting with SWE cold. Imagine how much more successful the meeting could have been if the group had rehearsed a bit with some people who were both friends and members of their intended audience, and had gotten feedback in time to make changes.

They should have tried out their presentation with some members of their intended audience, to see how the audience responded—before they tried it for real and found it didn't work.

#

And, finally finally, we discussed the long-term consequences of their mistakes in the presentation, and how communication creates relationships among composers of communication and their audiences.

Walter and his friend hadn't been able to figure out why they just couldn't back up in the meeting with SWE and correct their mistakes right then and there.

After some discussion, they realized that whenever we offend a person, it takes time for that person to overcome the offense. We have to let the person work through her or his feelings, and we have to show (and not just tell) the person that we understand our mistake and are willing to learn from it. That takes time. That can't happen in a few minutes, even if we want it to.

21

PUTTING THE PIECES TOGETHER:
A RHETORICAL PROCESS FOR DESIGNING COMPOSITIONS

All the pieces that we discussed on the preceding pages fit together into a process for composing:

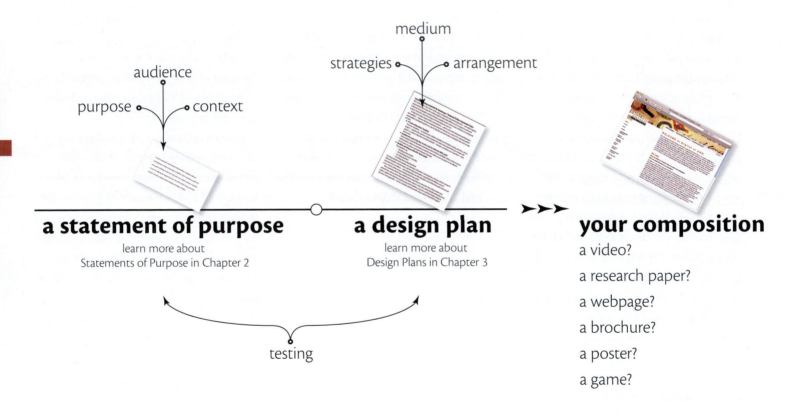

a statement of purpose

learn more about
Statements of Purpose in Chapter 2

a design plan

learn more about
Design Plans in Chapter 3

testing

your composition

a video?

a research paper?

a webpage?

a brochure?

a poster?

a game?

We began with Walter's story—and his and our reflections upon it—because it allows us to give you a concrete introductory description of the composing (and analyzing) process we develop in this book.

We think that learning this rhetorical process, seeing it at work in the communication of others, and practicing it yourself will help you strengthen your own abilities to communicate.

What we have begun to present on these pages is an overview of the process and of the pieces that go into the process. In the coming chapters, we describe the process and the pieces in more detail, with examples, so that you can start applying them.

If the pieces—and how they fit together—don't yet make sense to you in this introduction, don't worry: We discuss all this and more in the rest of the book—and it takes a bit of concrete practice with the process and pieces to start to feel confident and fluid with them.

Composing any text—whether a research paper or a video to promote a nonprofit organization—you will be on surer footing if you weave together your considerations of your purpose, your audience, and the context in which the audience will receive the text. By weaving these considerations together into **a statement of purpose**, you help yourself understand how purpose, audience, and context have to play off of and be attentive to each other.

A statement of purpose then helps you decide what strategies, media, and arrangements will help you compose an effective communication—and so helps you prepare **a design plan**, in which you think through and lay out for yourself everything you intend to do in producing your text.

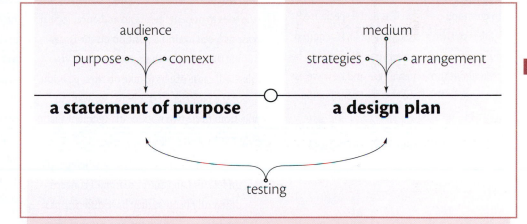

audience
purpose   context
a statement of purpose

medium
strategies   arrangement
a design plan

testing

Designers test their ideas as well as their final productions. They'll show a statement of purpose to members of their audience to see if it makes sense and to get feedback on other possibilities; similarly, they'll get feedback on a design plan. By **testing** their ideas with their audiences, before they do their final production, composers are more likely to develop effective communications.

Doing this work, you are doing analysis: You are analyzing your communication situation.

Whenever you take apart a process, situation, or text to see what pieces compose it, you are doing analysis. The rhetorical process we offer here asks you to think about your communication situation by thinking about it through its pieces—and so when you follow this process you engage in analyzing the situation in which you are communicating with others.

RHETORIC and ARGUMENT

Throughout this book you'll see "argument." In common use as well as in the specialized studies of rhetoric, "argument" has acquired different meanings over time. We want to be clear about those meanings—and how we use the word in this book—so that you'll understand our uses of it.

Everyday notions of argument

When you hear that someone was arguing with someone else, you might picture two people (or perhaps more) face-to-face (if not in each other's face), and perhaps raising their voices. This kind of argument is often acrimonious, when people vent their opinions and try to downplay—if not tear apart—the others' opinions.

"Argument" might also suggest debates to you, when two sides face off over an issue. Each side tries to present, before an audience, logical reasons for or against a position on the issue, hoping their words—their reasons made visible—will cause others to take on their position.

For the purposes of this book, we want to take from those two notions of argument that argument occurs only

- when people disagree (that is, when people understand an issue or matter of concern differently because they have differing past experiences, social positions, ways of identifying themselves, perspectives, beliefs, opinions, or values)

    and

- when people agree to make visible their reasons for understanding issues or matters of concern as they do.

Specialized notions of argument

Rhetoricians sometimes use a particular and focused definition of argument: They'll say that a speech or a piece of writing is an argument if and only if it presents premises, in logical order, in support of a stated conclusion.

For the purposes of this book, we won't hold such a narrow definition for "argument"—but we do draw on one aspect of the special definition: We will sometimes speak of formal (and informal) argument. Sometimes we identify an argument based on its structure—or form—because, sometimes, when composers want to be particularly overt about their intentions, they need to use formal logical structures. Most often, however, when we discuss argument, we will have in mind the more informal approaches, with a sense of "argument" as "any effort to move people through the deliberate choices one makes in shaping a text."

Formal argument is called "formal" because it uses logical "forms of argument," structures of organization that (generally) have explicit statements of premises and conclusion. "Formal" does not mean that the context in which the argument occurs is formal (like a prom), just that the argument uses particular logical structures to present premises in support of a stated conclusion.

Informal argument can simply be about directing others' attentions in new or different directions, or showing them a new possible position that they hadn't considered before, or shifting their values—without any explicit statement of premises and conclusions. (Keep in mind that "informal" does not mean without form; informal arguments simply use less rigid forms than formal arguments.)

Argument in this book

We all encounter situations every day when we need to make decisions with others or figure out how to act together. This happens between individuals, when we decide what video to watch with a friend or how to proceed with a partner on a class project. This happens in groups, when a sorority plans a fund-raiser or the delegates to a state political convention decide which candidate to support.

Decision making happens among people who know each other, but you can also be asked to make decisions or take action by strangers, such as when someone's radio commentary tries to persuade you what music is hot, an editorial about affirmative action tries to persuade you to have a particular position on the issue, or when a sitcom uses a character who learns that being thin and pretty does not bring happiness so that you too might believe that.

In such situations, those who speak, write, or otherwise make their positions visible might use formal argument—which is why there are sections of this book to help you analyze and use formal argumentative strategies. But a range of other strategies (including decisions about what media to use) is available when we want to shift someone's attention or help clarify what others are thinking—as we discuss throughout this book.

Notice, too, that in addition to emphasizing how arguments draw on strategies ranging from formal written or oral structures to the visible arrangements possible in a television production, we have been describing "argument" not as an event when you try to change someone's ideas 180 degrees. Instead, in this book we consider the overall purposes of argument to be presenting our positions to others in some kind of shape or arrangement so that others can see (or hear) and consider them. Only rarely do our words or other communications completely change the minds of others or cause them to storm out of the room determined to do what you think they should; most often, we might only strengthen or weaken their adherence to a belief, or we might move them closer to or further away from a possible action.

When we use "argument" in this book, then, we generally want you to have in mind a piece of communication that you hope will direct and shape an audience's attentions in particular ways.

RHETORIC, ARGUMENT, and ADVOCACY

Arguments—formal or informal—are possible only when disagreement exists. We don't often argue about the sky's color on a sunny day or whether we need to eat to stay alive. We argue when we believe that there are differing ways to act or understand a situation and that considering a range of possibilities will help us determine which is best.

And if we believe that the back and forth of argument is useful to us, then this tells us that we must value any individual's right to hold and discuss differing opinions: If we need the arguments in order to find the best actions in any changeable situation, and if arguments depend on people knowing and believing differing possibilities, then we need people to hold differing ideas and opinions.

We believe, therefore, that making arguments about what matters to you—being an advocate for what matters to you—makes sense only if you respect other people's rights to argue and advocate. This means you also should respect their actual efforts to argue and advocate, even when their choices are not ones you would make.

Nonetheless, people sometimes refuse to engage in argument. In the following list are reasons people often give for plugging their ears when those with whom they disagree talk.

1   Showing any doubt about the rightness (or righteousness) of a position shows weakness.

2   Showing any doubt about the rightness (or righteousness) of a position is wrong because moral values are clear and absolute, not up for debate or even questioning.

3   If you refuse to listen to others, that forces the others into a position where they have to give in more to you.

4   Others' positions just don't make sense.

5   It takes too long to listen carefully to others.

6   If they have power over you they won't listen to you.

7   If you have the power over them, why should you listen? What does it get you?

Do you want to live in a world where everyone holds those statements as beliefs? To believe, for example, that you don't need to listen to others if you are in power is not the stuff of democracy, which (we hope) continues to be a value worth holding and seeking.

Or look at the statement that if you refuse to listen to others, you force them into a position in which they have to give in more to you than you do to them. This statement might seem in line with much that is to follow in this book, for we do advocate an approach that helps you locate your purpose and context, take note of your audience, and plan strategies. *But we'll argue that you can plan communications so as to build or strengthen communities and social relations, not cut them down.*

Looking at the contexts in which you communicate involves looking at how acts of communication are embedded in what already goes on. If the social relations in which you are embedded are cut-throat, then planning what you say and how you say it in order to force others into a corner, no matter how it makes them feel in the long run, may make sense to you. But then you do not have a viable long-run vision; you are running a short-term game, the future (and respectful relations) be damned.

Any communication affects the future shape of our current communication contexts—our communities. If you accept the assumption that how you communicate echoes out into the contexts in which you will communicate, then—when you choose to communicate—you are responsible for the ongoing health of our communities.

Put otherwise, any serious discussion of argument leads us back to how we want to live with others and what we want to do to and in the world. Argument is an important, nonviolent way to advocate.

Conditions that make argument possible

The lawyer, philosopher, and rhetorician Chaim Perelman and his co-author, Lucie Olbrechts-Tyteca, in their book *The New Rhetoric: A Treatise on Argumentation*, asked what conditions make argument possible, if you assume (as we do here) the value of serious communication and argumentation. Their answer is long, and it is a list. And as we claim in other places in this book, lists can tell a story, a story you might have to construct. Below is our telling of their list of the conditions that make argument possible.

Anyone making an argument should:

- have an audience to address.

- make contact of some kind with the audience, through spoken or written words or visual means.

- have a sincere interest in gaining the adherence of the audience.

- have a certain modesty about his or her beliefs, not holding them beyond question or discussion.

- be concerned about the audience and be interested in their state of mind.

In their turn, audiences should:

- be willing not only to listen but also to try to understand.

- be committed to the argument, to its subject and its outcome.

- recognize how institutions like schools, churches, clubs, and so on both enable and inhibit how arguments happen.

- be willing to accept another's point of view, if only for the time of the argument.

Both the person making an argument and the audience should:

- recognize and accept that they may emerge from the argument changed, holding beliefs or knowledge or planning actions different than those held before the argument.

- always be aware that the person making the argument and the audience might not have understood each other.

TO ANALYZE

- **Discuss and then write:** When people write letters to the editor of a local newspaper or call in to a radio talk show, what are their responsibilities to their audiences and community? What about for someone creating a personal blog? Talk with others about their views, to consider how communications fit into the networks of communication in which we live and move, and then write down your observations about your responsibilities when you communicate with others.

- **Write informally:** What is your own definition of "argument"? In what ways does your definition align with—and differ from—ours?

- **Discuss with others:** Are the examples below "argument" as we've defined it? If you think not, can you imagine conditions under which they would be?

  - a public-service TV piece against marijuana use

  - a decision to wear blue jeans to school

  - a flyer on the wall about an upcoming fund-raising event

  - a refusal to buy clothing made in sweatshops

  - a radio interview with a political candidate

RHETORIC and PERSUASION:
Thinking about how texts work on us

Traditionally, those who study rhetoric have said that all texts have one of three goals: to persuade, to instruct, or to delight—with the main goal always being to persuade.

Traditionally, persuasion has been understood as a clear-headed, conscious, and mental activity: It has been seen almost as direct communication between minds. The belief is that, if I present a well-organized, logical, rational, clear-headed argument, it is bound to be persuasive.

More recently, though, rhetoricians and people concerned with communication have come to recognize that persuasion is not so simple or rational. We understand that people are not just minds but also are bodies that move through time and space and grow up into families, cultures, learned practices, and habits—and all of this, in addition to how we think, influences how persuasion works. While persuasion still requires well-organized, logical, rational, clear-headed argument with solid supporting evidence, it may require additional work, as we discuss to the right.

As you compose and analyze texts, then, keep an eye out for the range of ways texts can appeal to you through both rational and more embodied means.

Because of their logical structures and evidence

Over the last few pages we discussed argument and made a distinction between formal and informal arguments. In the chapter on writing—chapter 5—we discuss formal argument in some more detail, and how it can function persuasively in writing.

Evidence is another aspect of the logical side of argument. How effective would it be at a town hall meeting to claim, "We need a traffic light at the intersection of East Capitol and Oakland Avenues because too many people have been hurt there crossing the street!"? Wouldn't it be more effective to argue, "We need a traffic light at the intersection of East Capitol and Oakland Avenues because, over the past five years, an average of eight people a year have been injured there crossing the street—and I have in my hand the police reports showing this!"? Evidence fits into informal argumentation, whose workings we also discuss more in chapter 5.

Because we identify

The 20th century rhetorician Kenneth Burke emphasized *identification* in persuasion. Burke pointed out that we make, evaluate, and are moved by arguments logically but also through appeals to characteristics and qualities we share with others—how we move, dress, talk, look, sound, or smell alike.

Identification can happen in the movies, when we "connect" with characters who look and act like us. This is why there are "chick flicks" and "buddy movies": Moviemakers recognize that women want to watch movies about women and men want to watch movies about men. This is not to say that women and men don't watch movies with characters of other genders, but that identification is at work in how we respond to movies.

Similarly, when we read novels that take place in our towns or have characters close in age and situation to us, identification describes why we feel a heightened sense of connection and so interest—and are perhaps then more persuaded by what we read.

Identification may be less than completely conscious, Burke suggested. It may require us to attend to our learned habits of attention and to the power and influence that our social groups and roles have in our openness to persuasion.

Because of our cultural knowledge

When you look at the boy in the photograph on the right, your response depends on how your bodily experiences entwine with your experiences growing up in a particular culture. The attitudes you acquired growing up where and when you did will shape how you respond to people younger than you, to the color of someone's skin, and to how you interpret another's physical closeness.

Because of where and when you grew up, you will have cultural and media references that you share with everyone else in your culture or just with people close in age or interest to you. For example, most people now in the United States know the weight of a reference to "9/11," but only people interested in particular sports or music will get "Aaron Rogers" or "Wiz Khalifa." Different cultures use colors differently, so that, while in the United States we associate black with death and mourning, in China white is the color associated with death and mourning.

Such cultural elements encourage identification, as we discussed on the preceding page.

As you analyze elements in texts, or prepare to compose with them, ask how an audience's cultural knowledge and understandings are likely to shape their responses.

Because of our bodily experiences

Many visual elements do their work because they appeal to our experiences of moving through the world with our bodies. For example, the photograph above (from the webpage shown on page 318) draws on our understanding of how we feel when someone looks into our eyes from a close distance. Similarly, we can explain some of the effect of colors by our experiences of colors outside of pages and screen: Blue can look cool if not cold because of water and ice, while green can suggest grass or trees or nature more generally; red can suggest heat, making us think of sunburns or an angry face.

When we see the photograph of the boy above, we don't say to ourselves, "Oh, I know how it feels to look into the eyes of a boy with a serious expression"; we tend to react as though we were simply seeing the boy in front of us.

When we see a layout with elements organized in neat stacks, we respond based on our experiences of gravity and stability—as opposed to a layout in which elements look to be falling.

 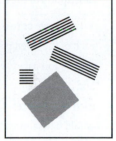

We have such bodily responses to written and oral texts, too. Think of how the rhythms of poetry can pull us into their swing, or of how a series of long sentences can lull us with their rhythm—until a short sentence pulls us up short. We respond to quiet or loud speaking as we respond to other quiet or loud sounds.

To analyze elements that appeal to bodies—and to start composing with such elements—you need to learn to react analytically. You need to ask how elements are appealing to your bodily experiences, and why a designer might want to draw on such experiences.

THINKING THROUGH PRODUCTION

- Several pages ago, before the analysis of what went wrong with the Fast Car group's attempt to appeal to women, we asked you to think of a communication situation you wish had turned out differently—and to keep that situation in mind as you read the description of the rhetorical process.

  Write a page or two in which you apply each of the seven pieces of the rhetorical process (on pages 19–21) to your situation, and describe what you would have done for each of the pieces. Then describe how you would have approached the communication situation differently had you done that analysis. How might things have ended up differently?

- Imagine that when you arrived on campus for the first time, you were assigned a dorm room and roommate. Your initial impression of your roommate was not good—the person seemed too worried about your having people over, about personal space, and about time alone—but you figured the relationship would work out over time. After four weeks, however, it's not any better—it's worse. Your roommate keeps leaving you nasty little notes about your dirty laundry and taste in music. You've decided to make a last-ditch effort and write your roommate a letter explaining your problems with the situation and what you see as the alternatives.

  Use the numbered steps in the rhetorical process to plan and produce the letter.

- Imagine you are on the membership committee for your church, skateboarding club, sorority, or fraternity—or any other organization close to your heart. Your organization has decided it needs to increase its membership. You've volunteered to help with this project, but as of now no one is settled on how to proceed. The group members have tossed around ideas for a brochure, for making "cold calls," for putting together an information table for an upcoming community open house, and for ads in the local paper.

  Use the pieces of the rhetorical process to help you decide what specific purpose you have and how best to go about achieving it.

composing
a statement of
purpose

CHAPTER 2

In this chapter, we start to develop the details of the rhetorical process from chapter 1. We focus here on the first three pieces of the rhetorical process: We show you how to approach purpose, audience, and context more thoroughly, and how to shape a sense of purpose, audience, and context into a full statement of purpose.

Read chapter 2 for a general sense of how to proceed in some communicative situation in the future, or apply these steps to any specific situation you now need to address.

In chapter 3 we examine the remaining pieces of the rhetorical process on the way to using a statement of purpose to develop a design plan, which is a concrete working out of many details of a text.

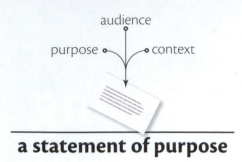

a statement of purpose

WORKING TOWARD A STATEMENT OF PURPOSE

What do you learn from this chapter—and why?

In this chapter we show you how to start applying the rhetorical process for composing from chapter 1.

We show you how to analyze a composing situation—for a class, for work, for a nonprofit organization where you volunteer—so that you develop a rich and useful idea of what you need to accomplish, for whom, and when and where. We offer you an organized approach for thinking about your purposes, audiences, and contexts so that you can confidently approach producing the texts you need to produce.

The process of analyzing purposes, audiences, and contexts ends with **a statement of purpose**: This piece of writing helps you tie purposes, audiences, and contexts together, see how they interrelate, and suggest concrete choices for production.

How does developing a statement of purpose fit into a composing process for writing?

People who study writers and writing have learned that all effective writers have processes they follow to develop their writing. From writer to writer, these processes differ in their particulars, but generally involve:

- Figuring out the project: *What are the project's purpose, context, and audience?*

- Considering and planning different approaches to the project: *What choices does a writer need to make to shape writing for its audience, given its purpose and context?*

- Writing a draft.

- Getting feedback from the intended audience.

- Revising the draft in response to feedback.

(Note that it looks as though the steps are linear, but writers usually move back and forth among the steps as they figure out more about what they are doing and as, sometimes, they figure out that they have taken a wrong turn.)

Developing a statement of purpose aligns with the first step of the process: By developing a statement of purpose, you can figure out, in a structured and useful way, what it is you need to accomplish with a text you are composing.

What's the difference between a statement of purpose and a thesis statement?

A thesis statement summarizes the argument of writing:

> *Modern language classes prepare students to live within the expanding global economy because modern language classes expose students to other cultures.*

A thesis statement can suggest the points a writer needs to make in a piece of argumentative writing and so is highly useful (as we'll discuss in chapter 4 on research). But a thesis statement does not help a writer think about tone of voice, how much emotion to fold into the writing, or what sorts of supporting examples (and in what order) will be most effective.

A statement of purpose, on the other hand, by helping a writer think deeply about purpose, context, and audience—and about their relations—sets a writer up to make those choices.

See pages 49, 139, 196, and 243 for example statements of purpose—and pages 124–125 for further exploration of the differences between thesis statements and statements of purpose.

Looking ahead: What do you do with a statement of purpose?

We've described how a statement of purpose ties together purpose, audience, and context, and so prepares a writer to make specific choices about writing or other composing projects.

Those choices start to happen when a writer develops a design plan out of the statement of purpose—as you will see in the next chapter. A design plan enables a writer to make direct connections between purpose, audience, and context and strategies, arrangement, and medium.

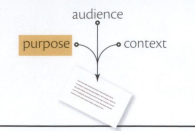

audience

purpose •——•———• context

---

a statement of purpose

PURPOSE

WHAT ARE YOU TRYING TO DO?

To develop a sense of your purpose for any text you are composing, ask yourself the questions and follow the prompts below. Write down your answers: You need to be able to come back to your ideas to see how you can change or add to them after you think about your audience and context.

1 What is your motivation in this communication situation?

In other words, why are you communicating? What do you hope to achieve by building the piece of communication you are approaching?

It might be that you are thinking about this question because you have to write a paper for a class, which is an external motivation. You will do your best work if you are also motivated from within: If you have to put time into building communication, work to find reasons that matter to you. Your own curiosity about a topic is enough, but also think about building communication that helps you make connections with others or that helps you learn something new.

2 What do you hope your audience will do or feel or think after having experienced the communication you will produce?

Do you want more people to vote, or do you want your audience to know more about the situation in Iraq, or do you want others to understand how your relationship with your grandparents, aunts, and uncles was critical to who you are today? Do you want your teacher to be dazzled by the thoughtful, critical, hard work you have done? Do you want people to stop driving cars and ride bikes more, or do you want them be better at doing mathematical word puzzles?

Do you want to educate, entertain, or inform others—or to do some mix of these?

The more specific you can be here about how you want your audience to respond to the communication you are building, the more easily you will be able to shape your communication toward those ends.

3 **If there is some event or situation that made you want to communicate with others, describe it in as much detail as possible.**

Sometimes we are motivated to write by seeing something happen to others, or by reading something with which we agree—or disagree—strongly. Because this is motivation, it is important for you to recognize this, so that you can be sure to help your audience understand where you are coming from; the audience will be more likely then to understand your reasons for communicating what and how you do… and when the people who hear you understand your reasons, they are generally able to make better judgments about your communication.

4 **What would be the best possible outcome of the communication?**

If you can imagine exactly what you would like to happen, then you can use what you imagine to guide and encourage you as you work.

What would be the worst possible outcome?

Knowing what failure looks like can help you figure out strategies for avoiding it.

5 **How will your communication change the situation in which you make the communication?**

That is, is your purpose worthwhile? When you picture the best possible outcome for the communication you are building, are you imagining effects that are worth striving to achieve? If not, perhaps you should rethink what you are contemplating.

practice with purpose…

The situations described below might seem obvious to you, but in working out a sense of purpose, you will clarify what it is you want to achieve—which will help you in thinking about audience and context in the next pages.

1   Imagine you've just found out your application to study abroad for a semester has been turned down by the committee that makes such decisions. You are thinking about appealing the decision. Use the questions above to write your sense of purpose in making the appeal.

2   A class you want to take is full, and you are planning to talk with the professor to try to get in. Use the questions above to write your sense of purpose in talking with the professor.

FURTHER DEVELOPING YOUR PURPOSE

The questions on the preceding two pages ask you to consider—regarding the text you are composing—where you are now and where you would like to be in the future. Thinking about purpose thus starts you toward "designing possible futures" for you and your audiences.

The future you envision needn't be a full-scale, fully worked out city, country, or universe. You can think about possible futures for your church, workplace, or neighborhood—changes like bike paths or recycling or fair access to resources or Sunday afternoon potluck dinners—and then work to compose communications to engage others with your imaginings.

developing your purpose for the present: complex motivations

Writing tasks often have "layers of motivation." Sometimes your motivation will seem simple—"I've been assigned a paper"—but it also can be more complex—"I want to build a webpage to teach others about neuropathic diseases because my father was just diagnosed and there's nothing available except in complex medical jargon and there's no way to communicate with others whose family members have this diagnosis."

It thus can be a good idea to try to separate the different parts of your motivation so you can be clear about your purposes.

For example, Martin Luther King Jr. wrote a now famous letter—"Letter from Birmingham Jail"—to eight clergymen explaining his partici-

pation in civil disobedience. As he composed, he realized that the letter would probably be published and read by more people. Dr. King thus had to make sure he spoke the language of the clergymen and connected his purpose to their beliefs and values, but he also had to keep in mind that arguments that might be effective with the clergymen might not be effective with others. In this case, Dr. King had to keep straight the different motivations for speaking to the two audiences, to make sure that his purposes in each case did not conflict.

Look at the motivation we described for the website about neuropathic diseases. There's strong and empathetic motivation in the desire to connect with and help others—but this also means the person building the website will need to be careful not to be too personal and not to make the website all about her experiences if she is to help others be comfortable.

developing your purpose for the present: when the motivation isn't yours

When you're asked to give a presentation or write a memo at work or for an organization at which you're volunteering, the motivation for communication comes from outside you; you will communicate not only for yourself but also for someone else. In such circumstances, you need to be clear about differences between your values and the institution's. If you cannot com-

municate the values of the institution without qualification, you must either find compromises acceptable to both you and the institution or you must back out.

developing your purpose for the future: how will you live up to your motivation?

Our actions have short- and long-term consequences, and it is easy to lose sight of one or the other—and to have our efforts then become tangled. Look at Dr. King's situation: In the short term he wanted the clergymen to understand how his civil resistance and desire to speak truth to power flowed from his religion, but he realized that in the long term his thoughts and actions needed to be answerable to a broader public, especially (in this case) to a white middle-class public that felt threatened by his actions. As you consider what you want to achieve with your communication, ask:

- Are my short- and long-term aims in harmony?

- Am I in a position to ask of my audience what I am asking of them? Do I have the proper authority, or have I built up the proper trust with them?

- Do I want to draw attention to myself and my cause at this time?

developing your purpose for the future: when the motivation isn't yours

We talked above about outside motivation when you communicate for someone else. But motivation can come from outside in another way, as when you are assigned a class paper. Sometimes you'll want to write such papers, sometimes not. And when you don't, this is how the future enters: If you cannot find internal motivation for writing, you plan a lousy future for yourself. You're planning frustration, boredom, or time you hurry through. If you can find a larger motivation for communicating—learning about written structures, perhaps, or trying out a creative approach—you'll make a much better future for yourself.

developing your purpose for the future: does it help to break your purpose into different parts?

When you plan communications, think incrementally about achieving the future you want. That is, you might break down what you want into steps and in each case ask: Is this step worthwhile? Can I achieve this?

This process may also help you discover strategies that get overlooked when you are focused on the big picture. You may need to think about making multiple or smaller communications rather than one big one.

YOUR RESPONSIBILITIES

■ As you work out your purpose in communicating, your responsibilities are to yourself, to the people with whom you'll be communicating, and to everyone around you:

1   *To yourself*, you are responsible for finding reasons to communicate that help you further your understandings of others and of communicating in general. There is no reason to do this work if you are not learning, if you are not gaining in competence and confidence in moving through and improving the world.

2   *To those with whom you are communicating*, you are responsible for finding purposes that are worth their time and attentions and that show that you care about the matters that lie between you and them.

3   *To everyone else...* Because communication is what binds us together and helps build—for better or worse—our communities, you are responsible for finding communicative purposes that respond to what is needed around you, that contribute usefully to the networks in which we all live.

TO ANALYZE

■ **Write informally for a few minutes:** List five things that matter to you in the world or that you like to do. Take an assignment that's been given to you, one for which you have either a printed or an online description. Rewrite the assignment to give it a purpose that helps you engage with at least one of the things that matters to you.

■ **Write informally for a few minutes:** Imagine tuition at your school is being raised. You probably have a straightforward and personal motivation to argue against the raise. You might not have the money or it might be hard to find (and you're already working two jobs). But administrators who make the decision about tuition will probably be unmoved by such a narrow purpose because it is so personal. In what ways can you make your sense of purpose more complex—to include effects on others or on the school or your community—so that it is more likely to engage others?

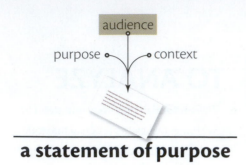

a statement of purpose

AUDIENCE

WHOM ARE YOU ADDRESSING?

Audiences are not one-dimensional and they generally do not want to be treated that way. The women with whom Walter spoke in the story we told back in chapter 1 did not want to be pictured only as secretaries. You probably do not like it when you are treated only as a student or as a young person who doesn't know anything or hasn't experienced anything in the world. You can probably remember times you were angered when someone spoke to you as though you were only a simple-minded stoner or metalhead or teenager or hair-club member. We are all more complex than any title or epithet can convey—and when we acknowledge that complexity in the ways we treat people, we shape better relations among us all.

Nor is any audience just three dimensional: We are all at least four dimensional, because we live in time. We all exist as bodies with histories, and we have particular identities, allegiances, roles, memberships, and commitments that have developed and shifted over time. All these qualities contribute to how we read, understand each other when we are talking, and look at all the paper and computer screens around us.

To develop a picture of your audience that can guide your other decisions in building communication, perform the following steps:

1 Generate a list of audience characteristics.

The idea here is to generate as full a list as you can of any and all characteristics shared by your intended audience. As you produce your communication, what may seem the oddest characteristics can sometimes suggest to you highly useful and persuasive strategies or arrangements.

There are many categories of characteristics you can think through to generate your list. Think of your audience's attitudes, beliefs, and habits. Think of audience members' backgrounds, how and where they grew up. Think of material qualities like age, race, gender, sexual orientation, and able-bodiedness. Think of their state of mind because of the time of day or place of communication.

2 Imagine your audience members at the moment they encounter the communication you make, no matter what you're making.

Try imagining using different media for your communication, to get the widest sense of the conditions under which your audience members can respond. What attitudes or moods are they likely to be in, and why? What might they be thinking? Why should they be interested in your communication? Why might they be disinterested, or hostile?

Add all your observations to the audience characteristic list you've made.

3 Filter your list.

Which characteristics are most relevant to the purpose you have so far developed? Cross out—tentatively—any characteristics that you can't see as shaping your audience one way or another toward what you hope to achieve.

If your purpose, as you've stated it so far, is to persuade women to join the "Fast Car" project (to use an example from the Introduction), then you know that your audience is composed of women: But it will also be important that you recognize that the women might be curious but also a bit apprehensive because they are being addressed by men on a primarily male campus and about a project that had in the past included almost exclusively men. The women might also be tired, if your meeting with them is at night, or late in the semester.

The idea is not to shorten your lists as much as possible, but rather to develop as complex and rich an idea of your audience as you can. By thinking of your audience complexly, you will treat it as being composed of the complex people they are.

practice with audience…

In the preceding section on purpose, we asked you to write your sense of purpose for two different situations, appealing a decision about studying abroad and trying to get into a closed class. For both situations, use the three steps on this page to write descriptions of the audiences for these situations. To write the most useful descriptions, ask others in your class what they know about these kinds of audiences on your campus; others may have experienced similar situations and have useful knowledge to share.

FURTHER DEVELOPING YOUR SENSE OF AUDIENCE

To begin: Complex and Shifting Audience Characteristics

First, go through the list below and think about or discuss with others how these characteristics—when made concrete in a particular person of a particular age, and so on—impinge on communication. Also use the list to help you start thinking about the particular audience(s) you are addressing in any particular situation.

But the list is just a beginning . . .

The list complicates how we often judge people by age and gender. When we also think about the values audience members hold and their emotional states (because of a national crisis or a personal achievement) or the relationships that matter to them, we are more likely to think in ways that help us address them respectfully and so develop good relations with them.

consider an audience's . . .

- ❏ age
- ❏ gender
- ❏ ethnicity
- ❏ level of education
- ❏ able-bodiedness
- ❏ sexual orientation
- ❏ class
- ❏ upbringing
- ❏ place of living
- ❏ place of work
- ❏ emotional states (tired, angry, receptive . . .?)

- ❏ past experience with the topic/issue/matter
- ❏ learned habits (how audience members have learned to look at the topic/issue/matter)
- ❏ values/beliefs/commitments relative to the topic/issue/matter
- ❏ possible questions about the topic/issue/matter
- ❏ self-identity: the kinds of relations people see themselves as having with others (mother ± unemployed ± daughter ± Republican ± leftist ± rich ± boss ± worker ± student ± teacher ± friend ± poor ± ambitious ± ??)

Think about how . . .

the people in your audience have eventful lives

The next time you walk through a crowded space—a cafeteria or an airport, for example—look at the people around you and imagine what their days have been like leading up to the moment you see them. Notice how your thinking about someone changes when you look at the person while thinking perhaps he or she just came out of a difficult interview on which a career depends, or has been up all night helping a friend who's had a death in the family, or is just leaving on a well-deserved vacation.

When thinking about your audience, think of it not as an "audience" but as being composed of people who are free to move about the plane, who bite off more than they can chew, who get tangled up in blue . . . you get the idea. This makes them less formidable than when they seem like a faceless list of characteristics and helps you think about them generously and humanely.

(Some designers, in developing software or furniture or tools, make up imaginary people who might use what they are making. The designers give these imaginary people names, ages, occupations—all the characteristics in our list. Then the designers work as hard as they can to keep these imaginary people in mind as they design so that they think as concretely and complexly as possible about their audiences.)

Think about how . . .

you have preexisting institutional relationships with your audience

Imagine you are writing a paper for a teacher you hardly know (big stretch, eh?). If the teacher thinks of you as a *mere student* and so does not expect much from you but you want the teacher to see you as more, how can you design this relationship so that the teacher doesn't see you as *just another student*?

Look at this situation from the other angle. Being a teacher sets limits on how you can relate to students: You have a certain authority and students are (mostly) predisposed to acquiesce. What can you do if you do not want students just to fall in line but rather want them to be responsible for their own learning? You may shift your authority by giving students a range of choices and responsibilities, or by setting up small group discussions so that you are not always the center. Even so, when teachers do things like that, they can still undermine all their efforts by referring to students (for example) as "my" students. The possessive "my" can imply a certain paternalism that repositions students as children and thus undercuts a teacher's effort to get students to take more responsibility for the classroom and their educations. It is easy to fall back into old habits, especially around the roles we have in the institutions where we live, work, and play.

These examples show that our communications happen within already existing institutional relations. In addition to school, we go to church and we work in offices, fast-food outlets, chain stores, auto repair shops, and web design studios. We live in different kinds of families. Each of these institutions gives us titles—*brother, employee, head fry cook, niece, citizen, deputy chief*—and titles have meaning only relative to other people and their titles. You cannot be a father without a child, a head fry cook without an assistant (otherwise you are just "fry cook"), an employee without a boss, or a citizen without there being many other citizens.

Any time you communicate within such institutional frameworks, you need to keep the particularities of the relationships in mind. How do others see you because of who you are within the institution, and how do you see them? What expectations of behavior do people have about you—and you about them—because of your roles or titles or names? How might these expectations shape what you can say or write or show?

And do you need to step outside the relationships or call attention to them to achieve what you hope? Teachers can do this when they ask students to talk about the experiences of being students and when students then suggest how the teacher can change classroom structures or practices—such as grading policies or seating—so students feel more responsible in the class.

Put otherwise, the fact that you have a preexisting relationship with your audience does not need to hamstring your efforts to communicate. By thinking about your role and what your audience knows about you as part of the context of communication, your role becomes tied to your sense of purpose and thus becomes a part of what you need to strategize about.

Think about how . . .

you often have primary and secondary audiences

In a complicated world, what you want to accomplish can get complicated.

For example, the U.S. *Declaration of Independence* has layers of purposes addressed to multiple audiences. It was a declaration to the King of England that the authors—representing the people of the 13 original colonies—believed they had the right to break away from England and form a sovereign nation. But for the *Declaration* to do all the writers intended, they had to think about several other audiences as well: the people of England, not just the King; foreign governments with whom the colonies had been doing business and who would be worried about trading with "radical" people; and future generations of Americans who might look back and wonder why the break with England was made. Neglecting any of these audiences would not only have made the

FURTHER DEVELOPING YOUR SENSE OF AUDIENCE, continued

Declaration of Independence less complex than it needed to be, but it would have excluded from consideration people who were being affected by the actions being declared.

Other texts can have multiple—primary and secondary—audiences. For example, you might be helping a domestic abuse shelter publicize its hotline, and, in working through this communication situation, you and the people at the shelter decide to put flyers about the hotline in restaurant and campus restrooms. But rather than just put the hotline's name and phone number on the flyer, you also describe all the different actions that count as domestic abuse, to help others understand whether they are in abusive relationships or perpetuating abuse. That is, your primary audience is those who have been abused and know it; your secondary audience is those who may not yet understand that they are in an abusive relationship.

Thinking long and hard about how your communication might have multiple audiences—sometimes hidden from view—is a good way to ensure that what you say is as complicated as it needs to be. It is also a good way to keep your eye on whom you are including and whom you are excluding (perhaps accidentally) by what you are saying or how you are saying it.

Think about how . . .

your audience is only ever your intended audience

You cannot compose communications that take into consideration every concern or feature of all audience members at the moment you communicate with them—even when you are speaking directly with them.

It is important, then, to keep in mind a distinction between your real audience and the audience you imagine as you prepare to communicate. As you plan and communicate you are living in the space between what you think, imagine, and believe about your audience members and who they actually are and how they actually respond.

It can be humbling to remember that at the end of the day, after all the planning in the world, the moment the words leave your mouth (or the paper gets turned in), your communication is out of your hands.

Even though we can never be certain we have anticipated our audience's reactions correctly, we still must try. In the final analysis our audiences are both real and intended, both imagined and actual, and we have a hand in how our relationship to them plays out.

Think about how . . .

audiences step into the characteristics you imagine its members to have

Two pages ago we asked you to remember when you felt someone addressed you as though you were only a student or only a young person. We asked you to recall such memories because they are most often unpleasant.

But also recall when someone said something complimentary to you or introduced you as "the smartest person I know" or "my best friend." Remember how you probably felt a bit of a glow and more capable and at ease.

Now extend such memories into how you—and other communicators—address audiences.

This should remind us that we are responsible for how we imagine—or construct—our audiences, how we position their members, and whom we include and exclude in the process. When we address audiences, we are asking them to step into the characteristics we imagine they have. If we imagine those characteristics from a less than respectful view, audiences either must take on those characteristics or actively resist them. If we imagine the audience in positive ways, they will generally respond likewise.

As you consider your audience, then, do keep in mind how your decisions shape what you ask your audience to be and to do.

YOUR RESPONSIBILITIES

- You are responsible for respecting your audiences as people who think and have good reasons for believing what they do.

- In order to make good on your responsibility to your audience, you need to listen carefully to what other people have to say about the piece of communication you are building. It is sometimes hard to hear critical feedback about what you produce, but it is important to acknowledge that others have good ideas about how you can strengthen what you make.

- You need to take seriously that any piece of communication you make—written, visual, oral, or any mix—affects other people. Take seriously that you can move other people for good or otherwise.

TO ANALYZE

- **Discuss with others:** David MacIntyre is a physics major. Here is his description of his audience and purpose as he was preparing to write a paper on space travel for a class:

The audience for this paper is a person who has given little thought to the space program and probably sees no outstanding reason why he or she should be paying for it—in other words, nearly everyone. This is the type of person I hope to persuade to support the space program in general and in particular to support the idea of human spaceflight. This leads to two general ideas I have to keep in mind throughout my writing: First, I need to show that the space program as a whole is a benefit to society and, second, why sending humans into space is a valuable part of that project. At the end of my paper, my readers should not be asking themselves, 'Sure, that's great, but why not just send robots?'

How does David's description connect his audience with his purpose? What more about his audience could David learn to help him achieve his purpose?

- **Write informally:** List the people with whom you have relationships shaped by the institutions within which you live and work. In your list, don't forget your religion, job, school, hospitals, civil institutions like the police and the Department of Motor Vehicles, your family, and the military. For each person you list, describe how your relationship shapes how you communicate.

- **Discuss with others:** Sometimes when you write papers you're told to consider your classmates as your audience—and yet you know you have to write to your teacher, too, since the teacher grades your writing. In such a situation, how do you think through these primary and secondary audiences? Who is primary to you—the teacher or the students? How do you address them?

Similarly, you might in some classes produce communication for a client, with the communication aimed at still another group of people: For example, you might produce a poster—aimed at attracting young people to an after-school program—for a local nonprofit. The client has to approve the project—and it will be graded by the class teacher. What can you do to work with these primary and secondary audiences?

43

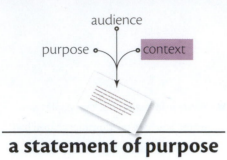

audience

purpose • • context

_____
a statement of purpose

CONTEXT

WHERE AND WHEN IS YOUR COMMUNICATION?

As you work toward an effective piece of communication consider:

1 the time of the communication

Just when will the communication take place?

Is there a specific occasion that motivates the communication, such as a funeral where you've been asked to give the elegy or a presentation you must make at a conference about research you've been doing? Do you have to imagine the occasion because you won't be there, such as when someone comes to a website you've made, or when your teacher reads a paper you've written, or your father receives the birthday card you've sent him?

Can you picture the time of day or year? Does it matter to your audience the time at which they'll be receiving your communication? (For example, are you giving an oral presentation to your class as the last person of five speakers or at night, so that your listeners are likely to be tired and having a little trouble being attentive? Are you developing a fund-raising campaign for a nonprofit around Christmas time when people are likely to be a little more generous?)

2 the place of the communication

Where, exactly, will the communication take place? Will you be there?

Will your audience be in a temple, mosque, or church? And, if so, is it a large, formal, and imposing structure, or an informal, comfortable place? How will this shape the attitudes and expectations of your audience, as well as your comfort or level of nerves?

Will your audience be sitting in uncomfortable folding chairs, or in rows of desks? Will your audience be sitting at home, comfortable at their personal desks (or likely to doze in an armchair)?

Or will your audience see your posters up on a wall where all others are hanging their posters, too, so that you need yours to be a different color or size—or else taped to the sidewalk or some other place where your audience will be more likely to see them?

3 the broader context of the communication

How do time and place shape your audience's expectations? It's probably obvious that an audience at a funeral in a Gothic cathedral has different expectations than an audience for a business presentation—but nonetheless it's worth asking why.

In our time, Gothic cathedrals are not new—but the people who built them saw them as engineering marvels and signs of a community's willingness to commit years and tremendous resources to construct a representation of their belief in a God. Some of this sense has carried down to us, in part because of how our bodies feel in the large, light, airy spaces of cathedrals and in part because, whether or not we attend such cathedrals, we have seen and heard about them. Also, they are, simply, churches, built by their communities as holy spaces.

Most business meetings do not take place in holy spaces. Instead, business spaces are usually functional, and we have probably grown up associating business with getting things done, with moving quickly and getting to the point.

Asking about the spaces in which we communicate, and about the perceptions of time we attach to those spaces, gives us a better sense of audience expectations.

practice with context...

In the sections on sense of purpose and audience, we asked you to consider two different situations, one in which you are appealing a decision about studying abroad, the other in which you are trying to get into a closed class. For both situations, describe the occasion of the communication you'll be making, its place, and its broader context of how and where decisions are made in schools. As with audience, if you find you need more information, describe what you need to learn and how you can learn it. You can ask others about their experiences in similar contexts on your campus.

FURTHER DEVELOPING YOUR SENSE OF CONTEXT

On the preceding two pages, we asked you to consider the occasion of the communication, the place of the communication, and the broader context of the communication. Figuring out the specific event, time, and place is generally pretty easy. Determining other factors that might weigh on your communication can be difficult: It's hard to decide how broad your context is—but you can always benefit from thinking broadly.

You'll be most successful with context if you visualize the moment of communication. The more real you make this moment beforehand, the more you'll be able to develop strategies for approaching your audience and determine what media work best.

Notice also how context and audience overlap, as (for example) when you present a paper late on a panel or late in the day when your audience is tired and needs you to be more energetic and humorous than you might otherwise be. Because of this, revisit your description of your audience after you work through this section on context so that you can add any important characteristics you might have missed.

As you move on to consider a more complex understanding of your context you might:

ALSO Think about . . .

. . . how audiences perceive the time of communication

Arguing with a friend over which movie to see, you might understand the temporal context for the discussion to be just this one evening, but your friend may include past disagreements in which you always won. You might be giving a presentation about pollution's effects on frogs to a fourth-grade class: For you, this is a special 20 minutes; for the children, you are just part of every day's science hour.

These are examples of how you and your audience might perceive the time of communication differently. How each of you understands this aspect of context affects how your audience attends to the communication.

. . . how audiences perceive the place of communication

Have you ever gone to a religious service for a religion not yours? How did you feel the first day of college, in your first class? Being in a place we know well or in an unfamiliar place affects how at ease we are and hence how well we listen to others. Often, people in new circumstances are too distracted by just figuring out where they are to see posters on a wall or hear a speaker. Sometimes people are uncomfortable in places they know well (perhaps something bad happened there), and some-

times they are relaxed. If you can learn about an audience's general response to the place of communication, you can better shape your communication to fit.

. . . the contexts of bodies in space

We've asked you to visualize the contexts of your communications and how they might affect how people receive your productions. For instance, if you make an oral presentation, how do you ensure your audience sees and hears you comfortably? Such decisions depend on your purpose, of course: It could be the case that to achieve your purpose you want your audience to feel odd, cold, or uncomfortable so they will be slightly off balance. Sleazy people know that sleazy actions put other people at disadvantage: Imagine communication contexts like having an interviewee sit in a chair lower than the interviewer's, shaking someone's hand limply, or speaking a little too softly for someone to hear. Unethical communicators take these actions when they want audiences to feel weak or powerless. But you can also help audiences feel comfortable and strong: You can ask them (even in a brochure) to sit if they are standing or take some deep breaths to relax. You can tell jokes. You can take care that a booklet you make has large enough type for their young or old eyes.

... institutional contexts

In addition to the physical dimensions of contexts, attend to the institutional dimensions. We talked in the section on audience about how audiences understand themselves through our institutions: families, religions, businesses and workplaces, and so on.

The contexts in which you communicate—classrooms, church halls, offices—might call to audience's minds some institutional relations more than others. When you give a speech in class, your audience sees you primarily as another student, an equal—but were you to present at a high school, students there would probably see you as a cool, older college person. If you are brought into a business or school to give a workshop about a topic you know well, your audience will see you as an authority, deserving respect for your knowledge.

The institutional relations audiences have with one another also affect how they respond. If you give a speech to family groups and talk only to the adults, they will notice that you ignore the children. Similarly, if someone in your class makes a comment during discussion and you ignore it and instead address only the teacher, other students can think of you as a snob or only out for a good grade.

Being alert to institutional contexts can help you think about whom to include as your audience and how to address it.

YOUR RESPONSIBILITIES

- If you have choices about where to communicate, be sure your audience will be comfortable, hear you, and, when possible, see and interact with you.

- The spaces within which we work with one another help or hinder our efforts to communicate effectively, so you will want to think about how you arrange such spaces. Is there room to move around? Is there plenty of elbow room? Are people isolated from one another? Lighting? Temperature?

- Context is more than just physical space, however. Contexts of communication also include what has led up to this point in time—peoples' histories as well as events that are happening around you (outside your building, or on the day before) and that may be relevant to you or members of your audience.

- Pay attention to the institutional context of your work as well. Do you have more authority than those you are speaking to, or less, and how will that affect what you can or cannot say and do? And how will your words—spoken with institutional force—affect those to whom you speak?

TO ANALYZE

- **Write informally:** Imagine you've been asked to give a speech to a group of 50 older people on the topic of what you learned about Indian art during your studies in Bombay. Sketch out—design—a space that would be the most conducive to their comfortable and attentive learning.

- **Write informally:** Consider an assignment on which you are now working for another class. Sketch out—design—the time and place in which you think that class's instructor would most generously respond to your work. How can you suggest that space and time through how you produce the assignment?

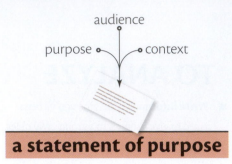

a statement of purpose

STATEMENT OF PURPOSE

With this step you will pull together what you have been writing and thinking about in the past three steps—purpose, audience, and context—into **a statement of purpose**.

A statement of purpose takes you beyond an initial sense of purpose because it asks you to tie purpose, audience, and context together. A statement of purpose should be detailed and specific enough to guide you through developing a design plan (see Chapter 3), for which you choose a medium or mix of media, decide on strategies, and then arrange, produce, and test what you compose. A final statement of purpose is usually about a half-page in length, depending on how concise you are.

To compose a statement of purpose

1 Look at what you have written about your sense of purpose, audience, and context and write one- to two-sentence summaries of each.

2 Write a one-sentence explanation of the relations among your purpose, audience, and context of communication. Use this as a draft of your statement of purpose.

3 Look at the one-sentence explanation you just wrote and ask these questions:

- Does this explanation show how your purpose is tied to your audience's characteristics and the communication contexts you have identified?

- Does this explanation make clear what the best possible outcome would be for your effort to communicate?

- Does this explanation make clear the main things that could go wrong with your attempt to accomplish your purpose?

- Does this explanation describe your responsibilities to other people as you move forward with this project?

4 Use your answers to these four questions to turn your one-sentence explanation into a paragraph—or more—that ties together your purpose, context, and audience.

AN EXAMPLE

Renee, from one of our classes, composed a statement of purpose to help her through a sticky but not unusual situation. Renee's sense of purpose, audience, and context are:

purpose	*I want to convince the Dean of Students that I should be allowed a late drop from the English class I'm failing. (It's my first semester, and Chemistry is harder than I thought, so I'm putting all my time into it—and not enough time into English. If I drop English then maybe I can get a better-than-passing grade in Chemistry.)*
audience	*My audience is the Dean of Students, who will demand strong reasons for my request—and will be reluctant to grant it—because the school has been tightening up on late drops.*
context	*The Dean will be in her office when she receives my request, and because there's only one month until the semester ends, everyone—including her—is probably pretty harried and rushed.*

- This is Renee's one-sentence explanation (from step 2 on the previous page) of how her purpose, audience, and context of communication tie together:

  I want to persuade a harried and reluctant Dean of Students that my circumstances warrant giving me a late drop in English.

- After asking herself the questions on the bottom of the previous page, Renee realized she hadn't considered the possible negative outcomes of her request: She hadn't thought about what might make the Dean of Students turn down her request. By working that thought into her planning, Renee developed this statement of purpose:

  I want to persuade a harried and reluctant Dean of Students that my circumstances warrant a late drop in English. I don't want her to think I'm only grade grubbing so that she turns down my request; instead, I want her to see I'm making the request because I'm serious about doing well and I learned a lot this semester about needing to manage my time.

By doing this revision, Renee sets herself up well to move into thinking about the next category of this rhetorical process—developing a design plan—and its steps of figuring out strategies, a medium, and arrangement. As we move through those steps in the next chapter, you'll see how Renee carried out her thinking, ending in a letter to the Dean.

49

FURTHER DEVELOPING STATEMENTS OF PURPOSE

As you continue working with the rhetorical process, and as your projects become more complex, your understandings of purpose, audience, and context will become more complex and your statement of purpose likewise will become more complex. For instance, since complex contexts sometimes mean that we have to juggle several purposes with respect to several different audiences, a corresponding statement of purpose will need to explain not only the relations among purpose, audience, and context but also the relations between different purposes and audiences.

composing a more complex statement of purpose

If you find yourself composing in complex situations, add the following questions to those listed under step 3 on page 48:

- Does this statement of purpose explain the relations between my main purpose and any secondary or subpurposes I may have?

- Does this statement of purpose reflect and respect the complexities of my audience? Does it take into account primary and secondary audiences?

- Is this a purpose everyone could share, or is it peculiar to my own interests or my social position?

- Is this a purpose I would want others to have?

- Is this purpose puerile, petulant, or petty? Am I base, brutish, or blind for having this purpose? Or is my purpose one that—when I achieve it—will help me feel proud and a useful member of the community I address?

recomposing a more complex statement of purpose

We hope you are seeing that even your statement of purpose is a strategy. How you state your purpose, how you represent your audience to yourself and to themselves, and how you envision your contexts are all strategic choices that shape how you think about and how you produce your communication—and will also shape how your audience responds.

YOUR RESPONSIBILITIES

- Since your statement of purpose connects your sense of purpose to your specific audience and context, you are responsible for making sure that the connections leave room for your audience to respond, if they need to. Be careful not to subsume the audience to the context and treat people like rocks or the ground you walk on.

- Try to use your statement of purpose to clarify for yourself how what matters to you connects with what matters to other people, given the contexts you share.

TO ANALYZE

- **Discuss with others:** It is often useful to stop and tinker with a statement of purpose to see how—by changing parts of it—the overall picture of your task changes. Below is a statement of purpose for a research project being undertaken by Stephanie Hill (a sociology major). Read through the statement of purpose, and then with a partner discuss the questions that follow.

Men in their late teens and twenties are my audience. I want them to learn just how much body-image is a problem for women because of how men look at women. I know most men think this isn't really a problem and that eating disorders are just personal issues for individual women. But I want men to be thinking about their sisters and girlfriends (and even potential daughters), and about how they probably don't want these people they care about to be spending so much time thinking about their bodyshapes— even to the point of starving themselves. I want to try to put my readers into the position of women, who see thousands of magazine covers of skinny women on them (or think of all the women on TV!), and about how the repetition of all those skinny women makes women feel... and then

I want my readers to think about what it's like to have a boyfriend or brother who constantly makes comments about how you look like you've just added a pound....

- Change the audience characteristics Stephanie describes. How does this change the overall statement of purpose?

- Stephanie doesn't say much about the context in which her audience will experience her communication. Imagine different contexts in which her audience could encounter her communication: How do the different contexts change your ideas about what media Stephanie could use? How do the different contexts suggest that the statement should be modified?

- Imagine Stephanie carrying out her purpose in several different media: How do different media change the context?

- What strategies does this statement of purpose suggest to you?

THINKING THROUGH PRODUCTION

- In preceding sections you've described a purpose, audience, and context for two different situations: appealing a decision about studying abroad and trying to get into a closed class. Use the model of Renee's statement of purpose to write a short statement of purpose for each of the two situations.

- Write a short, one-page paper in which you reflect on the following questions:

  - How is the rhetorical process we've laid out here for developing a statement of purpose different from how you usually approach composing?

  - What in the process do you think will be most useful to you given your strengths and weaknesses as a communicator?

  - What in the process can you see giving you trouble?

  - What in the process do you think will give you the most chances for being creative as you communicate with others?

- Choose a project assignment you know is upcoming in a class or a communication task you've taken on for a church group, sorority or fraternity, or other organization to which you belong. Take 30 minutes to apply the rhetorical process of developing— and writing—a statement of purpose for the assignment or task. Afterward, write a bit in reflection: *How is your sense of the assignment or task different from your very first thoughts about how you were going to proceed?*

composing a design plan

CHAPTER 3

In this chapter we speak generally about the strategies, media, and arrangement you can choose to achieve your statement of purpose. But also look closely at the individual chapters in section 2 on writing and on oral and visual communication for information about strategies that are appropriate for those particular modes.

Look at section 3 for many examples of texts made in different media to see how different authors use strategies of all kinds, including arrangement, in different kinds of communication contexts.

(And note that chapters 2 and 3 are separate in order to make the material in them into two more readily graspable parts. By splitting these chapters, we don't want you to think that first you think about audience, purpose, and context, and then you think about strategies, medium, arrangement, and testing. A design plan most often develops in a continual back and forth through all these steps; you need to be prepared to jump about between the steps, in whatever ways your thinking and your particular project catch your imagination.)

a design plan

WORKING TOWARD A DESIGN PLAN

What do you learn from this chapter—and why?

In this chapter we continue applying the rhetorical process for composing from chapter 1: Here, we discuss how to use your initial analysis of your purpose, audience, and context—and the statement of purpose you developed from that analysis—to make decisions about the strategies (including arrangement and medium) you'll use in the text you compose.

Pulling together your statement of purpose with the decisions helps you make **a design plan**. A design plan gives you concrete and specific guidance for producing your text.

How does developing a design plan fit into a composing process for writing?

You'll remember that at the beginning of chapter 2 we described how most experienced writers have a process like the following:

- Figuring out the project: *What are the project's purpose, context, and audience?*

- Considering and planning different approaches to the project: *What choices does a writer need to make to shape writing for its audience, given its purpose and context?*

- Writing a draft.

- Getting feedback from the intended audience.

- Revising the draft in response to feedback.

Chapter 2—developing a statement of purpose—addressed the first bullet point above; this chapter—developing a design plan—helps you focus on your choices and getting feedback.

What's the difference between a design plan and a thesis statement?

As we noted back in chapter 2, a thesis statement summarizes the argument of writing:

Modern language classes prepare students to live within the expanding global economy because modern language classes expose students to other cultures.

A thesis statement can suggest the points a writer needs to make in a piece of argumentative writing and so is highly useful (as we'll discuss in chapter 4, on research).

A design plan, on the other hand, helps a writer further develop the work of a statement of purpose, giving guidance for choosing how to shape an argument for a specific audience. For example, the above thesis statement could underlie a report to a college president recommending more modern language classes at the college; it could also underlie a brochure for encouraging high school students to take more language classes. A design plan would help you choose the different strategies that would be appropriate for those two different rhetorical situations.

Does this chapter tell me everything I need to know about design plans?

Design plans engage you with thinking about the specific strategies of a text you develop—including the strategies of medium and arrangement. With different media, however, we expect different arrangements and other strategic approaches: What works in an academic paper, for example, might not be appropriate in a poster, photographic essay, or graphic novel.

Because we have such different expectations, this book offers you—in chapters 5 to 7—information for how to work with audiences' expectations with writing as well as oral and visual texts. In each of those chapters, we show you how to work with such media.

In addition, in chapters 9 through 14, we demonstrate how to analyze texts that mix writing and visual approaches—posters, documentary photograph essays, editorial and opinion pieces, written essays, and comics—so that you learn how to combine written and visual approaches.

Examples of design plans in this book

- design plan for a letter to a dean requesting a late course drop: page 79

- design plan for a poster: page 80

- design plan for education materials: page 83

- design plan for an academic research paper: pages 162–163

- design plan for an oral presentation: pages 214–215

- design plan for a photo essay: pages 272–273

55

a design plan

STRATEGIES

WHAT CHOICES CAN YOU MAKE?

This step is really a mindset you need to acquire: You need to start looking at everything you do, say, or put in your communication as a strategy for helping you achieve your statement of purpose. A strategy is any part of your communication that you can change in order to better to achieve your statement of purpose.

In an essay, for example, strategies include the title, size of title, color of title, typeface of title, size of paper, color of paper, first word, placement of first word, second word, tone or mood set by first and second words, use of photographs, and so on—and so on.

To come up with strategies for your communication, you need to:

1 Generate a lot of different possible strategies.

To generate strategies, first think about an overall strategy. If, for example, you were going before the city council to propose a new traffic light in your town (a light you think they probably don't want), you might consider basing your argument on statistics about accidents at that stoplight or basing your argument on the stories of people who have been injured in those accidents—or maybe both statistics and stories together. After considering such large-scale strategies, generate possible smaller scale strategies: You could use overheads or handouts for the statistics, you could use a serious and formal tone of voice or a conversational tone of voice, you might lighten the seriousness with a little humor, you might wear a suit or casual clothes, and so on.

2 Use your statement of purpose to help you decide which strategies are most appropriate for your rhetorical situation.

To decide among strategies, always ask which will help you better achieve your statement of purpose. If, in the example about going before the city council, your statement of purpose helped you see that your audience is composed of people who are balancing budgets at the same time that they want to improve the quality of life in your city, then statistics about the cost of the car accidents, compared with statistics about the lower cost of the traffic light, will probably be more persuasive than only stories from accident victims.

Note that both medium and arrangement—the next two steps we'll examine—can be considered as large-scale strategies.

An example: How Renee thought through her strategies…

On page 49, you read Renee's statement of purpose—

I want to persuade a harried and reluctant dean of students that my circumstances warrant a late drop in English. I don't want her to think I'm only grade grubbing so that she turns down my request; instead, I want her to see I'm making the request because I'm serious about doing well and I learned a lot this semester about needing to manage my time.

—which helped her think about how to approach the dean strategically.

Here is what Renee wrote as she brainstormed about strategies for this communication:

I'm serious about this—I didn't mess up because I was lazy or not trying…. I really want to do well in school, especially my science classes, so I can get into med school. If I can persuade the dean I've really been trying, and really have learned a lesson from what happened, then maybe she'll be more sympathetic. So my main strategy has got to focus on how I've learned, and how I'll do better…. But what's going to make her see that I'm not just trying to make up for laziness? What will make her see that I've learned and I'm serious? Maybe if I can get my English teacher to put in a word for me because he keeps telling me he knows I could do better if I put in the time and focus. My adviser might help, too. Or maybe if I promise to sign up for time management or study skills workshops… I'm going to have to present this very carefully, too: I've got to approach her in a polished and serious way… and it would probably help if I let her know that I know she's busy and that I'm making a special request….

Out of this thinking-on-paper Renee pulled the following strategies:

1 *My overall strategy is to seem serious and aware of my mistakes: I will focus on my serious reasons for making the request. I have learned some very useful things about time management and the difficulty of college, and I do want to use what I have learned to do better in the next semesters so I can eventually make it into med school.*

2 *To support my overall strategy, I am going to demonstrate that I am serious by getting support from my teacher and/or adviser, and by signing up for time management and study skills workshops.*

57

practice with strategies…
Use the statements of purpose you wrote (in chapter 2) for the study abroad situation and for the situation of wanting to get into a closed class to develop strategies for addressing the situations.

THINKING FURTHER ABOUT STRATEGIES

Here we introduce traditional rhetorical concepts that allow us broadly to categorize strategies used in communication. These three concepts—*ethos*, *pathos*, and *logos*—allow us to categorize strategies as being based:

- in the character of the person(s) making an argument.
- in the emotions being engaged by the argument.
- in how the parts of an argument are ordered.

These strategies can be used for sentences or the colors in a photograph and they can structure a whole argument. You can use these terms both to generate arguments and to analyze others' arguments.

Like any other scheme, *ethos*, *pathos*, and *logos* cannot explain everything about arguments—but they can help you categorize and name what is going on in an argument and so help you think with some control about the strategic choices you use to engage others with your own compositions.

ethos, pathos, and *logos*

Ever since the philosopher Aristotle wrote *The Rhetoric* (a set of lecture notes handed down over the years and now printed in book form), people trying to improve their communicative strategies have distinguished among three strategies that Aristotle argued appear in all communication: *ethos*, *logos*, and *pathos*. These are Greek terms, and people continue to use the terms because there are no single English words that hold all the same meanings as in the Greek.

As we explain these terms, you'll see that even though the words look weird, you already know the basic ideas behind them and already have used them in your spoken, written, and visual designs. In this chapter and beyond, we want to help you use these strategies awarely in order to increase their power for you. We'll define the terms and then talk about how you can use these concepts as overall strategies.

ETHOS, or what your audience sees in you

Ethos is how you come across to your audience—how "you" fit into your communication as part of what you are trying to do. Everything you do or say not only conveys information to your audience but also sets up a relationship between you and them, and that relationship influences how things go. For instance, if as you approach a podium you say that on your way to give this speech you rescued a lost cat, the story is not only an explanation for your lateness; it also stirs the emotions of cat lovers in your audience and begins to incline them toward you. They begin to see you in a certain furry light, so to speak, and you can build on that.

Communicators create an *ethos* to give them authority to make the claims they do, as when Kimberly Wozencraft writes

> having seen the criminal justice system from several angles, as a police officer, a court bailiff, a defendant, and a prisoner, I am convinced that prison is not the answer to the drug problem, or for that matter to many other white-collar crimes.

The first part of the sentence states the experiences that, she believes, authorize her to make the claim of the second part of her sentence. But notice, too, that how Wozencraft writes—straightforwardly and with conviction—and what she writes shape our sense of who she is and so shape our willingness to be persuaded.

But communicators do not have to use "I" to tell us about themselves. The topics they choose, the tone of voice they use, their vocabulary—all these shape how we understand the communicator's character and hence the quality of our attention. For example, the words following, from Peter Singer, tell us nothing directly about him, but they tell us what matters to him, how he thinks, and how he thinks we should be in the world:

Elections can express the will of the people only if the people are reasonably well-informed about the issues on which they base their votes.

Singer says not a word about himself, and yet his words lead you to have a definite opinion about him and his character.

Ethos is in all communications, even when you cannot read or hear a communicator's words. Robert Nickelsberg's photographs in chapter 11, for example, show us a student graduating from high school in the U.S. To analyze ethos in these photographs, we must consider what sort of person would ask us to observe this student through the choices of framing, cropping, arranging, and captioning the photographs.

Ethos is a basic but complex strategy because so much affects it: tone of voice, gesture, stories one tells (or doesn't), how one smells, institutional roles, manner of approach, and so on.

PATHOS, or how your audience feels about what you are doing

Pathos is about how one communicates emotions in communication. Here Mary Pipher bases her argument on factual events as well as on fear, horror, and sadness:

I do believe our culture is doing a bad job raising boys. The evidence is in the shocking violence of Paducah, Jonesboro, Cheyenne, and Edinboro [school shootings before Columbine]. It's in our overcrowded prisons and domestic violence shelters.

It's in our adult bookstores and white supremacy groups. It's in our Ritalin-controlled elementary schools and alcohol-soaked college campuses.

Pipher evokes emotion not only through her examples but also through word choices ("shocking," "overcrowded," "alcohol-soaked") and the quick, repetitive rhythms of her sentences. Try reading Pipher's words aloud; listen to how the sentences have an urgent rhythm, which audiences will feel, awarely or not.

Another example of using emotion to shape your audience's responses is through photographs; in chapter 9 we discuss how this photograph, of a young person making direct eye contact with us, might work on the webpage where we found it:

A simple way to think about emotion is in terms of cause and effect. What you communicate can cause certain feelings in others, and there are many ways to influence feelings: Striking a confident pose might instill respect for you in your audience; a vivid example might shock them; a story with an unexpected but happy ending can delight; an analogy between drinking the local water and drinking poison can frighten them, and so on.

There are more complex ways of thinking about emotion, however.

For example, separate an audience's background emotions, or moods, from the more temporary emotions your work evokes. The same emotion can be a mood evoked in the moment of interacting with a text. Take fear as an example. When we say, "The country is in the grip of fear," we usually mean that we are operating within a "climate of fear"—a background emotion that many of us experience in some part of our days because of cultural events like wars or economic downturns. As a communicator you aren't responsible for such background emotions like this, but you need to be aware of such emotions that shape how audiences are feeling already. Fear also can be a target emotion—one you want to create at a specific time and place—as when someone shouts "fire" in a movie theatre (don't try this), or when a strong speaker invites you to resist your fears by saying, "The only thing you have to fear is fear itself."

Another more complex way to think about emotion is as a developing pattern or structure. Once you have encouraged someone to feel a certain way, you need to think about what that feeling prepares the person for, and how what you do and say next can lead to still other feelings. For instance, fear is closely related to anger. (If, while living with your parents, you ever came home way past curfew, you probably experienced how your parents' fear about you turned into relief—and then anger—when you returned). A communicator who evokes fear in an audience can then easily shift that fear into anger; this is often a strategy used by governments that want to go to war against another country, for example.

Here is an example of a writer, Jane Churchon, building a structure from simple to more complex emotions; she isn't asking us to feel fear but instead builds from sadness to grief, demonstrating the effort over time to control these emotions:

I once worked as a staff nurse in a neonatal intensive care unit. Whenever a baby died, I wrapped it in a blanket, and then around the blanket I wound a sky-blue disposable pad. I took the football sized package—baby, blanket, and pad— down to the morgue and opened the door of the refrigerator there and placed the package on the

glass shelf as gently as I could. Then I closed the door, pushing it until I heard the white seal grip, the way I might close the fridge door at home after putting away a chicken. There wasn't a way for me to close the refrigerator door with the reverence and honor the occasion deserved. This is a part of nursing we learn early: how to do the unthinkable without falling to our knees and wailing.

Look at Churchon's word choices ("package," "fridge"), and at the length of her sentences (notice that she repeats "and" in the third sentence, for example): Her words keep emotion present but on the edge in spite of the horrible task she must do, until her very last words. Notice, too, that as we read about what she is feeling we are taking stock of her *ethos*, developing a sense of her as a human.

As the preceding passage shows, *pathos*, like *ethos* and *logos*, develops over time, and in that development we see the intertwining of all three of the basic strategies. Over time, an audience's emotional responses result from what you have said (*logos*) and how you have come across (*ethos*), and yet how you come across in turn is influenced by the emotions being stirred (*pathos*) and the argument being made (*logos*). The audience is always feeling something, but what you say and do can redirect their mood and build emotional responses that influence how the audience hears your words.

LOGOS, or the reason and structure in arguments

You've seen the Greek word *logos*, usually attached to another Greek word such as "bio" (life) or "psyche" (spirit or mind). *Logos* is not the plural of "logo"; instead, for the ancient Greeks, *logos* meant word, structure, reason, thought, language, and argument—and so "biology" is the study of life, while "psychology" is the study of our internal mental workings; "logic" derives from *logos*. As a basic category of strategy, it includes all the strategies connected with the structure of an argument (including arrangement) as well as the kinds of reasoning you choose to use. Look at this passage, written by Jill McCorkle, about freedom of speech:

It's one of the most basic laws of human nature, isn't it? The more we are denied something, the more we want it. The more silence given to this or that topic, the more power. All you need to do is look to the binge-drinking or eating-disorder cases that surround us, the multitudes of church sex scandals, to show that the demand for abstinence or any kind of total denial of thought or expression or action can often lead to dangerous consequences. When we know we can choose to do this or that, we don't feel as frantic to do so, to make the sudden move or decision that might be the worst thing for us.

McCorkle takes on topics with much emotional weight in our time and place, and we certainly make judgments about her character based on what and how she writes, but her main strategy here is *logos*. McCorkle starts by making a claim (phrased as a question) about a basic "law" of human nature and logically builds consequences from that law. If you agree with her initial claim—or are pulled into a curious attitude by her question—then you're likely to follow along with the logical development of those consequences, and by the implied argument that we shouldn't absolutely forbid certain actions but should instead perceive them as choices.

Facts and numbers (like statistics) are also strategies of *logos*. In an essay arguing that the countries of Central Asia should be treated better by other countries, S. Frederick Stark presents facts about the area's history:

> *In chemistry, Central Asians were the first to reverse reactions, to use crystallization as a means of purification, and to measure specific gravity and use it to group elements in a manner anticipating Dmitri Mendeleev's periodic table of 1871. They compiled and added to ancient medical knowledge, hugely broadened pharmacology, and passed it all to the West and to India. And in technology they invented windmills and hydraulic machinery for lifting water that subsequently spread westward to the Middle East and Europe and eastward to China.*

This list of facts serves as evidence for the value of the region and hence for how the rest of the world should respect the region and its people. Facts and numbers carry persuasive weight in our scientifically minded culture—which is why, when we or others use them, we need to be alert to their careful use.

As with the other strategies, *logos* is not restricted to arguments made with words. While the war posters in chapter 10 may not use facts or statistics, their arrangements are examples of carefully constructed *logos*.

(Keep in mind that presenting yourself as a logical person in an argument isn't about *logos* but about *ethos*. *Logos* is simply about the structures and arrangements you choose as you build an argument, both in terms of overall and smaller scale structures.)

Some kinds of *logos* are appropriate only to writing or only to speaking or only to visual communication—as we discuss in chapters 4 to 7.

Choosing *ethos*, *pathos*, or *logos* as an overall strategy

You can choose *ethos*, *pathos*, or *logos* to be your overall guiding strategy for developing a composition. It might make sense for your overall guiding strategy to be putting emphasis on your character and qualities, on the emotional connections you can build with an audience, or on structure.

Earlier in this chapter, we imagined you making a presentation to the city council in favor of a traffic light at a dangerous intersection. We suggested that you could argue by using the stories of people who had been hurt in traffic accidents in the intersection; this would be to choose *pathos* as your overall strategy. You could argue from statistics about what accidents at that intersection cost the city, and this would be to choose *logos* as your overall strategy. We also described how the choice comes down to knowing your audience: A budget-minded city council is more likely to be persuaded by an argument based in *logos* than in *pathos*.

If you choose *ethos*, *logos*, or *pathos* as your overall strategy, keep in mind that you still have to address the other two strategies, shaping them in support of the overall guiding strategy. In this book, for example, the divisions of sections and chapters and our writing whose purposes are to help you learn about rhetoric show that our overall strategy is *logos*. Imagine then the effect if we developed an *ethos* that was silly or arrogant or plodding. Instead, we've tried to sound authoritative to you in our writing, so that you'll take our points seriously. We want you to understand us as thoughtful, enthusiastic, and concerned about your abilities as a communicator; we want to establish a relationship with you that invites you to consider these matters as seriously and with as much sense of possibility as we do. As for *pathos*, given that our overall strategy is *logos*, we couldn't very well write to evoke emotions of disgust, fear, or anger; instead, we've tried to write with a broad range of examples and with some humor, so that perhaps your intellectual curiosity will be piqued by what you can learn.

Other choices of one overall strategy shape how you use the other two. Imagine, for example, two editorials on affirmative action, one in favor and one opposed. Both use logos as their overall strategy, listing reasons why their readers should be for or against affirmative action and responding to criticisms others might raise—but attend to how differently ethos is shaped in each because of each's position. The first editorial is written by a man who benefited from affirmative action, and from the first sentence he identifies himself in this way, telling how he grew up poor and only went to college because he could take advantage of "minority outreach programs." Only after constructing an ethos that (he hopes) gives him the authority to speak from personal experience—and perhaps arousing in his readers the emotion of compassion—does he turn to his main logical points. In the second editorial, written by two men, the two tell us nothing about themselves; instead, they start their writing with claims about the effects of affirmative action and then give support for their claims. To be persuasive

about an issue that is so emotionally charged in this country, they cannot sound motivated by self-interest or anger in trying to deny benefits to others—and so they try to develop an ethos that sounds impartial, and they avoid strategies that will arouse much emotion. They use long words that slow down the rhythm of their writing, making it sound unemotional. Their sentences rarely describe individual people taking specific actions but instead often have abstract nouns as their grammatical subject, making the problem seem less emotional because less tied to real people.

Almost all the examples in the chapter on posters use the primary strategy of *pathos*, drawing us in by evoking romance or horror or by making a direct visual appeal to patriotism. But all these posters have to be arranged visually so that we can see and make sense of the emotional appeals, and so *logos* is at work. It may seem that there is no *ethos* in posters, because the person who designed the poster isn't ever present in it—but there are several ways viewers get a sense of *ethos*. When we look at the examples from wartime, we see that whoever designed the poster is trying to cause certain actions to happen, and we understand the designer's choice of action to indicate something about his or her character. We also judge the production qualities of a poster as a sign of *ethos*: Just as we make judgments about writers based on how

they've used spelling and grammar, we make judgments about others who produce communication based on the quality of attention they give to their production and how knowledgeably they've used their materials.

Remember that, although pieces of communication will have *ethos*, *pathos*, or *logos* as an overall strategy, they are always also shaped by the remaining two substrategies. Attend to this both as you analyze and produce communications. Note, too, how the *ethos*, *pathos*, or *logos* in a communication builds over time, over the course of the whole communication.

Choosing *ethos*, *pathos*, or *logos* as small-scale strategies

The overall sense a reader, viewer, or listener has of *ethos*, *pathos*, or *logos* in any piece of communication is built from all the different ways these strategies are used in the various elements that make up the whole composition.

In the chapters on written, oral, and visual modes of communication, and in the chapters of examples of many different kinds of texts, we'll point out how *ethos*, *pathos*, or *logos* are present in many different small ways appropriate to the different modes.

YOUR RESPONSIBILITIES

- Admit it when you don't have all the evidence you need for an argument (evidence is a strategy), and don't fudge your evidence.

- Be sure you use the kind of evidence that your context calls for. Some contexts call for logical proof and an airtight case, some call for the words of an expert, some call for concrete examples, and some call for evidence of passion (a sign that you really care).

- Consider the ideas and positions held by your audience or others who've written or talked about what you're discussing.

- Give appropriate attribution for any words, pictures, or other materials you use that have been made by others.

- Keep in mind the particularities and needs of your audience as you choose strategies. For example, be sure you use a larger typeface if you are designing for older people or children.

TO ANALYZE

- **Write to learn:** To understand *ethos*, *pathos*, and *logos* in communication using words, try restating the words to achieve different results. Look, for example, at the paragraph below about the 1994 U.S. crime bill. The paragraph was written by Bruce Shapiro, who along with several others that year had been stabbed, almost to death, by a "socially marginal neighborhood character" who believed his mother had been killed.

In early autumn I read the entire text of the crime bill—all 412 pages. What I found was perhaps obvious, yet under the circumstances compelling: Not a single one of those 412 pages would have protected me or Anna or Martin or any of the others from our assailant. Not the enhanced prison terms, not the three-strikes-you're-out requirements, not the summary deportations of criminal aliens.

We believe Shapiro is working to construct an *ethos* that is dispassionate and informed (look at what he's read), and deserving of readers' sympathies because of what he's undergone—but it's an *ethos* that might also gain persuasive strength for readers because they might expect him to want revenge for his injuries or tougher laws. Instead he's making an argument, based on painful personal experience, that tougher laws would

have made no difference. There seems to be little *pathos*: Shapiro applies no judgmental adjectives to his "assailant" (and look at the relative neutrality of that noun); there does seem to be emotion in the quick repetitive rhythms of the last sentence. There is an implied formal argument, which is a particular use of *logos*; that argument might be stated like this:

> *The crime bill is useful if it prevents crimes.*
>
> *The crime bill would not have prevented the attack on Shapiro and others.*
>
> *The crime bill is therefore not useful.*

You may not agree with the premises of this argument (or you might state them differently based on your reading), but something like this *logos* is at work in Shapiro's paragraph.

Rewrite Shapiro's paragraph to make him sound angry or vengeful. Increase the emotion by changing nouns, adding adjectives, or making all the sentences choppy and harsh. Take out the implied formal argument—or make it more obvious.

Give your revised paragraph to others. How do your changes shape how others read and respond?

a design plan

MEDIUM

OUT OF WHAT IS YOUR COMMUNICATION MADE?

Choosing a medium involves both creativity and common sense.

Creativity asks you to set aside or add to your first ideas. Sometimes the first idea about a medium is useful—but sometimes it is the "usual" solution, which might not be effective. If you think about media that are unexpected in your context—but appropriate—you might think up new and highly useful strategies to achieve your purpose. (For example, turning in a late paper gift-wrapped might just earn a little slack from a teacher, or at least some sympathetic laughter—but such a move requires careful judgment: You have to know your audience well!)

Common sense tells you the kinds of media that people most often use in similar contexts and with similar purposes and that your audience probably expects. Common sense reminds you to consider what is practical, too: Do you really have enough time and money—and competence—to make a music video that your teacher will accept in place of a written term paper?

Because you want to make communication that engages audiences and helps you achieve your purpose, it is generally a good idea to begin with creativity and then to judge your cool ideas with a healthy dose of common sense.

To figure out the best medium or media for achieving your statement of purpose:

1 Brainstorm different media you can use.

The more possible media you can imagine, the more likely you are to come up with something that will appeal to your audience effectively and appropriately.

2 Imagine each medium or media in use by your audience.

By imagining the media in use by your audience in context and by thinking about how you can shape your overall strategies through your possible media, you'll be able to decide which to use.

3 Think practically.

Which media can you handle in terms of time, resources, and experience? What will the medium or media demand of you?

An example: How Renee thought through her media....

Renee is the student trying to persuade the dean of students to give her a late drop from her English class. She's decided that her main strategies are to convince the dean that she's learned from her hard semester and that the late drop will help her do better.

Renee knows that she can send the dean an email or a letter making her request or that she can make an appointment to see the dean. She could also send flowers to the dean with the request written on an attached card.

Because she's trying to show that she's serious about the request and her schooling, Renee decides to send a letter *and* make an appointment. She thinks that an email is simply too informal for her purpose and that flowers might make her look just a little too goofy or like she was trying to bribe the dean.

She figures that if she drops a letter by the dean's office and sets up an appointment to see the dean at the same time, she'll look committed to her work and serious enough to make sure her case gets heard. (Renee also thinks she'd be a little too nervous to present her case to the dean only in a face-to-face meeting; if the dean has seen a well-crafted letter first, then Renee won't have to say too much but will need only to answer the dean's questions. Renee also hopes that the dean is someone who finds it harder to turn someone down in person.)

Renee also figures she needs to write a formal letter rather than a quick note to the dean—so she'll need some good paper and access to a computer (and software with a spell checker) and a good printer as well as access to some sample formal letters (which she can get from the handbook for her English class).

practice with medium...

Use the statements of purpose you wrote for the study abroad situation and for the permission to get into a closed class to help you determine media you could use in these situations.

and

Take an upcoming assignment you have in another class (a paper, report, or presentation, for example), and use the prompts on page 64 to come up with several unexpected but appropriate media you could use to satisfy the assignment's requirements.

CHOOSING YOUR MEDIUM

Is it appropriate to use a medium or media with which your audience is familiar or that is expected in the context?

That is, does your context suggest you will be most persuasive if you stick with a medium your audience knows well? For a class research assignment, for example, it will generally make sense to turn in a printed, double-spaced report on white 8 1/2" by 11" paper printed in black ink. If you are asked to give a eulogy at a friend's funeral, most mourners would think it inappropriate if you brought your guitar and amps and played a black metal anthem. If you're trying to persuade an audience to vote for your candidate because she has good economic policies, you're probably going to be most effective making a poster that's easy to read and states facts. How audiences attend to communication is shaped by their expectations of the context and purpose of the communication—and an odd or unfamiliar medium can distract or upset them and so get in the way of you achieving your purpose. Considering what your audience might expect in a given context can help you choose a medium.

Is it appropriate to use a medium or media with which your audience is unfamiliar or that is unexpected?

Suppose you're writing a research paper on the Scott expedition to the South Pole in the early 20th century, and—as you learn about the explorers' diets—you understand that your purpose is to argue that a better diet might have saved the expedition. To call attention to and support your arguments, it might make sense to turn in your paper with an attached ball of oatmeal and lard (which is what the explorers ate for months on end) with a note asking your teacher to have a taste to better understand why you think the explorers were undernourished. (And, of course, you probably have a good sense in this case of whether your audience—your teacher—will be receptive to such argumentative choices.) If you're asked to give a eulogy for a member of a metal band, then playing a black metal anthem (especially one she wrote) might be unexpected but probably not inappropriate. If you want to use an unexpected or unfamiliar medium, it needs to fit with and strongly support your statement of purpose.

How do you figure out a medium that might be unexpected but that works in the context?
At the end of this chapter, we describe a set of learning materials that Anne (one of the authors of this book) made for the National Civilian Community Corps. The materials were unexpected in that most previous materials used in the Corps had been in big binders; Anne made a series of small, colorful booklets in a plastic bag—and what led her to make such materials was the research that led to her design plan. In the course of figuring out who the audience was and how they needed to use the materials, Anne listened to people talking about how they'd like to have something they could carry with them to work, something small and easy to get to. It was Anne's audience who suggested the medium; she just had to listen.

You can also come up with unexpected but appropriate media through a kind of brainstorming. Go to a mall and wander, looking at and listing all the things that people make for each other to communicate: greeting cards, board games, stuffed animals, documentaries on audio cassettes or CDs, hands-on museum displays, fancily covered books, candy bar wrappers, skits, balloons, noisemakers, foldout photo albums, and on and on. Go to a bookstore and look at the different ways magazines and books are put together (look especially at children's books). Look at books and magazines about design. Looking at such varied material can suggest to you new media for carrying out your purpose, but do test your ideas with people who are likely to be audience members (by describing to them what you are considering) before you go into production.

Talking directly with people is just about as close as we can get; the intimacy of the situation will depend on how well we know the audience and how many people are in it.

Because they'll generally seem informal to an audience, unexpected media (fortune cookies are our example here) can feel like a gesture from someone known.

Handwritten letters feel very intimate; letters delivered directly to us can feel like a gesture of closeness.

Photographs of people we know will always be intimate; photographs of people in general will pull us in because of our connected sense of bodily experience.

Comics, because they carry with them both the sense of hand drawn production and illustrations of people, will feel close and informal.

Recordings of voices, film, or photographs seem one step removed from our actually being there.

Printed documents—because there's no visual presence of messy bodies in them and only a reduced sense of voice—can seem distant to audiences. Printed interviews and personal essays—because they're representations of individual voices—will seem closer than opinion pieces and editorials, which usually have a voice but also formal argumentative structures addressing groups of people. Academic articles—because they're supposed to be objective—can feel farthest away from audiences.

What kind of relationship—of closeness or distance, intimacy or objectivity—do you want to establish with your audience through the medium or media you choose?

The graphic above shows that differing media suggest differing, conventional relations with audiences. Some media—your voice or a handwritten letter—can give your audience a fairly direct sense of you: The audience will feel that the communication between you is personal and perhaps even intimate. Printed texts tend to feel more distant, and certain printed texts, such as academic articles are, by conventional design, produced to feel distant and consequently (their authors hope) more objective.

As you consider which media to choose, think about the sense of nearness and presence—or distance and objectivity—you want to have with an audience. There are other strategies for producing a sense of nearness or distance, as we describe in the section on strategies and in the chapters on strategies specific to written, oral, and visual communication. But the medium or media you choose—because of the conventional attitudes that audiences tend to carry about them—matter very much in the relationship you establish with your audience.

How do you choose a medium that is responsible to your audience, context, purpose, the environment, and your pocketbook?

- How many copies of this communication are needed? How much will each copy cost? Do you—or the people for whom you're working—have the money to produce as many as you need?

- What resources are required by the medium? Can you use recycled paper or soy-based inks? Can you make the piece so that it uses fewer resources?

- Does the intended audience have access to the medium? Can they access computers, for example, or computers that can handle memory-intensive animations?

- Is what you're making a size and shape that your audience will be able to use?

- Will your audience understand how to use the medium? Will you need to include instructions, or is it part of your purpose that they have to struggle a bit to understand?

- If you need multiple copies of the communication, is it easy and inexpensive to reproduce (on a regular copy machine) or does each piece require a lot of direct hands-on manipulation and expensive materials?

Can you responsibly make an effective production with the medium you're considering?

Do you know enough, for example, about the technical aspects of four-color print production to make a full color brochure? Do you have sufficient access to equipment for making a broadcast-quality public service announcement?

While you're working on a project, if it seems that the best medium to use is one with which you have little familiarity, your decision to go ahead will depend on the whole context: If you are producing a piece of communication within a class and your teacher is willing to let you try a new medium, then you are all set. But if, for example, you're working with a non-profit organization that asks you to produce a newsletter or four-color brochure for it (or you all agree that this is what is needed) and you've never had experience with such productions, tell the people with whom you are working. Since they are paying for the production of the piece, they need to be able to decide whether to proceed.

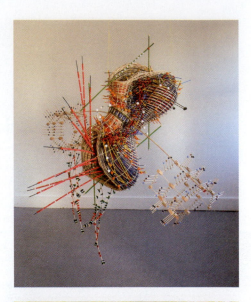

YOUR RESPONSIBILITIES

■ Keep in mind that all the members of your audience need to have access to the communication medium you are using. Keep your eye on who is included—and who is excluded—by the medium you choose. Not everyone has easy access to computers or to high-speed Internet connections.

■ Keep in mind also the resources required to produce the medium you're using, and try to waste as little as possible during production. (And do think about how people will use what you make: Flyers to put under windshield wipers might help you advertise an event, but most people will pull them off their cars and drop them on the ground.)

■ If you're using a medium that takes a lot of resources, ask yourself whether you're using your medium to its fullest potential to justify your choice.

■ Since choice of medium is also a choice of strategy, think about whether you're using the medium in ways familiar to you and your audience, or, when appropriate, whether you're challenging yourself and your audience by pushing the boundaries of the medium.

TO ANALYZE

■ **Write informally:** Over the course of a week, list every medium (or mix of media) you use, consume, produce, or encounter. Which of these media are within—or could be within with a little effort, creativity, or time—your capabilities to use?

■ **Write informally:** On the opposite page are two pieces of communication that use unexpected media.

The top photograph is of an art piece called "Warm Weather" by Nathalie Miebach. Made of "reed, wood, data" (to use Miebach's description), the piece weaves together complex weather information from the Gulf of Maine—air, water, and soil temperatures; wind speed and direction; and tides and moon phases—to help viewers think about the relations among all this data. Miebach writes that her work results from a "desire to explore the role visual aesthetics play in the translation and understanding of science information."

The second photograph is of a little cardboard robot—a "Tweenbot"—designed by Kacie Kinzer. Kinzer would set the robots moving through areas of New York City; the flag you can see in the photograph asks passersby to turn the robot toward a particu-lar destination. Kinzer expected the little robots to disappear, but they instead always ended up at their destinations: People guided the robots and in the process would talk to strangers about the robots or keep the robots from ending up in harmful situations. The robots show how strangers in urban situations can be encouraged to interact.

For these two objects, try to recreate the statements of purpose that would encourage the designers to come up with these uses of media.

strategies ● ──────── ● arrangement

a design plan

ARRANGE-MENT

WHAT WILL BE THE ORDER AND SHAPE OF YOUR ARGUMENTS?

Reading an essay takes time—as does reading a poem or a brochure or listening to someone give a speech or looking through a photo essay. Even communications that seem straightforward and simple—like posters, for example—have different parts (type and photographs) that require us to move our eyes through them in some kind of order, taking in the parts so that we can figure out what their relationships are.

Because almost all pieces of communication require an audience to move through them in time, the different parts of the communication have to be arranged. They have to be put in some order—and that order can be arranged to be more or less persuasive, more or less tied to your statement of purpose.

Several kinds of arrangement or structure occur in any piece of communication. In writing, for example, you'll be thinking about the arrangements of words in an individual sentence, but you'll also be thinking about how to order your different paragraphs to achieve your purpose. If you produce a photo essay, you'll be thinking about the arrangement—and resulting effects on an audience—of the elements within each photograph, but you'll also be thinking about how to arrange the photographs together on a page or across multiple pages.

Finding the most effective arrangement strategies for your purpose requires you to….

1 List the parts of your communication.

To figure out an arrangement to use, you need to know what you're arranging. If you have a statement of purpose and have thought about strategies and medium, then along the way you'll have developed a sense of the parts of your communication.

2 Brainstorm different possibilities.

Every medium has associated with it many possible arrangement alternatives. In chapters 10-14—the chapters of examples of different kinds of communication—we discuss the arrangements tied to different media.

3 Ask which possibilities best support your purpose and overall strategies.

An example: How Renee thought through her arrangement...

From thinking about strategies and media, Renee knows she'll write a formal letter to the dean. She also knows she needs to approach the dean carefully given how late it is in the semester, how the school is trying to give fewer late drops, and how stressed the dean must be at this time in the semester.

Renee also knows, from developing her statement of purpose, that she needs to address the following matters in her letter:

- a clear and concise statement of her request: that she wants a late drop
- what she's learned about time and college from the experience of her first semester and how she's going to take a workshop to help her with the challenges she's faced
- her reasons for wanting the late drop
- the situation that led her to want a late drop
- the support her English teacher and adviser are giving her (after talks with them) in seeking the late drop
- the dean's harried and busy state of mind

Because the dean's state of mind is not directly related—but still important—to her purpose, Renee decides it shouldn't be the center of her letter; it should come at the beginning or end—or maybe in both places, so that Renee can show her appreciation for the dean's personal attention.

The most important thing is the request for a late drop—but before that, Renee thinks she should probably explain the context of her request. She'll explain who she is and what happened in her semester, and then she'll ask for the drop, followed by her reasons, backed up by her commitment to taking a workshop and the support of her teacher and adviser.

71

practice with arrangement...

Use the statements of purpose you wrote for the study abroad situation and for the situation of wanting to get into a closed class to help you think about arrangements you could use for the different media you've described.

THINKING FURTHER ABOUT ARRANGEMENT

Here we discuss some general strategies of arrangement you can use to achieve your purpose. Turn to section 2 to learn more about strategies specific to written, oral, and visual communication. Section 3 has examples of arrangements in many media.

When you're figuring out how to arrange your argument or looking for an arrangement that might suggest possibilities for you, look through the suggestions and examples here. Can you work out how to use several of these different structures as overall strategies of arrangement to support your statement of purpose? Can you use these strategies at the sentence or illustration level to add interest to the details of your productions?

arrangements that move

If communication is about showing your audience how conditions could be better or different, then the arrangement of a communication needs to move an audience imaginatively from where they are now into the future conditions you—and they—think best.

You arrange your argument so that what the audience experiences first is what they know, ideas or images with which they are familiar or comfortable. Then, step by step, you move them into the unknown or unfamiliar; each step builds upon the previous one so that the audience never feels any gaps or that any step will take them in a direction they think is wrong, frightening, or ill-considered. You want the audience to follow your reasons, to move in their ideas from where they first enter your piece to where they leave.

small to big

In such a structure, you show your audience how something small they accept or understand can lead to bigger consequences that they may (or may not) want—as in this proverb:

> For want of a nail the shoe was lost,
> For want of a shoe the horse was lost,
> For want of a horse the rider was lost,
> For want of a rider the battle was lost,
> For want of a battle the kingdom was lost,
> And all for the want of a horseshoe nail.

Since at least the 14th century, people have used this proverb to argue—by analogy—that we ought to attend to small details because they lead to big consequences. Do an online search for "for want of a nail" and you'll find examples of this proverb and its arrangement of small to big used in car ads, history books, and computer programming examples.

In chapter 13, "Higher Education" shows "small to big" structuring an essay. "Higher Education" is about a black man who comes to a small, all-white, Mennonite town as a basketball coach and, after an initial awkward period, winds up having a strong effect on the town, its people, and its children—an effect the author, Gary Smith, calls a "miracle." The essay is an argument, in other words, about how one "small" human can have big effects.

big to small

With this structure, you can show your audience how something big that they accept may have hidden in it smaller consequences they may or may not want to accept. In an editorial titled "Who would call warrior 'squaw'?" for example, E. J. Montini writes about a Native American servicewoman, Army Pfc. Lori Piestewa, killed in the Iraqi war; Montini observes that in all the public writing and talking about her death no one called her "squaw." He argues that if it is inappropriate to use the term in the most careful and respectful circumstances, then it must also be inappropriate to use the term in less formal circumstances, such as when we name streets or mountains.

This strategy is also useful when you want to persuade others that a situation is less daunting or overwhelming than it might at first seem. For example, Google has come under government scrutiny because of its size and dominance online; Google's response has been that the company is (according to the *New York Times*), a "relatively small player in a vast market": By asking us to think of its size in terms of all the other companies doing similar work, it hopes not to seem such a large target.

best case to worst case (or worst case to best case)

These arrangements work along a continuum: You start at one end of a situation and show how what you propose moves the situation to or toward the other end. You can use these arrangements to argue that things are good now but will get bad if *x* happens—or that things are bad now but will get better if *x* happens. You hear such arguments if you read about state and national decision making: Legislators will argue for the circumstances they believe will improve some current situation—or will make the situation even worse.

before and after

"Before and after" arguments ask us to look at previous circumstances, compare them to where we are now, and to then judge whether they have improved. If circumstances are better, this is an argument for keeping things as they are; if not, this is an argument for change.

When Dan Kindlon and Michael Thompson wrote the introduction to their book *Raising Cain: Protecting the Emotional Lives of Boys*, they included this short argument:

> ....*unless we give him a viable alternative, today's angry young man is destined to become tomorrow's lonely and embittered middle-aged man.*

Looking from the present into the future, they show us the "before" of angry young men and the "after" of the miserably middle aged. If we accept this relationship, then we will agree with these writers that we need to do something now about boys' emotional education.

The essay "A Partly Cloudy Patriot" in chapter 8 uses this arrangement. Considering the events of September 11, 2001, the author, Sarah Vowell, reminds us how we heard over and over again on television and radio talk shows that "things will never be the same" after that date—but she asks us to compare now with then to persuade us toward particular attitudes.

We described above how the essay "Higher Education" in chapter 13 uses a "small to big"

structure. Entwined with that structure is also the structure of "before and after." "Higher Education" describes the town before the coach came, and then afterward; it needs to have this arrangement to help us feel the aftereffects of this encounter between a town and a man.

For now, here's a final small example. One of our favorite singers, Patsy Cline, sang the song "She's Got You," which contains the lyric, "I've got your picture, she's got you." There is an implied "before" in these words, a time when the singer had a sweetie, but now, after some changes, sweetie is with someone else; the singer ruefully suggests in this lyric that "before" (when she had more than just a photograph to hold) was much better than the present handful of Kodak.

near to far

We use this arrangement to put what is near into a larger context, showing how it carries more weight than we might have thought.

This strategy shapes an article by Stephen Katz titled "The Ethics of Expediency: Classical Rhetoric, Technology, and the Holocaust." In this article, Katz puts a simple memo in front of us—an example of technical or business communication—and examines it as a piece of writing, to conclude that it is well written, clear, and efficient. Then he moves the memo further away from us in time and moral purpose by showing that the memo was written by a Nazi bureaucrat instructing how to turn trucks into mobile gas chambers. Through this near-to-far arrangement, Katz constructs a compelling argument for questioning a noncritical attachment to the value of efficiency.

In a slightly different use of this strategy, the movie *The Wizard of Oz* starts at home in Kansas and takes Dorothy (and us) far, far away—so that, after our experiences there, we're happy to be back at home amid the chickens, scarecrows, and the little dog, too. This is using "near to far" to make what is near more valuable.

far to near

This arrangement helps tame what seems abstract, dangerous, or strange. Look at the "I want you!" poster on the right (and all its variations in chapter 10). One strategy at work in all of these is "personification": putting an abstract idea—patriotism, for example—into the guise of a person. This makes the abstract idea more concrete and not so distant for the audience.

Notice also that, once the idea is personified, the person in these posters can gesture to us, as though to pull us even closer. In all these posters, going to war—a horrible action even when justified—is changed from something we'd like to keep at a distance into something (the designers hope) closer and more acceptable.

arrangements that don't (seem) to move

Some arrangements seem to be about staying in one place, such as lists or arguments not to change conditions, or visual compositions that stay on one page or screen. But such arrangements can really be about moving audiences—maybe from an imagined future members don't want back to a fine present—when the arrangements are shaped for context and audience.

lists

Percentage change in U.S. labor productivity since 1972: +114

Percentage change in wages during that same period: -6

Percentage increase in food-stamp usage in 2010: 13

(Harper's Magazine, June 2011)

Some think lists exist only to help us buy food at the market, but we also make lists to compare objects or possibilities (which you might have done in deciding which college to attend). Sometimes lists can be argumentative, as with the above example, because they move you.

Why would someone put those three different statistics together (above) unless readers were to make some conclusions about them, or at least to question their implications? Isn't it hard not to ask why productivity has gone up so much but wages haven't? Isn't it hard not to wonder

why so many people need food stamps if U.S. laborers are working so hard? The list might prod us to do more research, not only into the veracity of the statistics but also into why the statistics don't jibe with our sense of how wages should match productivity.

comparison

Kate Winslet was the female lead, the figurehead and a very fetching cabin companion, in what is history's most successful film, Titanic. *But, of course, Mark Hamill was the lead in the* Star Wars *trilogy.*

Film critic David Thomson published those words before the *Lord of the Rings* trilogy replaced *Titanic* in the realms of success—but that doesn't undo the effect of his comparison of Kate Winslet with Mark Hamill. Thomson doesn't explicitly state the terms of his comparison, but he's arguing that even though Kate Winslet might seem to have an amazing career ahead of her, we need look only to the example of Mark Hamill, who once seemed similarly poised (following a blockbuster film) for a life of large film success.

Comparison asks us to see similarity between two (or more) people, situations, or events, so that we can judge the one by the other.

juxtaposition

When I was a soldier, I was often struck, as by a paradox, that at the very moment artillery was pounding somewhere, somewhere else men and women in soft clothing were touching glasses and carrying on flirtations; and that after and before this moment, but in this place, the peaceful pursuit of human purposes would go innocently forward, that families would picnic where men were killed.

Those words are part of an argument Arthur C. Danto makes that there has not yet been sufficient investigation into tensions in the Civil War—between the romantic view many had of war and and the deadliness (for the time) of the weapons—with the result that our memory of the war is inappropriate. The juxtaposition above, between fighting and the daily lives lived elsewhere, embodies both the forgetfulness and the tension Danto describes.

Juxtapositions are like comparisons in that they ask us to consider two situations at once—but juxtapositions hold two very different situations or conditions before our attentions so that we can feel the jangly and often disturbing differences.

arguments for not changing current conditions

Suppose your partner wants to move to another town—and you don't. As you and your partner go back and forth, trying to persuade each other, your argument will be for staying put—and so it may seem that your argument is one that goes nowhere. But it's only the conclusion of the argument (one you hope your partner accepts) that stays put; the argument itself has to move. One arrangement for such an argument is to start by describing all the good things about your lives now, with the jobs, opportunities, and friends you now have and to contrast them with the possible future you imagine in the other place. That is, you could paint a picture of an alternate future, one dependent on moving, and describe why that future will probably be worse than staying put. You'd obviously have to address your partner's particular concerns about staying, but moving into a possible alternate future—and not liking it—is a way of arguing to stay where you are now.

single page or screen visual arguments

We discuss visual argument in chapter 7, but we'll note here that some visual arguments don't appear to move because they're on a single screen or page. But consider the "I want you!" poster on the opposite page, and that it uses "far-to-near" strategies to pull us close and change our attitudes.

arguments that seem to repeat the same thing

Small children exhaust audiences into acquiescence when they repeat "I want ice cream. I want ice cream. I want ice cream…" Repetition in most adult arguments is more subtle: There will be slight variations in what is repeated, so that the weight of the argument is in the slight (or sometimes not so slight) differences.

Look at the two posters above. Through what they repeat and don't repeat, what sense do they ask you to take on about the art—and artmakers—that are the subject of the publicized exhibition? What relations do they posit between art and landscape?

Elie Wiesel, a concentration camp survivor, teacher, journalist, and author, gave a speech in the White House in 1999 on "The Perils of Indifference." In chapter 6, on pages 206–207, we show the speech's introduction and conclusion. Below is a section from the middle; notice how Wiesel repeats individual words but also uses sentences that repeat the same structure:

Indifference, after all, is more dangerous than anger and hatred. Anger can at times be creative. One writes a great poem, a great symphony. One does something special for the sake of humanity because one is angry at the injustice that one witnesses. But indifference is never creative. Even hatred at times may elicit a response. You fight it.

You denounce it. You disarm it.

Indifference elicits no response. Indifference is not a response. Indifference is not a beginning; it is an end. And, therefore, indifference is always the friend of the enemy, for it benefits the aggressor— never his victim, whose pain is magnified when he or she feels forgotten. The political prisoner in his cell, the hungry children, the homeless refugees— not to respond to their plight, not to relieve their solitude by offering them a spark of hope is to exile them from human memory. And in denying their humanity, we betray our own.

Indifference, then, is not only a sin, it is a punishment.

And this is one of the most important lessons of this outgoing century's wide-ranging experiments in good and evil.

What effects come from Wiesel's repetitions of words and sentence structures?

other arrangements

Later chapters focusing on written, oral, and visual communication suggest arrangements peculiar to those particular modes—although a creative approach is to rework a strategy that only seems to fit writing (for example) into a visual composition and vice versa.

Look also to section 3 of this book, where there are many examples of different communications: Mine those examples for arrangements you can use.

YOUR RESPONSIBILITIES

- Arrangements are not lifeless. Instead, they are social arrangements because they structure relationships between people. Arrangements arrange the pieces in a composition but they also form our needs, expectations, hopes, and desires. Take seriously the needs, expectations, hopes, and desires of those who read your writing or use what you design.

- Consider how the arrangements we examined in the preceding pages imply values, ways of seeing and feeling, and preferred ways of living. Think of the choice of arrangement as a moral choice.

- Make sure you arrange your composition so that it is accessible to everyone who may be in your audience. Consider ways of integrating multiple, alternative arrangements for complex audiences.

TO ANALYZE

- **Discuss with others:** In a small group, look through a stack of recent popular magazines. Try to identify in the advertisements any of the arrangements we've described in this chapter. Sometimes the arrangements will be in words, sometimes in photographs or drawings—and sometimes in how words and photographs play off each other.

- **Discuss with others:** With a partner, come up with a name for the arrangement strategy at work in any of the examples in chapter 14 on comics. Do you need to come up with differing strategies than we listed here?

- **Discuss with others:** How would you characterize the overall arrangement strategy of this book?

- **Write informally:** How would you characterize the overall arrangement strategy of the last paper you wrote?

strategies ○———————○ arrangement

a design plan

A DESIGN PLAN

Sometimes, as with Renee's letter on the next page, you needn't develop a long or formal design plan. When you're producing lengthy or complex texts, when you're producing texts that have important consequences for you (like a final class project on which most of your grade depends or an application to graduate school), when a teacher asks you for a sample design plan, or when (as in the example on pages 82–83) you need to produce a design plan for a client, you'll want to write a formal design plan.

A design plan lays out, on paper,

1 **your statement of purpose**

2 **a description of your overall strategies, with justifications based on your statement of purpose**

3 **your choice of medium or media, with justifications based on your statement of purpose**

4 **your ideas about arrangement, with justifications based on your statement of purpose**

5 **a description of how you'll produce the communication**

6 **a plan for testing the communication** (See pages 84–87 on testing.)

Design plans are always provisional. They help you get started and help you with a project's choices—but sometimes, when you're deep into production, a choice might seem not to be working. You won't need to start over, but you'll need to revisit and rethink your design plan. If you get stuck or confused, come back to your design plan to see if it hasn't shifted as you work more concretely with your text. If you need to fine tune your statement of purpose, as you gain a more concrete sense of audience or production, it's no big deal—and if you shift your statement of purpose, you probably need to adjust your strategies and thus your design plan.

An example: Renee's design plan—and the letter she wrote

I want to persuade a harried and reluctant dean of students that my circumstances warrant a late drop in English. I don't want her to think I'm only grade grubbing so that she turns down my request; instead, I want her to see I'm making the request because I'm serious about doing well and I learned a lot this semester about needing to manage my time.

My statement of purpose helps me see that my main strategy is to present a serious and focused ethos, to show that I am learning from my mistakes. I am going to demonstrate that I am serious by getting support from my teacher and/or adviser, and by signing up for time management and study skills workshops.

I think that a letter will be the appropriate medium (instead of an email) because it will show that I am willing to put in the time to write it, and a follow-up appointment will make the case even more. The letter needs to be respectful, but also real direct and honest because the dean is so busy.

I'm going to write the letter tonight, and then show it to my English teacher after class tomorrow to be sure I hit all the right tones and say what I need to say (this will be how I test it). I've set aside time tomorrow night to make any revisions I need—and I need to stop by the store tomorrow to pick up some good paper.

Box 3639
Calumet University
Calumet, MD 21400

November 18, 2013

Dean Gloria Meldrum
Calumet University
Calumet, MD 21400

Dear Dean Meldrum,

I know it is a busy time of the semester, so I appreciate the attention you are giving me.

I am a first-year student, finishing up my first semester. I've learned some hard lessons about time and college since I've come to the university—which is why I am asking you for a late drop in my English class (ENG 1000, section 22, taught by Professor Davidson).

I am failing English because I have been putting all my time into my Chemistry class. I want to go to medical school, and so Chemistry is very important. I know that English is important, too, but I always used to do so well in it in high school that I thought it would be easy here and that I could get caught up if I got behind. I've learned otherwise.

For next semester, I have signed up for two of the Learning Center's workshops—one on time management and one on study skills—so that I can get a better handle on doing well. I've also spoken with Professor Davidson about re-taking the English class, which he thinks is a good idea. Professor Davidson supports me in my request for a late drop, because he thinks I can do really well in the class—if I am able to be more focused and on top of the work. He has said he will call you about this, if you think that would help you make a decision about my request.

I hope you can see that I am serious about my schoolwork, and I want to have a good record for getting into medical school. I am trying to fix a bad start, so I hope you will grant my request.

I will make an appointment to see you when I drop off this letter, so that we can talk about my situation more if that would be useful.

Thank you very much for considering my request. I look forward to talking with you.

Sincerely,

Renee Saari

THINKING FURTHER ABOUT DESIGN PLANS

It may seem that we are asking you to do a lot with a design plan, but keep in mind :

- Design plans get easier as you go on. The steps become second nature, and what is most important is considering them.

- Design plans are never final. They change as you go along, and there is no way to figure out ahead of time every single detail of a project. Their purpose is to help you think richly about all the rhetorical potential available to you as you communicate with others so that what you produce will be as effective as possible. Before you start a project, try to have a design plan in which you've considered all the steps—but know that you'll modify and adjust your plan as you produce and work through the concrete details of production.

a design plan for a class project

The assignment for the project described below was to design a poster for a social issue about which the writer felt strongly.

Design Plan for a Poster

Atheists lead a life very similar to any person who believes in God. It's not until you dive deep into their thoughts and emotions that you see the difference. This difference is painful—to me, at least—and it segregates us from our Christian counterparts. Christians can say they'll see their loved ones when they die, and that their loved ones are in a better place. Atheists like me don't have this privilege, and it makes me grieve. This is what I would like to show in my poster.

Christians in the United States are my audience for this poster, and I want to increase the sympathy and understanding they have for atheists. I want them to understand that being an atheist isn't a choice but is just something that happens: I didn't try to become an atheist, but I just can't make myself believe in God—even though I'd like to have the confidence toward what happens after death as my Christian friends do.

Even though I've sometimes gotten angry at how some Christians I know yell at me or continually try to tell me what to do—even though I tell them nothing has worked—I don't think it will be useful if my poster is angry. I do want my poster to center on emotion, though: I'd like for my audience to feel compassion for atheists like me.

Because this is about emotion, I think it makes sense for me to make my poster black and white. I want the poster to be about ideas, too, so black and white are probably better for that. I want to keep it stark and strong, so that the strength of the emotion comes through.

I'm going to need some words—just a few—to make it clear to my audience what I'd like to happen. I think if I use words that address them directly, it'll help pull them in because it'll be more like I'm talking directly with them.

I have an idea for someone looking up at a church, sadly, to show the longing I feel—I hope that such a picture together with my words will evoke the emotions that will ask my audience to be understanding toward people like me.

the poster that resulted from the design plan on the right

Notice that Jacob Falk doesn't describe using the word "ATHEISM" in his design plan. Do you think the way Mr. Falk places the word in his poster supports or undermines the purposes he described in his plan?

I did not choose not to believe in God. In fact I wish I could.

ATHEISM

If you would like to help an atheist, listen and be kind.

designing for the government: a sample design plan

Several years ago, Anne (one of the designers and composers of this book) was asked to develop educational materials for the AmeriCorps National Civilian Community Corps (or NCCC), a government agency for those who want to be of service in this country.

The NCCC is a residential service program: People between 18 and 24 commit to a year of service, working on projects such as tutoring, building trails in national parks, organizing immunizations in rural communities, or helping communities rebuild after hurricanes. Corpsmembers needed to learn to use the tools for trailbuilding or the skills necessary for tutoring kindergarten children—but they also needed to learn about the contexts of their service: Why do schools in poorer communities have fewer resources than others and so stand in need of regular tutors, or how did the National Park Service come to be? Team leaders, often not much older than corpsmembers and rarely having formal teaching backgrounds, were to shape this learning with the assistance of trained education staff to fit the teams.

As Anne visited NCCC campuses, she interviewed corpsmembers, team leaders, education staff, and administrators. She gained an overall sense of the program—like the description we just gave you—but she also got to know corpsmembers and team leaders personally. She saw the conditions in which they lived and worked. She learned that there was formal time set aside each week for classroom work, and that teams often lived off campus for several weeks if (for example) they were working in a desert park several hours away to put in new trails. She saw the vans in which the teams traveled and the cafeterias in which they ate.

To develop a design plan for the educational materials she was to design, Anne first wrote out her descriptions of audience, context, and purpose, little of which she would have had if she hadn't talked directly with her audience.

- **audience**: *My audience is the team leaders who will be teaching and—through them—the corpsmembers. The team leaders are of all ages and educational backgrounds. Some are doing this work for the money, but most believe in the service goals of the NCCC (it's not as though anyone is going to get rich doing this). Team leaders have different commitments to education, but they are all smart and tough—and they have to be flexible in what they do. They're (for the most part) enthusiastic, idealistic, and energetic. The corpsmembers are similar, just younger or less experienced.*

- **context**: *The educational materials will be used all over the place. Teams might be on campus in a classroom, but they might be out camping or in a van. Sometimes teams set aside an hour or two for education, but often the education will be on the run, quick discussions.*

- **purpose**: *These materials are to help team leaders help corpsmembers think of their service broadly and think about how their service shapes our larger communities. The materials somehow have to address all the different kinds of service the teams are providing, but the materials also have to help team leaders, who might have no prior teaching experience, lead these teaching sessions.*

Here's the statement of purpose:

I want to help busy but enthusiastic and knowledgeable (in different areas) team leaders become enthusiastic shapers of experiential learning for corpsmembers—in all different kinds of contexts that do not include desks or tables.

By doing this writing, Anne could see that she couldn't just produce a binder of materials that described step-by-step things teachers could do in classrooms—although that was the image the people who hired her had (vaguely) in mind. Because her audience was constantly on the move and involved in all different kinds of work, she saw that she would have to develop very flexible—and portable—materials.

On the next page is a shortened version of the document—a design plan—that she sent to the people who hired her at the Corporation for National and Community Service.

Service-learning materials for Americorps National Civilian Community Corps

NCCC team leaders come from a wide variety of education and work backgrounds—and will be helping corpsmembers learn both the technical skills for doing their different service projects as well as the historical and geographic contexts that give meaning to their service. Teams will often be traveling and rarely in classrooms; they'll be living out of their backpacks and vans.

To help team leaders teach enthusiastically and comfortably in these circumstances, I propose that the educational materials I develop be a series of 12, small, back-pocketsized booklets (packaged together in a zip-top bag that can travel easily in a backpack) that cover a range of topics:

- *"Cycle of Questions" booklets*
  These are 4 booklets—an Introduction and then a booklet each for before, during, and after a service project—that describe a systematic questioning process team leaders and corpsmembers go through with each project, in order to help them structure and learn from their service.

- *Booklets for each of the four service areas in which the NCCC works*
  These booklets (*Education, Environment, Human Needs,* and *Public Safety*) contain resources (odd questions, videos to show, books to read) for team leaders to use on projects in the different service areas, to enhance and spark a team's learning.

- *Booklets on being an effective team leader*
  These booklets are *On Being a Team Leader, On Facilitating Service-Learning, On Asking Questions,* and *On Setting Goals & Reaching Them.*

By being separated into booklets, the materials will look less daunting than a big heavy binder. Seeing the different booklets and their topics will also help team leaders conceptualize the different areas of education they can address—and will help them see that education can be informal as well as formal, and can be relaxed, without always needing formal lesson plans.

These materials will also have colorful covers so that they are attractive. They will be written in an informal tone and use lots of informal hand-drawn clip art so that they will be friendly and inviting. Team leaders will feel that they can pick up any of the booklets at any time and flip through, picking up directions and suggestions—as the materials will also provide serious and rich educational support.

The design plan was approved, and production began. Notice that the plan describes the media—small, colorful printed booklets—and general strategies for arrangement (that the materials would be presented as booklets rather than in one big binder is an aspect of arrangement) into the various topics. The plan also describes some strategies.

The materials are shown above.

How can you tell if your piece of communication is successful?

How will you know if you achieve what you set out in your statement of purpose and design plan?

You can wait until your piece of communication is completely finished—after you've put in hours of work—and then see how your audience responds. But what if you find out that your design doesn't work, and in fact fails miserably, when it is too late to make any changes?

This is why designers use testing from the very beginning of their design process. They develop a thorough and thought-out statement of purpose, and then—before they start any production—they give the statement of purpose to their intended audience for feedback. They'll use the feedback to reshape the statement of purpose and so develop a stronger design plan. And then they'll show their design plan to their audience.

TESTING

If you involve your audience in designing your communication, you're much more likely to build a piece that the audience responds to well—and so you're much more likely to build a piece of communication that achieves your purposes.

To involve your audience in your composing processes, so that you test what you're producing in order to make it as effective as possible:

1 **Gather together people from your intended audience to go over your statement of purpose and give you feedback.**

2 **Get audience feedback to your design plan.**

3 **As you draft your project, get feedback.**

THINKING FURTHER ABOUT TESTING

WHAT TO TEST

In addition to testing your statement of purpose and your design plan, you can also test at other points of your design process:

- As you're considering a medium to use, observe how people from your audience use the medium. You'll see the patterns of use and thinking with which your audience approaches the medium. You'll also learn whether the medium is appropriate for your context and audience.

- As you're producing your communication, you can test parts of it. You can build just the first page of a website to test or ask others to read a paper's introductory paragraph. You can test the photographs you're considering for a brochure.

- You can test the whole communication. If you've done the previous testing we've described, chances are any changes suggested by testing at this stage will be minor.

Just what you test depends on the complexity and importance of what you're designing and your time. Chances are that you aren't going to have time to test a one-page response paper for a class (except to have someone else proofread). But for anything more complex, for anything on which a major grade or the reputation of a nonprofit or your job rests, be sure to make time to incorporate testing.

WHAT not TO TEST (or, rather, what not to test until last…)

You want to be sure any piece of communication is "mechanically" appropriate for its purpose, audience, and context. For a class paper, you want to be sure the paper has the expected-by-your-teacher level of grammar and mechanics. For a website for a nonprofit, you want all the links to work. But these are, really, minor things: You can ask someone else to double-check your grammar and mechanics or the links as the last test on your project, for these are qualities you can fix relatively quickly. We aren't saying that these qualities of a text aren't important, because they are: If the mechanics of a piece of communication don't function as the audience expects, this will frustrate an audience's understanding of the heart of your arguments. But you can and should test and adjust the mechanics only after everything else is in place.

When you're writing a paper or developing a website, the grammar, spelling, and links are the aspects of the communication that change most and that change up until the end; there is no point in testing or fixing them until you're sure all the other material aspects of what you produce are stable.

HOW TO TEST

How you test is as much about your attitude toward your audience as it is about the particular kinds of tests you use.

You can think of your audience as being less smart than you or as people you want to change without their realizing it. Think back to the pages on strategies in this section, where we asked you what relations you want to build with your audiences: If you denigrate your audience, you won't take their testing feedback seriously, you won't benefit from their responses, and your final composition will encourage adversarial and disrespectful relations.

On the other hand, if you think of your audience as participants in the design process then you are more likely to think of them respectfully and carefully.

Thinking of your audience as participants in the process can help you see that what you produce is always larger than just you: If your productions have effects—and have the effects you want—it's because they're able to take part in our ongoing conversations about what matters to us, in ways that show audiences they matter and are respected.

As you decide what testing strategies to use, figure out how to keep your audience participating in the process.

Kinds of tests

Remember that you need to test with several different people to avoid feedback that is idiosyncratically connected to just one person.

Observational tests

When you watch others use a piece of communication, you conduct an observational test. For example, if you've written instructions for your parents to help them text message, you'd watch to make sure they could use the instructions. When you watch them, you wouldn't speak: You'd just watch, to see if they could get by on their own. By watching, you might see where they run into trouble (if they do)—but you might also need to talk with them afterward to learn if they had any trouble.

When you observe people using more complex texts, or in more formal situations, you'll want to take notes as you observe, recording the actions people take. You'll also want to talk with them afterwards. Have prepared questions to ask, such as "Where did you get lost?" or "What parts of the communication were most helpful to you?" You might also want to give them a questionnaire, because some will write more openly than speak.

Watch for where your audience repeatedly has troubles, as well as for where they feel they moved easily through the text. Knowing what works well for them can indicate strategies you can apply to the not-yet-working parts.

Think-aloud tests

Think-alouds are observational tests with a twist: Tell those you're observing that they should speak aloud anything they think as they move through the communication. Because this is a bit odd for people, help by suggesting comments that will help you understand their responses, comments such as "I really don't understand this phrase" or "I'm looking for an index but I can't find one" or "This green looks like bad soup." But, as you suggest such comments, remind them that they should comment about anything in the text that stands out. If you are having people do a think-aloud with your writing, you can ask them to stop after each of your sentences to tell you what they understand and what they think will come next. This will help you hear whether others are catching the larger concerns of your writing, such as how you move from paragraph to paragraph or how you construct your overall argument.

Read-aloud tests

Read-aloud tests are a way to test writing, and are most useful for finding small-scale, sentence-level bumps. Have someone else read your paper while you follow along with your own printed copy. Underline or highlight any places where the reader stumbles or changes your words. Sometimes readers will correct your grammar without noticing it as they read: You need to be reading along to catch this.

How to respond to test feedback

Listening to feedback can be hard, especially when you've put a lot of time into what you're testing. The responses you collect can feel like criticism—but remind yourself that it's not criticism at all. You're not asking people to tell you whether your work is good or bad; you're instead asking whether it works in its context and how you can make it better.

How to help others in their testing

When you test the communications of others, it's of no use to the composer to say "I like this!" or "This sucks!" Instead, give a response that says "Given your purpose (which I understand to be [fill in the blank here]), I think the strengths of this piece are…. And I think this piece would be stronger if…." Give specific examples, pointing to specific parts of the plan or communication. The more detail you can give, the more helpful your responses will be, whether you're speaking or writing them. (And as you think about receiving feedback from others, imagine how much easier and more helpful it'll be to hear feedback in these ways.)

YOUR RESPONSIBILITIES

- Testing is ethical. The mere fact of testing allows you to show others that you don't presume to know everything, aren't able to see every consequence of your choices, and can't anticipate every way someone might respond to what you've made or composed. Testing shows that you trust and care about the judgment, ideas, and concerns of others.

- Remember that to test something is to ask other people how it works for them. As is the case with attending to your audience, good testing requires carefully listening—but not being so attached to your own work that you can't hear what others think.

- Testing is being responsible to yourself. Getting feedback to a draft for a class essay or a brochure for a nonprofit organization will help you produce work that makes you proud, that helps you gain more confidence, and that therefore helps you become a better, more effective communicator in general. (And if, like most people, you're nervous about giving speeches, testing parts of your speech will help you be less nervous when you really have to give it.)

TO ANALYZE

- **Write informally:** You've been asked to design a T-shirt for elementary school students that sends the message that smoking is unhealthy. Develop three different approaches for testing the effectiveness of your designs. Don't forget to consider when during the design process you'd do the testing.

- **Discuss with others:** Imagine you're producing a board game intended to help parents and their children talk relaxedly and learn—while playing—about drug use. What about this game will you need to test, to be sure it is effective?

- **Write informally:** Develop an approach for testing your own writing that helps you focus on and learn about what matters most to you in your writing.

- **Write informally:** Design testing strategies for another class you're taking, strategies that will help you see how well you are comprehending the material. Be creative: Consider multiple choice tests, but also think of how you could demonstrate your learning through a portfolio of your work, or through teaching others, or....

THINKING THROUGH PRODUCTION

- Collect examples of brochures and handouts meant to influence the behavior of people your age. For example, look at your campus or local health department for print materials meant to teach about sexual health, alcohol or drug use, or eating. Identify what you think the materials are supposed to teach, and then test the materials with their intended audience to see how effective they are. (This is using testing as a kind of research.)

  Based on what you learn from your testing, use chapters 2 and 3 to help you develop a statement of purpose and then a design plan (including a testing plan) for materials you think will work more effectively. (You needn't be constrained by a print medium: Your testing may suggest that it'll be more effective for you to produce a video or a game show type event.)

  Produce your communication.

  What in your design and development process do you think was most useful to you?

- Choose a topic that matters to you and that you'd like to teach others. Use chapters 2 and 3 to develop a design plan for producing a short piece of communication for teaching about this topic to children; then develop a design plan for teaching this topic to adults your age. How do the design plans differ? Why?

- Find a short piece—an editorial, a cartoon, a webpage—that you don't think is as effective as it could be. Use chapters 2 and 3 to develop a design plan for a revised text, paying particular attention to the statement of purpose. Re-produce the text, and test both its and the original's effectiveness with its intended audience. Write your observations about the effectiveness of your redesign: What did you learn from the redesign that might help you develop communication in the future?

- Develop a design plan (including a testing plan) for a board game intended to help parents and their children talk relaxedly and learn—while playing—about drug use. This is a complex audience situation, so carefully consider why parents and their children would want to play—and consider how your game would engage both parents and children in the playing. You'll also need to consider the complex role of drugs (including alcohol and medicinal drugs) in our lives, so you'll need to do research into this area.

  Produce the game, with the testing you planned.

  How effective is the game? What qualities make it effective—and what would you change, and why would you change it?

  What did you learn from this production that you want to remember for future productions?

researching

to support

composing

SECTION 2

8

WHAT IS IN SECTION 2:
USING RESEARCH AS A STRATEGY

FIRST, AN INTERLUDE

•

The next few pages give you background on how to think about the work of this section as well as how to generate ideas.

CHAPTER **4**

RESEARCHING FOR ARGUMENT AND ADVOCACY

•

Learn how and where to research

•

See the process of developing *an annotated bibliography*

CHAPTER **5**

ABOUT WRITTEN MODES OF COMMUNICATION

•

Learn strategies specific to writing

•

See the process of developing a design plan for drafting and producing *an academic research paper*

CHAPTER **6**

ABOUT ORAL MODES OF COMMUNICATION

•

Learn strategies specific to oral presentations

•

See the process of developing a design plan for drafting and producing *an oral academic presentation with supporting slides*

CHAPTER **7**

ABOUT VISUAL MODES OF COMMUNICATION

•

Learn strategies specific to visual texts

•

See the process of developing a design plan for drafting and producing *a photo essay*

CHAPTER **8**

ARGUMENT AND ADVOCACY

•

Learn what advocacy is and how to be an advocate—and how research supports advocacy

The next few pages together with chapter 4 ground you for the work of this section because researching is essential to the work of all the other chapters. In chapter 4, you will see a student start to research an issue; in chapters 5–8, you will see how the same research gets shaped into several different kinds of text. These chapters thus not only teach rhetorical researching and strategies particular to written, oral, and visual texts but also help you see how to apply research rhetorically.

From these chapters, you can learn procedures for producing texts; you can also use these chapters as reference to help you consider strategies you might use in producing written, oral, and visual texts.

BACKGROUND FOR THE WORK OF THIS SECTION

About design and communication

The New London Group, educators interested in making education more responsive to our lives in such fast-changing times, has recommended that those who teach literacies think of what they do as teaching design, specifically as teaching the design of social futures:

The notion of design connects powerfully to the sort of creative intelligence the best practitioners need in order to be able continually to redesign their activities in the very act of practice. It connects as well to the idea that learning and productivity are the results of the designs (the structures) of complex systems of people, environments, technology, beliefs, and texts. (20)

(The New London Group, "A Pedagogy of Multiliteracies." In *Multiliteracies: Literacy Learning and the Design of Social Futures.* Eds. Bill Cope and Mary Kalantzis. London: Routledge, 2000. Print.)

We talked in the Introduction about how we use "design" in communication. Because we see composing for others as advocating for change (whether in an attitude others have toward a new bike path or dropping all student debt), we believe that when you compose, you design different relationships people will have with each other and their worlds. When you compose, you are, that is, designing futures.

About argument, design, and communication

Arguing is a social activity. The aim of most arguing is to affect people through shaping their experience, influencing their attitudes, inviting them to consider an issue with you, or changing their minds.

Rarely, though, do we ever completely change someone's mind with an argument (and it is when we want to change people's minds completely that we most often have tooth-and-nail shouting matches). Instead, most arguments are about shifting someone's level of belief in or adherence to a position or attitude: Through argument, we most often strengthen or weaken people's beliefs or desires.

If we think of argument and communication as being about designing futures, then what argument can achieve is to give people ideas about what the future could be if their attitudes and beliefs—and hence actions—were to shift.

A NECESSARY DISTINCTION FOR HELPING YOU COMPOSE

When are you composing for yourself and when are you composing for others?
Understanding why that question matters—and understanding when you are doing
one of the actions instead of the other—will enable you to work with a clearer head
and a sharper focus and so will help you produce more effective compositions.

Composing to learn

When we wish to learn about what matters to us, we start by writing, sketching, or maybe even singing to ourselves, alone, not worrying about others. We stumble in this writing, drawing, or singing, and maybe we use quick handwriting that only we can read or pictures or phrases no one else will recognize. We wander if we write, not caring about grammar or English teachers with red pens. We make mistakes—who cares? We go down blind alleys, we find lovely expressions or neat ways to diagram an idea, we drift.

It takes writing, sketching, or singing our ideas privately to see them, to see how they connect and where they lead—and so to see if we want to adhere to the ideas and their consequences.

Composing in such ways is composing to learn.

This notion of composing to learn should matter to you if you care about communicating. Private production can live on its own—in notebooks and diaries and on scraps of paper—but it is also material that can be shaped into communication with others. There is no text in this book—our own writing and arrangements or the examples from others—that does not have its origins in jotted notes on scraps of paper or a sketch in a journal. There is no example in this book that did not start in someone's quiet, personal musing about an idea.

What you have composed in private musing, dreaming, sketching, and exploring is necessary—but it has to be shaped if others are to be able to understand it.

Composing to communicate

When you compose to communicate, you shape your ideas for others. You take the musings and ramblings from composing to learn and you create overt connections between ideas, explain your examples carefully, provide transitions between paragraphs, and make sure that illustrations or pictures will make sense to your intended audience.

In composing to communicate, you think of your ideas rhetorically, as a whole text whose parts and relations you need to arrange so that others will follow—will want to follow—and so will be able to discuss with you.

 When you compose, you move back and forth between these two attitudes.
If, while composing a research paper for class (for example), you realize that you don't have as good a hold on a major point as you thought, step back into composing to learn: Find a paper napkin on which you can sketch, or go for a walk—letting your mind run free a bit will help you find a solution, which you will then need to shape for your audience.

You cannot compose for others until you have composed for yourself and discovered your ideas.

FINDING A COMPOSING PROCESS THAT WORKS FOR YOU

Recognize that communication rarely develops in a straight line

You may be four pages into a five-page paper and think, sadly, "Nope, this isn't quite working …" and you'll need to come back to the thought-generating strategies we've described on the preceding page and elaborate upon on the next two pages. This is just how communication works: almost never in a straight line.

Every person who produces communication—writers, graphic designers, those who write the words the president speaks in formal situations—understands about the back-and-forth movements of composing. Needing to stop and find another approach is not a sign of failure or of loss of creativity, imagination, or intelligence. Instead, it is a sign that the communication matters to you and that you are producing something where all the parts fit together and work to a purpose. It is a sign that what you are producing is more likely to have the effects you desire because all the parts work.

How do you know when you're ready to move from *composing to learn* to *composing to communicate*?

When you have a statement of purpose that feels to you like a solid ground for moving forward, you are ready to start producing for the eyes (or ears) of others. When you have a statement of purpose that gives you good ground for choosing a medium or specific strategies or a particular arrangement, the chapters in Section 2 will help you find strategies and arrangements that are appropriate to your medium. Also be sure to look through the examples in section 3 for ideas about strategies and arrangements, and do collect for yourself other examples that you think do well what you want to accomplish.

The usefulness of composing to learn

Composing to learn needn't be something you do just to get started developing ideas and a statement of purpose for a big project. This kind of producing can be extremely useful in helping you study or work out other situations.

When you study for a biology exam, for example, stop every 10 or 15 minutes to jot down what you are learning. Just summarize informally the main ideas or a process you are trying to learn. This will help you see whether you indeed understand. If you are reading a book or article that flummoxes you, jot down ideas about what is going on. For example, when we (Anne and Dennis) were working on the essay chapter in this book, we came up with the rhetorical analyses we offer by jotting observations in the essay margins. Then, in not-too-careful and quick writing, we'd try to pull those observations together. When we could easily come up with three or four sentences that hung together, we knew we were on track.

When you write in a diary or journal about a struggling friendship or a dicey work situation, you are composing to learn. It may seem too organizational or scientific to put a name on something so personal, close, and emotional—but writing like this is thinking on paper.

DISCOVERING YOUR IDEAS

In previous chapters, we've offered you a framework for a rhetorical design process. We're about to fill in the framework more in section 2 by offering approaches to research and communicating research.

But (as we have been describing on the previous pages) creating communication is not a straightforward or linear process. Especially when you work on communications with complex audiences, purposes, or contexts, you may have trouble figuring out how to start; you may get stuck partway through. How do you find solutions?

Composing to learn is how you discover your ideas and their connections.

When you hit a sticking point in your work—at the beginning of figuring out a topic or at the end when you want the finest conclusion—step back into the approaches we describe on these next pages. These approaches will help you find what you need—and can also be deeply satisfying.

First: Make time for thinking

No matter the situation in which you need to produce communication, rarely can you just sit down and make the thing. Before you do anything else, set aside time to think.

Few people plan time for thinking. We plan time for buying food, for exercising, for studying, for hanging out with friends. But having a quiet time and place set aside for nothing but thinking is necessary if you are to produce communications that satisfy you and that are effective. We speak from experience here.

The amount of time you devote to percolating, composing for yourself, and just thinking depends on the project and how practiced you are in developing ideas. The more you make time to think (and the more you attend to your own processes of developing ideas in order to see which work best for you), the easier and often the quicker it becomes.

The amount of time should be proportional to the project: The bigger and/or more important the project, the more careful thinking you want to put into it. The more the project matters to you, the more you want to give it solid beginnings.

Second: Find strategies that help you think

How do you start thinking about what you need to do with a project? How do you find ideas, a purpose, and strategies? How do you figure out how one idea connects to another or what will work as the most effective introduction?

Try any (and any combination) of the following to see what works for you.

- **Freewrite**. Sit down with paper and a pen or at a computer and write about your project for 5 or 10 or 15 minutes. Do not stop, do not correct grammar, do not think about the writing—just let yourself write. The idea is to see what comes out, not to criticize it as you are going. (If you freewrite on a computer, try turning off the monitor so you can't see what you write; this will keep you from worrying about grammar or spelling and instead will keep you just generating ideas—the whole point.)

- **Brainstorm.** Write down any word or phrase that comes to mind about your project, and then write down any word or phrase that comes to mind in response to the first. Keep going as long as you can—but challenge yourself by setting a goal of 50 or 100 ideas. Brainstorming works only if you are not judgmental. Sometimes you'll come up with something that is just plain goofy or silly or dangerous and you'll know immediately that it won't work—but it may suggest something else that will work as well. So don't cut yourself off by thinking about how useless any idea is; just keep going knowing that the useless might lead to the useful. (Brainstorming is an activity that is fun and often highly productive when done in a group of two to four.)

- **Draw a picture.** Sketch out what you have in mind. Sometimes making your ideas into a picture opens up new ideas and directions. Try drawing a picture of your audience when and where they will encounter what you make. Try drawing a picture of what your audience will look like after they have read what you've made. This will help you make your audience—and your purpose—more concrete and so will help you (when you turn to it) make your statement of purpose more detailed and useful.

- **Collect photographs and pieces of words that suggest possible directions to you.** Go through old magazines or newspapers, or copy photographs off the web. (As long as you are using them just for yourself, you needn't worry about copyright infringement). Look for photographs and printed titles that suggest anything to you about your topic—or that you simply like. After you have a number, look to see what they have

(or don't) in common. The act of collecting matters because—when you see something that looks to be about your topic—you have to ask yourself how and why it connects, and so you have to define better what it is you are about. Don't stop with one object; the more photographs or phrases you collect, the more ideas you'll generate and the more potential you'll have for finding a new, interesting, and fruitful line of approach.

- **Do some preliminary research.** If you are composing a research paper, preliminary research is (obviously) absolutely necessary. We talk more about research in the coming chapter in the context of developing a research paper for a class—but to get started or to find a new direction or connection, skim sources with an open mind. Just look for ideas and possible directions: How have others approached your topic, what directions have they followed, and what do titles of articles or other materials suggest? Let yourself be led along, jumpily, waiting for something that catches your eyes and interests.

But even if you aren't composing a research paper, look for what people have made that relates to your sense of purpose. If you need to produce a text that will help draw young people to a new after-school program, see what materials you can collect or examine that have done this before: brochures, videos,

printed balloons, and so on. The more ideas you let yourself run into, the more likely one (or possibly more) will strike you as a potential direction to follow and modify.

- **Read poetry.** Sometimes looking into another genre of writing, especially one as expressive as poetry, can help you see connections and directions others have followed. Because poetry is often more emotionally full than some other types of writing and because a lot of poetry uses concrete descriptions or metaphors, looking to poetry for ideas can suggest how to make your topic concrete and real.

- **Watch a movie or listen to music with your sense of purpose in mind.** Watch any movie while trying to connect it somehow to your sense of purpose. Or listen to your favorite music while making the same effort. The action of doing this—often an amusing stretch—can lead you to odd ideas but also to new ways to connect audience and purpose or context or to some new ideas about media or arrangement.

- **Generate questions**. In chapter 4, in which we focus on research, we present a scheme for asking particular questions for developing a research focus. Use this scheme to help you spin out as many questions as you can about your purpose. In the process

DISCOVERING YOUR IDEAS, continued

of letting your mind move freely within the general guidance of the questions, you can have one of those eureka moments of discovering a direction.

- **Go walking.** The quotation to the far right is from the German-British writer W. G. Sebald, who wrote about how lives and events (both big and small) overlap in small, easy-to-miss ways. Sebald describes making finds while walking. His finds aren't random, but—because he was thinking about an issue while walking—he looked at what was around him through the frame of his thinking and his searching, and that helped him see how he could make connections between odd finds and the ideas moving in his mind. Even though walking and rambling can seem unsystematic, they feed our thinking.

We know that what we have just recommended might sound loopy—if not feeble—but what matters is finding strategies that allow you to think comfortably, widely, and without pressure about your project. Starting a project, you simply want to generate ideas, which often happens best when you are being loose and a little wacky; later you will judge and shape those ideas.

Third: Keep working toward a statement of purpose and a design plan

You've brainstormed or freewritten or drawn pictures … then what? How do you know whether you have anything useful?

Keep coming back to your sense of purpose and the audience and context for the communication you are developing; keep coming back to the medium, strategies, and arrangements you might use. Freewrite about context or find pictures of the context; brainstorm or read poetry about your purpose—then try to develop a statement of purpose and later a design plan, as we described in chapters 2 and 3 and examples of which you will see in the coming chapters.

Keep moving back and forth between the thought-encouraging strategies we've described in the previous pages and articulating a statement of purpose and a design plan. You'll know you have a useful statement of purpose and a design plan when you find yourself concretely visualizing some aspect of what you're going to produce, whether what you visualize is how your first paragraph is going to sound, the overall structure of the piece, or a particular photograph to use on a brochure.

"But then, as you walk along, you find things. I think that's the advantage of walking. It's just one of the reasons I do a lot. You find things by the wayside or you buy a brochure written by a local historian which is in a tiny little museum somewhere, and which you would never find in London. And in that you find odd details that lead you somewhere else, and so it's a form of unsystematic searching, which, of course, for an academic, is far from orthodoxy, because we're meant to do things systematically."

W. G. Sebald

researching for argument and advocacy

You do research in order to get yourself into a new position, to discover different views on a subject, or to learn about new and different possibilities for doing what needs to be done.

In chapters 2 and 3, we mentioned that as you plan your communication with others, you need to learn more about—to research—your purpose, context, audience, and the range of strategies available to you. But any time when you find yourself needing to make a decision, solve a problem, or begin a new phase in your life, you will do research: You will look for information or resources that challenge you to think, and to think critically, about your options.

In this chapter, we focus on the contexts of academic research projects—as you are asked to do in college—and on the products of such research: papers and reports, as well as photographic essays and oral presentations, as you will see in coming chapters.

The research you do in school can be as simple as performing a quick online search and checking out the results, or it can be as involved as designing and carrying out a laboratory experiment to fill a gap in existing knowledge. Often, however, classroom research contexts can seem vague—to whom are you writing, and why?—and so in this chapter, we try to make those contexts concrete and intriguing.

RESEARCH, ARGUMENT, AND ADVOCACY

Much advocacy requires research. It can be through research that you learn of the issues or organizations to which you want to devote time and energy. But anytime you decide to make change through the texts you produce—whether those texts be print, online, or spoken—you need solid support for what you advocate. You must communicate accurately about what has happened or is happening if others are to take seriously any recommendations you make. You can communicate accurately—and so you can responsibly represent others—only if you have done careful and patient research, if you have learned to the best of your abilities all that you can about a situation or issue.

Learning about a situation or issue requires more than just reading and recording what others have said and done. It requires your active engagement with others and with texts, materials, and events. You need to observe and report as well as to inquire and think critically about what you have read or observed.

It is by doing research that you come to understand how others have stood in the past—and so it is by doing research that you learn positions you can take or make in the world.

What research is

Consider "research" as "re-search": searching again. It might even be better if we had a word that meant "deep search" because when you research, you acknowledge that you do not know everything you need in a given context.

You research when you need more depth in an area. This involves studying the discoveries and conclusions of those who have worked in the area longer than you have. This also involves digging in and figuring out how something works or what has happened and where the hidden complexities are. What others have said and done starts you on an often messy journey, a journey in which you have to consider different perspectives on a situation, issue, or problem and then develop—creatively—your own interpretation and understanding.

You might think that research is only about going to the library or looking online for what others have written. That is certainly a part of research. But when you want to add depth to what you—and others—already know, your purpose should guide you: The library might be necessary, but so might an informal interview or taking photographs. When you purposefully and thoughtfully interview or take photographs to figure out or support your arguments, you are just as much researching as when you read an encyclopedia.

Research to complicate and to support argument

You ought to be able to tell from what we've written so far that the approach to research we offer seeks to help you develop arguments informed by research. Such arguments respond to what matters to others and take into consideration different possible perspectives on the situation at issue.

Your research is not aimed at supporting a position you already have; it should instead complicate what you already know by bringing what you know into dialogue with other perspectives. Research should test what you already know by helping you examine your assumptions, question your definitions, and consider what is at stake in the issue you examine.

Research is not about adding information. It is about learning and thinking critically.

The ethics of being a researcher

"Ethics" connects to "ethos" (a strategy we introduced earlier and discuss throughout this book). Both come from an Ancient Greek word meaning "dwelling." As we said, when you research, you are adding depth to what is already known—but with new knowledge you strengthen your ties to other people because knowing more changes how you dwell with others. Knowledge has effects—practical and moral—on yourself and on others.

It should be clear, then, that each step in this chapter has an ethical dimension. You need to represent others' positions accurately and to tell the truth about what you discover—and you need to consider that researching ethically means to tell the truth under difficult circumstances when others disagree. You need to respect your readers. And you need to adopt an ethical attitude as a researcher, which means being open to what the research shows you and being willing to change your position if your research does not support it. This means treating beliefs and positions like hypotheses, not like unassailable truths.

Put otherwise, research may feel like something you do alone in a dark library late at night away from the others—and that may be part of the process—but that does not mean that it is private. *Research is social action.* Through our research, we build stronger shared foundations with others and our communities.

Motivations for research

Motivations for research come from inside and outside. Are you going to the library for government documents because your supervisor asked you to write a report that requires examining the current governmental policies and laws? Or are you going to city hall to look for when and how often a piece of land has changed hands because your neighborhood community group wants to buy it for a park? Have you just discovered you like jazz music and want to learn more about where it comes from and how its sounds have changed over time—or do you have a class research project?

If the motivation to research does not feel like your own, then figure out how to get yourself excited about it. It may be enough motivation—if you are working for a grade—to aim for a good one. But you will do even better work—both for yourself and others—if you develop your own excitement. How will your research change your relations with others in the world?

Do not stop researching possible topics until you shape one that helps you learn what matters to you, that sets you up to build communications that do what you value.

TO ANALYZE

- **Write informally and then discuss:** Describe what you already know about research and list all the research you've already done—in school, at work, at home, and elsewhere.

  Combine your list with another person's list and then put the items of your lists into categories that show many different kinds of research you've done.

  Describe problems you've run into in the past doing research.

  Describe successes you've had with research.

- **Write informally:** Choose any of the examples from chapters 12–14 of opinion pieces, essays, or one of the longer comics examples. What sort of research did the people who composed the example do? How do you see their research reflected in what they produced? How does their research help persuade you (or not) to read and consider the arguments being made?

A RHETORICAL RESEARCH PROCESS

As with any process—but especially with research—the numbered steps that follow look neat on paper but are less so in reality. Sometimes you have to start over when a line of research leads you nowhere or when you simply cannot find interesting or motivating sources. Sometimes you have a purpose in mind, but when you get into the nitty-gritty of producing a text, you find that you have to change your purpose, do more research, and—maybe—even start all over again.

Modify this process to make it your own. Pay attention to the actions and ways of thinking (or productively procrastinating) that help you most in developing communications that matter.

1
Find a topic

2
Narrow your topic through initial research

3
Develop questions to guide your research

To note

- Each step of this process involves research, with the research becoming more focused as you proceed. Initially, you research just to get an idea of what's going on around a topic, but then you will be researching to deepen your sense of what's at stake and to determine what matters to you, and, finally, you will be researching to develop the evidence that supports and challenges the perspective you are developing.

- By helping you determine what matters to you, research helps you focus your purpose for any project—and it also helps you develop the strategies you need to shape your project. Research helps you develop evidence and examples, helps you determine your project's arrangement, and helps you complicate your purpose.

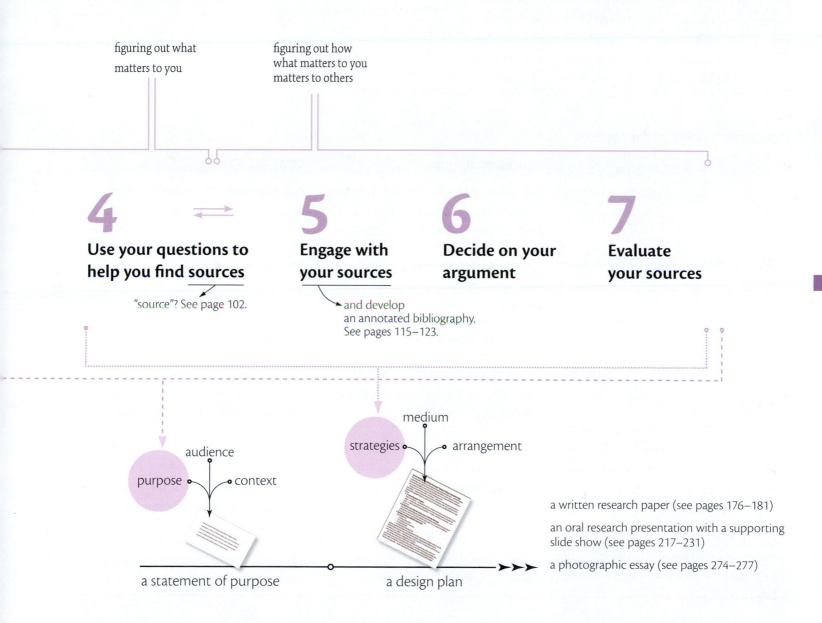

figuring out what
matters to you

figuring out how
what matters to you
matters to others

4
Use your questions to help you find sources

"source"? See page 102.

5
Engage with your sources

and develop
an annotated bibliography.
See pages 115–123.

6
Decide on your argument

7
Evaluate your sources

medium

strategies   arrangement

audience

purpose   context

a written research paper (see pages 176–181)

an oral research presentation with a supporting
slide show (see pages 217–231)

a photographic essay (see pages 274–277)

a statement of purpose   a design plan

WHAT IS A SOURCE?

A source is any text (a book, article, film, webpage, poster, video, photograph) or any person from which you draw information that you use in your own texts. Sources are useful when they help you develop and complicate your thinking and your arguments. To find the most appropriate sources to support their work, researchers need to understand the following distinction between kinds of sources:

Academic and popular sources

	ACADEMIC SOURCES	POPULAR SOURCES
Authority of writers	Authors have academic credentials: They have studied the topic in depth and know how to weigh and present different sides of the topic.	Authors are journalists or reporters, often without academic or extended study in the topic.
How these sources themselves use sources	The sources used by the writer are listed so readers can check that the sources have been used fairly.	The sources are not listed.
How topics are addressed	Topics are examined at length.	Topics are addressed briefly.
Purposes	Their purpose is to spread knowledge: These sources are usually found in libraries; they contain little or no advertising.	Their purpose is to be quickly informative or entertaining: You find these sources at newsstands and stores, and they contain advertising.
When to use	Academic sources provide the most authoritative support for academic research projects.	Popular sources provide stories and examples to use in introductions; they also can help you gain an overview of perspectives on a topic.
Examples	Academic journals (print or online), some reference works	Magazines, local and national newspapers, personal blogs

STEP 1: FIND A TOPIC

What is a topic?

A *topic* is a general area of interest, sometimes just a word or two:

- Being a parent
- Marijuana legalization
- Abstinence programs
- Terrorism
- Privacy
- The No Child Left Behind Act
- Economic policies
- Education
- Road rage
- Social networking
- The environment

A topic begins research but eventually must be more focused than any of the preceding descriptions, as we describe on the next pages. Rhetorical research requires that you find your own position on the topic while considering others—and so the next steps help you move on to determine the varying perspectives one could take on the topic you choose.

What matters to you?

The results of research matter most if you choose a topic that carries weight for you. What current issues or events impinge on your life or intrigue you? What events or situations have entangled a family member or friend? About what do you want to learn more?

Write for a few minutes, responding to the prompt, "What do I care about?" to get an initial sense of what matters to you.

What matters to others?

Your topic is probably not worth considering unless it is also of weight for others: You learn more by engaging with others, figuring out together what matters. As you consider a topic, ask yourself, "To whom does this topic also matter? What people are affected by this topic?" Talk to your classmates, family, and friends to learn their attitudes and concerns—but also imagine people beyond the circle of your familiars.

A step into research

To get a sense of a topic's value for further development, step into some quick research:

- **Talk to others.** Find out what others think about the topic, both to learn whether the topic interests them and to learn what attitudes and knowledge they have about it. This prepares you to understand what is at stake in the arguments you are just beginning to build.

- **Dip your toes online.** If you do an online search for "research paper topics," you will find webpages produced by schools and libraries that list possible research topics. If you do a Google search on the topic, you will find what general interest there is on the topic as well as what differing perspectives others take on the topic; you might also find other, related topics or suggestions of how to start narrowing your topic—as we discuss on the next pages.

FOR EXAMPLE

Ajay knows he wants to write something about education.

In this and chapters 5–8, boxes like this show how Ajay steps through the research process and uses his research to produce several different texts.

STEP 2: NARROW YOUR TOPIC THROUGH INITIAL RESEARCH

A narrowed research topic helps you focus your research and produce persuasive texts.

What kinds of research help you narrow a topic?

Using popular sources (a distinction we describe on page 102) as well as quick online searches—and searching widely—can help you learn possibilities for narrowing a topic.

FOR EXAMPLE

Ajay knows he wants to write about education and so carries out this initial research to help him narrow his topic:

Google search

On cnn.com, Ajay (who is attending a public university) finds the following: "Tuition and fees at public universities, according to the College Board, have surged almost 130% over the last 20 years—while middle class incomes have stagnated."

Reading the newspaper

An article in *The New York Times* describes how tuition at public universities in California will be raised 32% because the universities receive 50% less money from the state than they did 20 years ago. Another article in *The New York Times* describes how students who pay more tuition demand more for their money, wanting to be treated like customers.

Talking to others

In class, Ajay hears classmates complaining that—even though they are paying so much money in tuition—they are not getting As for their work. He asks them what they mean; they say that their money should be getting them good grades. He asks others about this, and learns that many of his classmates do wonder about what they get for all the money they pay.

YouTube

YouTube has a number of videos of television programs on the rising costs of college as well as videos produced by private organizations on how to budget for college—and there are also videos of students at some schools protesting about dramatic rises in tuition.

What a narrowed topic looks like

Narrowed topics usually relate a general topic (such as those listed on page 103) to specific places, times, actions, or groups of people.

Being a parent	>	The best age to become a parent now in the United States
Marijuana legalization	>	How marijuana legalization parallels the legalization of alcohol in the early 20th century in the United States
Abstinence programs	>	How abstinence programs affect the teen pregnancy rate
Terrorism	>	How the label of "terrorist" changes someone's legal status
Privacy	>	Online surveillance and the Bill of Rights
The No Child Left Behind Act	>	Effects of standardized tests on student creativity
Economic policies	>	Tax policy and income distribution in 2013
Education	>	Who benefits from an educated citizenry
Road rage	>	Connections between road rage and domestic violence
Social networking	>	How social networking shapes the abilities of first-year college students to solve interpersonal conflict
The environment	>	Relationships between invasive species and globalization

 FOR EXAMPLE

After the initial research shown opposite, Ajay could narrow his topic to:

• What students can do to affect the costs of college

• Whether students are customers

• How public education is funded in the United States and other countries

• Why tuition is going up so fast

• Whether people are getting priced out of college

• How people get the money for college

Ajay realizes that he is intrigued by what it means to think of students as customers; he has a hunch that this issue may tie in with some of his other possible narrowed topics—and so by researching "students as customers," he is hoping also to learn about broader issues of the cost of school. Importantly, though, his initial research also shows him that his topic matters to others, so he will find differing perspectives to push his thinking.

105

STEP 3: DEVELOP QUESTIONS TO GUIDE YOUR RESEARCH

Question types to guide research

People who study critical thinking have devised an organized approach to questioning; this approach is based on how courtroom lawyers have learned to focus the point they are arguing. This approach categorizes questions:

Using these question types

When you have a narrowed topic, simply brainstorm as many questions as you can on your narrowed topic, using the categories below as a guide.

questions of fact	**questions of definition**	**questions of interpretation**	**questions of consequence**	**questions of value**	**questions of policy**
What happened?	What is the thing in question?	How do we understand and make sense of what happened?	What caused what happened?	Is what is at stake good, useful, worthy of praise—or of blame?	What should we do?
Who was involved?	What is the accepted way of using the thing in question?	How are we to connect facts and definitions into a story that makes sense?	What are the effects of what happened?	What of our values are called on as we make judgments about what happened?	What rules should we make or enforce?
Where?			What might be the effects of what is proposed?		What laws should we write?
When?					

FOR EXAMPLE

After Ajay did the very initial research toward narrowing his topic, he realized he was intrigued by thinking about whether students are customers. Using the question types, he brainstorms the following questions:

questions of fact

Who thinks or writes about students as customers? When did people start thinking of students as customers?

questions of definition

What is a student? What is a customer?

questions of interpretation

If students are customers, what are they buying at the university? If students are customers, what are their professors? What motivates people to understand students as customers? If students are customers, does that mean the university is a business?

questions of consequence

What are consequences to students of thinking of themselves as customers? What are consequences for a university of thinking of its students as customers? What are the consequences of thinking of the university as a business?

questions of value

What values are implied by thinking of students as customers? What are the best ways to treat students who are *customers*? What are the best ways to treat students who are *students*?

questions of policy

What school policies should we develop if we think of students as *customers*? What school policies should we develop if we think of students as *students*?

TO ANALYZE

■ **Write and then discuss with others:**

Choose a topic for the whole class, and write as many questions as you can about it using the questions of fact, definition, interpretation, consequence, value, and policy.

Exchange your list of questions with several others in class. How many questions can you add to their lists?

After you've exchanged your list with several others, discuss how you each generated questions—and how you saw others generating questions—so you increase the range of questions you can ask.

■ **Write and then discuss with others:** Imagine studying the organization Mothers Against Drunk Driving (or another organization you know) in your economics class, your history class, and your composition class. With a partner, come up with questions about the organization using the questions of fact, definition, interpretation, consequence, value, and policy scheme we just described.

Compare your questions with others in class and decide which have the most research potential for the different classes we listed: Which seem to you like they might lead to interesting results in each of the different classes—and why?

STEP 4: USE YOUR QUESTIONS TO HELP YOU FIND SOURCES

Questions and sources, back and forth

As we implied with the research steps on pages 100–101, when you are researching, you will move back and forth between steps 4 and 5 until you can confidently state your argument.

You move back and forth because—as the two diagrams on the right indicate—you start by using your questions to find sources; then, as you engage with your sources, new ideas and questions will develop for you, and you will probably need to find still other sources for addressing your new ideas and questions.

In addition, you will probably start by turning up the sources that are easiest to find, which are usually popular sources (see page 102). Engaging with these popular sources helps you fine-tune your questions and concerns and helps you figure out how to ask increasingly sophisticated and focused questions—which will help you find and engage with academic sources.

Because they are considered more thoroughly researched and developed than popular sources, academic sources tend to provide you the most solid and dependable support for your arguments—so aim for finding a number of academic sources.

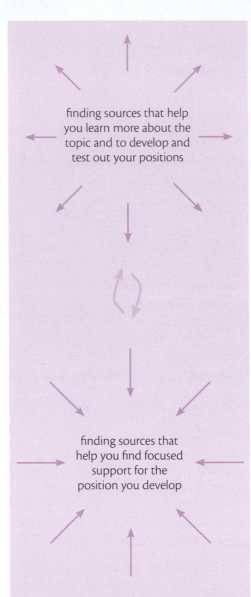

finding sources that help you learn more about the topic and to develop and test out your positions

finding sources that help you find focused support for the position you develop

Looking over your questions to see if you can start focusing your research

Sometimes doing the work of finding answers to all your questions will help you further focus your research. But sometimes just listing several questions for each of the categories listed on page 106 can help you start to sense a clearer focus for your research. How do you know?

Look for patterns in the questions or overlapping or repeated concerns. Perhaps one question seems to sum up all the others.

For example, when Ajay looks over the questions he generated (see page 107), he can see that what matters for him are issues related to thinking about students as customers:

His research will need to focus on learning the definitions of "student" and "customer"—but will also need to focus on the consequences of thinking of students as customers.

This tells Ajay that—although it will help him to find answers to all his questions in order that his thinking be as complex and informed as possible—he should work most diligently to find answers to his questions of definition, interpretation, and consequence.

Using the following chart

The categories into which your questions fit indicate the kinds of sources likely to provide the answers you need, as we show here.

On the next pages we discuss where to find these sources.

questions of fact	questions of definition	questions of interpretation	questions of consequence	questions of value	questions of policy
statistics	dictionaries	editorials	statistics	organizational mission statements	governmental decisions
"hard" news sources*	disciplinary dictionaries	opinion pieces	historical accounts	voting results	organizational policy statements
government or organizational documents		academic journals	photographs of event aftermaths	surveys and polls	business records
first-hand accounts (interviews, autobiographies)		partisan news sources	the items in the "interpretation" column	position statements	trial decisions
photographs of events		stories		the items in the "interpretation" column	academic journals
trial transcripts		artwork: films, novels, short stories			
surveys and polls		position statements			
government archives		biographies			
maps and atlases					
encyclopedias					

109

* "Hard" news stories tend to seek more factual approaches than "soft" news stores. Hard news stories ask: *What happened? Who was involved? Where and when did it happen? Why?* Soft news stories instead try to entertain.

The chart here is not all encompassing, and some may disagree over exactly where some of these sources fit or may point out types we've missed. Nonetheless, this chart can help you start finding useful sources.

STEP 4: USE YOUR QUESTIONS TO HELP YOU FIND SOURCES, continued

Where to find the sources you need?

If you just plug your questions into Google, you might find some initial answers—but without time and discernment, you are not likely to find credible sources easily or to find sources that will challenge you to develop your ideas to be most useful. (And, in fact, typing the full questions into Google or other search engines usually turns up much less useful results than carrying out a carefully crafted keyword search as we describe in our discussion of online searches on the next page.)

Keep in mind, too, that what we discuss on these pages will not address every place you can find useful sources. Sources are useful when they challenge you to think differently about your narrowed topic and when you can use them to support or complicate your arguments in your final research project. Be creative as you consider what kinds of sources you might use—and hence where to find them—so that you find the most useful ones (and encourage yourself to think actively).

Researching in the library

You probably know how to use the online catalogue at your school or local library to look for books that have something to do with your topic. But if you really want to take advantage of the library's riches, ask a reference librarian for help. Reference librarians know specific resources and strategies—and can therefore save you time while helping you find solid, useful sources. If you are shy about asking for help, keep in mind that reference librarians became reference librarians because they enjoy finding information and sharing their knowledge.

Preparing to work with a reference librarian

Your research questions set you up to get great help from reference librarians. For example, Ajay can use his sense that he needs to focus his research to ask a librarian for specific help:

- "I know I can check a regular old dictionary for definitions of 'student' and 'customer,' but can you suggest other resources where I might find more developed definitions?"

- "I'm trying to figure out some consequences for thinking of students as customers. I'm wondering what the consequences are for students and their attitudes about themselves but also for consequences if teachers and schools think of students as customers. Can you suggest academic sources that would help me learn about these consequences?"

- "I'm wondering what values are implied by thinking of students as customers—and I really don't know how to research that sort of question. I could probably use academic articles and editorials from respected newspapers to help me with this—but I'm not sure how to look. What can you suggest?"

By combining his research questions with the kind of sources that will help him answer the questions, Ajay gives his reference librarian information that will help the librarian more easily and quickly suggest—out of the wide range of sources in the library—those that will be most directly useful.

The reference librarian may point you to shelved books or journals or may help you in searching online databases of journal and magazine articles, abstracts, and newspapers. The reference librarian will help you find sources you wouldn't otherwise.

Library research to stretch your thinking

Use the library's catalog to get the names and locations of several books or magazines relating to your topic. Find the sources on the shelves, see if there is anything in them that might be useful—and then look at what is on the shelves right around them. Because library sources are organized by topic, what is on nearby shelves might be useful, too—and might be just enough off topic to suggest alternate approaches or a more fruitful direction for your questioning.

Researching online: Journal databases

If you are serious about your research and wish others to take it seriously, use online databases that give you access to scholarly journals.

When you present your research, the sources likely to be most authoritative for serious audiences come from scholarly journals for the following three reasons. First, scholarly journals contain articles by authors who have studied issues in depth. Second, before they are selected for publication, the articles are reviewed for their quality by scholars with expertise in the field. Third, articles in scholarly journals cite the sources on which they base their claims so that readers can check the sources themselves.

Most scholarly journals are now online—but although search engines such as Google or Bing may reference such journals and articles, access to them usually requires paid subscriptions. Your college library probably subscribes to services that give database access to journals. These databases sometimes give only basic bibliographic information—an article title, author name(s), date and place of publication, and journal name—and an abstract giving a brief description. Once you find this information, you have to learn whether your library has the journal on its shelves. More frequently, however, these databases provide full-text versions of journal articles and periodicals you can read online.

Learning to use databases requires patience, but the results make the patience worthwhile. Databases are convenient: Once you learn how to use them, you can get to them from wherever you have access to your library website, which for us usually means sitting at home in bed or at the kitchen table to find solid and useful articles we need for our own research.

Databases are not just for scholarly articles

Depending on the databases to which your school subscribes, they can also give you access to subscription-only newspapers and archives of academic conference presentations.

To learn how to use databases

Your teacher might set up a class session where you meet in the library so that a librarian can show you how to use databases. Such library sessions can be, um, dry, but pay attention: Once you understand the basics of databases, you can find the articles you need for producing the most interesting and useful projects.

If your class does not have a library day, ask a librarian if the library offers sessions in using its databases; most do.

Finally, as we suggested on the opposite page, most reference librarians will be happy to sit with you for a little while to help you start.

Steps in using databases

Searching databases is a lot like using Google or Bing: You need to enter your search terms. But first you have to find the searching tools for a database or set of databases.

1 *Find the database search page on your library website.* The library website's first page will usually have a link to the databases. Our library's link is titled "Search for articles"—but there are also links for "Resources by subject." If you cannot find a link, ask a librarian how to find the databases.

2 *Choose a database to search.* Many libraries help you choose databases by grouping them by subject. Don't limit yourself to the most obvious subject; try several related subjects to be sure you find a wide range of sources.

3 *Use the database's search features to find references to relevant articles.* Each database has different search features and will have a "Help" link to help you learn how to use them.

4 *Choose the references that seem the most relevant.* Your research questions help here: You know the kinds of answers you need (and that you want differing answers to the same questions), so have your questions in mind as you scan over sources.

5 *Once you decide on the most relevant references, get the articles.* If your library does not provide full-text access to a journal, ask a librarian how to get a copy of an article.

Researching online: Search engines

Search engines like Google and Bing or even library databases can look deceptively simple: Type in a word and receive thousands if not millions of results. More helpful to your research, however, are fewer, more focused results. To receive focused results:

Be specific.

Having a narrowed topic and research questions helps you find sources that specifically address your questions. Use the terms from your narrowed topic and questions for search terms.

Entering one word into a search engine is useless. Try two, three, or four words: For example, Ajay can search with "students as customers," but "students as customers university" focuses the results more usefully.

Try alternate terms.

Search using synonyms for your main terms. If you cannot think up synonyms for your main terms, use a thesaurus or ask someone else what other terms come to mind for your narrowed topic. The more terms you can use, the more likely you are to find helpful sources.

Check the search engine's help tips.

All search engines—the library's online catalog, a library database, or a general search engine like Google or Bing—have a help link or link to advanced search options. Read this information so that you can take advantage of the particular features of a search engine.

Use a familiar search engine to find sources you can then check in a more specialized search engine.

Library journal databases can have confusing interfaces; many people, including faculty, use Google (especially Google Scholar) to find a source and then check to see if it's in their library. For example, you might find through Google an academic article exactly on your topic. You can then enter into your library's journal database the journal name, author, and date to have access to a full-text version of the journal. (Similarly, some researchers use Amazon.com to find books because they can usually read some of the book and check reviews. If the book looks useful, they will then see if their library has it. This is most useful for recently published books.)

Search for visual or audio sources.

If you are searching for visual sources, both Google and Bing have options for specifying that you are searching for images or video.

If you are searching for audio sources, add "audio" or "podcast" to your search terms.

Ask for help.

Teachers, librarians, and people in your class who seem to be good at searching are usually happy to help.

Evaluate your initial online results.

When you are faced with a long list of sources onscreen at these early stages of research, use these strategies to evaluate results:

1 *Keep your research questions in mind as you scan the results.* The few lines of information about each potential source often give you just enough information to know whether the source might be useful. For example, as Ajay searches for "students as customers university," he can see quickly that many of the sites are about financial aid or the customer service offered by university offices; he need not click these.

2 *Look at the source's URL.* Is the source connected to a university (.edu) or to the government (.gov)? Does it come from a reputable newspaper or organization? Is "blogger" or "blogspot" in the URL? If you are looking for personal experiences to use as examples, blogs can be helpful; otherwise, the other sorts of sources are more likely to be credible for your audiences.

On pages 126–130, we give specific information for evaluating your sources once you have an argument and need to decide whether a source is relevant and credible for that argument.

Persist.

The more creative you are with your terms and the longer you search during this stage, the more information you will find that pushes you to weigh differing opinions. Your efforts here support you in developing the most effective and engaging research projects.

Researching in communities and neighborhoods

Your decision to research in a community or neighborhood depends on your research question. For example, were you researching the consequences of thinking of students as customers, you might want to research the relations between college students and their communities to see how students' day-to-day lives—shopping, commuting, working—shape how students think of themselves in and out of school.

Researching in communities and neighborhoods can mean researching in local government, but it often means talking with people. People who have lived in a community for a long time can tell you about the history of the community or about their perspective on the effects of past events. Almost anyone can tell you about the effects of present events or laws.

Look in chapter 6 for information on what to do to carry out helpful and respectful interviews with people.

What to look out for in communities and neighborhoods

When you move into and through a community or neighborhood for the purposes of researching, the most important thing you need to think about is how your actions affect others. The way you approach people positions them and you in specific ways: You set up a relationship of a certain kind, and you want to make sure you are paying attention to that relationship. If you walk up to someone on the street and say, "Hey, I want to study you!" (we know this is too obvious, but it makes the point), you not only come out of the blue and so potentially disorient the person but also position yourself as the one doing the studying and the person as an object of study. It might seem normal to you. It might seem normal to the other person. But it also might make that person feel weird.

Think about how you can talk with others so that they are *participants* in your research rather than distant objects of study.

In addition, be sure those you interview know exactly what your research is. Be sure that they give you permission to record their words (either through taking notes or using a recorder of some kind) as well as to use their words or any photographs or other objects that support your work.

Where to research in communities

- ❏ local archives
- ❏ local historians (some communities have people who write about the community, and some communities have people who will tell you stories they have collected—ask community members who has the best memory around)
- ❏ local newspapers
- ❏ records for local religious assemblies
- ❏ town hall and court records
- ❏ community libraries (librarians can often put you in touch with local historians)
- ❏ social and civic clubs

Researching (in) organizations

Sometimes your research questions indicate that you need to research an organization. Questions such as "How did the National Rifle Association become so powerful?" or "Why did Mothers Against Drunk Driving work to change the drinking age in 1984?" tell you that you need to learn about those specific organizations.

Most organizations now have websites where you can find information, but—nonetheless—sometimes you might need to telephone or write to an organization.

What to research about organizations

Below is a checklist of what you might need to learn about an organization in order to help yourself and your audience understand how and why the organization does its work. You may not need to look into everything, given your purpose, but it is always better to know a little too much about the organization rather than too little.

How organizations present themselves

Remember as you research organizations that most often they want others to have a positive view of them—which means that some materials may present only a positive view of the organization.

Research what others say about the organization

Given what we wrote above, keep in mind that, to get the widest possible perspective on an organization, you should also seek sources from outside the organization. Look for newspapers or magazine articles about the organization to learn what people outside the organization think of it and how accurately the organization represents itself in its own materials.

Also talk and listen to people affected by what the organization does. This will help you develop the fullest sense of how the organization works and how your audience might judge the organization.

Checklist for researching an organization

- ❑ history
- ❑ founding documents
- ❑ mission statement
- ❑ legal status
- ❑ structure
- ❑ leadership
- ❑ membership
- ❑ decision-making processes
- ❑ finances
- ❑ tax status
- ❑ promotional materials/publicity
- ❑ role in the community
- ❑ ways it is perceived by others
- ❑ adversaries and rival organizations
- ❑ affiliated organizations
- ❑ events sponsored
- ❑ projects undertaken
- ❑ past successes and failures
- ❑ vision for the future

TO ANALYZE

■ **Write and then discuss with others:** With a partner, develop a research plan for one of the research questions listed below. Plan what you would seek in the library or online for each question and what you would seek in (or about) an organization or neighborhood; also describe how you might use interviews for the research and the interview questions you would use. (As you work, modify your question as needed to help it better shape your potential research.)

- How has religious affiliation in the United States changed in the past century?

- Why did so many men move from the United States to Canada to avoid the draft during the Vietnam War?

- How is music downloading affecting musicians?

- How does one's high school education shape the careers graduates seek in later years?

- How do most families in the United States pay for their children's college education?

Compare your research plans to others': What can you learn from others to incorporate your plans?

Write a short reflection: What did you learn from this work that you would apply in any of your future research projects?

FOR EXAMPLE

Here is an abbreviated description of how Ajay searched for sources with descriptions of some of his results. On pages 118–119, we describe his initial engagement with these sources through an annotated bibliography he develops. Then on pages 176–181, 217–231, and 274–277, we show the research projects Ajay develops from his research.

Remember that on page 108 we described how Ajay, drawing on his research questions, determines that his research will need to focus on learning definitions of "student" and "customer"; he will also need to focus on the consequences of thinking of students as customers.

Using questions of definition

Ajay uses his college's library website to reference the *Oxford English Dictionary* after asking a reference librarian which dictionary would have the most authority for definitions. This dictionary defines "student" as "A person who is engaged in or addicted to study," and Ajay learns also that the word goes all the way back to the Latin *studere*, which meant "to be eager, zealous, or diligent, to study." This dictionary defines "customer" as "One who acquires ownership by long use or possession; a customary holder"—which helps Ajay realize that the word has its origins in the notion of "custom."

Using questions of consequence

As Ajay thinks about his questions of consequence and talks about them with both his teacher and a librarian, he comes to understand that his topic will be of most concern to people concerned with broad issues of education—and so he needs to seek academic books and journal articles as well as editorials and opinion pieces in newspapers that address education as a national (rather than local) issue.

Ajay uses his school library's databases to search for "student as customer" in databases in communication, education, and sociology (the librarian helps him choose those categories)—and finds many articles.

Ajay also does a Google search for "student as customer" and finds several editorials and opinion pieces in *The New York Times* and other newspapers that have a national reach. He also finds abstracts for several articles whose full text versions he finds back in the library databases; he also finds several webpages that discuss his topic.

As Ajay does an initial read of his sources, he discovers that many of his sources—in addition to addressing his questions of consequence—also address his questions of fact and value: The articles provide histories of how students came to be defined as customers and they discuss the values that drive the definition.

NOTE!

As you will see in chapters 5, 6, and 7 with Ajay's final projects, he will not reference every single source he found—and that is not at all unusual for a research project. On your way to enriching and complicating your understanding of a topic, you will need to read broadly; some sources at the beginning of research might help you find more useful sources, or your ideas might shift as you work. Researchers expect to read more sources than they reference.

STEP 5: ENGAGE WITH YOUR SOURCES

Set yourself up to read effectively

Many people think that just sitting down and reading is all it takes to learn what you need. But you can knowingly use strategies like those we describe below to help you focus, pull what you need from your sources, and be pushed to think productively and with pleasure.

Remember, too, that engaging with sources is not easy—and should not be. The pleasures of this work come from tussling with readings: Immense satisfactions arise from figuring out a source's arguments and from constructing your own responses.

Read to find answers to your questions.

To get the most out of your sources, read with a plan. You have your research questions: Use them to read for answers. Also read for what's new or provocative in a reading: What teases you to think in new or deeper directions?

Read rhetorically.

As we discuss in chapter 9, reading rhetorically asks you to ask about sources' purposes, contexts, and audiences. Ask, "With what events in the world is this writer concerned? To what events is this writer responding? With what other people does this writer engage?" In other words, your sources are not assertions about a topic; they are answers, counter-arguments, pleas, and responses to existing situations. Reading rhetorically reminds you that your project fits into and contributes to ongoing and shared concerns.

Read for opinions that differ—from yours and from each other.

Researching is learning, and learning happens only when you stretch what you know. If your sources only confirm or echo what you already know or believe, you do not learn.

And if your sources all agree with each other, you will not learn. If you cannot find sources that offer varied opinions, then you need to modify your topic.

Read actively: Annotate.

Chapters 12, 13, and 14 model approaches for annotating sources. Figuring out what to put in the margins of a source helps you think more about the source—and the act of annotating helps you remember the source's arguments. (If you are reading PDFs or docs, the software will provide some annotation tools; if you are reading webpages, have a writing application open in another window for your notes and for holding passages you wish to copy—but see page 120 for practices that help you avoid plagiarism as you copy quotations.)

Read actively: Take notes.

For each source that seems useful to you, write a short summary—even a sentence or two is more useful than nothing. If anything stands out to you in a source, record it—and if you have any questions following your reading, record them and see if you can find answers through other sources.

If you find words that you might want to quote in your project, record them—along with all the information you need to cite the source (see pages 121–123).

For every research project, make a place for keeping your notes together: Have a digital or paper folder with all your notes, or use an online reference manager such as Zotero or Mendeley.

☛ On pages 118–119, we show you how to produce an annotated bibliography, one strategy for helping you both remember and tussle with your readings.

What if a source is difficult?

Good researching often turns up difficult texts. They might be difficult because they use disciplinary vocabulary or methods or because they offer opinions we might not like. Getting used to reading difficult texts requires reading difficult texts; there are no shortcuts. Have patience, use a dictionary, use the questions on the next page to help you read, ask your teacher for help—but stay with it. Making the effort strengthens you.

Questions to ask of sources

Here we suggest questions to ask of each source so that you, thinking as a complex human, become richly tangled in your research.

What is at stake?

For each source, ask why the writer, speaker, or designer bothered: What motivated the person—both internally and externally—to produce the text? The answer not only helps you explain the composer's choices of strategies but also focuses you on the composer's purposes. Do those purposes agree with what you believe, suggest new perspectives, or indicate that you should modify your position?

How is the issue framed?

In chapter 10, discussing documentary photography, we discuss the concept of "framing": When you take a photograph, you have to decide what—out of all you see—will be in the viewfinder when you click the shutter button. Framing is not just for photography: All composers have to make decisions about what part of the world they will put in their text's frame.

For any source, then, ask, "Out of all possible attitudes or perspectives on this topic, which does this source offer—and why? What is left out? Why might the source's composer want to focus audience attentions on this and not something else?"

Framing also occurs when authors make distinctions. Authors make distinctions to offer two (or occasionally more) perspectives on a matter; then they can make judgments about the different perspectives, pointing you toward one and away from the other. Whenever you see a distinction in a source, ask what other distinctions could be made and what follows from the particular distinction in the text.

How is this source in dialogue with your other sources?

Your sources all address your narrowed topic, and your sources' authors probably discuss the opinions and ideas of others and may quote others' words directly. How do you respond?

The flattest and least useful-to-you response is simply to treat all your sources equally and to keep them separate. The paper that results from such a response simply jumps from one source to the next, describing each, and maybe offering a summary at the end.

A stronger and more useful response is to ask, "What if the author of source A really did talk to source B? And if both talked to source C?" For example, if two of your sources disagree, what can you learn from their disagreement? Or if they are almost in agreement, what can you learn from the "almost"?

Engaging with your sources' conversations will have you developing more complex and hence more useful responses.

What other possible sources does this source suggest?

Your sources will almost always cite or at least mention other sources. Do not hesitate to follow up on these possibilities: Not only is this an easy way to find sources, but also seeking out a source's sources can potentially help you find highly useful ideas and perspectives.

Does this source give you new questions?

In addition to looking for answers to your research questions, look for questions you hadn't yet figured out or known enough to ask. The more questions you have, the more details you will know … and, we promise, the stronger your own thinking and composing will be.

Does this source ask you to change your mind?

At least some of your sources should stake out positions different from yours. Obviously, you do not have to change your mind just because a source argues in a different direction than you had been heading—but do take seriously such arguments. You want to be pushed to question what you believe, and why, so that you can make the best possible case for what it is you believe and, more importantly, to learn the subtleties and complexities that underlie even what seem the simplest of topics.

117

STEP 5: ENGAGE WITH YOUR SOURCES, continued

An annotated bibliography

A *bibliography* is a list of the sources you use in a research project; an *annotated bibliography* lists those sources using the format you would in a bibliography but also includes a summary of each source—and perhaps questions and comments about each.

Annotated bibliographies help you summarize and reflect on your sources—and so are useful preparation for well-developed research projects. (They also help you keep track of your sources and provide information you might use in a paper.)

☛ See pages 121–123 for an introduction to citing your sources.

☛ See page 120 for ways to avoid plagiarism.

FOR EXAMPLE

The partial annotated bibliography on the right shows Ajay interacting with some of the sources he found.

☛ In chapters 5–8, you can see how Ajay turns his research into a paper, an oral report, a photo essay, and a slideshow to support his oral report.

Ajay Chaudry

Annotated Bibliography

Bejou, David. "Treating Students like Customers." *BizEd* Mar.–Apr. 2005: 44–47. Print. This article's author is "professor of marketing and dean of the School of Business at Virginia State University in Petersburg." He advocates that schools take up customer relations management (CRM) because it takes as a given that "While some administrators find it difficult to accept the idea of students as consumers, in reality, that's what they are. In today's competitive marketplace, schools are sellers offering courses, a degree, and a rich alumni life. Students are buyers who register for courses, apply for graduation, and make donations as alumni" (44). According to the article, most human relations go through four stages, "exploration, expansion, commitment, and dissolution" (44); the article describes how universities can apply these four stages to building long-term, profitable relations with their student-customers. (If I had not read the other sources I have, I would not have realized that nowhere in this article does the author discuss how education and learning fit into this model.)

Bousquet, Marc. *How the University Works: Higher Education and the Low-Wage Nation.* New York: New York UP. 2008. Print. This book is an investigation into the economics of higher education, giving a history of how we got to this point and how undergraduates are used as cheap labor. The purpose is to persuade tenured faculty to recognize that their interests are the same as those of other university laborers ("flexible" or "casual" labor and "contingent faculty"); rather than try to "manage" the shared problems, faculty should organize unions to "struggle in solidarity" with nontenured faculty. At stake for Bousquet in this issue is more than just equity for teachers but the independence of higher education from forces of the marketplace and from a "corporate model" of education.

Chaudry 2

Love, Kevin. "Higher Education, Pedagogy and the 'Customerisation' of Teaching and Learning." *Journal of Philosophy of Education* 42.1 (2008): 15–34. Print. This article is very philosophical, but I stayed with it. Although I do not think I understood everything—by far!—I think I got a lot out of this. I think there are two parts to Love's overall argument. First, he asks if a business model for education can cover everything about education. He mentions how ideas about what schools do shift over time and how schooling always is connected to the current economy. By asking such questions, I see him trying to be fair about business models. By asking such questions, he also sets himself up for the second part, to argue what "education" is and how we will miss the most important part of education if education follows a business model.

   Describing how a business model works, Love discusses "four fundamentals of customer service" that he thinks can help shape schooling well (19). But he does claim that the model has bad effects. It makes colleges put emphasis on student numbers, respond to students' immediate wants rather than basing education on knowledge from the past, and not provide time for reflection. He also says such a model "seems less concerned with the formation of citizens and more concerned with encouraging individuals to become consumers" (21).

   Then Love turns to asking what education should be. Here is where things got really tough for me. Love refers to a philosopher named Levinas, and a lot of the language gets a little too abstract for me. But some of it made sense, somewhat: "to be educated is to exceed oneself, to exceed the inadequacies of the oneself" (27). I am not going to claim that I get all of that, but it is neat to think that education is about "exceeding myself," stretching myself beyond what I thought was possible. My understanding seems to match another sentence: "More succinctly, to be educated is to be put in question" (27). I think Love is arguing that we need time to reflect, a sense of history, and to be challenged to be stretched. This appeals to my desire to understand how I got to where I am and why—and how I might be different.

To note about this annotated bibliography

- Each entry starts with a citation for the source being annotated. See pages 121–123 for an introduction to how these citations are formatted.

- The annotation starts immediately after the citation, *not* on a new line.

- The annotations are presented in alphabetical order according to the last names of the authors of the sources.

- The three sample annotations here show different ways that you can approach an annotation. The Bousquet annotation is the shortest, presenting a summary only. The Bejou annotation is summary supported by quotations with an ending evaluation. The Love annotation is informal and conversational in addition to providing a summary and some evaluation. If you are assigned an annotated bibliography, ask your teacher which approach to use.

STEP 5: ENGAGE WITH YOUR SOURCES, continued

Using your sources ethically: Avoiding plagiarism

What is plagiarism?

Plagiarism is using the ideas, words, or various productions of others as though they were your own without acknowledging that someone else produced them.

Plagiarism can happen inadvertently: While doing research, you might take notes or copy some text from a webpage and, in the rush to finish a paper, you lose track of where the words came from and put them straight into your paper. Plagiarism can also happen when you don't have enough confidence in your own ideas or the quality of your research to take your own positions; you let the words of others stand in for your words.

Plagiarism can also be purposeful, as when others buy an already written paper online and turn it in as their own. This happens when writers do not respect their own abilities or are too afraid to make the time and take the risks that learning requires.

WHAT words and ideas DON'T NEED TO BE CITED

- *Common and shared knowledge.* Most people will accept without question that a week has seven days or that Maryland's capital is Annapolis. To be sure whether you need to give a source, ask yourself if everyone in your audience will know. If the answer is *yes,* then you can write without citing a source. If you're unsure if what you are writing is common knowledge, find and cite a source for it.

- *Facts that are available in a wide range of sources.* If every encyclopedia or newspaper article you check states that Joan of Arc died in 1431 or that somewhere between 22 and 26 inches of snow fell in upstate New York on Monday, you can include these facts in your writing without citing any source for the facts.

- *The results of your own field research.*

WHAT words and ideas ALWAYS NEED TO BE CITED

- *Someone else's exact words* that you copied from a book, website, or interview.

- *Your paraphrase or summary of someone else's words or ideas.*

- *Facts not known or accepted by everyone in your audience.* For example, while global climate change is accepted by almost all scientists, some nonscientific audiences are still unsure. If you are writing to a nonscientific audience, provide sources for any evidence you offer that the climate is changing.

- *Photographs, charts, graphs, or illustrations.* In papers you write for school, give the source—and permission you have received from its copyright holder, if possible—for any visual object you place into writing or a webpage. Do this even if you made the object, to calm any concerns readers might have.

Tips for avoiding plagiarism

The best way to avoid plagiarism is to have integrity toward your sources and toward yourself as a researcher: Respect the words and ideas of others as you would like your own words and ideas respected.

Your work habits can help you: If you take notes carefully and record your research, you will know when you are using the words and ideas of others.

- Keep a working bibliography of all sources you might use. This will help you have at hand the information when you need it so that you can cite sources as others expect.

- If you record someone else's words because you might use them later, mark that they are someone else's words; this will help keep you from inadvertently using those words as though they were yours.

- If you copy words from a webpage into your notes, color-code the notes or put quotation marks around them; always record the information you need for citing the words.

Creating citations in MLA style

"MLA" stands for Modern Language Association, an organization that supports and represents scholars and teachers of literature, languages, and writing. The MLA has developed a style for creating citations for the sources you use in research.

As you work with MLA style citations, keep in mind the following words from the authors of the *MLA Handbook*, seventh edition:

> While it is tempting to think that every source has only one complete and correct format for its entry in a list of works cited, in truth there are often several options for recording key features of a work. ... You may need to improvise when the type of scholarly project or the publication medium of a source is not anticipated by this handbook. Be consistent in your formatting throughout your work. (129)

THE BASIC PATTERN OF MLA CITATIONS

Three elements make up any citation that goes into an annotated bibliography or a Works Cited list at the end of a research paper in the MLA style:

Author Name(s). Title of Text. Publication information.
1   2   3

Here is a sample citation for a book:

Tuchman, Gaye. *Wannabe U: Inside the Corporate University*. Chicago: Chicago UP, 2011. Print.
1   2   3

To note:

- In the MLA style, capitalize all the words in a publication title, except for articles, prepositions, and conjunctions—unless those words start the title or follow a colon.

- In the samples on this page and the next, pay close attention to punctuation and italicization of the differing elements.

- Include the medium for the publication: "Print" or "Web" are the main media, but you might need to mention another medium, depending on the sources you use.

☛ See MLA citations used in different kinds of research projects:

- a research paper, pages 176–181.

- an oral presentation with a supporting slide show, pages 217–231.

- a photo essay, pages 274–277.

On the next pages are patterns for making MLA citations for different kinds of sources ☛

STEP 5: ENGAGE WITH YOUR SOURCES, continued

MLA citations for BOOKS

> Laufer, Romain and Catherine Paradeise. *Marketing Democracy: Public Opinion and Media Formation in Democratic Societies.* Piscataway: Transaction, 1988. Print.

- The example shows how to cite a source by two authors.

- The publication information for a book generally appears on the book's title page and on the back of the title page.

MLA citations for PARTS OF BOOKS

> Noble, David. "Digital Diploma Mills." *Steal This University: The Rise of the Corporate University and the Academic Labor Movement.* Ed. Benjamin Johnson, Patrick Kavanagh, and Kevin Mattson. New York: Routledge, 2003. 33–48. Print.

- The example shows the format for a chapter from an edited collection. (An "edited collection" is a bound-together set of chapters written by different authors; the editor or editors have solicited the chapters, arranged them, and written an introduction.)

- Notice how the names of the editors follow the name of the book.

- Be sure to include the page numbers for the chapter or essay you cite.

MLA citations for ARTICLES FROM PRINT PERIODICALS (journals, magazines, or newspapers)

> Bejou, David. "Treating Students like Customers." *BizEd* Mar.–Apr. 2005: 44–47. Print.

> Lomas, Laurie. "Are Students Customers? Perceptions of Academic Staff." *Quality in Higher Education* 13.1 (2007): 31–44. Print.

- Put the name of the article in quotation marks and then put (in italics) the name of the journal from which the article comes.

- If there are volume and issue numbers, put them after the journal name as shown in the second example, followed by (in parentheses) the publication date; if no volume date is available, put the date of publication as shown in the first example.

- The page numbers of the article follow the dates; the citation ends with the medium.

MLA citations for ARTICLES FROM ONLINE SCHOLARLY JOURNALS AND DATABASES

> George, David. "Market Overreach: The Student as Customer." *Journal of Socio-Economics* 36 (2007): 965–77. *Science Direct*. Web. 10 Oct. 2011.

- Follow the exact format as for articles from print periodicals, EXCEPT: Following the page numbers, put (in italics) the name of the database you used to find the article, the medium, and the date on which you found the article. (Note the format of the date.)

MLA citations for WEBPAGES

> O'Doherty, Susan. "Succumbing to the Commercial Model of Education." *Mama PhD*. Inside Higher Ed, 5 June 2011. Web. 11 Oct. 2011.

> Reasonable Robinson. "Is a Student a Customer?" *Gullibility*. N.p., 20 Sept. 2010. Web. 21 Oct. 2011.

- The first example is for an essay written as part of an online academic periodical; the second comes from a blog.

- After the author name, put the webpage name (within quotation marks) followed by the website name (in italics)—then put the name of the publisher if there is one. In the first example, "Inside Higher Ed" is considered to be the publisher of the essay; in the second example, because there is no publisher, "N.p." follows the website name.

- After the name of the publisher, put the date that the webpage was posted or last updated; if there is no date, put "n.d." Then put the medium—"Web."—followed by the date you accessed the webpage.

GENERAL OBSERVATIONS

- Notice how, in citations that go onto a second line, the second line is indented by $\frac{1}{2}$ inch; this is standard formatting for an MLA citation.

- The book sample citation on the opposite page shows how to format a citation for two authors. For more authors, list them in the order they appear in the source, with the first author's name shown last name first; show each succeeding author's name in first name/last name order.

- For further help with citations, there are reputable online sources: Do a search for "MLA citations"—and look for university websites (websites that have ".edu" in the URL).

STEP 6: DECIDE ON YOUR ARGUMENT

Once you have read a range of sources (and—in order to get the best sense of the range of possible perspectives on your topic—you will need to read more than you will probably use in your final composition), you can help yourself by stating your argument. You cannot compose a coherent text until you have a coherent argument—and so trying to state an argument before you start composing (even though you will probably end up modifying it) helps give you concrete ground for your composition.

Trying to articulate a thesis statement is one way to decide on an argument.

What is a thesis statement?

Look at the example thesis statement on the opposite page: It summarizes the overall argument of a composition (and so is one aspect of logos at work in a composition).

A thesis statement has a very specific form that helps you see whether the parts of your overall argument make sense together.

Why write thesis statements?

Because thesis statements summarize your argument and because their form helps you see whether the parts of your argument make sense together, thesis statements help you figure out whether you have an argument and whether the argument works. Importantly, writing a thesis statement helps you see if you are engaging with others through your argument or are only repeating what you already believe.

In addition, the effort of writing a thesis statement helps you clarify your argument for yourself—and so helps you compose clearer and more focused arguments for others.

When should you write a thesis statement?

You need to have collected and read at least several different sources before attempting a thesis statement. You can write a thesis statement only if you have at least a general idea of the direction you want your argument to take; writing the thesis statement helps you know whether you even have an argument and then helps strengthen its direction.

But you should also revisit and rewrite your thesis statement as you read more sources and draft a composition: Rewriting a thesis statement helps you check that you are staying on track with your argument or can show you that your argument is shifting and needs revision.

Using a thesis statement

We've described various benefits of writing thesis statements, but you can use them to help you shape writing and other compositions:

☛ See page 149 on using a thesis statement to help figure out the logical structure of a piece of writing.

What a thesis statement doesn't do

A thesis statement helps you figure out the logical structure of your argument and can help you stay focused toward that end—but a thesis statement does not help you think about choices of ethos and pathos, or even about smaller logical choices of (for example) a title, word choice, or diction in writing. (See pages 155–157.)

Those other choices require a statement of purpose. A statement of purpose expresses your understanding of audience, purpose, and context—and so can guide your thinking about both logical and nonlogical strategies as you develop a design plan.

Keep revising your statement

As you keep finding and considering sources—and once you start composing—you may find that your thesis statement isn't as precise as you need, so revise it. But also check that you are staying focused by rewriting your thesis statement to see that it holds steady.

A thesis statement

Treating students as customers damages their education because **education requires students to take active responsibility for their learning, wait for rewards, and be challenged and uncomfortable in the process.**

The form of a thesis statement

A thesis statement is composed of two main elements (a claim and evidence) and a third element (a warrant) implied by the other two.

A CLAIM

is a statement about a condition, policy, or event that a writer believes should (or should not) come to pass. Notice how the claim is made up of two parts: (1) "Treating students as customers" and (2) "education."

EVIDENCE

states why the claim should come to pass. Notice how the evidence is made up of two parts: (1) "Education" and (2) "students to take active responsibility for their learning, wait for rewards, and be challenged and uncomfortable in the process."

A thesis statement offers a summary of the detailed evidence that would be offered in a developed argument.

125

FOR EXAMPLE

Ajay developed the thesis statement shown here based on the readings he has done.

☛ In chapters 5–8 you can see how Ajay turns this thesis statement into a paper, an oral report, a photo essay, and a slideshow to support his oral report.

A thesis statement also shows what you hope your audience will take for granted or accept easily once you write about it:

Treating students as customers does not ask them to take active responsibility for their learning, wait for rewards, or be challenged and uncomfortable in the process.

A WARRANT

is an idea or value that links the evidence to the claim. A writer believes the audience is likely to accept the warrant without much argument—and so, while the warrant is not stated explicitly in a thesis statement but is implied, the strength of the thesis statement depends on whether the audience does indeed accept the warrant. Notice how the evidence and claim each repeats a similar phrase about education; the warrant links the evidence and claim logically—by linking the parts that *aren't* repeated.

STEP 7: EVALUATE YOUR SOURCES

Sources should be both relevant and credible.

You have worked hard to narrow your topic, find sources to help you learn about it, and shape an argument—and now that you have an argument, you need to look back over your sources to check that they truly do help you build your argument. You also need to check that they will be persuasive for your particular audience.

Relevance has to do with the timeliness of a source for your topic.

Credibility has to do with whether your audience believes a source has sufficient authority for you to use it in supporting your argument.

While the criteria of relevance and credibility are equally important, use the questions shown at the right in order. Determining credibility often takes more effort than determining relevance, so you can save yourself some time by checking relevance first.

Audience?

☛ See Ajay's various statements of purpose in the coming chapters to see how he develops his sense of audience:

- research paper, pages 176–181
- oral report, pages 217–231
- photo essay, pages 274–277

Is a particular source relevant to your argument?

❑ *Is the source on topic?* This might seem too obvious a question to ask, but it isn't. You can save yourself a lot of time if you ask yourself whether each possible source really does provide information focused on your topic.

❑ *Does the source have a publication date appropriate to your research?* If you are researching a current and rapidly changing topic, you need sources dated recently; if you are researching a past event or past situations that have led to a current event, then you need sources from those time periods as well as from then until now.

❑ *Does the source bring in perspectives other than those of the sources you've already collected?* You do not want to collect sources that all take the same position, for two reasons. First, if all you can find are sources that take the same perspective, then your topic is probably not controversial or interesting enough to be worth your or your audience's time. Second, your audience is not likely to be persuaded by a composition that does not consider multiple perspectives on a topic.

❑ *Does the source provide something interesting?* Your audience wants to be intellectually engaged with your text. As you consider a new source, ask yourself if it contains ideas or information that are interesting—funny, provocative, puzzling, surprising—and that support your points. Quoting or citing such ideas or information in your writing helps you compose more engaging texts.

❑ *Does the source bring in data or other information different from your other sources?* Similar to the preceding, this question asks you to consider how much data or other information you need to construct a persuasive position.

❑ *Does the source suggest other possible directions your research could take?* We want you to stay on track in your research as much as you do, given that you have a deadline—but we also want you to stay open to the possibilities of reshaping or retouching your research and purposes as you discover potentially new and exciting approaches.

Is the kind of source credible to your audience?

❏ *Given your purposes and argument, what kinds of sources are likely to be most appealing and persuasive to your particular audience? What sources will show your audience that you have worked hard and with integrity to address the range of possible perspectives one could take?* When you are writing an academic research paper, your audience is composed of academic readers who tend to respect books published by academic presses, academic journal articles, and specialized encyclopedias. Academic audiences also respect the use of primary sources. (See page 102.)

Depending on your purposes, however, you might need to supplement such sources. For example, if you are writing about the role of women in space exploration, you might want to begin your essay with one woman's personal story about how she got into the U.S. space program; in such a case, you could look in popular periodicals or blogs for such stories—and those sources would be appropriate for your purposes.

Is a print source credible?

❏ *Who published the source?* Will your audience trust the source? If you do not know, your teacher should.

❏ *Does the author have sufficient qualifications for writing on the topic?* Most print publications tell you something about the author so that you can judge; you can also search online to learn about the author. If you cannot find an author or sponsoring agency, is that because no one wants to take responsibility?

❏ *What evidence is presented?* Is it a kind that fits the claims? What kind of evidence would be stronger?

❏ *Does the evidence seem accurate?*

❏ *Do the author's claims seem adequately supported by the offered evidence?*

❏ *Does the source try to cover all the relevant facts and opinions?* If you are at the beginning of your research, this might be hard to answer, but as you dig more deeply into your topic, you'll have a sense of the possible perspectives one can take on your topic, and you'll be able to judge how widely a source engages with the issues involved.

❏ *What is the genre of the source?* Is the source an advertisement (or does it contain advertisements)? Advertisers sometimes try to influence what is published near their advertisements to keep their appeal strong. But it also matters if the source is an opinion piece, a thought-experiment or essay, or a piece of scholarship: Writers and readers have different expectations for different genres regarding how much (unsupported) opinion is appropriate.

❏ *Does the source make its position, perspective, and biases clear?* When writers do not make their own biases clear, they often do not want readers to think about how those biases affect the writers' arguments.

❏ *Does the source make a point of seeking different perspectives?* If so, this is an indication that a writer is trying to understand a topic fully, not just giving a narrow view.

❏ *Does the writing seek to sound reasonable and thoughtful?* Inflammatory language in a piece of writing is a sign that the writer is trying to move you solely or mostly through your emotional responses without engaging your thoughtfulness.

On the next pages, we suggest questions for evaluating webpages, and we show example evaluations.

STEP 7: EVALUATE YOUR SOURCES, continued

Is an online source credible?

Use the criteria for evaluating print sources with the following additions:

❏ *Who published the source?* The domain name in the URL can indicate something about a publisher's credibility.(Example domain names are microsoft.com, whitehouse.gov, or lacorps.org.)

.gov A website created by an office of the U.S. federal government

.com A website created for a company that is seeking to publicize itself or sell products

.org A nonprofit organization—but anyone can register for the .org domain

.edu Colleges and universities

.mil U.S. military websites

.me.us A website for a U.S. state: The first two letters abbreviate the state name

.de A website created in a country other than the U.S.—but websites created outside this country can also use .com, .net, and .org

.net The most generic ending; Internet service providers (ISPs) as well as individuals can have .net websites

What websites will your audience find appropriate and credible given your purpose?

❏ *Does the author have qualifications for writing on the topic?* With some websites, you won't be able to answer this because you won't be able to determine the author either because no name is given or a pseudonym is used.

If you cannot find the name of an author or sponsoring agency, perhaps no one wants to take responsibility or someone is worried about the consequences of publishing the information. If you are writing on a controversial topic, you could use information from such a site to describe the controversy and support the fact that there is a controversy—but you couldn't use the site to offer factual support for anything else.

❏ *What evidence is offered?* In the most credible print sources, authors list the sources of their evidence; the same holds true for websites. If you cannot find the source of the evidence used, the site is not as credible as one that does list sources.

❏ *Does the source make its position, perspective, and biases clear?* Approach websites just as you approach print pages with this question—except that with websites, you can also check where links on the site take you. A website may give the appearance of holding a middle line on a position, but if the websites to which it links support only one position, then question the credibility of the original site.

❏ *What is the genre of the source?* Some online genres, such as newspapers and magazines, mimic print genres; approach them with the same questions as you would their print equivalents. But webpages can easily be made to look like any genre. For example, some websites look like the informational material you pick up in a doctor's office—and just as when you receive such material in a doctor's office, you need to look carefully: Is the website actually advertising treatments or products?

Also keep in mind that a blog is a tricky genre to use as a source. There are many well-respected blogs published by experts; if you want to cite one, you will need to give evidence why that particular blog is respected. On the other hand, if you are citing words from a blog solely to show a range of opinions on a topic, the blog's credibility will not be an issue.

❏ *How well designed is the website or webpage?* A site that looks professionally designed, is straightforward to navigate, and loads quickly suggests that its creators put time and resources into the other aspects of the site; these characteristics could also indicate that the site was published by an organization rather than an individual. Do these factors matter for your purpose and audience?

Sample source evaluation:
PRINT SOURCES

☛ We show evaluation of online sources on the next page.

George, David. "Market overreach: The student as customer." *The Journal of Socio-Economics* 36 (2007): 965–977. Print.

Kempen, Kayde. "With the State's Proposed Budget Threatening to Split the University System…" *Advance-Titan* [Oshkosh, WI] 17 Mar. 2011: A1+. Print.

Ajay is developing a research paper on the consequences of colleges and universities thinking of their students as customers. His audience is his class and his teacher.

This academic source is both RELEVANT and CREDIBLE for Ajay's audience. The article argues that, when marketing is given more weight in college education, "the role of the student in actively participating in the learning process is threatened" (965)—and so it is relevant because it helps Ajay learn and make arguments about his topic. The *Journal of Socio-Economics* is a peer-reviewed source, lists its own sources, and develops its arguments in depth—all qualities of academic sources—and so will be credible to an academic audience.

Ajay can use this source to make RELEVANT claims for his argument, but his audience will find this source NOT CREDIBLE if Ajay tries to use it to support his main arguments. This article ends with a comments about the results of making education only about money; Ajay might use these comments to show opinions about the effects of thinking of education only through an economic lens—but because this article is from a popular source, Ajay cannot use it as central in his arguments.

Nicole is writing an opinion piece for her college newspaper on relations among student success, student attitudes, and the amount of funding support her state provides her public university.

This source will be both RELEVANT and CREDIBLE for Nicole's audience and purposes. She can use the article's arguments to make connections between students feeling pressed by economic situations and their attitudes in school. She can also depend on the authority of this academic source to be persuasive to her particular audience.

Nicole can use this source to make RELEVANT and CREDIBLE arguments for her audience. Like Ajay, she can use this source to provide quotations about relations between economics and education. Because Nicole is writing an opinion piece, however, this popular source— with information about events on another campus—can provide Nicole facts and figures suitable for her context.

Sample source evaluation:
ONLINE SOURCES

 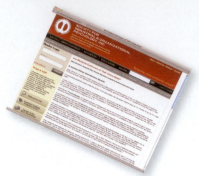

Saad, Gad. "I'll Have Large Fries, a Hamburger, a Diet Coke, and an MBA. Hold the Pickles." *Homo Consumericus.* Psychology Today, 28 Jan. 2009. Web. 21 Oct. 2011.

Schings, Stephany. "Are Students Customers of Their Universities?" *Society for Industrial and Organizational Psychology.* 2011. Web. 21 Oct. 2011.

Ajay is developing a research paper on the consequences of colleges and universities thinking of their students as customers. His audience is composed of his class and his teacher.	In this online article, the author discusses his perceptions of how thinking of students as customers has affected education in business schools—and so this article is RELEVANT to Ajay's work. But *Psychology Today* is a popular source with no evidence (in the form of supporting sources) given for the author's claims; while Ajay might use the author's perceptions as examples, this source is NOT CREDIBLE for his audience and so cannot be used as a major source for anything other than examples.	This article describes research done by industrial psychologists and the results that show how thinking of themselves as customers gets in the way of student success; this article is not in an academic source, however, because it is not peer reviewed and does not provide its readers any way to check the research being discussed. This source is therefore RELEVANT to Ajay's argument but will be NOT CREDIBLE to his audience. Ajay can use the article's examples as only the weakest of examples; he would need stronger sources to make his case.
Nicole is writing an opinion piece for her college newspaper on relations among student success, student attitudes, and the amount of funding support her state provides her public university.	This source will be both RELEVANT and CREDIBLE for Nicole's audience and purposes. While expecting logical and reasonable arguments, her popular audience does not expect the same level of source authority and evidence as an academic audience.	This source will be both RELEVANT and CREDIBLE for Nicole's audience and purposes for the same reasons as the *Psychology Today* article. But this source—because of its publication on an academic society's webpage and its references to research (even though no sources are given)—will probably carry more weight for Nicole's audience.

THINKING THROUGH PRODUCTION

■ Reflect on research practices you have used in the past. Write a short, informal paper in which you describe research practices you learned in high school or have used in other classes. What relations to other people and to thinking and academic work did your earlier practices encourage? How would you describe the ethics of your research practices?

How do your past approaches to research compare with what we recommend in this chapter? What is new, strange, or different for you in what we recommend? What makes sense to you in what we recommend—and what do you question?

■ Well . . . what did you expect here? The first suggested project has to be to start research on a topic that matters to you, using the steps we've laid out in this chapter.

With everyone in class, develop a rubric for giving feedback to each other on your research questions and on your annotated bibliographies.

Keep a journal on your process as you research. What will you do differently next time? What gave you pleasure? What didn't?

■ Use the steps in chapters 1–3 to plan and produce guidelines for high school students to help them judge the authority and credibility of websites to use in support of research.

■ At the end of chapter 8, the chapter on advocacy, there is a step-by-step description of using your communication and research abilities to assist a nonprofit organization in its work.

■ Use the steps in chapters 1–3 to plan and produce a "research scavenger hunt" that gets students into your campus library and using as broad a range of its various resources as possible.

As a class, develop a set of criteria for judging the creativity and effectiveness of the scavenger hunt.

■ On the next page are suggestions for "creative" research projects.

131

WHAT'S NEXT FOR AJAY?

a statement of purpose

purpose ● audience ● context

a design plan

strategies ● medium ● arrangement

a written research paper (see pages 176-181)

an oral research presentation with a supporting slide show (see pages 217-231)

a photographic essay (see pages 274-277)

ALTERNATIVE RESEARCH PROJECTS

In this chapter we gave you steps for producing an argumentative academic research project, one that most teachers would recognize. Here are other possible research projects:

■ *Produce an annotated visual timeline on an aspect of communication that has changed over time.* You could research how public spaces have changed over time, from the ancient Greek agora through the Roman forum and medieval and early American public squares to shopping malls; collect photographs or illustrations of these spaces (and more), and put them on paper or online with written explanations; produce an argument about how the nature of public space has changed depending on governmental, economic, or technological structures. To produce such a timeline, you would do research (with help from this chapter), produce a design plan (using chapters 1–3), and use the chapters on documentary photographs and visual communication to help you choose your illustrations and design your arrangements.

■ *Build a "museum" about a communication medium.* Choose a particular medium—brochures, postcards, newsletters, flyers, websites, magazines—and collect as many examples as you can. Build a "museum" display (which could be online) with explanatory signs: The signs should help your audience understand how you think the examples were produced—with different strategies and arrangements—to engage different kinds of audiences.

■ *Make a video about public communication practices on your campus.* Shoot video of the ways people on your campus communicate about social or political events. Out of the clips you collect, make an arrangement (with a voice-over or explanatory titles) that argues how public communication on your campus could be more effective or engaging.

■ *Demonstrate research in an unexpected medium.* Here are suggestions about how you can use research to build arguments in media where people might not expect to see arguments: Make a series of postcards from photographs you take: Use the postcards to document and build an argument about (for example) how people use clothing styles to communicate the group to which they belong. Produce a website that uses sound recordings of interviews with older and younger people in your community to argue how communication between people has changed as communication technologies change.

■ *Write a new chapter for this book by researching a kind of communication that we've not included.* Each chapter in section 3 discusses a particular kind of communication, such as posters, documentary photography, opinion pieces, and so on. Choose a kind of communication we haven't discussed (webpages for colleges, posters about movie Westerns, academic articles, billboards …), and use the chapters in section 3 as a model to produce your own chapter. Research the communication you choose, develop a design plan, and then produce a chapter that helps others learn how to analyze and produce that kind of communication.

about written modes of communication

CHAPTER 5

You've developed a statement of purpose for a project (as we describe in chapters 1–3), and you've decided that your project either needs to involve only written communication or needs writing along with other media.

This chapter focuses on helping you develop your initial ideas about writing into the appropriate and developed writing for your context and audience. We offer suggestions about writing processes here, and we offer arrangement strategies (both large and small scale) that are specifically appropriate for written texts.

We also focus in this chapter on writing academic essays because you are probably being asked to produce such texts in the class for which you are using this book— but we also discuss other kinds of writing you will encounter in different contexts.

THE PLEASURES AND CONNECTIONS OF WRITING

"You write it all, discovering it at the end of the line of words. The line of words is a fiber optic, flexible as wire; it illumines the path just before its fragile tip. You probe with it, delicate as a worm."

Annie Dillard

Annie Dillard's first nonfiction book, *A Pilgrim at Tinker's Creek*, was published when she was 29. In the book, Dillard describes how the woods and streams near where she lived in Virginia (and the animals of those woods and streams) helped her think about experience, life, pain, nature, and God. In addition to many other nonfiction books that explore those questions, she has published both poetry and fiction.

In the quoted paragraph, Dillard describes how her writing is invention and encourages invention. If you do not think of your own writing as helping you think and invent, what would you need to do to have writing help you think and invent?

Finding pleasure in writing

Anne (one of this book's composers) hates a blank page—but once she has some dependable words on a page, she loves moving them around; she delights in revising and in how written arrangement can suck people into reading. Anne likes final, finished writing best of all.

Dennis (the other composer of this book) hates moving out of reading and thinking: He generates page after page (after page) of notes and ideas because he likes where ideas lead him. But he too likes writing best when it is finished.

Writing's pleasures can come from cheering past experiences, from being caught up in an exciting project that happens to involve writing, or from having developed a feel for the sound of words. Some people learn early to love writing because they love reading or because they like to record their lives on paper; others come to writing later, when words open their pasts to understanding. Still others embrace writing intermittently, occasionally enjoying turning a stuffy memo into a joke or slipping a love note into a lunch bag. Writing's pleasures also come at different times in one's life, and at different times in the writing process itself, as we described for ourselves.

Find pleasure in writing if you want to find power in writing. Recognize that pleasure often comes in hindsight, after you have finished: There is nothing like success or a happy response from others to make a hard process pleasant and worthwhile in memory.

If you were told by a teacher earlier in your life that you can't write, don't despair—get angry. Writing can be hard, and in some contexts we do better than others—but anyone can learn to write with pleasure precisely because you can learn to write. Being a competent writer does not come with birth; it comes with practice.

In addition to all we have just described, perhaps the deepest pleasures of writing come from this: Writing makes your ideas visible to others—and to yourself. When you think through an issue or problem by writing for others, you figure out where you stand: You are, in effect, producing the position you take. You are not taking that position whole cloth from elsewhere but instead reworking others' ideas and opinions into what makes sense to you. You are creating yourself into relations with others, producing positions you've wrestled into shape.

When you have a finished and polished piece of writing, you get the pleasure of completion. But you also get to see yourself constructed in the writing; you get to decide whether you respect that person and that person's relation with the world.

How writing grows out of and in response to and sustains other writing

Good writing requires good reading because writing grows out of and responds to other writing. Nearly every example of writing in this book and elsewhere testifies to this. Look at the *Declaration of Independence*, for example. In the *Declaration*, Thomas Jefferson used the phrase "life, liberty, and the pursuit of happiness"—but he borrowed (today we would say "sampled") the phrase from the British philosopher John Locke, who in his own political writing had used the phrase "life, liberty, and the pursuit of property." Jefferson didn't mention Locke in the *Declaration of Independence* because he assumed anyone reading the document would recognize the words' origin. Over two hundred years later, Sarah Vowell (in an essay we reprint in chapter 8) quotes her favorite passage from the *Declaration of Independence*, including "life, liberty, and the pursuit of happiness," to show that Jefferson's writing in the *Declaration* is strong and beautiful—and that it resonates for us still. From Locke, to Jefferson, to Vowell, writing grows, responds, and sustains other writing.

Even what seems like everyday, unimportant writing—a letter sent home or a text to a friend—has its roots in other people's writing. Your letter sent home may have been occasioned by a letter received from home, but if not, the mere fact that it is a letter means it has ties to the history of letter writing and to letter writing as a genre. You know how to write a letter, email, or text because you have already seen and read many examples.

It might feel weird to describe such situations this way, but as you write a letter to your parents or a text to a friend, your hand is being guided invisibly by a multitude of hands extending back thousands of years across hundreds of cultures—all ghosts writing to each other, establishing the conventions that help us understand each other. To be familiar with a written genre like letter writing or text messaging means that we have built into our minds expectations about what a letter or text should look and sound like, based on past experience with the genre. And as you write, you add to, shift, and change the ways letters—or essays, texts, emails, or comics—are written, sustaining for others these ways of sharing.

> When one is writing, one is literally *writing into* and *writing from*, and those poles of *writing into* and *writing from*—inscribing and re-inscribing—situate the writer in a kind of interpretive and performative moment that allows the writer to be the mediator, to mediate between these two poles of invention.
>
> *Eric Michael Dyson*

In an article in the *Journal of Blacks in Higher Education*, Michael Fletcher described Eric Michael Dyson as "a Princeton Ph.D. and a child of the streets who takes pains never to separate the two" and as a "scholar and a hip-hop preacher." An ordained Baptist preacher, Dyson has published many books and has a radio show. Dyson's words quoted here describe his perspective on how his own writing comes out of earlier writing.

Why might Dyson think about writing this way—and how does this differ from, reinforce, or shift your sense of your own writing? If you would like your writing to engage you more deeply in our shared cultural past—and present—what do you need to do?

WRITING'S PURPOSES, AUDIENCES, AND CONTEXTS

"It is no less difficult to write a sentence in a recipe than sentences in Moby Dick. So you might as well write Moby Dick. "

Annie Dillard

Writing's purposes

Any writing has different and complexly inter-related purposes. For example, in a research paper, you may want to provide a large amount of information on a subject—but at the same time you want your audience to absorb that information *and* to finish reading invigorated and ready to think, see, feel, and act in new, perhaps unexpected ways.

Given the histories of writing in our culture and the resulting cultural expectations about what writing can do, purposes effectively addressed by writing can involve:

- Making our ideas visible to ourselves and others.

- Passing along large amounts of information.

- Providing detailed and emotion-full descriptions of people, scenes, objects, or events (fictional or non-).

- Interpreting through words otherwise complex visual messages (graphs, for instance) whose main point is not immediately clear.

- Making complex arguments while answering possible objections.

- Trying out new ideas to see where they might lead you. Ruminating. Musing.

The preceding list gives general purposes. Your actual purposes for any piece of writing (while perhaps fitting under one or more of the items listed) must have a greater specificity if you are to produce effective writing. If you need to pass along a large amount of information, for example, *why do you need to pass along the particular information, and to whom? What change should the new information offer its audience? How should the audience feel about the information? What are you trying to **do** by passing along the information?* The answers to these questions point to what is particular about your context and audience and so to what makes your purposes particular and challenging for you.

Finally, sometimes—especially these days when there are so many media among which you can choose—people who are thinking about writing a text have to ask themselves if what they are trying to accomplish can best be accomplished through writing or through other media. *Does your purpose require a shift in media from writing and toward composing in another mode (that might still require some writing)?*

As you work, then, attend to how your approach is supported by writing—and, as with all communication, continually ask how you can modify and experiment in order to build communication that reaches out to others and fulfills your purposes.

Writing's audiences

From a writer's perspective, a reader is an abstraction, a ghostlike presence hovering around while the writer writes. The reader to whom writers write is all-important—and yet writers rarely meet many or any readers.

It thus requires **imagination** to "see" your audience and it requires **practice** to see what is relevant about your audience to your writing task. The same holds true when you plan a talk, but when you give a talk you do eventually come face to face with your audience.

In the last 50 years, some theorists have made much of writing's odd independence from the time of reading: Once words are on paper, they can pass from hand to hand, so that writers struggle to imagine who the reader really will be. For some writers, this becomes a reason not to think at all about readers: Why worry about what you can't control? But we wouldn't have written this book if we didn't think effective writing comes out of trying to connect with and understand audiences—even though we believe that it is difficult to connect with and understand audiences. Not only do we never get to know others completely, but also tricky obstacles stand in our way, preventing us from hearing one another, or—if we hear—tricking us into thinking we understand someone when we really don't. And so we offer this rule of thumb for approaching other people: *If you feel comfortable that you understand others, beware.* And yet … keep listening, keep trying to hear, keep trying to understand. Productive communication is built not on any certain knowledge of who others are or what matters to them and why; productive communication is instead built on the sincere effort to figure out who others are and what matters to them and why.

And if readers are always hard for writers to know, the reverse holds true for readers: For a reader, an author also is a ghostly presence, a voice half heard behind the silently read words. The reader reaches out imaginatively to the writer similarly to how the writer reaches out to the reader. Again, this could become a cause to give up on ever understanding each another—but, in spite of that, we still think it is important for readers to try to understand (based on the many clues that a writer's strategies tell us) what the writer's purpose is. This is why we stress "rhetorical analysis." Rhetorical analysis (see chapter 9) is a way of searching for what the author/speaker/designer/composer is trying to do with a particular piece of communication (work we do while admitting the difficulties involved). By doing such analysis, you learn more about others' texts but you also strengthen your sense of how you, as a writer, can reach through your words to the audiences you engage.

So talk with potential audience members before, while, and after you write, testing your ideas and how they take shape in the words you do finally place on a page. You will never know your audiences completely or perfectly, and you will have to imagine them when it is just you and the keyboard or pen trying to make words—but it is those acts of imagination and practice (informed by discussion, listening, and respecting) that will best help you make decisions about what words to use.

Writing's contexts

Writing's contexts are strange compared to those of speaking. Speakers imagine standing before others—and then they really do later stand there. Writers can imagine a reader—but then never (or hardly ever) get to watch that other person quietly read. Put otherwise, the act of speaking to an audience unites production and delivery; the act of writing does not. Long stretches of time and many miles can separate your writing from its being read. Sometimes you'll know the context in which your writing is received (you can picture your mother reading your letter in her favorite chair), but most times you have to imagine a reader in some specific time and place.

But you also have to imagine more than that to avoid oversimplifying context. What (you need to ask) has happened in readers' lives, communities, or the world such that what you write matters to your readers? What specifically has agitated or intrigued your readers so that your writing matters?

Given what we have written, these approaches might help you think about context:

- Imagine the best possible place and time for a reader to read your words. Picture a lounge chair on a sunny vacation beach overarched by palm trees—or a rocking chair, cat, and cocoa in front of a glowing fireplace with a light snow out the dark windows. These contexts might give you a sense of a gentle, responsive reader.

- Imagine also the harder contexts, the after-work clang of subway cars, the cramped dorm rooms and blasting music of 2 a.m., or your teacher's dining room table covered with the 20 or 35 other papers to be read and responded to by tomorrow. These contexts give you a sense of the distraction and worries with which readers sometimes read.

- Imagine too, finally, the disconnect between the imagined beach (or subway) and specific and real recent or impending events such as a war, an economic drop, or a natural disaster. Such events always circle around us to inform what we write and why readers want to read—and how they read. Such background contexts do not consume the more immediate contexts of actual reading, but they *are* present. Consider what larger events shape our shared moods so you might reach readers through their worries or hopes.

We discuss these contexts not to befuddle but to encourage you: Address your readers as people whose hearts and minds are shaped by where they are bodily, emotionally, and mentally, and consider how your words shape the contexts of their reading. You can shape your words to slow down (or speed up) time to help the subway rider imagine a more comforting ride and life.

TO ANALYZE

- **Write, then interview, and then write with others:** List all your uses of writing in a day. Consider formal as well as informal writing, personal and official writing, paper and online writing: Any time you put words onto a page or screen, note it.

Interview at least three people with different jobs about the kinds of writing they do at work as well as at home. Try to interview one person who makes his or her living from writing.

With two others in class, combine all your lists to make three new ones: From your master list, pull out the purposes, audiences, and contexts in which writing happens.

Reflect on your list gathering in a short piece of informal writing: *Was there anything about writing and writing lives that surprised you? What does your list gathering help you learn about the writing that you will probably need to do in the years ahead?*

A STATEMENT OF PURPOSE FOR WRITING

Before you can think with any confidence about, much less decide on, the strategies you will use in writing, you need to know why you are writing and for whom: You need to have a clear sense of your purpose, audience, and context, as we have just discussed on the previous pages.

Remember from chapter 2 that a statement of purpose unites your sense of purpose with your thoughts about audience in the contexts in which you will communicate. Such a statement of purpose therefore supports you in making choices about your writing.

Writing a statement of purpose starts organizing your thinking. Because a statement of purpose is meant to move you toward other more formal writing, it needn't itself be particularly polished; it justs needs to be thinking that links purpose, context, and audience.

When you work on a research paper, some of your purpose is encapsulated in your thesis statement (as you can see from Ajay's statement of purpose on the right); a statement of purpose encourages you to think about your wider purposes in writing (as you can also see from Ajay's statement of purpose).

As you read the following pages about the strategies particular to writing, keep Ajay's statement of purpose in mind. If you were Ajay, what strategies would you shape out of this chapter's suggestions?

Statement of Purpose

For this research paper, my audience is everyone else in class and my teacher. My purpose is to persuade them that thinking of students as customers damages our education—but I also need to show that I can do a good research paper with an order that makes sense, with citations in the MLA style, and that ISN'T BORING. So—how do I make "thinking of students as customers is bad" interesting? How do I get others to care? I would like for my classmates to stop and think about how their actions and attitudes in class affect how we learn and how our teacher treats us—and so I want to persuade them that even simple actions and attitudes can have big consequences (my sources persuaded me). Everyone else will be reading this in class, but my teacher will be reading this in his home or his office (at the same time he is reading the other papers). When I think about these contexts, I think how everyone is already kind of bored by the old classroom where we meet—so can I do something to make them look around a little bit and think about how where we learn is tied into this?

139

FOR EXAMPLE

Now that Ajay has done the bulk of his research,* he is prepared to write a statement of purpose—as you can see here.

* Keep in mind that you may discover, once you dig into writing, that you need to find new or additional sources.

☛ See Ajay's design plan on pages 162–163.

ETHOS, LOGOS, AND PATHOS AS WRITING STRATEGIES

Each mode and medium has its own distinctive ways of embodying ethos, logos, and pathos as strategies to accomplish a purpose. Because writing is essentially about the arrangement of words, and words only, the richness and complexity of writing can be surprising: How many ways there are to establish relations with a reader, to structure an argument, and to influence the tight braid of emotion and judgment in which we all live!

The main point we make in this chapter about ethos in writing is that, as with speaking and visual communication, how you come across in writing is through the myriad of choices you make and how they reflect on you. Unlike speaking, though, writing cannot shape ethos through your physical presence— the gestures, tone of voice, manner of dress, way of carrying yourself. Ethos in writing relies on a more restricted range of choices. But that said, it always amazes us how numerous and complex is that range.

The main point we make in this chapter about logos in writing is that it spreads across writing in three ways: In the overarching arrangement of writing, in smaller pieces of discrete argument that fit together to make the whole, and in the little patterns of words and phrases that shape individual sentences and phrases.

The main point we make in this chapter about pathos in writing is that it is always there, even—or especially—when a writer is trying to hide or avoid it. Writing can seem less emotional than spoken or visual communication because it is simply abstract shapes on a page. And in the cultures that have developed out of western Europe (like that of the United States), we have a tradition of treating writing as the most objective, formal, rational, controlled, accessible, reliable, durable, explicit, and honest mode of communication. But writing is always shaped by emotions of one kind or another, always shaped by an individual or group with particular understandings of our world. Like speaking and visual communication, writing can convey only a limited range of emotions to others because it cannot possibly detail the full experiences of breathing, smelling, moving, swimming, singing, or being on the street. (And it's not as though we ourselves can ever attend to every sense and action around us even when we're not trying to communicate about it with others.)

It is worth questioning, then, always, what attitudes writing asks us to take toward emotion: How do writers evoke and so teach us about particular emotions, and how do they avoid or try to suppress it?

TO ANALYZE

- **Discuss with others:** When have you been persuaded by a piece of writing (including writing in advertisements, flyers, or brochures)? When has a piece of writing encouraged you to rethink your perspective on an issue or dig more deeply into thinking? When have you been persuaded to purchase (or at least to consider purchasing) something because of reading?

Given the times you've been persuaded, what strategies in the writing—ethos, logos, or pathos—seem to you in hindsight to have tipped you most toward being persuaded? Has it depended on how those strategies interact with the overall purpose of the piece? Has it depended on your age or who was around you when you were reading?

What do these questions suggest to you about how ethos, logos, and pathos do their work—alone and together?

Finally, consider how you *want* to be persuaded. Would you prefer to be persuaded by ethos, pathos, or logos? Why?

ETHOS IN WRITING

In chapter 3, we introduced you to ethos: Ethos is "the face you put on" for your audience. You already know—simply from living with others (and perhaps without thinking much about it)—how to shape yourself, your clothing, your actions, and your words so that you fit into Friday night's party, Sunday's church bench, Monday's classroom, or Wednesday afternoon's job. In each context, you speak a little differently—just as you do when you address your mother, your minister, a childhood friend, or a child. And in addition to modifying how you behave depending on your contexts and audiences, you modify yourself based on your purposes. A challenge when you write is to translate this knowledge of "real-world" strategies like clothing and tone of voice into words on a page or screen.

As with living day-to-day with others, you undoubtedly already often do this work when you write. Without too much thinking, you choose different ways to present yourself when you chat online, when you fill out job applications, and when you compose research papers.

If you study the writing of others, however, looking for how they construct themselves through words, you can expand your repertoire of strategies for engaging with others through how you—as a writer—come through. In chapters 12 and 13, we analyze the range of strategies writers can use to build an ethos.

Questions for seeing ethos

- What does the title suggest about the author and the relationship (friendly, distant, lecturing, seductive…) the author wants to build with readers?

- What do the words that begin the writing sound like and suggest about the author and how the author thinks about readers?

- What does the first sentence tell a reader about the writer? Is it a short, catchy sentence or a short, assertive sentence? Is it a long sentence that sounds accusatory or that sounds thoughtful and reflective?

- What does the structure of the opening paragraph suggest about the writer? Does the writer begin with a personal story or a list of facts? Does the paragraph move from sounding provocative to sounding conservative? Does the writer say outright what the writing is about or instead stay coy?

These questions get you started; modify them for later sentences and paragraphs (and check the questions we raise in chapters 12 and 13 about ethos for each piece of writing). Always tie your observations to this question: **What overall sense does this writing give me of this author—and why (given the contexts, audience, and purposes of the piece) would the writer construct this ethos?**

TO ANALYZE

- **Write with others:** In small groups, produce two different short letters to your college president concerning an issue of concern on your campus. (For example, perhaps your campus could use a walkway over a busy, dangerous street running through campus, or perhaps your campus has issues related to sports, tuition raises, or a proposed program.) In each of the two letters you produce, make your ethos the most important part of the letter because you are someone directly affected by the issue. In one letter, be playful, the epitome of the partying student; in the other letter, write as the student who is pale from library work. Do not be afraid to exaggerate your ethos in these letters; you want to experiment with stretching ethos to the limits in order to see the results. Share the letters with others, and ask what they think of the character written into the letters.

ETHOS IN WRITTEN INTRODUCTIONS

Ethos carries particular weight in the introductions of written pieces, just as logos (as you will see) does in the body of a piece of writing and pathos in conclusions. Of course, the three strategies are at work throughout every word, sentence, and paragraph of any writing, but they have a special emphasis in the parts mentioned.

Introductions are where readers and writers meet for the first time. Who you are as a writer and how you come across stand out as especially significant and worthy of attention when meeting and greeting—as with all first impressions.

Strategies for introductions

Stories

Cornel West, an African American philosopher, uses a story to start his book *Race Matters* (which argues that race matters in our country still). West tells us about a day he finished his work at Princeton University where he then taught. Princeton is in New Jersey, relatively close to Manhattan, so he and his wife drove together to Manhattan for appointments they each had. He took her to her appointment, parked their car in a lot, and tried to get a taxi to his appointment. His appointment was with a photographer who was shooting the cover of *Race Matters*, and so he was dressed in a nice suit (we can turn the book over and look at him

on the cover smiling in his suit, which adds to the effect of his story). He then tells us that he stood on a busy street where he knew there would be many taxis, and he watched as empty taxi after empty taxi passed by, refusing to pick him up. The tenth taxi stopped instead for (as he describes her) a "well-dressed smiling female fellow citizen of European descent." Stepping into the taxi, she said to him, "This is really ridiculous, is it not?" He finally had to take the subway and was late to his appointment, but he chose not to mention all this to the photographer because he did not want to dwell on it, preferring instead to have an enjoyable time. The fact that he did not dwell on it did not mean he was not angry. As we learn, this is not the first time this has happened to him: This is a regular occurrence for black men on streets in the United States.

This is one way to begin a piece of writing—with a story. In this case, the story is mostly about West himself. How do you imagine it sets up the subject of his book, *Race Matters*? How does it set West up to address his subject? What relations does he establish with his readers?

Quotations

We started this chapter with a quotation from Annie Dillard because she likes to write about writing and does so (we think) in lively detail. Our quotation use is thus a version of show-and-tell, showing our position on writing

through using the words of someone else, and so allowing us—and our ethos—to emerge from her authority.

An immediate turn to the writing's subject

Gary Smith's essay in chapter 13 begins, "This is a story about a man, and a place where magic happened." Smith turns our attentions away from himself (the essay is not about him, after all) and instead to his topic—but we get a sense of a writer who thinks he has something intriguing to tell us, who wants to engage us in this story. So even though he never uses "I" in this essay and starts right away directing our attentions elsewhere, we have an immediate sense of some qualities attached to this writer, qualities that shape our sense of how we trust him and respond to his words.

Clarissa Sligh's essay in chapter 13 begins, "I was a teenager when I first saw this group of photographs and the article that they appeared with, on June 1, 1956, in the *Washington Post and Times Herald*, the major daily newspaper in the Washington D.C. area." Opposite these words are the photographs she discusses; her words tell us where she lived and that she is looking back on her past. All those details, combined with the generally unemotional tone of the words, indicate that personal reflection is at work here—and personal reflection is often quiet and slow. But at the same time Sligh's words indicate that events larger than the personal are at work through her mention of a major newspaper. With one opening sentence, Sligh has immediately pulled us into a major thread of her essay—how personal and public lives entwine—and given us a sense of an ethos that is thoughtfully in between, thinking things through.

Other strategies for beginning

- *Open with a question.* Questions engage readers—but they can also help you pull readers immediately into your concerns while establishing you as someone who wants to engage readers. (Look at the editorial "Violence vs. Sex" or the opinion piece "Games People Play" in chapter 12.)

- *Fill in background knowledge readers need to understand what is to come.* (Many of the editorials and opinion pieces in chapter 12 do this.)

- *Give readers an image that will stick with them.* ("How to Look at the Periodic Table" in chapter 13 does this—but also look at the editorial "Court Majority Was Right" in chapter 12.)

How not to begin

One way, generally, not to start a piece of writing is with what writing teachers call the "In the beginning" start. Every teacher of writing has received a class assignment that begins, "In the beginning, humans invented fire …" or "From the dawn of time, people have always worn shoes. …" The paper could be arguing against gun control or for expanding the U.S. connection with the UN, but whoever wrote it clearly had trouble finding an opening to the argument. If you ever find yourself tempted to begin in this way, step back and ask yourself if this kind of beginning really is appropriate to your purpose. If not, go over the list of possibilities here for inspiration or read other writers. Take a look at the section on revision later in this chapter: Perhaps you are having trouble beginning because you still need to figure out your purpose or figure it out better.

TO ANALYZE

- **Discuss:** With a partner, compare the introductions of the editorials and opinion pieces in chapter 13. Describe how each author comes across: Does the author seem authoritative and distant, trying to be pals with the readers, or …? How old would you say each writer is, and how dressed? What sort of temperament do you think each writer has? As you discuss each question, point to what words or other features shape your response.

  Although we ask you here to describe writers more than you probably usually do, it's likely that you develop such senses of writers unconsciously any time you read. By articulating your sense of a writer and how that sense develops, you can gain more abilities to shape your own ethos in writing.

- **Write with others:** With a partner, rewrite the introduction to "How to Look at the Periodic Table" (in chapter 13). Rewrite it as though you were angry that most people don't know about the periodic table variations shown in the essay; also rewrite it as though you were bored with the whole topic. It's fine to exaggerate. Finally, rewrite the introduction as though the essay were aimed at 12-year-olds. What strategies did you use, and how might you use them in the future?

TO ANALYZE: ETHOS IN WRITTEN INTRODUCTIONS

■ **Discuss and write with others:** On the right are introductions to research papers written by students like you. With a partner, discuss the introductions, using the following questions to guide you:

- Which introductions do you like best and why?

- Describe the ethos that the writer is starting to develop in each introduction. Does the ethos seem trustworthy, knowledgeable, interesting, or…? How does each writer construct the ethos you describe? What word choices, tone of address, and examples help build the ethos you describe?

- What different relationships do these writers establish with you, their readers? Do you feel respected, trusted, hectored, or…?

- What do you expect the paper following the introduction to be about?

Based on your observations, list the characteristics of effective written introductions.

Customers listlessly drift through the fluorescent-lit aisles of any well-populated department store, pausing to contemplate whether or not their need for the latest television technology is greater than their need for the latest stainless steel kitchen appliance or celebrity fragrance. Smiling, interested faces can be seen all around, as people shop and blissfully choose the most fulfilling expenditures for their hard-earned currency. In the background, a smooth cocktail-jazz rendition of Nirvana's seminal "Rape Me" goes mostly unnoticed much in the way that Americans can just tune out television commercials. And even as they make their way toward the checkout lanes, a war is being quietly waged through the spacious, aesthetically pleasing expanses of the store. A war fought for control of customers' thoughts, moods, and behaviors. This war is a subtle, almost silent conflict between the subconscious minds of the shoppers and that inoffensive Nirvana song, which has been carefully chosen to shape shoppers' attitudes.

"The long arm of the law" is a clichéd and widely known phrase, but very representative of the reach of the law into our lives. The law tells you how fast to drive, when you can drink, how much you have to pay the government, and whom you can marry: The law impacts almost every aspect of your life. When the law has such a long arm it may become brittle and prone to breaking. In fact, there is such a major fracture, and it's called the Tort System.

There are many women who work as firefighters, law enforcement professionals, and soldiers and who protect our country every day. I would like to show that these women are necessary for the everyday functions and protection of our country. Some women may feel that they would like to pursue these occupations, but that they are not capable or would not be accepted in doing these jobs. Although the world is more accepting today than it was in the past, there is still the mindset that women might not be as able as men to perform these kinds of jobs. I hope to show, through facts and examples, why women should be encouraged to reach for their dreams if they are looking to become firefighters, police officers, or military professionals.

Ray guns. Rocket ships. Household robots, a family vacation to the moon, and an alien standing behind you in line to see the latest *Star Wars* movie. Everyone remembers that old "retro" vision of the future, from watching old episodes of *Star Trek* or *The Jetsons*, or newer parodies like *Futurama* on Cartoon Network. A few decades back, when Neil Armstrong had just taken that "one small step" into the future and it seemed that science and technology could produce new wonders every day, the idea of entering a "Space Age" world didn't seem all that unreasonable. But now, in today's world, we can laugh at Fry and Bender and their bizarre adventures, and think how silly all those old visions were....

So what happened? How could this futuristic vision, ridiculous as it may have been, simply vanish despite the spectacular achievements that inspired them?

The year is 1983 and you are hanging out with some hometown buddies having a good time. Being an eighteen-year-old is fun, right? You are basically able to do whatever you want now that you're an adult. Sure, you have responsibilities like jury duty or (if you're a guy) you have to register for the military draft; if you don't, you'll be fined by the government. But isn't it nice to enjoy an alcoholic beverage along with those cigarettes you're possibly smoking? Isn't it nice to have all sorts of privileges to go with your newly acquired responsibilities? Unfortunately, it's not going to last.

Imagine a desolate place where sheer destruction and pollution have occurred. Forests have been stripped bare, the water has been poisoned, the air makes it hard to breathe, and everything has become an essential wasteland. Would this be a place where you would want to live, raise a family, and work? Is this place the complete opposite of any place you would ever like to be? This mysterious place is soon to be our very own earth, and unless there's a dramatic change in how we live, we are headed on the fast track to turning our precious earth into this ecological wasteland.

Maybe you haven't noticed, but our planet looks much different than it did just ten years ago. Fortunately, most of you likely live in an area that has not changed dramatically. Because you are not directly observing some of the changes I'm going to discuss, you may be tempted to think that nothing is changing—and never will. You would be terribly wrong to think this in today's world. It could be the case that a place where you planned to vacation is now underwater, or that the office building where you planned to work is flooded because it was built too close to the ocean. Or maybe the place you thought you might live has a permanent water shortage because the city's reservoir is drying up. Each of these could become a reality for you or someone you know.

THREE LEVELS OF LOGOS IN WRITING

You can conceive of logos as applying to three levels in writing, as the diagram on the right (showing the *Declaration of Independence* as an example) shows:

1 There's the overall logos or structure of the whole piece of writing.

2 There are the various smaller arguments—such as syllogisms or lists—that a writer combines to build into the overall argument.

3 There are logical structures—such as definitions and other word choices—in every single sentence of writing.

① The *Declaration of Independence* has the overall structure of a syllogism.

② Building to that syllogism, the *Declaration* contains smaller logical structures, such as this list of grievances.

③ The *Declaration* shows very careful word choice at the sentence level.

LOGOS AS OVERALL STRUCTURE

Syllogisms

The composers of the *Declaration of Independence* chose to give it the overall structure of a syllogism, a kind of formal logical argument ("formal" simply means that the argument has a particular arrangement, or form). Syllogisms are often short arguments—but they can be used as the pattern for the overall argument of a piece of writing, serving like a skeleton for the writing on which all the other strategies are fleshed out.

A syllogism is (generally) formed of two statements (called "premises") and a conclusion:

> Socrates is a human.
>
> All humans are mortal.
>
> Therefore Socrates is mortal.

The example is old and probably overused, and it doesn't seem to show much: one person is mortal, will die—well, so what? We show that example to show you the form; when the form is filled in with other statements and conclusions, perhaps the point will be more apparent:

> If bad conditions exist between a ruler and those ruled, then those ruled have the right to declare independence from the ruler.
>
> Those bad conditions currently exist between us and our ruler.
>
> Therefore, we have the right to declare independence.

That is the overall form of the *Declaration of Independence*. The composers wanted their audience to understand that the audience was hearing from calm, rational, and educated people whose decision to seek independence resulted from careful reasoning and was the decision of last resort. Using a syllogism conveys that.

But the logical arrangement does still more.

When you use a logical arrangement such as a syllogism, it can be like saying to your audience, "Look, if you accept these two premises, then here is a logical outcome—you have to accept it." Such logical structures can therefore be compelling.

But of course logic isn't unassailable. The logic—and its ability to compel—holds only if an audience accepts the premises (or if using formal logic is appropriate for the issue at hand), and so—if we decide to use a syllogism as our overall structure—we have to make sure we present our premises thoroughly and in ways that make sense to readers. And that is precisely what the composers of the *Declaration of Independence* did in listing all the bad conditions that existed as a result of the king's rule—as we discuss next.

Parallels, juxtapositions, analogies, compare and contrast

The different structures listed in the title above function similarly: They ask us to understand one object, event, or situation through its similarities to and differences from another object, event, or situation. Such structures often blend the differing approaches we list in the title, as when a writer not only juxtaposes two situations but also asks us to look for analogies between them.

The Purpura essay in chapter 13 uses multiple parallel structures to create one overall sense of parallel. The essay is about a carnival exhibit titled "Smallest Woman in the World," and Purpura structures her essay around parallels between the woman in the traveling carnival show and her children (themselves small), between the experience of looking at the woman in the carnival show and the experience of looking at women in everyday situations, between being looked at as an exhibit in a carnival show and being looked at as a woman just walking down the street, between being a woman looking at a man walking down the street and being a man looking at a woman walking down the street, between being a younger woman being looked at by men and being an older woman being looked at by men… and there are other parallel

LOGOS AS OVERALL STRUCTURE, continued

structures besides these. Purpura uses these parallels in different ways for different purposes. The juxtaposition of the smallest woman in the world with Purpura's small children makes us face the difference between their fates: The smallest woman is trapped in this carnival show whereas the children are trapped only in the unexpected experience of seeing her and how that makes them feel. The analogy between looking at the woman in the carnival show and looking at women on the street reminds us (among other things) that men often look at women as exhibits they believe they have somehow paid for and thus deserve to see. The comparison and contrast between being a younger woman being looked at by men and being an older woman being looked at by men adds complexity to the other parallels and analogies by reminding us that these experiences and our attitudes toward them can shift with time—but that that does not mean that the pains and injustices go away.

Narrative

Narratives involve events unfolding over time, in chronological or nonchronological order. Gary Smith's essay "Higher Education" (in chapter 13), for example, tells the story of "Coach" and his changing relationship with the town of Berlin, Ohio; it begins after the coach has died and cuts back and forth in time to capture different aspects of the story.

Stories about other people engage us because we learn how the choices of others shape their lives—and how we might (or might not) make similar choices. Story arrangements work well, then, when our purposes tell us we need to pull audiences in close, encouraging them to reflect on their own actions as they parallel those of others. Narrative structures suggest the possibility of developing more pathos in argument, too, for stories can easily engage us with the rich emotions of others' lives.

Problem-solution arrangements

Almost any piece of writing can be seen as using a problem-solution format because this arrangement is ubiquitous to our thinking. One example we include in this book is Clarissa Sligh's "The Plaintiff Speaks" (in chapter 13). Sligh shows how the civil rights movement, like so many social movements, embodied painful paradoxes. In this case, the problem was that in order to attract the attention of people in power—white people—blacks had to compromise and often let whites take the lead and the spotlight in the movement. The solution is not so easy to come by, but Sligh's essay—her writing—tries to forge a solution out of the pain of her story by showing us how the events actually unfolded and how we all might consider implications of speaking for others.

TO ANALYZE

■ **Discuss with others:** There are many, many more ways of arranging or structuring a piece of writing than we can describe. In small groups, dig through the writing in this book looking for other examples. As you find examples, describe how the arrangement responds to the context and audience of the writing you are analyzing.

■ **Write informally:** From magazines, collect advertisements that have a paragraph or more of writing in them. What arrangements do these writings use? What arrangements do the writings and any photographs share?

USING A THESIS STATEMENT TO PROVIDE THE OVERALL STRUCTURE OF WRITING

On pages 124–125, we introduced you to the specific form of thesis statements; if you have read those pages on thesis statements and pages 147–148 on logos as overall structure, you might have begun to suspect that a thesis statement and a syllogism are similar creatures—and if you read ahead to pages 150–151, you'll really begin to suspect this.

If you craft a thesis statement carefully, following the form on page 125, the evidence is like the second premise of a syllogism and the claim is like the conclusion; the warrant, which you can construct from the premise and conclusion, becomes the first premise. Why does this matter? Because you can use the premises and conclusion to give you a good (although rough) sense of an overall structure for a paper—as we describe on the right.

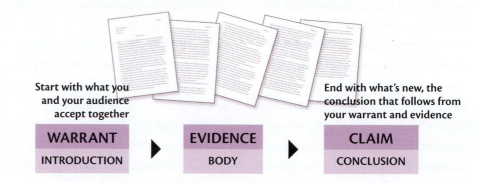

Start with what you and your audience accept together

WARRANT

INTRODUCTION

EVIDENCE

BODY

End with what's new, the conclusion that follows from your warrant and evidence

CLAIM

CONCLUSION

Those in ancient Greece who developed the rhetorical method noticed that the most persuasive speeches tended to begin with speakers discussing values or ideas the speakers and audience shared. When a speaker starts by being in agreement with the audience, in other words, the audience identifies with the speaker and so is more generous toward the speaker and the argument being made.

Because persuasive research writing is about moving audiences to consider differing perspectives than they might otherwise, those observations about persuasion suggest the structure for writing that we diagram above and explain here:

1 **INTRODUCTION: The warrant** is what you hope your audience will accept without much argument—and so it helps audiences move from your premises to your conclusion. When you write a thesis statement, use the warrant to determine what you believe your audience believes— and check that it is indeed the case that your audience will accept this. If you do believe your audience will accept your warrant, you can start your paper with the warrant because starting with the warrant means starting from a place of overlapping values or opinions.

2 **BODY: The evidence** is what you flesh out in the body of your paper, using it (you hope!) to move your audience from the warrant—what you all believe—to seeing some consequences of the warrant that they may not have previously considered.

3 **CONCLUSION: The claim** is the conclusion toward which your composition will be shaped: You want your audience to finish your composition inclined to accept the claim. In your conclusion, tie together for your audience how, if they accept the warrant and the evidence, your claim logically follows.

What thesis statements don't do

Remember, as we described on pages 124–125, that a thesis statement can help you with the overall structure of a composition—but it doesn't offer help with choosing ethos and pathos. For that, you need a statement of purpose; see page 139.

SMALLER LOGICAL STRUCTURES IN WRITING

Within the overarching arrangements of any writing are smaller pieces with *their* own arrangements. Scholars in the West—philosophers and rhetoricians—have for centuries identified, named, and studied these smaller logical structures. Whenever you choose as a persuasive strategy how your ideas are related to each other, you are relying on form—on arguments that depend on their formal arrangements for their force. When you say, "Hey, I was there, I saw it, and it was wrong," you are arguing formally. Likewise, when you say "Look, there's nobody on this planet who hasn't made a mistake at some time, and I live on this planet, so I'm entitled to some mistakes," you are arguing formally.

What follows are a few forms of argument that especially pertain to writing.

Deduction and induction

Deduction and induction are kinds of inference: They are ways of "inferring" a conclusion from reasons or premises.

- Deduction lets you infer a conclusion based on the formal relations between the premises (general and specific) and the conclusion.

- Induction lets you infer a conclusion based on the probability that all the (specific) premises add up to the (general) conclusion.

Each form of argument has its weaknesses—which you might expect, given that these are ways to make jumps between one belief and another—and the jumps might not always be safe or honest jumps.

Deduction's problem: Deduction requires us to accept the truth of a general statement in order to lead to a conclusion, but how are we to establish the truth of that statement?

Induction's problem: Induction requires us to leap from a list of examples to a generalization about those examples, but how do we know when we have enough examples?

It is easiest to see the difference between these forms of argument with examples, which we give next.

Deduction

Deductive arguments are also called "syllogisms." We discussed syllogisms two pages back as structures for shaping whole arguments, but you will most often encounter them as (and find them useful for making) shorter arguments within the body of a paper.

A syllogism is an argument that relates a general claim (such as "There's nobody on this planet who hasn't made a mistake at some time!") to a more specific claim (such as "**I** live on this planet") in order to make a conclusion: "I ought to be able to make mistakes without being made to feel like I'm the only person who ever has!" What makes a syllogism is its form, which is, generally, this:

A has some relation to B.

B has some relation to C.

Therefore, A is has some relation to C.

(This form is echoed in the warrant, evidence, and claim of a thesis statement; see pages 124–125.)

Often these two forms of argument are worded as "if-then" statements or as sentences, the last of which begins with "therefore":

> If Heather has threatened the United States, and if people who threaten the United States are potential terrorists, then Heather is a potential terrorist.

Or

> Modern language classes expose students to other cultures. Classes that expose students to other cultures prepare them to live in the expanding global economy. Therefore, modern language classes prepare students to live in the expanding global economy.

You can perhaps imagine these examples supporting wider arguments about what to do about Heather or about classes that ought to be offered at a university—but often syllogisms are entwined with ethos and pathos and need to be unpacked. For example, the following passage, which quotes a woman whose father was murdered when she was nine, contains at least one syllogism; see if you can identify it:

"A ten-year-old boy was raped and killed by two pedophiles in a suburb of Boston, and it raised a huge rallying cry for the reinstatement of the death penalty in Massachusetts," she says. "What helped defeat it—by one vote—was the testimony of survivors, going as a group before the legislature and urging it not to kill in their name. I met some of those people and for the first time started to sort out my feelings about the politics of murder. There's a whole crowd out there—certain prosecutors and demagogues—that presumes to speak for the survivors in murder cases. They trot us out as the almighty victim and tout the death penalty as our path to 'closure.' But they can't even begin to know what heals us. No one can, till they've been in our shoes and had their soul split open."

We see this syllogism in the quotation:

Most prosecutors have not experienced the murder of a loved one.

Not experiencing the murder of a loved one prevents one from knowing what heals the pain of murder.

Therefore, most prosecutors cannot know what heals the pain of murder.

Only by teasing out the syllogism in the above passage can readers decide whether they want to be persuaded by it. Also, imagine that the quotation had been presented only as a syllogism: Would it have held your attention as the quotation did?

Take away these ideas, then, from our presentation on syllogisms:

- Syllogisms can be wound up in other strategies, and—when you are a reader—you need to unwind them so you can decide whether you want to accept them.

- When you write, weave ethos and pathos together with the logos of syllogisms for your logic to be compelling for readers.

Induction

Induction relates a string of specific statements to a more general statement—to a generalization that is the conclusion you hope others will accept. Here is an example that caught on with philosophers and has been handed down from generation to generation:

Look, this crow is black!
And this crow is black!
And this crow is black!
And that crow is black!
And that crow over there is black!
so . . .
All crows must be black.

Inductive arguments can also be phrased as "if-then" statements:

If this crow is black, and that crow is black, and that crow is black … then all crows must be black.

Here is an example of induction from K. C. Cole's book *First You Build a Cloud, and Other Reflections on Physics as a Way of Life*, which explains physics to readers wary of its complexities:

What we see depends on what we look for. It also depends on our point of view. A house viewed from an airplane does not look at all the same as a house viewed from its own front door, or from the window of a rapidly passing car. A baby does not recognize a toy viewed from the top as the same toy that looked so very different when seen from the side. A rotating shadow of any three-dimensional object will take on an amazing variety of different shapes. Which is the "true" perspective? It may be that the only wrong perspective is the one that insists on a single perspective.

Cole gives three examples of how what we see changes based on the perspective from which we see—and uses those examples to support her conclusion that we ought always to acknowledge multiple perspectives. You ought to be able to picture yourself using similar strategies in your own writing.

Lists and repetition

Lists and repetitions are everywhere and in every bit of communication, as you can see if you start looking.

The body of the *Declaration of Independence* has the structure of a list of grievances against England's King George. The effect of the list is aggregative: As grievance builds upon grievance, the reader should feel what the colonists experienced under King George's rule and finally accept, as just, the decision to break away from England.

The opinion pieces and editorials on video games, violence, and the legislative policies in chapter 12 list supreme court justices, instances of violence by people who have played video games, and video games that have increasingly violent content.

Lists can be deceptive because they seem to present a simple set of items—information, nothing more. But the trick is always in the way the list is constructed.

...

Repetitions work like lists, but they have a slightly different effect. They seem to work on our bodies, making us feel the repetitiveness of the same thing. The editorial "Violence vs. Sex" in chapter 12 starts by pointing out that the Supreme Court is willing to limit children's exposure to certain—violent—ideas, but then observes:

> But not if the idea is sex. No, it would be wrong to expose children to the idea of sex without parental consent.

> But murder? Mayhem? Dismemberment? Cruelty? Outright sadism? OK, OK, OK, OK and OK—protected ideas all, sayeth the court.

The repetitions of the negative "not" and "no" reinforce the sense that "sex" is protected whereas violence is not. The repetitions of violent words—"murder," "mayhem," "dismemberment"—remind us that violence takes many forms and argues, perhaps, that violence should be treated as seriously—legally—as sex is treated. And the repetition of "OK"? What does it do? How do you feel as you read it?

Watch for lists and repetition and for how writers use these strategies as you read. When and how might you use them?

Arguing by example

The best way to explain this form of argument is to, well, give an example, or, better still, to give several examples. Of course, if we are to be effective explaining this form, we have to know how many examples to offer. How many is not enough? How many is too many? To answer those questions requires a judgment call on our parts (as it will when you write with examples) based on our sense of the context and on you, the audience. We don't think you'll need many examples to understand what an example is. But to understand that examples can function in different ways we suspect will require more than one example.

One way examples work is to substantiate a general claim. We will risk boring you by returning to the *Declaration of Independence*.

(U.S. citizens ought never to tire of their founding documents, yes?) The examples in the body of the *Declaration* serve to show or substantiate that King George was a lousy ruler for the colonists. James Elkins uses a different example in his essay in chapter 13 when he shows us multiple versions of the periodic table of the elements to support his claim that our ways of understanding the physical world have perhaps been too shaped by that table of the elements hanging in all our high school chemistry classes. (And this shows how visual examples can be used in writing to support claims.)

But there is an important difference between those two examples. In the *Declaration*, the grievances are listed, but they are not explained at any length. Once placed before us, they are pretty much taken at face value. Their nature as grievances seems easily understood. In Elkins's article, however, the examples do not and cannot stand alone. They require his expert analysis as well as his careful explanation of who made them, the circumstances in which they were made, how they were made, and most importantly, how they function to shape our understanding.

This may be the most important decision you make when using examples. How much surrounding explanation do the examples need—and what kind of explanation?

The form of "cause and effect"

When you start looking for this kind of argument, you find it everywhere. Western people seem obsessed with finding causes. To locate the cause of something is a form of power in our societies because it feels as though, once you have a cause in hand, you are half way to understanding or solving a problem. For example, here are words from an essay about Willa Cather, a novelist whose *My Antonia* you may have read:

> ... *Cather went off to Lincoln, the home of the University of Nebraska. The following spring, for her English class, she wrote a theme on Thomas Carlyle which so impressed her teacher that, behind her back, he submitted it to Lincoln's foremost newspaper, the* Nebraska State Journal. *One day soon afterward, Cather found herself in print. The effect, she said, was "hypnotic." She was no longer going to be a doctor; she was going to be a writer.*

This writing attributes Cather's life change to one event, one cause—neatly explaining how Cather became who she did.

When studying and using causal arguments, remember that causes vary in kind and degree, and they often must be argued for because we accept few cause-effect relations immediately—especially in the areas of social, historical, cultural, and political affairs.

Arguments from consequences

Related to cause-and-effect arguments are arguments from consequences. Cause-and-effect arguments assert a causal connection between one thing and another; an argument from consequences makes judgements about the effects of an action, process, or object.

Each editorial and opinion piece in chapter 12 argues about consequences of violent video games but also about laws or regulations that we could or should put in place regarding children and violent video games. As you read each editorial and opinion piece, attend to whether its argument hinges on a judgment about video games or on a judgment about the consequences of our actions in response to video games. Carefully teasing apart whether an argument tries to establish a cause (*Violent video games cause violence*) or the consequences of an action (*Laws restricting video games restrict our free speech*) enables you better to understand what is at stake and what you are being asked to accept.

As was the case with examples as a form of argument, arguments from consequences require explanation in order to be effective. It is only a first step to assert that something has had a bad effect; other steps are required to support that idea and to make the connection convincing to an audience.

TO ANALYZE

■ **Observe:** Pick up any book or magazine at random and see what logical forms you can identify in the writing. How do the forms support the overall purpose of the writing?

■ **Write creatively:** There are many more forms for arranging the smaller pieces of written arguments. Here are some others:

Argument from absurdity

Argument by elimination

Argument from authority

Argument from precedent

The names ought to suggest to you how these kinds of arguments function. Make up paragraphs that use these forms.

■ **Write creatively:** Follow the form of this list—"Argument from" and "Argument by"—and make up your own possible argumentative forms: "argument by headache," for example, or "argument from strength." Then write paragraphs that use these forms.

We hope you can see that, although many forms already exist on which you can draw as you produce writing, you are not limited to what is there. You need only what works appropriately for your context, audience, and purposes.

WRITTEN TRANSITIONS AS LOGOS

We have been writing about logos as the arrangements that structure an overall piece of writing and then as forms that structure the paragraphs or series of paragraphs that build the whole.

Now we look at logos at the level of sentences. We first look at the sentences that help readers make connections between paragraphs and then at sentences and phrases on their own.

Using transitions to signal structure to readers

Transitions in writing matter—big time. They orient readers to their place in the steps of an argument and they help readers understand how and why one sentence follows the next.

One major strategy for helping readers follow your ideas from one paragraph to the next is to repeat words and phrases from the end of one paragraph at the beginning of the next. The words can be synonyms, not necessarily the exact repetitions, but the conceptual repetition helps readers track how ideas move from paragraph to paragraph—and so helps keep them comfortable readers.

Because transitions are so important, we're going to jump (almost) immediately into asking you to work with them, in the "TO ANALYZE" column on the right.

Transitional words and phrases

- *To indicate sequence*: first, second, third, next, then, finally, after, afterward, at last, before, currently, during, earlier, immediately, later, meanwhile, now, recently, simultaneously, subsequently

- *To show position*: below, beyond, here, in front, in back, nearby

- *To emphasize a point*: even, indeed, in fact, of course, truly, above, adjacent

- *To provide an example*: for example, for instance, namely, specifically, to illustrate

- *To show addition of ideas*: additionally, again, also, and, as well, besides, equally important, further, furthermore, in addition, moreover, then

- *To show similarity*: also, in the same way, just as … so too, likewise, similarly

- *To show an exception*: but, however, in spite of, on the one hand … on the other hand, nevertheless, nonetheless, notwithstanding, in contrast, on the contrary, still, yet

- *To show cause and effect*: accordingly, consequently, hence, so, therefore, thus

- *To conclude or repeat*: finally, in a word, in brief, in conclusion, in the end, on the whole, thus, to conclude, to summarize

TO ANALYZE

- **Hands-on analysis:** Take a piece of writing you like because it is easy to follow—any piece of writing that is at least several pages in length—and make a copy of it. Circle (a thick colored pen helps) every transition you see. Use the list to the left to help you identify transition words and phrases, but circle any set of words or phrases that helps you understand what comes next or how one sentence or section connects with what comes before or after.

  After you do this, look to see whether any patterns emerge. Are there transitions clustered at the beginnings and endings of paragraphs or in the middles?

  Try this with several other pieces of writing. What overall patterns for transitions emerge for you? How can you copy these patterns into your own writing?

- **Hands-on analysis:** Take a recent piece of your own writing and give it to someone else to mark up as we described above. Are you providing enough transitions to help readers understand how to follow the logos of your writing?

LOGOS AT THE SENTENCE LEVEL

Words are resources. Words let us draw attention to objects or people, show existing connections among people and objects, and suggest connections between objects and people that aren't but should be. The more words we have to choose from, the richer we are in resources—but however many you have available, you still must care about your choices. Some choices are regional or tied to groups of people: *pop* and *soda*, *pan* and *skillet*, *bakery* and *baked goods*, *submarine* and *hoagie*, *dinner* and *supper*. Other choices are situational, such as when you say "What's up?" instead of "What has happened since we last met?"

Put otherwise, words do not just refer to objects and people, they fit (or not) into the contexts of our use. They fit (or not) our expectations, values, beliefs, and habits, and they fit (or not) the roles from which we speak. A classroom teacher may say, "Let's start," but in a courtroom, the words are, "All rise for the honorable Judge Hortense Johnson."

The humor newspaper *The Onion* often plays with word choice. For example, a recent headline was "Congress Passes Freedom from Information Act," as a way of pointing our attentions—subtly but with humor—to concerns the writers have about some governmental decisions.

Titles

Titles matter: They are what others see first when they come to a piece of writing (or to a movie) and because we assume they clue us about what follows. Titles are words set aside to frame the whole communication. Titles have a certain authority: They can sound solemn, even when they are funny, because, well, because they are titles.

Titles can begin the process of getting the audience in the mood, they can make a comment on what is to come, or they can begin the work of arguing by challenging the audience's expectations.

The power of titles is reflected in the following blog posting:

> When Hollywood movies are renamed for overseas audiences, the results can be literal or inexplicable, and sometimes remarkably apt. For example, Knocked Up *was released in China as* One Night Big Belly, *which makes perfect sense.* Austin Powers: The Spy Who Shagged Me *became* Austin Powers: The Spy Who Behaved Very Nicely Around Me *in Malaysia, which sounds like a scheme to get past censors. But what do you make of* Dragnet, *which was shown in Germany as* Floppy Coppers Don't Bite?

Would you be as drawn to the retitled movies as you were to the originals?

TO ANALYZE

■ **Discuss and write with others:** Following are titles from student papers. Which titles engage you and encourage you to want to read? How do they engage you? What sorts of audiences might be more likely to be engaged? Which titles aren't as interesting—and why? What do you think is going to happen in the body of the paper, based on the title?

Manufacturing Job Loss

The Quiet War for Freedom of Thought

Working Women and Society's View of Them

Earth: Used and Abused

A Story of Success

Youth of America

I'm 18. Give Me a Drink!

The Dilemma of Tort Reform

Same-Sex Marriage

Don't Hurt Fluffy!

Textbooks: The Other College Expense

With a partner, share your observations, and list the characteristics of titles that engage their audiences—and titles that don't.

155

Naming

The choice of a name can be as important as the choice of overall argument to make.

"child with Down syndrome" or "Down syndrome child"

Michael Bérubé, an English professor married to another professor, has two children, one of whom has Down syndrome. In a book he wrote about what he has learned from and about his son, *Life as We Know It: A Father, a Family, and an Exceptional Child*, Bérubé discusses the arguments swirling around what to call children like his son:

> As far as I understand the current status of our language, it's more proper to say "child with Down syndrome" than to say "Down syndrome child," on the grounds that the child should come first. We've even been known to have heated arguments that center entirely on an apostrophe, bickering over whether to say Down or Down's (the issue here having to with with whether our children should be semantically possessed by J. Langdon Down [who named the syndrome], as if they were DS versions of Jerry's Kids).

These arguments may seem petty, as Bérubé acknowledges, and yet he gives in to them: As a father of a child whose treatment is shaped by how others look at him—which is shaped by the names we use—he understands the delicacies and subtleties of how we approach others through the names we call them.

"undocumented immigrant" or "illegal alien"

A close look at the differences between these names is telling. Those who prefer "illegal alien" do so because they feel it captures the reality of the situation: The people who are in the country without the proper papers are in the country illegally. They disagree with the use of the term "immigrant," which implies that the people under discussion have come into the country through legal means. Those who prefer "undocumented immigrant" do so because they feel that the term "alien" is mean spirited and meant to dehumanize the people captured by the term. They feel that the term "undocumented" captures enough of the reality of the status of such people. Notice how each side has a term to vex the other.

TO ANALYZE

- **Discuss with others:** Following are names used to identify positions available to us in this country. Come up with new names that help reframe the debates that often separate—and polarize—those who take up these names.

pro-choice	pro-life
Democrat	Republican
liberal	conservative
homosexual	straight
gun rights	gun control

- **Discuss with others:** What attitude toward Muzak is the writer asking his readers to try on—and what strategies does he use to do this—in this research paper extract?

"Muzak" describes any music specifically designed to influence behavior and that is played in stores, offices, and other public places. Its name refers to the Muzak Corporation, which was the first company to develop such music and is also the chief supplier to the world. (There are several other competing companies, but none so successful as Muzak.) It's important to differentiate between Muzak and other forms of ambient music that you might hear in stores and workplaces; many stores simply tune in a radio station and play whatever is on. Such radio music is actual music, not engineered to influence customer behavior or mood.

Diction

Courtrooms, classrooms, the aftermath of disaster, funerals, festivals, parties, births—these are all contexts that can call forth communication from us. And as we've seen, different contexts bring with them different sets of expectations on everyone's part. Often the people involved agree in their expectations; sometimes they don't. At a funeral, most people expect silence, solemnity, and seriousness. They also expect that when someone does speak, the person will speak quietly, but above all, with a certain kind of dignity. To achieve the proper dignity when speaking of the deceased at a funeral is to achieve a certain level of diction: "Randy loved his friends and loved being with them," not (generally), "Randy liked hanging with his buds."

Diction is word choice made with an eye toward the particular context in which one is communicating.

Diction is tricky because it is not an exact science, and frankly, it often involves class- and culture-based norms, as the funeral example suggests. What is "proper" in a context? And for whom? And what is at stake if the "correct" level of diction is not achieved? These are questions with which we all struggle.

Most significant perhaps for us using this book is the level of diction many people expect in college classrooms but especially in college

writing. A good place to start is with the distinction between a conversational tone and a formal tone. It is common for students when they first start writing for school to write the way they have always talked, in part because it makes writing a little easier. But teachers often find such writing "sloppy" because when we talk, we are not as careful about word choice, phrasing, and punctuation as we are or should be when we write. For many of your teachers, what is at stake is exactness of meaning and the proper demonstration of care in your choice of words and expressions.

Differences in meaning that are not crucial in a casual setting can become exceedingly crucial in a research laboratory, an academic research paper, or a courtroom. (When would you write "It was about a half a glass of water" instead of "It was a litre of water"? When would you say "We went home," instead of "We drove Esmerelda's car back to my house at exactly 8:30 p.m."?)

TO ANALYZE

■ **Write creatively:** Following are the words someone used in thinking aloud about what to do with an introductory paragraph to a paper. Rewrite these words into a written introduction for a paper—but write two versions: Make the first version as though it were shouting rudely at its audience, and then write a second version so that its readers will imagine its writer is wearing a formal suit.

I am, like, interested in how people walk in different cultures and at different times. I've been reading about how, like, men in ancient Greece were supposed to walk with long strides while women were supposed to move in these small dainty steps. I've seen movies of women in Africa carrying heavy jugs of water on their heads, and they look like they are dancing—how do they do that? When I visited India it looked as though people moved gracefully like trees—but tourists like me from the United States looked like we belonged in the Army—we moved so stiffly! I have a Japanese friend who says the same thing about how people walk here. You just think people just learn to walk all the same—I mean, it's just walking!—and instead it looks more and more to me like how you walk reflects some kind of values of where you grow up.

PATHOS IN WRITING

Pathos in writing is

the stimulating

or avoiding

or managing

or directing

of emotion through your written arrangements and word choices.

We believe that western culture has (or rather, that certain western societies at certain times have) undervalued emotion—and undervalued the fact of emotion, the roles emotion plays in our lives, and expressions of emotion. But whatever your upbringing or cultural background, emotions are always present in all we do. We can't choose to "have" emotions or not. Emotions surround us unavoidably like space and air, necessary for a full and prosperous life.

The goals of "life, liberty, and the pursuit of happiness" in the United States *Declaration of Independence* would not make sense without emotion—or without thought, for that matter. If you're not sure you agree, that is fine. But as you read through this book, see if you can separate the emotions that move through the writing from the arguments being made.

Stimulating pathos through writing

Compare (in chapter 12) the editorial "Court Majority was Right" with the opinion piece "Separating Fact from Fiction in Video Game Debate." One appears to be highly emotional; the other, not. The opening of "Court Majority Was Right" describes "disgusting" (to use the editorial's word) video games; the fact that you can shoot President Kennedy or re-enact Columbine in a video game (and how that fact is presented using certain words and sentence rhythms) might appall you: Your heart might race or your breath quicken just at hearing about those games. "Separating Fact from Fiction in Video Game Debate" opens calmly with a statement of fact and a declaration of the writer's credentials; you probably feel no emotion in response to the writer's words.

If you compare these pieces in their entirety, however, you discover that "Separating Fact from Fiction in Video Game Debate" has plenty of emotion (even in that first paragraph) and that even though "Court Majority Was Right" seems to calm down as it moves along, it does not become "unemotional" but rather shifts its emotional tone.

The bulk of "Court Majority Was Right" manages and balances its readers' emotions, stirring them a bit and then reminding them that in the United States we value freedom of speech: Readers are asked to balance disgust with patriotism. The editorial even ends on a balanced note, suggesting that those who feel young people should be as legally protected from violent video games as they are from pornography might be right, but that that is just not who we citizens are now.

The bulk of "Separating Fact from Fiction in Video Game Debate" calms emotions that have been stirred by fears that violent video games damage youth—but it does so by countering with another fear, that government might be overstepping its bounds. Like "Court Majority Was Right, " "Separating Fact from Fiction in Video Game Debate" also works to balance its readers' emotions by the emotions it calls into play.

Notice that our analysis of these two short pieces points out how the writing in each shifts readers' emotions from the beginning of the piece to the end—in line with how each writer wants readers to be thinking at the end.

Managing or directing pathos through writing

"Separating Fact from Fiction in Video Game Debate" needs to avoiding sounding too emotional because its arguments depend on the ethos of the writer, who is a legal expert and so cannot not let his feelings blur his view of the scientific findings regarding the harm video games might or might not do; the writer also works to calm emotion in a vigorous debate. Notice, though, that none of this means emotion is absent; it is being managed and shaped in line with purposes.

Similarly, were you to read it, you would see that the *Declaration of Independence* appears to avoid emotion because of its complex context and purposes. The *Declaration* is a study in both the avoidance and the inciting of emotion—that is, in the managing and directing of emotion. Here's how to understand it as avoidance: Those who signed the *Declaration* wanted to be seen as Enlightenment rationalists, balanced in their judgment and prepared to take on the challenge of inventing a new government. The body of the document, however, is a long list of egregious actions mostly attributed to King George. The emotions weaving through the body of the *Declaration* are rich and complex. They involve fear and anger, frustration and righteousness, and disgust and hope among others. The line Jefferson walks in the *Declara-tion* is between rationally justifying the act of declaring independence from England and steeling himself, those signing the *Declara-tion*, and the colonists to revolt. In this way, we might say the *Declaration of Independence* appears to be avoiding emotion, but really is about managing and directing it—toward the proper objects: King George and securing independence.

As you write, then, consider:

- *What emotions are your readers likely to have already on your topic?* Will those emotions support or get in the way of your purposes? If the emotions support your purposes, how will you sustain them? If they get in the way, how will your writing work to shift readers' emotions to become more productive for your purposes?

- *What emotions do you wish your readers will have about your topic when they finish reading?* How might your words, paragraphs, and arguments move them toward having those emotions?

TO ANALYZE

- **Write:** Choose an emotion—joy, resentment, anger, contempt, love, compassion, sympathy, pity, grief, jealousy, pride, envy, hope, terror—and, for a week, look for that emotion in your daily life, in movies, and in what you read. Use your examples to write responses to the following questions:

  - What objects or events tend to evoke the emotion? (For example, jealousy can be evoked by other people who have qualities or possessions we would like.)

  - What do people say, do, or look like as they experience or feel the emotion?

  - To experience that emotion, what *beliefs* must someone hold? (For example, experiencing hope requires belief that our current situation can change.)

  - To experience that emotion, what *values* must someone hold? (For example, experiencing grief about the loss of another means that we valued the other's love or company.)

  - What relationships to other people does the emotion set up or suggest?

  - How might your observations help you in writing to evoke (or calm) the emotion?

159

PATHOS IN WRITTEN CONCLUSIONS

Pathos and conclusions traditionally have a special relationship: How a reader feels at the end of writing is how a reader feels later when remembering the writing. So: Can you end by getting under the skin of the people to whom you write? Leave them laughing or leave them crying, or (better still) leave them in a more complex emotional state that works with the more complex thinking you hope they'll do—but, no matter what, consider your writing's emotional ending.

With any ending, you can look back over what you have done, look at where you have gotten, or look ahead to what might or should come next. Most written conclusions do a little of each, and they differ in the emphasis they put on one or the other activity.

Strategies for conclusions

"The Partly Cloudy Patriot" in chapter 8 ruminates on "patriotism." The writer, Sarah Vowell, argues that she is uncomfortable with full-blown patriotism, with the kind of idealized patriotism whose single-minded focus can lead to civil strife; to support this, she quotes others from countries that have more recently suffered from civil war than ours. In her writing, she presents herself instead as a "partly cloudy patriot" who loves her country but wants room for disagreement and argument (and for argument based on respect and concern for others). Given all that, Vowell ends her essay with an example that sums up all her thinking, to demonstrate what she calls "the very epitome of civilization [and] good government." Vowell describes riding the New York City subways and seeing a sign that promises riders they will be cared for if they are sick. As a result of seeing that sign, she starts looking more closely at the people around her on the train. She ends, then, with an example rooted in pathos: Her conclusion is written to put us on the train with her, imagining our fellow passengers and imagining individuals who need care and feeling the complex weave of concern and empathy she feels. Readers thus finish the essay thinking about patriotism not as an abstract idea but as bound up in relations between us and real breathing others.

The essay "Higher Education" (in chapter 13) also ends with an example. The author of "Higher Education," Gary Smith, tells us that after "Coach" died, the people of the town of Berlin, Ohio, remembered him not in word only but also in deed. Smith concludes by describing the aftereffects of Coach's having been a loved member of that town because (Smith believes) the things the town did are like policies for a better life—such as one of Coach's student-athletes moving to a mostly African American neighborhood to do what Coach did "in reverse."

The two preceding paragraphs suggest ways to conclude—both tied closely to the purposes of the writing.

As you write, then, consider an ending that emotionally furthers your purposes.

TO ANALYZE: PATHOS IN WRITTEN CONCLUSIONS

■ **Write creatively:** Following are the last paragraphs of the essay "Save the Whales, Screw the Shrimp" by Joy Williams. Analyze this conclusion—its arguments, ethos, and pathos—by rewriting the paragraphs to drain all the energy from them and then seeing how others respond.

The ecological crisis cannot be resolved by politics. It cannot be solved by science or technology. It is a crisis caused by culture and character, and a deep change in personal consciousness is needed. Your fundamental attitudes toward the earth have become twisted. You have made only brutal contact with Nature, you cannot comprehend its grace. You must change. Have few desires and simple pleasures. Honor nonhuman life. Control yourself, become more authentic. Live lightly upon the earth and treat it with respect. Redefine the word progress and dismiss the managers and masters. Grow inwardly and with knowledge become truly wiser. Make connections. Think differently, behave differently. For this is essentially a moral issue we face and moral decisions must be made.

A moral issue! Okay, this discussion is now toast. A moral issue ... And who's this we now? Who are you is what I'd like to know. You're not me, anyway. I admit, someone's to blame and something must be done. But I've got to go. It's getting late. That's dusk out there. That is dusk, isn't it? It certainly doesn't look like any dawn I've ever seen. Well, take care.

■ **Discuss with others:** Following is the last paragraph of the whole book *The Magic of Reality: How We Know What's Really True* by Richard Dawkins. Why do you think Dawkins is trying to make "reality" seem "magic"? What sorts of emotion is Dawkins trying to attach to science—and why might he be trying to do this? What do you think he thinks his audience thinks about science, and why?

Miracles, magic, and myths—they can be fun, and we have had fun with them throughout this book. Everybody likes a good story, and I hope you have enjoyed the myths with which I began most of my chapters. But even more I hope that, in each chapter, you enjoyed the science that came after the myths. I hope you agree that the truth has a magic of its own. The truth is more magical—in the best and most exciting sense of the word—than any myth or made-up mystery or miracle. Science has its own magic: the magic of reality.

■ **Write creatively:** With a partner, rewrite in two ways the conclusion to any recent article you've read. First produce as awkward a conclusion as you can and then produce a conclusion that strives to fit its context as usefully as possible.

■ **Discuss with others:** Bring to class just the conclusion to a piece of writing you've read on your own. (Type up the conclusion, or make a copy of it.) In class, trade conclusions with someone else. From just the conclusion you've been given, try to reconstruct the rest of the writing. Describe the kind of writing (essay? opinion piece? academic writing?), the ethos of the writer, and the structure of the piece as best you can in an act of writing archaeology.

A DESIGN PLAN FOR WRITING

Remember from chapter 3 that a design plan integrates on paper:

- your statement of purpose. (See Ajay's statement of purpose on page 139.)

- a description of your strategies with justifications based on your statement of purpose.

- your choice of medium or media with justifications based on your statement of purpose.

- your ideas about arrangement with justifications based on your statement of purpose.

- a description of how you will produce the communication.

- a plan for testing the communication.

(Note that a design plan doesn't have to have all those elements in the order we've listed them. But you do want to consider all of them.)

The process of writing a design plan—precisely because you do this before you really start your paper—gives you a chance to think in a relaxed way about how all the pieces of your work might fit together.

A design plan is not a test and can be more or less formal. In fact, a fairly informal design plan will be of most use because you want to focus on your own thinking, not on how you are communicating to anyone else. You want to ask questions, write down possible ideas, and imagine the whole text you are about to produce.

A Design Plan for a Research Paper

In my statement of purpose, I say that I want my classmates (and teachers) to think about how their actions and attitudes affect how we learn and how a teacher treats us. This means that I am focusing less on the question, "Are students really customers?" and more on the question, "What are the consequences of thinking of students as customers?" Given all that, I think my overall strategies need to be:

- To shift the discussion away from whether or not students are customers to instead consider the effects in the classroom and around campus of thinking of them (of ourselves) as customers. What are the effects on how teachers treat us and how we treat teachers and learning?

- To change the question requires that I make sharp, clear, compelling distinctions between teaching and buying. I need to make my readers feel that there might be something wrong with just accepting this idea that we are customers.

My ethos: I need to avoid lecturing my readers (especially if I am arguing against ways of learning that just expect information that is packaged and bought). I need to show readers that we are in this together, exploring and looking for something better. I need to be excited in the way that people are excited when they are starting out on a new journey together. So how do I do that? How do I sound excited without sounding like a dork?Ask a lot of questions? Have tons of evidence? I want to sound thoughtful and smart, but not stuck up.

My logos: I need to make clear distinctions to change the questions being asked and to change what people feel is at stake. I need definitions of "learning" and "buying" in addition to definitions of "student" and "customer." Do I need a definition of "teaching"? Perhaps I need an argument that shows the shortcomings of the business model to demonstrate what the consequences are of thinking in this way (consequences that look silly if we really care about learning).

My pathos: From listening to other students talk about themselves as customers, I can tell that they are pissed off about the kind of education they are getting and ways that the university and some teachers treat them. They feel entitled to an education. But they also (rightly or wrongly) feel entitled to a degree and good grades. I think that on some level we all do care about learning, that all of us at some time have had a moment when we really enjoyed learning, seeing something unexpected and cool, etc. I also have seen teachers who are burned out and would just as soon think of students as customers. But I have known teachers who love to teach. How do I weave through that mix of my readers' emotions and what I need to do in this writing? What if I try to inspire pride in my readers about what they can achieve if they think of themselves as students instead of as customers?

Choice of medium: Well, I have to write a paper. I don't have a choice.

Ideas about arrangement: I have my thesis statement: *Treating students as customers damages their education because treating students as customers does not ask them to take active responsibility for their learning, wait for rewards, or be challenged and uncomfortable in the process.* The warrant tells me that I believe my audience will accept that *education requires students to take active responsibility for their learning, wait for rewards, and be challenged and uncomfortable in the process.* If I follow what Professor Wysocki says about how thesis statements work, that means I should probably start talking about my warrant, what an education is, because I think most people will accept that pretty easily. So I will start with definitions. (But I found such good information about what causes students to think of themselves as customers; where should I put that? Can I put that up front, too?) Then I need to spend my time giving my evidence about how thinking of students as customers gets in the way of their educations.

How I will produce my writing: I've done some good research, I think. (I got that *A* on my annotated bibliography, yay.) So now I just need to sit myself down and write—I think I have a pretty good idea now how to start.

Testing: I know we are going to have to share drafts in class and that we'll get feedback from Professor Wysocki—so that's probably most of what I'll need to test. But Aunt Camille has been helping me pay for school, and I know she cares, so maybe I could run it by her, too.

To note about Ajay's statement of purpose

Ajay asks lots of questions and proposes possible approaches in his statement of purpose—and that is fine. He is also not worried about writing formal and coherent paragraphs just yet because he is focused on developing ideas (although sometimes to write a second, more formal version of a statement of purpose can help you think still further about how your ideas and plans are working; a formal statement of purpose can also serve as a proposal for a text as we show on pages 82-83).

Keep in mind that statements of purpose do not mean you cannot make changes as you produce your text. You might find a new idea or connection in the middle of writing a paper, an idea or connection that strengthens or enriches or even changes what you had planned. And that is as it should be—but developing your ideas with a statement of purpose before you start to write will have helped you get to that change.

FOR EXAMPLE

Here is Ajay's statement of purpose. The first draft that follows from this begins on page 164; his final draft is on pages 176-181.

A FIRST DRAFT OF A RESEARCH PAPER

Give yourself enough time to write comfortably. Set aside a number of several-hour chunks—or an hour a day every day. Try writing in different locations; sometimes a change of scenery or different coffeeshop background chatter can help you see and hear your words freshly.

…

A design plan should give you solid ideas about how to proceed—but even with a solid design plan, sometimes it's hard to know where to start.

Just start.

If you are stuck on an introduction, look back over pages 142–145 for ideas.

Don't worry about making a draft perfect. Get your argument onto paper. The idea with a draft is to have one. You do get to revise.

…

Your teacher may or may not be particularly concerned about the format of a draft. If you are not sure about your teacher's desires about format, ask.

☛ On pages 121–123, we show formatting details for a paper in MLA style.

Ajay Chaudry

Professor Wysocki

English 102

May 21, 2012

Chaudry 1

DRAFT: Are Students Customers?

Here is a quotation from a college student:

> Students are most definitely customers. We pay don't we? And isn't that one of the definitions of a customer: "Someone who pays for a service"? We pay the university for the service of teaching classes, so we can attend the classes and earn a degree. (Denning)

I guess I had never thought about it before, but it was strange when I heard people in my class complaining about not getting good grades because they'd paid a lot of money to go to school. What does it mean to think of school as a place where we buy something, where we are customers?

According to the dictionary, students learn something, customers buy something. But when I read more about "students" and "customers" in academic journals, I learned that what they learn and what they buy are very different things—and I realized that most of the time we shouldn't think of students as customers.

According to my readings, it's the TQM movement that got people to think of students as customers. According to George O. Tasie, TQM started with businesses:

> The total quality management (TQM), born in the 1930s among the management circles in the United States and nurtured in post World War II Japanese business and industrial communities, has spread rapidly through higher education in various parts of the world during the past decade. There is no single theoretical formalization of TQM, but the American quality gurus, Deming and Juran, and the Japanese writer, Ishikawa, provided a set of core assumptions and specific principles of management which can be synthesized into a coherent framework.… TQM is a business discipline and philosophy of management which institutionalizes planned and continuous business improvement. The real test of quality management is its ability to satisfy customers in the marketplace. (310)

So that's how the notion of "student as customer" came into universities and colleges, along with some of how TQM works: The customer is placed first.

Some of the articles I read argue that sometimes it is right to think of students as customers. "The areas of institutions that conduct discrete business-like transactions—e.g., student services, registration, food services, mainte-nance—do seem amenable to streamlining and improvement via TQM meth-ods." (Schwartzman 216). But most of the articles I read on this topic argue that students should not be customers. "Students lack the expertise to judge exactly what constitutes quality in a particular subject, although they certainly have the competence to recognize degrees of courtesy, promptness, and reliability that generalize across disciplines." (Schwartzman 220)

When the writers I read argued about why we shouldn't think of students as customers, they started by asking how a student might be a customer. If a student is a customer, what is the product a student is buying? Some writers also ask who the customer of education really is.

But the most important question is how education is like the kind of products we all buy every day, like hamburgers or hair products. When I buy a hamburger, I don't have to do anything. I stand at the counter, place my order, and they give me a ham-burger. I eat it. That's it. But the articles I read argue that an education isn't consumed all at once—and that students have to have a part in making an education happen. Many of the articles I read also argue that education is a process, not a product:

> Business, typically speaking, is product oriented, although the product is often the delivery of a service. Education, by contrast, is process oriented in that it ideally seeks to train people to continue to educate themselves. Thus, a high quality experience or outcome can really only be assessed well over time and in multiple ways. Consumers engage in many discrete transactions, always with an identifiable product or service about which they can say, "I bought this." However, when seeking an education, students do not buy a specific product or service external to themselves, except for books and supplies. Further, the quantifiable results of educa-tion—salary earned, positions obtained, rewards gleaned—are not the only objectives here. Rather, our students contract with us to be chal-lenged and to exceed their previous intellectual limits. Unlike consumers,

■ As you read Ajay's draft, the following questions can help you consider how it works:

- How well does Ajay's current title prepare readers for what is to come?

- How well does Ajay's introduction prepare readers for what is to come? Does it give readers a sense of why the writing should matter to them?

- What strategies is Ajay using to help readers understand why he moves from one paragraph to the next?

- How do you think readers would summarize Ajay's overall argument?

- How is Ajay using his sources?

- Has Ajay cited all his sources and according to MLA convention?

- How well does Ajay's conclusion follow from the writing preceding it?

 FOR EXAMPLE

Here is Ajay's first draft. See his final draft on pages 176–181.

■ Compare these features of Ajay's draft to his final draft on pages 176–181. As you compare, ask how these changes between drafts have helped him strengthen his draft:

- Ajay's ethos

- How Ajay addresses his readers

- Transitions between paragraphs

- How quotations are introduced

- How quotations are woven into Ajay's writing

- How Ajay uses his sources to support and question his ideas

- How Ajay put his sources in dialogue with each other

- How Ajay has ordered his ideas in and through his paragraphs

students never really get an education. They, like all of us, are involved in the process of becoming wiser. (Cheney, McMillan, and Schwartzman)

My sources also argue that learning is very different from consuming because

Satisfying learners often runs counter to the conditions necessary for learning because learning often involves some discomfort, disequilibrium, and challenge. Students learn through the cognitive conflicts that occur when they face new points of view, new information, and new perspectives. Students learn when they are encouraged to reflect actively on the information that is unfamiliar and initially illogical or even threatening. In such situations, the dynamic tension created between the known and the new causes new thinking, analysis and reevaluation. (Tasie, 312)

Education is supposed to be uncomfortable because it challenges and changes us. "The teacher is not there to satisfy the student but to dissatisfy; not to provide but to demand." (Love, 28)

What are effects on students when they think of themselves as customers? Some articles argue that thinking of themselves as customers makes students more passive.

Students speak about how lecturers should be responsible for capturing and holding their interest. While lecturers have a clear responsibility to offer appropriate guidance and support and to present their material in interesting and pedagogically sound ways, there is a passivity implied in some of the students' responses that raises questions about how students are seeing themselves as learners. (White 599)

Or: "The stance is of 'the customer' who has minimal obligation to engage and contribute a satisfactory outcome, and who irrespective of the contribution made, has an entitlement to satisfaction with the service being provided." (White 600)

Other articles argue that when students think of themselves as consumers, they want immediate satisfaction, even though education takes time:

… with the business model comes this seemingly inexorable need to "get faster," resulting in a form of temporal disjunction between competing educational models. The business ideal, with its customer orientation, calls for constant change and rapid response, resulting in an educational sector that is "[o]bsessed by cultivating the ability to stay on top of the latest trends." Lasch points out that under such circumstances practitioners "find it difficult to imagine a community of learning that reaches into both the past and the future and is constituted by an awareness of intergenerational obligation." Education is divested of its heritage and revalued; it is deemed useful only in as much as it can respond to the business needs of the moment. (Love 21)

But the effect is not just on students. I found a blog comment where someone claimed that "When students are 'customers,' the academic institution becomes a business, seeking to maximize profits, rather than educate." When the university is a business, it becomes concerned with numbers: How many students can we teach?

All of this leads me to think that it is more important to ask: Who am I in school—and what am I becoming? What do I think I should be—what should my attitudes be—toward learning and a noble self? The readings, while frustrating, also seemed to call at me to push myself to be something other than someone who buys.

WORKS CITED

Cheney, George, Jill J. McMillan, and Roy Schwartzman. "Should We Buy the 'Student-As-Consumer' Metaphor?" *Montana Professor* 7.3 (1997): 8-11. Web.

Denning, Peter J. "Are Students Customers, or Not?" Oct. 12 2002. Web. 4 May 2012. http://cs.gmu.edu/cne/pjd/PUBS/StudentsCustomers.pdf

Love, Kevin. "Higher Education, Pedagogy and the 'Customerisation' of Teaching and Learning." *Journal of Philosophy of Education* 42.1 (2008): 15-34. Print.

Schwartzman, Roy. "Are Students Customers? The Metaphoric Mismatch between Management and Education." *Education* 116.2 (1995): 215-222. *Education Research Complete*. 3 May 2012.

Tasie, George O. "Analytical observations of the applicability of the concept of student-as-customer in a university setting." *Educational Research and Reviews* 5.6 (2010): 309-313. *Academic Journals*. Web. 5 May 2012.

White, Naomi Rosh. "'The Customer Is Always Right?': Student Discourse About Higher Education in Australia." *Higher Education* 54.4 (2007): 593-604. *Academic Search Complete*. Web. 5 May 2012.

■ You've seen Ajay's paper develop from his very initial thoughts as we showed them in chapter 4. How does his draft match (or not) the expectations you've formed as you've seen his ideas develop? What changes and developments have you noticed in Ajay's thinking as he's moved toward this draft? Is there anything you didn't expect in his draft?

GIVING FEEDBACK TO OTHERS' WRITING

To the right is feedback Ajay received from a classmate; the feedback follows the suggestions on the opposite page for giving feedback to a peer's writing.

Ajay,

I like how your paper starts off with words from an angry student. I can so identify. Your topic speaks to me. I've been angry about how much tuition we have to pay, and how classes keep getting bigger.

So I am interested in why you think we shouldn't think of ourselves as customers.

I have to admit, though, that I'm not yet persuaded by your writing. On page 2 is where you start to talk about this, but there are so many long quotes! You start to describe how an education might be like a product we buy (or not?) but I just am not seeing what the differences are yet. It's like a long list and I need some more explanation.

I do like all the questions you ask, especially in your conclusion. The questions in your last paragraph make me feel kind of gushy. They make me want to be better than I am. So that's all probably a good thing. But, those questions do kind of come out of nowhere. There isn't anything before the questions that's so idealistic or that appeals to what is supposed to be the better side of me.

Sorry. But I hope that helps.

Thanks!

Jenna M.

When asked to respond to another's writing:

❑ *Be sure you know what feedback the writer needs.* Perhaps the writer needs only grammar and spelling checked—but perhaps the writer needs feedback on the order of ideas, in which case correcting spelling is useless because the words you correct can go away in a revision. If a writer asks for help with a piece of writing but does not specify what kind of help—ask (and this can assist the writer in articulating what the writing needs).

❑ *Read the writing at least twice before you make any comments.* Take notes during a first reading, but use the first reading to get a sense of what the writer is trying to do given the feedback the writer requested; then reread to look for the parts in the writing that most support what the writing is trying to do and for the parts that aren't as supportive.

❑ *Prioritize your feedback.* Do not overwhelm the writer with a long list of suggested changes; pick your two to five most important observations and present only those so that the writer can focus.

❑ *Do tell writers what you like about their writing and why.* Writers (like any person) need to know what they do well. When we have a sense of what we do well, it gives us a ground on which we can stand as we start developing our other abilities.

❑ *If you are asked to give feedback on the main argument of a piece of writing, say first what you think the main argument is.* You may be seeing a different main argument from what the writer intends, and the writer needs to know; the writer can then reshape the argument to fit the original intention or can reshape it to pull out what you see. But if you give feedback on a different argument than what the writer intends, the writer will be revising at cross (and confusing) purposes.

❑ *Give reasons for your comments.* If instead of "I get lost in this paragraph," you say, "In this paragraph you started out writing about the effects of video game violence on children but then you ended by writing about television cartoons, and I couldn't see what connected those two ideas," you give the writer information useful for revision. (And if you articulate feedback in this way, you'll look at your own writing just as carefully; teachers of writing often talk about how useful to their own writing it is to have to formulate feedback to people in their classes.)

❑ *Describe how you read.* All writers, no matter how experienced, need help understanding how others read their writing. A good way to give feedback is to write something like, "The first sentence of this paragraph made me think you would focus on *x*, but then you started discussing *y*—and so I got confused."

❑ *Think about the most useful, respectful feedback you've ever received, and emulate it.* You might keep a collection of useful feedback and analyze what makes it useful. This will not only help you give good feedback to others, but also help you develop a stronger eye for reading your own words more critically.

❑ *Think about the most useful, respectful feedback you've ever received, and emulate it.* We repeat this advice because how you give feedback determines how others use it—and even whether they can use it. You know how it feels to put a lot of time and effort into any production, and then to get it back with only negative comments. You know how it feels when someone simply says about your work, "I don't like this," or, worse yet, "This sucks." Giving feedback is not a neutral process—it involves emotions. If you really want to help someone, be positive in your feedback. Say, "I think this could be stronger if …" or "It looks to me like you are trying to achieve *x*, so maybe a more effective way of doing it would be …"

169

RECEIVING FEEDBACK TO YOUR WRITING

On the right is feedback Ajay received from his teacher.

Receiving feedback can be hard if you've put a lot of effort into writing. You might not want to hear that you have more work to do. But it's important to know how to receive feedback because feedback is what helps you both develop your ideas and strengthen your writing to communicate what you need.

Read feedback as soon as you get it but then put it aside for a day or two. Read it again with a little distance, and you'll be in a better position to understand it.

When you receive feedback, keep in mind:

- *The feedback of others helps you become a stronger writer.* Only by hearing how others read and understand do you learn how your words communicate.

- *If readers do not understand your argument or believe it to be other than you intended, don't blame the readers.* If readers miss or misinterpret your argument, ask them why they see the argument they do. Ask readers to go through your writing sentence by sentence, explaining out loud what they understand, so you can learn the particular effects your words have—and so you can learn how to revise your words to do what you hope.

Dear Ajay,

Your writing works as a first draft. I can see that you are building an argument about why we need to pay more attention to differences between learning and buying.

I think your argument is a bit buried in your writing now, though, for three reasons:

(1) You use up a lot of space describing how the Total Quality Movement contributed to why schools think of their students as customers. How do you think that background helps your readers understand why thinking of students as students—and not as customers—matters?

(2) Right now, your writing is mighty close to being what writing teachers call "patch writing." Patch writing results when writers string together quotations they've copied from their sources. Often this happens when writers don't have the confidence they should in their own writing. But I know from all your preceding work that you have done good research and have a solid idea of why your ideas matter. So have the confidence your hard work deserves!

(3) Following from points 1 and 2, then: There are not yet enough of your ideas and argument in your draft. Given your thesis statement, I think you need to spend more time making clear to readers why we should be worried when students are seen—by themselves and by their schools—as customers.

I look forward to seeing your revisions, based on this good start and the ideas you have been developing.

Sincerely,

your professor, Anne Wysocki

A REVISION PLAN

When you receive written feedback:

- *Make notes on it.* Make marginal comments in any written feedback you receive, noting changes suggested by the feedback but also noting any questions or concerns you have.

- *Use your notes to ask for clarification or help you discuss revisions you are considering.* Take advantage of how someone else has read your work: Ask for further explication or explanation because listening to someone else's words on your writing helps you think with focus about how others hear your words.

- *Go to your campus Writing Center.* Writing Center staff are well trained to assist writers in strengthening drafts. Although they can certainly aid you with mechanics, the staff can also support you in understanding and applying feedback and in preparing for revision.

- *Say "Thank you."* Giving feedback is not easy for anyone, including teachers. We teachers fret that we are saying what you can hear and that it is useful, even though we've spent a lot of time learning about how to give feedback. (People who study how to teach writing often write articles on how to give feedback.) Like you, your classroom peers are learning how to do this work; give them the same respect you want.

Once you have received feedback, develop a revision plan: List the revisions you intend to make so that you keep track of what you should do. Revisit your design plan, too, to check that you haven't missed any of its ideas or to see whether your draft encourages you to rethink any aspect of it.

Ajay's revision plan follows.

> Given the feedback I received from Professor Wysocki and others in class, I think I need to focus on making my argument clearer. It's there in my writing—just not emphasized or visible enough.
>
> So here's what I need to work on:
>
> - Probably taking out the TQM information. It's really interesting how TQM has gotten picked up in schools. (And I'm also really interested from my sources in how TQM, tied to rising tuitions, encourages students to be more demanding of schools—and how rising tuitions have to do with how states are providing less money to schools so that schools have to raise tuitions.) All this fascinates me—but I guess it doesn't really fit in this argument. Maybe I can use it later.
>
> - Cutting the quotations and making them fit better into my own writing. I've learned that I need to introduce the quotations and explain how they help me develop my ideas.
>
> - Defining "education" more so that the differences between learning and buying become clearer.
>
> - Providing more reasons how thinking of students as consumers gets in the way of student education.
>
> - People liked my conclusion but didn't think it really followed from what preceded it. People liked how I asked questions, so maybe I need to ask more questions (which would help me develop the ethos I described in my design plan). But I also need to aim what comes before my conclusion to my conclusion.

☛ See pages 172–173 for the important differences among revising, editing, and proofreading.

THE WRITTEN STRATEGIES OF PROOFREADING, EDITING, AND REVISING

	Proofreading	Editing	Revising
what	A proofreader checks spelling, punctuation, and other mechanics.	In editing, you attend to sentences and sentence-level details. Are sentences readable? Have you cited and documented all your sources?	When you revise, you attend to large-scale persuasive aspects of texts, such as arrangement and style.
when	While you can pay attention to the details of mechanics and spelling throughout the development of a text, you also want to do this as the very last step. Whenever you edit or revise, you change words (and can add typos by mistake)—and so you want to be sure to catch all proofreading needs once and for all.	When your overall argument is solid and unlikely to change, it is time to focus on editing.	You start revising when you have almost a full draft.
how	**Ask the following questions:** • Is every word spelled and capitalized according to convention? • Did I leave out any words? • Have I used the right words? (For example, have I used "it's" when I mean "it is" instead of "its"?) • Is my punctuation conventional? • Are my quotations punctuated according to convention?	**Ask the following questions:** • Are my sentences easy to read? • Will my sentences engage readers? • Are my sentences grammatically appropriate for my audience and purpose? Does each sentence make sense on its own? • Have I integrated my quotations of others' work into my writing while making it clear when I am using others' words and ideas? • Have I documented my sources according to expected conventions?	**Ask the following questions:** • Am I clear about my argument? Can I present it as a thesis statement? • Do my claims reflect how complex the issues are? Have I offered well-supported evidence for all my claims? • Have I been fair and respectful toward other perspectives one could take on my argument? Have I considered everyone who might be affected by my conclusions? • Will my writing engage readers? • Does my introduction engage readers with my arguments and initial concerns? • Have I given appropriate emphasis for the main parts of my argument?

Proofreading	Editing	Revising
TIPS Leave yourself time to proofread. You need fresh eyes to see where you have left a word out or misspelled a word (because when you have worked closely with writing, your brain will often fill in or correct mistakes). If you work on a computer, proofread on screen but also proofread printed copy: You will see the words on screen and paper differently and are therefore more likely to catch what you need to fix. Proofread more than once. Each time focus on one aspect of grammar or mechanics: spelling or commas, for example. And if you know particular grammatical elements that tend to cause you trouble, proofread at least once just for them.	Leave yourself time to edit. As you schedule writing time for a paper, aim to finish writing at least a day before a draft is due: You want to put a paper aside for a while in order to see the paper again freshly—and so see changes you need to make. To understand how readers understand your sentences, read your writing out loud to yourself or a friend. Also ask another to read it out loud to you.	If your school has a Writing Center, the staff will be happy to help you at any stage of your writing process—but know that visiting them while you are working on revising is a particularly smart move. Writing Center staff are well trained to help writers clarify and strengthen drafts. After you have a first draft, talking with someone in your Writing Center will help you speed your process and focus on the most important revision steps you can take.

Why revising, editing, and proofreading are rhetorical

Few people produce, in a first pass, writing that others can understand readily—and so revising, editing, and proofreading are about making your writing make sense to others. And any time you are concerned about how your writing strikes your readers—any time you are concerned about the effects of your writing—you are being rhetorical.

But there is another dimension to the rhetoricality of revising, editing, and proofreading. You need to do these tasks to the extent that makes sense for the context and audience for which you are writing. When you compose a quick memo, you want others to be able to understand it—but they do not need to appreciate its careful sonorous language. When you compose a professional document, you want to be careful that it has no typos or odd grammatical elements. (We've known people who haven't been hired for writing jobs because there was a single typo in their writing samples.) When you compose a research paper, you want it to have a professional ethos in addition to it being engaging.

Revising, editing, and proofreading show that you care about your context and audience.

A SHORT EXAMPLE OF REVISION

On the right is the first draft of a letter to the editor written by Jacob Falk, who was taking a class with Anne (one of the composers of this book).

After reading the draft, other people in class who were Christian told Jacob that they felt a bit attacked by the draft: He describes Christians as "despising" others and just flatly states in the writing that he does not think they can understand or help him. They could see that his purpose was to encourage others to listen thoughtfully to him, but they didn't think that this writing yet achieved that purpose. They also told him that the first sentence of the draft right away made his ethos sound judgmental and angry—and that such an ethos would get in the way of their being able to think of the writer as someone to whom they would want to be attentive.

On the next page is Jacob's revision of this draft.

FIRST DRAFT

TO THE EDITOR:

Preachers of God really irritate me. Being an atheist, I cannot stand the thought of preaching about God with no viable proof as to if there really is a God. Questions such as, if there is a God then why do so many people suffer around the world? And if God forgives all sins then if I killed somebody and felt bad for it should I still be able to make it into heaven? Although I have many doubts about Christianity and its beliefs I also see that most church-goers are happy that they are part of it. They also have a group of people with whom they feel comfortable and have their religion in common. I understand that working for God can be an unbelievably rewarding thing and that many people experience this if and only if they have faith. This brings me to my point, how can Christians, or any faith for that matter, convert me so that I once again believe in something larger than myself?

Missionaries are very successful at converting people who are in third world countries to the Christian faith, so where are the missionaries in our country? At one time I was a Christian, I did not go to church but I believed in God and I knew if I lived correctly I would have a place in heaven after I died. Now I cannot ascertain how I am supposed to think those thoughts again without tremendous help from persuasive believers in faith.

Christians despise atheists because of their denial of God and the Bible. However I do not believe they understand the state in which atheists are in. Without hard proof or a miracle of some sort, I think it is extremely difficult to escape the atheist belief that there is no God. So how can I start to believe in something that has not shown itself in any way to me? Perhaps trying to go to church and talking with pastors and priests will help. I will try both; however I am doubtful that Christians can help a lost soul named Jacob Falk.

Sincerely, Jacob Falk

REVISION

TO THE EDITOR:

Being an atheist is not only painful it is a relentless pain that will not subside. I have the unfortunate luck of not believing in God and I have been both condemned and ignored for my beliefs. I once considered myself religious; I did not attend church, but I believed in God and I knew if I lived correctly I would someday find heaven. However, I have strayed from those former beliefs and have relied on science and facts instead of intuition and faith for my thoughts on religion.

Christian friends of mine have tried to convert me, ceaselessly telling me that I "just" have to believe and have faith. Faith is something I do not have and cannot possess at this time. Other Christians believe we, atheists, are blasphemers who will go to hell because of our refusal to believe in God and the Bible. These latter people do not understand our disposition. I would love to have faith and have a place in heaven where I will see all of my loved ones when I die, but I cannot.

Condemnation and people trying to convert me because of my honest doubt of religion do little to ease the anguish of my beliefs. Christians, Muslims, Jews, Buddhists, Hindus, and countless other religions of the world, please allow atheists to speak with you and ask questions about your religion. Give them space to think and do not berate them with questions or force upon them your beliefs. Listen to them and try to see religion from their perspective. I believe this is the only way for atheists to find the way in any religion. I know I need help and if there is anything I believe can help, it is support from others, not criticism and hatred.

Sincerely, Jacob Falk

TO ANALYZE

■ **Hands-on revision:** This exercise is productive when you have a solid draft of a paper and want to check how others are following your arguments.

In your word processor, set up your paper so that there is only one paragraph per page. Print the paper, shuffle the paragraphs, and give them with tape to a friend or classmate. Ask that person to read the pieces and then tape the paper back together in an order that makes sense. (And if your reader can't figure out where some paragraphs go, just leave them out.) Ask the reader also to write on each page to explain reasons for taping each page in its order.

175

Did the reader put your paper back into your same arrangement, or is the order different? Do the differences suggest that you need to clarify the transitions between parts of your paper, add more explanations, or change the order completely? Do the differences suggest that your introduction (or conclusion) does not yet do what an introduction or conclusion should do?

This is Jacob's revision of his original draft. What sort of ethos has he created in this writing—and how has he created it? What emotions does he raise in you as a reader? Do you think he has succeeded in revising his draft so that you listen more closely to his words—and think more about what he asks of his readers?

A REVISED RESEARCH PAPER

- This information—writer's name, teacher's name, class name and number, and date—is expected on the top left of the first page for any research paper in MLA style.

- Center the title above the body of the text for MLA style. Do not bold the title or put extra spaces above or below it.

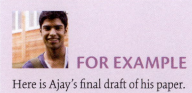

FOR EXAMPLE
Here is Ajay's final draft of his paper.

Ajay Chaudry   Chaudry 1

Professor Wysocki

English 102

June 4, 2012

Can You Buy an Education?

In college, do I want to be a student engaged with education—or a customer buying a product?

Until I read my sources for this paper, I did not understand that this question mattered. At first the difference between "student" and "customer" does not seem large: students learn something; customers buy something. Exploring the differences between learning and buying, however, and exploring the consequences of thinking of students as customers, has helped me learn that the differences do matter. If I really want an education, then I do not want to think of myself as a customer—and I certainly do not want my teachers or college to think of me as a customer.

Consider first the differences between learning and buying. When I buy a hamburger, I do not have to do anything. I stand at the counter, place my order, and they give me a hamburger. I eat it. That's it. To get into college, I had to do more than just pay money: I had to apply and show that I was prepared. As scholar David George describes in *The Journal of Socio-Economics*, "since flunking out is always possible, to remain a student and eventually earn a degree signals further that one had something besides money that made the degree possible" (George 971). Learning in college, then, requires more than walking in, putting down some money, and getting a degree; students have to prepare and make efforts to succeed in college. George does remind us that buying some products can also require efforts

1" ½" 1" 1" 1" 1 ½" 1"

from a consumer. If I buy a car, for example, I have to take care of it by changing its oil, keeping the brakes working, and so on; if I buy suntan lotion I have to pay attention to how I use it, and if I buy a book I have to put in effort to read it. George writes, however, that education "appears to be in a class by itself in requiring the demonstration of abilities prior to being accepted as a 'customer' and requiring the putting forth of effort before one can receive what one is ultimately seeking" (972).

And what is it we students are ultimately seeking? George says it is a diploma. Although a diploma is certainly important, I don't think anyone would be happy if someone described our school as "selling diplomas" (see George 970)—and I think that what we hope results from our efforts in college go beyond that piece of paper. As Laurie Lomas writes in *Quality in Higher Education*, a student is "only able to reflect fully upon the benefits of the knowledge and skills acquired and the attitudes that have been developed after a number of years when there has been sufficient opportunity to realise what they have learnt" (35). Getting a diploma means we have learned something, but I think Lomas is arguing that we won't really know what we have learned until we have time to put ourselves to the test in the real world.

But there is another aspect of education that my reading got me to think about. In the *Journal of Philosophy of Education*, Kevin Love builds an argument about what is essential to be educated; he writes that "to be educated is to exceed oneself, to exceed the inadequacies of the oneself" (27). This is odd language to me, but it pulls at me. The words suggest that education is about being stretched, being helped to push against our limitations, and trying to be and do more than I thought I could. I am in college, then, to learn what will help me get a good job

- For a research paper in MLA, put your last name and the page number at the top right of each page, including the first page. This will help readers in case the pages get out of order.

- We show, in blue, the conventional margins for a paper in MLA format.

- Papers in MLA format should be printed in a typeface like Times or Arial. (If a teacher does not specify a typeface for a paper, ask.)

- Papers in MLA format should be double-spaced. (Note that for space purposes we have not been able to show exact double-spacing here.)

- For a paper in MLA format, turn off hyphenation in your word-processing application.

- Note here, and throughout the paper, how Ajay introduces the sources he quotes. He does not quote any words from any source without providing some introductory information. (Also note that the first time he uses a source, he gives the source's full name; in any later uses of that source he uses only the source's **last** name.)

■ In MLA style, any quotation that would take up more than four lines should be indented as shown to the right. Such quotes are called "block quotes," and they are double spaced. Notice how the punctuation at the end of the block quote does not go after the source citation, as it would in a citation embedded in a sentence.

but also to learn how to keep stretching. As several Montana college teachers have written, "our students contract with us to be challenged and to exceed their previous intellectual limits. … They, like all of us, are involved in the process of becoming wiser" (Cheney, McMillan, and Schwartzman).

Those words help me see why Love and other writers describe how education is supposed to be hard. It is supposed to be hard because we are to be challenged and to challenge ourselves. I don't think wisdom comes easily. Love writes that a "teacher is not there to satisfy the student but to dissatisfy; not to provide but to demand" (Love 28). As George O. Tasie writes in *Educational Research and Reviews*:

2"

> learning often involves some discomfort, disequilibrium, and challenge. Students learn through the cognitive conflicts that occur when they face new points of view, new information, and new perspectives. Students learn when they are encouraged to reflect actively on the information that is unfamiliar and initially illogical or even threatening. In such situations, the dynamic tension created between the known and the new causes new thinking, analysis, and reevaluation. (Tasie 312)

When we buy something, we do not expect it to require much effort from us, to challenge us, or to help us exceed ourselves over the course of our whole lives—but we should expect that when we learn.

I hope I have made clear what I have been persuaded are differences between being a student and being a customer, between learning and consuming. What I hope to make clear next are consequences of not paying attention to these differences, of treating students as customers.

For anyone running a business, the primary question (as James C. Carey asks in his article "University or Corporation") is "Will this please the majority of my customers?" (443). When schools think of themselves as businesses and their students as customers, then they too ask the same question. The articles I read describe how colleges and universities, because they often compete for students and need tuition, want to please their students to keep them enrolled. Some consequences of trying to please students will trouble most of us, I think.

First, teachers who worry about pleasing their students can dumb down their classes or emphasize their entertainment value so students won't complain about hard work. Students can then come to expect such treatment, as these two quotations from university students show:

> I need a bit more motivation. . . . Basically, I don't want to study. I'm lazy…. I want [teachers] to excite me and make me want to be passionate about learning that subject. …If it doesn't grab my attention I'll just doze off, even though I might not be tired. My attention span is severely lacking in a subject that doesn't grab my attention at all. (qtd. in White 599)

And

> It gets kind of frustrating when [professors] … can't hold my attention. I don't understand why they should be so high and mighty and tell me off for keeping myself amused. … it's their own fault if they can't hold my attention and do an interesting lecture. (qtd. in White 599)

Although I think teachers should try to make their classes interesting, what I have written in earlier paragraphs about education and what students need to do

- Using the information on page 180, circle every transition Ajay uses in his writing. How might those transitions help readers follow Ajay's reasoning?

Are there places where you think Ajay could use transitions or clearer, more obvious transitions? Why?

implies that teachers shouldn't have to entertain us; we have responsibilities to make ourselves learn, too.

When students and schools both think of students as customers, grade inflation can happen. Grade inflation is when, over a number of years, the average grade given in the same class for the same work goes up. The writers I read explain that this happens for several reasons. Students think that what they are buying in school is a grade (see George 973 or White 600, for example). And when schools tell teachers that they have to keep students happy so that students will keep paying tuition, the teachers raise grades (White 594-595). Also, in such circumstances, schools evaluate teachers based on student evaluations, and so some teachers raise grades to make sure that their students give good evaluations (White 594-595).

Finally, when students and schools both think of students as customers, then that's all the students become through their education. All that I have read and presented above supports Love's argument that, when students become customers, the main consequence is that all of schooling "seems less concerned with the formation of citizens and more concerned with encouraging individuals to become consumers" (21).

When we are in college, then, we should ask ourselves who we want to be and become. Do we want our educations to be about becoming customers—people who are known for nothing but buying and wanting simple satisfactions? Or do we want our educations to be about becoming people who learn, who know how to stretch and take on hard work, who can be citizens, who seek wisdom?

Who do you want to be?

Works Cited

Carey, James C. "University or Corporation?" *Journal of Higher Education* 27. 8

(1956): 440-444+466. *Jstor*. Web. 7 May 2012.

Cheney, George, Jill J. McMillan, and Roy Schwartzman. "Should We Buy the

'Student-As-Consumer' Metaphor?" *Montana Professor* 7.3 (1997): 8-11. Web.

George, David. "Market Overreach: The Student as Customer." *Journal of*

Socio-Economics 36 (2007): 965-977. *Science Direct*. Web. 5 May 2012.

Lomas, Laurie. "Are Students Customers? Perceptions of Academic Staff."

Quality in Higher Education 13.1 (2007): 31-44. *Academic Search Premier*. 7

May 2012.

Love, Kevin. "Higher Education, Pedagogy and the 'Customerisation' of Teaching

and Learning." *Journal of Philosophy of Education* 42.1 (2008): 15-34. Print.

Tasie, George O. "Analytical Observations of the Applicability of the Concept

of Student-as-Customer in a University Setting." *Educational Research and*

Reviews 5.6 (2010): 309-313. *Academic Journals*. Web. 5 May 2012.

White, Naomi Rosh. "'The Customer is Always Right?': Student Discourse

About Higher Education in Australia." *Higher Education* 54.4 (2007):

593-604. *Academic Search Complete*. Web. 5 May 2012.

- For a formal paper in MLA style, put your Works Cited list on its own page at the end of the paper. Put "Works Cited" at the top center of the page. List only the sources that you cite in your paper.

- The Works Cited page is double-spaced throughout like all the other pages.

- See pages 121–123 on how to construct the Works Cited citations.

181

TO ANALYZE

- **Discuss with others:** Working with a partner, circle every change you see between Ajay's first draft and his final draft. Discuss each change together: *Why do you think Ajay made the changes he did? How did the changes make the draft stronger? (Did the changes make the draft stronger?)*

What observation about Ajay's changes can you turn into general advice for yourself on making revisions?

TESTING AND EVALUATING WRITING

When you ask others to read your writing before you consider it fully finished, you are testing your writing. There are different approaches you can use to help others read your work in more or less useful ways depending on where you are in the writing process. We've described some approaches on previous pages for how you can get assistance with the arrangement of your composition and with editing and proofreading.

Self-test for a writing draft

First, answer these two questions based on what you see in the writing:

❑ Describe your audience.

❑ What is your purpose?

If you cannot tell from the writing what the audience and purpose are, you know you have more work to do with focus and explanation.

Then, use these questions to determine the best approaches for strengthening your draft:

❑ What is strongest about this draft?

❑ What concerns you most about this draft?

❑ What sort of feedback would be most helpful to you now?

Finally, ask:

❑ Do I want to be the person I see emerging in this draft? Do I want to hold these opinions and ideas?

Testing your work during different draft stages

• When you complete your very first draft of a piece of writing, hand it to someone else to read for feedback, preferably to someone from the audience for whom you are writing—but don't just hand over your writing without explanation. Tell the person what you are trying to achieve and why so that she or he can read knowledgeably. You can write on a piece of paper the points to which you want your reader to attend, and ask your reader to write comments on the paper.

• Give your writing to someone else as in the previous point—but now ask your reader to summarize each paragraph in a phrase or sentence. Look over the list of sentences and see whether the order makes sense—the sense you thought your composition made before this exercise. You can do this yourself also.

• Give your writing to someone else, as in the two previous points—but now ask your reader to describe the relations among ethos, pathos, and logos in your writing. You can do this yourself also.

• Draw a map that shows the arrangement or structure of your composition.

• Design a plan for revising your composition.

A reminder: Before you decide which kind of testing to do, however, take a few minutes yourself to figure out the kind of feedback that will be most useful to you. Freewrite for a few minutes to figure out the kind of help you really need: Do you really just need someone to look over your grammar for you, or are you still working to figure out your main argument?

Qualities you can consider in testing a research paper

Following is a list of the many qualities that can characterize polished academic writing; the list can help you gain in confidence as a writer if you choose a few of these on which to focus at any time; move on to other qualities when you are comfortable with the first ones. (Some items might contradict others: Some apply only to certain kinds of writing depending on audience, purpose, and context.)

- ❑ The writing has one main argument.
- ❑ Any supporting arguments do indeed support the main argument.
- ❑ The writing acknowledges and responds to all who have a stake in the issue.
- ❑ The argument is understandable to its audience.
- ❑ The argument is worth making: It focuses on a topic or controversy that matters to its audience.
- ❑ The writing shows that the writer has tried to demonstrate to the audience that the topic matters to the audience.
- ❑ There is an appropriate level of support —such as examples (which can include personal experience), facts and/or figures, illustrations or photographs, charts and/or graphics—for the argument being made.
- ❑ The writing shows that the writer has made an effort to find appropriate and interesting sources.
- ❑ Sources are appropriately cited in the body of the paper.
- ❑ Any sections of the paper that appear to come from other sources show the source.

- ❑ All sources are appropriately cited at the end of the paper using one of the accepted citation styles.
- ❑ Any graphics used are clear and easy to understand.
- ❑ Any graphics used are appropriate to the argument.
- ❑ All graphics are treated appropriately as sources.
- ❑ Readers will easily understand why the paragraphs are ordered as they are.
- ❑ The writer has supplied transitions between each paragraph or section so that readers will understand why one paragraph moves into the next.
- ❑ Readers will be able to read the sentences easily because the grammar and spelling have been carefully checked.
- ❑ The grammar and spelling are rhetorically appropriate.
- ❑ The writing has a neat and easy-to-read appearance.
- ❑ The writing has an introduction that appropriately brings readers into the argument.

- ❑ The writing is as long as it needs to be to make its argument fully.
- ❑ At its conclusion, the writing sums up its argument in a manner that the audience both will understand and is likely to remember.
- ❑ The writing has a consistent ethos (if this is appropriate to the purpose of the paper).
- ❑ The ethos is appropriate to the purpose of the paper.
- ❑ The writing doesn't ramble, whine, or shout at its audience (unless rambling, whining, and shouting are appropriate to the purpose).
- ❑ The writing demonstrates that the writer has an appropriate level of authority and/or knowledge to write on this topic.
- ❑ The writer pays attention to the emotions of the audience.
- ❑ The writing shows that the writer respects the audience's intelligence and ability to think.
- ❑ The writing shows that the writer has tried to make the writing interesting to readers.

THINKING THROUGH PRODUCTION

■ Describe your writing process, what it looks and feels like, and the steps you go through in order to produce a piece of writing. Hold on to this. The next time you write something, keep a journal that describes each step as you go through it. Finally, compare and contrast the first account of your writing process with the second account in your journal. What is the reason for any differences between the two descriptions—and what would you like to change about your process?

■ Take the introduction to a paper on which you are working or have already written and write two more versions of it. In the first, combine ethos and pathos by showing your readers the passion you have for your subject (and so try to stir up a similar passion in them). In the other, combine ethos and logos by establishing your credentials: Prove why you are the person to write this composition.

Write a short paper in which you reflect on what you learned from writing these introductions: *By writing these introductions, what did you learn about how you have approached introductions in the past? What will you carry forward into your own writing and in what contexts?*

■ On page 138, we asked you to list all the kinds of writing you and others encounter and to draw up lists of audiences, contexts, and purposes.

Use your lists as the basis of a report for the local school board about how you think writing should be taught in high school. Develop a design plan for your report, and then produce your report—and ask your teacher to test it.

■ Write three different, short opinion pieces on an issue that matters to you. Each time you write, pick a new arrangement—a narrative, a problem-solution structure, juxtaposition, whatever makes sense given your purpose—and make it the overarching structure for the piece. How do each of the different structures shape what you are able to argue?

Give your pieces to others to read. Ask them to figure out your overall structure—and to say which structure seems most effective and why.

Write a short paper in which you reflect on what you learned from writing these opinions pieces: *How does making yourself write about your opinions affect your sense of what you believe? From writing these opinion pieces and trying different structures, what will you bring into your other writing in the future?*

■ Research the kinds of writing people produce with printing presses and/or for paper, and research the kinds of writing people produce for computer screens (writing to be read only on screen, not meant to be printed on paper). List the kinds of writing you can do with these different technologies, but also consider the relations these technologies allow composers to set up between themselves and their audiences. (For example, what different senses of an author come through a page as opposed to a blog?) Consider the contexts in which people read these different kinds of writing. What sorts of similar as well as different purposes can be achieved with these two technologies?

Do a library and/or online search for "writing technology," "writing technologies," and "history of writing." Read through a range of the materials you find.

Use your research to plan and produce an academic print essay that compares and contrasts the audiences, contexts, and purposes of the two technologies. In the essay, develop an argument about the differing relations we can establish with each other using these technologies. (And, if you have the abilities, also create an online version of the essay, including color, pictures, and video as appropriate.)

about
oral modes
of communication

People think speaking well is easy—or impossible. On the one hand, we grow up speaking, so what is there to learn? On the other hand, speaking before a group while keeping your thoughts straight for more than a minute feels like too much for anyone. It will not surprise you to hear us say that you can learn to be a more comfortable speaker if you approach speaking by thinking about context, audience, and purpose and if you consider some of the specifics of oral communication.

We cannot cover every aspect of oral communication in this chapter. We cannot cover all the kinds of speech or speaking occasions you may encounter. We do not go into the physiology of speech—how to breathe, the muscular expression of emotion, the chemical causes of speech anxiety—nor do we discuss radio and television broadcasting, debate, or parliamentary procedure.

We do address speaking (and listening) and what you can do to strengthen your oral—and aural—abilities. We offer you a base vocabulary for understanding speaking situations and listening, and we offer strategies for learning to speak publicly, with tips on delivering a speech. We touch on speech anxiety and ways to deal with it, the ethics of oral communication, and interviewing.

You may not emerge from this chapter a seasoned public speaker—but we do hope you will know more about what goes into a well-prepared speaking performance and feel a little more confident in your ability to talk to, and with, others.

PLEASURES OF SPEAKING...

...publicly and interpersonally

We've all been speaking since we were little kids. We have such long and varied and day-to-day histories of speaking with others—sometimes marred by some bad experiences—that it is easy to lose sight of speaking's distinct and distinctive pleasures.

The first pleasure? Speaking well gets things done. A few words in the right ear can work wonders. When we need to make a decision with others, for example, and we speak directly with them instead of sending an email, the sense of action—of making something happen—can feel both right and good. Speaking directly to people, in small or large groups, can quickly pull everyone together, especially when there is a sense of urgency to the occasion. Seeing what needs to be done and motivating others to act makes one feel connected and somewhat powerful.

And, then, well, there also are those personal pleasures of speaking. Consider those moments when you remember to attend thoughtfully and gently to the one listening to you, when you tilt your head and your words toward that one, and the response is a head tilted back toward you with a soft-spoken "yes"—well, that can be quite satisfying too, no?

We talk to other people because we live in the world with them. Even if, sometimes, we feel it is not worth all the trouble listening to other people and finding the right words to say back to them—be they friend, acquaintance, colleague, or just another person on the street—those should not be the single defining moments in our lives together. Stammering, discussing, conversing, shouting, rapping, schmoozing, whispering, arguing—altogether, those make some of the most pleasurable ways we live our daily lives together and remake our worlds.

Let us not overlook the range of possible joys in these basic aspects of our existence with others.

TO ANALYZE

■ **Write informally:** Call to mind a time in the past when you had to speak publicly—whether to a few people or many, to people you knew well or not—and the results made you happy. Also call to mind when such a situation had other results.

In writing, describe in detail what made the two situations different. *How had you prepared yourself for the two different situations? Who were the different audiences, and how did that shape the situation? What kind of talking was involved (that is, what were your purposes?)? What was the context: formal or informal, comfortable place or uncomfortable place...? In hindsight, what would you have done differently—in either situation—to have had more pleasing results?*

What can you learn from that short analysis to help you plan ahead for future speaking situations?

AND RESPONSIBILITIES OF SPEAKING

In the introduction to his book, *Democracy as Discussion: Civic Education and the American Forum Movement*, William M. Keith reminds us that American democracy has always relied on some notion of public forums and the practices that support such places and occasions. If we are to make informed decisions as citizens, he argues, we need to read, learn, talk, and listen. He describes his book as being about

> a broad educational and public project starting in the 1920s-1940s, the attempt to recast democratic discourse as discussion, and create a venue in which to discuss, the public forum. … Forums grew out of an American tradition of understanding democracy as embodied forms of communication, whether the speaker on the platform, the candidates debating, or something "new," discussion. (1)

Keith's book discusses a two-decades-long effort in the United States to rejuvenate public debate by reshaping how we teach public speaking, how we practice public deliberation, and how we talk to each other about political issues and our shared civic concerns. As you can tell from his emphasis on discussion, his book is about a shift in how we go about engaging one another: from *debating*, which is formal and performance oriented, to *discussion*, which is less formal but still learnable.

The preceding quotation draws our attention to three questions Keith argues that we need to ask when we start to consider what is distinctive and important about oral communication:

1 What role does oral communication play in our lives as citizens now?

2 What opportunities do we have for participating in public deliberation—political discussions—now?

3 What training in public speaking do we need and/or expect now?

Keith ends his book by suggesting that currently we are experiencing a similar effort both in American universities and beyond to "reinvent deliberative democracy," and he asks what we can learn from past efforts to do so. His answer, in a nutshell, is that "the actual details of interaction—who, what, when, where, and how?—will determine the success or failure of public deliberation" (331).

We hope that as you think about your purposes and strategies for speaking you will think not just about the specific contexts and occasions for your speaking. We hope you will also consider the broader context of public deliberation—the time and space we make, or do not make, for discussion with each other—in this, our shared and contested democracy.

be cool

By learning to be more comfortable speaking in public with others, you will learn to be more comfortable participating in the social and political discussions that create our country—and that also shape our relations with peoples beyond the geographical, political, and legal borders of our country.

ON LISTENING

After thinking about the pleasures of speaking, it makes sense to consider listening: Good speaking grows out of good listening. Listening also often provides the guidance we need to make decisions about what to say and when.

Most of us probably do not listen enough. We think speaking is how to get things done—and so listening can feel only like waiting for our chance to speak. We also have all learned ways to avoid listening without even realizing: Think about how those with whom you are close sometimes nod while you talk and then later you realize they haven't heard a word; no one does this purposefully. And, finally, listening (like seeing) seems deceptively easy and obvious: We've been doing it for as long as we can remember, and we think we've learned everything about it we need.

Listening provides so much more than meets the ear, however, and turning your attention to listening will help you understand how listening is a dynamic part of speaking. First, put aside your familiarity with listening and consider the possibility that you (like all of us!) do not really know how to listen and that over the years, we have all learned some bad listening habits we could stand to unlearn.

Communication theorists differentiate among various kinds of listening as we delineate next. The differences can be subtle, but so are listening and being an effective listener.

Participatory listening and passive listening

Most of us simply hear. If we are lucky, we have functioning ears and those ears just do their work. Sounds and voices come to us, without—it seems—our having to do any work. We can let the sounds pass through us, and if we don't pay attention, we can miss things and then sometimes we fill in the gaps with assumptions of our own. That is passive listening.

Participatory listening, by contrast, involves paying attention. You make yourself lean in. You think about what is being said. You make sure you are making yourself remember what is being said. You show you are engaged by nodding and saying "yes" occasionally—even if you disagree. Participatory listening shows that you consider a conversation or a talk to be an event between people.

Depending on your needs and occasion, you can choose to be an active or a passive listener. Choosing to be an active listener is especially appropriate when you are engaged in conversation with someone who matters to you or when you need to learn or to participate.

Empathetic listening and objective listening

Empathetic listeners *want* to understand those to whom they're listening. As they listen, they try to imagine what it is like to be in the speaker's position; as they listen, they ask what the speaker is feeling and why. Empathetic listening is charitable and supportive. Empathy, though, is hard, and sometimes when we think we have understood and empathized with someone, we really have not done so—as when we are too quick to say, "I feel your pain."

Objective listening tries to stay alert to the context. It balances what someone is saying against the listener's own (and developing) understanding of the speaker's context and purpose as well as to the perspectives of others.

Empathetic listening is useful in friendly contexts and when we want to give others our full support. Objective listening is appropriate in learning situations or when another is trying to persuade us.

Nonjudgmental listening and critical listening

Listening without making judgments or assumptions about what you are hearing is hard. In some circumstances, however, it is necessary to try.

Nonjudgmental listening involves keeping an open mind: You listen and work to hold in mind everything being said without making judgments. Nonjudgmental listening differs from objective listening, which involves positioning what you hear against what you already know or can see for yourself.

Critical listening is similar to objective listening in that you adopt a questioning attitude toward the speaker. Critical listening goes a step further because it involves concentrating hard to detect inaccuracies, biases, and mistakes. Critical listening assumes that people are not fully in control of their prejudices and deep-seated beliefs—and that listening can help us understand what prejudices and beliefs shape a speaker's words.

Surface listening and in-depth listening

Sometimes you just have to take what someone is saying at surface value because such acceptance builds trust and demonstrates that you may not know everything. Other times you just have to take what someone is saying at surface value because you know that pointing out the hidden or buried arguments underneath the surface will cause too much trouble or will lead a discussion in directions it simply doesn't need to go. Awarely deciding to listen in such a way requires discretion.

In-depth listening helps when you suspect there is a hidden message that the speaker cannot herself see or bring herself to acknowledge or needs you to acknowledge without her having to say it. Sometimes we think everything should be explicit and without secondary hidden messages, but that simply is not possible. Some things are better left unsaid—but still acted upon. In order to act upon them, you need to practice in-depth listening so that you will know what to do.

TO ANALYZE

- **Discuss with others:** In small groups, discuss differences between "listening" and "hearing." Can you tell by looking at others if they are listening or if they are hearing? What can you do to help others listen? What can you do to increase the chances you will be heard?

- **Write with others:** In pairs, list the obstacles, habits, and behaviors that get in the way of hearing and listening. Compile the lists in a large group to compare and to check that you've thought as broadly as possible. (As you do this, look around the room to see who is listening and who isn't; when you see someone not attending to the others in class, ask the person why. You can learn more concerning the decisions people make about listening.)

Together come up with a list of what you can do to improve your own listening and overcome the obstacles to others listening to you.

I am listening

SPEAKING'S PURPOSES, AUDIENCES, AND CONTEXTS

Speaking's purposes

Imagine, for example, that you've been asked to:

You probably can easily imagine yourself:

Toast a couple at their wedding. ⮕ Saying something funny and something warmly emotional about the couple.

Give a funeral eulogy. ⮕ Speaking respectfully and with warmth and heart about the deceased.

Speak at someone's 50th birthday party. ⮕ Telling funny but respectful anecdotes about the 50-year-old.

Accept an award at a banquet. ⮕ Humbly thanking those who gave you the award.

Make a presentation to co-workers explaining a project. ⮕ Laying out what the project is and describing each worker's part in it.

Confront a city council that has made a bad decision for your community. ⮕ Speaking formally and with moral strength at the city council.

Moving from general to specific purposes

Often a speaking occasion gives you your general purpose, as in the examples above. Because you have grown up in particular places and times where certain events always happen according to certain patterns, you can probably easily imagine about those examples the contexts, who would be there, and what it is therefore appropriate to say.

None of that is different from other kinds of communication. Asked to write a class paper, you know without too much thought that you want to sound smart, that you want your writing to support your arguments, and that your paper ought to look polished. If you make a brochure for a nonprofit organization, you know that it needs to make the organization sound solid and worthy, that it will have several panels of different information, and that it

needs to look professional. All these are general purposes.

In all these cases, you know enough about the general contexts of communications to have in mind what you can do—generally. You can probably see, though, how articulating these general purposes out loud to yourself can help you think more carefully about what you want to achieve more specifically.

So what you need to do, once you have a general context and purpose, is to get specific. You need to get specific about your purpose, and you need to think about how your purpose—grounded as it is within the particular mode(s) of your communication—can be developed and supported by strategies particular to the mode(s) you employ.

To get specific about your purpose in giving any kind of talk, use what we have written in

chapters 1 through 3. In chapter 2, we present actions you can take to generate—to invent—ideas about purpose. Look also to chapter 4, the chapter on researching. There we present questions to help you think about focusing the question that will guide a research paper—but the scheme we give for generating questions can help you focus in on exactly what you want to accomplish by helping you focus on exactly what question(s) you need to address through your speaking.

Purposes specific to speaking with others

Once you have a specific purpose, make it *even more* specific for the occasion of speaking, for being present in a room with others.

When you speak, you can see the faces of others, and judge their reactions—so use this to help you think about what you want to achieve.

For example, imagine that you have to make an oral presentation to a campus organization that you joined a year ago: You've been asked to help the organization think about how to increase membership. You want to persuade the others that you're losing potential members because the organization's activities have been, ummm, a bit on the boring side. Imagine yourself talking to the group: Given your purpose, do you want them to look at you with the devastated faces of people who have come to realize through your talking that they've been lackluster and dull? Or would you rather have them look at you with lights in their eyes, excited about the captivating possibilities you're creating for them as you talk?

In other words, although your initial purpose was to persuade the others that their lack of members was a result of their being boring, a more fine-tuned purpose and one more likely to succeed—more likely to get the others engaged—is indirect: Get them excited about the possibilities of what they might do while avoiding talking about their past failures.

The differences between the two ways of considering your purpose just mentioned may seem subtle, but they are crucial to the success of what you undertake.

TO ANALYZE

■ **Discuss with others:** Using the example to the left about reshaping the purpose of speaking to a campus organization about increasing membership, imagine the moment in which someone speaks about the following purposes to their audience. Restate or enlarge the purpose so that it considers how audiences look and respond during the speaking and how audience response might be best shaped for listening most attentively.

- You want to persuade your parents that changing your major from chemical engineering to French is in your—and their—best interests.

- You want to persuade your best friend why it might be better to use spring vacation to work on a Habitat for Humanity Blitz Build in the next state instead of going to Europe.

- You've been working with three others on a long-term class project that is due in three weeks. You think what you've all made so far has ended up taking you in a completely wrong direction. You want to persuade the others that you need to learn from your mistakes—and pretty much start over.

191

Speaking's audiences

In preparing to give a talk, you need to learn about your audience just as when you are preparing to produce any other communication. The approaches and questions of chapters 1, 2, and 3 are as useful and necessary here as for any communication. When you are preparing to speak, however, there are additional considerations.

Speaking with and listening to audiences

Just about any time we open our mouths, we position ourselves to speak *at* people—rather than *with* them. That is, if you initiate the speaking, you tend to see yourself as active, while you tend to see those to whom you are speaking as passive. This is the first challenge to overcome on the way to becoming a successful speaker (as opposed to being a "talker"): Find ways to listen to audiences.

There are at least two ways to listen to audiences.

The first concerns how you prepare to speak. When you research audiences and social contexts, you are, in essence, listening to your audience. You may be listening to them directly if you talk to potential audience members to learn what matters to them; you may also be listening indirectly when you research the background of a situation to learn how audience attitudes have been shaped by past events (even those of last week). As you prepare to speak, try starting as though you know nothing about your audience so that you have to build the most fundamental understanding of them, questioning how you know what you think you know. You can uncover assumptions on your part that you might need to work against, or you might find a new way of considering the people with whom you interact so that you work more easily together.

The second way of listening to an audience happens as you settle yourself in to talk with them. As you approach your audiences, see and think of them as whole people who think and feel and have material needs, who care about the world around them and yet can be blind to parts of it, and, above all, who listen and speak just as you do.

Researching audiences to encourage listening

Because audiences are complex, you can't prepare just once for the moments when you stand with them to talk. You need to start researching right away, research in stages, and continue up and through your actual talking. (Consider as research what happens while you speak, as you attend to the facial expressions of the people before you, modifying what you say in response to their responses.)

A simple questionnaire can help you begin your research. (Sometimes speakers bring brief questionnaires to a talk, hand them out in advance, and glance through them before they are scheduled to speak. Ideally, you would leave yourself more time to think the responses through.) When designing a questionnaire, you must know what you need to learn given your purpose and context. For example, what would Walter from chapter 1 have needed to ask potential audience members to find out what would have kept his group from failing in its approach to women on campus?

Even if such questionnaires do not provide useful information for helping you plan your talk, they bring your audience closer in concrete ways. Audiences need to be real for you, and so the more you can learn about their relevant characteristics, habits, tastes, knowledge, skills, and background experiences, the more likely you are to produce oral strategies that persuade audiences to consider what matters to you.

Another way to research people is to interview potential audience members—people like them, people who know them, or people who are familiar with people like them. You could read what people in a potential audience have written about themselves.

Finally, don't forget you are considering an audience that you will meet face to face—something that rarely happens with essays or posters. Look then especially for information that pertains to the context and purpose of speaking to your audience. Do people who have the characteristics of your audience attend talks often and so are used to giving their aural attentions at some length? Will the room be filled with tension, or will people be tired and need a lively talk? Do they know little about your topic, so that support materials—handouts, video, visual aids—might be especially helpful?

This is a short way of putting all that we've just written: *Make your audiences as real and human in your mind as possible.* Perhaps they are scarier this way, but then they are also concrete, like the people with whom you live. You know how to talk *with* (rather than *at*) the people directly around you because you know them so well and so complexly; the people in your audience are no different. They are like you, wanting to be respected, wanting to be treated complexly, wanting to be engaged with others.

Being an audience

If you've ever given a talk and seen in your audience a sullen face, a pouty expression, or a frown, you know how hard it can be to ignore. But often you can ignore it: Most people do not realize the faces they wear, and were you to ask them what about your speaking upset them so, they'd look at you quizzically and say that on the contrary, they were enjoying listening.

Keep this in mind as you speak with others— but also keep this in mind as you listen. If you

want to support communication among us all, listen generously and attentively. Smile (at least a little), make your eyes bright, nod. Let the speaker know that you are there, paying attention. This is how we build bonds with others. You can still disagree—but disagreement that stands on bonds of respect, generosity, and the willingness to listen and be moved is potentially productive. Disagreement built on the conviction that you are absolutely right and the other is without a prayer destroys friendships, families, and countries.

TO ANALYZE

■ **Discuss and write with others:** In groups of five to seven, draw up lists of your ages, genders, incomes, religions, educational backgrounds, majors, clubs, organizational affiliations, political affiliations, lifestyles, moral commitments, family lives, and so on. You don't need to get deeply personal—but try to get a sense of the characteristics that shape each of you as a *social being*.

After about 20 minutes, come back together with the full class and pool your results, putting them into categories on the board or a large sheet of paper.

Then pick a topic or issue that is of interest to the class, something you have been studying or discussing as a class already.

Go back through the various characteristics you've listed. How might someone with a particular characteristic respond to the topic or issue because of that characteristic? Are there any characteristics you did not mention at first but that in light of the issue chosen seem relevant now? (For instance, whether you own guns or cars, whether you vote, whether you have cats, and so on.) How might your observations help you think in the future about audiences you will need to address?

193

Speaking's contexts

Careful consideration of the physical and social contexts for your speaking helps you make the most appropriate choices for effective speaking.

The physical context of a speaking occasion includes the actual location of your talk as well as the time you talk.

Social contexts include everything that has happened in the world that leads up to your occasion to speak as well as everything you and your audience anticipate will come after—in part as a result of—your speaking.

Considering physical contexts

Whether you are being interviewed or are speaking to the campus skateboard club, try to visit the room where you'll speak. Get a feel for its lighting, size, furniture arrangement, and where you'll be standing or sitting. If you cannot actually visit, find people who can describe the space.

In thinking about the physical spaces in which you'll speak and how those spaces might shape your interactions with others, keep in mind that when we are together with others, we act (even if we are not aware of it) within **personal, social, and institutional senses of space**. These distinctions remind us that context includes more than lighting and temperature. As you think about where you'll talk—and how you'll place yourself and move within that space—keep these distinctions in mind both

because you can use them and because your audience will understand what you do in terms of them.

Personal space is our skin and the immediate area around our skin. When we are this close to others, space is intimate and sensuous, and so very comfortable—or uncomfortable. When we are this close to others, we are aware of the possibilities of touch—whether the touch be gentle, tender, and friendly or the opposite. In personal space we can often smell others and be smelled ourselves. Smell, like touch, shapes how we consider and respond.

In the United States, **social space** is roughly 2 to 7 feet around us. (If you've traveled to other countries, you may have experienced closer social spaces.) Social space is less intimate than personal space but is still close: It is the space of shared activities, of leaning in together to look at a car engine or shake hands. How we act in social space draws on the special (but perhaps not explicit) training we've had growing up to be sensitive to the proximity of people, actions, and events. Much of communicative interest goes on in this space. It is the space of whispering and significant eye contact. It may include the first row of your audience. You may find yourself talking in a large space: Given your purposes, is it appropriate to lean into your audience to create a sense of shared social space?

Institutional space includes the physical rooms and halls in which we meet and asks us to consider how those spaces shape our feelings and actions. For example, think of waiting rooms: They can be warm, relaxing places—or cold and awkward rooms that make us more nervous than we already were. Think of movie theater lobbies, which invite movement directed toward the theaters but also toward the snack bar (where you're encouraged to buy bite-size sweets). Grocery stores are usually designed to move you through colorful displays and tempting racks of little packaged goods. The spaces in which we make oral presentations to each other—classrooms, meeting rooms, city council chambers, convention center rooms—are rarely warm, comfortable, or personal spaces, but you can shape that space by drawing your audience's attentions to or away from the space by asking the audience to imagine other spaces or moving comfortably relative to it.

We mention these general kinds of dwelling space not because we picture you giving speeches in a movie lobby but because these examples indicate how space influences behavior—including communication. The distinctions among personal, social, and institutional spaces help keep our thinking about context complex enough to make thoughtful decisions about how to speak. By considering these different aspects of space as you plan what to say, you can figure out strategies for shaping the relation you want to build with your audience.

Similarly, our senses of the time in which we speak shape our—and audience—expectations. We cannot tell a long rambling story in five minutes. Audiences will be unhappy if they've come for an hour and we finish in 15 minutes—unless we give them good reason to understand.

In addition, however, audiences at the end of the day have a different sense of time than at the beginning of the day. Tired audiences are often impatient audiences, wanting to get away, and often will be more inclined to listen if you acknowledge their state of mind and the time. Rested audiences are generally more generous.

As you plan what to say, then, consider both how much time you have and when in the audience's daily rhythms that time comes.

Once you know or can concretely imagine the situation in which you will be standing, you will often know certain actions you will have to take. *Will the room be large?* You'll need to speak loudly and perhaps take effort to make the room feel less impersonal for your audience. *Will the room be cold?* You'll perhaps want to use words and arrangements that suggest warmth or that otherwise distract your audience from the cold. *Will the sound be good or just adequate? Will everyone be able to see you? And how much time do you have: 5 minutes? 10 minutes?*

2 hours? Answers to these questions tell you whether the audience will expect talking that is short and to the point or more languid, able to develop ideas in pleasurable detail. Once you know these factors, you can think about the appropriate relations you want to shape with your audience and how you need to prepare yourself and your words.

Considering social contexts

Think back to Walter's story in chapter 1: Walter and his group ran into the trouble they did—in a fairly simple and straightforward communication situation—precisely because they had not considered the social contexts of their speaking. They were speaking to a group of people—women at a technological university—who had already (and too many times) experienced being treated as less competent than they were. If Walter and his friends had taken time to think through the social contexts in which they were approaching their audience, they would not have tanked.

The more you research the social background of your reasons for speaking—and your audiences' understanding of that background—the more your words will be able to address your audience's specific concerns; the more you will be able to decide whether you need to continue developing lines of thinking that already exist or to strike off in new directions.

TO ANALYZE

■ **Discuss with others:** In small groups, pick a current event or controversial topic. Discuss different time frames for the research you might do in preparation to talk with others about this issue. That is, how far back in time do you need to look in your research and in what you say to address the issue or topic best? How far forward do you need to look as you consider the consequences of your position or conclusions? Do different time frames change the issue? Do different time frames change how people consider the issue?

What do your observations suggest about the contexts in which differing audiences will consider the topic or issue?

195

A STATEMENT OF PURPOSE FOR SPEAKING

FOR EXAMPLE

In addition to writing a paper based on his research, Ajay has an assignment to give an 8–12-minute-long oral presentation on his research.

As with producing any text in any medium, you cannot think with confidence about the strategies you will use to shape and deliver an oral presentation unless you know why you are speaking and to whom. You need to have a clear sense of purpose, audience, and context as we have described on the previous pages.

Remember from chapter 2 that a statement of purpose pulls together your sense of purpose with thoughts about your audience in the particular contexts in which you communicate. Such a statement of purpose therefore supports you in making choices about a presentation.

As you read the next pages about strategies particular to speaking, keep Ajay's statement of purpose in mind. If you were Ajay, what strategies would you shape out of this chapter's suggestions?

☛ See Ajay's design plan for his talk on pages 214–215—and see his talk on pages 217–231.

Statement of Purpose for Oral Presentation

My audience for this presentation is everyone else in class—and I will be giving this talk in class, so that's my context, the late afternoon when everyone is kind of snoozy and wanting to go home.

I know that the assignment says we can convert our research papers into our talks, but there was something from my research that got me curious (and I wasn't able to fit it into my paper). *WHY do students and colleges think of students as customers?* My research suggested that both the TQM movement and (probably much more importantly) rising tuitions in college are making students feel that, if they are paying so much, they should be treated like customers. So that's what I want to argue: How rising tuitions are causing this.

But as I write, I realize there's more: My research also showed me that public colleges aren't raising tuition just because they're trying to make more money. They're raising tuition because they are getting way less in money from their states. (I've found TONS of statistics on this.) And because of taxes: Who is paying taxes, and how do states spend taxes? And I am absolutely certain I don't want to get into having to argue with anyone about taxes—but given what I've learned about students thinking of themselves as customers and how much that messes up education for everyone, I want at least maybe to suggest that we should be thinking about how states spend their money.

So maybe my purpose is to get people concerned about students as customers, how rising tuition ties into that, and how schools have less money. Maybe I can get everything that far so that my audience will leave just thinking about what's going on. If I can make a strong case for how less money coming in to public colleges means students have to pay more and so get customer-y in class… would that be enough?

I think so. I think I'm willing to risk it, given what I learned about what's happening because of the student-as-customer thing.

ETHOS, LOGOS, AND PATHOS AS SPEAKING STRATEGIES

In preparing a speech, you can first approach ethos, logos, and pathos as you do in writing: You can sit alone at a desk looking at a piece of paper considering what ethos to project, playing with arrangements and arguments, and shaping sentences to evoke some precise emotion. After you've noodled this way with writing, you polish it, get feedback, make revisions—and then give it to your intended readers so they can sit alone out of sight to read.

But you have to perform a speech

You can practice a speech with comfortable friends or with a small group from a class, but eventually there's a moment when you have to stand in front of others and—in real time—perform. When you speak, you construct your ethos, logos, and pathos from all that you do during those moments of being in front of others.

The following sections help you think about what you do to construct your ethos, logos, and pathos in the presence of listening, watching others.

TO ANALYZE

■ **Write:** Think back to a time in the past when you had to speak publicly and weren't happy about it. Or visualize an upcoming occasion in which you need to speak before others.

In writing, describe in detail what you could have done or can do to make the occasion pleasurable. Don't settle for figuring out how to make the occasion tolerable; instead, think hard about what would make the occasion memorable and fulfilling through how you consider context, purpose, audience and your use of ethos, pathos, and logos.

We're not asking you to make the occasion "fun": Many speaking occasions—such as funerals—cannot ever be fun. But you can make funerals (like other occasions) feel right: You can help make such situations thoughtful and comforting and thus pleasurable and satisfying.

Consider how to make the occasion of which you are thinking pleasurable in those ways for yourself and for your listeners.

197

ETHOS IN SPEAKING

Have you ever developed a crush on someone just from hearing the person's voice on the phone? We make wonderful, and sometimes tragic, judgments about others based only on their voices. We believe that character resides in voices and that we can tell others' internal strength or seriousness from how they speak. Ethos just naturally feels a part of speaking.

In speaking, therefore, ethos is simply waiting for you. You can come as you are.

But ethos can also be a more complex and constructed part of verbal interactions. In the 1998 movie *Bulworth*, the senator played by Warren Beatty becomes disillusioned and suffers a nervous breakdown. He begins to deliver his speeches in hip hop rhythms, which is disconcerting because Beatty is (and is playing) an aging white guy. At first his (mostly mainstream and white) audiences are shocked: Hip hop (especially from an aging white guy) is unexpected and unfamiliar in such political contexts. As Beatty persists with his speeches and direct talk, some audiences begin to warm up. In addition to his refreshingly direct challenges to his audiences, his sincerity wins them over: He looks and sounds committed to what he is doing. His ethos shifts, but the shift doesn't lose his audiences because, finally, Beatty himself is convinced by what he does. He becomes a candidate who cuts through the crap and makes good sense.

From *Bulworth*, we can take several lessons about ethos in speaking. Ethos happens in the interactions of what we say and do and how others perceive what we say and do. Ethos is ethical: We connect to others through how we come across. And, finally, because we build ethos in each situation, we can unbuild and rebuild it within occasions and from occasion to occasion. Ethos is malleable in writing and visual communication but especially in speaking when you are facing others in the moment.

The following factors (among others) affect how audiences perceive you when you speak. Which factors can you shape?

- what audiences know about you already

- how you dress

- how you walk into the room

- how you stand

- the gestures you make

- your tone of voice—and how you vary it

- what you say and do not say

- how quickly you speak

- whether or not you tell jokes

How might your audience respond if you wear your baseball cap when speaking? If you talk about jobs in the United States and don't discuss globalization and industrial flight to other countries? If you scratch yourself or show up in a suit?

Sustaining ethos throughout oral communication

> "When I began going about by car I got just as angry at the carelessness of pedestrians as I used to be at the recklessness of drivers."
>
> *Sigmund Freud*

If ethos is a relationship between speaker and audience, then, as with all relationships, you need to keep an eye on ethos the whole time you are with your audience. If you set yourself up as being on the same level with your audience—as just working together, as opposed to your taking the lead—then make sure you do not later slip into ways of talking that imply you know more or better.

Sigmund Freud was always aware that much of what he had to say might seem like finger-pointing at his audience—and so he often used himself as an example to develop and sustain a more humble ethos. Rather than saying, "You probably don't get it that you judge others from a single, limited point of view, and you should think about that," he said what we quoted at the top of this column. He was aware that a relationship with his audience unfolded as he spoke and that a large part of that relationship depended on how he came across. He therefore paid steady attention to his place in his communications—and he used the fact of his presence to his advantage to emphasize how he and his audience were enmired together in the mess of life.

ETHOS IN SPOKEN INTRODUCTIONS

For all the reasons we wrote about ethos and introductions (see pages 142–145), introductions in speaking matter for your ethos. With more formal oral presentations, ask what general kind of opening would work best for you as you build the relationship you desire with your audience. In addition to the options we discussed for written introductions on pages 142–143, consider these for an oral presentation:

• a brief story, humorous or riveting

• a question that grabs your listeners

• an unexpected statement or declaration

• a long, uncomfortable pause, followed by a strong, short statement or declaration

• a quotation delivered with feeling

• a greeting

Here is how writer Virginia Woolf began a talk—titled "A Room of One's Own"—she gave at a women's college in the early 20th century:

> *But, you may say, we asked you to speak about women and fiction—what has that got to do with a room of one's own? I will try to explain.*

She seems to begin in the middle of a thought, as though she and her audience have already started talking. She also begins by raising what might seem a problem: The announced title of her talk does not obviously fit with the subject on which she was asked to speak. (It turns out that the title did indeed fit very well, and her talk was eventually published as a short book and is read to this day.)

We interpret Woolf's beginning ethos this way: She comes across as always thinking, and she positions her audience almost to eavesdrop on her. Her listeners are dropped midstream into her thoughts as though they are there with her. At the same time, she sends a clear signal that she respects her audience enough to anticipate an important objection that might be troubling them and to reassure them, she will "try to explain." There is even a hint of humility hidden in the word "try."

If you were to hear a speaker start as Woolf started, how might you respond?

TO ANALYZE

■ **Discuss with others:** Franklin Delano Roosevelt took office in the Depression's early years and delivered what became a famous rallying cry to the nation. Following is the speech's first paragraph. With others, discuss the relationship Roosevelt constructs with his audience. How does he come across, and what role does he prepare for his audience early on? What does he promise his audience—and what does he ask of them?

I am certain that my fellow Americans expect that on my induction into the Presidency I will address them with a candor and a decision which the present situation of our Nation impels. This is pre-eminently the time to speak the truth, the whole truth, frankly and boldly. Nor need we shrink from honestly facing conditions in our country today. This great Nation will endure as it has endured, will revive and will prosper. So, first of all, let me assert my firm belief that the only thing we have to fear is fear itself—nameless, unreasoning, unjustified terror which paralyzes needed efforts to convert retreat into advance. In every dark hour of our national life a leadership of frankness and vigor has met with that understanding and support of the people themselves which is essential to victory. I am convinced that you will again give that support to leadership in these critical days.

LOGOS IN SPEAKING

Your audience perceives your logos through the choices you make in structuring your talk. Structuring a talk is about the formal arguments and arrangements you choose as well as about word choices; in other words, the same levels of logos operate as with writing (see page 146).

Methods of presentation

Looking ahead to speaking, settle on whether you'll read a prepared speech off paper or talk through a planned speech performed from talking points (perhaps on 3 x 5 cards or PowerPoint slides). Or you might not have much choice because you must speak extemporaneously—as when you are invited to respond to questions.

Each of those methods presents its own challenges. Reading from a prepared script requires you to avoid the stiffness and droning that can accompany reading, sentence after sentence, without feeling or tone changes. Speaking from a set of talking points requires you be familiar with each point and how it leads to the next so that you don't forget the order and overall structure of the talk you planned.

We have not exhausted the possible methods of presentation here. We challenge you to be creative in developing methods that balance what your audience knows and expects with what new approaches best serve your purpose. Just be sure that your method fits your purpose—and that you are comfortable and at ease with what you choose.

Arranging a speech

We have included the reading "Constructing Connections" (which starts on page 202) because it argues that, when preparing to speak, you can think about using your arrangements to construct connections with your audience. "Constructing Connections" provides a list of such strategies for oral communication.

Because audiences are quick to pick up on the arrangement or structure you use—especially if you are sign-posting your connections—don't shift patterns in mid-stream. (But if you do, you need time to make it work. The shift needs to make sense within your overall purpose—and it needs to make sense to the audience. Normally you stay with one arrangement because of time constraints. Anytime you do something more interesting and complex—and don't get us wrong, we encourage that—you need to take care to make sure that those listening are in a position to fully appreciate what you are doing.)

Logos as word choice

Word choice and turning a phrase enliven a talk, especially a timed talk. If what you say and your structure are vivid, your audience will be able to remember—and so think about—your arguments.

We discuss word choice in chapter 5 (on pages 155–157), so you can turn there for inspiration—but do think particularly hard about how you shape words when you speak. In the contexts of speaking, a clever turn of phrase can catch an audience's ears and encourage members to listen more generously.

Read the following quotations aloud and then re-state them without the repetition of words or phrases that makes them almost musical. How likely are you—or any audience—to remember the different versions?

> It is above all by the imagination that we achieve perception and compassion and hope.
>
> *Ursula LeGuin*

> While you are experimenting, do not remain content with the surface of things. Don't become a mere recorder of facts, but try to penetrate the mystery of their origin.
>
> *Isabel Allende*

> We learn from experience that we never really learn from experience.
>
> *George Bernard Shaw*

At the 1984 and 1988 Democratic Conventions, Jesse Jackson gave two much-admired speeches that have been studied by people interested in how language works well. Jackson aimed to cast a wide net of unity over those at the conventions and those watching on TV; at the same time, he did not hide some very contentious issues. His theme was common ground.

In 1984 he said, "We must leave the racial battle ground and come to the economic common ground and moral higher ground." In 1988 he said, "Tonight there is a sense of celebration. Because we are moved. Fundamentally moved, from racial battle grounds by law, to economic common ground. Tomorrow we'll challenge to move, to higher ground. Common ground."

Common ground is both his core idea (he includes such variations as "common grave," "common table," "common thread," "common good," "common direction," and "common sense") and a formal verbal mechanism for unifying his argument. The combination of sound and meaning reminded people that spoken language can be both intelligent and pleasurable.

But spoken language can also give signs of not being so intelligent—by the standards of some. This is where grammar comes in. As we wrote about writing, grammar is rhetorical: You need to choose the kind of grammar that will persuade your audience you know what you are talking about, or you need to make it clear that if grammar matters to them you have a good reason for not satisfying their expectations. (Happily for us all, no one can see our spelling when we speak.)

There are contexts in which grammar doesn't matter. You might have heard the Wings song, "Live and Let Die," which intones "In this ever changing world in which we live in." There do not need to be three "in"s in that line—and the last "in" is guaranteed to make people crazy who care about hanging prepositions (which is why this line shows up on every website devoted to funky lyrics)—but did anyone not buy the album because of the prepositions? The Doors sang, "Till the stars fall from the sky/For you and I"—"correct" grammar would have killed this lyric with a final nonrhyming "me." Wilco sings, "I assassin down the avenue," substituting a noun for a verb, making English teachers quiver but giving us a very clear picture of how that walk looks. The point is that you can do wonderful things by playing with grammar, especially when you speak (or sing)—as long as you are in contexts in which this is expected—or unexpected but in harmony with your purpose.

"Constructing Connections"

On the next pages is a chapter—"Constructing Connections"—from Sonja K. Foss and Karen A. Foss's book *Inviting Transformation: Presentational Speaking for a Changing World*.

"Constructing Connections" is a compendium of forms—organizational patterns or arrangements—for speaking and oral presentations. Seeing and naming different ways of organizing your words and ideas gives you choices that will help as you plan talks—and even if you already know what a "causal pattern" is, or a narrative, having them all laid out together brings some back to mind that might have slipped out.

This reading on organizational patterns—overall arrangements for oral presentations—will be most useful as you begin planning what you will say. The forms or patterns do not just help prepare a talk, however; they also play a role in shaping the relationship you as a speaker develop with your audiences. Think of the differences between using a narrative format and using a problem-solution format: The latter sets, or can set, a no-nonsense, *let's get down to it* tone, while the former says, *let's take the time to hear the whole story*. Which relationships do you want to build with your audience, given your purpose and context—and the particularities of your audience?

Constructing Connections

by Sonja K. Foss and Karen A. Foss

Constructing connections is the process by which you formulate relationships among the major ideas of your presentation. ... The forms that result are organizational patterns; they are the basic structures in which you issue your invitation to transformation. There are no correct or right organizational patterns that will emerge from your attention to the relationships among your ideas. Let your own style—your personal, unique, characteristic way of constructing connections—guide you. You also will want to take into account any expectations generated by environmental factors for the form of your presentation. The subject you are discussing, your interactional goal, the genre of your presentation (a commencement address or a presentation at a staff meeting, for example), and the characteristics of your audience affect the choices you make in constructing relationships among your ideas.

Constructing relationships may be done in a variety of ways. Two common ways are playing cards and clustering. Playing cards is a technique in which you "play cards" with ideas or pieces of information. You put each idea you have generated or collected on a separate card or slip of paper and lay them out in various possible arrangements until a pattern appears that seems to you to encompass the information in a useful way. Cards that contain information or data that do not fit the emerging schema are discarded.

In clustering, a second approach to connecting your ideas, you start with key concepts and cluster some related concepts, images, and ideas around them. Some of the clustered concepts become the centers of new clusters and being to generate ideas for concepts and images associated with them. At some point in this process, you become aware of an emerging form or organizational pattern that connects your ideas.

Sometimes, you may find that you could use a little help in figuring out how to organize ideas for your presentation. In this case, you might want to turn to fixed forms of arrangement or organizational patterns as sources of possible ideas. These are common or conventional formats that others have considered to be useful ways of connecting ideas and, in fact, you may discover that you naturally tend to use some of them. They should not be regarded as ideal patterns into which you should make your ideas fit, however. These patterns simply may provide you with leads to follow in developing relationships among your ideas. Among these conventional organizational patterns are:

Alphabet. The alphabet can be used as an organizational pattern for a presentation. It involves arranging ideas in alphabetical order: this is the form used to organize this list of organizational patterns. A variation of this pattern is the structuring of a presentation around an acronym such as SAFE to discuss earthquake preparedness. S might stand for securing the environment, A for advance planning, F for family meeting place, and E for emergency supplies.

Category. A category format is suggested by a set of categories that either is relatively standard for your subject or naturally arises from it. The major components, types, questions, functions, or qualities of a subject can be used as its organizational schema. The subject of leadership, for example, readily breaks down into the categories of different models of leadership or the categories of qualities of a good leader; either could be used to organize your ideas.

Causal. A causal organizational pattern is structured around a series of causes or contributing causes that account for some effect. This pattern can be organized either by discussing how certain causal factors will produce a particular effect or by suggesting that a particular set of conditions appears to have been produced by certain causes. In a presentation on the condition of the American educational system, for example, educational consultant David Boaz spent the first part of his presentation establishing that schools do not work (the effect) and the second part establishing that there is no competition and thus no incentive to improve the school system (the cause).

Circle. In a circle organizational pattern, ideas are structured in a circular progression. One idea is developed, which leads to another, which leads to another, which leads to another, which then leads back to the original idea. You might suggest to your co-workers, for example, that greater cooperation is needed among staff members. To achieve this, you propose that the group come up with some goals for working together, such as being honest with each other. Honesty may contribute to a greater feeling of trust which, in turn, may contribute to an environment in which staff members are more likely to cooperate.

Continuum. A continuum organizational pattern is structured by gradation; objects or ideas are linked by some common quality but differ in grade, level, or degree. Using this pattern, you move from one end of the continuum to the other. You might organize a presentation using a continuum pattern by discussing ideas in the order of, for example, small to large, familiar to unfamiliar, simple to complex, or least expensive to most expensive. For a presentation on absenteeism in a company, you might talk first about the department with the highest rate of absenteeism and end with a discussion of the one with the lowest rate to discover what can be learned about the factors that contribute to absenteeism.

Elimination. An organizational pattern of elimination begins with a discussion of a problem, followed by a discussion of several possible solutions to the problem. The solutions are examined in turn and eliminated until the one preferred remains. In a presentation on the state's budget deficit, for example, you might suggest solutions such as imposing an additional tax on cigarettes, implementing a sales tax, cutting state programs, and raising property taxes. You dismiss the first three solutions for various reasons and devote your presentation to advocating an increase in property taxes.

Location. Ideas are assembled in terms of spatial or geographical relationship in an organizational pattern of location. In a presentation on the closing of military bases in the United States, for example, a speaker could discuss the bases to be closed in geographical order, beginning with the Northeastern part of the United States and moving to the Southeast, the Midwest, the Southwest, and the Northwest.

Metaphor. Metaphor, a comparison between two items, ideas, or experiences, can be used as an organizational pattern that structures a presentation. One example of this use of metaphor is a presentation by Richard R. Kelly, the CEO of Outrigger Hotels Hawaii. He used the metaphor of a cold to organize his ideas on how the company could survive in recessionary times in a presentation entitled "Prospering in '92: How to Avoid a Cold When the World Is Sneezing."

Motivated Sequence. The motivated sequence is a five-step organizational pattern designed to encourage an audience to move from consideration of a problem to adoption of a possible solution:

1 *Attention*: the introduction of the presentation is designed to capture the attention of audience members. In a presentation to high-school students on the sexual transmission of AIDS, for example, a speaker might begin by citing statistics on the number of high-school students who have AIDS and who have died of the disease in the United States.

2 *Need*: In the need step, a problem is described so that the speaker and audience share an understanding of the problem. At this point, the speaker describes the transmission of AIDS through sexual intercourse and suggests there is a need for young people to engage in honest, explicit discussion about sex and sexual practices with their partners.

3 *Satisfaction*: A plan is presented to satisfy the need created. The speaker might suggest various ways young people might initiate talk about sex with their partners.

4 *Visualization*: In visualization, the conditions that will prevail once the plan is implemented are described, encouraging the audience to visualize the results of the proposed plan. The reduced risk of AIDS and more open communication in the relationships would be results the speaker could encourage the audience to visualize.

5 *Action*: The audience is asked to take action or grant approval to the proposed plan—in this case, to use the techniques offered to discuss sex more explicitly and openly with their partners.

Multiple Perspectives. An organizational pattern created around multiple perspectives is one in which an idea is developed or a problem or object analyzed from several different viewpoints. In a presentation at a PTA meeting on how to deal with the drug problem in schools, for example, you might examine the problem from several different perspectives—medical, social, legal, and educational—in order to understand it fully and to generate creative and workable solutions to it.

Narrative. In a narrative organizational pattern, ideas are structured in a story form, using characters, settings, and plots. Communication professor Sally Miller Gearhart's presentation, "Whose Woods These Are," for example, consisted solely of a story that vividly conveyed her ideas about the violence implicit in many forms of communication.

Narrative Progression. The organizational pattern of narrative progression consists of the telling of several stories, one after another, with the speaker following the leads or implications of one story into the next. Photographer Anne Noggle's commencement speech to the Portland School of Art provides an example of narrative progression as an organizational pattern: the presentation consisted of one story after another about her life, loosely connected by the notion that life is a feast.

Perspective by incongruity. Qualities or ideas that usually are seen as opposites or as belonging to different contexts are juxtaposed to create an organizational pattern of perspective by incongruity. This form works particularly well in presentations in which discovery of knowledge is the focus because juxtaposing opposing concepts often generates new perspectives. Feminist theorist Ti-Grace Atkinson, for example, used an organizational pattern of perspective by incongruity in a presentation at Catholic University when she juxtaposed religion and law and judged the Catholic church guilty of a number of crimes.

Problem/no solution. In the organizational pattern of problem/no solution, a problem is developed and its significance is established, but no solution to the problem is suggested by the speaker. A solution is seen as desirable and actually is anticipated, but it either comes as individual audience members draw their own conclusions or through group discussion by those present. Using this organizational pattern, a supervisor might discuss, with the staff, the morale problem in the office and then ask everyone to join in coming up with solutions to it.

Problem/solution. A problem/solution organizational pattern begins with a discussion of a problem and concludes with a suggested solution or solutions. In a presentation to the Central States Communication Association, for example, communication scholar Samuel L. Becker began by establishing as a problem the "loss of our ability—and even apparently of our desire—to work out our disagreements in a thoughtful way, in a way that seeks understanding, a way that brings others in rather than locking them out, a way that builds community instead of destroying it." He then went on to propose that teachers of communication take more responsibility for developing the kinds of discourse needed to deal effectively with social problems.

Rogerian. This organizational pattern, derived from the work of Carl Rogers, is based on the belief that if people feel they are understood—that their positions are honestly recognized and respected—they will cease to feel threatened. Once threat is removed, listening is no longer an act of self-defense, and people are more likely to consider other perspectives. This pattern begins with a demonstration of understanding of audience members' positions. This means you must discover what your listeners' positions are—either prior to or at the beginning of the presentation—and demonstrate that you really understand and respect them. In the second part of the presentation your own ideas are presented, taking into account what you have learned from the audience.

Space between things. The essence of this organizational pattern is consideration of the opposite or the reverse of what usually is accorded attention or viewed as important. This pattern is particularly useful for generating new vantage points for viewing and understanding a subject. In this approach, you attend to whatever is not typically considered—the time between notes of music or the space between buildings, for example. You might focus, in a presentation on communication between the sexes, on what happens in the spaces between talk—in those silences when neither person is speaking.

Stream of consciousness. Stream of consciousness is an unfocused organizational pattern that does not contain easily identifiable connections among main ideas. It is held together by a central idea, but this idea is not as explicitly stated as it is in other organizational patterns. Careful examination of the presentation, however, usually reveals the system or idea that unites the seemingly irrelevant fragments. Garrison Keillor's monologues on his radio program, "A Prairie Home Companion," are examples of a stream of consciousness organizational pattern. In one monologue, for example, he discussed the sights he would show visitors to Lake Wobegon on a Flag Day celebration in 1958 in which the town created a living flag: he described gardens, porches, air conditioning, a ritual of greeting people from porches, and the Lunberg family and their sleepwalking habits—in that order.

Time. When the ideas of a presentation are organized according to their temporal relationships, an organizational pattern of time is used. Ideas presented in this form usually are organized chronologically—from past to present or from present to past. In discussing the economic relationship between Japan and the United States, for example, a speaker could show the chronological progression of the relationship and how it has changed over time.

Web. A web organizational pattern revolves around a central or core idea, with other ideas branching out from the core; each branching idea is a reflection and elaboration of the core. In the web form, you begin with the central idea and then explore each idea in turn, returning to the core idea and going out from it until they all have been covered. Judaic studies professor Jacob Neusner's commencement speech at Brown University in 1981 provides an example of this organizational pattern. His core idea was that higher education had failed to prepare students for the outside world. The major ideas he discussed were the faculty's lack of pride in the students' achievements, the high grades earned by students for poor performances, the forgiving world created by professors for the students, and professors' disdain for students. Before Neusner developed each new idea, he reiterated the core idea.

In the connection step to the forming process, you construct the relationships among your major ideas, resulting in an organizational pattern in which the ideas you are generating are presented. Your next task is to elaborate on those ideas.

TO ANALYZE

■ **Discuss with others and then write:**

Imagine you are having trouble with your roommate. Things have gotten so bad you both agree you need to bring in a third party (a resident assistant, say). You think your roommate has been using your stuff without asking and she brings her boyfriend around too much. Your roommate thinks you are standoffish and do not act like a real roommate. The plan is for each of you to take 5 minutes and present your case to the mediator. The mediator then will find a way of reconciling your conflict.

With a partner, discuss the pros and cons for each roommate of at least five of the organizational patterns described in "Constructing Connections."

Individually, choose a pattern and use it to sketch—in writing—your presentation to the mediator.

205

PATHOS IN SPEAKING

When we hear others speak, we not only make (often unaware) judgments about their characters but also hear and respond to the voice's emotions. In speaking situations, therefore, pathos, like ethos, is simply waiting for you—the speaker—to shape. Audiences are likely to take on your sadness if you speak quietly and with a catch; they are likely to take on your joy if you speak gleefully.

What is the overall emotion you wish your audience to feel, to remember in their bodies, as they walk away? Ask that as you prepare to speak, as you decide what words and tones of voice to use. With what emotions is your audience likely to come to your topic, and what sorts of actions on your part might persuade them to shift their feelings to the emotion you believe appropriate?

Considering where your audience starts emotionally and where you hope to move them will help you consider *how* to move them. Will you rely on tone of voice? Examples? Photographs? Starting with a quiet and slow rhythm of voice and becoming progressively quicker and more heart felt?

Born in Hungary in 1928, Elie Wiesel was deported to the concentration camps as a teenager. Having afterward become a teacher, journalist, and author, Wiesel was invited to talk at the White House on April 12, 1999, as part of a series of presentations called "Millennium Evenings" aimed at commemorating the change of the 20th into the 21st century. The following paragraphs are the introduction to Wiesel's talk, which is titled "The Perils of Indifference." What emotions might his audience develop as he talks, and why?

......

"Fifty-four years ago to the day, a young Jewish boy from a small town in the Carpathian Mountains woke up, not far from Goethe's beloved Weimar, in a place of eternal infamy called Buchenwald. He was finally free, but there was no joy in his heart. He thought there never would be again. Liberated a day earlier by American soldiers, he remembers their rage at what they saw. And even if he lives to be a very old man, he will always be grateful to them for that rage, and also for their compassion. Though he did not understand their language, their eyes told him what he needed to know —that they, too, would remember, and bear witness.

And now, I stand before you, Mr. President —Commander-in-Chief of the army that freed me, and tens of thousands of others—and I am filled with a profound and abiding gratitude to the American people. "Gratitude" is a word that I cherish. Gratitude is what defines the humanity of the human being. And I am grateful to you, Hillary, or Mrs. Clinton, for what you said, and for what you are doing for children in the world, for the homeless, for the victims of injustice, the victims of destiny and society. And I thank all of you for being here.

We are on the threshold of a new century, a new millennium. What will the legacy of this vanishing century be? How will it be remembered in the new millennium? Surely it will be judged, and judged severely, in both moral and metaphysical terms. These failures have cast a dark shadow over humanity: two World Wars, countless civil wars, the senseless chain of assassinations (Gandhi, the Kennedys, Martin Luther King, Sadat, Rabin), bloodbaths in Cambodia and Algeria, India and Pakistan, Ireland and Rwanda, Eritrea and Ethiopia, Sarajevo and Kosovo; the inhumanity in the gulag and the tragedy of Hiroshima. And, on a different level, of course, Auschwitz and Treblinka. So much violence; so much indifference.

What is indifference? Etymologically, the word means "no difference." A strange and unnatural state in which the lines blur between light and darkness, dusk and dawn, crime and punishment, cruelty and compassion, good and evil. What are its courses and inescapable consequences? Is it a philosophy? Is there a philosophy of indifference conceivable? Can one possibly view indifference as a virtue? Is it necessary at times to practice it simply to keep one's sanity, live normally, enjoy a fine meal and a glass of wine, as the world around us experiences harrowing upheavals?"

PATHOS IN SPOKEN CONCLUSIONS

Which of the following options suggest how you can purposefully end your talk?

- a funny anecdote capturing your main point

- a suggestion for further research or a list of questions that are still to be answered

- a description of consequences following from your argument

- a summary of what you already said

- a challenge to the audience

Here are the closing paragraphs of Wiesel's talk, whose opening paragraphs we gave you on the opposite page. With what emotions does Wiesel hope his audience will leave? Why?

......

" And yet, my friends, good things have also happened in this traumatic century: the defeat of Nazism, the collapse of communism, the rebirth of Israel on its ancestral soil, the demise of apartheid, Israel's peace treaty with Egypt, the peace accord in Ireland. And let us remember the meeting, filled with drama and emotion, between Rabin and Arafat that you, Mr. President, convened in this very place. I was here and I will never forget it.

And then, of course, the joint decision of the United States and NATO to intervene in Kosovo and save those victims, those refugees, those who were uprooted by a man whom I believe that because of his crimes, should be charged with crimes against humanity. But this time, the world was not silent. This time, we do respond. This time, we intervene.

Does it mean that we have learned from the past? Does it mean that society has changed? Has the human being become less indifferent and more human? Have we really learned from our experiences? Are we less insensitive to the plight of victims of ethnic cleansing and other forms of injustices in places near and far? Is today's justified intervention in Kosovo, led by you, Mr. President, a lasting warning that never again will the deportation, the terrorization of children and their parents be allowed anywhere in the world? Will it discourage other dictators in other lands to do the same?

What about the children? Oh, we see them on television, we read about them in the papers, and we do so with a broken heart. Their fate is always the most tragic, inevitably. When adults wage war, children perish. We see their faces, their eyes. Do we hear their pleas? Do we feel their pain, their agony? Every minute one of them dies of disease, violence, famine. Some of them—so many of them—could be saved.

And so, once again, I think of the young Jewish boy from the Carpathian Mountains. He has accompanied the old man I have become throughout these years of quest and struggle. And together we walk towards the new millennium, carried by profound fear and extraordinary hope. "

TO ANALYZE

■ **Write:** Circle the words and phrases in the introduction and conclusion to Wiesel's speech that seem designed to strongly affect the listening audience's emotions.

List the specific emotions Wiesel names or suggests. List the emotions you think Wiesel hopes his audience will feel—or assumes they already feel.

In writing, describe what Wiesel does with the emotions the audience is presumed to be experiencing or may be experiencing as a result of what he says. Discuss how Wiesel builds on emotions over the course of the speech.

■ **Write:** Rewrite the first paragraphs of Wiesel's speech to evoke different or more intense emotions in the listening audience.

■ **Discuss with others:** Have several different people read aloud the introduction and conclusion of Wiesel's speech. Do you respond differently to hearing this speech rather than reading it? How do the different readings shape your sense of the emotions of the speech?

PREPARING (YOURSELF) TO TALK

Speech anxiety

Speech anxiety hits us all—and, as a result, much useful information exists for dealing with it.

FIRST, know that there are different kinds of speech anxiety. Some kinds derive from your context: You may be easygoing when you talk with lunchtable friends and you may have no trouble standing up and speaking your mind in a student organization where you know everyone—but you may have more trouble standing up in class and giving a formal or informal presentation because you know you are being graded, or you may have trouble in an interview for a position you really want.

Other kinds of speech anxiety are more personal. You may have had bad experiences in the past or you may have always been unhappy with the idea of getting up in front of people and talking, and you are not about to suddenly feel great about it now, just because, once again, you are being asked to do so.

SECOND, speech anxiety rears its ugly head in generally recognizable stages:

1 Setting out to speak, you get a jolt of adrenaline and your body tells you to bolt. Your heart races (not unlike being around the one you love), and you might even start breathing funny and notice sweaty palms. You know the routine.

2 Then you become conscious of your feelings—sweaty palms are hard to ignore—but that only exacerbates the problem because it starts a cycle: feeling anxious, being self-conscious about it, getting more anxious ….

3 And what is worse, once you recognize the reaction you're having, you start talking to yourself about yourself and saying unkind things. You "internalize" the experience and the fact of having reacted that way, and you start telling yourself that this is who you are. You become a sweaty-palmed person instead of just a person with sweaty palms. This sets you up for further, even more intense, negative experiences in the future. Isn't it fun to be a human being? We are, of course, joking about what is a serious matter, but joking, it turns out, is one way of dealing with speech anxiety. Try to distance yourself from yourself. Try not to take it as seriously as you are taking it. Try to relax.

THIRD, many approaches exist for working with speech anxiety. The approaches vary depending on the kind of anxiety you experience, the intensity of your experience, and the extent to which you have entered into a feedback loop of fear and self-deprecation. Here is a brief list of coping strategies:

- **Deep breathing.** Take long, slow breaths on a regular basis and really let yourself feel the air moving deeply into your lungs. Stand in a doorway and press your arms against the jambs, slowly, and then with gradually more force. When you stop pressing, concentrate on how your muscles feel. Feel them relax. These are bodily efforts, and they remind us that our mental states are also bodily states. If you know how to use breathing to relax and you know how your body feels when you are relaxed, you can more easily re-create these feelings, even when you are about to speak formally.

- **Other kinds of relaxation exercises** also help, such as tensing your feet, relaxing, tensing your calf muscles, relaxing, tensing your thighs, relaxing, and so on, moving up through the muscles in your body. This works best lying down in the dark—but, again, knowing what relaxation feels like can help you be relaxed in many situations.

- **Talk to yourself about how you are making too big a deal out of this speaking thing.** Remind yourself that worrying about having to speak only reinforces the problem. At the very least, remind yourself that at such times you need to stress the positive. Remind yourself of the many good things in your life—and when you are getting ready to give a speech, tell yourself, "I can do this; I can do this… !" Remind yourself that what you are experiencing is normal and that lots of people feel the same way in similar circumstances. The odd thing is that feelings like these isolate us just at the moment we most need to connect with others.

- **Sometimes knowing something about the physiology of speech anxiety can help** because we can think about that instead of about the speech. That is why we described the stages your mind/body goes through so that anxiety does not take you by surprise but rather seems normal—and manageable. Speech anxiety is an adrenaline rush that sends us into a flight-or-fight response. Adrenaline rushes last about 20 minutes, so if you get anxious just before speaking, the anxiety won't go away quickly. But you can use that extra energy. For instance, research shows that once you start speaking, the tension caused by the adrenaline rush seems to lessen. One strategy then is just to plunge into the speech, like swimming in cold water. If you do this, though, it is even more important to make sure you are prepared and know what you want to say.

- **Preparation is another way to lessen stress levels.** If you are so stressed about speaking in front of others that you put off thinking about it, then you will find yourself with nothing to say when the time comes. So remember that preparation, planning, and

practice will accustom you both to the idea of speaking in front of other people and to actually speaking. Preparation, planning, and practice give you confidence that you know what you are doing and can pull it off. Practicing also gives you positive feedback because when you practice in front of your goldfish, you are guaranteed a sympathetic audience response.

One last word to those of you who, like us, are a bit nervous about speaking in public: You may or may not think of yourself as a "shy" person, but in either case, it helps to set yourself small, achievable goals; if you do this, you can build them into the larger goals you seek. For example, if you are nervous about speaking in a class, promise to say just one thing during each class discussion for the first two weeks—and then do it and relax. Make sure you also have a plan for when you will challenge yourself to move on to two contributions each class, and then three.

Finally, remember that we are all different—and some of us really do have strong apprehensions about speaking before others. You probably already have some sense of this about yourself, and you may need to pull your teacher aside and discuss the matter. You may want to talk to other professionals on campus. We are in this together. Even when it feels like we are alone… especially when it feels like we are alone.

Visualization

Visualizing yourself giving a stupendous, knockout speech combats speech anxiety, especially if you do it several times in order to let the experience—the feeling of success—sink into your heart and bones.

But anxiety aside, visualizing yourself giving a talk or a speech, or conducting an interview, helps in several other ways. First, it is a form of practice, and practice is essential to working out the kinks and becoming comfortable with the material and the rhythms of delivery. Second, visualizing puts a kind of imprint in the back of your mind that then gets activated as you start to give the real thing and in a sense guides you through it. (And if you know where you will present and can visualize yourself in that space, in front of some of the people you know will be there, the actual presentation will feel familiar and comfortable.) Visualization substitutes for not having actually given this particular speech, or one like it, before.

Many professionals use visualization techniques to enhance their chances of success. Surgeons visualize an operation the night—or for days—before an important or unfamiliar surgery. Musicians visualize a performance. Sports figures visualize a game or specific moves in a game or event. And teachers visualize classes, setting up class activities, leading class discussion, and so on. So visualize your talks.

Delivery: Wording, gestures, smells

When you consider how to deliver your speech, an entwined set of questions arises. What voice will you choose for speaking, how will you make the divisions in your talk clear to those listening, how will you use gestures, and how will you hold yourself?

People have studied how to speak, gesture, carry yourself, and dress while performing a speech for thousands of years in the west, going back, we know for sure, at least to 400 B.C.E. in the Mediterranean societies of ancient Greece, Rome, and Asia Minor. What follows grows out of this rich background of experiences.

It is a good rule of thumb to vary your tone as you speak (volume, pitch, pace). But if you speak in a monotone out of habit, it will not help matters to vary your tone in a mechanical way. You need to practice varying your tone in conjunction with what you want to say and the effect you want to have. You need to think and talk at the same time, like walking and chewing gum.

How you carry yourself into a room or up to a podium, how you stand up from a table to speak, and how you turn to someone who has just introduced you are all modes of communication. Your body talks and people listen. Often your body talks behind your back, if you can picture that, and then you are not only not in control of your communication but also may be communicating the very thing you do not want to communicate. Coming out of high school, all Dennis (one of the composers of this book) wanted to do was keep his head low and pass unnoticed—even when he was called upon to speak. These combined acts, speaking and keeping his head low, always struck people as confusing and made it such that he might as well not have spoken at all. If you need to speak, you need to speak, and that becomes the primary force behind decisions you make. You have to face up to that and change the head-hung-low behavior because it's not in step with your overall plans.

What we just said is good advice, generally, in some contexts in the United States. But depending on the culture in which you grew up, not speaking or being silent can mean different things. What to Dennis felt like his head hanging low might to someone else feel like a sign of respect. We need to be careful how we read other people's body language, even as we learn to read—and change—our own.

There is too much to say about bodily movement and communication. We encourage you to observe, to think about what you see, to talk with others about it, and to read the studies others have done. Stop and think about facial expressions, for instance. They are fascinating in their complexities. You can learn to see more in people's expressions than you currently register. And you can train yourself to better express what you want to express through a smile, a raised eyebrow (look at Hollywood actors), or a taut forehead.

Formal occasions call for a stiff posture, but sometimes you can achieve a good effect by relaxing a little. If the occasion is solemn and you do not have a complicated role to play, getting up stiffly and saying a few words may be just fine. If the occasion is a ritual, you may want to be serious but not too stiff. Imagine yourself as a second-year college student asked to speak to incoming first-year students; you may want to balance between being official, more knowledgeable, and being cool. Stiff but not too stiff is the stuff of practice.

Finding the appropriate and comfortable expressions, postures, or ways of moving is a slow, experimental process that begins and ends with what you can do, comfortably.

A word to the wise:

Many verbal mannerisms force their way into how we speak in front of others, and when we are nervous they often become exaggerated. Here are some that are generally worth avoiding: "ah," "er," "um," "like," "you know," "whatever."

Delivery: Using support materials

When you give a speech, consider using support materials such as statistics, examples, pictures, graphs, charts, stories, quotations, or testimony. There is a practical reason for using such materials: audience attention.

When we discussed context earlier, we encouraged you to think about the time you have to talk. This helps you think about someone in your audience sitting for that time, listening. Even a well-rested, eager audience can hold on to only part of what you say. Research suggests people do not retain everything they hear in a speech; researchers have charted the attention span of audiences over an hour or so and have discovered that retention is sharp initially, wanes after about 10 minutes (unless listeners find ways to resist this tendency), and returns when the audience senses the end. This tells you that in planning a speech you need to keep your audience's bodily attentions in mind: If you want to hold their attentions (especially in a longer speech), then you need to vary how you present your ideas in line with your purposes.

Once you have gathered appropriate support materials, attend to their use. What will be effective—and ethical? Statistics are often expected and can win the day—but they can cause people to feel lost in a sea of numbers, and nearly everyone agrees they can easily be ma-nipulated. Likewise, charts and graphs can be a breath of fresh air—or they can nastily obscure the issue by presenting misleading information or skewing the issue. Audiences must hear you explain how and why you've used the statistics you do.

Examples and stories are pleasing to audiences, but they have their drawbacks. One example or story, harped on over and over, can be boring but can also present itself as the way things really are and thus can squeeze out other relevant examples and stories. One picture repeatedly pushed at an audience or just prominently displayed can dominate people's thinking unfairly. Testimony, often coming as narrative, is vitally important to making a case—but testimony too can be fabricated or one sided and so is in and of itself no guarantee of true support.

You can be creative with support materials, bringing in interesting objects to pass around the audience or playing music in the background—but use these materials thoughtfully, purposefully, and with respect for your audience.

TO ANALYZE

■ **Discuss with others:** Richard Wilkinson was a professor of social epidemiology at the University of Nottingham in England. He coauthored *The Spirit Level*, a book published in 2009 on how societies with unequal distributions of income have problems with the health of citizens, violence, drug abuse, teenage pregnancies, mental illness, and other social concerns. Following is an introduction to his speech, "How Economic Inequality Harms Societies." Using the information we give on these pages, discuss what sorts of gestures and tone of voice would help make this introduction most persuasive to a general audience; also discuss what sorts of support materials you think would also best support this introduction. Finally, analyze the words for the ethos they construct for Wilkinson.

You all know the truth of what I'm going to say. I think the intuition that inequality is divisive and socially corrosive has been around since before the French Revolution. What's changed is we now can look at the evidence, we can compare societies, more and less equal societies, and see what inequality does. I'm going to take you through that data and then explain why the links I'm going to be showing you exist.

A CHECKLIST FOR A DESIGN PLAN FOR A TALK

Use the following observations (that come from what we wrote in chapter 3)—together with other observations you generate about context, audience, and purpose from your statement of purpose—to deepen your statement of purpose and develop your design plan.

As with any checklist, do not let this one suggest it encompasses everything. It covers a lot and can help you see potentials for communication you might not otherwise—but it is you being attentive to your time, place, and audience that will help you know how best to proceed.

Context

PHYSICAL CONTEXT

❏ Describe the room where you'll present. What of its characteristics might shape how your audience listens and responds?

❏ How much time do you have for speaking? How does the amount of time constrain what you can say?

❏ What time of day will you speak? How might this shape your audience's abilities to listen?

SOCIAL CONTEXT

❏ How will intimate space play into your talk? How should you address or shape intimate space to help you achieve your purpose?

❏ How will social space play into your talk? How should you address or shape social space to help you achieve your purpose?

❏ How will institutional space play into your talk? How will your audience understand the space in which they hear you? How should you address or shape institutional space to help you achieve your purpose?

Audience

❏ You've developed an initial sense of your audience through your statement of purpose, but now is really the time to imagine them. Do your best to picture how they look so you can imagine them sitting in front of you, listening. Give them attentive, generous expressions—and imagine how you will engage them.

❏ After you have researched the room where you'll speak, imagine yourself speaking to your audience in this space, looking into their faces. Describe what you'll see.

❏ What approaches can you use to listen to your audience before you speak?

❏ What approaches can you use to listen to your audience as you speak?

Purpose

❏ You've developed an initial sense of your purpose through your statement of purpose, but now that you are closer to giving your talk, does the context of your speaking—as you imagine yourself speaking—help you enrich your sense of what you need to do?

❏ How do you want the audience to respond as you talk? After you talk?

❏ What would you like your audience members to be saying to each other as they leave your talk?

Strategies

ETHOS

❏ What sort of ethos do you want to build through tone of voice, body posture, and so on? Describe the ethos—and then describe what sorts of tone of voice, posture, and gestures will help you achieve that.

❏ What sort of ethos do you want to build through your word choices, vocabulary, and length of sentences?

❏ What level of grammar in your speaking will help you achieve the ethos you think appropriate for your audience and purpose?

❏ What sort of introduction will start you toward achieving your purpose?

PATHOS

❏ What sort of emotions can you evoke through tone of voice, body posture, and so on, that will help you achieve your purpose?

❏ What sort of emotions can you evoke through the particular words you use and the rhythms and modulations of your voice?

❏ Try to develop one or two memorable phrases (or, if you are using slides, memorable graphics) for the parts of your talk that you most want your audience to remember and consider later.

❏ What sort of conclusion will leave your audience with the closing thoughts, ideas, or emotions most in support of your purpose?

LOGOS

❏ What overall arrangements for your talk seem most appropriate to your purpose? (Look at the article "Constructing Connections" on pages 202–205 for suggestions on arrangements.)

❏ What word choices—and repetitions of words and of figures of speech—will help your audience hear and so remember the relationships you are building among ideas?

A DESIGN PLAN

FOR EXAMPLE

Here is Ajay's design plan, which grows out of his statement of purpose on page 196—and which also grows out of the research you saw him developing in chapter 4.

You can see his notes and slide for his presentation on pages 217–231.

On pages 274–277 is a photographic essay Ajay developed out of the same research.

A Design Plan for an Oral Report

PURPOSE: Thinking about the strategies for my presentation helped me get clearer about my purpose. I would like for my audience to leave with the following logic in their heads: (1) When students think of themselves as customers, it's bad for their educations; (2) Students think of themselves as customers because they have to pay so much tuition; (3) Tuition is so high (at public colleges at least) because states are funding colleges at much lower levels than they used to—and so (4) When states don't fund colleges well, one result is that our educations suffer.

When I finish talking, I want my audience to be thinking both about their attitudes toward their own educations as well as about how we fund college education in this country. I want them to leave not with a new or fixed opinion but with questions about these issues.

AUDIENCE: Our class meets late in the day and it's almost the end of the semester—and I am one of three presentations. I can just picture people nodding off. We won't know the order of our talks until that day, so I sure hope I am not last. No matter what, though, I had better be lively—which causes me problems, because my topic is not exactly lively (although it sure matters to my audience) and I want to be thoughtful about it. I need to think that through some more.

MEDIUM: I want to figure out how to make that logic above be memorable for my audience. I was already thinking about using slides with my presentation to make my points more visible, so I think I need a slide that lays out my logic in a memorable way. (And in my slides, I think I can use photographs from the ones I've taken to use in my photographic essay.) But the rest of my slides probably need to be pretty straightforward, so that my information comes across straightforwardly, too—but because of the time of day, I can't overload the slides with stuff.

ETHOS: Because I am arguing about how states spend money, which is very touchy for everyone these days, I don't want to come across as a hardhead. I want to be maybe even delicate about how I talk about this, and to have a very questioning tone. I do want to sound thoughtful and to come across as having done my research—so I guess my slides have to be lively and my ideas to the point.

I also want to be sure that I make as much eye contact as possible, and not look down—so I'm going to risk going with talking points as much as I can. I also want to compose my presentation so that I don't read slides to my audience and so I need to be sure that my slides and my talk play off each other.

I also want to figure out what to do with my hands. We don't have a podium in class (I'm glad I'm thinking about this now) so I can't stand behind something. But I get so nervous that I either put my hands behind me stiffly or swing them around. If I have pages to hold, maybe that will help me settle down.

PATHOS: I want to be sure to have my audience's attention from the start—and I've got all kinds of statistics to use. Which statistics speak most directly to the other people in class? Ha: the statistics about the loans we are all taking out. I think that will pull people in while also setting me up to start into the steps of my argument. But statistics can be so deadly and boring. How can I get them across without putting everyone to sleep (especially given the time of class already)? Can I get Martha (I'm so lucky to have a math whiz as a friend) to help me make some charts or graphs? I think seeing a graph for how tuitions have risen will help people see the changes so much easier than a bunch of numbers—and the same with the changes in state support for colleges. But I need to have the numbers somewhere to back me up. Speaking them will put people to sleep. The professor said we can use handouts, so I could make a handout with my statistics. I could also put my longer quotations into the handout, too—and so my audience will leave with my main evidence.

LOGOS: Reading "Constructing Connections" made me realize that the steps in my logic make a kind of circle—which I think will be a memorable slide graphic for my audience. And I know the logic gives me an order to my points, so I can just follow that.

What sorts of words do I need to use? I need to be lively and quick but thoughtful—so I think my sentences need to be short but full of good information. How can I summarize my argument into something more memorable than the four steps of my logic so that my audience leaves holding on to my main idea and able to think more about it? I need to work on that.

TO ANALYZE

- **Revise:** Ajay's design plan for his oral presentation is written informally; he is using the writing to "think on paper" and so is proposing ideas and thinking them through—and it seems to have helped him work out a lot of what he needs to do.

Imagine that Ajay's teacher had asked him to turn in this design plan as a formal piece of writing. Revise the words to the left to make them less conversational and more formal. Revise the words to make the writing sound as though Ajay has settled on all the different aspects of his oral presentation.

AN ORAL PRESENTATION

You may have had a speech class before, in which case you will have learned various approaches to the actual steps of preparing words to say (in addition to preparing yourself physically and emotionally to speak, which we've addressed on pages 208–211).

If you've not had a speech class, the following are considerations for preparing your words; starting on the opposite page, you can see the physical stuff one student (Ajay, whom we've been following since chapter 4) composed to prepare for an oral presentation.

How many words do I need?

If you were to read from a written paper, estimate approximately 2 minutes of reading for each page. (Double-spaced pages average 250 words per page.)

Should I write it all beforehand?

Writing out a talk can ease your nerves, since—when you first present—standing in front of a group and remembering what you want to say is hard (if not scary). Unfortunately, writing out your talk ahead of time means you are likely to read your talk to your audience. People who read their talks tend to look down at their pages, not at their audiences; they tend not to speak with engaging tones of voice; they are likely to look up at the end to see disengaged (and, at worst, dozing) audiences.

If I don't write it all out, how will I know what to say and do?!?

Talking points

Experienced speakers have talking points. Talking points are the points you want your audience to remember when you finish.

Experienced speakers work hard to develop three to five talking points. You can think of talking points as the skeleton of your paper around which you shape everything else. And it's generally pretty easy to remember (even in front of an audience) three to five points.

Get those points down, and then figure out what to say to explain and connect the points. (Talking points can help speakers shape shorter or longer talks: They don't subtract from or add to the points; instead, they shorten or lengthen the explanation they give to support and connect the points.)

The following pages shows that Ajay came up with four main—logically connected—points and shaped his talk around those points.

Visual aids

In addition to giving audiences something to look at and ponder, visual aids can help you remember what you need to say.

Look at Ajay's slides on the following pages: Many of the slides contain the information Ajay wants to convey, so he can work off them.

When you use slides, you do not want to turn your back to your audience to read them. First, you do not want to turn your back on your audience because you do not want to lose eye contact and so emotional engagement, but, second, you also generally don't want to read exactly what's on the slides because audiences will wonder why you just didn't give them your slides to read on their own.

Instead, look on the following pages to see how Ajay printed his slides on paper with his notes underneath. (Most presentation software allows you to do this.) In his notes under the slides, Ajay has written ideas about what he wants to say. In the places where he is most nervous about remembering, he has written his actual words so that he can fall back on them if he needs to—but he has tried mostly to suggest to himself what he needs to say so that he will talk *with* rather than *at* his audience. In his notes, he has also written reminders to himself about where to pause and the kinds of gestures he would like to make.

How often do I need to practice a presentation before I give it?

As often as you can. The more you practice (and the more you practice standing up, using your visual aids with others in front of you [which can include pets and other family members]), the more comfortable and at ease you will be when you give the talk to its "real" audience.

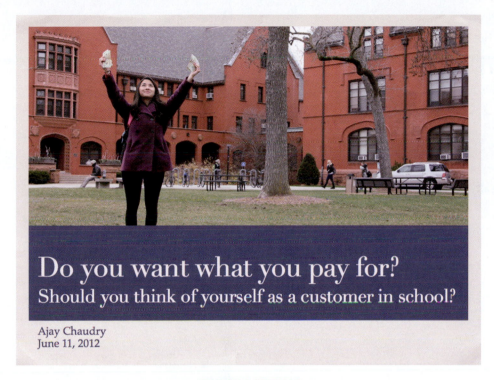

Do you want what you pay for?
Should you think of yourself as a customer in school?

Ajay Chaudry
June 11, 2012

SLIDE 1 NOTES

- *Have this slide up while I wait for everyone to settle in or to finish their feedback from the previous talk and turn their attention to me.*

- *Say the title out loud… with emphasis on the second question, looking out and around at everyone: Make eye contact!*

- *Then ask if people can hear me well enough.*

- *Tell them that I have a handout with my data, longer quotations, and sources—and that I'll hand it out at the end of my talk so they can check over my information.*

- *Take a deep breath…go to the next slide.*

FOR EXAMPLE

Ajay was required to produce an 8–12 minute oral presentation growing out of his research (which we presented in chapter 4).

On this and the next pages are Ajay's materials for his presentation: You can see the printouts of his slides and his notes for talking. On these pages are also comments about why he made the choices he did and questions to help you think about producing your own presentation.

To learn more about producing slides to accompany an oral presentation, see the comments that accompany Ajay's presentation as well as pages 280–281 in chapter 7.

217

On the left and the next pages are Ajay's slides for his talk and, beneath them, his notes for talking. (Note that the slides are small; projected, they will be much larger. Also note that most presentation software allows you to print your slides and notes like this.)

Average student debt in 2010:

$25, 250

- This is the average amount of debt among all students who graduated with debt. This does not include loans taken out by parents. This is for students at public and private non-profit colleges and universities.

- A 5% increase from the previous year.

- (Information from Project on Student Debt 1.)

SLIDE 2 NOTES

Look at people in the audience: How many of you think you are paying too much for college? *PAUSE.* How many of you will graduate with more than $25,250 in debt?

That's the average carried by students who graduated with debt from nonprofit private and public universities in 2010. It's a 5% increase over the preceding year.

I bring this up because my research paper made me curious about something. In my paper, I argued that when students think of themselves as customers and when schools think of students as customers, our education is damaged.

In a minute I'll lay out quickly what I argued in my research paper, but my paper got me curious about why students and colleges think of students as customers.

The answer surprised me—but it is tied to that debt.

☞ On pages 280–281, we suggest how to design effective slides for oral presentations.

■ For this slide, Ajay has written in his notes what he wants to say: He's worried about trusting himself to work off the slide and his memory at the beginning of his talk when he might be most nervous. As long as Ajay doesn't do this for every slide, this shouldn't be a problem—but, also, the more he practices saying these words aloud, the easier it will be for him to remember them.

■ Note that Ajay starts by asking his audience questions that (he hopes) will immediately make his classmates interested in his talk; the questions are meant to link his talk with audience concerns.

■ Ajay prepares his audience to hear what is to come by explaining how he came to this topic and initially describing the broad organization of his presentation.

■ Why do you think Ajay ends this short introduction with "The answer surprised me"?

MY 4 POINTS

1 When students—and colleges— think of students as customers, it damages our educations.

2 Students and colleges think of students as customers because public colleges have had to raise tuition — a lot — in past years.

4 When states give less money to public colleges, it encourages students— and colleges—to think of students as customers.

3 Public colleges have to raise tuition because they receive less money from states than they used to.

SLIDE 3 NOTES

Here are the points of my argument. *(Read them a bit slowly to let them sink in.)*

You may have some concerns about these points now, but I will be going over each of the points in my talk. If I don't address your concerns during my talk, please bring them up during the time for questions at the end.

■ Why might Ajay want to start the body of his talk with his four main points? How might this help his audience better understand and hold onto his argument? (Would having the points be animated, to appear one by one, make them more memorable?)

■ Do you think Ajay's points might be too controversial for his audience, his classmates?

■ In his notes for presenting, Ajay includes reminders to himself to slow down as he presents—especially in places where he wants his audience to remember his information.

■ How might Ajay's audience respond to his words, "You may have some concerns..."? Why do you think Ajay put in these words here?

■ Note that having his presentation notes attached to pictures of his slides helps Ajay remember when to move to the next slide.

AN ORAL PRESENTATION, continued

POINT 1

When we buy	When we learn
Buying is about immediate satisfaction.	School requires effort to get in, stay in, and finish.
	Often you don't know what you've learned until years later.
Customers are supposed to be pleased and never upset.	Teachers challenge students to learn—which means learning can be hard.
"The customer is always right"—and so never challenged.	Learning challenges us to stretch, to become more than we are.

SLIDE 4 NOTES

I won't read you my whole paper, but let me summarize it. It depends on the differences between customers and students—which you can see in this slide.

• When you are a customer buying a hamburger, I bet you expect to stand at the counter, place your order, and get a hamburger quickly. You eat it. That's it. If you don't like the hamburger, you complain; you are the judge of what is good or bad.

• With school, you have to put in effort to get in. And you have to work hard to stay in and graduate. Teachers decide what it is we are to learn, and they grade us on it. What we learn can't be handed over all at once, and—according to many of my sources—we students often aren't able to understand or use what we've learned until years later. Schooling is not about getting a product but about becoming wise: We are supposed to be challenged to change and to learn—so school is supposed to be hard.

■ For a slide like this, presenters are often tempted to use animations to bring out the different points. Given how much time Ajay has to give his talk, and the main points he wants people want to take from his talk (as he expresses in his notes below the slide), do you think Ajay should use animations to bring out these points one by one, moving left to right across the slide?

■ Note that what Ajay intends to say along with this slide does not exactly repeat what is on the slide. Instead, Ajay summarizes the slide, trusting his audience to make the connections. He hopes what he says will work with the slide's points to make these points more memorable and persuasive for his audience.

POINT 1

Consequences of student-customers

* Classes being dumbed-down

* Students expecting entertainment rather than learning

* Grade inflation

* Schooling "seems less concerned with the formation of citizens and more concerned with encouraging individuals to become consumers." (Love 21)

■ Ajay helps his audience remember where they are in his talk by putting "Point 1," "Point 2," and so on at the top of each slide.

221

SLIDE 5 NOTES

Explain the points from the information in my research paper:
Schools need to keep students (because they need student tuition—which I'll get to shortly in my talk) and so:
• Teachers make classes easier so that students will want to stay in school.
• Students then come to expect that things should be easy—and entertaining, too.
• Teachers don't grade as hard in order to keep students happy; that's grade inflation.
In my paper, all this led me to end by asking "Do we want our educations to be about becoming customers—people who are known for nothing but buying and wanting simple satisfactions? Or do we want our educations to be about becoming people who learn, who know how to stretch and take on hard work, who can be citizens, who seek wisdom? Who do you want to be?" *Pause before next slide.*

■ Ajay's explanation of the slide's bullet points follows the order of the slide so that his audience will attach his words to what is on the slide, giving more emphasis to his points.

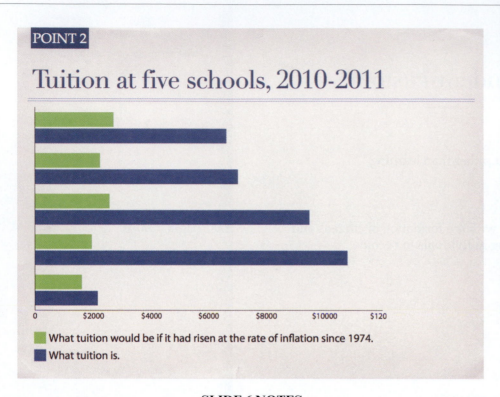

POINT 2

Tuition at five schools, 2010-2011

■ What tuition would be if it had risen at the rate of inflation since 1974.
■ What tuition is.

(x-axis: 0, $2000, $4000, $6000, $8000, $10000, $120)

SLIDE 6 NOTES

I think the main reason students think of themselves as customers is because of how much tuition they have to pay now.

My father talks about paying almost nothing when he was a college student in the 1970s. I thought he was doing the usual Dad-thing. But then I started my research.

As this slide shows, tuition has gone up. A lot.

The slide shows tuitions at a range of public schools—from community colleges to what are called "flagship" state schools and in between. The green bars show what tuition would be at each school if—between 1974 and 2010—tuition had gone up only with the rate of inflation. The blue bar shows actual tuition. Big difference, hey?

(The exact figures for all this and the names of the school are on the handout I'll give you at the end, so you can look at the details later.)   *Take a breath.*

■ Ajay chose to put this graph on his slide rather than the chart you can see on his handout on page 230. Do you agree with his choice? Why?

■ Ajay is careful to repeat—in short statements—summaries of his main points as in his first sentence here.

■ Why do you think Ajay decided to mention what his father says about what he paid for tuition in the 1970s?

■ Do you think this slide of evidence helps Ajay make his point about the rise in college tuition?

■ Ajay's handout is on pages 230–231.

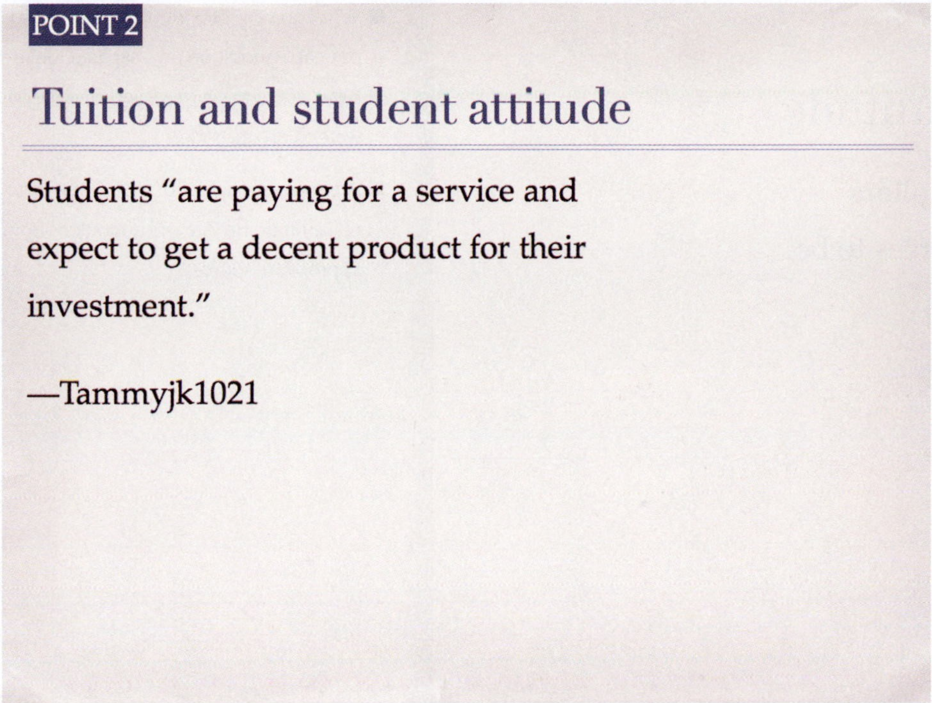

POINT 2

Tuition and student attitude

Students "are paying for a service and
expect to get a decent product for their
investment."

—Tammyjk1021

SLIDE 7 NOTES

How does that intense rise in tuition change how students think of learning?
PAUSE.

The quotations on this slide and the next three slides suggest what happens when students have to pay a lot of tuition.

This quotation is a comment I found in response to a newspaper article on the rise in tuition.

Wait a second or two—and breathe!!!!

Next slide.

■ What do you think of Ajay's use of a question to introduce this slide?

POINT 2

Tuition and student attitude

"…for the 10s of thousands of dollars that are spent we do expect degrees to be somewhat catered to us …"

—Asia Victim

SLIDE 8 NOTES

Here is another comment I found in response to a newspaper article on the rise in tuition.

Wait a second or two—and breathe!!!!

Next slide.

■ What do you think of Ajay's decision to put each quotation on a separate slide? How would these have worked if they were all on one slide?

■ Are there enough quotations for Ajay to make his point? Are the quotations from appropriate sources?

POINT 2

Tuition and student attitude

"It appears that students demand a level of 'entertainment' from faculty commensurate with the price of tuition."

(Delucchi and Korgen 104)

SLIDE 9 NOTES

This quotation comes from an academic article titled "We're the Customer; We Pay the Tuition."

Pause—then next slide.

POINT 2

Tuition and student attitude

"…the student believed that, for $40,000, he deserved an instructor who would keep him entertained with information he found pleasing."

(Delucchi and Korgen 104)

SLIDE 10 NOTES

This quotation also comes from the same academic article, "We're the Customer; We Pay the Tuition."

I think you can see how attitudes like this and those on the other three slides play into how (as I described a few slides ago) students thinking of themselves as customers damages their education.

The students who speak or who are described in these slides feel that they deserve something, should be entertained, should be catered to.

Do I want to sound like that? Do you want to have those attitudes?

(Wait a second or two—and breathe!!!!)

So… why has tuition gone up so much to cause these attitudes?

Pause—then next slide.

■ How do you think Ajay's strategy of using all these questions here will work with his audience? How might they respond?

Why has tuition gone up?

It's not what you think!

Schools are not finding new ways to spend money and are not increasing salaries outrageously.

Instead, "Public universities have been reining in overall spending per student in recent years. … Spending at public colleges has generally not exceeded inflation." (Clark)

SLIDE 11 NOTES

Let audience see the title while I say this:

I bet you are thinking that tuition has gone up because schools are finding new ways to spend money or are raising teacher salaries, or other things like that.

Click to animate on "It's not what you think"—read that aloud—then click to bring on the last two lines—and say:

Public colleges have not raised their spending beyond inflation as this quotation from *U.S. News and World Report* shows.

Pause—breathe—next slide…

■ For this slide, Ajay decided to use animations: First, his audience will see just the title and then, quickly, he will bring on "It's not what you think," and then, finally, he will animate the last two paragraphs. What sort of animation do you think Ajay should use? Why do you think he might want to do this (and do you think his animation strategy will be effective)?

☞ On pages 280–281, we suggest how to design effective slides for oral presentations.

227

■ Why might Ajay introduce this slide with the statement "I bet you are thinking…"?

■ Notice that, while Ajay's notes help him remember what to do, he should practice working with this slide so that he can comfortably and without stumbling click through it exactly as he wants.

AN ORAL PRESENTATION, continued

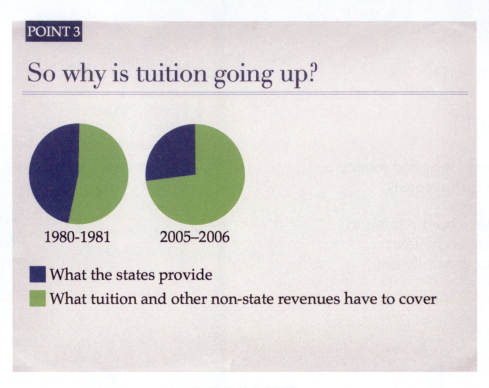

SLIDE 12 NOTES

I made this chart based on data I found in a booklet on the costs of college. In the booklet, I found this quotation: "In 1980-1981, on average, states provided 47% of the revenues needed by public colleges but by 2005-2006 they provided only 27%." (This is on my handout, so you can see the source.)

In the 25 years from 1980 to 2005, states dropped their funding for schools by almost half. (On the handout I have some other quotations about how funding has dropped even more in recent years—I could have filled pages with such quotations!)

Public colleges are not businesses: They don't make profits. They have very limited ways to make money: donations and tuition. If donations don't go up, or don't go up enough, tuition has to go up. And so we pay more and owe more.

■ How different would this slide be if Ajay had put on it the quotation that he reads (shown in the notes below)—instead of the two pie charts? Imagine that other slide with only the quotation on it; how might audiences respond to that slide as opposed to the slide to the left?

■ Different software—presentation or spreadsheet software—can help you take any data you find in your research and convert it into charts and graphs. If you do not know how to use such software, ask around to find someone who can help you.

■ Ajay's handout is on pages 230–231.

■ Do you think Ajay has provided enough evidence for his audience to accept the conclusions he makes here?

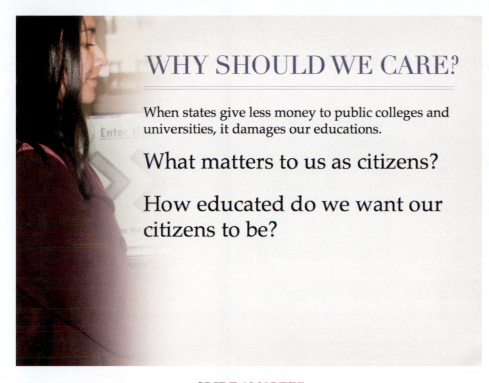

SLIDE 13 NOTES

If students thinking of themselves as customers damages our educations because of grade inflation and classes being dumbed down—and if students think of themselves as customers when they have to go into big debt to pay for rising tuitions—and if tuition (and our debt) is rising because public schools receive less funding from their states—then shouldn't we be questioning where our state money goes? Do we want the best possible educations? Do we want to be thoughtful citizens?

Shouldn't we be discussing these issues together?

LONG PAUSE. Here's my handout. Thank you for listening so well. I hope you have questions to help me see where my argument could be stronger—and to talk about what we all might do to change the situation I've described here.

■ Ajay decided he wanted a memorable last slide, so that his audience would remember his questions. Do you think he's succeeded?

■ What do you think of Ajay's strategy of ending with the questions on his slide?

■ How do you think Ajay's last paragraph—"Here's my handout; I hope…"—might shape his audience's response?

Ajay Chaudry

June 11, 2012

Do You Want What You Pay for? Should Students Think of Themselves as Customers?

HANDOUT

Slide 6: Changes in tuition

What would tuition be now if tuition rates from 1974-1975 had risen only with the rate of inflation? (I've included 1994-1995 data for your information.)

	1974-1975	1994-1995	2010-2011	2010-2011 with inflation
Eastern Kentucky University	na	$1790	$6624	$2691
University of Colorado at Boulder	$476	$2216	$7018	$2225
University of Minnesota—Duluth	$546	$3213	$9482	$2552
University of Virginia	$415	$3616	$10782	$1939
Metropolitan Community College	$112/qtr	$345/qtr	$720/qtr	$533/qtr

NOTE: I found the above information on each school's website. The figures above do not include fees, which vary widely. All amounts shown are for in-state undergraduate students, for the academic year— except MCC, which shows per quarter charges. I used the Inflation Calculator at http://www.dollar-times.com/calculators/inflation.htm to determine the values in the final column.

Slide 8: So why is tuition going up?

- "In 1980-1981, on average, states provided 47% of the revenues needed by public colleges but by 2005-2006 they provided only 27%." (Blum and Ma 14)
- The chief operating officer of the California State University (CSU) system said the system "had no choice but to raise tuition because the new state budget reduced CSU's allocation by $650 million, rather than the expected $500 million." (Asimov)
- "In 2009-2011, [Washington State University] lost over $132 million in state funding. Even with two tuition rate increases of 14 percent each, $57 million more was needed to balance the core education budget. [University President Wise] points out that 2010 was the first year that students paid more for tuition than what the state provided in financial support." (Delucchi and Korgen)

■ As he described in his design plan on pages 214–215, Ajay decided to put his complex data and quotations on this handout; he also decided to give his audience the handout after his talk so they wouldn't be distracted by reading it while they talked. (He also hoped that they would take this information home to think about it.)

How effective do you think this handout strategy is for Ajay?

Ajay Chaudry
HANDOUT—page 2

Works Cited

Asia Victim. Comment to "Are They Students? Or 'Customers'?" *New York Times*. New York Times. 3 Jan. 2010. Web. 5 May 2012.

Asimov, Nanette. "CSU Tuition Now Twice 2007 Cost." *SFGate*. Hearst Communications. 13 July 2011. Web. 5 May 2012.

Blum, Sandy and Jennifer Ma. *Trends in College Pricing 2009*. Washington, DC: The College Board, 2009. Print.

Bosworth, Angelo and Hector Cordon. "Drastic Cuts, Tuition Increases Loom for Washington State Universities." *World Socialist Web Site*. World Socialist Web Site. 8 Mar. 2011. Web. 4 May 2012.

Clark, Kim. "The Surprising Causes of Those College Tuition Hikes." *U.S. News & World Report*. U.S.News & World Report. 15 Jan. 2009. Web. 4 May 2012.

Delucchi, Michael and Kathleen Korgen. "'We're the Customer–We Pay the Tuition': Student Consumerism among Undergraduate Sociology Majors." *Teaching Sociology* 30.1 (2002): 100-107. JSTOR. Web. 9 May 2012.

Love, Kevin. "Higher Education, Pedagogy and the 'Customerisation' of Teaching and Learning." *Journal of Philosophy of Education* 42.1 (2008): 15-34. Print.

Project on Student Debt. "Student Debt and the Class of 2010." Oakland: The Institute for College Access & Success, 2011. Print.

Tammyjk1021. "Customers." Comment to Lane, Marcia. "Proctor: College students can expect higher tuition." *St. Augustine Record*. St. Augustine Record. 9 Sept. 2011. Web. 10 May 2012.

■ Ajay has created a works cited page just as he would have for a research paper. There are no settled conventions for how to handle citations in a slide presentation as there are for papers; for example, Ajay could have put his citations onto a last slide (which means he would have had to go to that slide—rather than staying on slide 13—during the question and answer time).

Your teacher should let you know how to approach citations for an oral presentation.

TO ANALYZE

■ **Practice with others:** Using Ajay's notes, you give his presentation to 3–4 others. What of his strategies work for you—and which would you change to fit your style? What do you want to remember from Ajay's approaches to use in your own presenting?

TESTING AND EVALUATING ORAL PRESENTATIONS

Testing and evaluating your oral presentations can be awkward because it can feel so personal: It is you, speaking, being tested and evaluated. But, really, you just have to get over it—and you can help yourself do this by remembering that when you test and evaluate speeches, the point is for you to learn what works well and to strengthen what could be more effective. That's all.

But, meanwhile, here are...

Ways to address evaluation fairly and humanely.

❏ Make the evaluation criteria as clear as possible.

❏ Come up with the criteria as a class.

❏ Talk through the criteria with those evaluating a talk: Discuss how you all understand the criteria and what kinds of responses will be most helpful from those doing the evaluation.

❏ Practice applying the criteria with everyone involved and then discuss differences in your responses.

❏ Err on the side of being positive in your responses to one another.

❏ Emphasize verbal feedback over numerical evaluations.

❏ Use a variety of evaluations (self, peer, instructor, written, verbal).

Questions and prompts for evaluating a speech

THE INTRODUCTION

❏ How did the introduction capture audience interest? How could it have been stronger?

❏ Describe your understanding of the speech's purpose from what you heard in the introduction.

❏ What did you think the speech's arrangement would be, based on the introduction?

THE BODY

❏ What were the main points you heard? What offered evidence supported the main points?

❏ How did the evidence persuade you? Could it have been more concrete or more detailed?

❏ How did the arrangement of the speech support the purpose?

❏ What were the strengths of the language used in the speech?

❏ What suggestions do you have for how the language of the speech could be more engaging?

THE CONCLUSION

❏ How did the conclusion help you remember the purpose of the speech?

❏ How does the conclusion give you closure? How might it do this more effectively?

DELIVERY

❏ What were the strongest qualities of voice to support the purpose and engage the audience?

❏ How did the postures and gestures contribute to the effectiveness of the speech? How might they have been more effective?

❏ How did the speaker's eye contact engage you with the speech?

❏ What was the overall manner of the speaker (enthusiastic? reserved?)—and how did it support the purpose?

❏ How aware were you of the speaker's use of notes?

OVERALL

❏ How could the topic be narrowed to be more appropriate for the speech's time?

❏ How persuasive to its audience was the speech? How might it be more persuasive?

ETHICAL CONTEXTS OF SPEAKING—AND LISTENING

Sonja K. Foss and Karen A. Foss, who wrote the article "Constructing Connections" that we used earlier in this chapter, also wrote an article titled "Inviting Transformation." In "Inviting Transformation," Foss and Foss argue that the ethics of the speaking context suggests speakers should try to invite transformation when they speak to an audience rather than do whatever they can to ensure change in the audience. To reinforce this idea, Foss and Foss urge speakers to resist seeing themselves as the active partner in communication and seeing audiences as passive. Instead, they urge speakers to learn to be better listeners in order to be better speakers, to build better relations with audiences.

Speech communication scholar Karlyn Kohrs Campbell builds on Foss and Foss's argument in an article titled "Hating Hillary." To build her argument, Campbell examined all the speeches given by Hillary Rodham Clinton during the first term of the Clinton presidency in order to consider how effective a speaker Clinton was at that time.

Campbell was particularly interested in Clinton's speeches on health care reform because that was a project on which Clinton worked closely. What Campbell discovered is interesting and complex: Clinton's speaking manner was sharp, direct, and at times aggressive. Clinton was no more sharp, direct, or aggressive than any other politician—but,

Campbell argues, women in politics must walk a fine line between being aggressive and strong and coming across as feminine or motherly. Campbell refers to this as a double-bind because women are expected to be both aggressive and not aggressive at the same time—quite a trick.

Campbell concludes that Clinton was not a wholly successful speaker. Clinton tended to ignore the double-bind in which she was caught and, instead, she spoke forthrightly. As a result, many people responded negatively (in some cases very negatively) to her "manly" way of speaking and carrying herself. Campbell also concludes, however, that much of the fault for Clinton's lack of success can be laid at the feet of her audience because they unselfconsciously, uncritically, and unfairly expected Clinton to give in to the double-bind and both be and not be the proper woman speaker.

Campbell thus tries to nudge her readers into admitting that they listen to men and women speakers differently, to the unfair advantage of male speakers. Campbell argues that the ethics of the speaking context suggest audiences (at times) should acknowledge when speakers are caught in a social double-bind not of their own making; Campbell argues that speakers should not blindly reinforce the double-bind by going along with superficial expectations.

We made a related point earlier in this chapter when we urged you to be more self-conscious about how you sit in an audience and how responsive you are to a speaker's efforts. We were raising the question of the ethical responsibilities of audiences, just as Campbell has done.

In addition, then, to being a careful listener while you are speaking, having integrity in your arguments, and being an attentive audience while you are listening, do consider how attitudes of which you may not always be aware shape how you listen and evaluate. If, while you listen, you find yourself responding negatively and you can't honestly pin your response to the speech's long-winded phrasing, obvious faulty logic, or mean-spiritedness, then consider whether unspoken assumptions are at play.

And even if you think you can point to such faults as we listed, it is sometimes worthwhile (especially in politics or when a speaker comes from a differing background) to consider whether you are judging based on your own attachments rather than on the merits of the speech.

233

INTERVIEWING

You can learn about your audience through interviewing, and interviewing is also a useful way to gather information or supporting material for the body of a talk.

As you plan for an interview, remember that you are looking for the specific information you can use in shaping your talk or as material for your talk. But also remember that interviewing someone about the subject of your talk gives you an opportunity to try out your ideas and check the response you get.

Interviewing is an essential for research. Like listening and seeing, it can seem so easy and obvious you hardly need to think about it—but just sitting down and asking questions will not help you learn what you need. Here we will sketch some basic interviewing strategies that should help with your research.

Many of the subjects we address in this textbook, interviewing among them, can themselves be the subject of a book-length study. For more detailed information on interviewing, we recommend Shirley Biagi's *Interviews That Work: A Practical Guide for the Journalist* (Belmont: Wadsworth Publishing Co., 1986). Even though Biagi steers her advice toward journalists, she has much to offer anyone who needs to plan and carry out a successful interview. We have drawn much of what we have to say about interviewing from Biagi.

Rule 1

Prepare for your interview.

An interview can feel and move like a conversation—which is deceptive. You should expect interviews to take unexpected turns as conversations do, but don't decide that you therefore don't need to plan. What you plan will be useful even as the discussion twists unexpectedly because as it twists away from what you anticipated, you will know how it is deviating. Knowing what you expected helps you understand and hold on to the unexpected.

To prepare, get very clear about your purpose. *What do you want to get out of the interview? Are you looking for specific knowledge or someone else's particular take on a situation?* Work up questions to achieve that purpose. You need an opening question to set the tone of the interview, a set of questions to follow, and concluding questions. You also want to prepare follow-up questions.

Prepare your questions and think about the context of the interview: location, possible distractions, length of time needed, the mood the person may be in, and so on. Attend to what you say through your nonverbal actions—and show up on time and sit straight and lean forward to display your interest and concern. You do want to establish a relaxed atmosphere, but concentrate on what the person is saying.

Rule 2

Interviews are interactive.

Of course you listen carefully during the interview and take notes when appropriate, but attend to what else is going on. Pay attention to the gestures and expressions of the person you're interviewing. If you are in the person's home or office, check out the paintings, posters, or awards displayed; these can give you topics for "small talk," the kind of conversation that eases relations between people.

What helps interviews be interactive

❑ Smile. Introduce yourself calmly but enthusiastically.

❑ Set an agenda early by stating what you want to get out of the interview.

❑ If possible, establish a shared goal with the person you interview.

❑ If you use technical words or special references to people, places, or institutions, make sure that you both understand the words similarly: Define what you mean when you talk, and ask the person you interview to define words about which you are not clear.

❑ Give the other person time to answer. It's fine to let pauses go a little longer than when you are talking with friends because the person you are interviewing may need a little time to think. When it seems as though the person you are interviewing has finished speaking in response to your questions, ask if she or he is finished.

❑ Once you have a sense of the other person's rhythms in speaking, keep the discussion moving. This is especially important in phone interviews.

❑ Try to sense early on whether the person really doesn't want to talk.

In the middle of an interview, these approaches help you learn more or be sure you understand:

• Restate an interviewee's answer to ensure you heard correctly or to invite qualification.

• Ask the person to expand on a point or enlarge on a specific incident if it will help you better understand what happened.

Rule 3

Establish respect and trust as best you can.

Even when an interview is strained and you are seeking information the informant is not willing to give, treat the person as you want to be treated. The hard part about being moral is that it is your responsibility that matters. If someone is not responsible to you in return, you have to let it go. All you can do is be the interviewer you know you should be: open, thoughtful, prepared, critical, and respectful.

Rule 4

End the interview.

With the person you are interviewing, go back over what has been said to double-check your grasp of the interview's main points. If you are taking notes, put away your notebook toward the end and keep listening. Ask if follow-up questions, perhaps over the phone, are acceptable. Be sure to say "Thank you."

Thank you.

235

Preparing questions to ask

In chapter 4, we distinguished some basic kinds of questions: fact, definition, interpretation, value, and policy. Read about these questions because they will help you know what questions to ask and in what order. As you consider possible questions, ask yourself whether the person you are interviewing is qualified or otherwise in the appropriate position to answer what you ask.

• Begin with an open-ended question.

• Concentrate on *how?* and *why?* questions because these lead to fuller answers than *yes* and *no* questions.

• Ask the person you are interviewing to define any terms that matter to the discussion.

• Ask questions that invite the interviewee to rank or evaluate something.

• Give an either/or choice in a question when you want to know the interviewee's position on an issue.

• Ask for a chronology of events. This often brings out details to an event that an interviewee might otherwise miss.

• Avoid two-part questions, overly long questions, unfocused questions, clichéd questions, leading questions, yes-no questions, and absolute questions (using qualifiers such as certainly, positively, or absolutely). Such questions do not encourage thoughtful or detailed responses.

THINKING THROUGH PRODUCTION

■ Take this Langston Hughes poem home with you and read it aloud to yourself at least 10 times. Commit it to heart. Find a way to read the poem—where to pause, where to change tone, where to put emphasis—that lets it do for a listening audience what you think Hughes wanted it to do.

DREAMS

Hold fast to dreams

For if dreams die

Life is a broken-winged bird

That cannot fly

Hold fast to dreams

For when dreams go

Life is a barren field

Frozen with snow

Present the poem to the rest of your class. Compare your reading with that of others in class.

As you listen to others, consider what you would liked to have done differently in your presentation. What do you want to remember from this short presentation for any future oral presentation?

■ Using the design process from chapters 2 and 3—and the interview sections in this chapter—plan and conduct an interview about the civic side of life with an older relative, older friend of the family, or someone you know at school who is at least 10 years older than you. Cover the activities in which they are involved outside of work and home, what they think being a good citizen means, how they divide private and public life, and relevant commitments, attitudes, and beliefs.

Use the interview as the basis of a 5-minute talk you design and then deliver to class about your interviewee's civic life.

After your presentation, write a short paper in which you reflect on what you learned: *Did your interview shift your understanding of the person you interviewed? How? Did your interview shift your sense of your own civic life? How? What might you do differently in our day-to-day life in response or think would be good to change in your community?*

In your writing, also reflect on your presentation. Using the criteria on page 232, describe what you did well and what you would like to do better in future presentations. *How can you prepare yourself to do better?*

■ Remember a time you gave a speech or talk that didn't go as well as you would have liked. Describe how you would redesign the physical context in which you gave that speech so that the audience would have been as comfortable and supportively listening as possible and so that you would have been as relaxed and confident as possible.

What can you take away from your redesign to help you shape the physical contexts in which you speak in the future?

about visual modes of communication

Do you think you need a degree in art or design to include photographs effectively in a research paper or to compose a poster for a fund-raising event?

There is certainly much more to learning to be a professional visual communicator than we present in this chapter. For example, we do not give any history of design, which could give you a sense of how visual conventions have changed over time and place. We do not ask you to spend a semester drawing lettershapes—by hand—so that you have the smart expressiveness that calligraphic work requires. We do not discuss how to prepare a document for printing or how to design interactive online interfaces: Both processes can be highly complex and require extensive technical knowledge.

What does make sense for us to offer you, however, are basic but sufficient vocabulary, concepts, and methods to help you start being as rhetorical with the visual aspects of texts as with the verbal. Almost all the texts you compose—in school or out—require you to make visual choices (even if your choices are typeface, the size of margins, and alignment). Almost all texts you encounter have been designed to have visual effects on you; you can respond to those texts analytically only if you have vocabulary and concepts to help you see how the texts are working.

We don't intend to make you an expert in this chapter; we do intend to give you resources that will help you move thoughtfully through our visually full and varied environments.

THE PLEASURES—AND COMPLEXITIES— OF VISUAL COMMUNICATION

eeing so often brings delight. Think of how parents look at their children and of how people who are in love look at each other. Think of how enjoyable a walk in the woods is, whether we see the bright greens of early spring or the stark soft shapes of an overnight snowfall. These visual pleasures seem easy: We just open our eyes and, automatically and effortlessly, there is the world to touch with our eyes. Seeing, that is, can seem to be only physiology, a result solely of the physical processes of our bodies, unaffected by who we are, where we live, or how we've been raised.

This easiness of seeing appears to extend to the visual texts we make for each other. When we take photographs or videos or try to capture an "exact likeness" in a drawing, we might think we are capturing a bit of reality; anyone anywhere should understand what the picture is about without explanation. Think of how children's books are composed only of pictures with little or no text and how we take it as a sign of maturity when a child can read words-only books.

Because seeing and understanding photographs and drawings can seem so effortless and can be so pleasurable, some people think that visual texts are not as serious as verbal texts, which by comparison appear to require more abstract and conceptual thinking. Because of this, some people look at the increase in visual texts in this country and time—advertising, comic books, music videos, webpages, movies— and believe we are all becoming less thoughtful and complex people because we spend less time than ever reading.

In this book, however, we argue that visual texts are complex—and can be as complex and thoughtful as any purely verbal text. If someone thinks they are not, it is in no small part because our educations have encouraged us to have that attitude: We have grown up in places and times that have valued verbal texts as being more serious and worthy of educated attention than other kinds of texts.

But every visual text involves choices—just like every written text. A photograph requires the photographer to frame the picture, to decide what to emphasize and what not, what level of focus to use, and so on … and we can understand photographs only if we have some understanding of the contexts in which they are shown.

We are not arguing that our understandings of the visual aspects of texts have no connections with how our bodies work. For example, our eyes are of a certain size, they cover a certain angle of vision, and they have a certain range of focus, which changes as we age. Anyone who is designing visual objects must keep these matters in mind when making compositions for others: If you compose a poster, you want to be sure others can see its main elements from a distance; if you design a booklet for older people, you will use larger typefaces and colors that help people see contrast more clearly.

We are arguing, however, that if we don't learn to analyze and understand the complexities of visual texts and to compose thoughtful, complex visual texts ourselves, then it can seem as though we just perceive visual texts naturally and easily … and then we won't read visual texts critically, as texts made by people who arrange the text's elements to achieve specific purposes.

On the following pages, we present strategies for analyzing and composing visual texts, strategies based both on how we see physically and on how we see as participants in our cultures.

66Daniel Simons, a professor of psychology at Harvard, has done a … dramatic set of experiments. … He and a colleague, Christopher Chabris, recently made a video of two teams of basketball players, one team in white shirts and the other in black, each player in constant motion as two basketballs are passed back and forth. Observers were asked to count the number of passes completed by the members of the white team. After about forty-five seconds of passes, a woman in a gorilla suit walks into the middle of the group, stands in front of the camera, beats her chest vigorously, then walks away. 'Fifty percent of the people missed the gorilla,' Simons says. 'We got the most striking reactions. We'd ask people, "Did you see anyone walking across the screen?" They'd say no. Anything at all? No. Eventually we'd ask them, "Did you notice the gorilla?" And they'd say, "The what?"' Simons's experiment is one of those psychological studies which are impossible to believe in the abstract: If you look at the video (called 'Gorillas in Our Midst') when you know what's coming, the woman in the gorilla suit is inescapable. How could anyone miss that? But people do. In recent years, there has been much scientific research on the fallibility of memory—on the fact that eyewitnesses, for example, often distort or omit critical details when they recall what they saw. But the new research points to something that is even more troubling: It isn't just that our memory of what we see is selective; it's that seeing itself is selective. 99

from "Wrong Turn: How the Fight to Make
America's Highways Safer Went Off Course."
By Malcolm Gladwell. *The New Yorker*, June 11,
2001 (pp. 50–61).

Figure provided by Daniel Simons. For more information and to view the video, visit http://www.theinvisiblegorilla.com

239

VISIBLE PURPOSES, AUDIENCES, AND CONTEXTS

Visible purposes

When should you use visual strategies for argument instead of or in addition to written or oral strategies? Whenever it is appropriate to your purpose and when the visual strategies support your purpose.

Like writing and speaking, visual communications and the purposes they can fulfill are complex and interesting because—as we discussed in chapter 1—they draw on what we know about the world because we have bodies and because we grow up in cultures. Consider how the following characteristics of visual texts shape possible purposes:

■ In our culture, photographs and drawings of people can seem automatically to carry more emotion than writing. We respond because we know or can imagine what it is like to have the expression and be in the body posture shown. Including photographs or drawings in a written composition can thus attach emotions and bodily sensations to the writing—but do be alert to how different audiences can respond in very different ways.

■ When we see photographs and realistic illustrations, we see and assume much more than we often are aware because of our knowledge about people and culture. We make judgments about people's ages and character and relationships, about when

and where photographs were taken, and so on. These are good reasons to check how your intended audiences understand any photographs or illustrations you are considering for a composition. How we respond to photographs and illustrations also suggests that we can use them to lead audiences to think of particular times and places and of the associations they have with those times and places.

■ Often when people say "image," they think only of paintings or photographs. But consider technical illustrations, charts and graphs, logos, and so on. Technical illustrations or photographs are designed to show us only the details we need to understand a process or machine. Charts and graphs show us the relations that their composers want us to see among numbers or other data. When they compose logos (the plural of "logo"), designers try to compress into them the values they want audiences to associate with a company. Each of these kinds of visual communication has purposes that can help you with particular communications you produce.

■ When we learn to write, we rarely learn about visual potentials of writing. We do understand differences between handwritten and printed documents: The former seem more personal, and we often make judgments about people based on their handwriting (for example, how do you feel about the letter *i* when the dot above it is a circle or a heart?). Printed documents have the feel of being formal and professional and so distanced from us. But what about differences in the typefaces and colors you can use on a page? Like photographs and illustrations, typefaces and color can add emotional associations to a page (and, as with photographs and illustrations, this means you should always test your choices with audiences). Typefaces and color also can help with the logos of a page, helping readers differentiate levels of argument on it. Much of this chapter will help you make such choices.

In this chapter, we focus primarily on how you can use visual elements of pages (print or screen) to produce arguments. In chapters 10 and 11 we consider the compositional strategies of posters and photographs; in chapter 14, we look at comics and how words and drawings or photographs can work together to achieve purposes that either alone cannot.

Visible audiences

I am 55 years old as I write this (this is Anne, one of your authors), and my eyes are different than they were when I was 20. I am one of those people you see in the aisle at the supermarket trying to read the small type on the sides of vitamins. I move the bottles nearer and farther, and eventually end up quite close—closer than my glasses can handle so I look out from underneath my lenses. I am one of those people you—who are most likely not 55 years old—should have in mind when you design visual communication for general or older audiences. If you assume that anyone can read what you design because you can, you might leave me out.

So even though writing and visual communication are the same in that you rarely see your audiences at the time they engage with your productions, there are additional attentions you need to give to your audiences when you design visual communications.

I've already mentioned eyes—and their age-bound abilities—but also consider how different audiences respond to different photographs and drawings. Not too many years ago, a software company producing page layout software put a graphic on screen while the software was opening; the graphic included the symbol at the top left of this column, the circle with perpendicular lines over it, which you might sometimes see if you use page layout applications. When a book, poster, or other text is printed on a press in hundreds or thousands of copies, its pages are often printed on paper that is larger than the document's final size and then trimmed. (This is how we get pages that have photographs that run off the edge of a page: The photograph "bleeds" off the edge of the page as it is designed to do, and then that bleed is cut away when the page is trimmed to its final size.) The symbol on this page is a registration mark that printers use to ensure that pages are all aligned properly up and down when they go to trim big stacks of the pages.

The point of all this information is that many people who bought the software we've just described complained about the registration mark because they didn't know what it was. Christians complained that the software company was profaning the cross; non-Christians complained that the software company was trying to force Christianity down their throats. Were these audiences for the software being too sensitive? Were they just stupid?

No.

You can never expect others to know everything you know—just as you hope others do not expect you to know everything they do. Judging what others value is also a dicey proposition: Even when you disagree, you probably would like others to respect what you value and not to call your values stupid or not worthy of care. Look back at the list of conditions that make argument possible on page 27; if you want arguments that do indeed engage you with others, you do need to respect their beliefs and values.

Because we cannot often predict the associations others will have with the photographs or drawings we use, it is crucial when you are making decisions about using photographs or drawings to test them with your intended audiences. Ask people what associations or ideas come up for them as they look at the photographs or illustrations or the colors you're considering. You can learn if audiences think the graphics are too childish for them, incomprehensible, or potentially distracting from your purposes.

As you design and produce visual communications, think of audiences as people with beliefs, values, and opinions you want to engage, not to alienate.

Visible contexts

Like writing but unlike speaking, you never or rarely get to be there when audiences see visual communications you have made. And so you have to be imaginative as you produce communication that is primarily visual. Imagine the moment when others see what you produce—but also get out there observing how others look at similar productions. Find people from your audience who will help you test your productions in the contexts where they'll be seen.

One of the biggest—and most avoidable—failures of visual communication is communication that people can't see because it's been poorly designed for its context. Have you ever noticed road signs that were impossible to read as you drove by at 60 mph because they were detailed and pretty—rather than large and simple? Most failures, however, are the ones you don't see because they are easy to overlook. The next time you pass that wall on your campus or those telephone poles plastered with announcements, notice how many of the announcements you don't notice—and pay attention to how the ones that do grab your eyes do their work. If you make posters or flyers, test one (before you print 400) by hanging it in a place where it would be hung and ask someone from your intended audience to walk by: Does the person even see it? Posters and flyers are seen by people walking by 5, 6, or 10 feet away: There must be something large—really large—on the page that can catch their attention. If your page has a single feature that interests audiences from a distance, they will come closer to read the more detailed information in smaller type.

For visual communications like signs, posters, and flyers, there's an aspect of context that writings and talks don't have to work with: Signs, posters, and flyers are placed where they compete with other signs, posters, and flyers. For them to be noticeable, they have to stand out against the background of all the others. This is where you need the principle of contrast, which we discuss in this chapter. Consider the strategies for creating contrast to help you design communication that others can see.

Other visual communications—or communications that require some visual attentions, such as any printed or onscreen piece of communication—will be seen in the same contexts as people reading books or magazines. Go back and look at what we wrote about context in the writing chapter for encouragement and ideas. Most importantly, research contexts.

Or make contexts. If you have a poster, in what unexpected places can you put it so that people will see it? On the ground? Tucked into visible but uncluttered corners?

Always consider how you can shape the contexts in which your productions are seen.

TO ANALYZE

■ **Discuss with others:** Bring your favorite or an interesting picture postcard to class. In groups of two or three, look at someone else's postcard—but don't look at the back.

List as much as you can about the photograph on the postcard based just on what you see. When and where do you think the photograph was taken? What can you say about who or what is in it?

After about 5 minutes, share your observations with the whole group. Tell why you make the guesses you did about the postcards. (Turn over the postcard to see what information is there—how close were you?)

Were you surprised by how much everyone could say about the postcards? What can you learn from this about how we see and understand photographs?

A STATEMENT OF PURPOSE FOR A PHOTO ESSAY

Remember that in a statement of purpose, you bring together your initial sense of purpose with your knowledge about your audience and the context in which your audience encounters your text. By doing this, you sharpen your sense of what it is you hope to achieve with your text, and so you set yourself up to make crisper decisions about the strategies you will use.

FOR EXAMPLE

In addition to writing a paper based on his research, Ajay has an assignment to compose a short photo essay using his research; his first focused thinking on this assignment is on the right in his statement of purpose.

Ajay's design plan for the photo essay is on pages 272–273 and the photo essay is on pages 274–277.

Statement of Purpose for a Photo Essay

My audience includes my classmates and my teacher, and the context will be class on the next to the last day of classes (yay!) when we're going to post our photoessays on the wall. Everyone's going to be a bit wiped out from the semester and from having finished our final papers and doing our presentations, so I think everyone's looking forward to having a little fun experimenting with pictures.

But this is still graded (the professor made that very clear) based on the following qualities: The photoessay has to grow out of our research paper/oral presentation and has to creatively use at least four photographs (and captions if we want) to make a point tied to our paper/presentation. It also has to be understandable to others in class with no help from us. (The professor said the essays can be printed or online and that on the day they are due, we will post them on the wall or move from computer to computer to look at them.)

So part of my purpose is to meet those expectations—but then I also have to have a purpose specifically tied to the photoessay. As I was imagining what I could do with my argument from my research paper about students as customers, I tried to picture what students as customers looked like—and I realized how hard it is to show this. I mean, it's easy to picture someone buying a soda—but what does it mean to buy a grade? Okay, I know you can picture handing money over for a grade, but such a photograph would look weird, wouldn't it? Wouldn't such a photograph sort of creep us out because we would know that buying grades isn't right?

I need to think a bit more on how to make this work, but I think my purpose is to use photographs to show just how weird it is to try to photograph students being consumers as students—and by doing that, to suggest that (while we may try to act as customers when we are students), the reality of what we do shows that we can't really purchase a grade, a diploma, or an education.

I'm hoping that I can do all that but also maybe have my photo essay seem a little funny or weird, to work for it being almost the end of classes.

243

VISIBLE ETHOS, LOGOS, AND PATHOS

As with written and oral communication, visual texts have their own particular strategies we can use to compose ethos, logos, and pathos, strategies that have developed over time and through the shaping of particular cultures. Keep in mind, then, that what we offer you here about ethos, pathos, and logos in visual arrangements is appropriate for arguments that meet audience expectations in the early 21st century United States.

In visual communication—as in the general U.S. approach to how we use space and time—efficiency is now valued. Historians of visual design argue that the rise of efficiency as a value in visual communication paralleled the linked rise of industry and advertising in the 20th century. As industrialists strove to produce as many objects as possible as quickly as possible, they also needed to produce consumers for those objects. Advertising was born to encourage people to desire things and to desire them quickly, and visual communication in general therefore took on the values of quickness and directness.

What we present in the sections on the logos of arrangement in visual communication, especially, will help you compose layouts whose order supports the efficient communication of information, but keep in mind that ethos and pathos can also be visually shaped into efficiency. A photograph, for example, can show a person having a single clear emotional response to an event or can indicate more complex emotional responses. You can visually compose an ethos that shows you to be singularly focused on efficiency or you can compose an ethos that shows you to value generosity as well.

Because efficiency has been so highly valued, it can seem not to be a value but simply how things are and always ought to be. Many books that teach about visual communication teach layout principles as though efficiency—with its concordant layout values of coherence, unity, and a clear hierarchy of informative elements—is the value that should underlie all choices in layout. In the pages that follow, we hope to teach you the ability to use those values well, precisely because they are the values many of your audiences will hold. But as you read through the next pages, keep in mind that many other possible values can go into how you compose ethos, logos, and pathos on a page or screen.

Because visual communication has such strong ties to advertising, many people think that advertising is all that visual communication can do. It doesn't take much looking—whether back in time or in different places in the present—to see visual texts that use other values to shape ethos, logos, and pathos: Look at stained glass windows, weather charts, biology textbooks, tattoos, or the pages of Bibles or Korans to see those other values at work. We challenge you—both as a composer and as audience for others' compositions—to look in visual texts for ethos, logos, and pathos that advocate values such as compassion, respect for complex thinking, diversity, simplicity, and self-awareness.

Precisely because we have grown up in a culture in which such values are rarely taught through visual communication, they may look odd to us when we see them made visible. But if we wish to see more of such values in our communications, we need to make those values visible ourselves, and we need to show generosity toward the designs of others who are trying to make those values present.

ETHOS IN PHOTOGRAPHS

Which of the photographs on this page draws your attention? How have the elements been arranged or treated so that you notice one element first and then another second or third?

Photographs tend to direct our attention to other people and objects, to the "outside" world. In that way, even if they are about family members or intimate events, photographs resemble scientific essays. We would like them to show us the world just as it is.

How then could there be any ethos? What in these photographs asks you to think about the character of the photographer?

Along with showing us people or objects, photographs (even those made with automatic cameras) show us the photographer's decisions. They show us the position the photographer chose for the camera, the exposure time, and the use or not of a flash or filters—and they show us that the photographer thought there was something worth photographing.

Learning to interpret photographs, then, means acknowledging that such decisions have gone into them. Learning to interpret photographs means listing the decisions—the strategies used to take them—and asking what they tell us about the photographer and what the photographer wants us to see.

For photography, such a line of questioning matters more than for other media because photographs ask us to become the photographer. Whenever we see a photograph, we see it from the position the photographer did. Every photograph asks us to see the world as though we were seeing it through the photographer's lens and through the series of judgments the photographer made in setting up the shot and then working with the photograph because of how much can now be done digitally. In looking at any photograph, then, we need to ask why a photographer wants us to see a particular scene arranged as it is.

What sort of person would look at the world—would make the particular choices about framing and displaying—in the way the photograph asks us to look?

245

WHAT YOU ALREADY KNOW BECAUSE YOU LOOK— AND A PROFESSIONAL ETHOS

If you find rest or distraction in flipping through TV channels, you can probably tell, almost immediately, whether you've hit an infomercial or a network series. Without thinking, you probably register the difference in production values—in the lighting and in the quality of sound and the set—between the two genres because you've seen so many different kinds of TV shows that you've learned almost automatically what looks polished and professional and what doesn't.

Two useful-to-understanding-visual-texts qualities reside in your ability to distinguish between infomercials and other shows.

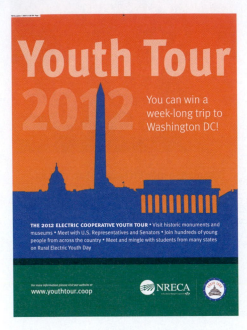

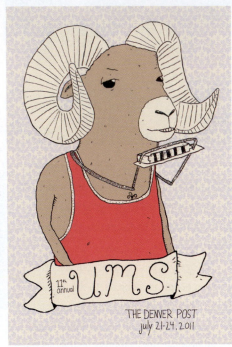

First, you make judgments about the quality of different visual texts all the time—

often without being aware of the judgments. If you want to start producing your own visual texts or being even more alert to how such texts have the effects they do, noticing your existing judgments and tastes about visual texts can help you. The vocabulary and concepts we offer in this book can support you in such work.

Second, the qualities of "polished and professional" are valued in our day and place.

As a culture, we often value communicative visual texts if they get to the point efficiently and demonstrate that their composers know how to use their materials well. A director who lets a microphone show in a scene or an actor who speaks in a monotone are the stuff of comedy for us. When texts do look "polished and professional," we tend to place a certain trust in the makers of the text and hence in the persuasiveness of the text—in most contexts.

Producers of visual texts can rhetorically use the distinction between what is considered professional and what isn't. Precisely because alt bands want to look outside the mainstream, posters for their shows are often hand drawn and, in comparison to a poster for a Katy Perry concert, they can look gentle and edgy rather than slick and mechanical.

Danny Gregory drew the page above, showing pictures of his son, Jack. The page comes from a (published) diary in which Gregory used drawing and writing to reflect on and come to some understanding about his life. When Jack was a baby, Gregory's wife had been run over by a subway train and paralyzed from the waist down. Gregory writes that his book "is about how art and New York City saved my life." Gregory's pages do not look "professional" because they are handwritten, but they are handwritten precisely because computer-generated pages—while professional looking—would not at all convey the heart- and hand-tied emotions Gregory needs.

As you analyze and produce visual texts, you need to learn what is generally considered professional looking, so that you can produce professional texts and can decide when nonprofessional strategies are useful.

TO ANALYZE

■ **Observe, then write:** Because "professional" is such a noticed quality in visual texts of our time and place, it is useful for you to be able to say explicitly what qualities make different texts professional or not.

Collect at least 10 samples of a certain kind of visual text. For example, you could collect examples of brochures, flyers for events on your campus, business cards, Power-Point presentations, or resumes. For each, list any adjectives you would attach to the ethos of the composers of the sample. Do you think the composers present themselves and their work professionally? Do they seem friendly and inviting or formal and distant? Do they seem cheerful or neutral? Also decide which of your samples look most professional and which look less.

Write down the qualities of the different texts that encourage you to make your judgments. As you look and judge, consider how the samples use type as well as the quality of writing, the kind of paper used, any use of color, the size of graphics, what any photographs depict, and so on.

As you work through this chapter, you will learn other terms and concepts to use in adding to your judgments. Your lists of what visual decisions help persuade audiences to see a particular ethos in a text can help you analyze visual texts in more detail in the future—but they can also help you if you ever need to produce any of these kinds of texts in the future. Any time you need to produce a kind of text that is new to you or that you've seen many times but have never made yourself, it is useful to collect and analyze a wide range of examples of that kind of text.

PATHOS IN PHOTOGRAPHS

Obvious pathos

When we see people in a photograph, we might identify with them: We understand the situation they are in through our own experiences. When we see happy (or sad or angry) people, we can feel similar emotions in response because we know the emotions ourselves. It is probably an obvious point to you, but this is why advertisements for cars or cookies show happy rather than perplexed people: The advertisers want you to believe you too will be happy in possession of that car or cookie.

Less obvious pathos

The two photographs above right are also composed to evoke emotional response from us.

When we see only part of an object, we mentally fill in what isn't shown, which can get us more engaged with the object—especially when it also takes a little time to understand what the photograph is showing us. A photograph of a storm might invoke memories of being caught in the rain, but it might also invoke the feelings of summer afternoon beauty. The context in which you see such a photograph—printed on a Christmas card or on a postcard from someone's overseas trip—and your specific cultural background will shape your own specific response.

Neither of the photographs on the right are meant to evoke the emotions of happiness, sadness, anger, or fear, but they do evoke bodily feelings—and therefore can be used rhetorically. To analyze and use the potential pathos of photographs, don't be afraid to name the emotions or bodily responses you yourself feel—just be alert to how the different backgrounds of others might lead them to respond differently.

PATHOS AND COLOR

When you analyze or choose colors for communication, keep in mind that we respond to colors because of our experiences within both the natural and cultural worlds—but our associations with color are not fixed. For example, we might associate light blue with a warm summer sky or the glow of winter ice. Black is the color people in the United States associate with death; in some Asian countries, white is the color for mourning. How people understand or respond to colors thus depends on the contexts in which they see the colors.

The colors of a photograph or page layout contribute substantially to our emotional responses. Our responses are not random but instead have much to do with what we have learned to associate with different colors.

To analyze and use color rhetorically, you need not only your cultural knowledge but also some vocabulary. "Color" is analyzed in terms of hue, saturation, and brightness:

Hue

"Hue" describes what most of us think of as color: When you name the hue of a color, you are saying whether it is red or blue or yellow or…. Hues are often represented in a wheel, as above: You can use those that are next or close to each other on the wheel when you want color schemes that seem harmonious; hues that are opposite have the most contrast.

Saturation

"Saturation" describes how much of a hue is present in a color. In the colored bar directly above the colors toward the left end are unsaturated; they have no blue in them. As you move to the right in the bar, the colors become more and more saturated: They have more and more blue in them.

Brightness

"Brightness" (sometimes also referred to as "value") describes how light or dark a color is. In the colored bar directly above the color at the extreme left has no brightness; the color at the extreme right is as bright as it can be.

Hue, saturation, and brightness are present in all colors. In the three examples here, the leftmost color chip is red hued with as much saturation and brightness as possible. The color chip in the middle is not very bright but is still a saturated red hue. The color chip on the right has a blue hue, is fairly bright, but is not very saturated.

PATHOS AND COLOR, continued

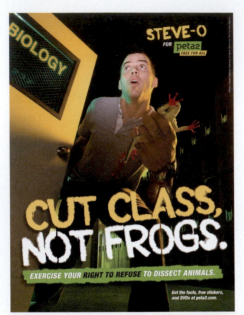

Analyzing the rhetorical effects of color

The two posters to the left are the same except for their colors. The poster's purpose is to persuade people not to use dissection in biology classes. The poster's composers decided to use photographs instead of drawings or technical illustrations; they decided to use a photograph of a television personality instead of a scientist, teacher, or student; they used informal type-faces and an informal layout, with very few and large shapes.

The poster's composers thus seem to want to address their audience in a nonthreatening and humorous way about the topic—and so the poster's visual presentation should almost tickle the audience into considering the topic. Which colors best support that overall purpose?

The first example uses bright and saturated yellow and green. The second uses less bright and less saturated blues and browns. Which uses hues that you associate with humor? Which poster seems to pull you in more, and why, in terms of color? Which do you think uses color appropriately for the poster's purpose? (Notice that were you just to discuss hue you couldn't account for how the colors work fully. You need to consider brightness and saturation together with hue.)

TO ANALYZE

■ **Write:** Choose any poster in this chapter or in chapter 10. Write a short rhetorical analysis in which you explain how its overall colors (be sure to address hue, saturation, and brightness) support (or not) the purpose of the poster.

■ **Discuss with others:** Discuss our use of color in this textbook. We've tried to differentiate sections and functions of the book through our use of color—color as logos—and we've also used color to (we hope) give the book appeal and depth to your eyes and to give it a look that is up-to-date—color as pathos. How effective do you think our color choices have been for these purposes? What would you change, and why?

250

TO ANALYZE: PATHOS AND COLOR

■ **Observe and then write:** The "Eat at Bill's" examples on the right use hue, saturation, and brightness differently to create their effects. Apply one or two adjectives to each example: hard, soft, inviting, exciting, shouting, cheery, loud, energetic, quiet, and so on. Make a chart like the one below to connect the adjectives with how the color qualities are used. Because your observations depend on your own associations with color, the chart can help you decide how to use color to achieve effects for audiences that share your general background.

Adjective	Color Qualities
hard	the colors have the strongest possible contrast in hue and brightness but have similar saturation

■ **Write:** Use the discussion of pathos in photographs as well as what you've learned about color to write a short rhetorical analysis comparing the emotional effects of two of the photographs below. First, describe how you respond to each photograph, and then describe how you think what is shown in each photograph shapes your response (be sure to mention the kinds of associations you have with what is shown in the photographs); then describe how the colors contribute to your response.

Compare your analysis with those of others in class: Do you bring the same associations to what is in the photographs as well as to the colors? When you find someone with different responses, work together to figure out how you have come to your different understandings.

THE PATHOS OF TYPE

Typography is the study of how letter shapes—on paper or on screen—work functionally and rhetorically. You need to know about typography to compose effective visual compositions with words.

In some visual compositions, such as school papers, type should not, by convention, call attention to itself: Such type should be designed so readers heed your ideas and not the letters' appearance. Such type design results from convention and our bodily practices. When you are told to turn in double-spaced pages in Times 12 point size, for example, it is because this is a typeface and a size of type that—when double spaced—many people have become accustomed to reading in school papers.

In other visual compositions—brochures, posters, webpages—we have learned to expect that type will evoke emotion and feeling. We expect to see typefaces that look boisterous, edgy, or loud because they work with the composition's other elements to create an overall effect in support of some purpose.

If you look at pages printed in earlier centuries, they look different from those printed today. In hand-calligraphed manuscripts, pages have large ornate letters. These manuscripts were usually meant to be read slowly aloud. The purpose of the type wasn't to ease the speed of an individual reading alone and quietly, which is the purpose of functional typography today.

How does type evoke feeling and emotions?

Letters' curves and straight lines can be arranged to suggest bodies or abstract shapes. Type can be:

graceful friendly **loud** relaxed childish goofy formal old-fashioned easy 3D staid light-hearted

Describing lettershapes

Knowing the names of parts of letters and of the qualities of different typefaces can help you differentiate among typefaces, which can help you make thoughtful rhetorical choices.

A fundamental distinction with typefaces is that between serif and sans serif typefaces. Serifed typefaces have little lines at the ends of the letter strokes; sans serifed have none ("sans" means "without" in French). In the United States, serif typefaces are considered more formal and easier to read than sans serif typefaces.

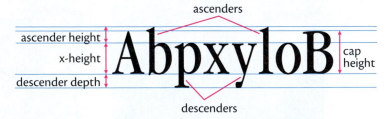

counter · serif · ear · Tsgvaf · counter · bowl · serif

ascenders · ascender height · x-height · descender depth · AbpxyloB · cap height · descenders

Styles of type

Typefaces often come in sets with lettershapes that have the same basic structure but different vertical orientations and visual weights. When you want to compose a page or screen on which the elements look harmonious because they look similar, use the different styles of one typeface.

Minion

Minion Italic

Minion Semibold

Minion Semibold Italic

Minion Bold

Minion Bold Italic

Minion Black

Categories of type

The following chart describes categories of typefaces. If you are deciding which typefaces to use in your compositions—or trying to figure out why someone else chose the particular typefaces of a layout you are analyzing—If you are deciding which typefaces to use in your compositions—or trying to figure out why someone else chose the particular typefaces of a layout you are analyzing—distinguish first between *typefaces we see in books and other situations where we have to read at length* and *typefaces that are used to emphasize short passages like titles or a line or two.* When you produce visual communication, divide typefaces into one of these two categories first. When you produce visual communication, divide typefaces into one of these two categories first.

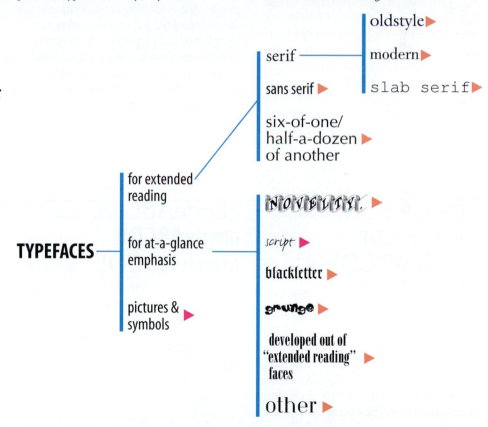

the arrow means: *look on the next pages to learn more about this category*

TYPEFACES FOR EXTENDED READING

OLDSTYLE

abcdeABCDE   Galliard

abcdeABCDE   Garamond

abcdeABCDE   Janson

abcdeABCDE   Jenson

This category goes back to the 16th century when people were designing typefaces for the relatively new printing press and were paying attention to creating regularity among letters' appearance. Oldstyle typefaces always have serifs and usually wide and rounded lettershapes. Notice how the serifs at the tops of the letters are usually slanted, and that the strokes are not all the same weight but have some transition from thick to thin. These typefaces look formal.

MODERN

abcdeABCDE   Bodoni

abcdeABCDE   Fenice

abcdeABCDE   Onyx

"Modern" typefaces were modern in the 17th century when mechanization picked up its pace and printing technologies supported people's desires for more precision and clarity. New printing technologies allowed type designers to make typefaces with very thin lines. Modern typefaces always have serifs— but their serifs don't slant. Modern typefaces mix very thick and very thin strokes, whose contrast can give them an elegant feeling.

SLAB SERIF

abcdeABCDE   Courier

abcdeABCDE   Lubalin Graph

abcdeABCDE   Officina Serif

In the early 19th century Napoleon invaded Egypt. His army included historians and artists who brought back samples of Egyptian art and writing to France. This started a craze in Europe for all things Egyptian—including typefaces that looked like they came from the Nile area. These typefaces were originally called "Egyptienne." Notice how the serifs are straight slabs with no curves softening how the serif joins the body of the letter. These typefaces often look informal.

254

SANS SERIF

abcdABCD   Avant Garde

abcdeABCDE   Bailey Sans

abcdeABCDE   Helvetica

abcdeABCDE   Officina Sans

In the 19th century, type designers wanted typefaces that looked modern and up-to-date to echo the streamlined mechanical wonders that were filling western factories and streets. Note how the lines in most of these typefaces are all the same weight, and that there is no ornamentation to the letters. These are straightforward-looking typefaces.

SIX-OF-ONE

abcdeABCDE   Optima

abcdeABCDE   Poppl-Laudatio

abcdeABCDE   Zapf Humanist

In the "for-extended-reading" category, you will occasionally find a typeface that has mixed features of serifed and sans serifed faces, like the ones above, with varying weights in their strokes. These faces tend to have an informal feeling.

PICTURES & SYMBOLS

Animal

Good Dog Bones

Insect

SchneeFlaken

Sugar Coma

Zapf Dingbats

Instead of lettershapes, these typefaces have pictures or symbols attached to each letter. These characters can be used as bullets or paragraph markers or decorative elements or… Be creative with them.

TYPEFACES FOR AT-A-GLANCE EMPHASIS

NOVELTY

ABCDEABCDE — Almonte Snow

ABCDEABCDE — Baby Jeepers

abcdeABCDE — Bailey's Car

ⒶⒷⒸⒹⒺ — Dialtone

ABCDEABCDE — Elwood

abcdeabcde — Jingopop

ABCDE — Shrapnel

Novelty typefaces are usually cute and lively; you might associate them with circus posters or old-fashioned advertising.

SCRIPT

abcde ABCDE — Avalon

abcdeABCDE — Caflisch

abcdeABCDE — Cezanne

abcdeABCDE — Handwriting

abcdeABCDE — Kidprint

abcdeABCDE — Visigoth

Script faces look as though they were hand-drawn with a pen. Sometimes they look drawn by someone with a long-practiced hand and sometimes by a three-year-old. They can therefore give a feeling of relaxed elegance to a page—or of playfulness.

FROM EXTENDED-READING FACES

abcdeABCDE — Bell Gothic

abcdeABCDE — Bodoni Poster Compressed

abcdeABCDE — Futura Extra Bold

abcdeABCDE — Garamond Bold

abcdeABCDE — Officina Serif Bold

Sometimes a typeface intended for blocks of extended reading is modified to make the face bolder for using as a headline, title, or other function. If you use one of these typefaces with the typeface from which it was developed, the look will generally be harmonious because the lettershapes echo each other—but do not use these typefaces for long text blocks.

255

BLACK LETTER

abcdeABCDE — Ancient Bastard Secretary Hand

abcdeABCDE — Ancient Formal Text Hand

abcdeABCDE — Notre Dame

You now see black letter typefaces in goth settings, but these typefaces go back to the Middle Ages, when monks and other scribes used quill pens to write. These typefaces can look formal and elegant—or dark and oppressive—so use them carefully.

GRUNGE

abcdeABCDE — BBQ Cow Moo

AbCDEABCDE — Devotion

abcdeABCDE — Dyslexia

abcdeabcde — Fragile

abcdeABCDE — Industrial Schizophrenic

ABCDEABCDE — Osprey

As you might expect from their name, grunge faces appeared with grunge music: The typefaces and the music share the same quick, hard-edged garage aesthetic.

OTHER

abcde — Bayer Type

ABCDE — Bermuda Squiggle

abcdeABCDE — Journal Text

abcdeABCDE — Katfish

Because typefaces in the "at-a-glance emphasis" category are used in so many different kinds of documents, designers develop new typefaces all the time, and sometimes they don't fit into the other divisions of this category. These typefaces tend to be playful and energetic.

THE LOGOS OF ARRANGING VISUAL ELEMENTS

Some use "shaping someone else's attention" as a definition of rhetoric—which helps us consider aspects of logos in visual composition. Because we see where we focus our eyes, seeing is very much about attention. If we are asked to put our visual attention on one thing, we often miss other things going on. (Look back to the description on page 238 of how much we can miss seeing because of how we focus.)

And so: When you make any kind of visual layout, you work to draw your audience's eyes—and hence their attention and thinking—through your presentation in a certain order: You want the order to persuade them to take the action, think about the matters, or have the experience you hope they will. Composing visual layouts, you order your elements (alphabetic symbols, photographs, drawings, shapes, and so on) that your audience follows visually—and hence conceptually—to arrive where you want them to.

This all means, then, that your visual compositions must be arranged:

1

Your visual compositions generally should have a limited number of elements so that your audience is not overwhelmed by detail and can see the point of your composition.

2

Your visual compositions should have a visual hierarchy—a visual path—that indicates to your audience what to look at first, what to look at second, what third, and so on … .

3

Your visual compositions must look like a set of unified pieces so that your audience understands that the pieces are meant to work together to make one main argument.

Questions (in order) that help you arrange your visual compositions:

▶ What elements do you need to include in your composition?

▶ What visual hierarchy—created from contrast and repetition—supports your purposes?

▶ What visual unity—created from repetition—can you create?

THE LOGOS OF ARRANGING VISUAL ELEMENTS
HOW MANY ELEMENTS TO INCLUDE

Which of the two layouts above feels to your eyes as though all the elements come together into one unified layout?

We're hoping you agree that the layout on the left—with a limited number of elements and a consequent visual simplicity—requires less effort from eyes and mind: When we look at it, we feel as though our eyes can take it in all at once.

With the layout on the right, however, our eyes feel pulled all over the place, not quite sure where to stop and focus. It is consequently hard to understand the relationships among the elements of the layout.

Audiences comprehend layouts like that on the left more easily because they do not require the audiences to make much visual effort. That is why the layouts seem straightforward: Audiences can look and easily see what element you want them to see first, which second, and which third; there's no need for them to figure out which element you intend to be fourth in their attentions, or fifth, or sixth, or seventh … .

Imagine you've brought home a pet rat and you have a choice of printed instructions to read about caring for the rat. Which of the two rat examples above look like instructions you could read easily and quickly? Which looks like you could find what you needed without much trouble?

The first sample has three elements—a rat, a series of lines (which you might interpret as a block of text), and cheese; the other example has those same elements plus 8 or 10 or 12 more. The second example might look as though it has more information, but could you find out on it quickly what to do when your rat starts nibbling its way through your clothes?

As you produce visual compositions, notice that many layouts use a limited number of elements to achieve their purposes. Flip through the examples in this chapter, look at the poster examples in chapter 10, and look at examples in magazines to analyze how many elements layouts tend to use.

When you start producing visual compositions, limit yourself to three to four elements (one picture, perhaps, a title, and one text block). This helps you to learn how to control the relationships among the elements so you can achieve your purposes straightforwardly. Doing this also shows your audience that your purpose is straightforward.

- You can have more than three to four elements, but use the strategies of repetition and proximity (which we discuss in the next pages) to make different elements look closely related. This reduces the apparent number of elements.

- Simple layouts are conventional in the sense that we see lots of them in magazines and on television. This means that, like most audiences we will address, we are accustomed to not having to do much work in figuring out visual compositions.

257

CREATING A VISUAL HIERARCHY

For each set of page thumbnails below, circle the composition that looks to you to have a clear visual path for your eye to follow. That is, in which of the two compositions do you have no question as to which element you are to look at first, which second, and so on?

a1   a2

b1   b2

c1   c2

d1   d2

e1   e2

f1   f2

We're guessing you circled a2, b1, c1, d1, e2, and f1. In each of those, you should be able to tell which element you are intended to notice first, which second, and so on. In those layouts, in other words, there is a clear visual hierarchy. You can see immediately which elements are given most visual weight and which least.

Contrast—a design principle we discuss in the next pages—helps one element stand out against a background of repeated elements, while the repetition creates visual unity.

- Notice that the element that first draws your attention is usually largest and darkest. When you start building visual hierarchies, begin by making obvious contrasts.

- Notice how the elements you are to see first are often in the top left or top middle. Because we learned to read from top to bottom and left to right, we are accustomed to start reading at top left. Use that to your advantage to create a clear and unambiguous visual starting point on a page.

- Notice how the number of elements helps you see a path. As we recommended on the preceding pages, limiting yourself to three to four elements can help you create compositions that are easy for your audiences to comprehend.

CONTRAST AND REPETITION FOR VISUAL HIERARCHY

Notice in the examples on the facing page that, in general, one element (at the top left or center) attracts your attention first, telling your eyes where to start looking. Creating one element that stands out by using contrast is easiest to do by thinking about contrast analytically, if—when you produce visual compositions—you describe in words to yourself how you create contrast. The following illustrations should help you figure this out; circle the one in each set that has one element that stands out.

g1

g2

h1

h2

i1

i2

j1

j2

k1

k2

l1

l2

m1

m2

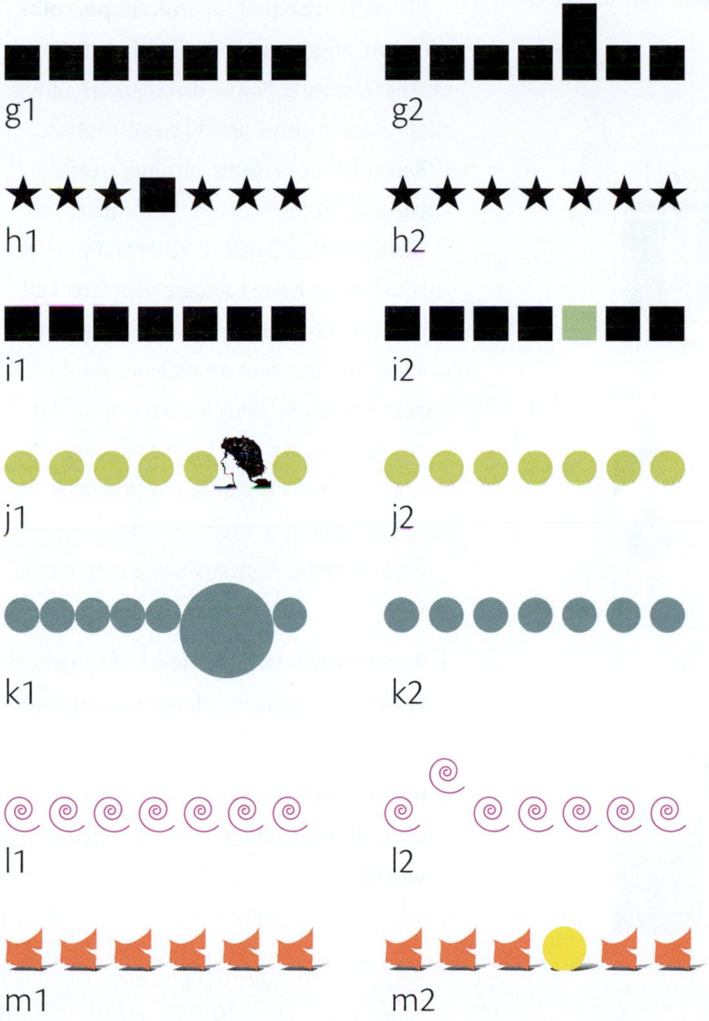

We're guessing you circled g2, h1, i2, j1, k1, l2, and m2. In each of those sets, one element contrasts with all the others.

The element contrasted because of how its **size**, **shape**, **color**, **position**, or **level of abstraction** contrasted with all the other elements. ("Level of abstraction" refers to what is going on in the "j" set: Notice how the abstract shapes create a background against which the more "realistic" face can stand out.) Contrast draws our attention to parts of visual compositions (although contrast isn't a principle for visual composition alone. Musical composers play with contrasts of tone or rhythm to create aural interest just as writers vary their voice, rhythm, or word sound).

When you compose, attend to this odd aspect of visual composition:

> **No single element can stand out unless the other elements blend together, appearing all the same.**

When you want to create contrast, therefore, attend carefully to creating a background of sameness against which an element can stand out. This means also that you can't make too many things different—or none will stand out.

THE LOGOS OF ARRANGING VISUAL ELEMENTS
CREATING VISUAL UNITY THROUGH REPETITION

In our time, we value unity and coherence. Newspapers put similar articles together into sections (world news, entertainment, sports), people dress in coordinated outfits, car colors do not vary much, and we expect politicians to base their decisions on a coherent set of values. Just as in those situations, unity and coherence extend to visual compositions. Unity in a visual composition isn't magic. You can design unified layouts by attending to certain concrete visual principles.

Circle the thumbnail layouts below that look to you as though all the elements are unified and built into a coherent visual composition.

n1

n2

o1

o2

p1

p2

q1

q2

r1

r2

s1

s2

We're guessing that you circled n2, o2, p2, q1, r1, and s2. In each of those layouts, the different elements are visually linked with each other, and each element repeats something from the other elements.

Elements can repeat the **size**, **shape**, **color**, **position**, **alignment**, or **level of abstraction** of other elements. Notice that these are almost all the same qualities used to create contrast.

Repetition of elements' qualities creates visual relationship between the elements just as when you meet a friend's sister and you can tell the two are related because their faces look alike. Repetition matters in writing or speech-making, too: You show an audience you are staying on topic by using the same or similar words, phrases, and tone of voice throughout—except when you use contrast to emphasize what you want people to remember.

Repetition therefore serves two purposes in layouts:

1 **Repetition creates the level of sameness against which some elements can stand out.**

2 **Repetition helps create the sense of unity that ties the elements together visually.**

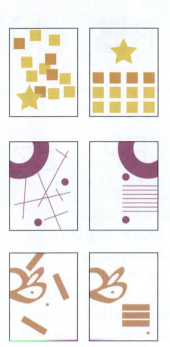

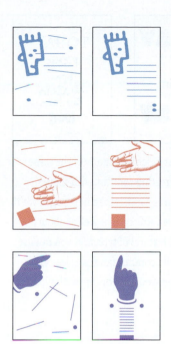

261

Repeating alignment

Of all the elements you can repeat, alignment most often gets overlooked—but alignment always matters for creating a unified page. Each composition on the left above follows the guidelines we've described on the preceding pages: Each has only a few elements and strong contrast in size and shape, with a background created by color repetition. Notice, though, how the right-hand composition of each pair looks more orderly and is aligned with at least one (if not more) other element.

In the illustrations in the third column, we have added the lines to which each composition's elements align: Every element aligns with at least one other element. Alignment is thus a strategy of logos, for creating compositions whose elements have an obvious visual relationship because they all line up with each other.

Two kinds of alignment

• **"Backbone" alignment.** The composition with the star and the one with the pointing blue hand have central alignment. It's as though all the elements hang off a single line, like a backbone, at page center. When you choose one line on a page as the backbone and hang everything off it, you compose layouts with a high degree of unity.

• **Alignment with the edges of the page.** Notice that the elements in the aligned compositions align not only with each other but also with the edges of the page: Every element is positioned vertically or horizontally, and so all the elements of these thumbnail compositions—including the pages they are on—are aligned. You may think, "Well, duh… I've been doing this all my life because this is what comes out of the printer," but if you consider this kind of alignment as a choice, you can use it alertly and purposefully in your visual compositions.

THE LOGOS OF TYPE ARRANGEMENT

The same strategies for making shapes stand out in a composition apply to typefaces: A background of sameness enables you to emphasize the words you want to emphasize.

For example, imagine that the thumbnail sketches of flyers above were posted together on a wall. Which are most likely to catch your eye? Which help you most clearly see—and differentiate—the information being presented?

Notice how clear differences in size and shape of the letterforms help you more easily see differences in what the words are conveying. Notice also how differences in color (here, whether a typeface looks black or gray) also help you see and differentiate among the elements of the layouts: This helps you more clearly tell what the flyer is about.

As we've just described, many of the same strategies for creating contrast with shapes apply to typefaces—and, on the next pages, we'll write about these strategies as well as about a few additional features of typefaces you can use to help you build contrast (and, so, clear visual hierarchy) when you are working with type:

- **category**
- **size**
- **shape**
- **position**
- **color**
- **weight**

When you start to produce visual compositions and try to choose and use different typefaces together, choose faces that have a lot of strong contrast—and then you want to arrange the typefaces so that the contrast is clear to your audience.

How the different *categories* of type can help you choose typefaces with strong contrast

Earlier in this chapter, you learned that typefaces can be divided into two large categories: those for extended reading and those for short blocks of text. You learned further that those categories can also be separated into serif and sans serif and then novelty, grunge, and so on. When you are choosing typefaces for strong contrast, a handy—but not foolproof—rule of thumb is to choose typefaces from different categories. That is, you can generally count on a serif and a sans serif contrasting well (but rarely will the different kinds of serifed typefaces contrast enough for you to be able to use them without some additional work).

Look at the pairs of typefaces shown above and circle the ones you think have the most contrast. Then identify the categories of those pairs to see what works for you.

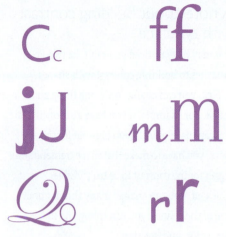

Using the *size* of typeface to create contrast

Size is probably the most obvious differentiation you can make between different pieces of type. Look at the examples at the top of this column. Which of the sets of letters has the most contrast between the two letters?

As with any use of difference in type size, be sure that when you are sizing typefaces you make the contrast clear and bold; it is generally better, as you are starting out, to err on the side of more rather than less contrast. In the beginning, go for bold rather than subtle: It's easier to learn subtlety after you have the broad moves down.

"I have never let my schooling interfere with my education."
Mark Twain

"I have never let my schooling interfere with my education."
Mark Twain

"I have never let my schooling interfere with my education."
Mark Twain

"I have never let my schooling interfere with my education."
Mark Twain

Using the *shape* of typefaces to create contrast

When you want to build strong contrast between two or more typefaces, look closely at how the *shapes* of individual letters contrast. This will help you choose typefaces that, on the whole, contrast strongly.

For example, look at the differences in the **g**s above; try to describe (using the names for parts of typefaces on page 252) the differences between the letters in each of the different pairs. Then look at the phrases from Mark Twain, each of which uses the two letterfaces in one of the sets above: Do the phrases show strong contrast between "Mark Twain" and the other words? Can you account for at least some of the contrast by the differences in the shapes of the different letters?

"If men and women are in chains, anywhere in the world, then freedom is endangered everywhere."
John Fitzgerald Kennedy

John Fitzgerald Kennedy
"If men and women are in chains, anywhere in the world, then freedom is endangered everywhere."

"If men and women are in chains, anywhere in the world, then freedom is endangered everywhere."
John Fitzgerald Kennedy

"If men and women are in chains, anywhere in the world, then freedom is endangered everywhere."
John Fitzgerald Kennedy

"If men and women are in chains, anywhere in the world, then freedom is endangered everywhere."
John Fitzgerald Kennedy

"If men and women are in chains, anywhere in the world, then freedom is endangered everywhere."
John Fitzgerald Kennedy

Using the *position* of type to create contrast

Position refers to how one piece of type is placed relative to another. In the examples at the top of this column, notice that position can also involve type's direction. Which of these examples develops the clearest contrast to your eyes—and why?

Notice that you have to make quite distinct changes in direction for this strategy to be effective.

THE LOGOS OF TYPE ARRANGEMENT, continued

This typeface is Caecilia Light.

This typeface is Caecilia.

This typeface is Caecilia Bold.

This typeface is Caecilia Heavy.

Using the *weights* of typefaces to create contrast

If you've chosen typefaces on a computer, you may have noticed that you can sometimes choose Roman (meaning generally that the typeface is a serif face) or light, bold, or ultra versions of one typeface. Notice, however, that in the example at the top of this column there is little contrast between the light and Roman versions or between the bold and heavy versions. If you were to use these typefaces, you would probably want to use the light and the bold versions together, or the regular face with the heavy version.

When you are using different weights of typefaces, be sure that the differences in the weights are clearly visible.

Yet I cannot speak your tongue with ease,
No longer from China. Your stories
Stir griefs of dispersion and find
Me in simplicity of kin.
—Shirley Geok-lin Lim

Yet I cannot speak your tongue with ease,
No longer from China. Your stories
Stir griefs of dispersion and find
Me in simplicity of kin.
—Shirley Geok-lin Lim

Yet I cannot speak your tongue with ease,
No longer from China. Your stories
Stir griefs of dispersion and find
Me in simplicity of kin.
—Shirley Geok-lin Lim

Using the *color* of typefaces to create contrast

Color can be red, green, blue, puce, lavender, or flesh—but it can also mean the range of grays from white to black. You can apply different colors to individual letters of words to build contrast, but when you are choosing typefaces to use together, look at the "color" of the whole typeface. Designers do this by comparing paragraphs printed out in different typefaces to see how light (or dark) one typeface looks relative to another; the greater the differences in color between the typefaces as a whole, the more likely the typefaces will contrast well.

Notice how different the phrases at the top of this column look—even though the type is all set in the same size. You can use the color of type to choose typefaces that contrast well; you can also use a typeface's color to add a light or heavy mood to a visual composition.

A note about building contrast with typeface

You may have noticed you can take two approaches to building contrast with shapes:

First, you can change only one thing about a shape. For example, if you have a set of circles, you can make one of them big—but for this to work, you have to make that shape tremendously bigger for the contrast to be truly visible.

Second, you can change many things about one of the shapes: you can change its shape, size, color, and position.

The same holds for working with type:

1 You can build contrast by changing only one aspect of the type with which you are working, such as the color—but you have to make big changes for this to be visible.

2 You can build contrast by being sure the typefaces you choose take advantage of three or more of the ways to build type contrast that we've discussed in this section. If you do this, you are more likely to build effectively contrasting type.

TO ANALYZE:
Rhetorical type arrangement

■ **Write:** Write a short rhetorical analysis of the visual composition on the right. Use the evidence of the poster—its words as well as its arrangements and typefaces—to develop an idea of the audience the designer had in mind as she composed it. Characterize the audience in as much detail as you can: Describe not only the age you think characterizes the audience but also where they might live and the values and beliefs they might hold. Use evidence from the poster to support any claim you make.

These tips from Women In Media & News (WIMN), a New York-based media-monitoring, training, and advocacy group, can help you make the leap from righteous indignation to effective critique.

how to write a
PROTEST LETTER
by Jennifer L. Pozner

You flip to your local Clear Channel station to find a shock jock "joking" about where kidnappers can most easily buy nylon rope, tarps, and lye for tying up, hiding, and dissolving the bodies of little girls. Reuters run an important international news brief about a Nigerian woman sentenced to death by stoning for an alleged sexual infraction—in its "Oddly Enough" section, where typical headlines include "Unruly Taxi Drivers Sent to Charm School."

When California Democrats Loretta and Linda Sanchez became the first sisters ever to serve together in Congress, the Washington Post devotes 1,766 words in its style section to inform readers about the representatives' preferences regarding housekeeping, hairstyles, and "hootchy shoes." (Number of paragraphs focusing on the congress women's political viewpoints: one.) Nearly a million demonstrators gather in cities across the country to protest impending war on Iraq; America's top print and broadcast news outlets significantly undercount protestors' numbers...again.

So, what else is new? Sexist and biased fare is business as usual for all too many media outlets - but what do you do when hurling household objects at Dan Rather's head just isn't enough?

Be firm but polite Make your case sans insults, rants, and vulgarity. Nothing makes it easier for editors and producers to dismiss your argument than name-calling. Good idea: "Your discussion of the rape survivor's clothing and makeup was irrelevant, irresponsible, and inapropriate. Including those details blames the victim and reinforces dangerous myths about sexual assault." Bad idea: "Your reporter is a woman-hating incarnate of satan!"

Be realistic but optimistic Calling for the New York Times to transform itself into a socialist newspaper will get you nowhere; suggesting that quotes from industry executives be balanced by input from labor and public-interest groups is more likely to be taken seriously.

Choose your battles While we'd all like to see fewer female bods used to sell beer, asking the networks to reject such ads is a waste of time. (A letter-writing campaign to the companies that produce those ads is another matter.) However, its worth the effort to pressure telecom and cable giant Comcast to air the antiwar ads it censored during Bush's State of the Union speech.

Correct the record For example, remind media outlets discussing "partial birth abortion" that this imprecise and inflammatory term doesn't refer to an actual medical procedure but is, rather, a political concept fabricated by conservative groups to decrease public support for abortion rights. Focusing on facts is more persuasive than simply expressing outrage: "Christina Hoff Sommers's quote contained the following inaccuracies…" is better than "Anti-feminists like Christina Hoff Sommers should not be quoted in your newspaper."

Expose biased or distorted framing Look at whose viewpoint is shaping the story. In light of the Bush Administration's assault on affirmative action, for example, Peter Jennings asked on World News Tonight: "President Bush and race: Does he have a strategy to win black support?" Let ABC producers know that you'd rather they investigate the economic, academic, and political implications of the president's agenda for African-Americans then the effects of race policy on Bush's approval rating.

Keep it concise and informative If your goal is publication on the letters page, a couple well-documented paragraphs will always be better received than an emotional three-page manifesto. Sticking to one or two main points will get a busy editor to read through to the end.

Avoid overgeneralization Don't complain that your local paper "never" reports on women's issues or "always" ignores poor people. Even if stories on topics like workfare are infrequent or inaccurate, their very existence will serve as proof to editors that your complaint doesn't apply to their publication.

Address the appropriate person Letters about reportorial objectivity sent to editorial columnists or opinion-page editors will be tossed in the circular file.

Proofread! Nothing peeves an editor faster than typos or bad grammar.

Finally, give 'em credit Positive reinforcement can be as effective as protest. Be constructive whenever possible, and commend outlets when they produce in-depth, bias-free coverage.

Jennifer L. Pozner is WIMN's founder and executive director.

THE LOGOS OF USING WORDS AND PICTURES TOGETHER

When you use words and photographs or illustrations together, they can interact in three ways:

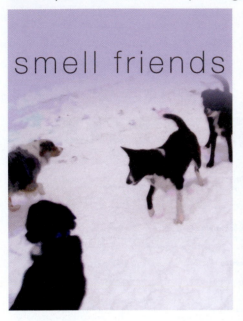

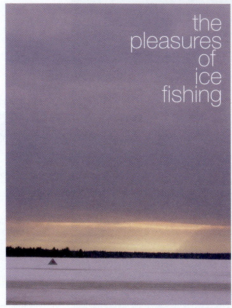

1

The photograph or illustration "explains" the words. The words, that is, wouldn't make much sense without the photograph or illustration.

For example, does "smell friends" make sense to you as anything other than a very odd command—until you see the words paired with an illustration of dogs? Then, based on your knowledge of how dogs interact, the words probably make perfect sense.

2

The words "explain" the photograph or illustration.

In the middle example above, would you have any idea what that triangle on the ice is if you didn't see the words? (In case you have only lived in warm climates, know that the triangle is an ice fishing tent.) Notice also how the words direct your attentions away from the light and clouds to focus on the tent.

3

The words and photograph or illustration work together to have a stronger effect than either alone has. In the third example, the connection between the word and the photograph is not quite as direct as in the first two. Instead, you—the viewer—have to figure out whether the word asks you to think of the leaves as clothing for some animal or to rethink your notion of clothing (as covering) based on the leaves, or both. There is more room for viewer interaction when the connection between word and photograph is not so obvious.

Naming the relationships

French theorist Roland Barthes named the first two relationships on the facing page "anchors": The words and pictures tie each other down in the same way an anchor keeps a boat in one place. "Relay" is how Barthes named the relationship shown in the third example where, as in a relay race, the function of the pairing is to move us along rather than tie us down.

Rules for putting words and pictures together?

Because our responses to photographs and illustrations depend on our bodily and cultural experiences of the world, there are no hard and fast rules for using words and pictures together. Instead, attend to their rhetorical functioning: How do particular audiences in particular contexts respond to particular combinations of words and pictures? Testing your compositions—through asking audiences how and why they have the responses they do—will show you if your word + picture combinations work.

TO ANALYZE

■ **Write and discuss:** Under the two bird photographs above, write captions that encourage others to understand the photographs as differently as possible.

My biggest pet peeve is bad grammar.

Is this the life I hoped I'd lead?

■ **Discuss with others:** Use the three categories of word and photograph interaction to analyze the strip above. If you were to see just the photograph or just the words, how would you respond? How do the words typed on paper scraps contribute to the overall effect? Imagine different typed words; what words will most change your response to the strip?

267

ANALYZING VISUAL ARGUMENTS

Visual analogies

Analogies compare two objects, events, or processes so that the more familiar can explain the less familiar. The two posters on the right help us see how this can work visually.

The red poster is from Great Britain in the 1940s, during World War II. As in the United States, so many men were away at war that factories needed workers; efforts were directed at women to encourage them to leave home and go to work constructing war equipment—work traditionally considered inappropriate for women. By showing women patching fabric, sewing, and peeling potatoes and then showing the women in almost exactly the same postures but working with drafting tools and industrial equipment, this poster argues that because the postures are the same, women have the abilities to do industrial work. The argument of this poster isn't "You can do it!" but—by analogy—is "You are already doing it, so get yourself into the factories!"

The second poster is also from the 1940s but from the United States. You can probably see how its purpose, like the previous example, is to get women into factories: Similarly to the first poster, women are shown doing two different tasks to demonstrate that, if they can do one, they can do the other. Here, however, the analogy works across time, showing a woman in clothing from the time of the

Revolutionary War loading a musket to argue that contemporary women could work with power tools. This poster uses pathos—evoking the emotion of patriotism—to bring women into the industrial workforce.

In the first poster, the viewer is directly addressed as "you," Women are the audience, and the argument for going to work is aimed directly at them. In the second poster, audiences are to understand the words as spoken by women ("us") but addressed to men ("Mister!"). Perhaps this poster is addressing two different audiences: Women are asked to identify with others across time who have

done patriotic work so that they have justification for going to work, while men—husbands, fathers, and brothers who might resist women working—are asked to see industrial work as a patriotic tradition.

In these examples, visual analogies are used to help a composer encourage an audience to look differently (literally and figuratively) at a situation. The analogies help audiences understand what would have been strange and unseemly—factory work—is equivalent to the work of home or the work of defending the country.

Visual symbols

If you've ever left soup to bubble on the stove for a while, you've experienced how flavor intensifies as the soup condenses. Symbols are like that left-to-bubble soup: They contain emotions and understandings condensed into a drawing or object.

For example, Valentine's Day is awash in the symbol of the heart, meant not only to evoke thoughts of love but also the diffuse but usually lovely emotions connected with love.

The flag of the United States—like that of any country—is a symbol. It can represent the emotions of patriotism or the country's strength. Its colors represent blood and valor; the stars represent not only the states but all that stars can evoke—aspiration, light, glory. The number of stripes represents the original 13 states. Even when the flag is represented inaccurately, its power as a symbol still holds, and it can be used to bring people together around common causes or to cause divisiveness as people argue over what counts as allegiance. Because symbols condense so much emotion and understanding, they have that power to unite or divide.

When you use visual symbols, recognize that they will not mean the same thing to everyone. Different cultures have different symbols, and the symbols with which we have grown up are usually ones we do not question because they have been such a part of our lives.

Symbols are linked to what they represent through resemblance (the way the majesty and power of the bald eagle are supposed to represent the majesty and power of the United States) or convention (as the apple is meant to represent temptation). You cannot make your own symbols; you can only use the symbols you inherit through living in a particular time and place.

The poster on the right demonstrates a symbol working visually. Without explanation and with only a few words, the poster links sex with the devilish evil of Eve's temptation in the Garden of Eden. The poster overlays sex with a Biblical history and the loss of paradise. The poster can do this because chances are that—if you've grown up in the United States—you've learned that an apple and a snake together mean that original temptation. With the addition of "AIDS," the poster makes clear its purpose: The designer wants viewers to see the danger lurking around the red pleasure.

A question to ask about symbols in visual arguments, then, is whether you think the linking of symbol with its purpose is appropriate. Regarding this poster, we can ask whether sex should be linked with the original temptation. Because symbols work without explicit statement of their emotional weight, they can cause us to carry away many more associations and

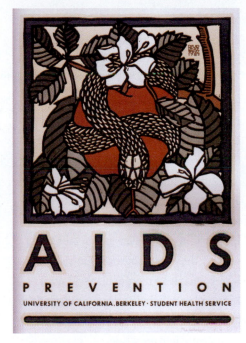

emotions than might really be necessary for the argument to be made. When you compose arguments that use symbols, you need to ask yourself whether you are doing too much.

Visual arguments using symbols work because they equate some situation (in this case, AIDS) with a whole set of undescribed emotions and understandings we've learned by growing up in a particular time and place. When you want to bring the weight of a culture's beliefs or emotions to bear on an issue, then consider what symbols you can use.

ANALYZING VISUAL ARGUMENTS, continued

Visual accumulation

To *accumulate* is to pile up objects that are similar or the same.

The photograph on the right is of an artwork titled "Whale" from the series "Running the Numbers II: Portraits of global mass culture"; its original size is 44" x 82". The person who made the piece, Chris Jordan, uses photography to document human resource consumption. The artwork uses "50,000 plastic bags, equal to the estimated number of pieces of floating plastic in every square mile in the world's oceans"; the words come from Jordan's website, where you can see more of his work: www.chrisjordan.com. In the closeup following the photograph, you can see how plastic bags have been shaped into the whale.

What might such an accumulation of plastic bags, so photographed, tell us about our use of plastic? What might it tell us about our consuming habits? Why might Jordan have shaped the bags into the whale?

How would the effect of this visual argument be different if Jordan had photographed each bag separately and hung all the photographs on a wall?

Visual accumulation can make visible and concrete a large number of elements or make visible a pattern that can then perhaps be broken. In this artwork, a number is given emotional weight.

In what argumentative contexts do you think such strategies will be most effective?

TO ANALYZE: VISUAL ARGUMENTS

■ **Observe, then write:** Look through magazines and online sites to find other examples of visual analogy, accumulation, or symbols. Do the examples you find support our descriptions of when these different arrangements seem most effective? See if you can find examples that show other arguments that these arrangements can help build, and then write a short paper that argues how these visual arguments work, as we did with the examples in this chapter.

■ **Discuss with others:** Look through writing examples—essays, poems, opinion pieces—to find word examples of analogy, accumulation, and symbol. When these arrangements are built of words, how are the arguments of which they are part similar to or different from visual arguments that use these structures?

■ **Write:** Look at the websites of candidates running for national office, members of Congress, or the presidential administration. You'll find many symbols at work in the websites, including (often) the U.S. flag. Write a short rhetorical analysis of one such site, arguing how any symbols used support its overall purposes and focusing on how you think the site designers thought about their audience(s). Use your analysis as a lens for considering the website of someone who takes different political positions.

271

■ **Discuss with others:** The photograph above shows an accumulation of photographs that are all the same size and that are mostly in the same format, a closeup of someone's face.

General Augusto Pinochet was president of Chile from 1973–1990; during this time, thousands of people were detained by the military, never to return. In 1998, General Pinochet was arrested under an international warrant issued by a Spanish judge and charged with the crime of torture. The photograph above, printed in *The New York Times*, shows a 2003 exhibition in Chile of photographs of the missing. The accumulation of so many similar photographs allows the audience to see—literally see—at once how many people are missing. The audience can see individual faces and think about individuals who are missing, but always as part of the accumulated weight of how many all together are missing. How is seeing this exhibit different from reading, "Thousands of people disappeared during General Pinochet's presidency"?

(Notice too how the photograph has been structured so that you cannot see how high up the wall the photographs go, or how long the walls are. Why do you think the photographer chose this particular framing? To learn about *framing* as a rhetorical strategy for directing attention, see chapter 11 on documentary photography.)

A DESIGN PLAN FOR A PHOTO ESSAY

Remember from chapter 3 that a design plan integrates the following in the order that makes sense to you:

- your statement of purpose. (See Ajay's statement of purpose on page 243.)

- a description of your overall strategies with justifications based on your statement of purpose.

- your choice of medium or media with justifications based on your statement of purpose.

- your ideas about arrangement with justifications based on your statement of purpose.

- a description of how you will produce the communication.

- a plan for testing the communication.

You write a statement of purpose to help you think about how to proceed with a text, so a statement of purpose is not a test and can be more or less formal. Generally, however, a fairly informal statement of purpose will be most useful because you want to focus on your own thinking, not on how you are communicating your thinking to anyone else. You want to ask questions of yourself, get possible ideas down, think about what others have said about your concerns, and start to imagine the whole text you are about to produce.

Design Plan for a Photo Essay

PURPOSE: As with all my research for this class, I want mostly to raise questions about how we think of ourselves while we are in college. *Are we students—or consumers? How are we supporting students in college so that everyone gets the best possible education? What happens when students think of themselves as consumers?* Because of what I wrote in my statement of purpose, I know that I want to use photographs to show that we can talk as though we are consumers when we are in school. But looking at pictures of "buying a grade" or "buying a diploma" will show (I hope!) how weird it is really to do that. I hope that, by seeing how weird it is really to show what it looks like to buy a grade, maybe we'll think differently about how we earn our educations.

MEDIUM & PRODUCTION: I am using photographs. I am not the best photographer, but—because of my purpose—I know that I need to focus on someone buying things. I need to show someone buying regular stuff and then someone buying a grade. I need to figure out how to show buying a grade or an education because it's just so hard to picture what that actually looks like. (And I need to plan: Pictures of people buying stuff will be easy, but I'm going to have to find a teacher—oh, and I think my friend Mia will help me by being the student in the photographs.) I also will probably need to take a whole bunch of photographs in order to get a couple that work. I need to ask Jamshed if he will help me learn how to get photographs off my phone so I can print them.

STRATEGIES

ETHOS: Even though I am raising serious questions, I don't want to come across as someone who thinks my position is the only one or as though I'm yelling about my position. I think the ethos that best supports my purpose—to get others to question—will have me come across as questioning rather than assertive.

PATHOS: What I wrote about purpose and ethos makes me think I should keep the essay simple and focused. But also I'd like it to seem kind of lighthearted and funny (especially since it's the end of the semester). I want the essay not to look too polished because I want people in class to be sucked into thinking that this is all easy and the questions are relaxed. Maybe then they'll take the questions home with them. (And I was thinking about using captions—so I want them to look handwritten.)

LOGOS: My argument is based on comparison. I am going to put a photo of someone buying regular stuff next to a photo of someone "buying" a grade. I hope the comparison makes people think about how weird the second photo is.

But as I picture all this in my head, I think I am going to need to put a caption with each comparison because the second photograph in the comparison won't make sense on its own: We just don't see people buying grades. And because I know I want to have a questioning rather than a demanding or yelling ethos, I think I need the captions to be questions—and that also means that people might really ask themselves the questions and go home thinking about them (which is my purpose). I wonder how many sets of comparisons will be enough? The assignment says at least four photos, but that's only two sets; I don't think that's enough. I think I need at least three sets—three comparisons—in order to make enough of a pattern for people to remember.

ARRANGEMENT

Because writing about logos helped me see that my argument is about comparison, I will probably have four pages for my essay: A title page and then three pages, each of which has two photos on it for comparison. Having the photo sets on separate pages means my audience has to move through them page by page, so they will move through the photos more slowly rather than see them all at once.

TESTING

If Mia will be in my photos, I'll show them to her after I put them on their pages with their captions to make sure she can understand what is in them. She'll know what I am trying to do and so can help me test the wording of my captions.

TO ANALYZE

■ **Compare with others:** With a classmate or two, compare Ajay's design plan for his photo essay with his design plan for his research paper (pages 162–163) and his oral presentation (pages 214–215).

What do you see in the design plans—in both what Ajay wrote and also how he wrote the plans—that most seemed to help him? How might such approaches help you in your own composing work?

273

FOR EXAMPLE

To the left is Ajay's design plan for his photo essay—which you can see on pages 274–277.

A PHOTO ESSAY

how alike are buying and learning?

photo essay • Ajay Chaudry • June 8, 2012

- Here and on the next pages are Ajay's photographs and captions for his photo essay. Given what he wrote in his statement of purpose (on page 243), we know that the assignment for which he made the essay says that these pages are meant to be understandable to others without help from Ajay. Do you think he has achieved that?

- Given what Ajay wrote in his design plan (on pages 272–273), do you think his essay's opening page appropriately prepares his audience for his purposes? Do you think the photograph and title are appropriate for his purposes?

Is how you get your coffee just like how you get your education?

■ Do you think Ajay has framed and cropped his photographs to help his audience see what he wants them to see? What might you have done differently with these photographs if you were making his essay?

(See pages 353–355 on framing and cropping in photographs.)

A PHOTO ESSAY, continued

Is how you get your gum just like how you get a grade?

- ■ Are Ajay's captions doing the work he hoped they would do as he described in his design plan (on pages 272–273)?

- ■ How would Ajay's captions have worked as statements or assertions rather than questions? Would the photographs have worked without captions?

- ■ Would you change any of Ajay's photographs?

Is how you get your soda just like how you get your diploma?

■ Do you think Ajay has enough photographs to achieve the purposes he described in his statement of purpose (page 243) and design plan (pages 272–273)? Why?

■ How well has Ajay achieved the overall purposes he set for himself?

TESTING AND EVALUATING VISUAL TEXTS

A self-test for visual texts you produce—and the fundamental questions to ask of any visual text

As with any text in any medium that you produce for communicating with others, look at the text when you think it is finished (or almost finished); pretend that you are a member of your audience and answer the following questions based on what you see in the text.

❑ Who specifically is the audience for this text? Does the text treat the audience as appropriately complex people? (For example, has the text avoided defining the audience simply as adults or teenagers?)

❑ What is this text's purpose? What is this text trying to do?

If you cannot answer those questions from what you see in the text (and not based on what is in your head), then your text needs more work to clarify its purpose for its audience.

Also always ask:

❑ Do I want to be the person whose ethos is constructed in this text? Do I want to hold these opinions and ideas? Do I want to have the relationships with other people that this text establishes?

Because different kinds of visual texts depend on different visual strategies, here are other questions you might use in evaluating particular visual texts whether you or someone else has made them.

Some of the following criteria can be used for multiple kinds of texts.

A **brochure** designed for a nonprofit organization

❑ Has writing that develops an appropriate ethos for the nonprofit organization.

❑ Has writing that addresses its audience using pathos appropriate to the purpose.

❑ Uses strategies that address the audience respectfully.

❑ Has writing that has been visually presented to be easy to read.

❑ Uses photographs or illustrations that are clearly relevant to the brochure's purpose.

❑ Makes thoughtful and purposeful use of contrast, typefaces, color, and so on.

❑ Is crisp and professionally produced.

❑ Uses verbal text that is all correctly spelled and grammatically appropriate.

A short **comic** on a social issue

❑ Uses comic book/graphic novel conventions appropriately in developing its purpose.

❑ Uses comic book/graphic novel conventions creatively in developing its purpose.

❑ Has text that treats its audience as people who think and feel.

❑ Uses writing that is respectful of its audience (even when humorous).

❑ Reflects the composer's ethos, which is appropriately authoritative and thoughtful but nonetheless fits the comic medium.

❑ Uses illustrations and/or photographs that are appropriate for the argument being made.

❑ Uses a layout that encourages the audience to approach the material thoughtfully.

❑ Uses writing and illustrations that have appropriate pathos appeals for the audience.

❑ Uses appropriate grammar and spelling.

A **documentary photography** book

❑ Has an argument that makes a statement or claim about its topic and supports the statement or claim with reasons.

❑ Has an argument that is worth making, is new for its audience or creatively presented, or offers an old argument in a newly compelling manner.

❑ Orders photographs to build an argument over time.

❑ Uses visual strategies (typography, page arrangement, etc.) that are appropriate to the argument.

❑ Presents photographs that are relevant to the argument.

❑ Includes only text that is relevant to the argument.

❑ Has text that supports the photos, not vice versa.

❑ Introduces its audience to its topic appropriately.

❑ Has text or captions that are perfectly spelled and use appropriate grammar.

An argumentative **poster**

❑ Shows that thought has been given to how the poster's appearance support its purpose.

❑ Uses pictures or other visual strategies that are unambiguous and easy for its audience to understand.

❑ Includes pictures that are clearly relevant to the poster's purpose.

❑ Uses words that are unambiguous and easy for its audience to understand.

❑ Makes thoughtful and tied-to-its-purpose use of contrast, typefaces, color, etc.

A short **video** public service announcement

❑ Is created so that, after seeing it, the audience will know the sponsoring organization and how to contact it.

❑ Develops an appropriate ethos for the organization being represented.

❑ Doesn't put an overly emotional spin on its topic.

❑ Uses only audio and video effects that support the purpose of the video.

❑ Uses audio that is clear and easy to understand.

❑ Is engaging for its audience, who will want to see it again.

TO ANALYZE

■ **Evaluate and reflect:** According to the assignment Ajay was given for his photo essay, his essay would be evaluated on the following criteria:

❑ The photo essay has to grow out of the research paper and/or oral presentation (which you can see on pages 176–181 and 217–231).

❑ The photo essay has to make a point tied to the paper and/or presentation.

❑ The photo essay has to creatively use at least four photographs (and captions if needed).

❑ The photo essay has to be understandable to others in class with no help from us.

What evaluation would you give Ajay's photo essay based on these criteria?

What other criteria to the left might you use to evaluate Ajay's photo essay? Why?

■ **Evaluate:** Find samples for any of the visual texts listed to the left. Evaluate the samples using the criteria on the left.

What on other criteria might you use for evaluation?

279

DESIGNING SLIDES **TO SUPPORT** ORAL PRESENTATIONS

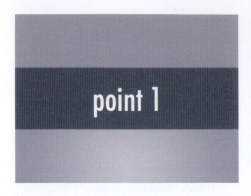

The title at the top of this page gives the most important advice for designing slides: Slides should rhetorically support the arguments you make. Slides should not stand alone but should come to life only with your words and explanations.

Put on a slide only the absolute minimum for making your point. You want what is on the slide to be memorable for your audience.

Your audience has come to hear you talk, not to read your slides. If your slides are full of stuff, the audience will read and look, not listen.

Choose (or make) and stay with a slide template that works with your purposes. Unless incoherence suits your purposes, using the same theme throughout gives your presentation coherence.

Choose typefaces that are easy to read and large enough to be readable at the distance where your audience will sit. Test your slides by projecting them ahead of time and trying to read them from your audience's distance. (See pages 253–255 on choosing type.)

Choose colors to support your purposes. Make sure that the type color contrasts crisply with the slide's background color so that your audience can read the type. (See point 6 for advice on checking the readability of slides, and see pages 249–251 for help with color.)

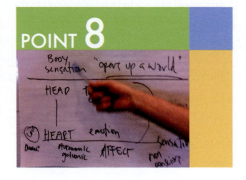

Photographs that are large and uncluttered generally are the most easy for audiences to understand—and all photographs should relate to your purposes.

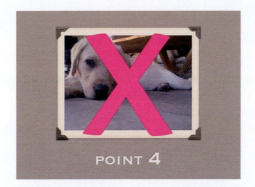

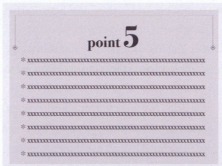

Your slides should contain only elements that are relevant to your presentation. You do not need to decorate slides—although a relevant graphic can help explain or make information memorable.

Go easy on bullet points. If you must use them, keep them short and do not use more than three to four. (Remember point 2, to the left.) (Go easy on text, in general.)

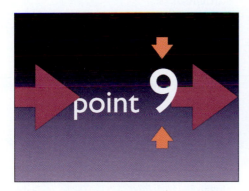

Slide transitions are fun—but they can make audiences dizzy. Transitions *between* slides should support your argument's movement: For example, does your argument seem to move up, or down, or sideways? Transitions *on* a slide—as bullet points come on, for example—should also tie to your purposes.

Just as a beginning memorable slide will help pull your audience into your presentation, a final slide should offer a memorable takeaway. What is the last point you wish your audience to remember about your presentation?

TO ANALYZE

■ **Develop criteria:** Using the points we have listed here as well as the criteria for testing and evaluating visual texts on pages 278–279, develop a rubric for evaluating slides for a presentation.

■ **Evaluate:** Look back over the slides that Ajay used to support his oral presentation (on pages 217–231).

How well do Ajay's slides take into account the advice we offer on these two pages? If you developed criteria in response to the prompt above, use your criteria to evaluate Ajay's slideshow.

■ **Reflect:** From your experiences watching others' presentations, do you have other points to add to what we have listed on these two pages? Are there aspects of those slideshows—and the presentations they supported—you would like to remember for your own work in the future?

281

THINKING THROUGH PRODUCTION

■ Using any technologies available to you, produce two to three posters for an upcoming event. (Be sure to compose a statement of purpose and design plan as you work.) Each poster should have exactly the same illustrations or photographs, the same text, and the same layout—but choose very different color schemes for each poster. Ask your classmates to describe their responses to the colors. Record the strategies that seem most effective for the context, audience, and purpose of the poster.

■ Use whatever materials and technologies you have available to produce your own visual argument—for any purpose, context, and audience—based on analogy, accumulation, or a symbol. Look again at the examples and our analyses of them to think about the contexts in which these formal arrangements are most effective, in order to decide which to use for the audience and purpose you choose.

■ Look at the "Spoof Ads" at the Adbusters website (http://www.adbusters.org/spoofads). (Look especially at the tobacco, fashion, McDonald's, and corporate spoofs.) Choose two or three of the spoofs that you find most successful, and write a short analysis of what you think makes them successful. Then use whatever materials you have available to you to make your own ad spoof.

■ Produce a visual timeline* that presents the changes over time in some aspect of our lives. You could show how a company's logo has changed since the company began, how women's dresses or men's pants differ from generation to generation, or how the design of cars, cereal boxes, or newspapers has varied over decades. But don't just show pictures of the changes: Annotate them to argue how the changes are in response to other cultural or technological changes.

You'll need to do research. Find examples of the visual artifact you're studying, and research why it has changed. Come to your own position on why the changes you see have occurred and support it with evidence.

When you produce the timeline using any medium available to you, integrate into your presentation annotations that explain what the visual aspect is, how it has changed, and why you think it has changed. (Be sure to take advantage of the layout of your timeline to help you make your argument.)

* An example of a timeline to help you think about what you might do is in the chapter "Graphic Design in America" in *Design/Writing/Research* by Ellen Lupton and J. Abbott Miller, which your library might have or can get for you. Many examples of interactive timelines are online.

■ Take a short paper you've already produced, and re-produce it twice. Each time, use a very different typeface (you might use a sans serif typeface in one and a grunge face in the other) as well as different spacing between the lines of type. If you have headers in the paper, make them be a very different typeface from the body of the paper. Revise the visual structure of the paper, keeping in mind what we've described about using layout rhetorically. Give your papers to others for reading and response. Compare the responses you receive: Do readers appear to give less serious attention to papers printed in typefaces that are unusual in academic circumstances?

■ Take a short paper you've already produced and re-produce it as best you can by using photographs. Afterward, write a short paper in which you reflect on differences between writing and photography: *Given your paper's arguments, what were you able to show photographically—and what not? What do you think you were able to argue more effectively through words, and what through photographs? What was impossible to do in photographs?*

Compare your conclusions with others in class. As a group, try to develop some general statements about how we use words and pictures differently in our time and place, and why.

about argument and advocacy

CHAPTER 8

Some people think that the desire to advocate just wells up passionately inside, regardless of where and when we are. Passion certainly strengthens advocacy, but effective advocacy is also about determining what is worth caring about in the situations around us. Effective advocacy also requires figuring out how to design the futures we seek.

This chapter is about contexts of advocacy: There are readings about others who think strategically about advocacy, and there are many questions about what constitutes advocacy for whom and when. We hope to support you in thinking more about your potential to advocate through argument and to help you strengthen what you already do.

In the *Declaration of Independence*, Thomas Jefferson included the "pursuit of happiness" as one of our unalienable rights. "Pursuit" implies that happiness is something we have to seek actively. But do we pursue happiness as individuals, as citizens, or as both, together? What are our responsibilities in and to this country that grounds itself on a belief in our ability to pursue (if not reach) happiness?

Our first questions to you in this chapter, then, are these: How is your happiness bound up with the happiness of others—friends, family, and fellow citizens—both now and in the future? How is it bound up with the health of your communities? What is the happiness that you pursue—and does advocacy have any part in it?

BECOMING AN ADVOCATE

In this book's introduction, we wrote of advocacy: "When we consider oral, written, and visual communication in this book, we always treat composing and designing as actions that DO something in and to the world."

Every time you communicate with others, you shape your relations with them. If you speak, your tone of voice indicates the respect or friendship you have (or don't have) for them and so strengthens how you feel toward each other. You've probably realized that someone likes you (or not) based on the person's way of speaking to you and choice of words.

Communications also show what communicators value. You can ask a friend to go to a basketball game—or you can ask the friend to help out with a Saturday car wash raising money for Big Brothers, Big Sisters. In either case, you tell something about what you value in the world without explicitly stating your beliefs and concerns. You start a ripple effect around you because your actions ask others to accept that what you do is worth doing.

Similarly, communications aimed at multiple people tell us what the communicators value and how they think the world should be. This is often easiest to see in communications not aimed at us, because in communications directed to us, the values just seem so normal and accepted that they can be invisible. But look at TV shows, newspapers, and radio programs: When people speak about or show you certain topics, they are choosing and so emphasizing those topics over all others. Chances are that your local newspaper has some kind of regular section about the stock market but not about blue- or pink-collar work. Look at magazines on a supermarket checkout line: *What values are repeated in what is shown on the covers? What isn't shown? Whose lives are not being considered?* The values underlying how all these communications are designed and what they choose to emphasize all shape your sense of what is important and worth doing—or not.

To talk about argument, and so to talk about advocacy, is to talk about how we can and should live our lives. It is to talk about what we should do as communities and as individuals. *What position do you want to have in the world? What do you want the world to be? How do we live together well?* To answer these questions is to become an advocate for what matters to you. It is to start shaping the world in ways you—having grown up in your local and national communities—believe will better all your communities.

TO ANALYZE

- **Write informally:** Make a list of

  - qualities you have that make you proud and could be useful in the communities around you.

  - everything you are able to do that might be useful to others.

  - ways you've already participated in your communities.

  - situations in local communities or at your school that need changing for the better.

- **Interview an older friend or relative:** Ask that person about her or his understanding of advocacy. Ask also about when and how the person participated in public or civic life and what caused the person to take the actions that most shaped her or his life.

- **Discuss with others:** Throughout this book, we've been arguing that all arguments—because they advocate particular positions on issues or ways of seeing the world, because they do something in the world—are advocacy. Is it possible to make the converse claim, that all advocacy is argument?

SITUATING YOURSELF TO ADVOCATE

In this book's introduction we wrote of advocacy that it is important for you to "recognize the power you have as a result of the communications you compose and design—a power that exists because of what communication simply is—and that you take responsibility for the effects of your communication."

We also wrote that "Time—the time you are in, the time you have, and the time that stretches out before you—defines who you are, what you want to do, what you are doing, and what you plan to do."

The analytic activities described in the columns to the right seek to help you think about how you have become the advocate you are and how you might become the advocate you would like to be.

TO ANALYZE

■ **Write reflectively:** Collect 5–10 pieces of writing you have done in the last several years. Reread them, looking for what you advocate. Although in your writing you may never explicitly state, "I advocate for this," look for the values you uphold through your writing and the changes you endorse or seek. For example, although you might not advocate for any direct action in any of your writing, perhaps your writing shows how much you value generosity, family, friendship, being alert to what is happening more broadly in the work, being responsible only to yourself, or careful critical thinking.

Write a short two- to four-page reflection in which you describe what values you see yourself having advocated in your writing, whether you realized it or not. In your writing, also consider what values, actions, or change you would like to advocate and how your writing might shift to advocate for those values, actions, or change. *How would you like to affect others' actions— and how are you willing to be affected by others' advocacy?*

■ **Compose a timeline:** Using any media available to you, compose a timeline in which you link your life and its major events with major cultural, political, technological, and environmental events. On your timeline enter your life events (whichever you do not mind sharing with others)—and then add to the timeline events like wars, presidential elections, natural disasters, the release of songs or movies, the development of new technologies, or any other event or ongoing situation you noticed that had local, regional, national, or international weight.

Compare your timelines with those made by others in class. *What nonpersonal events have they put on the timeline that you have not—and vice versa?* Discuss why. Also discuss with others how you think these various events have shaped who you are, what you value, how you see yourself in the world, and how you understand how people work together (or not) in the world.

Write reflectively on what you have learned. *How have your values been shaped by what has happened around you? How do you see larger societal values as having been shaped by these events or situations? What seems right to you— and what would you like to change, and why?*

ADVOCACY IS RHETORICAL

Because advocacy seeks to change situations, it seeks to shift others' attentions and attitudes. Advocacy is therefore always rhetorical, and so all advocacy can be based on the rhetorical process we first described in chapter 1—with some particular emphases, as we number in the following graphic and describe on the facing page.

① ② ③
audience

④ ⑤   **⑥**
purpose ●   ● context

⑦ ⑧   medium
strategies ●   ● arrangement

a statement of purpose
What do you want to make happen?

a design plan
How will you make it happen?

►►► **ADVOCACY**

testing

Audience: Be alert to the differing audiences in advocacy.

Distinguish between the people for whom advocacy is being carried out and the people to whom the advocacy is addressed. For example, Ajay, whose research and compositions we saw in chapters 4 through 7, has been researching and starting to advocate about rising college tuitions. Will his ongoing advocacy be to help students learn more about why tuition is rising, to persuade those who control tuitions not to raise them, or to encourage students to contact those who control tuitions? (Notice that purpose and audience are inseparable here: Each description of audience in the preceding sentence also partially describes a purpose.)

Do not forget audiences who might resist what you advocate. Who does not want the situations you want, and why? How might you address them or their arguments?

 Audience: Are you "for" or "with"?

Advocacy is always on behalf of someone. As Ajay moves forward, will he work alone to advocate for other students, or will he advocate to bring students together so that he works with them as a group? Which is more likely to help him achieve his purposes?

 Audience: Can you help others change from audiences to rhetoricians?

Helping audiences move from what can seem to be a passive listening position to the more active position of advocating on their own behalf can be a purpose for advocacy.

 Purpose: Choose carefully among the wide range of possible purposes for advocacy.

You can choose to inform others; you can choose to ask others to stop and think; you can choose to try to change how people define an issue or others; you can choose to bring people together for discussions; you can choose to change laws and policies. No matter your purpose, be as clear as possible about what you want to achieve. Because (as we describe in the considerations about audience to the left) advocacy can complicate our notions of audience, it can also complicate notions of purpose—but you are most likely to achieve your purposes when you can state them, and how they matter to others, with laserlike focus.

 Purpose: Should you break a complex purpose into parts?

Will smaller, short-term purposes help step you most effectively toward a larger purpose?

 Context: Be creative.

Successful advocacy gets others interested and moving, so which (perhaps unexpected) contexts for your communications will energize and engage your audience?

7 *Strategies:* Be creative.

What media and arrangements will appropriately engage as well as energize your audience?

8 *Strategies:* Do not forget ethos, logos, and pathos.

Ethos, pathos, and logos all matter in any kind of communication and so in any kind of advocacy. How is the ethos of an organization or corporation shaped? How do organizations and corporations address their audiences emotionally and by what logics?

RESEARCH AND ADVOCACY

As with any rhetorical pursuit, research—both broad and focused—tends to move you toward the most effective work. When you research for advocacy, you often research about shared concerns as well as for facts and data.

The following questions (in combination with the points we raise on the preceding page) suggest what to research in developing any advocacy project.

While developing a statement of purpose

Purpose

- On what problem would you like to have a positive effect? What are the causes of the problem?

- Is the project you are considering worthwhile? Will it have real effects through helping others? Will its effects spread?

- Is there a need for what you consider?

- Does the project support your values and those of your community? Does it connect you with others?

- Do you have the resources, abilities, time, and support to carry out—successfully—the project you are considering?

- Is the project well defined?

- Is the project sustainable? Will its effects end quickly or linger and spread?

Audience

- Who is in the best position to bring about the change you seek? Who else can be persuaded to help you communicate with those who can make the change you seek? In other words, who is your primary audience, and who is your secondary audience?

- What are your audience's opinions, beliefs, and values around the issue for which you advocate?

- How might you engage with those on whose behalf you advocate? How can you help them become advocates themselves? How have you situated yourself to learn from them?

- Who might be left out of your considerations? Why?

Context

- What understanding of the past will best help you understand the current situation you hope to change?

- How far into the future do you need to look?

- What in the physical location—local, regional, or global—shapes people's current understanding of the problem or issue?

While developing a design plan

Strategies

- What strategies will best help you establish the relations you seek with your audiences and between your audiences and others affected by the problem?

- Do you have reliable and authoritative data and information for supporting your recommendations?

Arrangement

- How do the arrangements of your text echo the actions you wish to encourage among people? (Should the arrangements of a text do this?)

- How do your arrangements help others see the problem or issue in a new and helpful way?

Medium

- Can everyone in your audience access the medium you are using?

- How does your medium help others see the problem or issue in a new and helpful way?

WHO CHANGES AND WHO BENEFITS WHEN YOU ADVOCATE?

Some think of advocacy as a one-way street. One does something, it affects others—and that's that.

The actions of advocacy, however, move in multiple directions. They come back to us and unexpectedly move off and around.

Precisely because the arguments involved in advocacy shape the attitudes of others and show what we value—and because we are talking about a process involving people—our arguments often have much more than a single effect. When we advocate, we enter the web of human conversation and work, and so we open ourselves to the actions and thinking of others. It is therefore not always (or even often) possible to know who changes and who benefits when we advocate. What is certain is that, if you think the only thing happening is that you give and someone else benefits, you are wrong.

Situation 1 to the right is probably the way a lot of people look at taking action. Situation 2 is a more accurate description of what can and usually does happen.

For these reasons, humility, openness to surprise, and generosity are usually the best attitudes for approaching the arguments underpinning advocacy.

1  He makes a workbook to help children develop literacy abilities through learning about recycling.

2  He makes a workbook to help children develop literacy abilities through learning about recycling.

His enthusiasm for working with kids pulls others into volunteering.

By watching children use his book and listening to their feedback, he learns that they already have literacies tied to community contexts, and so he learns how to become a more effective teacher.

The children develop a school recycling program.

He is moved by how many children grow up without health care or whose parents' work schedules don't allow them to be there when children come home from school, so he starts learning more about health care policy and workers' rights.

His work with the children helps him decide to become a science teacher.

The children think he's cool and want to be like him; they make him a big end-of-the-year thank-you card.

BEING AN ADVOCATE, BEING A CITIZEN, AND BEING A CRITIC

Preparing to read "The Partly Cloudy Patriot"

On the next pages is an essay written by Sarah Vowell, who lives in New York City, publishes smart and humorous essays about contemporary life in American (she's written six books on American history and culture), and was for eight years a contributing editor to public radio's *This American Life*. In 2004, she provided the voice of Violet in the movie *The Incredibles*. In late 2011, she joined *The Daily Show* as the senior historical context correspondent. All that work shows how Vowell communicates on different levels with her audiences.

The essay "The Partly Cloudy Patriot" comes from an essay collection that addresses a wide range of topics: visiting Civil War sites, being poor in California, Buffy the Vampire Slayer, political and other kinds of nerds, and former president George W. Bush's inauguration. In "The Partly Cloudy Patriot", Vowell starts by talking about her response to the Mel Gibson movie *The Patriot* (from 2000) as a way of thinking through what it means to be a patriot. She moves on to talk about the events of September 11, 2001, with the same concern about patriotism. As the essay title indicates,

Vowell has an ambivalent relation to the idea of patriotism—not that she is against it—but she wants to know what others think it means to be patriotic and whether she agrees with their style of patriotism.

In this essay, Vowell speaks in a personal tone, drawing on her own experiences—and so it may seem that, if she is advocating something, it is focused around herself; it might seem she is engaged in a style of selfish advocacy. Selfish advocacy—advocacy based on personal experiences or personal grievances— is not necessarily bad. We all need to figure out what matters to us, to draw on our experience of suffering, and to connect with others who share similar ideas about what might make society better. As Vowell argues, however, a fine line separates knowing what is right from seeing yourself on a journey of discovery with others as a result of an event that hit us all.

Much had happened in and to the United States after September 11, 2001, even by the time Vowell wrote this essay, and she clearly feels the need to do something to influence the direction people are moving.

As you read, look for what Vowell is advocating for us all.

The Partly Cloudy Patriot

by Sarah Vowell

In the summer of 2000, I went to see the Mel Gibson blockbuster *The Patriot*. I enjoyed that movie. Watching a story line like that is always a relief. Of course the British must be expelled, just as the Confederates must surrender, Hitler must be crushed, and yee-haw when the Red Sea swallows those slave-mongering Egyptians. There were editorials about *The Patriot*, the kind that always accompany any historical film, written by professors who insist things nobody cares about, like Salieri wasn't that bad a sort or the fact that Roman gladiators maybe didn't have Australian accents. A little anachronism is part of the fun, and I don't mind if in real life General Cornwallis never lost a battle in the South as he does rather gloriously in the film. Isn't art supposed to improve on life?

Personally, I think there was more than enough historical accuracy in *The Patriot* to keep the spoilsports happy. Because I'm part spoilsport on my father's side, and I felt nagged with quandaries every few minutes during the nearly three-hour film. American history is a quagmire, and the more one knows, the quaggier the mire gets. If you're paying attention during *The Patriot* and you know your history and you have a stake in that history, not to mention a conscience, the movie is not an entirely cartoonish march to glory. For example, Mel Gibson's character,

Benjamin Martin, is conflicted. He doesn't want to fight the British because he still feels bad about chopping up some Cherokee into little pieces during the French and Indian War. Since I'm a part-Cherokee person myself, Gibson lost a little of the sympathy I'd stored up for him because he'd been underrated in *Conspiracy Theory*. And did I mention his character lives in South Carolina? So by the end of the movie, you look at the youngest Mel junior bundled in his mother's arms and think, Mel just risked his life so that that kid's kids can rape their slaves and vote to be the first state to secede from the Union.

The Patriot did confirm that I owe George Washington an apology. I always liked George fine, though I dismissed him as a mere soldier. I prefer the pen to the sword, so I've always been more of a Jeffersonhead. The words of the *Declaration of Independence* are so right and true that it seems like its poetry alone would have knocked King George III in the head. Like, he would have read this beloved passage, "We hold these truths to be self-evident, that all Men are created equal, that they are endowed by their Creator with certain unalienable Rights—that among these are Life, Liberty and the pursuit of Happiness," and thought the notion so just, and yet still so wonderfully whimsical, that he would have dethroned himself on the spot. But no, it took a grueling, six-year-long war to make independence a fact.

I rarely remember this. In my ninety-five-cent copy of the *Declaration of Independence*

and the *Constitution*, the two documents are separated by only a blank half page. I forget that there are eleven years between them, eleven years of war and the whole Articles of Confederation debacle. In my head, the two documents are like the A side and B side of the greatest single ever released that was recorded in one great drunken night, but no, there's a lot of bleeding life between them. Dead boys and dead Indians and Valley Forge.

Anyway, *The Patriot*. The best part of seeing it was standing in line for tickets. I remember how jarring it was to hear my fellow moviegoers say that word. "Two for *The Patriot* please." "One for *The Patriot* at 5:30." For years, I called it the P word, because it tended to make nice people flinch. For the better part of the 1990s, it seemed like the only Americans who publicly described themselves as patriots were scary militia types hiding out in the backwoods of Michigan and Montana, cleaning their guns. One of the few Americans still celebrating Patriot's Day—a nearly forgotten holiday on April 19 commemorating the Revolutionary War's first shots at Lexington and Concord—did so in 1995 by murdering 168 people in the federal building in Oklahoma City. In fact, the same week I saw *The Patriot*, I was out with some friends for dessert. When I asked a fellow named Andy why he had chosen a cupcake with a little American flag stuck in the frosting, I expected him to say that he was in a patriotic mood, but he didn't. He said that he was "feeling jingoistic."

Well, that was a long time ago. As I write this, it's December 2001 in New York City. The only words one hears more often than variations on "patriot" are "in the wake of," "in the aftermath of," and "since the events of September 11." We also use the word "we" more. Patriotism as a word and deed has made a comeback. At Halloween, costume shops did a brisk business in Uncle Sam and Betsy Ross getups. Teen pop bombshell Britney Spears took a breather during her live telecast from Vegas's MGM Grand to sit on a piano bench with her belly ring glinting in the spotlight and talk about "how proud I am of our nation right now." Chinese textile factories are working overtime to fill the consumer demand for American flags.

Immediately after the attack, seeing the flag all over the place was moving, endearing. So when the newspaper I subscribe to published a full-page, full color flag to clip out and hang in the window, how come I couldn't? It took me a while to figure out why I guiltily slid the flag into the recycling bin instead of taping it up. The meaning had changed, or let's say it changed back. In the first day or two the flags were plastered everywhere, seeing them was heartening because they indicated that we're all in this sorrow together. The flags were purely emotional. Once we went to war, once the president announced that we were going to

retaliate against the "evil-doers," then the flag again represented what it usually represents, the government. I think that's when the flags started making me nervous. The true American patriot is by definition skeptical of the government. Skepticism of the government was actually one of the platforms the current figurehead of the government ran on. How many times in the campaign did President Bush proclaim of his opponent, the then vice president, "He trusts the federal government and I trust the people"? This deep suspicion of Washington is one of the most American emotions an American can have. So by the beginning of October, the ubiquity of the flag came to feel like peer pressure to always stand behind policies one might not necessarily agree with. And, like any normal citizen, I prefer to make up my mind about the issues of the day on a case by case basis at 3:00 A.M. when I wake up from my *Nightline*-inspired nightmares.

One Independence Day, when I was in college, I was living in a house with other students on a street that happened to be one of the main roads leading to the football stadium where the town's official Fourth of July fireworks festivities would be held. I looked out the window and noticed a little American flag stabbed into my yard. Then I walked outside and saw that all the yards in front of all the houses on the street had little flags waving above the grass. The flags, according to a tag, were underwritten by a local

real estate agency and the Veterans of Foreign Wars. I marched into the house, yanked out the phone book, found the real estate office in the yellow pages, and phoned them up immediately, demanding that they come and take their fucking flag off my lawn, screaming into the phone, "The whole point of that goddamn flag is that people don't stick flags in my yard without asking me!" I felt like Jimmy Stewart in *Mr. Smith Goes to Washington*, but with profanity. A few minutes later, an elderly gentleman in a VFW cap, who probably lost his best friend liberating France or something, pulled up in a big car, grabbed the flag, and rolled his eyes as I stared at him through the window. Then I felt dramatic and dumb. Still, sometimes I think the true American flag has always been that one with the snake hissing "Don't Tread on Me."

The week of the attack on the World Trade Center and the Pentagon, I watched TV news all day and slept with the radio on. I found myself flipping channels hoping to see the FBI handcuff a terrorist on camera. What did happen, a lot, was that citizens or politicians or journalists would mention that they wonder what it will be like for Americans now to live with the constant threat of random, sudden death. I know a little about what that's like. I did grow up during the Cold War. Maybe it says something about my level of cheer that I found this notion comforting, to remember that all those years I was sure the world might blow up at any second, I somehow managed to graduate from high school and do my laundry and see Smokey Robinson live.

Things were bad in New York. I stopped being able to tell whether my eyes were teary all the time from grief or from the dirty, smoky wind. Just when it seemed as if the dust had started to settle, then came the anthrax. I was on the phone with a friend who works in Rockefeller Center, and he had to hang up to be evacuated because a contaminated envelope had infected a person in the building; an hour later, another friend in another building was sitting at his desk eating his lunch and men in sealed plastic disease-control space suits walked through his office, taking samples. Once delivering the mail became life-threatening, pedestrians trudging past the main post office on Eighth Avenue bowed their heads a little as they read the credo chiseled on the façade, "Neither snow, nor rain, nor heat, nor gloom of night stays these couriers from the swift completion of their appointed rounds."

During another war, across the river, in Newark, a writer turned soldier named Thomas Paine sat down by a campfire in September 1776 and wrote, "These are the times that try men's souls. The summer soldier and the sunshine patriot will, in this crisis, shrink from the service of their country; but he that stands it now, deserves the love and thanks of man and woman." In September and October, I liked to read that before I

pulled the rubberband off the newspaper to find out what was being done to my country and what my country was doing back. I liked the black and white of Paine's words. I know I'm no sunshine patriot. I wasn't shrinking, though, honestly; the most important service we mere mortal citizens were called upon to perform was to spend money, so I dutifully paid for Korean dinners and a new living room lamp. But still I longed for the morning that I could open up the paper and the only people in it who would irk me would be dead suicide bombers and retreating totalitarians on the other side of the world. Because that would be the morning I pulled the flag out of the recycling bin and taped it up in the window. And while I could shake my fists for sure at the terrorist on page one, buried domestic items could still make my stomach hurt—school prayer partisans taking advantage of the grief of children to circumvent the separation of church and state; the White House press secretary condemning a late-night talk show host for making a questionable remark about the U.S. military: "The reminder is to all Americans, that they need to watch what they say, watch what they do, and that this is not a time for remarks like that." Those are the sorts of never-ending qualms that have turned me into the partly cloudy patriot I long not to be.

When Paine wrote his pamphlet, which came to be called "The American Crisis," winter was coming, Washington's armies were in

retreat, the Revolution was floundering. His words inspired soldiers and civilians alike to buck up and endure the war so that someday "not a place upon earth might be so happy as America."

Thing is, it worked. The British got kicked out. The trees got cleared. Time passed, laws passed and, five student loans later, I made a nice little life for myself. I can feel it with every passing year, how I'm that much farther away from the sacrifices of the cast-off Indians and Okie farmers I descend from. As recently as fifty years ago my grandmother was picking cotton with bleeding fingers. I think about her all the time while I'm getting overpaid to sit at a computer, eat Chinese takeout, and think things up in my pajamas. The half century separating my fingers, which are moisturized with cucumber lotion and type eighty words per minute, and her bloody digits is an ordinary Land of Opportunity parable, and don't think I don't appreciate it. I'm keenly aware of all the ways my life is easier and lighter, how lucky I am to have the time and energy to contemplate the truly important things—Bill Murray in *Groundhog Day*, the baked Alaska at Sardi's, the Dean Martin Christmas record, my growing collection of souvenir snow globes. After all, what is happiness without cheap thrills? Reminds me of that passage in Philip Roth's novel *American Pastoral* when the middle-aged, prosperous grandson of immigrants marvels that his own daughter loathes the country enough to try to blow it up:

Hate America? Why, he lived in America the way he lived inside his own skin. All the pleasures of his younger years were American pleasures, all that success and happiness had been American, and he need no longer keep his mouth shut about it just to defuse her ignorant hatred. The loneliness he would feel if he had to live in another country. Yes, everything that gave meaning to his accomplishments had been American. Everything he loved was here.

A few weeks after the United States started bombing Afghanistan and the Taliban were in retreat, I turned on the TV news and watched grinning Afghans in the streets of Kabul, allowed to play music for the first time in years. I pull a brain muscle when I try to fathom the rationale for outlawing all music all the time—not certain genres of music, not music with offensive lyrics played by the corrupters of youth, but any form of organized sound. Under Taliban rule, my whole life as an educated (well, at a state school), working woman with CD storage problems would have been null and void. I don't know what's more ridiculous, that people like that would deny a person like me the ability to earn a living using skills and knowledge I learned in school, or that they would deny me my unalienable right to chop garlic in time with the B-52s' "Rock Lobster" as I cook dinner.

A few years back, a war correspondent friend of mine gave a speech about Bosnia to an international relations department at a famous Midwestern university. I went with him. After he finished, a group of hangers-on, all men except for me, stuck around to debate the finer points of the former Yugoslavia. The conversation was very detailed, including references to specific mayors of specific Croatian villages. It was like record collector geek talk, only about Bosnia. They were the record collectors of Bosnia. So they went on denouncing the various idiotic nationalist causes of various splinter groups, blaming nationalism itself for the genocidal war. And of course a racist nationalism is to blame. But the more they ranted, the more uncomfortable I became. They, many of them immigrants themselves, considered patriotic allegiance to be a sin, a divisive, villainous drive leading to exclusion, hate and murder. I, theretofore silent, spoke up. This is what I said. I said that the idea of Memphis, Tennessee, not to mention looking down at it, made me go all soft. Because I looked down at Memphis, Tennessee, and thought of all my heroes who had walked its streets. I thought of Sun Records, of the producer Sam Phillips. Sam Phillips, who once described the sort of person he recorded as "a person who had dreamed, and dreamed, and dreamed." A person like Elvis Presley, his funny bass player Bill Black, his guitarist Scotty Moore (we have the same birthday, he and I). Jerry Lee Lewis. Carl Perkins. Hello, I'm Johnny Cash. I told the Bosnian record collectors that when I thought of the records of these Memphis men, when I looked out the window at the Mississippi mud and felt their names moistening my

tongue, what I felt, what I was proud to feel, was patriotic. I noticed one man staring at me. He said he was born in some something-istan I hadn't heard of. Now that my globe is permanently turned to that part of the world, I realize he was talking about Tajikistan, the country bordering Afghanistan. The man from Tajikistan looked at me in the eye and delivered the following warning.

"Those," he said, of my accolades for Elvis and friends, "are the seeds of war."

I laughed and told him not to step on my blue suede shoes, but I got the feeling he wasn't joking.

Before September 11, the national events that have made the deepest impressions on me are, in chronological order: the 1976 Bicentennial, the Iran hostage crisis, Iran-Contra, the Los Angeles riots, the impeachment trial of President Clinton, and the 2000 presidential election. From those events, I learned the following: that the *Declaration of Independence* is full of truth and beauty; that some people in other parts of the world hate us because we're Americans; what a shredder is; that the rage for justice is so fierce people will set fire to their own neighborhoods when they don't get it; that Republicans hate Bill Clinton; and that the ideal of one man, one vote doesn't always come true. (In the U.S. Commission on Civil Rights' report "Voting Irregularities in Florida During the 2000 Presidential Election," the testimony of Dr. Frederick Shotz of Broward County especially sticks out. A handicapped voter in a wheelchair, Dr. Shotz "had to use his upper body to lift himself up to get up the steps in order for him to access his polling place. Once he was inside the polling place, he was not given a wheelchair accessible polling booth. Once again, he had to use his arms to lift himself up to see the ballot and, while balancing on his arms, simultaneously attempt to cast his ballot.")

Looking over my list, I can't help but notice that only one of my formative experiences, the Bicentennial, came with balloons and cake. Being a little kid that year, visiting the Freedom Train with its dramatically lit facsimile of the *Declaration*, learning that I lived in the greatest, most fair and wise and lovely place on earth, made a big impression on me. I think it's one of the reasons I'm so fond of President Lincoln. Because he stared down the crap. More than anyone in the history of the country, he faced up to our most troubling contradiction—that a nation born in freedom would permit the enslavement of human beings—and never once stopped believing in the *Declaration of Independence's* ideals, never stopped trying to make them come true.

On a Sunday night in November, I walked up to the New York Public Library to see the *Emancipation Proclamation*. On loan from the National Archives, the document was in town for three days. They put it in a glass case in a small, dark room. Being alone with old pieces of paper and one guard in an alcove

at the library was nice and quiet. I stared at Abraham Lincoln's signature for a long time. I stood there, thinking what one is supposed to think: This is the paper he held in his hands and there is the ink that came from his pen, and when the ink dried the slaves were freed. Except look at the date, January 1, 1863. The words wouldn't come true for a couple of years, which, I'm guessing, is a long time when another person owns your body. But I love how Lincoln dated the document, noting that it was signed "in the year of our Lord, one thousand eight hundred and sixty-three, and of the Independence of the United States of America the eighty-seventh." Fourscore and seven years before, is the wonderfully arrogant implication, something as miraculous as the virgin birth happened on this earth, and the calendar should reflect that.

The *Emancipation Proclamation* is a perfect American artifact to me—a good deed that made a lot of other Americans mad enough to kill. I think that's why the Civil War is my favorite American metaphor. I'm so much more comfortable when we're bickering with each other than when we have to link arms and fight a common enemy. But right after September 11, the TV was full of unity. Congressmen, political enemies from both houses of Congress, from both sides of the aisle, stood together on the Capitol steps and sang "God Bless America." At the end of the memorial service at the National Cathedral, President and Mrs. Carter chatted

like old friends with President and Mrs. Ford. Rudolph Giuliani, the mayor of New York, kissed his former opponent Senator Hillary Clinton on the cheek as the New York congressional delegation toured the World Trade Center disaster area.

In September, people across the country and all over the world—including, bless them, the Canadians, and they are born sick of us—were singing the American national anthem. And when I heard their voices I couldn't help but remember the last time I had sung that song. I was one of hundreds of people standing in the mud on the Washington Mall on January 20 at the inauguration of George W. Bush. Everyone standing there in the cold rain had very strong feelings. It was either/or. Either you beamed through the ceremony with smiles of joy, or you wept through it all with tears of rage. I admit, I was one of the people there who needed a hankie when it was over. At the end of the ceremony, it was time to sing the national anthem. Some of the dissenters refused to join in. Such was their anger at the country at that moment they couldn't find it in their hearts to sing. But I was standing there next to my friend Jack, and Jack and I put our hands over our hearts and sang that song loud. Because we love our country too. Because we wouldn't have been standing there, wouldn't have driven down to Washington just to burst into tears if we didn't care so very, very much about how this country is run.

When the anthem ended—land of the

free, home of the brave—Jack and I walked to the other end of the Mall to the Lincoln Memorial to read Lincoln's Second Inaugural Address, the speech Lincoln gave at the end of the Civil War about how "we must bind up the nation's wounds." It seems so quaint to me now, after September, after CNN started doing hourly live remotes from St. Vincent's, my neighborhood hospital, that I would conceive of a wound as being peeved about who got to be president.

My ideal picture of citizenship will always be an argument, not a sing-along. I did not get it out of a civics textbook either. I got it from my parents. My mom and dad disagree with me about almost everything. I do not share their religion or their political affiliation. I get on their nerves sometimes. But, and this is the most important thing they taught me, so what? We love each other. My parents and I have been through so much and known each other for so long, share so many in-jokes and memories, our differences of opinion on everything from gun control to Robin Williams movies hardly matter at all. Plus, our disagreements make us appreciate the things we have in common all the more. When I call Republican Senator Orrin Hatch's office to say that I admire something he said about stem cell research, I am my parents' daughter. Because they have always enjoyed playing up the things we do have in common, like Dolly Parton, ibuprofen. Maybe sometimes, in quiet moments of reflection, my mom would

prefer that I not burn eternally in the flames of hell when I die, but otherwise she wants me to follow my own heart.

I will say that, in September, atheism was a lonely creed. Not because atheists have no god to turn to, but because everyone else forgot about us. At a televised interfaith memorial service at Yankee Stadium on September 23, Muslim, Christian, Jewish, Sikh, and Hindu clerics spoke to their fellow worshipers. Placido Domingo sang "Ave Maria" for the mayor. I waited in vain for someone like me to stand up and say that the only thing those of us who don't believe in god have to believe in is other people and that New York City is the best place there ever was for a godless person to practice her moral code. I think it has something to do with the crowded sidewalks and subways. Walking to and from the hardware store requires the push and pull of selfishness and selflessness, taking turns between getting out of someone's way and them getting out of yours, waiting for a dog to move, helping a stroller up steps, protecting the eyes from runaway umbrellas. Walking in New York is a battle of the wills, a balance of aggression and kindness. I'm not saying it's always easy. The occasional "Watch where you're going, bitch" can, I admit, put a crimp in one's day. But I believe all that choreography has made me a better person. The other day, in the subway at 5:30, I was crammed into my sweaty, crabby fellow citizens, and I kept whispering under

my breath "we the people, we the people" over and over again, reminding myself we're all in this together and they had as much right—exactly as much right—as I to be in the muggy underground on their way to wherever they were on their way to.

Once, headed uptown on the 9 train, I noticed a sign posted by the Manhattan Transit Authority advising subway riders who might become ill in the train. The sign asked that the suddenly infirm inform another passenger or get out at the next stop and approach the stationmaster. Do not, repeat, do not pull the emergency brake, the sign said, as this will only delay aid. Which was all very logical, but for the following proclamation at the bottom of the sign, something along the lines of "If you are sick, you will not be left alone." This strikes me as not only kind, not only comforting, but the very epitome of civilization, good government, i.e., the crux of the societal impulse. Banding together, pooling our taxes, not just making trains, not just making trains that move underground, not just making trains that move underground with surprising efficiency at a fair price—but posting on said trains a notification of such surprising compassion and thoughtfulness, I found myself scanning the faces of my fellow passengers, hoping for fainting, obvious fevers, at the very least a sneeze so that I might offer a tissue.

TO ANALYZE: "A PARTLY CLOUDY PATRIOT"

- **Discuss with others:** Why do you think Vowell starts the essay with her discussion of the movie? What do we learn about how she thinks from her discussion of the movie, and how does that set us up for the rest of her essay?

- **Discuss with others:** Vowell moves from talking about the movie to talking about the attacks on the World Trade Center and the Pentagon on September 11, 2001. In the first two paragraphs of this part of her essay, how does she approach the events of that day and their aftermath? What is the issue she addresses in those paragraphs?

- **Discuss with others:** Vowell tells us she went to George W. Bush's inauguration and was patriotically moved. Look at the details of the story. How does what she tells us affect our view of her?

- **Discuss with others:** If Vowell's view of patriotism is "partly cloudy," does that mean she does not have a clear understanding of what patriotism is?

- **Write informally:** Vowell ends her essay talking about a sign she read in the New York subway instructing people how they might help a fellow passenger who's sick. Why might she end an essay on patriotism with this story?

- **Write informally:** Toward the end of the essay (and several times) Vowell says that her "ideal picture of citizenship will always be an argument," yet in the last few pages, she implies that kindness toward strangers is connected to patriotism in some way. Is this a contradiction? Assuming that it is not a contradiction in her eyes, explain how she might reconcile these two ideas.

GROUNDS FOR ADVOCACY—AND FOR LIVING

Preparing to read "The False Idol of Unfettered Capitalism"

As you will know as soon as you start reading the following essay, the author—Chris Hedges—is a foreign correspondent. Called "correspondents" because the position started when hand-written letters were what they had to send, foreign correspondents work for a newspaper or a radio or television station, contributing observations from other countries. Foreign correspondents often live in those other countries for some period of time and, unlike reporters, usually include more explanation and context in what they write.

Chris Hedges has an undergraduate degree in English literature and a Master of Divinity degree. He speaks Arabic, French, and Spanish and knows ancient Greek and Latin. He has been a foreign correspondent for many years, writing for many different and much-respected news sources and writing from Central America, Africa, the Middle East, and the Balkans.

In 2002 Hedges was part of a team that won the Pulitzer Prize for their reporting in *the New York Times* on global terrorism networks. Hedges received the Amnesty International Global Award for Human Rights Journalism in 2002; *The Los Angeles Times* named him the Online Journalist of the Year in 2009 and gave him the Best Online Column award in 2010 for his essay "One Day We'll All Be Terrorists."

Hedges has also taught at Columbia University, New York University, Princeton University, and The University of Toronto, and now teaches inmates at a New Jersey prison.

Hedges has also written 11 books. His 2002 book, *War Is a Force That Gives Us Meaning,* was a best-seller as well as a finalist for the National Book Critics Circle Award for Nonfiction. The Academy Award-winning 2009 film, *The Hurt Locker,* opened with a quotation from Hedges's book: "The rush of battle is often a potent and lethal addiction, for war is a drug."

The title of the essay on the next pages, "The False Idol of Unfettered Capitalism," should immediately give you a sense of Hedge's positions and ways of writing. The title is a strong declarative statement that judges economic policies when they are treated like religious idols; if you had a Christian upbringing, the term "false idol" should call to mind the Ten Commandments—which is part of what Hedges discusses in his essay.

The essay asks us to consider how we live. What do we value? How do we value others and the communities in which we live? What, the essay asks, are the "core rules that, when honored, hold us together, and when dishonored lead to alienation, discord, and violence"?

The False Idol of Unfettered Capitalism

by Chris Hedges

When I returned to New York City after nearly two decades as a foreign correspondent in Latin America, Africa, the Middle East, and the Balkans I was unsure where I was headed. I lacked the emotional and physical resilience that had allowed me to cope as a war correspondent. I was plagued by memories I wanted to forget, waking suddenly in the middle of the night, my sleep shattered by visions of gunfire and death. I was alienated from those around me, unaccustomed to the common language and images imposed by consumer culture, unable to communicate the pain and suffering I had witnessed, not much interested in building a career.

It was at this time that the Brooklyn Academy of Music began showing a ten-part film series called *The Decalogue*. *Deka*, in Greek, means "ten," and logos means "saying" or "speech." The Decalogue is the classical name of the Ten Commandments. The director was the Polish filmmaker Krzysztof Kieślowski, who had made the trilogy *Three Colors*, consisting of the films *White*, *Blue*, and *Red*. The ten films of *The Decalogue*, each about an hour long and based on one of the commandments, were to be shown two at a time over five consecutive weeks. I saw them on Sunday nights, taking the subway to Brooklyn, its cars rocking and screeching along the tracks in the darkened tunnels. The theater was rarely more than half full.

The films were quiet, subtle, and often opaque. It was sometimes hard to tell which commandment was being addressed. The characters never spoke about the commandments directly. They were too busy, as we all are, coping with life. The stories presented the lives of ordinary people confronted by extraordinary events. All lived in a Warsaw housing complex, many of them neighbors. They were on a common voyage, yet also out of touch with the pain and dislocation of those around them. The commandments, Kieślowski understood, were not dusty relics of another age, but rather a powerful compass with vital contemporary resonance.

In film after film he dealt with the core violation raised by each of the commandments. He freed the commandments from the clutter of piety and narrow definitions imposed upon them by religious leaders and institutions. Magda, the promiscuous woman portrayed in *Decalogue VI*, the film about adultery, was not married. She had a series of empty, carnal relationships. For Kieślowski, adultery, at its deepest level, was sex without love. Michal, the father in *Decalogue IV*, the film about honoring our parents, was not the biological father of his daughter, Anka. The biological mother was absent in the daughter's life. Parenting, Kieślowski knew, is not defined by blood or birth or gender. It is defined by commitment, fidelity, and love.

In *Decalogue V*, the film about killing, Jacek, an unemployed drifter, robs and brutally murders a cab driver. He is caught, sentenced, and executed by the state. Kieślowski forces us to confront the barbarity of murder, whether committed by a deranged individual or sanctioned by society.

I knew the commandments. I had learned them at Sunday school, listened to sermons based on the commandments from my father's pulpit, and studied them as a seminarian at Harvard Divinity School. But Kieślowski turned them into living, breathing entities.

"For six thousand years these rules have been unquestionably right," Kieślowski said of the commandments:

> And yet we break them every day. We know what we should do, and yet we fail to live as we should. People feel that something is wrong in life. There is some kind of atmosphere that makes people turn now to other values. They want to contemplate the basic questions of life, and that is probably the real reason for wanting to tell these stories.

In eight of the films there was a brief appearance by a young man, solemn and silent. Kieślowski said he did not know who the character was. Perhaps he was an angel or Christ. Perhaps he represented the divine presence who observed with profound sadness the tragedy and folly we humans commit against others and against ourselves.

"He's not very pleased with us," was all the director said.

The commandments are a list of religious edicts, according to passages in Exodus and Deuteronomy, given to Moses by God on Mount Sinai. The first four are designed to guide the believer toward a proper relationship with God. The remaining six deal with our relations with others. It is these final six commands that are given the negative form of You Shall Not. Only two of the commandments, the prohibitions against stealing and murder, are incorporated into our legal code. Protestants, Catholics, and Jews have compiled slightly different lists, but the essence of the commandments remains the same. Muslims, while they do not list the commandments in the Koran, honor the laws of Moses, whom they see as a prophet.

The commandments are not defined, however, by the three monotheistic faiths. They are one of the earliest attempts to lay down moral rules and guidelines to sustain a human community. Nearly every religion has set down an ethical and moral code that is strikingly similar to the Ten Commandments. The Eightfold Path, known within Buddhism as the Wheel of Law, forbids murder, unchastity, theft, falsehood, and, especially, covetous desire. *Om*, the Hindus' Sacred Syllable, said or sung before and after prayers, ends with a fourth sound beyond the range of human hearing. This sound is called the "sound of silence." It is also called "the sound of the universe." Hindus, in the repetition of the Sacred Syllable, try to go beyond thought, to reach

the stillness and silence that constitutes God. Five of the Ten Commandments delivered from Mount Sinai are lifted directly from the Egyptian *Book of the Dead*. No human being, no nation, no religion, has been chosen to be the sole interpreter of mystery. All cultures struggle to give words to the experience of the transcendent. It is a reminder that all of us find God not in what we know, but in what we cannot comprehend.

The commandments include the most severe violations and moral dilemmas in human life, although these violations often lie beyond the scope of the law. They were for the ancients, and are for us, the core rules that, when honored, hold us together, and when dishonored lead to alienation, discord, and violence. When our lives are shattered by tragedy, suffering, and pain, or when we express or feel the ethereal and overwhelming power of love, we confront the mystery of good and evil. Voices across time and cultures have struggled to transmit and pay homage to this mystery, what it means for our lives and our place in the cosmos. These voices, whether in the teachings of the Buddha, the writings of the Latin poets, or the pages of the Koran, are part of our common struggle as human beings to acknowledge the eternal and the sacred, to create an ethical system to sustain life.

The commandments retain their power because they express something fundamental about the human condition. This is why they

are important. The commandments choose us. We are rarely able to choose them. We do not, however hard we work to insulate ourselves, ultimately control our fate. We cannot save ourselves from betrayal, theft, envy, greed, deception, and murder, nor always from the impulses that propel us to commit these acts. These violations, which can strike us or be committed without warning, can leave deep, often lifelong wounds. There are few of us who do not wrestle deeply with at least one of these violations.

We all stray. We all violate some commandments and do not adequately honor others. We are human. But moral laws bind us and make it possible to build a society based on the common good. They keep us from honoring the false covenants of greed, celebrity, and power that destroy us. These false covenants have a powerful appeal. They offer feelings of strength, status, and a false sense of belonging. They tempt us to be God. They tell us the things we want to hear and believe. They appear to make us the center of the universe. But these false covenants, covenants built around exclusive communities of race, gender, class, religion, and nation, inevitably carry within them the denigration and abuse of others. These false covenants divide us. A moral covenant recognizes that all life is sacred and love alone is the force that makes life possible.

It is the unmentioned fear of death, the one that rattles with the wind through the heavy branches of the trees outside, which frightens us the most, even as we do not name this fear. It is death we are trying to flee. The smallness of our lives, the transitory nature of existence, the inevitable road to old age, are what the idols of power, celebrity, and wealth tell us we can escape. They are tempting and seductive. They assure us that we need not endure the pain and suffering of being human. We follow the idol and barter away our freedom. We place our identity and our hopes in the hands of the idol. We need the idol to define ourselves, to determine our status and place. We invest in the idol. We sell ourselves into bondage.

The consumer goods we amass, the status we seek in titles and positions, the ruthlessness we employ to advance our careers, the personal causes we champion, the money we covet, and the houses we build and the cars we drive become our pathetic statements of being. They are squalid little monuments to our selves. The more we strive to amass power and possessions, the more intolerant and anxious we become. Impulses and emotions, not thoughts but mass feelings, propel us forward. These impulses, carefully manipulated by a consumer society, see us intoxicated with patriotic fervor and a lust for war, a desire to vote for candidates who appeal to us emotionally or to buy this car or that brand. Politicians, advertisers, social scientists, television evangelists, the news media, and the entertainment industry have

learned what makes us respond. It works. None of us are immune. But when we act in their interests, we are rarely acting in our own. The moral philosophies we have ignored, once a staple of a liberal arts education, are a check on the deluge. They call us toward mutual respect and self-sacrifice. They force us to confront the broad, disturbing questions about meaning and existence. And our callous refusal to heed these questions as a society allowed us to believe that unfettered capitalism and the free market were forces of nature, decrees passed down from the divine, the only routes to prosperity and power. They turned out to be idols, and like all idols they have now demanded their human sacrifice.

Moral laws were not written so they could be practiced by some and not by others. They call on all of us to curb our worst instincts so we can live together, to refrain from committing acts of egregious exploitation that spread suffering. Moral teachings are guideposts. They keep us, even when we stray, as we all do, on the right path.

The strange, disjointed fragments of our lives can be comprehended only when we acknowledge our insecurities and uncertainties, when we accept that we will never know what life is about or what it is supposed to mean. We must do the best we can, not for ourselves, the great moralists remind us, but for those around us. Trust is the compound that unites us. The only lasting happiness in life comes with giving life to others. The

quality of our life, of all life, is determined by what we give and how much we sacrifice. We live not by exalting our own life but by being willing to lose it.

The moral life, in the end, will not protect us from evil. The moral life protects us, however, from committing evil. It is designed to check our darker impulses, warning us that pandering to impulses can have terrible consequences. It seeks to hold community together. It is community that gives our lives, even in pain and grief, a healing solidarity. It is fealty to community that frees us from the dictates of our idols, idols that promise us fulfillment through self-gratification. These moral laws are about freedom. They call us to reject and defy powerful forces that rule our lives and to live instead for others, even if this costs us status and prestige and wealth.

Turn away from the moral life and you end in disaster. You sink into a morass of self-absorption and greed. You breed a society that celebrates fraud, theft, and violence, you turn neighbor against neighbor, you confuse presentation and image with your soul. Moral rules are as imperative to sustaining a community as law. And all cultures have sought to remind us of these basic moral restraints, ones that invariably tell us that successful communities do not permit their members to exploit one another but rather ensure that they sacrifice for the common good. The economic and social collapse we face was presaged by a moral collapse. And our response must include a renewed reverence for moral and social imperatives that acknowledge the sanctity of the common good.

The German philosopher Ludwig Wittgenstein said, "Tell me *how* you seek and I will tell you *what* you are seeking. " We all are seekers, even if we do not always know what we are looking to find. We are all seekers, even if we do not always know how to frame the questions. In those questions, even more than the answers, we find hope in the strange and contradictory fragments of our lives. And it is by recovering these moral questions, too often dismissed or ignored in universities and boardrooms across the country, laughed at on the stock exchange, ridiculed on reality television as an impediment to money and celebrity, that we will again find it possible to be whole.

TO ANALYZE

■ **Discuss with others:** Although it may not seem the case because his writing is so passionate, Hedges has a syllogism at the core of his writing. (We wrote about syllogisms on pages 146–147). With others in class, try to reconstruct Hedges's syllogism.

If we accept Hedges's arguments in this essay, what sort of life would that imply we should each be living? Where do you agree or disagree?

■ **Discuss with others:** Compare Hedges's ethos with Vowell's ethos. First, describe each separate ethos with adjectives that characterize it for you (cheery? passionate? angry? morose?) and then point to specific features in each essay that lead you to label it with the adjectives you do.

■ **Write:** In a three- to five-page paper, compare the purposes and supporting strategies of "The Partly Cloudy Patriot" with "The False Idol of Unfettered Capitalism." First describe what you take to be the purpose(s) of each essay, and then consider how each writer's ethos, use of pathos, and other strategies support the purposes you have named. (You could, for example, focus on how each writer starts by writing about movies: What do you think Vowell hopes to achieve by discussing *The Patriot*, and how is that similar to and/or different from what Hedges hopes to achieve by discussing *The Decalogue*?)

■ **Write for yourself and then for others:** You might find yourself uncomfortable with Hedges's essay: You might be uncomfortable with how he equates the ethical groundings of differing religions; you might believe capitalism is the best economic system available to us; you might not believe in any god or transcendent being.

Nonetheless, we can respect Hedges's efforts to find grounds for how we can live together ethically.

On your own, write an explanation to yourself of what you believe about why you are alive. What do you believe and what relations do your beliefs encourage you to have with others? What would your life look like—what sorts of relations would you build with others—if you were able at every moment to live by your values? What would you advocate, for whom and with whom?

Then rewrite your words so that your reasons are clear to others. Your purpose is not to persuade others to take up your reasons and values; instead, simply write so that others might understand why you live the life you do and so that they might understand the life you hope to live in the future.

THINKING THROUGH PRODUCTION

- Develop a design plan and then produce a materials kit that elementary school children can use to understand and to start being advocates for an issue that matters to them.

- Research the organizations on, connected to, or near your campus that provide opportunities for civic involvement and advocacy. Put together a list of the organizations to help someone new to campus decide where to get involved; on the list, describe what the organization does, its values, and how someone else could connect with the organization. Produce the annotated list as a website, extended brochure, or small booklet.

- The readings in this chapter discuss the ideas of citizenship, ethics, and freedom—sometimes overtly, sometimes implicitly.

  Pick one of those three ideas, and look for how it is discussed or used as a guiding value through the readings. Write a paragraph summary of what the readings say about the idea. Do summarize; try to keep your own opinions out of this writing.

  Break into groups based on the idea you want to discuss further and talk about your response to how citizenship, ethics, or freedom was discussed in the reading: *With what do you agree? What do you find lacking? What you find just plain wrong?*

  Also discuss what role you see visual, oral, and written communication playing in the creation/promotion/continuation/suppression of the idea in our daily lives. Report back to class.

  Use what you learned to design a visual explanation of citizenship, ethics, or freedom. (Consider a poster, flyer, comic, drawing, painting, photomontage, photo-essay, video, or …).

- Research the life of someone no longer living whom you and others consider to be a strong advocate. Design, produce, and test a memorial to that person and her or his work and use the memorial as a means for persuading others of the value of advocacy.

  Be creative with "memorial." Research the genre. Look at statues on your campus and in your town, but also look at television shows, encyclopedia entries, bulletin boards, or websites that honor individuals. What media will help you best engage others with the life and work of the person you research? What media will help you best persuade others to themselves become advocates?

Thinking about advocacy through producing texts

■ Collect examples of brochures and handouts meant to influence the behavior of people your age. For example, look at your campus or local health department for print materials meant to teach about sexual health, alcohol or drug use, or eating. Identify what you think are the values the materials advocate, and then test the materials with their intended audience to see how effective they are. (This is using testing as a kind of research, and the section on testing in chapter 3 can help you.)

Also identify the values you think the materials should advocate, according to your own understanding of the issue as well as what you learn from your testing.

Based on what you learn from your testing, use chapters 3 and 4 to help you develop a statement of purpose and then a design plan (including a testing plan) for materials you think will work more effectively. (You needn't be constrained by a print medium: Your testing may suggest that it will be more effective for you to produce a video or a game-show event.)

Produce your communication.

What in your design and development process do you think was most useful to you?

■ Find a short text of some kind—an editorial, a cartoon, a webpage—that you don't think is as effective as it could be in advocating the values it is trying to advocate. Use the resources of chapter 3 to develop a design plan for a revised text, paying particular attention to the statement of purpose. Re-produce the text, and test both its and the original's effectiveness with its intended audience. Write your observations about the effectiveness of your redesign: What did you learn from it that might help you develop more effective communication for advocacy in the future?

■ Revise an academic paper you have already written so that it more explicitly advocates the values implicit in the original essay. *Can you make the paper do something other than just report on your research?*

Write a short reflection on the revised paper. *How did you have to change your writing to make its advocacy more explicit? What strategies might you carry forward from this writing into future writing, and why?*

■ Develop a design plan (including the use of testing) for a board game intended to help parents and their children talk relaxedly and learn about drug use while playing. This is a complex audience situation, so carefully consider why parents and their children would want to play and how playing your game would engage both parents and children. You'll also need to consider the complex role of drugs (including alcohol and medicinal drugs) in our lives, so you'll need to do research into this area.

Produce the game with the testing you planned.

How effective is the game? What qualities make it effective, and what would you change and why would you change it?

What did you learn from this production that you want to remember for future productions?

THINKING THROUGH PRODUCTION, continued

Producing a useful piece of communication for a nonprofit organization

The following steps describe one way you can use research and the rhetorical process of design to produce communication for a nonprofit organization. This project can be particularly effective if you work with others from your class in small teams, or a whole class can participate in this project, dividing the research and recommending different communication possibilities to the organization.

1　Contact a nonprofit organization whose work you respect. Explain to its representatives the process you are undertaking. You want to be sure that they are willing to work with you and that they need you to do the work described here.

2　To gain background for designing communications that best support the group, research its purpose and history. You can do this by reading materials produced by the group and/or interviewing directors, employees, or volunteers. (Use pages 234–235 of this book to help you prepare for interviews, and be sure you talk with the group's director(s) to let them know your purposes and to check that interviewing is okay.) Look for a mission statement in the group's materials. Also look online and in the library for anything that people outside the group have written about it.

3　To know how the group has represented itself in the past and to see where and how it might communicate more effectively, collect the group's brochures, flyers, or posters; explore its website. Depending on the group, you might be able to find speeches made by people within it. Any communication produced by or about the group will help you.

4　If you can, interview people served by the group who are the audience for the communication you have collected. Ask questions that help you understand how the audience members respond to the communication.

5　Analyze all the information you have collected through your research with the goal of making recommendations to the group about how it could improve the communications it already has or about how it could open new directions. This is rhetorical analysis—examining communication in light of its audience, purpose, and context—so use chapter 9 to help you do your analysis.

6　Write a formal research paper for your class— alone, or in a small team—in which you use your analysis as a basis for recommending a specific new text the group could use. (For example, you could recommend that the

group add to its website a section specifically addressing teenagers or that it could produce a brochure better explaining its application process.)

7　Use feedback you receive to your paper to prepare a short (10- to 15-minute) oral presentation with supporting visual materials for the director and/or other members of the group. In the oral presentation, recommend how the group can improve its communications with the specific text you propose. Use chapter 6 on oral communication to help you prepare your presentation, and develop a full and formal design plan (using the design plan on page 83 as a model).

8　At your oral presentation, ask for feedback to help you strengthen your proposal. Unless you have interviewed and worked with the audience for the communications you recommend, the group's director or other workers are in the best position to help you refine how to address that audience.

9　If the group approves what you recommend, produce and test the communications you have designed.

Section 2 focused on research of a certain kind: *How do you learn what others think on certain issues and about how and why people differ on issues so that you might explore possible positions and perspectives for yourself?*

Section 2 also provided specific background for working with different modes and media. It should help you understand (for example) why and when to give a speech instead of write a paper. Section 2 should also help you understand how to compose that speech or that paper.

Section 3 supports you in a different kind of research. *What can you learn—about issues and the world but also about what you can do in your own composing—by closely reading others' texts rhetorically?*

We're supposed to be producing communication, so why are we analyzing others' arguments?

How easy it would be to produce communications if we could just say or make whatever we felt like saying or making—if, in other words, we didn't have to think about audiences. But communication is precisely about audiences—and because communication is about audiences, we have a lot to learn from others' communications.

Let us explain.

First, why is communication about audiences?

Communication is about audiences because mind meld does not exist.

If you could put your thoughts directly into the minds of others—and, along with those thoughts, put the experiences and education that give your thoughts their particular weight and reasons—there would be no need to shape your thoughts for others. There would be no need for rhetoric.

But because we do not ever have the same experiences, education, or expectations—because we do not and cannot live inside each other's heads and bodies—we have to figure out how to shape what we say or make for others. You undoubtedly do such shaping already, often unconsciously, when you address yourself differently to your parents, your friends, your siblings, your teachers, or your employers.

For any communication situation, then, as we have been discussing in all the earlier chapters of this book, you need to consider how to shape your communications for those you are addressing.

Second, what can you learn from analyzing others' arguments?

You speak differently to your parents, friends, teachers, and employers because you've learned—explicitly or not—conventions for speaking with different audiences. Similarly, different kinds of texts have conventions, too. You know to start a letter with "Dear ..." and to put your name on assignments.

In the following chapters are examples of many kinds of texts: posters, documentary photographs, editorials and opinion pieces, essays, and serious and not-so-serious comics. The purpose of these examples is twofold.

First, we use these examples to point out conventions for media and communication contexts. The examples can be a kind of checklist for you to which you can refer as you produce your own work. As you become observant about such conventions, you strengthen your abilities to make communications that meet audience expectations. By becoming attentive to conventions, you also become attentive to when and how you can break them so as to be more interesting or engaging and, ultimately, more persuasive.

Second, we use these examples to demonstrate rhetorical approaches for analyzing texts so that you will have more support for doing rhetorical production of texts.

ANALYSIS, RHETORIC, AND CRITICAL THINKING

What is analysis?

"Analysis" means "taking apart." "Analysis" is to communication what disassembling is to bicycles or car engines. If your bicycle or car is broken—or if you want to figure out how it works—you take it apart to look at the parts and to see how they are shaped and how they connect into a whole. It helps to remember that there are pieces within pieces—that some of the pieces of a bicycle or car form subgroups with special functions of their own (a braking mechanism, for example). The same is true for communication: Speeches, essays, and posters all have their own pieces within pieces.

How to carry out rhetorical analysis

In the next chapter—chapter 9—we offer steps for doing rhetorical analysis of texts of all different kinds. To do rhetorical analysis, you consider how texts work in terms of the audience and context envisioned by the text's creators (which is, in essence, a way to use the rhetorical composing process of the earlier chapters of this book backward)—and such consideration gives you a systematic and organized way to observe communication conventions, strategies, arrangements, and effects.

As we've written on the opposite page, by observing how others texts work, you yourself gain abilities and ideas for your own work.

Producing and analyzing texts is a circular process: As you yourself produce texts, working out how to relate audience and context to purpose through your strategies and arrangements, others' texts should become more interesting to you because of how they have been produced to achieve their purposes. You'll find yourself wanting to adapt others' strategies and arrangements to your own ends—and you'll find yourself better understanding how documents made by others are trying to shape your responses.

Analysis is critical thinking

Because rhetorical analysis involves naming the choices you see a text's composer having made and then examining the relations among the choices in light of the text's purpose, audience, and context, you are thinking critically when you do this work. And when you do this work, you are also thinking about the text as something whose pieces could have been otherwise; this too involves thinking critically.

When you treat your own initial sense of a text's purpose as a hypothesis, as an idea that might require modification (in response to other evidence from the text), you treat your own thinking critically, as something that could be wrong or only partially right. To risk being wrong and being willing to admit it is (a part of) critical thinking—as is revising your thinking to better account for your evidence.

☛ On the next pages are explanations of why we chose the kinds of examples we did for the following chapters; there are also descriptions of what we hope you will learn from each of the chapters.

309

ABOUT THE EXAMPLES IN THIS SECTION

Before we get into particular examples of different media used for communication and before we talk about how you can analyze the examples, here is a description of the kinds of media we are presenting to you and why we've chosen them.

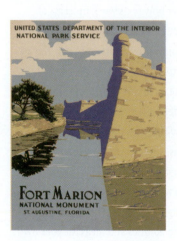

POSTERS

Because posters are single pages, they are straightforward places to begin talking about the logos of visual composition. We show you posters from different times and places so that you can see how both time and place—history and culture—affect audiences' expectations about visual composition.

DOCUMENTARY PHOTOGRAPHY

Rather than relying on a quick visual hit such as posters, documentary photography—multiple photographs building arguments—relies on time (and usually somewhat more complex compositions) to make arguments. This medium builds directly out of posters but expands the possibilities of strategies for visual argumentation.

EDITORIAL & OPINION PIECES

The writing of editorial and opinion pieces (whether online or in print) is public writing that strives to change public opinion. The purpose of changing public opinion means that this medium usually involves a more explicit statement of arguments than the previous examples—as well as an emphasis on ethos and pathos for supporting opinion— from which you can learn how to approach these strategies in your own writing.

ESSAYS

Essays are the most "writerly" of the examples in this section. Like documentary photography, essays build effects upon effects over time, and like editorials and opinion pieces, essays bring the author's ethos into focus. With the rise of new printing and on-line technologies, writers are experimenting with essays, and so we can raise questions of how and why one would "play" with existing conventions.

COMICS

With this medium, we hope you'll see some of the argumentative potentials that are opening up (primarily because of changes in technologies of publication and distribution) for composers who are competent in both visual and verbal strategies.

THINKING THROUGH PRODUCTION

■ **Learning to see conventions that shape communication**

Choose a kind of text from the list in the right-hand column of this page or come up with another, and then look at no fewer than 10 examples of that kind of text. Generate a list of characteristics people expect to be in a text that they can recognize as fitting that type of text—and get as detailed as possible. If you are looking at texts that involve writing, for example, look at tone of voice, whether the composer uses first or third person to write, logical structures of arrangement, typefaces, color, choice and placement of photograph or illustration, and so on; use the descriptions of media, strategies, and arrangements in the earlier sections of this book to help you get as detailed as you can.

After you've generated your list of defining characteristics for the kind of text you've chosen, do one or all of the following:

1 Print your list in a format easy for someone else to read but in which the kind of text you've analyzed is nowhere given. Give your list to someone else, and have the person try to guess the kind of text from your list.

2 Use your list to produce your own example. For some kinds of texts, you'll have to be creative: You don't, for example, have a budget for making a Hollywood horror film—but you can write a plotline and storyboards (do a Google search for "storyboard" to see examples).

3 Make a new chapter for this book, following the model of the other chapters in Section 3, to teach others how effectively to analyze and compose the kind of text you've analyzed.

possible kinds of texts

Hollywood horror film

office memo for a large company

hip-hop track

popular science magazine article

country western song

history thesis (check your campus library for copies of theses written in different departments)

romance novel

coffee-table documentary photography book

advertisement for an SUV

instruction for using small electronic devices

store sign

e-mail or instant messaging

sympathy card

front page newspaper article about foreign events

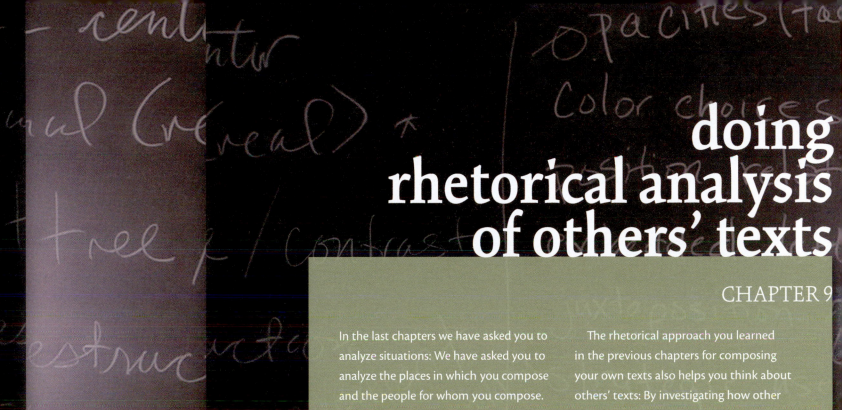

doing
rhetorical analysis
of others' texts

In the last chapters we have asked you to analyze situations: We have asked you to analyze the places in which you compose and the people for whom you compose.

In this chapter, we ask you to analyze others' texts. What can you learn from other texts to help you produce your own?

In this chapter you will turn from considering *your* audiences, purposes, and contexts to thinking about how other composers built texts to respond to *their* audiences, purposes, and contexts.

The rhetorical approach you learned in the previous chapters for composing your own texts also helps you think about others' texts: By investigating how other composers work with audiences, purposes, and contexts to choose strategies, media, and arrangements, you expand what you can use in your own work.

ANALYZING OTHERS' TEXTS
Reading like a writer, watching like a filmmaker, looking like a graphic designer…

> "… the essence of cinema is editing. It's the combination of what can be extraordinary images, images of people during emotional moments, or just images in a general sense, but put together in a kind of alchemy. A number of images put together a certain way become something quite above and beyond what any of them are individually."
>
> *Francis Ford Coppola*

> "I am always chilled and astonished by the would-be writers who ask me for advice and admit, quite blithely, that they "don't have time to read." This is like a guy starting up Mount Everest saying that he didn't have time to buy any rope or pitons."
>
> *Stephen King*

Writers read for the pleasures of story or argument; they also read for what they can learn from other writers. They attend to others' writing to learn what can happen when sentences have particular rhythms, evidence is presented as story not fact, or an essay starts with what startles.

Similarly, filmmakers watch others' films to lose themselves in pleasure but also to learn new possibilities for how to relate close-ups to long shots or a soundtrack to a character's walk down the street.

Graphic designers study others' page and screen layouts to see what typefaces are currently popular or to learn new strategies for using photographs or staples.

Part of the work of becoming a composer, then, is to learn to look at other compositions so you can learn from them. This is why analysis—and having a systematic approach to how you analyze—matters for composing. If you tease apart the components of another text and then contemplate the relations among the components, you will learn:

1 **New possible components you can use in your own texts.** You can learn new words, new possibilities for sentence structures, new approaches to color or sound or….

2 **New possible relations you can build among the components of a text.** As Francis Ford Coppola said in the interview we quote to the left, cinema depends on editing: Which bits of film are put next to which others, and what are the transitions between those bits? Writing and speaking and composing visual texts work in the same way: The relations you build among the components of a text build the overall effect. How should your introduction work to build emotion or evidence, for example, and what tone should the next paragraph take, and how do you build a connection between those two paragraphs?

By analyzing the texts of others, you learn how other people have composed such effects, and you learn how you can too.

A COMPARISON: ANALYZING COMMUNICATION SITUATIONS AND ANALYZING OTHERS' TEXTS

Analyzing a communication situation

When you are *analyzing to compose*, you figure out all the pieces of purpose, context, audience, strategies, arrangement, and medium so that you can put them together into one text.

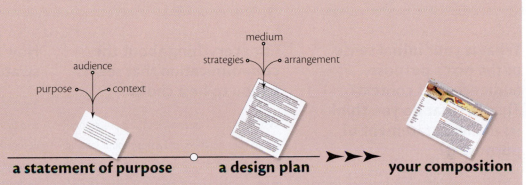

Analyzing someone else's text

When you are *analyzing to learn*, you reverse the steps in the chart above: You start with a complete text, figure out its strategies (which include arrangement and medium), and then determine what sort of audience, context, and purpose are implied by the strategies.

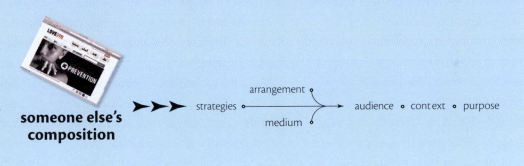

STEPS FOR RHETORICAL ANALYSIS

1

What is your initial sense of the text's purpose, audience, and context? That is, what do you think its maker's statement of purpose is?

After you read a letter or essay, watch a movie, or stand before a sculpture, you usually have some sense—even if it's a hesitant, initial sense—of what the person who composed the piece wanted you to feel or think in response. Put this "sensation" of understanding into words. Say aloud or write down what you think the main point is or the main experience you are supposed to have. *This statement is a hypothesis*, and your analysis from here on out is about testing this hypothesis. (If you do not have a clue what the thing you are reading or viewing is about, then proceed to step 2—start identifying the strategies at work in what you analyze.)

The steps that follow are about testing and revising your initial sense of the purpose, audience, and context for the object you analyze.

2

List everything about the communication that seems to you to be a choice.

When you read an essay, look at a poster, or listen to your neighbor tell a story about joining the army, certain aspects will stand out: a funky tone of voice, a scary scene in the background, some strange words, or an example that makes you blink. Your attention might be drawn to a joke, a lovely photograph of snow, or a jarring color or word. Note what surprises you, irritates you, doesn't seem clear—anything that stands out. Gather these observations in your mind or on paper.

If something stands out, it probably is an important choice the author made and so is a good place to start your analysis. Ask why the author chose what catches your attention.

Start with what stands out, and then list—and try to make a long list—every strategy you can identify, every aspect of the communication that you can identify as a choice the composer would have had to make.

3

How are the choices used strategically?

The idea behind analyzing any communication is to figure out how it works: How do the pieces fit together and work with each other to affect a reader or viewer in a particular way? To begin analysis, simply ask yourself what effect each choice you identified (in step 2) might have on someone.

Also ask how the choices fit together. If the background photo to an advertisement is of a poor U.S. inner-city neighborhood, how does the mood it creates work with the other pieces of the ad? And how does that mood fit with your initial hypothesis?

As you begin to explain why the pieces are there and how they fit together, you will find yourself making further observations, which will lead to further explanations about what effect these choices have and how they fit—or don't—the overall picture. Don't let this bother you. If you feel you are getting lost in the details, keep going back to what you originally sensed and hold on to what seems most obvious. Then venture out again.

4

Test your observations: Are there any anomalies?

While looking closely at the pieces of the text you are analyzing and asking how they fit together, you may run into pieces that do not seem to fit with your initial sense of what the author is trying to do. Maybe there's a title that does not fit the story, maybe there's an example that goes on for too long, maybe there's a large empty space in the middle, or maybe there's an unexpected interruption in the flow of the story. Looking closely at these pieces—these anomalies—can show you where your initial hypothesis about an author's statement of purpose falls short and where you might look for a more complete, more accurate hypothesis.

If your other observations have not already forced you to do this, these observations about anomalies should help you revise your earlier statement about the purpose, audience, and context of the piece—that is, they help you move to the next step.

5

Revise your original statement about the text you are analyzing.

Although steps 2 and 3 ask you to have this in mind, revisit with full attention now your initial sense of the purpose, audience, and context of the piece. How have your focused attentions to the pieces of the text—naming them; tying their use to purpose, context, and audience; checking for anomalies—changed your sense of what the text is trying to do, for whom, and when and where?

Restate—out loud or on paper—your sense of the text's audience, purpose, and context; include in your restatement evidence from the text in the form of the choices you noted.

☞ See these steps applied on the next several pages.

examples of rhetorical analysis in this book

We offer you samples of student writing that rhetorically analyzes:

- a website, page 323
- movie posters, page 324
- a photographic essay, page 358
- editorials, p. 384 and page 390
- two opinion pieces, page 398
- an essay, page 417

APPLYING THE STEPS TO A WEBPAGE

On this and the facing page we show how one student applies the steps for rhetorical analysis from pages 316–317: The student talks in response to each step's question while looking at the Love146 webpage shown on the right.

Love146 is a nonprofit organization whose purpose (as explained under its logo on the top left of the webpage) is to "end child sex slavery and exploitation."

On the Love146 website, the group explains the origin of its name and offers lots of information—through a blog, through a digital booklet, through videos, through FAQ (Frequently Asked Questions) pages—about child sex slavery and exploitation, primarily in southeast Asia but also in the United States.

The website also asks viewers to participate in the work of the group: People can volunteer to help in local offices or can join a "Love146 Task Force," which is a group that meets monthly to educate themselves about human trafficking, raise awareness and become activists about this issue in their communities, introduce others to the work of Love146, and help raise money for the organization. The information on the website makes it clear that people cannot volunteer to help with the work the group does in southeast Asia because of the particular long-term needs of the young people with whom the group works.

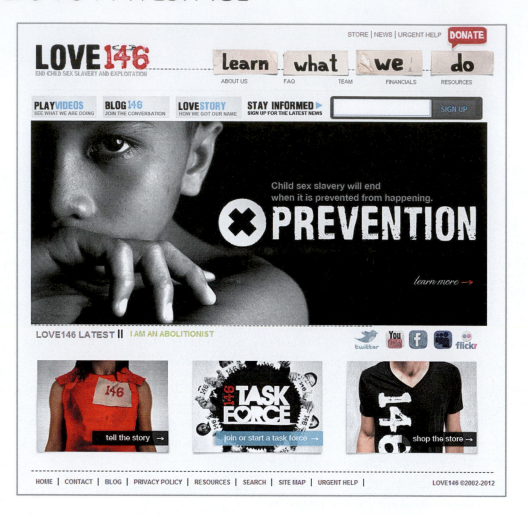

1 What is your initial sense of the the piece's purpose, audience, and context?

"It's a nonprofit organization that wants to end child sex slavery and exploitation. It wants to raise money to do this work. So the purpose is to get people to donate money. The audience is people who can read English. The context is the web."

2 **List everything about the communication that seems to you to be a choice.**

Here are choices I see:

First, there's the organization name, at top left, kind of big.

Second, there's a series of what look like clickable links at top right. They're little slips of messy paper, and the words on them are handwritten in bold black lettering.

Third, there's a big photograph of a child looking straight at us close up. He's serious.

Then there's the word "PREVENTION," really big. It's been made white on a black background and is the biggest thing on the page. It's in a kind of messy typeface.

Fifth, there are links to learn about the "latest" and about how "I am an abolitionist"—and links to different social networking sites.

Then there are pictures (I assume they're links) to shop, "join or start a task force," and to "tell the story." The pictures are of young people.

At the bottom of the page is a list of links to more detailed information about the organization.

The designers have made all the elements of the page line up with each other, too, I realize when I look at the whole page.

☛ See this analysis presented more formally on page 323.

3 **How are the choices used strategically?**

Hmmm. When I look at all those strategies together, what stands out for me is that there's a fair amount of quick and big emotion—in the hand drawn or messy typefaces and the little slips of paper—but at the same time everything is organized.

The messy and hand drawn stuff makes me think the designers want to reach young people by making the organization look hip. (All the links to the social networking sites kind of say that, too.) It's as though the organization wants to look youthful and energetic, too, so you'll know it's going to get the work done. (And if you can't really volunteer with it, this seems really important.)

I guess if I were going to give money to an organization I would want to know that it's reliable and on top of things. So you need the page to look solid and organized.

And I'm looking at that boy looking at us. That sure seems meant to make the webpage seem personal and compelling, like it's making direct contact with me through those eyes.

So, now I guess I'd say this page is aimed at young people who need to be sucked in to caring about this project and who want to trust that their money will be well spent by dedicated folks.

4 **Are there any anomalies?**

I don't think so. I think I can explain every choice in terms of the audience and purpose I just described—even that sort of stodgy line of links at the very bottom that looks like the line of links at the bottom of every corporate webpage. The designers are trying to make this look professional and reliable at the same time they're trying draw us in emotionally.

5 **Revise your original statement about the text you are analyzing.**

Well, the webpage's broadest purpose I'd still say is to get people to donate money. But after thinking about the context of how people can't really volunteer and how then the group needs to build other emotional connections with people to help them want to give, I'd say that the purpose also includes getting people to *feel* committed: The page looks like it's coming out at you with all those bold elements, there's that large face looking right at you, and there are all the hand drawn and messy elements. And the organization makes itself look youthful and energetic, so you get a sense it's going to go out there and get stuff done.

People still need to feel that they are contributing to a reputable organization, though, so there are choices that make the site look stable and dependable underneath the emotion.

APPLYING THE STEPS TO A DIFFERENT WEBPAGE

On these two pages we show how one student applies the steps for rhetorical analysis from pages 316–317: The student talks in response to each step's question while looking at the Habitat for Humanity webpage shown on the right.

According to its website, Habitat for Humanity is a "nonprofit, ecumenical Christian housing ministry" whose work involves "those in need of adequate shelter working side by side with volunteers to build simple, decent houses."

Also on the Habitat for Humanity website, the group explains its history, tells about its founders, and offers lots of information—through a blog, through videos, through FAQ (Frequently Asked Questions) pages—about how, why, and where the organization builds houses.

The website also asks viewers to participate in the work of the group. People can join local affiliates of Habitat and help with building houses, or they can travel within the United States or internationally to help with both short-term and long-term projects. People can donate building materials and, of course, money.

1 What is your initial sense of the the piece's purpose, audience, and context?

"It's a nonprofit organization that wants to help people in need have good housing. It wants to raise money to do this work. So the purpose is to get people to donate money. The audience is people who can read English. The context is the web."

2 List everything about the communication that seems to you to be a choice.

Here are choices I see:

First, there's the organization name, at top left, with nothing else around it so that we are not distracted from seeing it.

Second, there's a series of what look like clickable links at top right. They're organized in a straight line on a dark blue background.

Third, there's a big photograph of someone working with "Partnership News" over it. "Partnership News" is the biggest thing on the page, so it seems like it wants us to see that first, almost.

Then to the right of that are some really simple links on a beige background. These links take us to more information, or to help with the work of the organization—or to give.

Fifth, there are some small photographs. I assume you could click them and the big photograph would change, to show other things about the organization.

Then there are some ways to search to find your local organization or sign up for a newsletter.

At the bottom of the page are links for information about the organizations.

The page looks pretty simple and plain, overall. Everything is organized and straightforward.

3 How are the choices used strategically?

There's nothing that stands out about this webpage. It all looks organized and quiet. The colors are muted. Nothing calls out to me. I look at this page and it looks like a quiet, confident person.

The webpage doesn't appear to be calling out to anyone in particular. It's as though the organization expects you to know about it: It doesn't have to grab you in any way to say "Here's what we do!" or "Here's who we are!"

The page has all the links I think you need in order to understand that this organization knows what it's doing. It all looks official and calm, and it's sort of like "We are busy doing our work; here's how to contact us."

It's got the links to social networks all in a neat, boxed-in row. It's got a picture of North America to let you know where it operates. You can get information immediately about your local organization. It's as though the organization expects you to come here knowing about it and knowing that you want to participate in some way, and it gives you options.

The whole organization comes off as thoughtful, quiet, and organized, just getting business done, and if you want to join it, you can.

4 Are there any anomalies?

I don't think so. I think I can explain every choice in terms of how the organization wants the audience to think about it as a serious, down-to-earth, getting-things-done kind of place that you can join if you want.

5 Revise your original statement about the text you are analyzing.

I'm not so sure I'd say anymore that the main purpose of the webpage is just to get people to donate money. That's still important, but because of all the choices the designers made, I'd say that educating audiences and encouraging them to learn more are just as important. The design of the page is quiet and so kind of gentle: I feel like I can explore it on my own time. I feel comfortable clicking and looking around and so learning about the organization. (Even the person in the photograph is looking away from me and toward the work that needs to be done—as though that's what's most important.)

So the page design is about making the organization look solid and at ease, completely dependable and nonflashy, and so comfortable and inviting, so that I will trust it and feel comfortable getting to know it better—which means that I might be more likely to work with it, not just donate.

WRITING A RHETORICAL ANALYSIS

You may be asked to turn an informal discussion that involves rhetorical analysis into formal writing. Here are approaches for writing about a single text and for writing about several texts. (Writing about several texts can support you in carrying out cultural analysis).

ANALYSIS OF ONE TEXT

You know well that, when you carry out a class assignment, the writing needs to be more formal than notes and jottings. Teachers generally want to see writing that appears organized and has a purpose. The purpose of a summary rhetorical analysis is not simply to give a description of a reading or an advertisement or a poster; a summary rhetorical analysis instead condenses what you see to be the purpose, context, and audience for the piece and describes the major strategies you believe demonstrate that the piece's composer was working toward the purpose, context, and audience you describe. You can arrange such a summary by first stating what you see to be the purpose, audience, and context of a text and then describing what you see to be the major strategies and how they support your understanding of purpose, context, and audience.

☛ An example of such writing is on the facing page.

ANALYSIS OF MULTIPLE TEXTS

Rhetorically analyzing individual texts (as we have discussed in the left column) helps you learn about how composers make choices about single texts and about how they think about audiences; you also learn about yourself as an audience and how you respond to various strategies.

But no individual piece of communication functions on its own: As you've already experienced and will read about in other chapters of this book, texts make sense to us because they work in contexts. An author or designer can make strategic choices because our time and place provide us ranges of choices that different audiences understand. Rappers, for example, choose rhythms that identify their songs as hip-hop to their audiences, and they write about subjects that others understand to be appropriate for their music. (Have you ever heard a rap about vacuuming or writing a rhetorical analysis?)

Because of our social and cultural (not to mention political, economic, religious, and other) contexts, texts affect us as they do because we have the experiences we do. Because we experience all the repeated parts of texts (such as the repeated rhythms and topics of hip-hop), texts can teach us, in very quiet ways, what to expect about the larger world and ourselves. We are the people we are because of the things we do over and over every day. How we tend to respond to and treat others and the actions we think are appropriate or moral shape us into who we are—and we learn much of this through watching and experiencing what our families and friends do day in and day out and through what we see in all the media that surround us.

If you analyze a range of similar texts, or a number of texts by one author or designer, you can often see repetitions of strategies—and these repetitions can suggest patterns of thought or behavior that audiences can pick up.

☛ On pages 324–329 is an example of a rhetorical analysis of several similar texts that then makes a larger argument about cultural conditions.

READING AND RESPONDING RHETORICALLY
A written analysis of one text, a website

Chantel Shepherd writes about the website whose first page is on page 318.

Chantel Shepherd

September 22, 2012

Encouraging Commitment with Website Design

Imagine you are designing the website for a fairly new non-profit organization, one dedicated to ending child sex slavery and exploitation, with a focus in southeast Asia. Imagine also that people in the U.S. can't volunteer to help with the work of your organization, not only because the work takes place in Asia but also because helping children who have been rescued from brothels requires special training and years of commitment to stay with the same children. How do you design a website to encourage people to care enough to support this organization? It seems to me that this context suggests that at least part of the purpose of the website would be to encourage the audience to become as emotionally committed as possible and to identify with and trust the work of the organization as much as possible.

The website for this organization—Love146—employs many strategies to encourage emotional commitment. On the first webpage we encounter for Love146 (see page 318), there is a central photograph of a young man looking directly at us; he is also photographed close, as though we were only inches from him. The typefaces used for headers and links are big and bold (and some even look handwritten), as though the page is moving toward us, speaking loudly, urgently grabbing our attention. When you click one of the first links on the page—the one labeled "LEARN"—you go to a digital book, with the same bold and energetic typefaces and rich colors: The book has photographs of and drawings by young children who have been in slavery, tells their stories, and offers statistics about child sex slavery, all presented in small snippets so one can read quickly, sense the urgency of the situation, and get sucked in to what is happening. There are also videos in which survivors tell their stories.

When you click the link to learn about the organization and its staff, you see a page of photographs of each staff member, smiling and holding a small chalkboard with "Love" written in the person's handwriting. The staff look at you and smile, making it easy for you to identify with them and catch their energy. There are also links to see the organization's financial information and program impact reports, so you can see easily how they are spending the money someone gives them and exactly what they are doing with it. How can one not trust an organization that seems so personable, energetic, and honest?

I hope I have argued that, in the contexts of their work, it makes sense for Love146 to have a website that focuses on engaging us emotionally and building identification and trust.

READING AND RESPONDING RHETORICALLY

For his rhetoric class, Bill Lincoln wrote the rhetorical analysis to the right. His analysis, about movie posters, makes an argument that the posters help shape cultural patterns.

Bill Lincoln

Lincoln 1

Professor Lynch

English 102

May 15, 2012

Attack of the Monster Movie Poster:

How to Be a Man or a Woman in the 1950s

Why do four horror-movie posters from the 1950s all focus on a scene of attack involving women? Through a rhetorical analysis of the posters, I argue that the posters place their viewers in positions where they are asked to imagine themselves taking action to save a woman . . . or to do something about a woman causing trouble. The posters ask viewers to become imaginatively involved with the attack scene, which seems like a good strategy for getting people interested in seeing the movies. It also seems to me, however, that getting people involved is also a kind of teaching: It is a way of teaching men and women about their proper roles.

The four posters I analyze were made for these movies:

- Creature from the Black Lagoon (1954)
- Attack of the Crab Monsters (1957)
- Attack of the 50 Ft. Woman (1958)
- The Wasp Woman (1959)

These movies were made after World War II and the Korean War. The United States was building in prosperity, and people had time to go to the movies. But people were also uneasy about the world situation: The Cold War was beginning, and there were fears of potential nuclear war. There have always been monsters in the stories people tell each other, but in the fifties such stories took on particular urgency because of fears about mutations caused by radiation—mutations that would turn people into fish or insects, or that would make people or animals grow to ungraspable size.

I will analyze each of the posters individually—in the order they were produced—to support my arguments.

About each of the movies

The Creature from the Black Lagoon poster has the movie title at the top, large, so that we see it first. What we see next—centered and large—is the creature carrying, underwater, a woman in a skintight swimsuit. Although the woman isn't struggling with the creature, her expression shows that she isn't happy about being dragged down below the surface of the water, which is made darker (and so scarier) toward the poster's bottom. At the top left of the poster are two divers—drawn to look like they are farther away—coming toward the creature and the woman. The divers have a knife and a gun, so we can perhaps assume that they are coming to save the woman. The bottom of the poster shows three scenes from the movie that set up the main scene of the poster: There is a boat sitting calmly in tropical waters, then a scene of a male diver being attacked by the creature, then a scene of the woman clutching a man with a gun. We get the sense that the people have come to this place, been attacked, have tried to protect themselves—and now the woman has been carried off.

Because the main scene of the poster—the woman being carried off—spills off the edges of the poster, the poster makes it look as though we, the audience, are there in the water with the creature. The creature comes toward us with the woman, and because we are closer than the divers at top left, we are in a better position to act. The design of the poster shapes the audience then as another potential rescuer, someone who has come upon this scene and can—probably should—do battle with the monster to save the woman.

This paper shows one way to insert photographs or illustrations into a paper for a class: If you can insert the illustration so that it is close to the writing that discusses it, and if it will be obvious to readers which photograph or illustration is being discussed, then you do not need to label the illustrations. In the example to the left, because the movie posters contain the movie titles, it will be easy for readers to link the writing with the poster.

CHAPTER 9: Rhetorical analysis

325

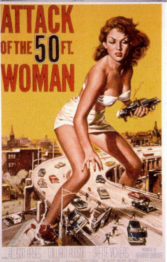

The poster for *Attack of the Crab Monsters* has a similar visual composition to the poster for *Creature from the Black Lagoon*. The title is at the top and directly underneath is another unhappy, unstruggling woman (in another skimpy bathing suit) being carried off by an unnatural being; this poster also shows potential rescuers at top left. Like the poster for *Creature from the Black Lagoon*, this poster is mostly in dark colors, with the title and the woman's flesh lighter. Also as in the poster for *Creature from the Black Lagoon*, the visual composition of this poster makes the scene of the attack spill off the page to make us imagine we are in the scene. The woman is again placed between us and the monster, with the potential rescuers far away: again, the visual composition of the poster designs the audience into the poster, so that we feel we are there, about to do battle.

Attack of the 50 Ft. Woman turns the tables on the previous two posters. It does not show us an apparently helpless woman being carried away by a monster; instead, she is the monster. Although this woman is in a skimpy bathing suit as the others, she is huge and threatening: She straddles a freeway, posed as though caught in the middle of picking up and destroying cars, with a truck that has crashed into her leg smoldering at the lower left—but she apparently isn't hurt.

She isn't looking at us; instead, her heavily made up eyes are turned slightly to the side, with lowered lids, as though she's thinking about what to do next; her right arm is poised to pick up another vehicle, her sharply pointed and painted nails like the talons of a huge predator bird. There is a potential rescuer shown in this poster as in the others, but this time the rescuer is a tiny policeman at the lower left of the poster, aiming his gun: Given his proportions to the woman, he looks like a feeble, powerless ant.

But we, the audience, are not placed to be feeble in this poster. The poster isn't designed to make us look up at the woman as though she were towering above us, as though we were as tiny as the people in the poster. The poster is instead designed so that we are facing the woman: When we see the poster, it is as though our eyes are at almost the same level as her face, so that we must be almost as big as her. As with the other posters, once again the scene fills the whole space of the poster and spills off the page, so it is as though the whole scene extends around us. Here, then, we are placed to be in the scene, the same

size as the woman: Once again the audience is visually composed as rescuers—but this time, not rescuers of the woman but rescuers of all the people she is menacing. The designs of this poster again place us to do battle with the monster—it's just a very different kind of monster this time.

The Wasp Woman also uses a different kind of monster. A wasp much bigger than a human, but with a woman's face, she menaces a man over a pile of bones and skulls. In the poster for this movie, the title of the movie is again at top, along with "A beautiful woman by day—A lusting queen by night." The

Notice that the inserted reproductions of the movie posters are aligned with the edges of the text, so that they fit well within the body of the paper.

wasp's wings are under the title, and lead our eyes down into the huge body. The woman's face has an expression like that of the 50 Ft. Woman: Her eyes are heavily made up, but almost closed, as though she is contemplating what to do next with the man in her grip. And once again, the visual composition of the poster places us as though we were in the scene. This time, however, there is no potential rescuer shown in the poster: Only the audience is in any position to do battle with the consuming wasp.

Conclusion

The visual compositions of the posters all position the audience as potential rescuers. The designers of the posters probably did this so that we would find ourselves imagining ourselves in the movie, being the hero who saves the day: This gets us emotionally involved with the movie before we even see it—and so probably heightens our desire to see the movie, to be able to feel ourselves even more as heroes.

But the heroes—the rescuers—in these movie posters are always shown as men. The audience for these posters—and so for these movies—is therefore asked to imagine themselves as men, even if they are women. If a woman looking at these posters instead tries to identify with the women shown, look at the positions she is allowed to take up: She can either be the passive victim who is carried away by the monster and who must await others to save her, or she can be the destructive monster who must be destroyed.

I don't think horror movies are supposed to be subtle or complex: They are meant to scare us, perhaps to let us experience our fears in the safe environment of the movies so that we can go to our non-movie lives feeling that our fears can be faced. But, unfortunately, what my analysis of these movie posters shows is that the ways men and women are asked to think about themselves aren't subtle and complex, either. Men are asked to think of themselves as heroes and protectors who will do battle with horrors; women get to be passive and weak—but, if

You may have noticed that this paper is written in the first person, with the author often using "I." In the past many believed that academic writing should be written as though the ideas in the writing were universal, which argued for not using "I." In the last decades, however, many academics (even in the sciences) have recognized that this belief in universality can exclude people who are not in powerful enough positions to assert their authority and ideas as though they were universal; it is now believed by many that a writer using "I" and explaining why the writer holds particular values, beliefs, and opinions helps readers better understand the limitations and hence the appropriate usefulness of the writing.

Because these positions about using "I" are up for disagreement, there are no hard-and-fast rules about using "I." If an assignment does not make clear whether you can use "I" in writing, be sure to check with the teacher about the policies for your class.

they have any power, it is seen as horrible. Men are asked to look at women as needing protection—but if they don't need protection because they are strong, then they are to be destroyed.

These posters are certainly not the only ways that men and women were taught about what their proper behaviors were to be in the United States in the 1950s. But imagine how seeing these posters week after week (there are hundreds more like them!) would contribute to how a teenage boy, for example, would think about himself and about women.

I hope I've shown, through a rhetorical analysis of how these posters visually shape their audiences, how the posters shape the ways men and women were to think about how they were to behave in the world of the 1950s.

Works Cited

Attack of the 50 Foot Woman. Movie poster. Woolner Brothers Pictures Inc. 1958. Print.

Attack of the Crab Monsters. Movie poster. Los Altos Productions. 1957. Print.

Creature from the Black Lagoon. Movie poster. Universal International Pictures. 1954. Print.

Wasp Woman. Movie poster. Film Group Feature. 1959. Print.

For a formal paper in MLA style, the Works Cited listings would be on their own page; we have put them here to save paper. Check with your teacher about policies for your class.

HOW CHAPTERS 10–14 HELP YOU WITH RHETORICAL ANALYSIS

THE STEPS FOR RHETORICAL ANALYSIS

1

What is your initial sense of the text's purpose, audience, and context? That is, what do you think its maker's statement of purpose is?

2

List everything about the communication that seems to you to be a choice.

3

How are the choices used strategically?

4

Test your observations: Are there any anomalies?

5

Revise your original statement about the text you are analyzing.

In chapters 10 through 14, we focus on what is unique about each chapter's texts: We help you see the range of choices a composer can make with that kind of text and how those choices work strategically within a text.

Chapters 10 through 14, then, help you in particular with steps 2 and 3 of all the steps we originally discussed on pages 316–317.

THINKING THROUGH PRODUCTION

■ How do the steps for rhetorical analysis we offer in this chapter set you up to read differently than your usual approaches? Write an informal, short (one- to two-page) paper in which you compare how you tend to read with the approach to reading we have just presented.

The following questions might help you reflect on these differing ways of reading:

- What pleasures do you take from reading? How do different approaches to reading support those pleasures, offer different kinds of pleasure, or deny pleasure?

- To what uses do you put your reading? Do you use reading to help you understand relationships with other people or how the world works? Do you use reading to gain a critical perspective on events or institutions? Do you read to help you fall asleep at night? How might a rhetorical approach support these uses or offer different uses to you?

- What do you see to be the benefits and limitations of these different kinds of readings? What does each of these different kinds of readings help you do in the world?

■ In this chapter we apply a rhetorical approach to websites and posters, but—as chapters 10–14 demonstrate—you can apply a rhetorical approach to any communication. Test this out by analyzing a short text from another medium: your favorite song, a short poem, a TV commercial, a short video on YouTube, an assignment for a class, a flyer for an upcoming event, or . . . .

Apply the rhetorical analysis steps to the text and write your analysis as a short paper.

At the end of the paper, reflect on your analysis—and on the process of doing analysis. The following questions might help you reflect:

- Why did you choose the text to analyze that you did?

- Do you think differently about the text than you did before? What has shifted in your thinking, and why?

- What do you think you missed in your analysis? Are there aspects of the text whose purposes you still can't explain? What would you need to do to better explain those aspects?

- What was smooth in your process of analysis and what was hard? What more do you wish you knew in order to do this more easily?

■ To practice using analysis to help your own composing processes, find and analyze a sample of a text you will have to produce for an assignment in another class. If you have a lab report coming due, find a sample of a successful lab report; if you have to write a research paper, find an exemplary research paper; if you have to produce a lesson plan, find a strong lesson plan.

Apply the analysis steps from this chapter to the text—and then, through writing a short report, consider what you can learn from the analysis to help you produce your own text:

- Which of the text composer's choices seemed to you to contribute most to its being a strong example?

- What did you see in the text that you hadn't expected? Why was it unexpected for you?

- What do you want to remember from what you observed about this text to help you with your own assignment?

Strategies we emphasize in chapter 10

In chapter 10 our rhetorical analysis grows out of the general observations we made about persuasion back in chapter 1 and from our observations about rhetorical analysis in chapter 9. We also draw on the discussions in chapter 7 about the rhetorical workings of visual texts.

That background helps us consider how posters use the following primary strategies:

- **How posters work because they draw on what we already know**

- **How posters work because they create visual hierarchies—paths for our eyes to follow**

- **How posters work because they address our bodies and emotions**

analyzing posters

CHAPTER 10

Throughout the 19th century and into the early 20th, the bare spaces of cities—the sides of buildings as well as specially built kiosks—were covered with posters advertising auction agencies, health remedies, women's wigs, or theatrical performances; the posters might also call people to political meetings or inform them about political decisions. Posters—large color printed sheets—appeared when they did in cities for several reasons: Printing technologies allowed for large color prints, for the first time enough people could read to justify the costs of such publications, and cities had sufficient population massed together that it made sense to publicize ideas, events, and products using posters.

Without public spaces—and without a public moving about in those spaces—posters make no sense. Posters were an early kind of mass communication: They were a way for someone who could afford the costs of printing and who wanted to reach a large audience to contact that audience. For the first time, audiences didn't hear news and information from others in one-to-one conversations or in large meetings. Instead, posters could address many people one at a time in public.

Because posters usually are used in public spaces where people are passing by quickly, they are usually designed to be scanned and read quickly. People who make posters consciously design them to get across one idea quickly and easily.

On the next pages, you'll learn something about how the visual elements of a poster are chosen and arranged to catch your attention and hold it long enough for you to understand the poster's purpose. You'll see how posters work both because they attend to how we experience the world through our bodies as well as because they draw on concepts and ideas we already understand because of where and when we live.

HOW POSTERS WORK: Drawing on what you know

People use public space differently now than they did in the 19th century, when color posters were first published. Now in the United States, you probably see posters most often if you live in a large city: Walls around construction sites are often plastered with posters for plays, concerts, or political events. On some college campuses, telephone poles and bulletin boards are covered in letter-size flyers advertising group meetings, band performances, and sorority rushes.

We'll start analyzing posters with the example to the right.

■ What visual aspects of this poster tell you that it is probably for a movie?

■ When do you think the movie publicized by this poster was made? Why do you guess the time period you do?

■ What kind of movie is being publicized here, a comedy, a horror film, or a sci-fi film or . . .? What visual aspects of the poster encourage you to make the judgment you do?

Look at how much you knew in order to understand what's going on with this poster.

List all you had to know—about the medium of posters, about the place of movies and moviegoing in the United States, about the kinds of pictures used in posters, about genres of movies, and so on—in order to understand what the designers of this poster were hoping to achieve rhetorically with the poster.

> ☞ In chapter 1, pages 28–29, we discuss the interpretive scheme we use here—understanding visual texts, first, through how they resonate with our experiences of moving in the world and, second, through the cultural knowledge we bring to them.

334

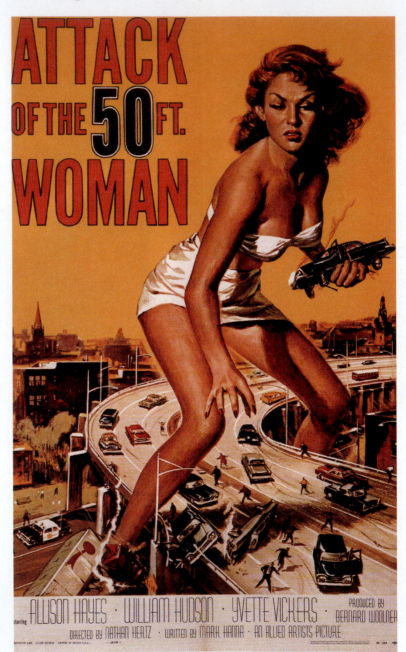

HOW POSTERS WORK: Principles of visual composition

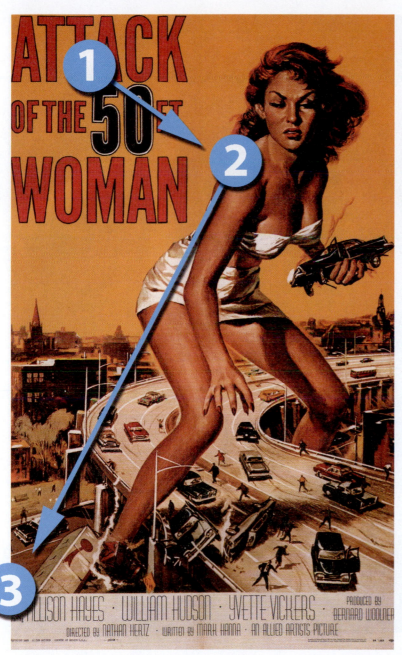

Like most posters of any kind, this movie poster does not have many elements: The poster has a title and then a representational image (a painting in this case, but you've probably also seen posters that use photographs), and then more text. Those are the only components of this poster, and so a viewer can scan the poster quickly and understand its purpose.

The poster's elements have been arranged logically to create a path through the elements that your eyes probably follow—a visual hierarchy (see pages 256–259) as the numbered elements to the left show:

1 The title is at the top left of the poster—at the spot we expect if we have learned to read in the top-to-bottom, left-to-right motions of English. The title is large relative to the other elements, and it is in a simple sans serif typeface.

2 The woman has been made much larger than the other elements (so much so that she would be much taller than 50 feet if she were real) and placed so that we see her second. Notice, however, that the colors of the poster do not contrast very much, so that the woman doesn't "pop" out of the poster as she would were she (for example) tinted blue. Notice too how the shape of the woman's body draws your eyes down the page: Chances are your eyes move from the title to her face and then down her right arm to her right leg—which leads your eyes down to the left bottom edge of the poster, where you see a car crash and the remaining typographic information.

3 Finally, at the very bottom of the poster, in an unobtrusively thin typeface, is the information about who is in the movie.

HOW POSTERS WORK: Drawing on what you know

At right is a poster for a movie you may have seen.

■ Why do you think the poster's designers chose green and black as the main colors? How would the poster be different if it were bright pink and white or violet and black?

■ Why might the designers have chosen to show the people turned with their backs to viewers and their bodies fading away at bottom—but with their faces turning toward us? What sense of space does this help create in the poster? What sort of emotions does this help create?

■ Why might the designers have decided to mix a photographic with a painterly style? Why might the poster not have as much to look at as the poster for *Attack of the 50 Ft. Woman*?

■ What do the poster designers expect audiences to know about the earlier *Matrix* movies?

■ What are all those slanting lines? How do they contribute to your understanding of the poster?

Again, look at how much you already knew in order to understand this poster: You know about how we use black and a certain shade of green in our culture and how we think about turned bodies and about illustrations instead of photographs.

The Matrix Revolutions poster is publicizing a movie that has some similarities to *Attack of the 50 Ft. Woman*: Both movies are about situations that (most of us believe) do not happen in real life. Does one poster look scarier to you than the other, or does one look sillier? How do the posters encourage you to think differently about the two movies?

HOW POSTERS WORK: Principles of visual composition

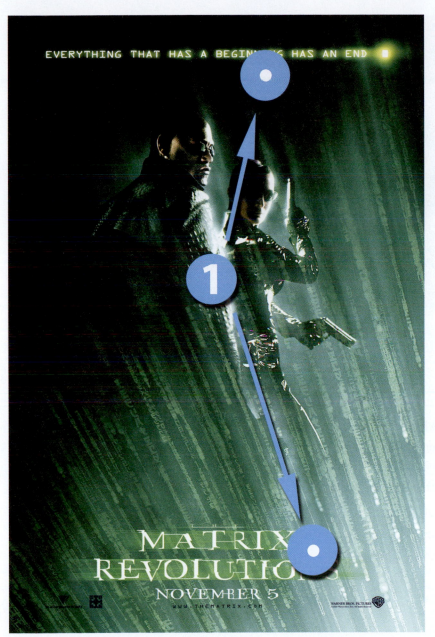

We think the poster for *Matrix Revolutions* is composed to have a visual hierarchy something like this:

1 Unlike the poster for *Attack of the 50 Ft. Woman*, this poster has no large words at the top. Instead, we think this poster's center has been designed to catch our eyes first: The poster's main colors divide it in two diagonally; in the middle of the poster, placed on top of that dividing line, are the two people. No other people are in the poster, only text—and so our eyes are probably drawn to the center by our interest in people and by their placement.

2 After we see the people, the poster's design suggests two other directions our eyes can follow:

- The text at the poster's top gets brighter to the right, ending in a flash of light. The line of the second character's head and up-pointed arm move in the direction of that light. These two features direct our attentions upward.

- The poster gets lighter at the bottom right, so our eyes will be drawn there. The lines of "rain" all point in that direction—and the movie title is there at the bottom, too.

To us, this poster seems to have been designed to keep our eyes moving back and forth from the top to the bottom, from darkness into light and back again—and the light is on the bottom right, suggesting both the ground as well as where the story is moving, since we are used to reading from right to left. If you have seen the movie, how does this movement fit with what you know about it?

TO ANALYZE: Movie posters from the United States

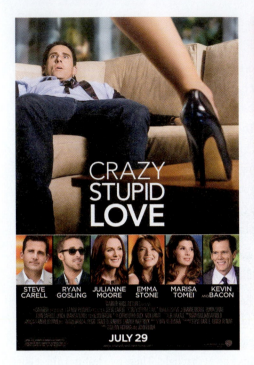

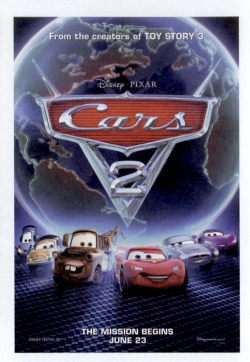

■ **WRITE:** Above are several movie posters from the United States. Use what you know and what you read on the preceding pages to write a short paper in which you answer the following questions about at least three of the posters:

• When do you think these different movies were made? On what visual evidence or other knowledge do you base your estimates?

• What genres of movies (comedies, romances, sci-fi) are being publicized by these posters? What evidence do you use for making your judgment?

• Why do you think the designers of each poster chose the colors they did for their poster?

• What is the visual path your eye follows through these posters? Why do you think the designers "ask" you to see the elements of the posters in the order you do?

• Try to explain the overall effects of each poster by bringing together your responses to the previous questions.

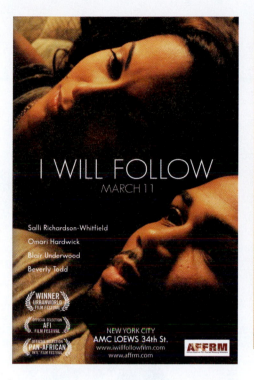

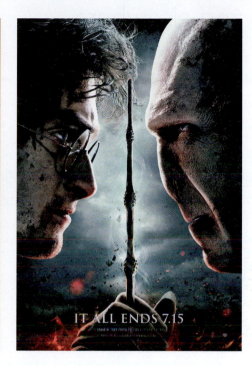

■ **WRITE:** From the examples here or others you find, choose two or more posters for the *same* film genre. (For example, you could look at posters for comedies or for romances.) Analyze each poster's visual arrangements and what the designers expect you to know already in order to understand it. The following questions can help you with your analysis.

• What differences in the posters do you see? What do those differences explain about the distinctive effects the designers of the posters sought?

• How do the different strategies used in the posters connect to the varying purposes of the posters?

Then ask what the posters have in common:

• What similar strategies used in the posters help you see that the posters are in the same genre?

TO ANALYZE: Wartime posters from the United States and elsewhere

AN APPEAL TO YOU

Allons-y.. CANADIENS!
ENRÔLONS-NOUS

I WANT YOU
for THE NAVY
PROMOTION FOR ANY ONE ENLISTING
APPLY ANY RECRUITING STATION
OR POSTMASTER

Keep us flying!
BUY WAR BONDS

■ **Discuss with others:** These posters were printed during different wars in the United States and elsewhere. Use what you know and what you read on the preceding pages to respond to the following:

- When do you think these different posters were made? On what visual evidence or other knowledge do you base your estimates?

- From what countries do the different posters come? Try to use visual clues other than language to support your judgments. (Just because a poster is printed in English doesn't mean it comes from the United States!)

- Why do you think the designers of each poster chose the colors they did?

- What is the visual path your eye follows through each poster? Why do you think the designers of each poster "ask" you to see their elements in the order you do?

HOW POSTERS WORK: Using faces

Notice the way the various wartime posters on the preceding pages use similar—but not the same—strategies of visual composition as the movie posters.

For example, the wartime posters have very few elements, and their elements are arranged to provide viewers a clear visual path from top to bottom.

Notice, however, that the first element in the wartime posters you see—the element at the top—is a face (or, in one case, a hand) instead of words.

Why do you think the designers of these posters decided to place a face as the first element for you to see?

HOW POSTERS WORK: Considering more closely what we already know when we look at posters

The "I Want You" poster with Uncle Sam was first designed just as the United States was entering World War I, and it was such an effective poster that not only were more than four million copies printed between 1917 and 1918 but the poster was brought out again during World War II. In addition, the representation of Uncle Sam (the poster designer, James Montgomery Flagg, used himself as the model) has been reused in many different ways—as in the examples on the preceding pages.

Uncle Sam's pose in this poster was derived from a British poster that used an illustration of

Lord Kitchener, a military hero in 19th century Britain because of his campaigns in Africa. The illustration of Kitchener pointing directly at the viewer appeared on a magazine cover in 1914, and the British Parliamentary Recruiting Committee (in order to make a poster to encourage men to enlist) changed the wording to turn the magazine cover into the poster you can see on the middle of page 340.

The success of the Kitchener poster in Britain led to the "I Want You" poster in the United States and then to all the other posters that have appeared since that draw on Uncle Sam's pose.

As with the movie posters, understanding these wartime posters thus requires us to understand (whether knowingly or not) many things before we can respond to the posters in the way their designers were hoping. As we wrote earlier, you can think about what we need to know about posters—as about any visual composition—as fitting into two general categories:

1 what we already know because we have bodies

2 what we already know because we live in particular places and times with other people

HOW POSTERS WORK: What we know because we have bodies

The effectiveness of the Uncle Sam poster—and of the Kitchener poster on which it was based—depends in large part on how the figure is positioned to appeal to a viewer.

In the full-size poster, Uncle Sam is almost human size. His body is painted to seem close to the poster's front—as though he were leaning toward a viewer—and his facial expression is serious, with his eyes focused a few feet directly in front of the poster. The poster would hang on a wall at almost eye level, and so—if we were to walk by—it would be hard not to feel that Uncle Sam is looking us directly in the eyes. Those caught up in the patriotic fervor prevalent in the United States going into World War I must have felt emotionally compelled by Uncle Sam's closeness and gestures.

Designing this poster, James Montgomery Flagg thus used his understanding of how the poster would be hung and, importantly, of how we tend to respond to gestures aimed directly at us (even when they are printed). We understand some of what is going on in this poster because we know—from our embodied physical experiences—what Uncle Sam's gestures and (perceived) physical closeness indicate.

HOW POSTERS WORK: What we know because we live in particular times and places

To analyze the Uncle Sam poster, we need to understand not only the postures of human bodies but also who Uncle Sam is.

Just what do you know about Uncle Sam, and how did you learn it? And what do you have to know to understand why Uncle Sam is dressed in red, white, and blue? Will those colors carry the same emotional weight for someone in (for example) Italy as for a citizen of the United States?

In addition, Uncle Sam is an older white male. How do you think your responses to this poster would change were Uncle Sam *Aunt Sam* instead? There is one poster on pages 340–341 that has a woman in it, but notice that she is not the same age as Uncle Sam—why do you think that is? How is the appeal built by these posters changed when the person shown in the poster is not older or male? What cultural expectations about gender shape your understanding of the appeal being made in the poster?

Why do you think Uncle Sam is white? What cultural understandings of ethnicity seem to be at work in these posters' representations of people?

We bring our understandings of gender and ethnicity—like our understandings of class—to making sense of these posters. In addition, what people are wearing as well as our knowledge of what was happening at the time these posters were made certainly shape how we understand them.

As you look back over the posters made for audiences outside the United States, what (in addition to language) do you think you need to know about the other country and its culture if you are to better understand how the posters work?

TO ANALYZE: Wartime posters

■ **Discuss with others:** Look at all the posters on the preceding pages and analyze how the body positions of the people represented in each are intended to appeal to the poster's audience.

Which posters attempt to pull you closer, and which come out at you? Describe how the body positions, gestures, and facial expressions create these effects and why you think the posters' designers would make these particular choices. What overall purpose do you think the designers of each poster had so that they chose the design strategies they did? (These are primarily strategies of pathos, as we discussed in chapter 3.)

■ **Discuss with others:** Make a list of all that you need to know to understand the different wartime posters. What does this suggest to you about considerations you need to hold as you design for others?

■ **Discuss with others:** How would the wartime posters be different, do you think, if they had used photographs instead of drawings and paintings? What associations do you have with photographs as opposed to paintings and drawings? How might this change the kind of appeals the posters are making?

■ **Write:** Look back to the "I want you" poster with a woman on page 341.

Write a short paper in which you analyze the similarites and differences between the poster with a woman and the original Uncle Sam poster.

Use your analysis to argue whether the two different posters seek the same purpose through different means or seek different purposes through different means.

■ **Write:** Look back to the "I want you" poster with a skeleton on page 340.

Because it uses the same overall arrangement and words, this poster in some way asks its audience to respond to it as they would to the original poster with Uncle Sam. By using the skeleton, however, it also asks its audience to think differently about the purposes of the original poster or to respond differently to the original poster's call.

Write a short analysis paper in which you compare the original poster with the skeleton poster, using your analysis to explicate how the similarities and differences in the posters point to different purposes.

THINKING THROUGH PRODUCTION

■ Reread the description of the meeting of the Fast Car team in chapter 1. Given the purpose of the group and their audience, design a poster that will encourage women to come to a meeting. Then write a short paper justifying your design decisions (especially your decisions about what words to use as well as all your decisions about the visual aspects of your poster).

■ Use the conventions of the Uncle Sam recruitment poster to design a poster that presents your position on the draft.

■ Use the discussion of typography on pages 252–255 and 262–265 in chapter 7 to analyze how the typography and illustrations of any of the posters in this chapter—or a poster for a current movie or event in your community—work together to create an overall rhetorical effect. If you have access to a scanner or digital camera and image-processing software, scan in the poster and modify its typography or illustrations to see how changes in one or the other change the overall effect.

■ Design a poster to interest people on your campus in a nonprofit organization that matters to you. Use the steps in chapter 3 to develop a design plan; also use the research recommendations in chapter 4 to help you learn as much as you can about the organization so that your poster can be appropriately informative.

Produce your poster using the technologies available to you.

■ Redesign one of the posters shown on these pages (or another to which you have access) as an announcement that would fit on a webpage. Given the relatively small size of webpages, and the possibilities of creating links to other pages, what changes do you need to make to the original poster to keep its original purpose but to make it work well online? Write a justification of your choices.

■ On the following page are posters from different countries for the Alfred Hitchcock movie, *Vertigo*. There are also questions to help you think about how the visual composition of posters—and what you need to know to understand them—changes from country to country. Use the questions to make observations about these single examples from different countries, and use your observations to speculate about what the designers think will appeal to audiences in each country. Pick two of the countries to compare, and—in the library or online—find at least five other examples of movie posters for the same (or a similar) genre from each country. (Online you can find many examples of posters from other countries.)

Write a paper comparing the posters from the different countries, using your analysis of all the posters to see if your speculations are supported.

■ Write a rhetorical analysis comparing the visual compositions of the posters on this page, all for the Alfred Hitchcock movie *Vertigo*; in your analysis, also consider the *Vertigo* poster on page 338. These questions can guide your analysis:

- What differences do you see between the examples from other countries and the example from the United States?

- Compare the photographs and drawings shown in the different posters. What various senses of the movie do the different photographs and drawings give to an audience?

- What changes in these posters when a designer chooses to use a photograph instead of a drawing or vice versa?

- In the posters that use photographs, compare the relationship shown between the man and the woman. What do the different posters—with their various relationships—lead audiences to expect about the movie?

- Based on what you know about color and how it works, what do the different color choices in each of the posters indicate to an audience about the movie?

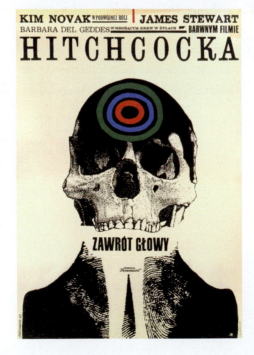

The posters come from the following countries:

Top left: Japan

Bottom left: Poland

Top right: Italy

analyzing documentary photography

CHAPTER 11

Since Aristotle, people have known that light passing through a pinhole could be focused into an image. In the Renaissance, artists fitted lenses into the hole to improve the cast image; they traced the image and used it as a base for painting. By the 17th century, people had observed that some silver compounds darkened in sunlight, and in the 19th century, inventors tried to stop the silver from darkening so they could "capture" an image focused on it. In 1826, in France, Joseph Niépce first "captured" such an image after an eight-hour exposure onto a metal plate; Louis Daguerre built on Niépce's work, so that—in 1839—he announced the "daguerreotype," a kind of photograph made after a few minutes' exposure onto silver-plated copper. A Briton, William Henry Fox Talbot, also announced in 1839 (three weeks after Daguerre) that he had fixed images from a lens—but Talbot's method, which gave rise to the processes of photographic printing used prior to digital photography, used paper instead of metal plates.

Before photography, only painters could "capture" images, requiring time and considerable money; afterward, cities and towns in Europe and the United States filled with photography studios. There were enough people to support these studios (in 1853, approximately three million daguerreotypes were taken in the United States alone) and to encourage studios to sell photographs of other countries and of parts of the United States that few people in cities had seen. Photographers also started going to war (a British photographer recorded the Crimean War in the 1850s, and Mathew Brady's studio recorded the death fields of the U.S. Civil War). In the early 20th century, photographers started recording social conditions, hoping that others, after seeing the lives of the poor, would work toward improvement. All these practices have led to what is now called "documentary photography": photographs that record—document—conditions of a place or time.

HOW PHOTOGRAPHS WORK

Photographs do not "capture" reality, as though "reality" were just standing around waiting for someone to make it fit, unchanged, onto a small piece of paper or a computer screen.

Not only is "reality" at least four dimensional while individual photographs are two dimensional, but every photograph has had someone or something (a tripod) hold a camera pointed in a particular direction; someone has also made decisions about what is included (and how it is arranged) within the space open to the lens. The capabilities of the lens to focus closely or at great distances, the time chosen for the exposure—these all shape the final photograph we see, whether the photograph is shot on film or is digital. Photographers have to decide whether to shoot in black and white or in color, and—in developing or in digital retouching—have to decide how much to brighten or darken parts of a photograph, and where (perhaps) to crop.

This is a long way of saying that *photographs are always rhetorical*: Photographs are always about a photographer making decisions about how an audience's attention will be directed and shaped as the audience looks at a photograph.

Because photographs are rhetorical—are about directing the attentions of an audience just as posters are—we can use the same basic scheme and ideas for analyzing photographs that we used for analyzing posters. That is, you can look at photographs by asking not only what you are meant to see first and what second, and so on—but also by asking how a photograph addresses your body and experiences to shape your responses.

In this chapter we fine-tune strategies for looking, as we list in the box to the right. The strategies we show you in this chapter for analyzing photographs—the strategies of "vectors of attention," "framing," and "cropping"—are also strategies you can use for composing your own photographs as you draw attention to what you want others to consider and think about; they are also strategies you can apply to drawings and paintings. (When you finish this chapter, you might go back and use "vectors of attention" and "framing" to analyze the posters in the previous chapter.)

Strategies we emphasize in this chapter

In this chapter we start by considering how individual photographs work, by considering the following:

- **How photographs direct our eyes and so thoughts by creating "vectors of attention"**

- **How photographs focus our attentions on particular aspects of a scene by using the strategy of "framing"**

- **How photographs focus our attention on particular aspects of a scene by using the strategy of "cropping"**

After we consider individual photographs, we turn our attention to series of photographs—photographic essays—to consider how groups of photographs build their effects.

HOW PHOTOGRAPHS WORK: Drawing on what you know

You've probably been photographed and you've probably used a camera. You understand—even if you haven't thought about it—how the photographic situation almost always means that there's someone or something holding a camera while facing some sort of scene. And, of course, there's always something or someone being photographed.

Until digital photographs, we generally believed that what is in a photograph existed at the time the photograph was taken (although, with considerable effort, photographers using film could use darkroom techniques to bring together in a photograph what had never been in the same place at the same time in "real" life). We have tended to assume, therefore, that what is in a photograph is tied to a particular time and place, and that we can infer things about what is in a photograph without too much worry.

In fact, when we see photographs, we often infer quite a lot, probably not consciously, just because we know what it is to be in a photograph and what we assume about the photographic situation.

To start analyzing photographs, it's useful to see just how much we infer—and can infer—about almost any photograph.

We'll start analyzing photographs by using the example above right.

- When do you think this photograph was taken—both year and season? Where might it have been taken—both a specific kind of place and a general region?

- What relationships might exist among these people?

- What sorts of lives might these people live? What kinds of personalities might they have?

- Why do you think this photograph was taken?

Look at how much you were able to infer about this photograph, based on what you know about photographs, the world, and people's lives.

List what helped you make your inferences. Think about what you know about clothing—and how its style can reveal a time period and perhaps someone's class. Think about what you know about the occasions for taking photographs, and about photographic technologies (for example, how the look of this photograph probably helped you date it), and about people's ages and the ways they stand next to each other depending on the relationships they have.

HOW PHOTOGRAPHS WORK:
Vectors of attention

Notice how vectors of attention work like the visual paths we described in posters—but note also that vectors of attention can work within and across several photographs, as you will see on the following pages.

You're wondering at what all the people in the photograph to the far left are looking—and, as we discussed on the previous page, you've probably already made assumptions about when this photograph was taken, where these people are, and the relationships among them.

This is a fairly dramatic photograph for making the point we want to make here, but all photographs do this: They direct your attentions by the way the people—or objects—in the photograph are arranged.

In this photograph, each person's body is turned to the right, as are the faces. The man is even pointing—and notice how he is the tallest person, with everyone else arranged around him: Like us, you probably assume he is the father of this family, shepherding them carefully on a tour in a city, being responsible for directing their—and our—attentions.

Arrangements in photographs suggest lines of direction for our eyes to follow; these lines of directed attention can be called "vectors of attention" (or just "vectors"), and it is useful to look for them (and even draw them) in a photograph in order to see how the photograph has been arranged and how, therefore, the photographer is trying to direct our attentions, thoughts, and concerns.

You've probably made assumptions about when and where the photographs to the right were taken, and about the relations between the people shown. Notice how your sense of those relations probably depends on who is looking where in the photographs, that is, on the vectors of attention arranged in the photographs.

The assumptions you make about what vectors of attention tell us are based both on what you know because you have a body and on what you know because you live with others. Because you have a body, you understand where your attention is directed when you turn or bend your eyes, head, or body. Because you live with others in particular places and times, however, it is possible that assumptions you make about photographs of people who live in other places and times might not be correct: Your understanding of relations between people shown in photographs—based on your understanding of different bodily positions and ways of looking—might not be the same as the people who are in the photographs. The people might have been posed by someone outside their culture (as is the case here), and their sense of relation to others might be based in understanding a religion or family different from yours.

Draw the vectors of attention in these photographs.

Vectors of attention, continued

Based on what we have written on the preceding two pages, there are several important things to note about how visual composition works.

Limitations of analysis

Separating what we know because we have bodies from what we know because we live with others can be difficult—and sometimes we can't be sure if what we know because we live with others here and now applies to those who live in different times or places.

Keep these limitations in mind as you analyze photographs—or any kind of visual text—so that you do not make assumptions that you cannot support or that lead you in unfruitful or unhelpful directions.

Vectors of attention and you

Look back at the photographs on the previous three pages and note how in some photographs several of the vectors of attention come directly out at you and how in other photographs you are not addressed directly by any of the vectors.

How is your sense of a photograph shaped when someone in the photograph is looking directly at you? How about when no one is looking at you?

When a vector of attention is directed toward the audience, it is a way for the photographer to pull you into the scene of the photograph, to build an (often) emotional connection between you and who or what is in the photograph. When the vectors of attention do not include you, you are an onlooker, an outsider, an observer, someone eyeing the relationships shown within the photograph by the vectors of attention among whoever is in it.

Vectors of attention are thus about arrangement—the logos of a photograph—and about emotional connections within the photograph as well as between the photograph and the audience—the pathos of the photograph. What the photograph shows certainly affects how you think about and respond to it, but you cannot separate your responses from how the photograph's vectors direct your attentions and connect you to what the photograph represents.

TO ANALYZE

■ **Discuss with others:** Because you live with others in a particular time and place, you know about relationships between others based on what you have learned about how particular people in your time and place (such as mothers) should or do act toward particular other people (such as children). You know, through experience, the socially acceptable distance you should place between you and family members, you and friends, you and very close friends, and you and strangers.

Do you think that what you know from your time, place, and experience necessarily or completely applies to the people in the photographs on the previous page? What kinds of judgments can you make about those photographs—and what kinds of judgments should you be careful about?

HOW PHOTOGRAPHS WORK: Framing

While vectors are about a photographer's choices in arranging a photograph's elements, framing is about a photographer's choice of what elements to include in the first place. What does a photographer include (or not) from a scene as she frames a photograph through her camera's viewfinder?

Because framing cuts off what is around a photograph when it is taken, framing focuses your attentions on parts of an event or situation; you rarely know exactly what else was going on around the photograph—but you make assumptions, consciously or not.

Framing puts you into an odd relation with a photograph: Framing asks you to take on the physical perspective of the photographer relative to what's photographed. Are you placed close to the action, far away, or at middle distance? Are you looking up or down at the event, or is it occurring at eye-level? How does each of these possible placements shape your relationship, as viewer, to what is happening in a photograph? Each of these differences asks you to take up a different spatial relation— intimate or distant—with what is shown, and so shapes how you are likely to respond.

To start thinking about framing, list your assumptions and thoughts about the photographs above, which were all taken on the same day at the same event. What was the larger scene in which the above photographs were taken? On what evidence or photographic suggestions do you base your judgments?

HOW PHOTOGRAPHS WORK:
Cropping

354

Take a minute or two to list your assumptions and thoughts about the photograph above (and be sure to use vectors of attention and framing in your observations)…

…then look at the photographs on the next page, all of which are simply different ways of cropping the one above. Pick three or four of the photographs on the next page, and write for a minute or two about what they encourage you to think about generally or what they encourage you to think about the people in them.

Probably your writing will show that your sense of what each of those photographs is about will shift a fair amount depending on its cropping.

The photographs above are "cropped" versions of the photograph on the previous page. After taking a photograph, a photographer can choose to crop it in any number of ways to focus your attentions.

When you are thinking about how a photograph is arranged, try moving pieces of paper over it so that you crop it in different ways and see only parts of it; this can help you not only think about the photograph's cropping but also about how its details work together to make a whole.

When you look at any photograph, you generally cannot tell whether a photographer cropped what he saw through the camera viewfinder. Nonetheless, pay attention to how the framing or cropping positions you relative to what has been photographed. We pointed this out in our discussion of framing, but it is worth repeating because so much of how we respond to photographs depends on what they show and the relationship we are asked to take with them.

For example, look at how the close photographs of hands and faces above can make you feel closer to the photograph—and so to the people. The cropped photographs can seem more intimate because they place you—as viewer—closer to what is shown.

Go back to the earlier pages of this chapter, and look at how the photographs have been framed or cropped to direct your attention in particular ways. Draw on the photographs (or do this in your imagination) to think about what isn't included.

A PHOTOGRAPHIC ESSAY

Frequently—but not always—photographs can seem to freeze time: They are small enough that your eyes can take them in all at once, catching all that happened in the instant the shutter snapped. Although your eyes do move from element to element—person to person or facial feature to facial feature—and you do need time to look at a photograph, it can seem that the temporality of sequence or moving time is missing from any single photograph.

In the rest of this chapter, we'll look at several series of photographs. We'll be looking at photographs that people have arranged to be seen together with others in order to have a larger or different effect than a single photograph can. We call such series "photographic essays" or "visual essays."

☛ We'll start by looking at the series of photographs to the right, which we have composed, in order to introduce ways of analyzing series of photographs; on the next two pages is an analysis of this essay.

After that, we'll look at other photographic series made by different photographers.

Being a family in the United States in the early 20th century

READING AND RESPONDING RHETORICALLY
A written analysis of a photographic essay

Having used the steps for rhetorical analysis from pages 316–317, and focusing on vectors of attention, framing, and cropping, Hiroko writes an informal rhetorical analysis of the photographic essay on the previous pages, "Being a family in the United States in the early 20th century."

Hiroko Bridgewell
November 10, 2012

Being Isolated inside the Picture

As I was first looking at this visual essay, I was surprised by the picture of the family working. The pictures on the left are of families doing leisure things—as are the two pictures on the bottom right—and I realize that when I think about "family" I just pretty much picture in my head a mother and father and children doing family things together: eating, going on Sunday drives, watching television, or celebrating a holiday of some kind. At first I thought the family in the third picture was eating together because they were gathered around a table, but whatever they were eating is kind of strange: When I looked closer, it appeared to me as though they were assembling something, and I thought—given the way the room around them looks, which is not very fancy, with clothes hanging up above and everything pretty cluttered—that they must all have been working, even though the children all look like they are between 4 and 10 years old. Because this picture is so different from the others (it is also the only picture where the family is inside), it makes me wonder if the person who made this essay intended for this photograph to stand out in this way: Because the photograph stands out, and makes me realize that I think about families as doing leisure or pleasant things together (and not working), the essay makes me wonder what else I take for granted about families, and what isn't shown here.

For example, I think that families are units to do things together, but in these photographs it's not just that families are doing things together; instead, they are all taking on similar behaviors. In all of the photographs except one (which I'll discuss in a moment), everyone has almost the same expression and is looking in the same direction; all the vectors of attention go to the same place. There is the family looking off into the sky together, the musical family looking at the photographer together, the family concentrating on their work, and the family in the grass all looking back to the left together. The one family that isn't all looking in the same direction appears to me to be the wealthiest family because of the way they are dressed; I am assuming (because the title tells us these photographs are about families) that this photograph shows a grown daughter with her parents. The father is in the middle with his arms around both women, but his head is turned to his wife; the women both look at the camera.

The father looks as though he has just said something, and his wife has tilted her head to listen. The two women look almost like mirror-images of each other, like bookends to the father. This is the only family framed as though they are no place, not doing anything, just being for the camera or paying attention to each other—and this is also the only family where anyone has anything like a smile on their faces. One way I guess I could interpret this photograph, based on its differences from all the others, is that because these people are wealthy they do not have to focus together on the same things, that they just get to relax and be who they are without having to concentrate on something together. It's almost as though the other families have to work hard at doing the same things in order to hold together, to survive as families … and perhaps just to survive.

I'm also struck by how all the white families are on the left, while the one black family is off to the right but looking back in. The expressions on the different family members in this photograph are thoughtful and serious; I wonder what they would think were they really to find themselves in such a situation, looking at all the other families. The direction of their eyes asks me to look in the same direction and so I wonder what it would be like to be one of them, and to see all those other white families, and to be so separated. This makes me think again about families in the United States, and how different they are: How it is that we are all in the same place, but so different, as though each of the photographs in the essay contains its own little world, separated from the others? People can look across at each other, but the framing of all the photographs mostly holds them all in place, kind of stiffly.

Perhaps the person who composed this essay was aiming at that: Perhaps the person is arguing that families in the early part of last century were separated, cut off from each other, because of having to be families in order to hold on together.

This preliminary analysis leaves me with several questions. Would it be possible to make a photographic essay that showed people not being so separated by the boxy edges of the photographs? Would someone who didn't have my suburban background with my family see this differently? What kinds of families from that time period aren't included in this essay—and how would that change my sense of families, both then and now?

A PHOTOGRAPHIC ESSAY:
excerpt from "American Muslim Students"

The next seven photographs come from Robert Nickelsberg's series titled "American Muslim Students." The series has 28 photographs composed into shorter subsequences about individual high school students and their day-to-day lives.

Nickelsberg was under contract to TIME magazine for 25 years. For 12 of those years he was based in India, photographing conflicts in southeast Asia and documenting the early rise of the Taliban in Afghanistan and Pakistan. Now living back in New York, he continues to travel, having photographed the U.S. invasions of both Afghanistan and Iraq. Nickelsberg serves on the advisory board of the Kashmir Initiative at the Carr Center for Human Rights Policy at Harvard University.

The next seven photographs focus on one student, Mohamed Amin, as he goes to school and prepares to leave home for college. Nickelsberg wrote the captions under the photographs.

As you look through the seven photographs, first analyze them individually using the approaches we discussed earlier. But then consider how the photographs work together: *What is repeated from one photograph to the next, and what are differences among the photographs?* For example, does each photograph have the same visual arrangement, with a single centered subject, or do the photographs differ from one to the next in their overall arrangements? Are the photographs all close-ups, or do they show their objects at middle or far distance? Do the photographs all happen in the same place, or are there different settings?

As you observe these similarities and differences, ask how Nickelsberg is shaping and directing your attentions because of these repeated and different strategies. Keep moving back and forth between asking yourself *what* and *why*.

What do you think Nickelsberg's purposes are in the arrangements within the sequence's individual photographs as well as in the larger overall arrangements of the sequence? How has his framing put you into positions for thinking about Mohamed Amin? What attitudes toward Mohamed Amin is he shaping?

What does the title of the overall collection suggest about Nickelsberg's purposes?

Mohamed Amin stands in front of the Subzi
Mundi market July 8, 2010 in Jackson Heights,
Queens, New York. Mohamed, a Bangladeshi-
American, graduated from Bronx High School
of Science and now attends the University of
Wisconsin in Madison.

Mohamed changes subway trains while traveling
90 minutes to high school June 7, 2010 in New
York.

Mohamed reads a Henrik Ibsen play while traveling by subway to school June 7, 2010 in New York.

Mohamed presents his environmental sciences project on pollution in China to his Bronx High School of Science class June 14, 2010 in New York. Mohamed now attends the University of Wisconsin.

Mohamed Amin speaks on his cell phone at
New York's Lincoln Center where his June 21,
2010 Bronx High School of Science graduation
ceremony was held.

Mohamed is photographed with his South Asian classmates at New York's Lincoln Center June 21, 2010 following their Bronx High School of Science graduation ceremony.

Mohamed gathers his bags before leaving his
Jackson Heights home August 28, 2010 for a flight
to begin classes at the University of Wisconsin in
Madison.

TO ANALYZE: photographs from "American Muslim Students"

■ **Plan:** Imagine you were going to describe these photographs to a friend who cannot see. What would you emphasize about each photograph—and how would you help the friend understand how all the photographs work together?

■ **Discuss with others:** What is your initial sense of Nickelsberg's purpose for this set of photographs? Why?

What are the three to five most-used strategies you see Nickelsberg using? Why do you think Nickelsberg would emphasize those strategies, given your understanding of his purpose?

■ **Discuss with others:** Why do you think Nickelsberg chose to include captions with these photographs? (See pages 266–267 for help thinking about how photographs and captions work together.)

■ **Discuss with others:** What responsibilities do you think Nickelsberg has to Mohamed Amin?

What responsibility do you think any photographer has to the human subjects of the photographs she takes? Do these reponsibilities differ if the photographs are to be published or not?

■ **Write:** If you were to add another five photographs to this series, what would you add to further enhance what you see to be Nickelsberg's purposes? Write a list of these new photographs, describing for each what it would be and why you would include it.

■ **Discuss with others:** Can you look at these photographs and know immediately what they are about and where they were taken? Can you tell easily in what sort of place the photographer was standing when he took the photographs? Why might a photographer choose to show photographs like this?

■ **Plan and write:** Imagine you were going to take photographs to document the day-to-day life of someone your age who lives in your area but in a different kind of community.

What sorts of relations would you need to develop with that person so that you could take photographs? Would you discuss your plans for individual photographs with that person, or not?

■ **Write:** Imagine a photographer came to you, asking to document your life as a student. How would you feel about having your life so documented? Would you agree to this, or not—and why?

Imagine that you decided to participate in this project. What aspects of your life do you think the photographer would want to photograph, in order to emphasize how it is for you to be a student?

In several paragraphs, write your responses to the questions above, and then list and describe in detail five to seven photographs that you think could do the work of documenting your life as a student. What would these photographs enable someone to learn about your life as a student?

Finally, write about what would be left out of such a photographic essay. What aspects of your life and activities wouldn't be addressed by such an essay?

A PHOTOGRAPHIC ESSAY:
photographs from *A Civil Rights Memorial*

Jessica Ingram says she photographs because of a "desire to understand how people relate, what they long for, and what motivates the choices they make." On the next pages are photographs from her series "A Civil Rights Memorial." Here are Ingram's words about that series:

Five years ago, I wandered downtown Montgomery [Alabama] in the sweltering heat, picked up a walking tour trail, and found myself facing a large, ornate fountain, situated on a brick pavilion. A historical marker said that I was standing on the former Court Square Slave Market, where slave traders sold men, women, and children to the highest bidder. It presented cold facts, detailing dollar values for slaves at the time and how none were given last names.

I was speechless. The fountain was erected at a time when this site was not considered for its history, the sign placed in a gesture of reconsideration. Moreover, the language printed on the sign was so void of sentiment—in no way testifying to the experience and meaning. I am from the American South, aware of the devastating history of slavery, but this site moved something in me that caught fire. I watched people pass by and wondered if they knew or thought of the history beneath their feet.

Curious about other histories and sites (marked and unmarked) I may be passing by in the American South, I began to research.... Over the next several years, I traveled repeatedly through Mississippi, Tennessee, Georgia, Alabama, and Louisiana, and documented sites where Civil Rights era atrocities, Klan activities, and slave trade occurred. In Money, Mississippi, I visited the remains of the store where 14-year-old Emmett Till allegedly whistled at a white woman, and the Tallahatchie River, where he was dumped after being tortured and disfigured. I traveled to Midnight, Mississippi, the birthplace of Rainey Poole, and saw the Sunflower River, where Poole was dumped after his murder in 1970. There are no markers in these places.

The Southern landscape is swallowing up these and other sites, as time is also burying these histories and leaving families without a sense of closure or justice....

I have found each of the sites included here through research, and more importantly, have met and talked to family members and local people about the person who was lost, and the effects it had on both the family and the community.... These histories are fresh for the people that lived them. In the majority of these cases, there was no justice, or justice came late, when cases were reopened in the 1990s and 2000s. The justice system failed, and this history must also be considered and called to account, as the effects of this history still linger.

My larger body of work is about families and communities. This project is absolutely about that. It is a meditation and a recapturing. These images are renewed representations of these events, some of which have been excluded from the collective and mediated retelling of this period in American history.

As you look at the photographs on the next pages (which are accompanied by Ingram's captions) ask what history the photographs suggest. How do the photographs ask you to think about the people involved in the events that took place at the sites of the photographs? What thoughts and emotions do the photographs encourage? What memories do the photographs ask viewers to construct? What sorts of shared cultural memories or history might these photographs hope to construct?

(You can see more of the photographs from "A Civil Rights Memorial"—and more of Ingram's other work—at http://jessingram.com)

Store, Money, Mississippi

In 1955, Emmett Till, a 14-year-old boy from Chicago, was dragged from his uncle's cabin in Money, Mississippi and beaten, shot, and dumped in the Tallahatchie River by two men who accused him of whistling at a white woman in this store. Roy Bryant and J.W. Milam were acquitted by an all white jury in 1955, but later confessed to *LOOK Magazine*. Both men have died, but the Justice Department reopened the case in 2004 to investigate if anyone else was involved.

Koinonia Farms, Americus, Georgia

Koinonia Farms was founded in by Clarence Jordan in 1942 in Americus, Georgia as an interracial community where people could live and work. During the Civil Rights Movement, both black and white children from Koinonia were not allowed to attend segregated schools. Koinonia withstood firebombing, night riding, Klan intimidation, and economic boycotts. Koinonia still exists today as an interracial community, dedicated to affordable housing for all. Habitat for Humanity was founded at Koinonia in the 1960s as a response to poverty in the rural American South.

Site of James Chaney, Andrew Goodman, and Michael Schwerner's murder, Neshoba County, Mississippi, near Philadelphia

Civil Rights workers James Chaney, Andrew Goodman, and Michael Schwerner were murdered by the Meridian Klan and Neshoba County Klan, with the help of members of the Neshoba County sheriff's office on June 21, 1964. Schwerner and Goodman were shot once, and James Cheney was beaten and shot three times.

The murders received national attention. Charges were brought and several men were found guilty in 1967 and given sentences that ranged from 3-10 years.

In 2005, Edgar Ray Killen was convicted on three counts of murder for coordinating the murder of Chaney, Goodman, and Schwerner. Jerry Mitchell, a journalist at the *Clarion Ledger* in Jackson, Mississippi was instrumental in discovering Killen's involvement and reopening the case.

Medgar Evers' Backyard, Jackson, Mississippi

In 1963, Medgar Evers, the first NAACP field secretary in Mississippi, was gunned down in his driveway in Jackson, Mississippi. Byron De La Beckwith was tried in 1963 and 1964, with both trials ending in hung juries. He was convicted of murder in 1994.

Prayer Helps, near Meadville, MS

Henry Hezekiah Dee and Charles Eddie Moore were kidnapped by Klansmen in 1964, taken to Homochitto National Forest near Meadville, Missippi where they were beaten, then taken to the Mississippi River, where they were thrown in, alive, with Jeep motor blocks tied to them. Authorities found their bodies in a bayou while searching for the bodies of civil rights workers Chaney, Goodman and Schwerner. This site, formerly the Tasti-Freeze, was the last place Dee and Moore were seen alive.

TO ANALYZE: photographs from *A Civil Rights Memorial*

If you can, look at all the photographs from "A Civil Rights Memorial" (online at http://jessingram.com/section/36249_A_Civil_Rights_Memorial.html).

- **Plan:** Imagine you were going to describe these photographs to a friend who cannot see. What would you emphasize about each photograph—and how would you help the friend understand how the photographs work together?

- **Discuss with others:** What is your initial sense of Ingram's purpose for this set of photographs? Why?

  What are the three to five most-used strategies you see Ingram using? Why do you think Ingram would emphasize those strategies, given your understanding of her purpose?

- **Discuss with others:** Why do you think Ingram chose to include captions with these photographs? How do the captions encourage you to understand the photographs? Under what conditions—for whom, or where, or when—might these photographs not need captions?

- **Reflect and then discuss with others:** On your own, name and describe the emotions you feel as you look at these photographs.

  With others, list your emotional responses. Try to describe why you think you have these emotions both as an individual but also as someone who grew up in a particular place and time and received a particular education in U.S. history.

  Where there are differences in your emotions, try to figure out what in your backgrounds set you up to respond differently to these photographs.

- **Discuss with others:** Use the following questions to start a discussion with others:

  Why do you think the photographer, Jessica Ingram, chose to show no people in the photographs?

  Why do you think Ingram stood where she did when she took her photographs? How does her position as photographer shape your position as viewer?

  How do these photographs function as a "memorial"? What is being memorialized in these photographs?

  What sort of attitudes toward the events being documented in these photographs do you think Ingram might be encouraging?

- **Plan and write:** Imagine you were curating an exhibit of these photographs. Compose a design plan for such an exhibit.

  As you plan, consider the following: Given your sense of how these photographs work as memorials, what would be the best floor-plan through which viewers should walk to see these photographs, in what order? How would you introduce the exhibit to its audience? How big would you want the photographs to be? How would you print the captions and mount them relative to the photographs? How would you advertise the exhibit?

- **Plan and write:** Imagine you were developing a memorial for an aspect of our history that you think is usually overlooked or is in danger of being forgotten. Compose a design plan for such a memorial. In your design plan, describe the aspect of history you are memorializing and why. What medium would you use for the memorial? Where would it be most appropriate to put this memorial? What memories and history do you want to construct? What kinds of objects should be in the memorial? If the memorial needed words to help its audience understand, write the captions and describe where they would be placed.

THINKING THROUGH PRODUCTION

■ If you have access to a camera and printing, compose your own photographic essay about an issue that matters to you. Your audience and context are your classroom, so consider carefully your purpose: What sorts of attitudes or ideas do you want others in class to take toward what matters to you?

Plan the arrangements of the individual photographs for your purpose, keeping framing, cropping, and vectors of attention in mind.

Also think about how you can arrange the sequence of photographs, having in mind the kinds of considerations the photographers in this chapter did. Will you, for example, have photographs that use captions or repeat overall arrangements?

(You can also arrange your photographs into an online essay, if you know how to work with digital photographs and webpages.)

Before you produce your essay, write a design plan in which you use your statement of purpose to justify the choices you make in arranging your essay.

■ If you don't have a camera, use photographs you have from your family or from trips, or use photographs you cut from magazines you own, to make a photographic essay. If you have access to the Web, or want to work with photographs from another time or with those you probably wouldn't be able to take even if you had a camera, use ones you can download from government websites. (For the most part, these photographs are fair use, either because they were taken more than 75 years ago [the length of time that copyright now extends] or they were taken in the service of the U.S. government—which cannot copyright photographs or any document.)

Look at the photographs available to you, and then compose a design plan and photographic essay as we described in the column to the left.

■ In chapter 13, the essay "Higher Education" is accompanied by a number of photographs.

Using the analytic tools we introduce in this chapter—framing, cropping, and vectors of attention—analyze the photographs in that essay. Analyze the photographs both individually and as a collection. Also analyze the words in the essay and the photographs together: What arguments do the photographs and the words make together?

Write a rhetorical analysis comparing how photographs and words play off each other in the essay. How can photographs and words be used together to build arguments they can't build on their own? What strategies for using words and photographs together can you describe for your own future use?

analyzing editorials and opinion pieces

CHAPTER 12

Before the invention of the printing press, handwritten newsletters—with information about events, places, and people—circulated among merchants in Europe, who passed the newsletters back and forth as they traveled. After the invention of the printing press in the 15th century, people published news pamphlets and broadsides about particular events, but only irregularly. It was in London in the 17th century that regularly published newspapers were first printed.

Newspapers, like posters, thus came to the shape we recognize as a result of technologies and publics. For newspapers to be possible, there had to be enough people in one place—a city like London, then the largest in the world—and a fast, cheap, and reliable means of reproduction. (In the mid-19th century presses were developed that could print 10,000 newspaper copies in one hour.)

Editorials have been written from the beginning of newspapers. "Editorials" are so named because they are written by newspaper editors; editors are responsible not only for the news being correct but also for deciding the approach—conservative? liberal? or . . .?—a newspaper will take. Editorials represent the opinion of the newspaper and have the authority of the newspaper behind them.

But others as well contribute their opinions to newspapers and magazines—hence "opinion pieces," often structured similarly to editorials; these are written by individuals who often claim no authority beyond being a member of a particular community. Similarly, "letters to the editor" respond to what is printed in newspapers.

How do you think the online publication of newspapers—and so of editorials, opinion pieces, and letters to the editor—changes how people share their opinions?

HOW EDITORIALS AND OPINION PIECES WORK

Because opinions are expressed—and argued—in this chapter more explicitly than in earlier chapters, prepare to encounter ideas that may not sit well with you. The point of looking at these opinions is not immediately to make up your mind whether you agree or disagree, but first to see how these arguments are constructed and supported and what they ask you to do and become. After such analysis it makes sense to ask, "Do I want to be persuaded by this argument?"

Also, recognize that your responses to these essays come because, unlike many of the examples in other chapters, a lot of these editorials and opinions are directed at you: Many of the writings in this chapter have a general audience of people living in the early 21st century in the United States. You can analyze these writings as though you—not someone else—are addressed by them, because you are.

THE PURPOSES OF EDITORIAL AND OPINION PIECES— and the consequent general characteristics of editorial and opinion pieces

Editorial and opinion pieces help us communicate with each other about what we ought to do, about specific actions we ought to take.

This is *writing as deliberation*: We use this writing to deliberate over possible future actions; such writing is also sometimes *writing as judgment*, asking us to decide whether our actions in the past have been correct.

In such editorial and opinion pieces, we are addressed always as members of some community: We may be addressed as citizens of our neighborhood, town, city, county, state, or country; we may be addressed as members of a church or a civic or advocacy organization. And when we are so addressed, we are most often being addressed by someone who situates herself within the same community and who wants to show us that, given our common goals, there is some action that follows logically out of those goals, given some particular context.

This is *public writing*, meant to bind us together more strongly, so that we will act together.

Strategies we emphasize in this chapter

Because the public writing of editorials and opinion pieces focuses on persuading others to particular action, this kind of writing usually involves explicit statement of arguments. Also, because this kind of writing requires writers to show that they share community and concerns with their readers, this kind of writing can help us see strategies writers use to persuade us that we can trust them and ought to listen closely.

In this chapter, then, we focus on the following strategies:

- **How writers persuade us that we ought to read them attentively and be open to being persuaded by them. In other words, we will be focusing on written ethos in this chapter, as we described it in chapter 5.**

- **How writers structure arguments following particular kinds of forms—or the logos (see chapter 5) of these kinds of arguments.**

How we understand editorial and opinion pieces because we live in particular times and places

Because editorial and opinion pieces are deliberative or judgmental as we described on the preceding page, they ask audiences to act. Writers of such pieces need to persuade their audiences that the actions they advocate are worthwhile—which means that these writers must appeal directly to their audience's values and beliefs. Before they write, these writers must therefore pay particular attention to their times and places, to who values or believes what, and why. (If you read editorials from even 10 years ago, or from communities different from yours, you might be struck by how values and beliefs shift over even small differences in time and space.)

But editorial and opinion pieces do more than respond to a community's values and beliefs: These pieces actively shape values and beliefs. Because those who write editorial and opinion pieces can emphasize only some of the values and beliefs of a community, and because the writers often connect those values and beliefs in new ways to argue why their audiences should act, the writers can create new values and beliefs or shift relations between values and beliefs. By emphasizing some things over others, the writers can redefine what a community cares about.

How we understand editorial and opinion pieces because we have bodies

Values and beliefs are ideas, but they are not things we keep in a mind's cool dryness: As much as they are intellectual constructs, values and beliefs are emotional, too, and they dwell in our hearts and bodies. Values and beliefs result from how and with whom we grew up, and from what the people around us think, feel, and do. When we discuss values and beliefs about which we care strongly, we can respond bodily: We can shake, forget to breathe or breathe quickly, jump up and down, sweat, yell, or become silent.

Editorial and opinion pieces are precisely about what we value and what we believe—and so they appeal to our emotions as well as to our intellects. Be alert, then, to how the examples of this chapter—or of any editorial or opinion piece—address your intellect *and* your emotions. We discuss our emotions much less than our thinking and we generally know less about how our emotions play in us and connect with others' emotions. Therefore, even though our analyses in this chapter focus on ethos and logos, attend to how editorial and opinion pieces address us emotionally. You want to be sure you are willing to have your values and beliefs—and your emotions—shaped in the ways a text asks.

THE CONTEXTS OF OPINION PIECES AND EDITORIALS

A "broadside" is any publication on a large sheet of paper. To the left is a sample, with a small enlarged excerpt so that you can grasp a sense of the language. Printed on one side only, broadsides were posted in public places so that many people could see them; they carried information about meetings or things for sale; they also carried—as in this sample—opinion.

This broadside was published November 5, 1799, by Thomas Cooper, the editor of the *Sunbury and Northumberland Gazette of Pennsylvania*. He gave his judgment of then-president John Adams, criticizing him for "a stretch of authority which the Monarch of Great Britain would have shrunk from; and interference without precedent, against law and mercy!"

We found this broadside in the collections of the National Archives of the United States, where it has been stored because it was used as evidence against Mr. Cooper when he was charged by the United States with sedition for his criticism of the president. At his trial, Cooper defended himself on the grounds of the First Amendment's protections of free expression, but—given the political climate of his time—he was found guilty, fined $400, and sent to prison for six months. He was later pardoned by Thomas Jefferson.

We show you this broadside not only to demonstrate how opinions made public (remember that "publication" simply means to make something public) can have strong consequences and that those consequences depend on the contexts in which opinions are published. If Cooper had not published his broadside when there was tension in the country—and in the government—over the degree of the government's authority, his broadside might have been seen simply as opinion, not as words meant to incite others to revolution.

Because anyone who publicizes her or his opinions—like all the writers in this chapter—risks the strong responses of others, writers of editorial and opinion pieces put themselves at risk. The risk can simply be others' nasty or thoughtless responses but it can also be—as for Thomas Cooper—imprisonment. There are several things to note about this risk:

- Writers of editorial and opinion pieces have to attend very carefully to the contexts in which they publish their opinions if they are to be persuasive.

- If we value our own rights to hold our opinions, we readers of editorials and opinion pieces can help shape the contexts in which opinions appear by insisting on the rights of everyone to an opinion, no matter how unpopular.

The media and publication of opinion pieces and editorials

We also show you Cooper's broadside because it does not look like today's newspapers. Its columns do resemble the columns of today's newspapers, but you can probably tell from the small excerpt how different the writing is. And were you to travel back in time to see this broadside posted on a small town public wall, with people clustered around, reading, you'd be struck by how differently the media and methods of publication then and now ask us to read each other's public words.

On some college campuses today there are spots where people speak their minds publicly, and there are traditions of posting news and events on telephone poles and campus bulletin boards. But mostly we get our news alone, with a newspaper and, increasingly, online.

Because so many newspapers now publish online or are archived in online versions for researchers, we use this chapter (in addition to our other purposes) to think a bit about how words look on the Web.

We have not magically embedded a working Web browser into the following pages—but we wanted to include editorials that we found online. We made screenshots of various editorials in order to translate them to print but still keep a flavor of reading online in their original contexts.

As you read the "online" texts, consider how it is to read online as compared to reading on paper. Ask the following questions to ponder the differences and similarities between the context of reading online and the context of reading print material, especially books and magazines:

- How is scrolling through a one-screen online text different from turning the pages of a book?

- How is following links in an online text different from turning a book's pages?

- How is your body positioned differently when you read a newspaper or magazine than when you read or surf online? What effects—if any—do these shifts in body position have on how you read or your relationship to a text?

- Do you think print texts are more "serious" than online texts or carry more prestige for writers? Why or why not?

There are certainly more questions to ask about differences between reading on screen or paper, and we do not mean to imply here that these questions work only for editorials.

A SHORT EDITORIAL ON A CONTROVERSIAL TOPIC

As we described on the preceding pages, opinion pieces and editorials are about the explicit statement of arguments and about how writers must persuade readers that those arguments are (or should be) of shared concern. To show this, we analyze the editorial on the right by labeling its logos appeals (in yellow) and its ethos appeals (in blue).

Notice the pattern of logos in this editorial: The author makes a claim, follows it with different pieces of supporting evidence, considers differing viewpoints, and then gives a conclusion. How is that pattern repeated or modified in the other editorials and opinion pieces in this chapter?

CLAIM

EVIDENCE 1

EVIDENCE 2

EVIDENCE 3

ANTICIPATING OBJECTIONS

CONCLUSION

STATEMENT OF VALUES

alestlelive.com
50 years of student journalism at southern illinois university edwardsville

home   news   opinion   a&e   sports   archive   multimedia   advertising   info   login

Menu ▼   Go   Search

Home > Editorial

Student denounces video game violence

Issue date: 7/19/06 **Section:** Editorial

 Print   ✉ Email   ⊕ Article Tools   Page 1 of 1

Video games are becoming more and more violent and they are part of the reason children are doing more violent things.

One example is the study of aggression done by the National Institute of Media and Family, which stated that studies measuring aggressive behaviors after playing violent video games (compared with behaviors displayed after playing nonviolent games) have shown that violent games increase aggression.

In one study of college students, students played either a violent or nonviolent game. After playing this game, they were given a competitive reaction time task in which they played against another student. If they beat the other student, they got to deliver a loud "noise blast," and were able to control how loud and how long the noise blast would be. Students who had previously played the violent video game delivered longer noise blasts to their opponents.

Children with the lowest hostility scores are almost 10 times more likely to have been involved in physical fights if they play a lot of violent video games than if they do not play violent games (38 percent compared 4 percent). In fact, the least hostile children who play a lot of violent video games were more likely to be involved in fights than the most hostile children who do not play violent video games.

Some may say the video game industries should not have to censor video games. Parents need to educate their children and let them know that what they play on video games is not real because as long as children have easy access to these games they will continue to play them.

I propose that the industry makes their games less violent and parents take responsibility and make sure their child doesn't have access to these games.

I believe that if my solution is not put into effect then the industry will continue to sell violent video games and aggression in children will continue to rise. The principle that is at stake is that violence among children needs to be decreased.

Charmaine Walker
Freshman
Elementary Education

ETHOS in "Student denounces video game violence"

1 The preceding editorial was published in a campus newspaper—which implies that the editorial was read and approved by the newspaper's editorial staff. What sort of authority do you think this gives to the editorial's writer, and what sort of authority might the newspaper's readers give to the editorial?

2 The editorial's writer probably did not choose this title—but what sense of the writer do you take from this title?

3 The very first sentence of the editorial is a strong statement of the writer's argumentative claim. What sense of the writer do you take from such a strong and clear statement, from such a tone of voice?

4 The words "Some may say…" demonstrate that the writer listens to those who hold other opinions and to potential objections to her position. How do these words shape your sense of the writer?

5 This is the writer's first reference to herself, with "I." Why might the writer have waited to use "I" until this paragraph?

6 The writer's final statement expresses her fear that violence among children will continue unless the video game industry changes. What opinion of the writer does this final expression of fear encourage you to have?

LOGOS in "Student denounces video game violence"

CLAIM

This editorial begins with an explicit statement of the claim it will be arguing, that an increase in the violence in video games is causing an increase in children's violence. How do you think such an explicit statement will affect the attitude of those already inclined to agree with this claim? How might those inclined to disagree respond?

EVIDENCE 1

The writer offers a study done by the National Institute of Media and Family as evidence in support of her claim. How compelling do you find this evidence? How might someone inclined to agree with the claim respond to this evidence, and how might someone inclined to disagree with the claim respond?

EVIDENCE 2

The writer references another study in support of her claim. How might the addition of more evidence shape a reader's response?

EVIDENCE 3

The writer references what appears to be a third study, and this time draws on statistics from that study. How might the addition of a third piece of evidence shape a reader's response?

ANTICIPATING OBJECTIONS

After she has made her claim and offered all her evidence, the writer addresses a possible objection, another possible recommendation one could make for addressing children and video games.

CONCLUSION

Rather than argue for her position exclusively, and argue that this is an *either/or* situation, Walker argues for *both/and*: *Both* the video game industry *and* parents need to be held accountable.

STATEMENT OF VALUES

Rather than having her conclusion be her final argumentative move, this writer chooses to end by making a final claim, a statement of the value she believes is "at stake" in this argument. Why might a writer choose to make such a statement rather than simply end with the conclusion?

☛ For more discussion on logos in writing, see chapter 5. For definitions of "claim" and "evidence," and the other terms we use in this chapter, see pages 124–125 in chapter 4.

READING AND RESPONDING RHETORICALLY

To the right is a short, informal rhetorical analysis of the editorial on page 382.

Notice that the first time Aisyah refers to the editorial's writer, she uses the writer's first and last name; in any following reference, she refers to the writer by her last name. This is the academic convention for referring to other writers: The first reference uses the first and last names; following references use the last name only.

Aisyah Musa Merican
June 11, 2012

A Brief Rhetorical Analysis of the Editorial "Student denounces video game violence"

Precisely because arguments surrounding the connections between violent acts and violent video games are about violence, this is a highly emotional issue. One of Charmaine Walker's main strategies in her editorial, interestingly, seems to me to be about treating the issue unemotionally, to ask us to back away from the emotion and to consider evidence about the connections between violent acts and violent video games.

Walker's ethos in this editorial is firm and straightforward. Her sentences do not contain many emotional words. She does not bring herself explicitly into the editorial until her next-to-the-last paragraph, where for the first time she uses "I"; until then, her writing is mostly the reporting of other people's studies. When she does use "I," it is when she makes her conclusion—and her conclusion shows her to be trying to balance the claims of those who would censor video games and those who say parents should bear the full weight of responsibility in this issue. This balancing shows her to be a reasonable person seeking the best, balanced solution that addresses everyone's concerns. Her final sentence also helps develop her ethos, for the last thought she wants her readers to have is that what is at stake, after all, is children.

When I turn my attentions to how Walker uses logos in this editorial, I see how strongly she relies on a very straightforward structure and approach to her argument: She states her claim up front, offers three studies in support of her claim, gives a nod to an opposing argument, and then concludes by arguing for both industry and parents to be responsible. As with her ethos, there are no frills to the logos: Walker presents her points in an order that makes sense and that builds some weight of evidence for her conclusion.

It is interesting to me how Walker's ethos and logos work together in this editorial. The straightforward, no-nonsense ethos parallels and also grows out of her no-nonsense use of logic; it is hard to imagine how she could have constructed a different ethos while keeping the same logical structures.

MORE OPINIONS ON VIDEO GAME VIOLENCE

On the following pages are five more opinion pieces and editorials that consider violence and video games—but these next writings consider violence and video games against the background of legal events, as the next paragraphs describe.

In 2005, the California State Legislature, with the governor's approval, passed a law that made it illegal to sell violent video games to minors. A *New York Times* editorial (from May 2010) discusses that law and how it has been challenged:

> California went too far in 2005 when it made it illegal to sell violent video games to minors. Retailers challenged the law, and a federal appeals court rightly ruled that it violates the First Amendment. Last week, the Supreme Court said that it would review that decision. We hope it agrees that the law is unconstitutional. California's law imposes fines of up to $1,000 on retailers that sell violent video games to anyone under 18. To qualify, a game must, as a whole, lack serious literary, artistic, political, or scientific value for minors.

On June 27, 2011, the Supreme Court ruled against the California law, finding it unconstitutional—that is, finding that California's law violated the protections described in the First Amendment.

In the months leading up to the Supreme Court hearing, the media's coverage of this issue heated up. The *New York Times* editorial we quoted here both laid out some of the main questions the California legislation had raised and (as you can see from the passage we quoted) argued against California's legislation and for the Supreme Court to find the legislation unconstitutional. The editorial interpreted the law for readers by describing what it thought the law was intended to do, why, and what its consequences would be for the video game industry, the businesses that distribute and sell the videos, and consumers and parents.

At stake from a legal point of view was whether or not California's law against selling violent video games to minors is a violation of free speech. That has been the ground upon which most censorship cases in the United States have been fought (another ground being national security). The *New York Times* editorial points out that the argument for the law likens violence in video games to obscenity laws that ban the sale of sexually explicit materials to minors. The *New York Times* editorial praised the appeals court for rejecting this argument, saying that it "rightly refused to extend that doctrine to violent games."

The analogy between laws against selling violent video games to minors and laws against selling "sexually explicit" materials to minors plays a central role in the legal—and public—discussion of this issue. But, as you will see in the editorials to come, it is not the only way people have of framing this issue.

The First Amendment to the United States Constitution is part of the Bill of Rights, and its exact wording is:

Congress shall make no law respecting an establishment of religion, or prohibiting the free exercise thereof; or abridging the freedom of speech, or of the press; or the right of the people peaceably to assemble, and to petition the Government for a redress of grievances.

☛ Of the five opinion pieces and editorials that follow, we will analyze one quite closely, as we did the first editorial; for the remaining, we will provide questions and support to help you take over the analysis.

OPINION: "Separating fact from fiction in video game debate"

The opinion piece below was published well after the California law had been passed (although the law never took effect because it was immediately appealed)—so why was the opinion piece written? One reason: The Supreme Court had just begun hearing the case (although its final ruling would not be issued for another seven months). Another reason: The *Tampa Bay Tribune* had just published an editorial, "Videos kids shouldn't play," that supported the California law. The author of the editorial below, Christopher Ferguson, wanted to counter what the *Tampa Bay Tribune* editorial board had argued, by arguing that the California law was wrong and that we should shift our attentions in the debate.

Remember that the blue circles indicate places where we see ethos emphasized; the yellow rectangles indicate where we see logos emphasized.

"Separating fact from fiction in video game debate" continues on the next page.

1

Opinion

COMMENTARY

Separating fact from fiction in video game debate

By CHRISTOPHER FERGUSON
Published: November 15, 2010

2 Recently The Tampa Tribune Editorial Board published an editorial backing California's efforts to ban the sale of violent video games to minors ("Videos kids shouldn't play," Nov. 9). I am a psychologist **3** and video game researcher whose work was referenced by the Supreme Court; as such I take great interest in these matters.

4 Although I respect the editorial board's views, I believe several issues warrant further discussion. `CLAIM?`

5 First, I and 81 other scholars filed an amicus brief with the Supreme Court opposing the California law. Our concern was not merely that there are a few inconsistencies in the research on video games, but rather that California had ignored wide swaths of literature that demonstrate absence of even correlational relationships between video game violence and harm to minors. `CLAIM 1`

Ethos in "Separating fact from fiction in video game debate"

1 What sort of authority does publishing in the *Tampa Bay Online* give this author?

2 Ferguson establishes his credentials—his authority on this topic—immediately: He describes himself as a psychologist who researches video games, and his work "was referenced by the Supreme Court." How do you respond to this immediate statement of authority?

How would you describe Ferguson's tone of voice throughout this editorial—and how do you imagine readers will respond?

3 We want to note that Ferguson tells us he takes "great interest in these matters." He's already told us his credentials, implying that he should take interest. Why might he want explicitly to state his interest?

4 Why might Ferguson want to state, early on, that he respects the editorial board's views? What effects on Ferguson's ethos do you think such a statement might have?

5 Ferguson adds to his credentials by pointing out that he is one of 81 scholars who oppose the California law. *

Logos in "Separating fact from fiction in video game debate"

CLAIM?

Ferguson doesn't make a claim here about the specifics of the issue being considered, but instead makes a claim about how the argument should proceed, with "further discussion" of several of the issues. What sort of effects do you think such a claim about what the argument should be about has on an audience's sense of the opinion piece's progression?

CLAIM 1

Ferguson makes the claim that the California legislature ignored "wide swaths of literature" that demonstrate that video games don't harm children. Given how he has constructed his authority—through the ethos used we describe to the left—do you think readers are likely to accept this claim, even though he offers no specific evidence from this literature and names none of it?

* In his writing, Ferguson mentions an "amicus brief." "Amicus" means *friend* in Latin, and an "amicus brief" is information given to a court by someone who is not involved in a specific case; the information is intended to assist the court in making its decision.

6 Our overriding concern is that the science has been poorly communicated to the general public, exaggerating the notion of harmful effects and giving rise to urban legends such as that the "interactive" nature of video games makes them more harmful (not one iota of evidence to support such a belief) or that media violence effects are similar to smoking and lung cancer research (an obviously absurd claim).

CLAIM 2

EVIDENCE?

As video games have soared in popularity, youth violence has plummeted to 40-year lows. Of course, video games are probably not the cause of this decline, but we now know video games have not sparked a youth violence crisis. The best studies that are coming out - those that carefully consider youth violence or youth mental health, find little to no evidence of harmful effects.
It's probably time to discard this hypothesis.

7 The state of California (and the Tribune) makes references to a single game, Postal. Indeed, this is a vicious game morally unsuitable for minors. However, I've reviewed research databases of my own and colleague Cheryl Olson and the Pew Research Foundation in which children report on games **8** they play. Of approximately 2,500 children, not one reported playing Postal or its sequel. So California is paying millions of dollars (which could have gone to children in need and families at risk or used to not lay off thousands of teachers) to prevent children from playing a game they already don't play.

EVIDENCE 1

CLAIM 3

A voluntary Entertainment Software Rating Board (ESRB) rating system (much like the voluntary movie rating system, which is not government regulated, contrary to misunderstanding) already exists and is working well. Both the Federal Trade Commission and the Parent Teacher Association, as well as many state attorneys general, have praised this system.

EVIDENCE 2

9 Government is at its worst when it tries to fix something that isn't broken.

CLAIM 4

We can look into the past and see these kinds of moral panics about media. Scholars in the 19th century warned that women shouldn't read "dime novels" because women couldn't distinguish reality from fiction.

EVIDENCE 3

In the 1950s experts testified before the U.S. Senate that Batman and Robin were secretly gay, leading youth into delinquency and homosexuality.

It's time to learn from these mistakes. Some video games may be offensive, but being offensive and harmful are two different things.

DISTINCTION

A law that distracts us from real causes of youth violence and diverts precious money from education and mental health into a law that will help no one is what is truly harmful.

CONCLUSION

Christopher J. Ferguson is an associate professor in the Department of Behavioral Sciences at Texas A&M International University.

Ethos in "Separating fact from fiction in video game debate," continued

6 How do you think the phrase "Our overriding concern"—an expression of what matters to Ferguson and his colleagues—will affect readers' sense of Ferguson? What does the phrase "poorly communicated to the general public" tell you about how Ferguson situates himself relative to the ordinary reader, that is, to the general public?

7 "Indeed, this is a vicious game morally unsuitable for minors": What does Ferguson's word choice tell a reader about him? Why would Ferguson want to say these words about the video game?

8 While presenting evidence in support of his main claim, Ferguson uses the phrase "I've reviewed research databases" to remind us that he is a researcher who understands the science behind this issue. What understanding of "science" underlies Ferguson's writing, and is it an understanding likely to resonate with his readers?

9 Ferguson makes a short, sharp judgmental statement about government. How might different readers respond? How might their responses shape their attitudes toward Ferguson?

Logos in "Separating fact from fiction in video game debate," continued

CLAIM 2

Ferguson claims that "the science has been poorly communicated to the general public." What sort of evidence do you think readers would need to accept this claim?

EVIDENCE?

As support for claim 2, Ferguson states that there is no evidence that the interactivity of games makes them "more dangerous" and states that it is "absurd" to equate smoking and its effects with video games and their effects. Does Ferguson offer any studies or other sort of authority to support what he offers as evidence?

EVIDENCE 1

Ferguson offers the results of his own studies of databases to demonstrate that children do not play "Postal," the "vicious game" Ferguson says is the only game mentioned by California. Do you think this will be sufficient evidence for readers to accept his claim about "Postal"?

CLAIM 3

Based on the evidence from his studies that he offers, Ferguson claims that the California law is not only based on misunderstandings but also is wasteful of taxpayer dollars. Given the evidence he offered, do you think most readers will accept this claim?

EVIDENCE 2

Ferguson offers as evidence that the law isn't necessary because there exists a rating system developed by the video game industry. Included in the evidence, however, is a claim that the rating system is working well; does Ferguson offer any evidence to support this additional claim?

CLAIM 4

Ferguson states that "Government is at its worst when it tries to fix something that isn't broken." How does this claim help him move toward his conclusion?

EVIDENCE 3

As evidence that restricting video games isn't a good action, Ferguson offers evidence from past attempts to restrict popular media. How persuasive do think readers will find such evidence?

DISTINCTION

Ferguson makes a distinction between video games being offensive and being harmful. How does he (or does he?) use this distinction to help him move toward his conclusion?

CONCLUSION

Ferguson's conclusion: The California law distracts us from the real causes of youth violence. Has Ferguson suggested what those "real causes" might be? Should he?

READING AND RESPONDING RHETORICALLY

To the right is a short, informal rhetorical analysis of the editorial on pages 386 and 388.

Sheila Martin
June 18, 2012

A Brief Rhetorical Analysis of "Separating fact from fiction in video game debate"

I am inclined to agree that legally restricting minors' access to video games is going too far, but this opinion piece did little to help me better understand my reasons or develop new reasons. I am unmoved by this writing because its primary strategy for persuasion is the author's ethos; the logic of the opinion piece is, to me, undeveloped and not persuasive.

If I had to describe the author's ethos, it would be "Trust me! I am an authority!" The construction of this ethos starts in the first paragraph: The author describes his occupation and that the Supreme Court has referenced his work. That's impressive, and I am inclined to give him credit. He re-emphasizes his stature when he mentions that he filed an amicus brief with "81 other scholars." There's nothing wrong with any of this.

But look at the claims he makes and the evidence he offers. He claims that he and the other scholars filed their brief because there are "inconsistencies in the research on video games" and that California "ignored wide swaths of literature" showing no connection between video games and violent actions. I understand there isn't room to give detailed evidence, but Ferguson offers *no* evidence. He does not explain what the inconsistencies are and gives no suggestions for how we might check the literature. He could have provided a link to a list of literature, but instead we have to trust him on this.

Ferguson's next claim is that "the science" has been poorly communicated to "the general public"—but, again, he offers no evidence. He claims that in place of "the science" we have been given urban legends. If he is concerned about the quality of the information we have been given, he could help out: He could, as I suggested above, provide links to what he considers to be the best science so that we can learn.

The one place where he does offer more specific evidence is when he claims that California based its law on only one game, "Postal." He states that his review of databases and research showed that no children included in the databases or the research had played the game, and he concludes that California paid millions of dollars to develop a law "to prevent children from playing a game they already don't play." He gives no source name in this paragraph that would help me check his information about "Postal"—but I do know that there are other violent video games in addition to "Postal" and would want to know that children aren't able to get to them, either.

In the next paragraph, Ferguson seems to anticipate my question. He mentions the Entertainment Software Rating Board rating system meant to help parents know what games are appropriate for their children. But without offering any evidence, he claims that this system is working. Again, I have to trust his claim that this system works.

I do appreciate that he offers a distinction between "harmful" and "offensive," which might help me better understand my thinking about video games—but I wish Ferguson had spent less time mentioning his authority and more time giving us more evidence for his claims. Then I might have really learned something useful.

TO ANALYZE

■ **Mark it up:** Find an opinion piece or editorial on any topic that matters to you. If it is in a newspaper, tear it out or copy it; if it is online, print it.

Using two different colored pens or pencils, mark up the opinion piece or editorial as we did our examples on the preceding pages: Use one color to circle or highlight anything that seems to you to be about constructing the author's ethos; use the other color to box in or highlight anything connected to logos.

Number each of your circles, boxes, or highlights. On a separate sheet of paper, write a short description of each numbered item, describing it, explaining it as best you can, and asking questions of it.

Use your annotations to help you write a short analysis of the opinion piece or editorial.

(The approach we describe above is exactly the approach used to produce the short rhetorical analyses on pages 384 and 390.)

A CHECKLIST FOR ETHOS

Generalizing our observations from analyzing the last two editorials, we offer a checklist to help you analyze ethos in others' writing and to help you construct ethos in your own.

The checklist

❏ **The context of the composition.** A writer's publication in a recognized newspaper—or by a recognized publisher—indicates that someone with authority believes in the writer. (Ask yourself, as a reader, how much you accept the authority of the publisher.)

❏ **The composer's knowledge of the topic.** How does a composer show that he knows the topic? What kind of depth of knowledge does the composer display? (And does the composer appear to be showing off knowledge or, instead, quietly demonstrating authority?)

❏ **The composer's connection to the topic.** Look for the reasons why someone writes. Understanding a writer's motivation helps us decide if we accept those reasons.

❏ **The composer's connection to the people affected by the argument.** Are you more persuaded by an argument written by someone who has a personal stake in an argument or by an argument written by someone without such a stake?

❏ **The words a composer chooses to present herself.** Does a writer use "I" or "we"? Does a writer even mention her- or himself? As with all the strategies we discuss here, we cannot say that using "I" will always sound selfish while "we" won't: How these words sound to us always depends on the other strategies working in a composition.

When you are analyzing a composition—or designing one yourself—keep in mind that there are other strategies for self-presentation than just pronoun choice. Look for any words composers use to give you a sense of who they are.

❏ **The way a composer addresses the audience.** Some composers address audiences directly (think about how the posters in chapter 10 stare or point at their audiences) and some don't. In different compositions, this will encourage us to experience different kinds of relations with a text.

❏ **Tone of voice.** Does a composer sound gentle or strident, confused or ambivalent, or absolutely certain? Trust your ears on this when you are deciding about tone of voice: Read sentences and paragraphs aloud, and name the sense you get of the composer's tone as precisely as you can. Once you name the tone you can start trying to pin down why you hear the tone you do and what its effects are.

EDITORIAL: "Violence vs. sex"

This editorial was published June 29, 2011, immediately after the Supreme Court handed down its decision on the constitutionality of the California law banning the sale of violent video games to minors. Note that, as is often the case with editorials, no name is given for an author because the editorial is considered to come from the newspaper itself.

What sorts of authority will this newspaper carry, and for whom?

What sense does the title give you about why the editors are writing this editorial? What sense does it give you about the editors?

If we rework the first five sentences of this editorial, the claim being made is something like "the Supreme Court is willing to limit children's exposure to sex but not to violence." Does that seem an adequate summary to you?

The evidence for the claim just identified is, apparently, a fact: the recent Supreme Court decision. But how does the decision have to be described for it to serve as evidence for the claim?

The editorial summarizes the California law in order that the editors might make arguments about it. How else could they have summarized the law to change how readers think about it?

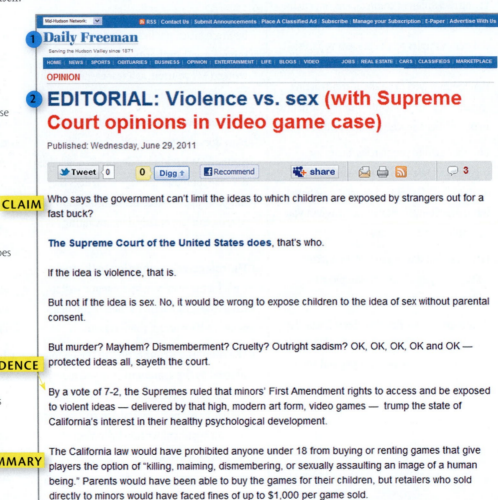

1 **Daily Freeman**
Serving the Hudson Valley since 1871

Mid-Hudson Network | RSS | Contact Us | Submit Announcements | Place A Classified Ad | Subscribe | Manage your Subscription | E-Paper | Advertise With Us

HOME | NEWS | SPORTS | OBITUARIES | BUSINESS | OPINION | ENTERTAINMENT | LIFE | BLOGS | VIDEO | JOBS | REAL ESTATE | CARS | CLASSIFIEDS | MARKETPLACE

OPINION

2 **EDITORIAL: Violence vs. sex (with Supreme Court opinions in video game case)**

Published: Wednesday, June 29, 2011

Tweet 0 | 0 | Digg ↑ | Recommend | share | 3

CLAIM Who says the government can't limit the ideas to which children are exposed by strangers out for a fast buck?

The Supreme Court of the United States does, that's who.

If the idea is violence, that is.

But not if the idea is sex. No, it would be wrong to expose children to the idea of sex without parental consent.

But murder? Mayhem? Dismemberment? Cruelty? Outright sadism? OK, OK, OK, OK and OK — **EVIDENCE** protected ideas all, sayeth the court.

By a vote of 7-2, the Supremes ruled that minors' First Amendment rights to access and be exposed to violent ideas — delivered by that high, modern art form, video games — trump the state of California's interest in their healthy psychological development.

SUMMARY The California law would have prohibited anyone under 18 from buying or renting games that give players the option of "killing, maiming, dismembering, or sexually assaulting an image of a human being." Parents would have been able to buy the games for their children, but retailers who sold directly to minors would have faced fines of up to $1,000 per game sold.

Note that we won't give detailed analyses for this editorial and the following two pieces as we did with the first two. Instead, we have highlighted some ethos and logos uses, so that you can complete the highlighting and start the analysis on your own.

By nature, we're not inclined to argue for censorship.

And it's by no means clear that the playing of violent video games affects healthy development in children. **3**

But the parent in us just can't shake the feeling that there are some things children simply ought not be exposed to.

It boils down, then, to whose job it is.

The court says, in effect, it's not the state's job. By default, that puts the decision in the hands of parents — after the fact of purchase by a child.

Good luck, with that.

Ultimately, however, we're just puzzled by how the majority reconciles its position on video game content with prior rulings upholding bans on the sale of pornography to children.

As Justice Stephen Breyer, in the minority, put it:

"What sense does it make to forbid selling to a 13-year-old boy a magazine with an image of a nude woman, while protecting the sale to that 13-year-old of an interactive video game in which he actively, but virtually, binds and gags the woman, then tortures and kills her? What kind of First Amendment would permit the government to protect children by restricting sales of that extremely violent video game only when the woman — bound, gagged, tortured and killed — is also topless?"

What sense, indeed?

CONCLUSION

Why might the editors make these statements about their attitude toward censorship, violent video games, and children? How might this shape readers' attitudes toward the editors' motivations in writing?

CLAIM & EVIDENCE

The claim: Children shouldn't be exposed to some things. Evidence: We believe this because we're parents. How might readers respond to these editors offering their experience as parents—worried about what their children see and experience—as evidence?

CLAIM

The claim, implied: The Supreme Court could have —and should have—decided for the California law.

EVIDENCE

The editors offer as evidence for their claim the fact that the Supreme Court has ruled that children can be protected from pornography; they also point out Justice Breyer's objection. How persuasive might readers find this evidence?

This short ending implies, strongly, that the editors agree with Justice Breyer and that his statement regarding their claim therefore serves as their conclusion. Why do you think they end with this implied, and with a question?

How would you characterize this editorial's tone of voice? Why might the editors have chosen it for this particular argument, and how does it ask readers to think of the editorial ethos?

393

OPINION: "Games People Play"

This opinion piece was published July 2, 2011, roughly a week after the Supreme Court made its decision about the constitutionality of the California law banning the sale of violent video games to minors. Look at the last paragraph of the opinion piece to learn more about its author.

What authority is given to this piece by being published in the *New York Times*?

Why might there be such a light-hearted title for this opinion piece? How does this title set up a reader to approach the opinion piece?

A QUESTION

Why do you think Bakan would start his writing with this question, which he uses to shape his argument?

A DISTINCTION

Bakan distinguishes between "casual" and other types of games. How does he use this distinction to help him build his argument?

CLAIM & EVIDENCE

Bakan claims that young people don't have to buy or rent violent games, because—his evidence—such games are available for free. Is this evidence readers are likely to accept?

---

1 The New York Times

Sunday Review | The Opinion Pages

| WORLD | U.S. | N.Y. / REGION | BUSINESS | TECHNOLOGY | SCIENCE | HEALTH | SPORTS | OPINION |

OPINION

2 ## Games People Play

By JOEL BAKAN
Published: July 2, 2011

THE Supreme Court's decision to strike California's ban on selling and renting violent video games to young people raises the obvious question: what are children and teens playing on their computers and digital screens?

How Many Kills Can You Rack Up?

The answer isn't pretty. Among the most popular "casual" games (so called because they are quick and simple to play) are twisted, violent games with names like Beat Me Up, Bloody Day and Boneless Girl.

Young people don't need to rent or buy casual games. They are available on computers, tablets and cellphones — free. (California's law wouldn't have applied to these games, even if it had survived the court's scrutiny, because they are not rented or sold.)

RECOMMEND

TWITTER

LINKEDIN

E-MAIL

PRINT

REPRINTS

SHARE

Related in News

Justices Reject Ban on Violent Video Games for Children (June 28, 2011)

Remember that the blue circles indicate places where we see ethos emphasized; the yellow rectangles indicate where we see logos emphasized.

Many popular casual games contain as much violence as notorious video games like Postal 2 and Grand Theft Auto 4, if not more. But they tend to exist under the radar; they're part of an obscure world into which teenagers and children escape and about which parents are often in the dark. (I learned about them only after I asked my 12-year-old son what he liked to do online.)

Nickelodeon's addictinggames.com, a premier casual game site, calls itself "the largest source of the best free online games." It attracts 20 million unique monthly users, mostly children and teens. Though violent games aren't the only type of games on the site, they are well represented — and many appear on the site's list of most popular games. A quick look at the list supplies a sense of what entertains many of us.

Like other leading casual game sites, addictinggames.com makes money by running advertisements. According to Viacom, the site's corporate owner, the aptly named site allows "junkies" to "gorge themselves" and to "fuel their addiction."

Viacom's interest in promoting addiction helps explain why Nickelodeon, the award-winning children's network, might want to push brutal, violent entertainment. Violence sells. And it continues to sell to children, teens and tweens "hooked" at an early age and hungry for more. The games at addictinggames.com and other premier game sites may be casual, but their use of graphic violence to generate profit is strategic and calculated.

Joel Bakan is the author of the forthcoming book "Childhood Under Siege: How Big Business Targets Children."

We do not have room to label every ethos move or every aspect of logos of this or any of the opinion pieces and editorials on these pages. Please feel free to mark and consider what we have not been able to highlight.

3 How would you categorize the overall tone of voice of this writing?

How does your knowledge that Bakan is a parent shape your sense of his relation to his argument—and hence of his argument? What **4** authority does being a parent give Bakan in building toward his conclusion?

EVIDENCE

The self-proclaimed "largest source of the best free online games" offers many violent games, Bakan claims. How does a link to the addictinggames.com website help the persuasiveness of this claim?

CONCLUSION

Bakan concludes that video game makers are not innocently or unknowingly making video games available to children, and—in fact—that they are pushing addiction. Given this conclusion, how do you think Bakan would respond to the Supreme Court ruling?

5 Bakan is about to publish a book on the subject. How does this shape your sense of his ethos?

395

EDITORIAL: "Violence, Video Games, and What We're Not Playing"

The editorial below was published on June 30, 2011, the same day as the Bakan opinion piece on pages 394–395, and it was written as a direct response to Bakan. The precipitating event for this editorial thus isn't only the Supreme Court ruling but also the appearance of Bakan's piece in the *New York Times*. Online publications such as *Gamepro* allow for such quick editorial response.

GamePro is a website for those professionally involved in the video game industry. How does this shape a reader's sense of Plante's ethos?

The short abstract for this editorial claims that anyone who doesn't understand games as this editorial does will produce "ignorant, misplaced arguments." How do these words reflect on the writer?

Plante speaks directly to his readers. What might those readers think of his ethos if they're "part of the minority of Americans who do not play video games"? What if they are video game players?

CLAIM

The Supreme Court decision was correct, Plante claims, because the video game industry polices itself.

EVIDENCE

Is this sufficient evidence for readers to accept that the video game industries adequately police themselves?

Editorial: Violence, Video Games, and What We're Not Playing

Until the mainstream media understands what games are, we're going to face ignorant, misplaced arguments that seek to stifle the industry's creativity.

- by **Chris Plante**
- July 15, 2011 15:15 PM PT

In a recent Sunday edition of the New York Times, author Joel Bakan reacted to the Supreme Court's recent 7-2 decision, which struck down a California law that sought to ban the sale of violent video games to minors.

If you're part of the minority of Americans who do not play video games, Bakan's ire for both the Court's decision and addictinggames.com -- a popular website that hosts, amongst other things, cartoonishly violent games -- might very well sound sensible.

After all, a fraction of video games are violent. In a recent episode of The Daily Show that lampooned the Court's vote, host Jon Stewart wryly illustrated this point by playing a clip from the M-rated fighting game Mortal Kombat, in which one player's character ripped another asunder like a human banana.

But the Supreme Court was right to rule in favor of the industry, because the industry, more so than that of any other media, competently polices itself. Just as film has the MPAA, the games have the Electronic Software Ratings Board, or the ESRB, a non-profit, self-regulatory body that "assigns computer and video game content ratings, enforces industry-adopted advertising guidelines and helps ensure responsible online privacy practices for the interactive entertainment software industry."

Publishing a console video game without an ESRB rating is nigh impossible. Microsoft, Sony, and Nintendo only allow ESRB-rated titles to be published for their platforms. And ESRB compliant stores like Gamestop, Wal-Mart, and Best Buy refuse to sell non-rated games. Of course a voluntary rating system is only good as its volunteers' willingness to commit.

* Plante describes how Bakan cites 10 games in his opinion piece. Bakan does this in a separate graphic that we do not include here in the reproduction of his opinion piece.

In 2010, the Federal Trade Commission conducted its annual "secret shopper" survey, in which undercover minors attempted to buy adult content from popular retailers. The FTC found that stores sold "M" or "AO" rated games to underage shoppers 13% of the time. By comparison, R-rated movies were sold 38% of the time. And 47% of the time shoppers were able to purchase Unrated DVDs, think *Girls Gone Wild* or the extra gory "Director's Cut" of *Hostel II*.

Casual games can be browser games, but not all browser games are casual games.

Bakan never mentions the ESRB, its effectiveness, or even the massive popularity of console games. Instead he focuses exclusively on browser games, which he erroneously categorizes as casual games. Casual games are the Angry Birds, Farmvilles, and Bejeweleds of the world; novel, easy distractions that target a mass audience. Browser games are generally free and can be played on host websites like addictinggames.com, candystand.com, and even Facebook. Casual games can be browser games, but not all browser games are casual games. Neither are the culturally degrading medium Bakan imagines.

* In regards to addictinggames.com, Bakan claims owner Nickelodeon and parent company Viacom knowingly promote excessively violent games to turn a profit. To prove the point, he cites 10 games, representing the most popular and also most grotesque distractions. But of those 10, none depict violence on realistic looking characters; instead, players shoot or punch stickmen.

He also brazenly highlights a game called "Don't Shoot the Puppy." A grim title, no doubt. No picture was included for context, because the reader would have seen a 6 pixel high cartoon dog blasted by an Elmer Fudd hunting rifle, comically disappearing into black dust. If this is the threat, someone start shoveling the Merry Melodies catalogue into the furnace.

Worse, only 2 of Bakan's 10 "most popular games" are actually amongst the site's 25 most popular of all time -- add 1 more to that if you expand to the site's top 50. Instead a majority of the popular games on addictinggames.com involve sports or car racing. A handful are puzzles. The 14th most popular game is a geography quiz for the United States. The first level: Place New Hampshire correctly onto the US map.

If any parent wishes to prevent their children from taking this quiz, or playing any game on addictinggames.com, they should be encouraged to block the website from their home computer. The function is included in all the top browsers, and should be used liberally. After all, the internet can be a dark place. Even Google has the power to conjure haunting images and video of an actual puppy being shot.

There are some sick, twisted, deviant things happening in games today. I know, I review a lot of them. But there's plenty of everything else too, ranging from frivolous to educational. The ESRB rating system begins at E for everyone and ends at AO for adults only. In 2010, 55% received an E-rating, while less than 5% were rated M. No titles were rated AO.

Perhaps the real threat isn't websites trying to profit off violent video games, but authors monetizing parental fear.

4 Throughout all these paragraphs, how do Plante's use of statistics, his knowledge about particular games, and his mentioning that he reviews video games shape readers' responses?

EVIDENCE

Here is more evidence that the video game companies police themselves. Do you think this additional evidence will be persuasive for readers?

5 Plante implies, through his various points in this paragraph, that he knows video games better than Bakan. Has he presented enough—and the right kind—of evidence for this ethos?

6 Plante continues his rebuttal of Bakan in these two paragraphs. How might readers respond to so much response to one person, with the word choice used here?

397

CONCLUSION

In these two paragraphs, Plante pulls his points together, implying that parents should take more responsibility and reminding us of the rating system. How would you summarize Plante's overall argument?

7 How might a reader's sense of Plante's ethos be affected by this last sentence calling Bakan's motives into question?

READING AND RESPONDING RHETORICALLY

To the right is an informal comparative rhetorical analysis of the two writings on pages 394–395 and 396–397.

Benita Okojie
June 24, 2012

How Editorials Relate Ethos, Pathos, and What's at Stake

For Joel Bakan, the author of a *New York Times* opinion piece "Games People Play," what is at stake are the lives of children. For Chris Plante, the author of the *Gamepro* editorial "Violence, Video Games, and What We're Not Playing," what is at stake is the health and creativity of the video gaming industry. Given their respective concerns, it is not hard to understand how each constructs his ethos and makes the various choices that come under the overall strategy of logos.

Bakan makes clear from his first paragraph that his concern is young people. In his writing, he tells us nothing about his occupation except that he is a parent. He gives his writing—and so his argument—a sense of urgency by using short sentences and paragraphs and by claiming that video game companies promote addiction. Given his ethos of concern for children above all, it makes sense that he would call readers' attentions to how the original California law that would have prevented minors from buying violent video games would not have prevented them from playing such games online—as, he claims, young people already do. It makes sense that his logos moves interact with his ethos: His claims, evidence, and distinctions are all about arguing that children are playing such games and that companies want them to. What he does not address—what he seems to take for granted and what his urgency implies—is just what the bad results are of children playing the games to which he so urgently calls our attentions.

Plante makes clear from the beginning of his writing that he is on the side of video games and the video game industry. He uses his detailed knowledge of games, gaming sites, and the gaming industry to construct an expert ethos. And given his ethos and concerns, no wonder Plante's choices about logos cannot be separated from his ethos: What he can offer as logos are the details he knows because he is an expert. By constructing himself as such an expert, he claims for himself the authority to dismiss Bakan's claims by showing, in detail, what Bakan doesn't know about video games. And also then no wonder that Plante says nothing about whether there might be connections between playing violent video games and violent action; this is not within the realm of being an expert about making or playing video games. Knowing that the most popular games at addictinggames.com are not violent does not address what might be effects of playing the ones that *are* violent—even cartoonish ones like "Don't Shoot the Puppy." Finally, given Plante's ethos, it makes sense that he would end his arguments by reminding parents of their responsibilities for what their children play and by calling Bakan's motives into question, directing us away from the game industry.

In each case, we see how what is at stake for a writer is inseparable from the writer's ethos and logos.

TO ANALYZE

■ **Write:** The comparative rhetorical analysis on the opposite page makes arguments about (as it states in its last sentence) "how what is at stake for a writer is inseparable from the writer's ethos and logos." Turn to the "Violence vs. sex" editorial on page 392. Compose your own analysis of that editorial: Identify what is at stake for the editorial's writer and how the ethos and logos of that editorial then follow.

■ **To discuss with others:** Sometimes what makes opinion pieces and editorials thought-provoking is that they offer us new perspectives or bring in unexpected but related concerns. Notice, for example, how the five preceding pieces move from arguments about how violent video games cause violent actions to arguments about the First Amendment; sex, violence, and what is offensive versus what is harmful; government intrusion into business; creativity in industry; and what protections we should offer children.

With others, choose a topic of current concern (not video game violence!) and discuss the usual opinions people have on the topic. Then brainstorm how you might consider the topic from other perspectives and what other concerns could be related. How might you use such brainstorming in the future?

CRITICAL THINKING: Evaluating the logos of editorials and opinion pieces

So far in this chapter we have focused on identifying ethos and logos in opinion pieces and editorials and analyzing how they work together. There has been, of course, some evaluation of those uses of ethos and logos, but now we want to focus on how to evaluate logos.

step 1
Identify the logical elements of the opinion piece or editorial just as we did with the pieces on earlier pages in this chapter.

step 2
Ask these questions of each logos element.

CLAIMS

• What other claims are possible about the issue at stake? Why might the writer choose the claims presented in the writing, given other possibilities?

• How do the claims direct readers' attentions toward or away from particular aspects of the issue at stake?

• Will each claim seem reasonable to a reader?

EVIDENCE

• Does the evidence support its related claim?

• Is the source for each piece of evidence credible? Does the writer provide you enough evidence (names, weblinks) so that you can check it at its source?

• Is the evidence relevant; that is, does it support the claim being made?

• Does the writer provide ways for you to check the evidence on your own, such as providing names of sources or links to websites offered as sources?

ASSUMPTIONS

• When the writer states a claim, what does the claim suppose we already believe?

• When choosing a certain word (such as "obscenity" or "intrusion" or "freedom"), what does the writer hope we will associate with the word, or what ideas we will accept without question?

CONCLUSIONS

• Do the conclusions follow from the claims and evidence?

☛ On the next two pages, we apply these questions to a new editorial on video game violence.

EVALUATING THE LOGOS OF AN EDITORIAL:
"Court majority was right"

There seem to be two claims wound up in this editorial's opening: First, that the Supreme Court was right to overturn the California law and, second, that the Supreme Court's decision was unfortunate.

By separating these two claims, we can ask "what" questions about each. About the first, we know, from the other editorials, what other claims could be made about the Supreme Court decision; we will read forward to ask how the editors defend this claim with evidence.

TWO CLAIMS

About the second, we are confused. How could the decision be both correct and unfortunate? We need to read ahead.

EVIDENCE

The editors' evidence for their first claim seems to lie with their judgment of Judge Scalia's observation: They say it "best" sums up the situation. The editors must therefore agree (and assume that readers agree) that "disgust is not a valid basis for restricting expression." Is this enough—or the right kind of—evidence for readers to agree with the first claim?

The Register-Guard
http://www.registerguard.com/

EDITORIAL: Court majority was right

But parents still need to monitor video game violence

Published: **Thursday,** *Jun 30, 2011 05:01AM*

In one video game, the player tries to fire a shot into the head of President Kennedy as his motorcade passes the Texas School Book Depository. In another, players can re-enact the killings at Columbine High School and Virginia Tech. In another, the goal is to rape Native American women or kill ethnic or religious minorities.

Disgusting? Yes. Allowed by the U.S. Constitution? Yes, according to Monday's 7-2 decision by the U.S. Supreme Court, which struck down a contested 2005 California law intended to curb minors' exposure to graphically violent video games. But did the court get it right? Unfortunately, yes.

Five of the seven justices voting in the majority agreed that video game violence — like that in books, plays and movies — is covered by the freedom of speech protections in the First Amendment. Writing for the majority, Justice Antonin Scalia summed it up best with the pithy observation that "disgust is not a valid basis for restricting expression." Justice Samuel Alito Jr. and Chief Justice John Roberts voted with the majority but did not join in Scalia's opinion, which upheld a lower court ruling.

Justice Clarence Thomas dissented, saying the First Amendment's freedom of speech protections "does not include the right to speak to minors without going through the minors' parents or guardians." Justice Stephen Breyer, noting that the court had upheld prohibitions in the past on exposing children to nude pictures, dissented and said violent video game images are at least as damaging. He appended a 15-page list of studies on the effects of video game violence on children.

This editorial was published June 30, 2011, just three days after the Supreme Court handed down its decision on the constitutionality of the California law banning the sale of violent video games to minors.

At issue was whether the state could bar the sale or rental of violent video games to customers under the age of 18. It defined violent as "killing, maiming, dismemberment or sexually assaulting an image of a human being." Had the law gone into effect, stores that violated it would have been subject to a $1,000 fine. Nothing in the law would have prevented an adult from buying such a game and giving it to a minor.

Scalia noted that only a few kinds of speech — obscenity, incitement and "fighting words" — are not covered by the First Amendment. He said the drafters of the California law were seeking to "create a wholly new category" of regulation for speech aimed at children. "That is unprecedented and mistaken," he wrote.

The justice was right that we don't need to add any more categories of speech that would be unprotected by the First Amendment, which, as it stands, is magnificent in its clarity, simplicity and respect for the individual.

But the extreme violence depicted in many of today's video games — Alito warned that new gaming technology may soon allow a player to "actually feel the splatting blood from the blown-off head" — should continue to concern parents. Representatives of the video game industry, which currently takes in $10 billion per year, were crowing Monday about how the court's ruling protects the "constitutional rights" of its customers but in reality, all they care about is their bottom line, and they're not the least bit shy about appealing to some of our basest instincts to fatten it up.

Breyer was right to note the hypocrisy in the court protecting young people from viewing nudity but standing back and giving a free pass to an industry that seems bent on feeding them a steady diet of blood-letting and mayhem. That's a reflection of a puritanical streak in our society that dates back to the landing of the Mayflower.

Maybe a time will come when such gory images will rank right up there with sexual content on the scale of things too awful for your young people to see, but don't hold your breath. Until then, minors' only effective protection against video-game violence will be parents, not laws.

Copyright © 2011 — The Register-Guard, Eugene, Oregon, USA

CONCLUSION

This conclusion seems to imply that the editors really do wish that the Supreme Court had ruled the California law to be constitutional by finding we have the right to protect children from violence just as we have the right to protect them from pornography. Does this conclusion follow from the claims and evidence of the rest of the editorial? Do you think readers will be confused by how this conclusion seems to contradict the first claim we identified at the beginning of the editorial?

The editors offer the First Amendment's "magnificence" in its clarity as further support for their first claim. Will this, combined with the first evidence we identified, be persuasive to readers? To which readers?

EVIDENCE

CLAIM

Is this how we are to understand the "unfortunately" from the editorial's beginning, with this more developed claim? Although the Supreme Court decision was right, it doesn't—unfortunately—do away with the problem that led to the original law.

EVIDENCE

The evidence for the revised claim is, in part, implied: Because the California law was overturned, nothing has changed about the situation of young people and violent video games. In addition to that implication, however, the editors point to the monetary motives of the gaming industry; this, they imply, will keep the violent games coming. (Are they also assuming that, freed from worrying about the possible censorship, the industry will produce even more violent games?)

THINKING THROUGH PRODUCTION

■ Write a new editorial on game violence. Use the various arguments and perspectives offered in this chapter to help you shape your own attitude on the issue, and use those arguments as evidence in addition to what you find on your own.

■ Pick a recent major national or international event that stirred controversy. Then, as we did in this chapter, find at least five opinion pieces or editorials on a single topic. (If you choose an international event or a national event of international interest, look at international as well as domestic newspapers. This link gives you access to online newspapers from the United States and around the world: *www.refdesk.com/paper.html*)

Analyze the individual pieces as we did here by marking and commenting on their ethos and logos.

Write a five- to seven-page paper in which you use your analysis as the basis for considering the following:

- What are the most important concerns regarding the topic?

- What are the most common arguments and conclusions about the topic?

- What is at stake for the different writers, and how does that shape their approaches to ethos and logos?

■ Pick a topic that matters to you, and write two versions of an opinion piece on it. First, research your topic so that you have facts to support the position you take. Write a version of the opinion piece in which you construct a knowledgeable, thoughtful, appealing ethos. Then, using all the same logical arguments and arrangements, write a version in which you construct an unreliable, nonauthoritative, rude, and obnoxious ethos.

Many people think that logos always wins out; producing these two editorials will help you see how ethos can very much affect how people take in all other parts of writing.

(For audience and context, plan this opinion piece as though you were writing it for your school paper. After you describe audience and purpose to yourself, use this information to help you make decisions about strategies and arrangement.)

■ Develop a design plan for an online editorial that you write on a topic that matters to you. As you work out your plan, make choices about the typeface and colors you will use and whether you will include any photographs or other illustrations. How do you think your choices will contribute to the ethos and logos readers will see in the piece?

If you have access to and knowledge about making webpages, produce the editorial and test it with various readers to see if your ideas about ethos and pathos are accurate.

analyzing essays

Essays are short writings that teach us something interesting, useful, or fun—or all three at once. We find essays in magazines and journals, collected in books, and, these days, on the Web. The word *essay* goes back at least as far as the sixteenth century, when the French writer Michel Montaigne used the French word *essai* (which literally means *to try*) to describe his short writings on subjects such as friendship and hate. In his essays, Montaigne used his writing to work through ideas or understand aspects of his life—like friendship—that are familiar and yet come in many odd forms.

Essays can be more or less argumentative and more or less long. Many thousands have been written, and in them you find a dizzying range of strategies and arrangements: comparisons, assertions of cause and effect, storytelling, logical arguments, accounts of personal experience, historical reconstructions of events, imaginative reconstructions of events, ethnographic studies, facts and figures, interviews, dialogue, self-interrogation, poetry, puns, and pictures.

HOW ESSAYS WORK

" Baudelaire wanted to call a collection of his essays on painters 'Painters Who Think.'

This is quintessentially the essayist's point of view: to convert the world and everything in it to a species of thinking. To the reflection of an idea, an assumption—which the essayist unfolds, defends, or excoriates. "

Susan Sontag

Susan Sontag was a 20th century novelist, essayist, and political activist whose books include *Against Interpretation, On Photography, Regarding the Pain of Others,* and *The Volcano Lover*. Charles Baudelaire was a nineteenth-century French poet and essayist.

How we understand essays because we live in particular times and places

Essays, like opinion pieces and academic articles, are cultural objects. Unlike drawings and photographs, where using our eyes and bodily experience of the world helps us figure out in large measure what is going on, essays require us to have undergone a tremendous amount of overt, particular, and focused instruction. Think about your years in classrooms being taught the alphabet and how to read. Think about your first picture books and how, over many years, your teachers helped you take on progressively more complex texts.

Through this process you were taught—directly or not—that words are important and that (in our time and place) being able to express yourself in words is a sign of being cultured or civilized—or able to think at all. This is certainly implied in the quotation at the left from Susan Sontag, who herself wrote many essays and novels.

Essays thus carry a lot of cultural weight: They are meant to be popular so that anyone can (and will want to) read them, but they require you to have had a long and particular training (which is continuing in this book, yes?) in order for you to understand them or take pleasure from them.

How we understand essays because we have bodies

Because essays are so tied to culture and to thinking—to notions that thinking is abstract—they can seem far away from bodily experience. Essays can be about topics that seem very intellectual (on how to think systematically about the elements) but they can also be about very bodily things (on playing basketball and living in a small town). Obviously, we need to have had bodily experiences to understand the pleasures and potentials of basketball, but we also need to have bodies and senses to understand what elements are. So bodily experience is necessary, to some degree or another, in being able to understand particular essays.

But what about understanding essays in general? Where does the pleasure of reading essays come from? We argued in the preceding column that you have to learn this. And some argue that the form of the essay is precisely about learning to turn away from your body, to shift from experiencing your body as a body to experiencing it as a thought or an abstraction. Keep this tension in mind as you read by being alert to how you understand what you read. In the essays of this chapter, *where is your body? Where is your culture?*

How essays differ from opinion pieces

Opinion pieces share some qualities with essays: They are generally one person's opinion about a particular topic, event, or possible action. But opinion pieces also differ from essays in several ways.

Opinion pieces are most often deliberative, meaning that they are intended to spur a community to action of some kind or another, with fact and reason; they can also be judgmental in that they look back to the past and argue that an action taken by a community was right or wrong, should be upheld, or should be changed. Opinion pieces are also public writing in that they are aimed at moving community members toward decisions about the community's actions.

Essays, on the other hand, tend to be reflective and often personal. They do not try to persuade readers to take particular action in the world but to think about and dwell on events or questions. Essays are public insofar as they are published, certainly, but they address readers as individual thinkers and ponderers rather than as members of a community considering action.

Strategies we emphasize in this chapter

Ethos is often central to essays, but because in chapter 12 we considered how writers develop ethos, you can apply from that earlier chapter all that you learned about analyzing ethos to this chapter's essays.

But then, because the purposes of essays vary so broadly, there is little overlap in other strategies from one essay to the next. *Learning to analyze essays rhetorically is thus about learning to notice strategies as strategies*—and so in this chapter we focus on your strategies as a reader who reads like a writer (as we discussed in chapter 9).

In this chapter, then, we focus on the following strategies:

- **How do you as a reader learn general approaches for identifying strategies?**

How this chapter is arranged

In addition to offering you a range of examples of the essay, we wish (as we wrote in the column at the left) to continue supporting you in learning to analyze rhetorically.

There are five essays in this chapter. With the first, we ask many questions of the essay and then step you through a student's analysis, showing how the student identified strategies and then wrote a rhetorical analysis from those observations.

With the second, we point out several general approaches you can use for identifying strategies and then, following the essay, discuss what we learned from those approaches.

With the third essay, we step back a bit, adding to our suggestions for identifying strategies but leaving more of the analysis up to you—an approach we continue with the fourth and fifth essays.

"THE PERIODIC TABLE"

This chapter comes from James Elkins's book *How to Use Your Eyes*, which has sections on looking at "Things Made by Man" and "Things Made by Nature." The sections have chapters on (for example) "How to look at an oil painting," which is followed by "How to look at pavement," and chapters on "How to look at the inside of your eye" and "How to look at nothing."

Elkins teaches art history and theory at the School of the Art Institute of Chicago. He has written many books—some very scholarly, some popular—about painting, the workings of sight, words and pictures, and how we respond to the things we see, art and otherwise. *How to Use Your Eyes* continues in this tradition: It is a popular text with many small chapters, and each of the chapters—like the one here—attempts to get the book's audience to use their eyes more carefully and thoughtfully.

As you read, look for strategies Elkins uses—with words and visual examples—to get you to look at and think about the periodic table in ways he thinks you haven't. At the end, we offer a rhetorical analysis of this essay to model how you might do this yourself.

■ Why do you think Elkins starts his essay by asking his readers—indirectly—to think back to high school? Into what sort of mood or frame of mind do you think he is hoping this will put readers?

how to look at

the periodic table

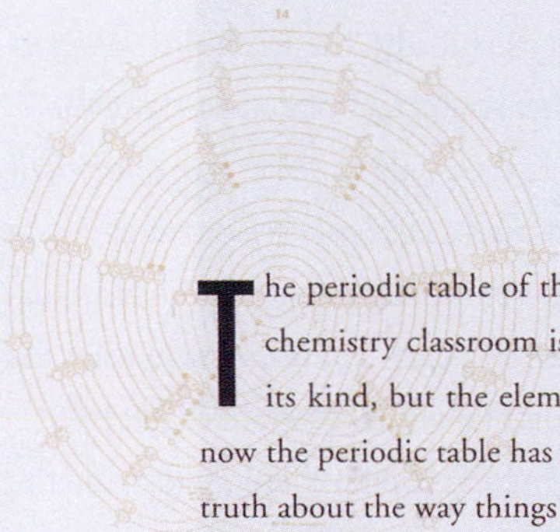

The periodic table of the elements that hangs on the wall of every high school chemistry classroom is not the only periodic table. It is the most succesful of its kind, but the elements can be arranged in many different ways, and even now the periodic table has its rivals. In other words, it doesn't represent some fixed truth about the way things are.

The table arranges the chemical elements into periods (the horizontal rows) and groups (the vertical rows). If you read it left to right, top to bottom, as if it were a page of writing, you will encounter the elements in order from the lightest to the heaviest. The top left number in each cell is the element's atomic number, which is the number of protons in its nucleus and also the number of electrons that orbit the nucleus. If you read any one column from top to bottom, you will encounter elements that have similar chemical properties.

Figure 16.1 is a version of Dmitri Ivanovich Mendeleev's periodic table, the one that has become the standard. It serves many purposes well, but it is also full of drawbacks. Just looking at it, you can see that it has an unsatisfying lack of symmetry. There is a big gap at the top, as if a chunk had been taken out of it. And at the

figure 16.1

The periodic table.

- How complex is the language Elkins uses to describe the periodic table? Does the writing sound like a college textbook? What does this tell you that Elkins is assuming about the kind of education his audience has had?

- Why might Elkins use a German example of the familiar periodic table?

- In the writing, Elkins says that this periodic table "has an unsatisfying lack of symmetry," and then he goes on to describe the "big gap at the top" and "elements that couldn't be fitted onto the table." As you read, see whether Elkins argues—gives reasons—why an asymmetric periodic table should be unsatisfying.

- This reproduction of the periodic table is printed on its side in Elkins's book. Why do you think the book's designers decided to do this?

As you read our questions, see what patterns you can note in where we ask questions. What tends to catch our eye and get us pondering? Paying such attention can help you figure out the sorts of questions you might ask.

Periodensystem der Elemente

- These pages from Elkins's chapter are arranged in our book just as they are in the original book where these two illustrations come in between pages of text. What are the effects on you, as a reader, to come upon these visual examples in the middle of turning the page to continue reading? Do they break your attention to the reading, or do they help you see Elkins's points about how "the elements can be arranged in many different ways"?

- How persuasive would Elkins's claims that "the elements can be arranged in many different ways" be if he did not include these examples?

figure 16.2

Detail of a portion of the periodic table.

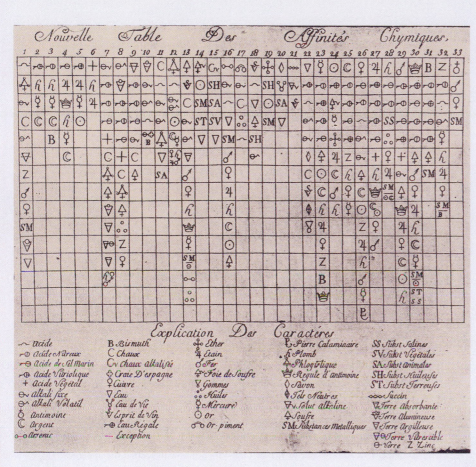

figure 16.3

J. P. de Limbourg, an affinity table of substances and elements.

- Elkins writes that a "physicist might say the periodic table should really be separated into three blocks. . . ." Why do you think he chose to write this rather than to quote a physicist?

- Do you think Elkins's intended audience will grant him enough authority to believe that any physicist would say something like that? How has Elkins built his authority in this chapter? (Consider both his writing and the visual examples he uses.)

bottom there are two extra strips of elements that couldn't be fitted onto the table. They would attach along the thick red line toward the lower left. So really the table is not two-dimensional—rather, it is two-dimensional with a flap attached near the bottom.

From a physicist's point of view, the periodic table is only an approximation. A chemist looks at elements for how they behave in test tubes; a physicist looks at them for what they say about the exact arrangements and energies of the electrons in the atoms. When electrons are added to an atom, they can occupy only certain "shells" (orbits) and certain "subshells" within those shells. (That information is given at the lower right of each cell.) A physicist might say the periodic table should really be separated into three blocks, comprised of the left two columns, the middle ten, and the right-hand six. Then each row would represent a single subshell in an atom, and if you were to read left to right across one row of one of the blocks, you would be seeing electrons added, one by one, to a single subshell.

A tremendous amount of information could potentially be added to this simple arrangement. This table distinguishes elements that are ordinarily solid (printed in black) from those that are liquid (green) and gaseous (red), and it notes which are radioactive (white). Each box has a fair amount of information: the key names atomic number, electronegativity, boiling point, melting point, atomic mass, and electron configuration. Yet if this chart were bigger, it would be possible to add much more. Figure 16.2 is a small section from an expanded periodic table with even more detail.

Before modern chemistry and physics, no one had an inkling of such complexities. The forerunners of the periodic table were "affinity tables" (Fig. 16.3). The idea was to list substances across the top and then group other substances underneath them according to how much "affinity" they had—that is, how easily they would combine. This affinity table by J. P. de Limbourg begins with acids at the upper left and runs through a miscellany of substances, including water (denoted by the inverted triangle ∇), soap ($\Diamond$), and various metals. Affinity tables have a logic, since any higher symbol will displace any lower one and combine with the substance given at the head of the column. They were criticized by Antoine Laurent Lavoisier for their lack of any real theory, but it has also been said that they were not intended to exposit any single theory.

In the late eighteenth century, there were a growing number of proposals for tables that would capture some underlying theory. People began to want something

figure 16.4

Charles Janet's helicoidal periodic table.

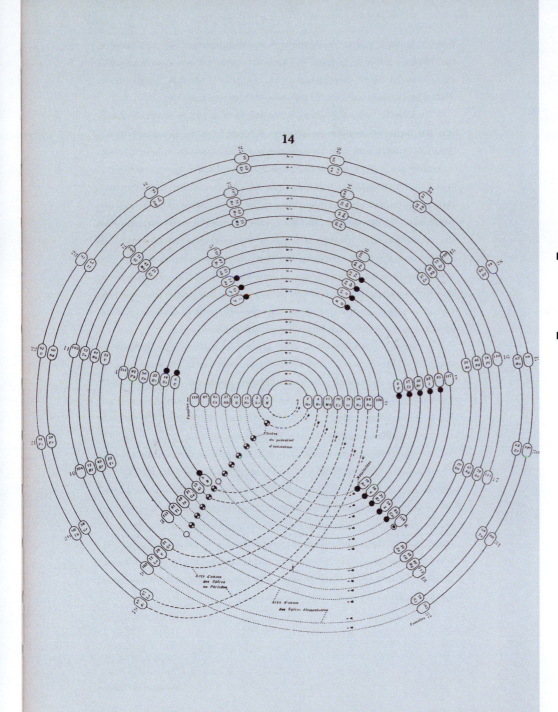

■ When you see this chart for the first time, coming as it does in Elkins's text before he explains it (on page 124 of his book), what do you think it is? Does it look like any other kind of chart or diagram with which you have experience?

■ What adjectives would you use to describe this chart? Is it boxy and thick or light and graceful—or are there other words you would use? Given the adjectives you have chosen, how do you think the arrangements, shapes, and quality of lines of this chart ask you to consider the elements? You might be helped to respond by imagining this chart with thicker, heavier lines, or colored rectangular shapes instead of ovals. You can also compare this chart with the more familiar periodic table opposite the first page of Elkins's essay.

411

■ In the second full paragraph, Elkins writes that the periodic table shown to the far right "has the virtue of being a single piece instead of a stack of blocks like the familiar periodic table." Why, for Elkins, is this a virtue? What strategies has he used to try to persuade his readers that this is a virtue?

■ This essay ends with Elkins writing that "there seems to be an inbuilt notion that something as elemental as the elements should obey some appropriately simple law. It's a hope that animates a great deal of scientific research. The periodic table, in all its incarnations, appears to be a glaring exception to that hope."

How has Elkins prepared his readers for those statements?

Based on these final sentences, what do you think Elkins is hoping his readers will think or do when they have finished this essay?

that was rigorously true and could not be shifted and rearranged like the affinity tables. We have settled on a version of Mendeleev's table, but many others continue to be proposed. There are polygonal tables, triangular "scrimshaw" graphs, three-dimensional models, and even old-fashioned-looking schematic trees.

Charles Janet's "helicoidal" classification, proposed in 1928, is a typical elaboration (Fig. 16.4). He imagines the elements all strung together on a single thread. The chain spirals upward as if it were wrapped around a glass tube, and then it leaps to another glass tube, winds around a few more times, and leaps to a third tube. Janet asks us to imagine the three tubes inside one another. At first the helix is confined to the smallest tube, but it spirals out to the middle tube and occasionally the largest tube. The diagram gives the helix in plan, as if the three tubes were squashed flat. Actually, he says, it is very neat because the three imaginary glass tubes all touch on one side (as they would if they were laid on their sides on a table). The problem is that to draw them, he has to cut the chain—hence the confusing dotted lines. In Figure 16.5, the whole thing is spread apart, as if the glass tubes had been removed and the chain were splayed out on a table. That makes it clearer that all the elements are on a single thread wound around three different spools.

It looks odd, but Janet's periodic table has the virtue of being a single piece instead of a stack of blocks like the familiar periodic table. The beginning of Mendeleev's periodic table is at the center of Janet's smallest spool, in Figure 16.4. If you follow the thread, you encounter the elements one after another in the same order as in Mendeleev's table. The middle spool is the middle "block" of the periodic table, separated from the others the way a physicist might do it.

Why don't people adopt schemes like Janet's? Partly from force of habit, because we are all accustomed to Mendeleev's chart. Maybe knots and helices are intrinsically harder for people to imagine. (I certainly have trouble thinking about Janet's helices and trying to picture how they work.) Still, there seems to be an inbuilt notion that something as elemental as the elements should obey some appropriately simple law. It's a hope that animates a great deal of scientific research. The periodic table, in all its incarnations, appears to be a glaring exception to that hope. It seems that when it came to the elements, God created something massively complex and very nearly without any satisfying symmetries at all.

figure 16.5

The same, spread out.

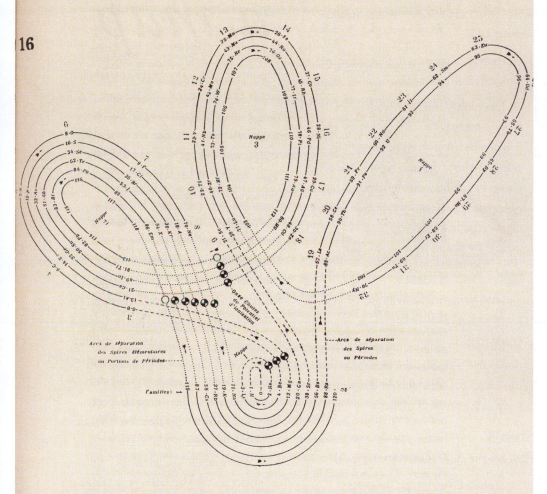

■ Is this a "satisfying" diagram for you when you know that it is supposed to represent how all the elements in the universe are related?

413

A RHETORICAL ANALYSIS OF "THE PERIODIC TABLE"

These next few pages show one person's thinking process as she worked her way through the preceding essay using the steps for a rhetorical analysis that we described on pages 316–317.

Step 1

What are the piece's purpose, audience, and context?

"When I first read the essay, I thought Elkins just wanted us to learn that there is more than one version of the periodic table. I figured he was speaking not to experts (because he speaks about them) but to nonexperts, people who have been to high school and remember that big periodic table on the wall in chemistry class.

The context for this essay is the book where the essay was published but the context also includes the fact that Elkins knows more about the periodic table and about seeing than we do. His relation to us is something like a teacher to a student. I think Elkins wants to expand our nonexpert view of the periodic table."

Step 2

List everything about the communication that seems to you to be a choice.

"As I read (and reread) the essay, certain things stood out:

1 Right away, Elkins invokes the image of a periodic table hanging in a high school classroom.

2 He begins the essay by pointing out that the periodic table we know—the Mendeleev table—is not the only one.

3 He shows us a German version of the Mendeleev table.

4 He shows us three (actually four!) other versions of the periodic table.

5 He interrupts his discussion of the Mendeleev table by having us turn the page and find not the rest of his discussion but two other versions of the periodic table. We do not get back to his words until we turn the page again (that is, until we are done lingering over the new tables).

6 He uses much time (for a short essay) discussing the last example, the Janet version.

7 He poses the question, "Why don't people adopt schemes like Janet's?"

8 He titles the essay "How to look at the periodic table"—but his point seems to be that there is not one ideal table but many actual and possible periodic tables."

Step 3

How are the choices used strategically?

"1 Right away, Elkins invokes the image of a periodic table hanging in a high school classroom. *Why?* Perhaps because he wants to pique our interest or get us to think, "I remember the periodic table being a bunch of squares. What do these other ones look like? Why do we need more than one version? Who is making them? Why are they making them? What can we learn by looking at these other versions?"

2 Elkins begins the essay by pointing out that the periodic table with which we are familiar —the Mendeleev table—is not the only one. *Why?* Perhaps he wants to signal early on that he assumes that readers are somewhat familiar with this table—at least with how it looks—and he will be using this fact about his audience to move his essay forward.

3 Elkins shows us a German version of the Mendeleev table. *Why?* I do know that Elkins wants us to learn about other versions of the table, and (as we know from the next observation) he criticizes the Mendeleev table for being asymmetrical and for being in crude blocks. So maybe there's something special about the German version? Is it more symmetrical and less crude? When I look back at the essay to check these ideas out, I don't find Elkins talking about the German vs. the English version at all. It is just there, as asymmetrical and in crude block form as he describes the Mendeleev table being. So—another idea—perhaps he wants us to look at the German Mendeleev table, assume it is the one we are familiar with, then do a double-take and say, wait a minute, that

looks odd—hey, it's in German! Perhaps he wants the familiar version suddenly to look a little strange. *But why?*

4 Elkins shows us three (actually four!) other versions of the periodic table. *Why three? Why these three, in this order?* For a short essay, three or four versions would be enough to give us a sense of a range of other versions. The three he shows us are—in order—a detail of one like the Mendeleev table but with more information, an older version called an affinity table, and (two views of) Janet's periodic table.

I think he chose these three because the first one is similar to the Mendeleev table, the second looks similar but also includes odd symbols and looks musty and mysterious, and Janet's looks very different in either of its views. I think maybe Elkins put them in this order because—if you only know the Mendeleev table—the others move from the more familiar to the less familiar, from the simpler to the more complex.

5 Elkins interrupts his discussion of the Mendeleev table by having us turn the page and find not the rest of his discussion of it but two other versions of the periodic table, and we do not get back to his words until we turn the page again after looking at the new tables. *Why?* I think maybe Elkins thinks that, by this point in the essay, he has put a little distance between us and the familiar version because he's pointed out its flaws

and showed us a German rather than an English one—and now he wants to build on that distance by showing us still other versions.

The fact that he shows us first one that is quite similar (the detail) and then one whose column form is familiar but whose content is strange suggests that he still thinks we may be a little resistant to these other versions and that we need to be eased into looking at them. Maybe he arranged them as he did in order to move us gradually into the less familiar—to get us comfortable being uncomfortable, so to speak.

But what's interesting is that he interrupts his own words and leaves us to look at these two versions on our own. This implies he wants us to see for ourselves.

6 Elkins uses much time (for a short essay) discussing the last example, the Janet version. *Why?* I think the answer lies in what he tells us about the other two versions and then about Janet's version: The table with more information than the Mendeleev version is better suited to physicists while the Mendeleev version is better suited to chemists. Physicists look at elements in terms of electron orbits, but chemists look at elements in terms of their reactions in test tubes. It is about organizing information usefully. Janet's version similarly organizes information about the elements according to Janet's purpose, which is to show that elements

form a continuum as though joined by a single thread. Janet's version is not fanciful, though: It is based on knowledge of modern science. It just invites us to look at the relations between the elements differently than we do the other tables.

Elkins also tells us that the Mendeleev table took hold at a time (the late 17th century) when people wanted a single version of the table that captured the truth, that is, the modern scientific truth that was just emerging—as opposed to the partial or mixed truths found in versions like the affinity table.

7 Elkins poses the question, "Why don't people adopt schemes like Janet's?" *Why? And why should we care?* Again, it looks to me as though the beginning of an answer is in what Elkins tells us: He answers his question by saying, "Partly from force of habit." All along we have seen him use strategies that imply he thinks we—his readers—might be stuck in a rut because we've seen only the Mendeleev table. He wonders how—even whether—we will look at these other versions. And when he gets to the Janet version, he admits that he himself has trouble looking.

The other reason people don't adopt schemes like Janet's, Elkins argues, goes back to the 17th-century desire for a single straightforward table that presents modern scientific truth. So he tells us that even scientists—who know the difference between chemistry and physics—assume that "something as elemental as the elements should obey some appropriately simple law."

The reason people resist schemes like Janet's, then, is twofold, according to Elkins: We resist out of habit and because we assume there should only be one, true, simple version.

8 He titles the essay "How to Look at the Periodic Table"—but his point seems to be that there is not one ideal table but many actual and possible periodic tables. *Why?* I should have begun with this question because the title is the first thing we see when we read the essay, but now I think I sense why he titles the essay as he does. After answering my other questions, I see that Elkins not only wants us to learn something new about the periodic table but also that, by doing so, he also wants us to learn something about the connection between sight, habit, and assumptions. He wants us to learn that we do not just see; rather, we learn to see, and what we learn affects what and how we see. "

Step 4

Test your observations: Are there any anomalies?

"I'm noticing two things now.

One, my initial sense of Elkins's purpose—that he just wanted us to see other versions of the periodic table—didn't mention anything about learned habits or assumptions. So my initial statement was based on a partial view of the essay: It was based only on Elkins showing us different versions and inviting us to look at them. But it ignored important parts of the essay, such as how Elkins ordered the versions he showed us and his concern that out of habit we might resist looking at new versions. Taking these details into account, I need a new statement of purpose, audience, and context.

Two, I noticed that his title seems odd given what his purpose is. In the title he refers to the periodic table as though there were only one, but any reader ought to realize quickly that Elkins wants us to see that there are many periodic tables, many possible versions, some of which have not even been designed yet. "

Step 5

Revise your original statement about the piece.

"If we ask now what about his audience most concerns Elkins, I see that it is the way they—we—have learned to see the periodic table and how our habits and assumptions influence how we look at anything new or unfamiliar. The purpose is to make us aware of the role that habits and assumptions play in how we look at objects. The audience is people who are familiar with only the Mendeleev table, and what is important about the audience is that they have learned to look at the periodic table in a certain way and need some help to look—to see—differently.

Here's some evidence in my favor. First, the context of the essay supports my statement that Elkins does not just want us to look at the periodic table differently but from now on to look differently at anything new and unfamiliar. Part of the context is the book title, *How to Use Your Eyes*, which suggests right away that he wants to achieve more than simply changing how we look at the periodic tables. And, second, it just makes more sense to me that Elkins would be concerned more about how we look at things generally than about how we look just at the periodic table (though he cares about that too, and it serves him as a useful example to make his larger argument about how we see and how we understand the world).

But I'm still troubled by why Elkins brings God into the story at the end. Why does he write that it seems "when it came to the elements, God created something massively complex and very nearly without any satisfying symmetries at all"? It is as though all the periodic tables are just fruitless attempts to get at something more complex than we have models for understanding ... and maybe that's part of his point, too, that these tables (and other scientific models?) are just attempts and can never be complete and that we need to use them without thinking that we are getting to the "real" truth ...? "

☞ On the following pages is an essay that takes many of the observations and conclusions from the preceding analysis and builds them into a coherent paper that most composition and rhetoric teachers would like.

READING AND RESPONDING RHETORICALLY

To the right is an informal rhetorical analysis—that makes an argument—of the essay on pages 406–413. This essay grows out of the analysis on pages 414–416.

Reg Wiedmeyer
March 21, 2012

A Rhetorical Analysis of "How to Look at the Periodic Table"

I think James Elkins wrote his essay "How to Look at the Periodic Table" to get us to understand how we organize the world through charts. That's why Elkins shows us not just one periodic table, but several, each one giving us a different possible way of seeing, and so understanding, what's out there. By encouraging us to question how charts like these shape how we see, Elkins asks us to think about our sight in larger ways, too.

Let me describe some of Elkins's strategies, in the order he gives them to us, to show how I think his strategies support my interpretation.

First, the way Elkins addresses his readers shows us that he is not trying to teach us about elements. Instead, Elkins begins by asking us to think about the periodic tables we might have seen in high school because I think high school is the experience he assumes everyone in his audience shares. This indicates the knowledge level he imagines his audience has (and in doing so he also calms any fears a reader like me might have that this essay will be beyond us). Elkins also doesn't use abstract scientific language or math, which also indicates he doesn't think his audience is highly-trained scientists. For example, when he talks about how elements are arranged in the periodic table, he uses expressions like "lightest to heaviest" and "similar chemical properties"—again, language that is easy to follow.

While he is putting us at ease as I have just described, Elkins shifts how we look and what we look for. He opens the essay with a negative statement: He tells us that the familiar periodic table is not the only version and so prepares us to consider the others' merits. Elkins ends the first page by offering evidence of the familiar version's "unsatisfying asymmetry," yet before he has finished with the thought, the reader turns the page and finds two other versions of the table—and they are intriguing enough to make one pause. What Elkins does is to interrupt our reading and to substitute looking; he also interrupts consideration of the familiar version of the table and substitutes other versions, just at the point where the familiar version's asymmetry is being established. The effect can only be (I argue!) to get us not only to look at and see two other versions but to do so with the question of symmetry in mind. On the surface, each of the two new versions has greater symmetry. The first has two neat rows, without any "big gaps" (such as the one that makes the Mendeleev version "unsatisfying"), and the second runs left to right with thirty-three columns and no gaps. Some of the columns run longer than others, and the general "look" of the thing is antiquish and funky, but still it feels more symmetrical—and that is what one has been set up to look for.

This sets me up to look in a new way at the fourth version. Before this, I would have thought Janet's "helicoidal periodic table" looked like a weird Japanese board game. But having been alerted to the question of symmetry, and having been told by Elkins that different tables capture different interests, I am prepared to see the relatively satisfying symmetry of this version.

And, messy or not, Janet's version has virtues for Elkins that the Mendeleev model does not: Janet's version captures and displays more and better information. As Elkins remarks, "It looks odd, but Janet's periodic table has the virtue of being a single piece instead of a stack of blocks like the familiar periodic table" (124). If we did not get his point earlier, that the more familiar Mendeleev periodic table's appeal is based only on its familiarity and that other versions have their virtues too, despite being unfamiliar and seemingly complex, we certainly get it when he contrasts the "blocks" of the Mendeleev table to the "beads" and "single piece" of Janet's table.

At some point during this tour of periodic tables, the reader most likely will ask what the point is. Elkins does not want us to see one particular table as better than all the rest. He makes it clear (as I said above) that different tables serve different purposes, and if value is related to purpose, each will have its value. A reader might then ask, if each has its value, why does Elkins seem intent on trashing the Mendeleev periodic table?

But is this what Elkins is trying to do?

By asking "Why don't people adopt schemes like Janet's?," Elkins begins to answer our question regarding his overall point: We don't adopt the other schemes, he writes, "Partly from force of habit, because we are all accustomed to Mendeleev's chart." Elkins has come full circle back to the essay's opening, reminding us that, if we are familiar with a periodic table at all, we are probably only familiar with "Mendeleev's chart." Admitting that the other charts have potentially confusing "knots" and "helices," he nevertheless wants us to stretch beyond the familiar to appreciate the others. The others may be "intrinsically harder for people to imagine," he tells us—and he makes common cause with a reader who feels that way by adding about himself that "I certainly have trouble thinking about Janet's helices and trying to picture how they work"—but by essay's end, Elkins hopes we are more inclined to accept the twisted "knots" and "helices" of the unfamiliar.

Put otherwise, Elkins hopes we are more inclined to accept that not everything obeys simple, easy laws, that not everything easy is good, and that not everything good is simple. In case a reader is still wavering, uncertain there is room for messiness in the world God created, Elkins gently closes the door with his final sentence: "It seems that when it came to elements, God created something massively complex and very nearly without any satisfying symmetries at all" (124). If it is good enough for God, it should be good enough for us, Elkins seems to be saying.

Learning to see and appreciate requires at the very least that we learn to feel our way beyond the familiar and in the process learn to put up with complexities beyond easy comprehension. I assume the lesson is supposed to reach beyond our appreciation of periodic tables to all our eyes happen upon.

WORKS CITED

Elkins, James. "How to Look at the Periodic Table." *How to Use Your Eyes*. New York: Routledge, 2000. Print. 118–125.

TO ANALYZE:
"HOW TO LOOK AT THE PERIODIC TABLE"

■ **Write and discuss:** Write a one- or two-sentence summary of Elkins's essay. Then write several paragraphs in which you use examples of Elkins's words and illustrations to support your summary. Compare your summary and supporting examples with those of two or three other people in your class to see how differently you use Elkins's words and illustrations to support your summaries.

■ **Discuss with others:** Do you think that Elkins's strategies in this essay, overall, rely primarily on logos or pathos—or a mix? How might his overall purpose shape his choices of strategy?

■ **Produce a museum:** Using a mix of library and web research, find examples—besides those Elkins uses here—of how the elements are (or have been) represented. On paper or online, construct a "museum" of the examples for beginning high school chemistry students. You'll need to include commentary to help orient your audience. What do you want them to see and think about as they look at your examples? What strategies will help you focus their attentions on what you think is most important in your collection?

(One resource for finding other periodic tables is "The Internet Database of Periodic Tables" at http://www.meta-synthesis.com/webbook/35_pt/pt_database.php)

■ **Make a presentation:** Find other charts or diagrams (besides the periodic table) with which you've grown up or that you see around you frequently. (The food pyramid put out by the U.S. Department of Agriculture [online at http://www.nal.usda.gov/fnic/Fpyr/pmap.htm] is one possibility; the constellations and a calendar of the months are others.) Using a mix of library and web research, gather together other representations of the same information. Compare the examples, as Elkins does in this essay, to think about how the different configurations of the charts or diagrams ask their audiences to consider the information. Develop an oral presentation in which your examples support an argument about which chart or diagram seems the best or fairest representation to you—or why none of them alone achieves what you think should be represented.

PREPARING TO READ THE ESSAY "HIGHER EDUCATION"

About the essay's author

The author of the next essay, Gary Smith, is a senior writer for *Sports Illustrated* magazine and a three-time winner of the National Magazine Award for feature writing; he has also won Excellence in Sports Journalism awards presented by the organization Sport in Society and Northeastern University's School of Journalism, and he has won a Women's Sports Journalism Award. His works have appeared numerous times in *The Best American Sports Writing* collections. "Higher Education" has been reprinted in *The Best Spiritual Writing of 2002* and *The Best American Nonrequired Reading*, and Jerry Bruckheimer and his production company bought the rights to turn it into a film.

As a writer, Smith takes great care not only to say what he wants to say but also to say it in such a way that he will affect his readers in a thoughtful way. He cares about his readers. And his readers care about his writing—hence, all the awards and attention given to him as a writer. But we should be careful not to put him on too high a pedestal, for we can learn much from him that will help us improve our own communication abilities.

What stands out as you read?

In chapter 9, on pages 316–317, we laid out the steps for reading (or listening or looking) rhetorically.

Of all those steps, perhaps the most difficult is the second: Making detailed observations, especially observations that will lead you to useful questions, takes practice. What if, when you read, nothing stands out? What if the words just sit there on the page flat and mute?

Making detailed observations requires reading more than once. The first time through, pay attention to where—and how—a composer wants to direct your attentions. As you read the first time, attend to strategies composers can use to make a word or phrase or paragraph stand out, so that you will "hear" it. Strategies such as the following help writers place emphasis where they want it:

- **Titles**. Titles give you a sense of the topic as well as (often) the emotional mood.

- **Beginnings**. First paragraphs are like first meeting a person: Your first impressions carry with you through all your experiences of and with that person, coloring how you think about each other.

- **Endings**. This is like a goodbye, the last view you have that lingers, the last view through which you look back on all that preceded.

The last paragraphs of any writing tell you what thoughts or emotions the writer hopes audiences will carry away.

- **Repetitions**. Anything repeated—a word, a phrase—shows you that a composer wants that word or phrase to stay with you, to shape how you think while reading.

- **Breaks between sections**. Section breaks mark off the conceptual chunks through which a composer wants you to think about the essay; the words at the beginning and end of the sections likewise gain importance from being set off.

Read "Higher Education" looking for the strategies listed above (and anything else that sticks out to you). Afterward, we'll show you how and why various strategies stood out to us, and how we built them into an interpretation.

(We'll ask questions alongside this essay to indicate where something stood out to us, using items from the list on the preceding page but also making other observations we'll explain in more detail after this essay. You might read the first time without paying any attention to our questions, noticing instead what stands out to you; then come back and see where our questions fit with yours or point in other interpretive directions.)

■ What does "higher education"—the title of this piece—make you think the first time you see it? By the end of the essay, do you think Smith is working with a different sense of "higher" than simply that which invokes a college education?

Interlude Jason Mishler will always carry, on his body and in his heart, the image of his greatest teacher.

Higher Education

In the unlikeliest of places— Ohio's Amish country—a high school basketball coach changed a community's ideas about race, and about life

BY GARY SMITH   PHOTOGRAPHS BY LYNN JOHNSON

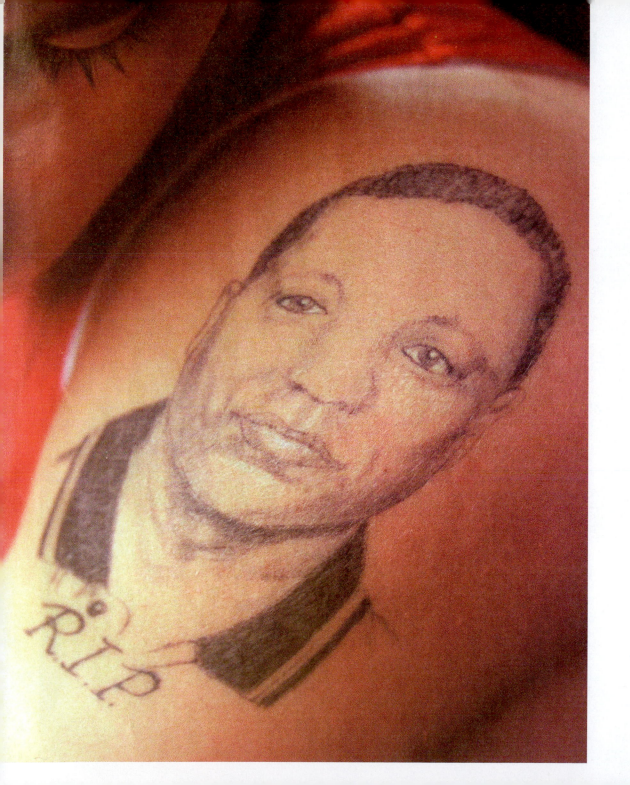

- Why might Smith use "magic" twice in the first paragraph? Into what mood or frame of mind might he hope this will put readers?

- Smith never uses "I" to refer to himself—but what sense do you develop of him? Do you trust his observations, opinions, and conclusions? What strategies does he use to encourage you to trust his observations? (And why do you think Smith keeps the attention off himself? Where instead does he ask you to direct your attentions?)

- What are we supposed to think about Willie? Why does Smith choose to tell us what he does about Willie here?

- Notice how, after several descriptive phrases about Charlie's assistant coach, Smith gathers them together in a summary description: "an unmarried, black, Catholic loser." How does this compare with what we just learned about Willie? Does Smith ever give us another descriptive list for "the black man" and is the description similar to or different from this one?

THIS IS a story about a man, and a place where magic happened. It was magic so powerful that the people there can't stop going back over it, trying to figure out who the man was and what happened right in front of their eyes, and how it'll change the time left to them on earth.

See them coming into town to work, or for their cup of coffee at Boyd & Wurthmann, or to make a deposit at Killbuck Savings? One mention of his name is all it takes for everything else to stop, for it all to begin tumbling out. . . .

"I'm afraid we can't explain what he meant to us. I'm afraid it's so deep we can't bring it into words."

"It was almost like he was an angel."

"He was looked on as God."

There's Willie Mast. He's the one to start with. It's funny, he'll tell you, his eyes misting, he was so sure they'd all been hoodwinked that he almost did what's unthinkable now—run that man out of town before the magic had a chance.

All Willie had meant to do was bring some buzz to Berlin, Ohio, something to look forward to on a Friday night, for goodness' sake, in a town without high school football or a fast-food restaurant, without a traffic light or even a place to drink a beer, a town dozing in the heart of the largest Amish settlement in the world. Willie had been raised Amish, but he'd walked out on the religion at 24—no, he'd peeled out, in an eight-cylinder roar, when he just couldn't bear it anymore, trying to get somewhere in life without a set of wheels or even a telephone to call for a ride.

He'd jumped the fence, as folks here called it, become a Mennonite and started a trucking company, of all things, his tractor-trailers roaring past all those horses and buggies, moving cattle and cold meat over half the country. But his greatest glory was that day back in 1982 when he hopped into one of his semis and moved a legend, Charlie Huggins, into town. Charlie, the coach who'd won two Ohio state basketball championships with Indian Valley South and one with Strasburg-Franklin, was coming to tiny Hiland High. Willie, one of the school's biggest hoops boosters, had banged the drum for Charlie for months.

And yes, Charlie turned everything around in those winters of '82 and '83, exactly as Willie had promised, and yes, the hoops talk was warmer and stronger than the coffee for the first time in 20 years at Willie's table of regulars in the Berlin House restaurant. They didn't much like it that second year when Charlie brought in an assistant—a man who'd helped him in his summer camps and lost his job when the Catholic school where he coached went belly-up—who was black. But Charlie was the best dang high school coach in three states; he must've

known something that they didn't. Nor were they thrilled by the fact that the black man was a Catholic, in a community whose children grew up reading tales of how their ancestors were burned at the stake by Catholics during the Reformation in Europe more than 400 years ago. But Charlie was a genius. Nor did they cherish the fact that the Catholic black was a loser, 66 times in 83 games with those hapless kids at Guernsey Catholic High near Cambridge. But Charlie. . . .

Charlie quit. Quit in disgust at an administration that wouldn't let players out of their last class 10 minutes early to dress for practice. But he kept the news to himself until right before the '84 school year began, too late to conduct a proper search for a proper coach. Willie Mast swallowed hard. It was almost as if his man, Charlie, had pulled a fast one. Berlin's new basketball coach, the man with the most important position in a community that had dug in its heels against change, was an unmarried black Catholic loser. The *only* black man in eastern Holmes County.

It wasn't that Willie hated black people. He'd hardly known any. "All I'd heard about them," he'll tell you, "was riots and lazy." Few had ever strayed into these parts, and fewer still after that black stuffed dummy got strung up on the town square in Millersburg, just up the road, after the Civil War. Maybe twice a year, back in the

Berlin wall Reese used basketball to bridge the gap between Amish traditions and those of the modern world.

1940s and '50s, a Jewish rag man had come rattling down Route 39 in a rickety truck, scavenging for scrap metal and rags to sell to filling stations 30 miles northeast in Canton or 60 miles north in Cleveland, and brought along a black man for the heavy lifting. People stared at him as if he were green. Kids played Catch the Nigger in their schoolyards without a pang, and when a handful of adults saw the color of a couple of Newcomerstown High's players a few years before, you know what word was ringing in those players' ears as they left the court.

Now, suddenly, this black man in his early 30s was standing in the middle of a gym jammed with a thousand whites, pulling their sons by the jerseys until their nostrils and his were an inch apart, screaming at *them*. Screaming, "Don't wanna hear your shoulda-coulda-wouldas! Get your head outta your butt!" How dare he?

Worse yet, the black man hadn't finished his college education, couldn't even teach at Hiland High. Why, he was working at Berlin Wood Products, the job Charlie had arranged for him, making little red wagons till 2 p.m. each day. "This nigger doesn't

know how to coach," a regular at the Berlin House growled.

Willie agreed. "If he wins, it's because of what Charlie built here," he said. "What does he know about basketball?"

But what could be done? Plenty of folks in town seemed to treat the man with dignity. Sure, they were insular, but they were some of the most decent and generous people on earth. The man's Amish coworkers at the wood factory loved him, after they finally got done staring holes in the back of his head. They slammed Ping-Pong balls with him on lunch hour, volleyed theology during breaks and dubbed him the Original Black Amishman. The Hiland High players seemed to feel the same way.

He was a strange cat, this black man. He had never said a word when his first apartment in Berlin fell through—the landlord who had agreed to a lease on the telephone saw the man's skin and suddenly remembered that he rented only to families. The man had kept silent about the cars that pulled up to the little white house on South Market Street that he moved into instead, about the screams in the darkness, the voices threatening him on his telephone and the false rumors that he was dating their women. "They might not like us French Canadians here," was all he'd say, with a little smile, when he walked into a place and felt it turn to ice.

Finally, the ice broke. Willie and a few pals invited the man to dinner at a fish joint up in Canton. They had some food and beers and laughs with him, sent him on his merry way and then . . . what a co-incidence: The blue lights flashed in the black man's rearview mirror. DUI.

Willie's phone rang the next morning, but instead of it being a caller with news of the school board's action against the new coach, it was *him*. Perry Reese Jr. Just letting Willie know that he knew exactly what had happened the night before. And that he wouldn't go away. The school board, which had caught wind of the plot, never made a peep. Who *was* this man?

Some people honestly believed that the coach was a spy—sent by the feds to keep an eye on the Amish—or the vanguard of a plot to bring blacks into Holmes County. Yet he walked around town looking people in the eyes, smiling and teasing with easy assurance. He never showed a trace of the loneliness he must have felt. When he had a problem with someone, he went straight to its source. Straight to Willie Mast in the school parking lot one night. "So you're not too sure about me because I'm black," he said, and he laid everything out in front of Willie, about

- "Nigger" is a word crusted over with hate. When used by white people, it is most often meant to cause pain. Smith—and his editors at *Sports Illustrated*—must have given long and deep thought to including the word here because it causes so much pain when used by whites. Why do you think Smith and his editors decided to use the word? Do you think they think there are no black people in their audience? Do they think their audience thinks that only people who haven't benefited from "higher education" would use the word, and that the essay shows one (long, hard, and personal) way people are so educated?

- Why does Smith tell us the man's name (Perry Reese Jr.) at the precise moment he does, only after we've heard others talk and think about him through (hateful) stereotypes? Why does Smith then keep referring to him as "the black man"? Does this change?

Perry Reese Jr.

- Smith comes back to the idea that what happened in the town was "magic," and yet an important part of this story is about religion. What connection do you think Smith want us to make with these two terms ?

- Here is where Smith chooses to describe differences between the Mennonites and the Amish. How is the difference important to the essay? How does it shape how you understand the people described in this essay?

racism and how the two of them needed to get things straight.

Willie blinked. He couldn't help but ask himself the question folks all over town would soon begin to ask: Could I do, or even dream of doing, what the coach is doing? Willie couldn't help but nod when the black man invited him along to scout an opponent and stop for a bite to eat, and couldn't help but feel good when the man said he appreciated Willie because he didn't double-talk when confronted—because Willie, he said, was real. Couldn't help but howl as the Hiland Hawks kept winning, 49 times in 53 games those first two years, storming to the 1986 Division IV state semifinal.

Winning, that's what bought the black man time, what gave the magic a chance to wisp and curl through town and the rolling fields around it. That's what gave him the lard to live through that frigid winter of '87. That was the school year when he finally had his degree and began teaching history and current events in a way they'd never been taught in eastern Holmes County, the year the Hawks went 3–18 and the vermin came crawling back out of the baseboards. Damn if Willie wasn't the first at the ramparts to defend him, and damn if that black Catholic loser didn't turn things right back around the next season and never knew a losing one again.

How? By pouring Charlie Huggins's molasses offense down the drain. By runnin' and gunnin', chucking up threes, full-court pressing from buzzer to buzzer—with an annual litter of runts,

> The Hawks' Nest, Hiland's old gym, became a loony bin, the one place a Mennonite could go to sweat, shriek and squeal.

of spindly, short, close-cropped Mennonites! That's what most of his players were: the children, grandchildren and great-grandchildren of Amish who, like Willie, had jumped the fence and endured the ostracism that went with it. Mennonites believed in many of the same shall-nots as the Amish: A man shall not be baptized until he's old enough to choose it, nor resort to violence even if his government demands it, nor turn his back on community, family, humility, discipline and orderliness. But the Mennonites had decided that unlike the Amish, they could continue schooling past the eighth grade, turn on a light switch or a car ignition, pick up a phone and even, except the most conservative of them, pull on a pair of shorts and beat the pants off an opponent on the hardwood court without drifting into the devil's embrace.

The Hawks' Nest, Hiland's tiny old gym, became what Willie had always dreamed it would be: a loony bin, the one place a Mennonite could go to sweat and shriek and squeal; sold out year after year, with fans jamming the hallway and snaking out the door as they waited for the gym to open, then stampeding for the best seats an hour before the six o'clock jayvee game; reporters and visiting coaches and scouts sardined above them in wooden lofts they had to scale ladders to reach; spillover pouring into the auditorium beside the gym to watch on a video feed as noise thundered through the wall. A few dozen teenage Amish boys, taking

Hoops fever A run-and-gun attack—this year including Chris Miller (21, opposite)—and rabid fans are part of Reese's legacy in Berlin.

advantage of the one time in their lives when elders allowed them to behold the modern world, and 16-year-old cheerleaders' legs, would be packed shoulder to shoulder in two corners of the gym at the school they weren't permitted to attend. Even a few Amish men, Lord save their souls, would tie up the horses and buggies across the street at Yoder's Lumber and slink into the Nest. And plenty more at home would tell the missus that they'd just remembered a task in the barn, then click on a radio stashed in the hay and catch the game on WKLM.

Something had dawned on Willie, sitting in his front-row seat, and on everyone else in town. The black man's values were virtually the same as theirs. Humility? No coach ever moved so fast to duck praise or bolt outside the frame of a team picture. Unselfishness? The principal might as well have taken the coach's salary to pep rallies and flung it in the air—most of it ended up in the kids' hands anyway. Reverence? No congregation ever huddled and sang out the Lord's Prayer with the crispness and cadence that the Hawks did before and after every game. Family? When Chester Mullet, Hiland's star guard in '96, only hugged his mom on parents' night, Perry gave him a choice: Kiss her or take a seat on the bench. Work ethic? The day and season never seemed to end, from 6 a.m. practices to 10 p.m. curfews, from puke buckets and running drills in autumn to two-a-days in early winter to camps and leagues and an open gym every summer day. He out-Amished the Amish, out-Mennonited the Mennonites, and everyone, even those who'd never sniffed a locker in their lives, took to calling the black man Coach.

Ask Willie. "Most of the petty divisions around here disappeared because of Coach," he'll tell you. "He pulled us all together. Some folks didn't like me, but I was respected more because he respected me. When my dad died, Coach was right there, kneeling beside the coffin, crossing himself. He put his arm right around my mom—she's Amish—and she couldn't get over that. When she died, he was the first one there. He did that for all sorts of folks. I came to realize that color's not a big deal. I took him for my best friend."

And that man in Willie's coffee clan who'd held out longest, the one given to calling Coach a nigger? By Coach's fifth year, the man's son was a Hawk, the Hawks were on another roll, and the man had seen firsthand the effect Coach had on kids. He cleared his throat one morning at the Berlin House; he had something to say.

"He's not a nigger anymore."

THE MAGIC didn't stop with a nigger turning into a man and a man into a best friend. It kept widening and deepening. Kevin Troyer won't cry when he tells you about it, as the others do. They were brought up to hold that back, but maybe his training was better. He just lays out the story, beginning that autumn day 10 years ago when he was 16, and Coach sat him in the front seat of his Jeep, looked in his eyes and said, "Tell me the truth."

Someone had broken into Candles Hardware and R&R Sports and stolen merchandise. Whispers around town shocked even the whisperers: that the culprits were their heroes, kids who could walk into any restaurant in Berlin and never have to pay. They'd denied it over and over, and Coach had come to their defense . . . but now even he had begun to wonder.

A priest. That's what he'd told a few friends he would be if he

JAMIE SABAU

- Smith tells us that the Amish boys, and "even a few Amish men, Lord save their souls," were drawn to the basketball games. Is he suggesting that they are being led into temptation? Are Perry and the game of basketball undermining the religious values of the community?

- Are all the values Willie sees Reese sharing with the community religious values? Any? All? Most?

- Smith tells us that the man in Willie's coffee clan who held out the longest against "Coach" announced one morning, five years after Reese had settled into the town, "He's not a nigger anymore." How are readers supposed to hear that?

weren't a coach. That's whose eyes Kevin felt boring into him. How could you keep lying to the man who stood in the lobby each morning, greeting the entire student body, searching everyone's eyes to see who needed a headlock, who needed lunch money, who needed love? "Don't know what you did today, princess," he'd sing out to a plump or unpopular girl, "but whatever it is, keep it up. You look great."

He'd show up wearing a cat's grin and the shirt you'd gotten for Christmas—how'd he get into your bedroom closet?—or carrying the pillow he'd snagged right from under your head on one of his Saturday morning sorties, when he slipped like smoke into players' rooms, woke them with a pop on the chest, then ran, cackling, out the door. Sometimes those visits came on the heels of the 1 a.m. raids he called Ninja Runs, when he rang doorbells and cawed "Gotcha!", tumbling one family after another downstairs in pajamas and robes to laugh and talk and relish the privilege of being targeted by Coach. He annihilated what people here had been brought up to keep: the space between each other.

His door was never locked. Everyone, boy or girl, was welcome to wade through those half dozen stray cats on the porch that Coach gruffly denied feeding till his stash of cat food was found, and open the fridge, grab a soda, have a seat, eat some pizza, watch a game, play cards or Ping-Pong or Nintendo . . . and talk. About race and religion and relationships and teenage trouble, about stuff that wouldn't surface at Kevin Troyer's dinner table in a million years. Coach listened the way other folks couldn't, listened clean without jumping ahead in his mind to what he'd say next, or to what the Bible said. When he finally spoke, he might play devil's advocate, or might offer a second or third alternative to a kid who'd seen only one, or might say the very thing Kevin didn't want to hear. But Kevin could bet his mother's savings that the conversations wouldn't leave that house.

Coach's home became the students' hangout, a place where they could sleep over without their parents' thinking twice . . . as long as they didn't mind bolting awake to a blast of AC/DC and a 9 a.m. noogie. There was no more guard to drop. Parents trusted Coach completely, relied on him to sow their values.

He sowed those, and a few more. He took Kevin and the other Hawks to two-room Amish schools to read and shoot hoops with wide-eyed children who might never get to see them play, took the players to one another's churches and then to his own, St. Peter, in Millersburg. He introduced them to Malcolm X, five-alarm chili, Martin Luther King Jr., B.B. King, crawfish, Cajun wings, John Lee Hooker, Tabasco sauce, trash-talk fishing, Muhammad Ali.

And *possibility*. That's what Coach stood for, just by virtue of his presence in Berlin: possibility, no matter how high the odds were stacked against you, no matter how whittled your options seemed in a community whose beliefs had barely budged in 200 years, whose mailboxes still carried the names of the same Amish families that had come in wagons out of Pennsylvania in the early 1800s—Yoders and Troyers and Stutzmans and Schlabachs and Hostetlers and Millers and Mullets and Masts. A place where kids, for decades, had graduated, married their prom dates and stepped into their daddies' farming or carpentry or lumber businesses without regard for the fact that Hiland High's graduating classes of 60 ranked in the top 10 in Ohio proficiency tests nearly every year. Kevin Troyer's parents didn't seem to care if he went to college. Coach's voice was the one that kept saying, "It's *your* life. There's so much more out there for you to see. Go places. Do things. Get a degree. Reach out. You have to take a chance."

The kids did, more and more, but not before Coach loaded them with laundry baskets full of items they'd need away from home, and they were never out of reach of those 6 a.m. phone calls. "I'm up," he'd say. "Now you are too. Remember, I'm always here for you."

He managed all that without raising red flags. He smuggled it under the warm coat of all that winning, up the sleeve of all that humility and humor. Everyone was too busy bubbling over the 11 conference titles and five state semifinals. Having too much fun volunteering to be henchmen for his latest prank, shoving

■ We learn about Reese's antics, such as waking his players up at 7 a.m., or rousting whole families out of bed at 1 a.m. What does this intrusion into their homes tell us about his relationship to the townspeople? Can you think of other places in the article where our attention is turned to the relation of the public to the private?

■ For a while now, Smith has been referring to Perry as "Coach." When did he start to do this? How does this differ from what Coach was called before? Why do you think Smith made this change without calling attention to it?

Mr. Pratt's desk to the middle of his English classroom, removing the ladder to maroon the radio play-by-play man up in the Hawks' Nest loft, toilet-papering the school superintendent's yard and then watching Coach, the most honest guy in town, lie right through all 32 teeth. He was a bootlegger, that's what he was. A bootlegger priest.

"Kevin . . . tell the truth."

Kevin's insides trembled. How could he cash in his five teammates, bring down the wrath of a community in which the Ten Commandments were still stone, own up to the man whose explosions made the Hawks' Nest shudder? How could he explain something that was full of feeling and empty of logic—that somehow, as decent as his parents were, as warm as it felt to grow up in a place where you could count on a neighbor at any hour, it all felt suffocating? All the restrictions of a Conservative Mennonite church that forbade members to watch TV, to go to movies, to dance. All the emotions he'd choked back in a home ruled by a father and mother who'd been raised to react to problems by saying, "What will people think?" All the expectations of playing for the same team that his All-State brother, Keith, had carried to its first state semi in 24

"Most of the petty divisions around here disappeared because of Coach," Mast says. "He pulled us all together."

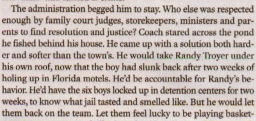

years, back in 1986. Somehow, busting into those stores in the summer of '91 felt like the fist Kevin could never quite ball up and smash into all that.

"I . . . I did it, Coach. We. . . . "

The sweetest thing eastern Holmes County had ever known was ruined. Teammate Randy Troyer, no relation to Kevin, disappeared when word got out. The community gasped—those six boys could never wear a Hawks uniform again. Coach? He resigned. He'd betrayed the town's trust and failed his responsibility, he told his superiors. His "sons" had turned to crime.

The administration begged him to stay. Who else was respected enough by family court judges, storekeepers, ministers and parents to find resolution and justice? Coach stared across the pond he fished behind his house. He came up with a solution both harder and softer than the town's. He would take Randy Troyer under his own roof, now that the boy had slunk back after two weeks of holing up in Florida motels. He'd be accountable for Randy's behavior. He'd have the six boys locked up in detention centers for two weeks, to know what jail tasted and smelled like. But he would let them back on the team. Let them feel lucky to be playing basketball when they'd really be taking a crash course in accountability.

Kevin found himself staring at the cinder-block wall of his cell, as lonely as a Mennonite boy could be. But there was Coach, making his rounds to all six lost souls. There was that lung-bursting bear hug, and another earful about not following others, about believing in yourself and being a man.

The Berlin Six returned. Randy Troyer lived in Coach's home for four months. Kevin walked to the microphone at the first pep rally, sick with nerves, and apologized to the school and the town.

Redemption isn't easy with a 5' 11" center, but how tight that 1991–92 team became, players piling into Coach's car every Thursday after practice, gathering around a long table at a sports bar a half hour away in Dover and setting upon giant cookie sheets heaped with 500 hot wings. And how those boys could run and shoot. Every time a 20-footer left the hands of Kevin Troyer or one of the Mishler twins, Nevin and Kevin, or the Hawks' star, Jr. Raber, Hiland's students rose, twirling when the ball hit twine and flashing the big red 3's on their T-shirts' backs.

Someday, perhaps in a generation or two, some Berliner might not remember every detail of that postseason march. Against Lakeland in the district championship, the Hawks came out comatose and fell behind 20–5, Coach too stubborn to

429

- What does Smith mean when he calls Reese a "bootlegger priest"? If that seems an odd description to you, try to explain why Smith might combine those two words.

- Smith returns here to the scene of Reese confronting Kevin (with "Kevin … Tell me the truth."). What did we learn in the past few pages and what does it add to the story? Why does Smith interrupt Kevin's story?

- Smith gives us Kevin's perspective on the break-in. Does he want us to think what Kevin did was okay? Why give us such a compelling view from inside Kevin's head?

- Smith shows us that we have now come 180 degrees: Reese quits, and the "administration begged him to stay." Are we supposed to feel that Reese and the town are now fully reconciled? What role does this story (about the break-in) within a story play in the overall story?

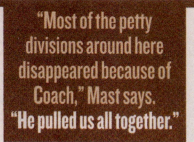

- How does Smith create suspense in his description of this state semifinal game? (Look, for example, at his use of time at the beginning of the paragraphs in the second column of this page. What other strategies do you see?)

- There are quite a few paragraphs focused on one particularly exciting basketball game. You might argue that Smith puts this into the article just to keep the interest of his *Sports Illustrated* readers, but how does it also fit into the other rhythms of the story? Why tell about the game here?

call a timeout—the man could never bear to show a wisp of doubt. At halftime he slammed the locker-room door so hard that it came off its hinges, then he kicked a crater in a trash can, sent water bottles flying, grabbed jerseys and screamed so loud that the echoes peeled paint. Kevin and his mates did what all Hawks did: gazed straight into Coach's eyes and nodded. They knew in their bones how small his wrath was, held up against his love. They burst from that locker room like jackals, tore Lakeland to bits and handily won the next two games to reach the state semis. The world came to a halt in Berlin.

How far can a bellyful of hunger and a chestful of mission take a team before reality steps in and stops it? In the state semifinal in Columbus, against a Lima Central Catholic bunch loaded with kids quicker and thicker and taller and darker, led by the rattlesnake-sudden Hutchins brothers, Aaron and all-stater Anthony, the Hawks were cooked. They trailed 62–55 with 38 seconds left as Hiland fans trickled out in despair and Lima's surged to the box-office windows to snatch up tickets for the final. Lima called timeout to dot its *i*'s and cross its *t*'s, and there stood Coach in the Hiland huddle, gazing down at a dozen forlorn boys. He spoke more calmly than they'd ever heard him, and the fear and hopelessness leaked out of them as they stared into his eyes and drank in his plan. What happened next made you know that everything the bootlegger priest stood for—bucking the tide, believing in yourself and possibility—had worked its way from inside him to inside them.

Nevin Mishler, who would sit around the campfire in Coach's backyard talking about life till 2 a.m. on Friday nights, dropped in a rainbow three with 27 seconds left to cut the deficit to four. Timeout, calm words, quick foul. Lima's Anthony Hutchins blew the front end of a one-and-one.

> Something had dawned on everyone in town. The black man's values were **virtually the same as theirs.**

Eleven seconds left. Jr. Raber, whose wish as a boy was to be black, just like Coach, banked in a driving, leaning bucket and was fouled. He drained the free throw. Lima's lead was down to one. Timeout, calm words, quick foul. Aaron Hutchins missed another one-and-one.

Nine ticks left. Kevin Troyer, who would end up going to college and becoming a teacher and coach because of Coach, tore down the rebound and threw the outlet to Nevin Mishler.

Seven seconds left. Nevin turned to dribble, only to be ambushed before half-court by Aaron Hutchins, the wounded rattler, who struck and smacked away the ball.

Five seconds left, the ball and the season and salvation skittering away as Nevin, who cared more about letting down Coach than letting down his parents, hurled his body across the wood and swatted the ball back toward Kevin Troyer. Kevin, who almost never hit the floor, who had been pushed by Coach for years to give more, lunged and collided with Anthony Hutchins, then spun and heaved the ball behind his back to Jr. Raber as Kevin fell to the floor.

Three seconds left. Jr. took three dribbles and heaved up the impossible, an off-balance 35-footer with two defenders in his face, a shot that fell far short at the buzzer . . . *but he was fouled.* He swished all three free throws, and the Hawks won, they *won*—no matter how many times Lima fans waiting outside for tickets insisted to Hiland fans that it couldn't be true—and two days later won the only state title in school history, by three points over Gilmour Academy, on fumes, pure fumes.

In the aisles, people danced who were forbidden to dance. The plaque commemorating the crowning achievement of Coach's life went straight into the hands of Joe Workman, a water and towel boy. Kevin Troyer and his teammates jumped Coach before he could sneak off, hugging him and kissing him and rubbing his head, but he had the last laugh. The 9 a.m. noogies would hurt even more those next nine years, dang that championship ring.

SOMEONE WOULD come and steal the magic. Some big-cheese high school or college would take Coach away—they knew it, they just knew it. It all seems so silly now, Steve Mullet says. It might take Steve the last half of his life to finish that slow, dazed shake of his head.

Berlin, you see, was a secret no more by the mid-1990s. Too much winning by Coach, too many tourists pouring in to peer at the men in black hats and black bug-

gies. Two traffic lights had gone up, along with a Burger King and a couple dozen gift shops, and God knows how many restaurants and inns with the word *Dutch* on their shingles to reel in the rubberneckers. Even the Berlin House, where Willie Mast and the boys gathered, was now the Dutch Country Kitchen.

Here they came, the city slickers. Offering Coach big raises and the chance to hush that whisper in his head: Why keep working with disciplined, two-parent white kids when children of his own race were being devoured by drugs and despair for want of someone like him? Akron Hoban wanted him. So did Canton McKinley, the biggest school in the city where Coach had grown up, and Canton Timken, the high school he attended. They wanted to take the man who'd transformed Steve Mullet's family, turned it into something a simple and sincere country fellow had never dreamed it might be. His first two sons were in college, thanks to Coach, and his third one, another guard at Hiland, would likely soon be too. Didn't Steve owe it to that third boy, Carlos, to keep Coach here? Didn't he owe it to all the fathers of all the little boys around Berlin?

Coach had a way of stirring Steve's anxiety and the stew of rumors. He would walk slow and wounded through each April after he'd driven another team of runts to a conference crown, won two or three postseason games, and then yielded to the facts of the matter, to some school with nearly twice as many students

World of their fathers At Mullet's auction barn, Berlin's future Amish farmers can get early lessons in the value of horseflesh.

and a couple of 6' 5" studs. "It's time for a change," he'd sigh. "You guys don't need me anymore."

Maybe all missionaries are restless souls, one eye on the horizon, looking for who needs them most. Perhaps Coach was trying to smoke out even the slightest trace of misgivings about him, so he could be sure to leave before he was ever asked to. But Steve Mullet and eastern Holmes County couldn't take that chance. They had to act. Steve, a dairy farmer most of his life, knew about fencing. But how do you fence in a man when no one really understands why he's there, or what he came from?

Who was Coach's family? What about his past? Why did praise and attention make him so uneasy? The whole community wondered, but in Berlin it was disrespectful to pry. Canton was only a 45-minute hop away, yet Steve had never seen a parent or a sibling of Coach's, a girlfriend or even a childhood pal. The bootlegger priest was a man of mystery and moods as well as a wide-open door. He'd ask you how your grandma, sister and uncle were every time you met, but you weren't supposed to inquire about his—you just sensed it. His birthday? He wouldn't say. His age? Who knew? It changed every time he was asked. But his loneliness, that at last began to show.

■ We learn that the town—after a successful season—is worried Coach may get lured away by another team that wants a good coach and Coach seems to feed their concern. Smith speculates that "[p]erhaps Coach was trying to smoke out even the slightest trace of misgivings about him. . . ." Is that a fair speculation? Does it make Coach seem ungrateful, or . . . ?

Perry Reese Jr.

Coach's teasing and advice, on his cards and flowers and prayers when their loved ones were sick or their children had them at wit's end, and they did what they could to keep him in town. "I wish we could find a way to make you feel this is your family, that this is where you belong," Peg wrote him. "If you leave," she'd say, "who's going to make our kids think?" The women left groceries and gifts on his porch, homemade chocolate-chip cookies on his kitchen table, invited him to their homes on Sundays and holidays no matter how often he begged off, never wanting to impose.

But they all had to do more, Steve decided, picking up his phone to mobilize the men. For God's sake, Coach made only $28,000 a year. In the grand tradition of Mennonites and Amish, they rushed to answer the community call. They paid his rent, one month per donor; it was so easy to find volunteers that they had a waiting list. They replaced his garage when a leaf fire sent it up in flames; it sent him up a wall when he couldn't learn the charity's source. They passed the hat for that sparkling new gym at Hiland, and they didn't stop till the hat was stuffed with 1.6 million bucks. Steve Mullet eventually had Coach move into a big old farmhouse he owned. But first Steve and Willie Mast had another brainstorm: road trip. Why not give Coach a couple of days' escape from their cornfields and his sainthood, and show him how much they cared?

That's how Steve, a Conservative Mennonite in his mid-40s, married to a woman who didn't stick her head out in public unless it was beneath a prayer veil, found himself on Bourbon Street in New Orleans. Standing beside Willie and behind Coach, his heartbeat rising and stomach fluttering as he watched Coach suck down a Hurricane and cock his head outside a string of bars, listening for the chord that would pull him inside.

Coach nodded. This was the one. This blues bar. He pushed open the door. Music and smoke and beer musk belched out. Steve looked at Willie. You could go to hell for this, from everything they'd both been taught. Willie just nodded.

They wedged into a whorl of colors and types of humanity. When Steve was a boy, he'd seen blacks only after his parents jumped the fence, became Mennonites and took the family in their car each summer to a city zoo. Nothing cruel about blacks was ever said. Steve's parents simply pulled him closer when they were near, filled him with a feeling: Our kind and theirs don't mix. Now there were blacks pressed against his shoulders, blacks on microphones screaming lust and heartache into Steve's ears, blacks pounding rhythm through the floorboards and up into his knees. People touching, people gyrating their hips. You could go to hell for this. Steve looked at Willie as Coach headed to the bathroom. "I can't take this," Steve said.

"It's Coach's time, bub," Willie said.

Coach came back, smelled Steve's uneasiness and knew what to do. "Liven up," he barked and grinned. They got some beers, and it was just like the Hawks' radio play-by-play man, Mark Lonsinger, always said: Coach stood out in a room the instant he walked in, even though he did everything to deflect it. Soon Coach had the folks nearby convinced that he was Black Amish, a high-

■ Why does Smith spend so much time on the trip to New Orleans? How does he set up this story? That is, what has Smith told us just prior to the New Orleans story that prepares us for the story and its purpose within the overall story?

Tough love Reese's players—and their parents—took his tirades in stride.

There were whispers, of course. Some claimed he'd nearly married a flight attendant, then beat a cold-footed retreat. A black woman appeared in the stands once, set the grapevine sizzling, then was never glimpsed again. Steve and his pals loved to tease Coach whenever they all made the 20-mile drive to Dinofo's, a pizza and pasta joint in Dover, and came face to face with that wild black waitress, Rosie. "When you gonna give it up?" she'd yelp at Coach. "When you gonna let me have it?"

He'd grin and shake his head, tell her it would be so good it would spoil her for life. Perhaps it was too scary, for a man who gave so much to so many, to carve it down to one. Maybe Jeff Pratt, the Hiland English teacher, had it right. Loving with detachment, he called it. So many people could be close to him, because no one was allowed too close.

A circle of women in Berlin looked on him almost as a brother—women such as Nancy Mishler, mother of the twins from the '92 title team, and Peg Brand, the school secretary, and Shelly Miller, wife of the booster club's president, Alan. They came to count on

COURTESY OF TOM MULLET

ly obscure sect, and Steve, swallowing his laughter, sealing the deal with a few timely bursts of Pennsylvania Dutch, had them believing the three of them had made it to New Orleans from Ohio in a buggy. Before you knew it, it was nearly midnight, and Steve's head was bobbing, his feet tapping, his funk found deep beneath all those layers of mashed potatoes. You know what, he was telling Willie, this Bourbon Street and this blues music really aren't so bad, and isn't it nice, too, how those folks found out that Mennonites aren't Martians?

When they pulled back into Coach's driveway after days filled with laughter and camaraderie, Steve glanced at Willie and sighed, "Well, now we return to our wives."

"You're the lucky ones," said Coach. "Don't you ever forget that."

Steve realized something when they returned from the road: It wasn't the road to ruin. He felt more space inside himself, plenty enough room for the black friends his sons began bringing home from college for the weekend. He realized it again the next year, when they returned to Bourbon Street, and the next, when they went once more, and the one after that as well. "Some things that I was taught were strictly no-nos . . . they're not sins," Steve will tell you. "All I know is that it all seemed right to do with him."

Funny how far that feeling had fanned, how many old, deep lines had blurred in Berlin, and what occurred in a dry community when Coach overdid it one night four years ago and tried one last time to leave. "I screwed up," he told school superintendent Gary Sterrett after he got that second DUI, 14 miles up the road in Sugar Creek. "You need to take my job."

What happened was sort of like what happened the time the ball rolled toward the Hawks' bench in a game they were fumbling away that year at Garaway High, and Coach pulled back his leg and kicked the ball so hard that it hissed past a referee's ear and slammed off the wall, the gym hushing in anticipation of the technical foul and the ejection. But nothing happened. The two refs had such enormous respect for Coach, they pretended it away.

He apologized to every player and to every player's parents for the DUI. Steve never mentioned it. The community never said a word. It was pretended away.

THEY'VE COMBED through the events a thousand times, lain in bed at night tearing themselves and God to shreds. There were clues, after all, and it was their job to notice things Coach was too stubborn to admit. They thought, when he holed up in his motel room for three days in

Spreading the gospel Players on the Hiland bench wear reminders of Reese's teachings on their backs during games.

> "I wish we could make you feel this is your family," Brand wrote to Reese. "If you leave, who's going to make our kids think?"

Columbus last March, that it was merely one of his postseason moods, darker than ever after falling one game shy, for the third straight year, of playing for the state title. They thought he was still brooding two months later when, preoccupied and suffering from a cold he couldn't shake, he started scrambling names and dates and getting lost on country roads.

It all came to a head one Saturday last June, when he climbed into another rented tux because Phil Mishler, just like 50 or 60 kids before him, had to have Coach in his wedding party. At the reception, Coach offered his hand to Tom Mullet and said, "I'm Perry Reese Jr., Hiland High basketball coach." Tom Mullet had been Hiland's assistant athletic director for 10 years.

Phone lines buzzed that Sunday. People began comparing notes, discovering new oddities. On Monday night two of Coach's best friends, Dave Schlabach and Brian Hummel, headed to Mount Hope and the old farmhouse Coach had moved into just outside Berlin, the only house with lights in a community of Amish. They found him shivering in a blanket, glassy-eyed and mumbling nonsense.

Their worst possible fears . . . well, it went beyond all of them. Brain tumor. Malignant. Inoperable. Four to eight months to live, the doctors at Canton's Aultman Hospital said. You can't bring down a sledgehammer faster than that.

Jason Mishler, Coach's starting point guard the past two years, was the first kid to find out. He stationed himself in the chair beside Coach's bed, wouldn't budge all night and most of the next day. His cousin Kevin Mishler, from the state championship team, dropped his vacation on Hilton Head Island, S.C., and flew back. Dave Jaberg, who had played for Hiland a few years before that, dropped the bonds he was trading in Chicago and drove for six

- What is the connection between what Smith refers to as the "magic" and this notion of "pretending" things away?

- Why do you think the essay doesn't end when we learn of Reese's brain tumor, or shortly thereafter?

- Smith says that the townspeople, upon learning Reese has cancer, prayed for a "Big M, a miracle." Why not just say "a miracle"? Are readers supposed to see a difference between magic and miracles in the story?

- Smith tells us that Reese had two half-sisters and a sister and a brother whom he had been visiting all along but had kept from the townspeople. Smith also tells us that Reese's relation to the townspeople was like family, and that the student athletes were his "sons." How do you square these two parts of the story? What does it suggest about the relation of the public to the private?

hours. Jr. Raber was on the first plane from Atlanta. Think a moment. How many teachers or coaches would you do that for?

The nurses and doctors were stupefied—didn't folks know you couldn't fit a town inside a hospital room? Coach's friends filled the lobby, the elevator, the halls and the waiting room. It was like a Hiland basketball game, only everyone was crying. Coach kept fading in and out, blinking up at another set of teary eyes and croaking, "What's new?"

What do people pray for when doctors don't give them a prayer? They swung for the fences. The Big M, a miracle. Some begged for it. Some demanded it. A thousand people attended a prayer vigil in the gym and took turns on the microphone. Never had so much anger and anguish risen from Berlin and gone straight at God.

Steroids shrank the tumor enough for Coach to return home, where another throng of folks waited, each telling the other tales of what Coach had done to change his life, each shocked to find how many considered him their best friend. When he walked through his front door and saw the wheelchair, the portable commode, the hospital bed and the chart Peg Brand had made, dividing the community's 24-hour care for Coach into six-hour shifts, he sobbed. The giving was finished. Now all he could do was take.

Go home, he ordered them. Go back to your families and lives. He called them names. They knew him well enough to know how loathsome it was for him to be the center of attention, the needy one. But they also knew what he would do if one of them were dying. They decided to keep coming anyway. They were family. Even more in his dying than in his living, they were fused.

They cooked for him, planned a trip to New York City he'd always dreamed of making, prayed and cried themselves to sleep. They fired off e-mails to churches across the country, recruited entire congregations who'd never heard of Coach to pray for the Big M. Louise Conway, grandmother of a player named Jared Coblentz, woke up three or four times a night, her heart thumping so hard that she had to drop to her knees and chew God's ear about Coach before she could drop back to sleep. People combed the Internet for little-known treatments. They were going to hoist a three at the buzzer and get fouled.

Coach? He did the strangest thing. He took two radiation treatments and stopped. He refused the alternative treatments, no matter how much people cried and begged and flung his own lessons in his face. Two other doctors had confirmed his fate, and damned if he was going to be helpless for long if he could help it. "Don't you understand?" he told a buddy, Doug Klar. "It's O.K. This is how it's supposed to be."

He finally had a plan, one that would

How much, in the end, was changed by this one man? In Berlin, they're still tallying that one up.

make his death like his life, one that would mean the giving wasn't finished. He initiated a foundation, a college scholarship fund for those in need, started it rolling with his $30,000 life savings and, after swallowing hard, allowed it to be named after him on one condition: that it be kept secret until he was dead.

He had no way to keep all the puzzle pieces of his life in boxes now; dying shook them out. Folks found out, for instance, that he turned 48 last August. They were shocked to meet two half sisters they'd never heard of. They were glad finally to see Coach's younger sister, Audrey Johnson, whose picture was on his refrigerator door and who was studying to be a social worker, and his younger brother, Chris, who helps run group homes for people who can't fend for themselves and who took a leave of absence to care for Coach.

It turned out that Audrey had made a couple of quiet visits a year to Coach and that the family had gathered for a few hours on holidays; there were no dark or splintering secrets. He came from two strict parents who'd died in the '80s—his dad had worked in a Canton steel mill—and had a mixed-race aunt on one side of the family and a white grandfather on the other. But there were never quite enough pieces of the puzzle for anyone to put them together on a table and get a clean picture.

Coach's family was shocked to learn a few things too. Like how many conservative rural white folks had taken a black man into their hearts. "Amazing," said Jennifer Bethà, his half sister, a supervisor for Head Start. "And so many loving, respectful, well-mannered children around him. They were like miniature Perrys! Our family was the independent sort, all kind of went our own ways. I never realized how easy it is to get to Berlin from Canton, how close it is. What a waste. Why didn't we come before?"

Coach had two good months, thanks to the steroids. Berlin people spent them believing that God had heard them, and that the miracle had come. Coach spent the months telling hundreds

Coaching change Jordan (right), adopted by the Millers, plays with his brother Cameron as sister McKenzie and mother Shelly look on.

of visitors how much he cared about them, making one last 1 a.m. Ninja Run and packing his life into 10 neat cardboard boxes.

The first week of August, he defied doctors' orders not to drive and slipped into the empty school. Gerald Miller, his buddy and old boss at the wagon factory, found him later that day at home, tears streaming down his cheeks. "Worst day of my life," Coach said. "Worse than finding out about this thing in my head. I cleaned out my desk. I can't believe it. I'm not gonna teach anymore. I'm done."

In early September the tumor finally had its way. He began slurring words, falling down, losing the use of his right hand and leg, then his eyesight. "How are you doing?" he kept asking his visitors, on blind instinct. "Is there anything I can do for *you*?" Till the end he heard the door open and close, open and close, and felt the hands, wrapped around his, doing that too.

On the day he died, Nov. 22, just over a week before the Hawks' first basketball game and 17 years after he first walked through their doors, Hiland looked like one of those schools in the news in which a kid has walked through the halls with an

> ## Hard to believe, an outsider becoming the **moral compass** of a people with all those rules on how to live right.

quit going to church for months, then figured out that it might be greedy to demand a miracle when you've been looking at one all your life. Tattoo parlors added Mennonites to their clientele. Jr. Raber stares at the R.I.P. with a P beneath it on his chest every morning when he looks into the mirror of his apartment in Atlanta. Jason Mishler rubs the image of Coach's face on the top of his left arm during the national anthem before every game he plays at West Liberty (W.Va.) State.

The scholarship fund has begun to swell. Half the schools Hiland has played this season have chipped in checks of $500 or $600, while refs for the girls' basketball games frequently hand back their $55 checks for the pot.

Then there's the bigger stuff. Kevin Troyer has decided that someday, rather than teach and coach around Berlin, he'll reverse Coach's path and do it with black kids up in Canton. Funny, the question he asked himself that led to his decision was the same one that so many in Berlin ask themselves when they confront a dilemma: What would Coach do? Hard to believe, an outsider becoming the moral compass of a people with all those rules on how to live right.

And the even bigger stuff. Like Shelly and Alan Miller adopting a biracial boy 10 years ago over in Walnut Creek, a boy that Coach had taken under his wing. And the Keims over in Charm adopting two black boys, and the Schrocks in Berlin adopting four black girls, and the Masts just west of town adopting two black girls, and Chris Miller in Walnut Creek adopting a black girl. Who knows? Maybe some of them would have done it had there never been a Perry Reese Jr., but none of them would have been too sure that it was *possible*.

"When refugees came to America," the town psychologist, Elvin Coblentz, says, "the first thing they saw was the Statue of Liberty. It did something to them—became a memory and a goal to strive for your best, to give your all, because everything's possible. That's what Coach is to us."

The mourning season This year's Hawks struggle with their grief in different ways.

automatic weapon. Six ministers and three counselors walked around hugging and whispering to children who were huddled in the hallway crying or staring into space, to teachers sobbing in the bathrooms, to secretaries who couldn't bear it and had to run out the door.

AN OLD nettle digs at most every human heart: the urge to give oneself to the world rather than to only a few close people. In the end, unable to bear the personal cost, most of us find a way to ignore the prickle, comforting ourselves that so little can be changed by one woman or one man anyway.

How much, in the end, was changed by this one man? In Berlin, they're still tallying that one up. Jared Coblentz, who might have been the Hawks' sixth man this year, quit because he couldn't play for anyone other than Coach. Jason Mishler was so furious that he

At the funeral, just before Communion, Father Ron Aubry gazed across St. Peter, Coach's Catholic church in Millersburg. The priest knew that what he wanted to do wasn't allowed, and that he could get in trouble. But he knew Coach too. So he did it: invited everyone up to receive the holy wafer.

Steve Mullet glanced at his wife, in her simple clothing and veil. "Why not?" she whispered. After all, the service wasn't the bizarre ritual they had been led to believe it was, wasn't all that different from their own. Still, Steve hesitated. He glanced at Willie Mast. "Would Coach want us to?" Steve whispered.

"You got 'er, bub," said Willie.

So they rose and joined all the black Baptists and white Catholics pouring toward the altar, all the basketball players, all the Mennonites young and old. Busting laws left and right, busting straight into the kingdom of heaven. □

■ Smith tells us in the final pages all the aftereffects Reese had on the town and townspeople. How would you sum up the effects Smith points to?

■ Smith tells us that Kevin decided after Reese's death to "reverse Coach's path" and teach "black kids up in Canton." Does Smith think this is a simple reversal? Do you?

■ Smith ends saying "Busting laws right and left, busting straight into the kingdom of heaven." What does he mean? Which laws were being busted?

LOOKING BACK AT "HIGHER EDUCATION":
What we noticed—and why

Developing an initial sense of the purpose, context, and audience of "Higher Education" isn't hard. The article was written for *Sports Illustrated* and is about a black, African American high school basketball coach in a small Ohio town populated by people mostly of the Mennonite faith, a Christian sect related to the Amish. Smith tells how the coach came to the town, about his initial rejection by many of the townspeople, and how the town slowly came to accept, appreciate, and even love him. It is an essay with a lesson to teach about how we can learn to live with people who have religious and cultural backgrounds different from our own; Coach already appears to have known, but the townspeople didn't.

So far, so good. But how do we test, extend, qualify, or change this initial assessment? We know we need to start by making more careful observations—by looking more closely at what is said and the way it is written—and by turning those observations into questions about Smith's purpose, audience, and context. We need to be able to ask of the moves we see Smith making, *Why did he do that, there? What is it supposed to do to and for the reader? How does it work as a single strategy within Smith's overall plan and purpose?* But how do we know what to look at, what to observe, in order to respond to those questions?

Put otherwise, when we get to the second step in a rhetorical analysis—where we make observations about a text in order to test our hypothesis about the purpose, context, and audience of the text—what if nothing really stands out for us? Or what if too many things stand out, and we don't know how to choose what matters to our hypothesis?

Next we go over what stood out for us in this essay and why; much, as you'll see, comes from the list we gave you on page 421.

The essay's title

Smith's title draws attention to what seems like a small part of the essay: What does higher education have to do with relations between people with different cultural and religious backgrounds? But look at how "education" is treated throughout the essay. Who learns what and why? How does the education happen? How is our usual notion of "higher education"—college—changed or turned on its head?

What is repeated in the essay

Writers repeat names and phrases to draw attention to them.

The first repetition we noticed in Smith's essay is that, in the beginning, Smith keeps referring to the person we will come to know as "Coach" or "the black man" before we learn his real name. Smith could alternate between the name and "the assistant coach," but chooses to emphasize "the black man" at this stage. We wondered why, though not for long: The essay is about the relationship between this black man and a town that had never experienced a black man in the community, much less in a prominent position. Referring to him repeatedly as "the black man" keeps front and center the main obstacle between him and this town.

The next repetition we noticed was that in several places Smith calls Reese a "bootlegger priest" without explanation. Given that what Smith calls Reese ("the black man" or "Coach") seems important, "bootlegger priest" must also be important, but we are not sure why—so we file this away to keep in mind as we read on.

Placement in an essay

Once we observe a repetition—for instance, of "bootlegger priest"—we then look to see where in the essay, exactly, Smith calls Reese that. By considering what comes before and after the words we want to understand, we might better understand Smith's strategy.

We observe that Smith first calls Reese a "priest" on page 53 of the essay, at the very end of a digression within the essay, where Reese confronts Kevin about the break-in. The point of calling Reese a "bootlegger priest" here seems to be to tell us that the coach is a paradoxical mix, part bootlegger (Smith also calls him a "prankster") and part priest (Smith also says Reese was like a father to his students). The second time Smith calls Reese a "bootlegger priest" is on page 54, in the middle of the story of one of Reese's biggest wins as a coach, and specifically at the point in the essay where Reese turns around a losing game with a rousing locker-room speech. Here Smith seems to be saying that Reese was effective in turning the game around both because he had a special relationship with the players, and because, well, he had a certain "magic."

Small changes in repetition
The second time Smith calls Reese a "bootlegger priest," Smith seems to imply something different from the first time: It is not that Reese embodies paradoxical qualities as that he embodies both natural (or normal) and magical qualities. We don't yet know what to do with this observation, though, so we file it away, too.

Other repetitions
Another repetition: Smith tells us how Reese confronted Kevin, one of his student athletes, about a break-in at the local hardware store; Reese says to Kevin, "tell me the truth." After this, though, Smith interrupts the story about

Kevin to give us more background information about Reese's developing relationship with the town. After a few pages (and immediately after the first "bootlegger priest"), Smith returns to the story of Kevin and repeats the line "Kevin … tell me the truth." This repetition draws our attention to how Smith feels the need to interrupt the story about Kevin; it led us to wonder why he uses the repetition in this way, to mark an interruption. Again, we were not immediately sure why Smith does this, but it did cause us to look at what he includes in the interruption that could not wait until later in the essay. Put otherwise, we noticed that the suspense created between the two times coach says "Kevin … tell me the truth" put a special emphasis on what came between them, on the content of the interruption.

How lists draw our attentions
We have learned over time that lists look deceptively straightforward—but lists have to be ordered, and the order shapes readers' attentions. In "Higher Education," Smith, for instance, early on calls Reese an "unmarried, black, Catholic loser." This list of adjectives names what the town initially finds troublesome with Reese and focuses them all on "loser."

Smith's list strategy works straightforwardly, we think: It sets up the terms that change in

value through the essay. Once Reese starts winning games and championships, "winner" replaces "loser" and retroactively makes the list adjectives ("unmarried, black, Catholic") more tolerable and, finally, positive.

Moments that seem odd because they contrast with what's around them
We mentioned that our attention had been drawn to what Smith tells us about Reese during the interruption of Kevin's story. Some of what Smith tells us struck us as odd, given the story's direction. Smith seems to go out of his way to describe Reese as a likeable, forthright, honest guy. In the passage Smith inserts into Kevin's story, however, we learn about Reese's antics and pranks, such as toilet-papering the superintendent's house. These are relatively harmless revelations about Reese, and they hardly contradict the picture of him as a good, honest guy. But it seems odd that Smith would concentrate his account of the oddest parts of Reese's behavior into one section—and then emphasize that section by placing it in the middle of Kevin's story, arguably the most dramatic moment in the whole essay.

We have already mentioned the oddity of calling Reese a "bootlegger priest." Not only was the word choice odd—purposefully odd, we felt—but it does not fit with the general direction Smith has been taking us. We are trying to understand Reese and what happened in the town—and suddenly Smith uses an expression clearly designed to confuse more than illuminate. What might he be telling us about confusion and its role in essays like this?

Yet another oddity: Smith spends a long time telling us about a trip Reese took to New Orleans with Willie and a other townspeople. Why such a big deal about a vacation? This struck us as odd because it seemed overly emphasized given the circumstances. The focus of the essay is on Reese's relation to the town as a basketball coach. We expect attention to be paid to the games and trips to play other teams but not to a vacation Reese takes. We quickly understood, though, why Smith does what he does: Telling us about the New Orleans trip fits with much else in the essay, such as Reese's odd behavior and his occasional foul-ups (drinking and driving, among them). Taken together, these parts of Reese's personality are the more difficult things the town had to put up with. What Reese had to put up with was obvious: the town's racism and strict values.

Pulling all those observations together …

Remember that our initial sense of Smith's purpose was to offer an inspiring example of people overcoming their differences in order to live well together. Based on what we observed—and the questions brought up by our observations—we now think that Smith's purpose is a little different though still compatible with our initial idea. As sometimes happens, our initial idea now strikes us as only a part of Smith's overall purpose.

When we look carefully at what we noted—at the odd interruption of Kevin's story, at the New Orleans story, at phrases like "bootlegger priest," and that Smith keeps saying (a repetition we left out here but we noted alongside the essay) that what happened was "magic"—we began to think that Smith wants not just to show us a shining example. Instead, we think Smith is working to tell us what is needed if more such stories are to be told—if what happened in Ohio is to happen again. Two things at least have to happen:

1 People have to find ways of, first, putting up with what seems strange or uncomfortable and, second, coming to appreciate exactly what felt strange or uncomfortable. The townspeople came to appreciate and indeed truly enjoy some of Reese's antics. They not only made room for the antics but also began to look forward to them. According to Smith, then, tolerance alone is not enough to pull off the magic this town experienced.

2 People have to find gray areas in their values and learn to live in them. The differences between us are real and uncomfortable—but become even more uncomfortable the more sharply defined they are. For instance, the townspeople chose to look for overlaps between their values and Reese's rather than use the occasion to make ever sharper distinctions. They said, in effect, "He is hardworking and values family, just as we do" rather than, "The way he values family is different than the way we do, and he works harder at different times and on different things than we do."

The town had been suspicious of higher education and the effects sending their children to college might have on their values and community, but they also value the discipline that goes along with learning. When Reese pushed their kids to go to college, they embraced it rather than digging in their heels even more. They also did not approve of drinking, but—in order to keep Reese in their community—they took him to New Orleans and some drank beer with him. The others approved of the action, though, even if they did not participate. Such division of labor is a strategy for being flexible and again puts the emphasis on living in gray areas as opposed to finding excuses to make ever sharper distinctions.

TO ANALYZE: "HIGHER EDUCATION"

■ **Write:** If you have observations about the essay that do not fit with its purpose as we describe on the preceding page—or if you have observations that make our description richer or fuller or more complex—write a short rhetorical analysis of the essay in which you use both our and your observations to support your reading.

■ **Write:** We purposefully did not write anything about the photographs in this essay. Use what you know from earlier chapters about documentary photography and about how words and photographs work together to write a rhetorical analysis of the photographs and their relationships to the words of the essay. Be sure to consider why whoever designed the layout for this essay would have put particular photographs where they are. How is this analysis different from an analysis of words alone?

■ **Discuss with others:** To the right is a scan of a page from the book *The Best American Nonrequired Reading* (edited by Dave Eggers, Boston: Houghton Mifflin, 2002), in which "Higher Education" was reprinted—without any of the photographs. What do the photographs add to (or take away from) how you read, analyze, and understand the essay? You could focus on just the two opening pages of the essay from *Sports Illustrated*: With what sort of thoughts or emotions does the close-up picture of Jason Mishler and his tattoo encourage you to start reading the essay? How does that change when—as in the example to the right—there are no photographs?

GARY SMITH

■

Higher Education

FROM *Sports Illustrated*

THIS IS A STORY about a man, and a place where magic happened. It was magic so powerful that the people there can't stop going back over it, trying to figure out who the man was and what happened right in front of their eyes, and how it'll change the time left to them on earth.

See them coming into town to work, or for their cup of coffee at Boyd & Wurthmann, or to make a deposit at Killbuck Savings? One mention of his name is all it takes for everything else to stop, for it all to begin tumbling out . . .

"I'm afraid we can't explain what he meant to us. I'm afraid it's so deep we can't bring it into words."

"It was almost like he was an angel."

"He was looked on as God."

There's Willie Mast. He's the one to start with. It's funny, he'll tell you, his eyes misting, he was so sure they'd all been hoodwinked that he almost did what's unthinkable now — run that man out of town before the magic had a chance.

All Willie had meant to do was bring some buzz to Berlin, Ohio, something to look forward to on a Friday night, for goodness' sake, in a town without high school football or a fast-food restaurant, without a traffic light or even a place to drink a beer, a town dozing in the heart of the largest Amish settlement in the world. Willie had been raised Amish, but he'd walked out on the religion at

PREPARING TO READ THE ESSAY "THE SMALLEST WOMAN IN THE WORLD"

About the essay's author

The essay that starts on the next page comes from the 2006 collection *On Looking* (a finalist for the National Book Critics Circle Award and winner of the Towson University Award in Literature). The collection's author, Lia Purpura, teaches writing and writes essays and poems. In addition to the awards mentioned, she has been awarded an NEA Fellowship, a Fulbright Fellowship, an Associated Writing Programs Award, three Pushcart Prizes, a grant from the Maryland State Arts Council, and residencies and fellowships at the MacDowell Colony, Blue Mountain Center, Millay Colony, and The Virginia Center for Creative Arts.

What stands out as you read?

Even though "The Smallest Woman in the World" differs considerably from the preceding two essays, as you will soon see, you can still focus your attentions on the same author choices we described for "Higher Education":

- **Titles.**

- **Beginnings.**

- **Endings,** of both the whole essay but also of sections.

- **Repetitions.** In the preceding essay, we noticed repetitions of specific words and phrases; in "The Smallest Woman in the World," look instead for repetitions of ideas—seeing, attitudes, mentions of gender—but also for repetition of arrangement, such as how the author ends each section or brings in observations about her past and her relations to how men and women look at each other and are themselves looked at.

- **Breaks between sections.** In this essay, the breaks can be abrupt. As you read, keep asking how those abrupt breaks work.

Another strategy you can use

By asking you to look closely at the author choices we described in the preceding column, we ask you to do "close reading": We are asking you to lean in close to the writing and to consider carefully how its details build into a whole.

Another strategy for close reading is to track how authors use similar phrases and concepts. This is like looking for repetitions, as we've described, but taken to the next step. You can learn a lot by tracking a phrase or concept through an essay, carefully attending to how it changes from beginning to end and how readers' attentions are therefore shifted.

In "The Smallest Woman in the World," watch for any descriptions of *looking* or *seeing* or *a person's age*—even if those exact words are not used—but also look for any observations Purpura makes about *gender*, about men and women, males and females, even if (again) she does not explicitly call your attention to those terms.

Finally, try to chart how looking, age, and gender entwine through this essay: Can you chart how the ideas are introduced and set into relation? Into what relations are the ideas put?

The Smallest Woman
in the World

...said the red letters on the painted measuring stick at the Maryland State Fair. It was a hot, darkening day, the sky holding off rain. Between the play-till-you-win fishing game and made-to-look-old carousel, there was her booth. The Smallest Woman in the World.

Do you want to see her, I asked Joseph and his friend, Denis. Yes, they said. It was only fifty cents. Ania, who just told us that she was afraid of big characters in costumes and so would never go to Disney World, figured she was not going to like a very small person either, and stayed out. The man at the entrance returned her fifty cents, in dimes.

Joseph and Denis went into the tent and peeked behind a cubicle, gray and fabric-covered like in an office. I saw them waving. Waving *back*, since at seven, they wouldn't have thought to do so on their own.

Yes, a heart can sink. A heart can drop as fast as a white rock in a clear river, a dry leaf in white water. A heart can sink far from sight, the misstep above chipping the rock, the pieces hitting each outcrop down the steep cliff: there was a folded blue wheelchair in the

■ You probably noticed that the first sentence of the essay is only a sentence if you read the title as part of it—and that doing this reading tells you that the title of the essay comes directly from the sign that instigates much of the thinking in this essay. Why might a writer start with such an unconventional move?

■ Who are Joseph, Denis, and Ania? How do you learn about them, and what do you learn about them? Why do you think Purpura does not tell you immediately, or directly, about these people?

■ Why do you think Purpura positions herself outside the tent? When she does this, she also positions readers there. Why might she do that?

■ The first time you read it, how did you respond to—and understand— the sentence "Yes, a heart can sink"? The sentence seems not to follow from what precedes it, but by the end of the paragraph, we should understand that the writer is describing her own heart. Why do you think she might describe her feelings in such descriptive ways rather than write, "As the boys walked into the tent, my heart sank when I saw that wheelchair that must have carried the Smallest Woman"?

- Why is the writer hoping the boys do not see the wheelchair? Why do you think she never says this more directly?

  What does her response to the wheelchair tell you about what she was hoping the boys would see and the memories they would take away with them?

- Why does Purpura let us know of her predicament in which she needs to stay outside the tent with Ania but also wants to be in the tent holding the boys' hands?

- Where in the essay does Purpura use the words "The Smallest Woman in the World"? Why do you think she repeats the title where she does?

442

- What emotions and attitudes has Purpura described or involved so far in her writing? How does the movement between these attitudes and emotions structure this essay?

corner. There was a cheap wheelchair I was hoping the boys wouldn't notice.

Because then she'd be small-because-hurt. Small-due-to-problems. Not little-pal small. Not hold-her-in-your-pocket-magically-small, like a coin or a frog. Not small as a secret, or the very idea of a dog waiting all day outside the school fence—just for you.

Hoping they didn't see *what?* The way the chair leaned into the makeshift corner? Its blue, tarplike back? Its own terrible smallness? How its careless placement broke the illusion of small-for-small's sake?

I stayed out of the tent. I wasn't going to leave Ania alone, with her fear of large characters transforming. I could not let her stand there while I went with the boys, who of course, also needed to hold a hand while looking.

Looking at what?

The Smallest Woman in the World.

Now, weeks later, Joseph still can't sleep and comes calling: *I'm thinking of the smallest woman in the world. Why?* And: *When will I stop thinking of her?*

When I was eighteen, and in college, I began to think a lot about being seen. I remember not wanting to be seen "as an object." And that we insisted on being called "women." But just a few weeks ago, walking past some old, drunk guys on the stoop of a neighborhood bar, I reversed my position. I let them look. I allowed them the sight of me. I mean I did not scowl and did not turn sharply away. At eighteen, I'd have been edgy and hard; I'd have walked past with my shoulders angled to cover my body. But I walked by them thinking, "If this is all you have, if all you can do is look, then here, *look*. Take it all in." It was easy to do, though not enjoyable. If it was some sort of sacrifice, it was not hard—first profile, then a full frontal view. What do you want to see—some ass passing by? The swing in my walk? And you, some breast? I was on the way to meet a friend and had been singing a John Pryne song I like these days: "Somebody said they saw me, swinging the world by the tail, bouncing over a white cloud, killing the blues."

You're seeing me killing the blues, I thought—you're seeing that, right?—the white cloud, the world by the tail? Because I'm in deep, and somehow that's clear to you three, who have been drinking, it must be, for hours already, though it's still early morning. I'm killing the particular blues I've got by laughing a little at your stupid, raw comments, by turning toward and not away, and the amber liquid is tilting a line, like—so clearly it comes back—the cross section of a glacial lake up against its perpetual glass in the Museum of Natural History back in New York. What you're holding in your hands, in that bag, is terrain. What I am is—terrain. Map me, then, Sailor. Lay me out. Say you're just passing through and want to see a sweet thing before you leave port.

But she wasn't passing through. The boys were. They walked up to the cubicle and waited and waved. And stood for a moment and waved again. And then turned to go—as she must have turned from them, and back to something at hand, at rest in her lap. *Enough*, her eyes must have indicated. *That's all you get.*

I did not see what my son saw. He went out without me and now he's lost there, in the scene, with her, though she was *nice*, he assures me. She had a plastic jack-o'-lantern of candy she was eating from. A *jack-o'-lantern*, I asked? Yes, he said, with her hand digging in it. It was August. And that gesture, that image, will displace him for weeks: the jack-o'-lantern in summer. The candy unoffered. Her own private stash. And was there a book, tableside, she was reading? A tiny TV? My own questions keep coming. Does that man make her sit there, my son asks and asks. Is he mean? Is she happy? Does she want to be there? Mom, why am I sad? Is it because I looked at her like she was a sculpture? Why is he advertising her?

Purpura shifts our attention from the two boys going into the tent to see the small woman to her experiences and understandings of being looked at. What sense do readers gain of the writer from her description in these paragraphs?

And why might she describe how she feels to be looked at, as a woman, after she has described the boys going to look at the "Smallest Woman in the World"? Why might she be contrasting the boys and the men, too?

Why mention a museum here? What kinds of looking—and relations between lookers and objects—happen in museums?

Why might Purpura decide to use such an abrupt transition here? We go from her talking about herself to talking again about "The World's Smallest Woman" without explanation or even naming the subject: We are given, simply, "she."

Why might Purpura not describe the "Smallest Woman in the World" any more than she does, even though she could draw on Joseph's description of what he saw? Why do we learn of the woman only through her son's responses? Why do we know that the woman had her hand in a "jack-o'-lantern of candy" but not how small she was or what she was wearing or what her face looked like?

Why might Purpura have her questions turn into her son's questions?

- Here is another abrupt transition. What effects might these transitions have for readers? How do they shape a reader's sense of time and place in the essay?

- In this paragraph Purpura repeats the experience of walking down the street and being aware of her body. But now no one else is watching her. How does what she thinks and experiences contrast with the earlier walk?

- How do you understand why Purpura wants to be "that guy"?

- It's starting to look as though Purpura ends each of her sections by returning to her son's questions. How does this repetition shape a reader's sense of the rhythm of the essay—and what does this repetition suggest to you about what Purpura wants to emphasize?

- Men (usually) go to strip joints to watch the bodies of others (usually women)—and they look at *Playboy* for similar reasons. What do these experiences of looking—and being looked at—have to do with what else Purpura has described in the essay? (And how do her descriptions of her friends work to set up audience attitudes toward strip joints and *Playboy*?)

- More repetition: This is the second time Purpura has told readers that she sees things differently than she did at 18. Why does she want us to think about how our ways of seeing relate to age?

The other day, in the early September sun, I walked for a block or so to try this out: hands behind my head and elbows out, to take up a lot of room, like the guy who had just passed me. He was walking down a wide, shady street, at home in the ease of his body's expanse. And yes, walking that way, I take up a lot of room, as he did, but there's this: when my hands are behind my head, my breasts lift up. Am I freer because I take up more space, or less free because now I'm even more seen? Do I provoke more attention, erode my own space, invite, by the provocation I cannot help being, another's gaze into the scene?

I just want to be that guy, arms up in the cool air, my shoulders and neck stretching, lungs open, ribs rising.

I want to lift my shirt and scratch my stomach as a friend of mine does wherever he likes. "I do that?" he asks. Yes, you do, I point out—in the kitchen, in the store. On a walk. Wherever you like.

When will I stop thinking of her? my son asks and asks.

I have a friend who goes to strip joints. (And who, by the way, has written surprise compassion into those scenes, real compassion, the kind that shows he knows the below-deck of all the whirling hers in the dark surround: working mother, or artist, activist, would-be accountant. How formal and graceful his words become when touching, yes, touching, that other.) I have another friend who subscribes to *Playboy*. (Who thinks it's more the anticipation—article, article, article: photo!—than the photos themselves that . . . do it for him.) What do I think about that, he asks. What do I think of his subscription. I tell him: why not? As in: go ahead. Live it up. I say *why not?*—because I, too, like to look. At everything. To see myself. To see myself being seen. Though *Playboy* certainly used to bother me. A lot, when I was eighteen. My son, reading his cousin's 1970 collector's edition one morning this summer when we were visiting, woke me saying "This is disgusting! Why are their clothes off?" At five a.m., this was all I could muster: I said it isn't disgusting, that the body is beautiful and it's natural to be naked, but the magazine isn't for kids. Not at all, hand it over.

My son still thinks, by way of the perspective in photos or drawings in magazines that some people are really *very* small—say, two inches high, and you can hold them in your hand. Just pluck them out of the photo and pocket them. He wants to know where they live. A boy in Sudan on a tiny barren hill. Can I take him? he asks. *Home*, he means, and *can I hold him here safely?*

There's a scene I remember from college, an image so sharp and clear and impressive I remember thinking, *you'll retain this*. It was my last year and I was standing outside the militant vegetarian co-op with a friend, talking. And I stopped, just stopped midsentence, and she looked in the direction I was looking. "He's *cute*," she said. But that wasn't it at all. I was aware of his beauty, and of my easy desire, but more powerful still, I wanted to *be* him. I wanted the angular frame and slim hips, low belt and button-flys resting just so. I wanted the T-shirt's sharp fall from his shoulders to fall from my shoulders. For a long moment he didn't even have a face. I couldn't unravel the two desires: I wanted to look and to touch, yes. But more than that, really, I wanted to *be* him.

I look now, at forty, more like him than ever. I've pared down. I wear my pants low, with a belt and I tuck in my T-shirts, simple white T-shirts or green or black ones. And though I've lost the wide hips of a new mother and the full breasts for feeding, the lines of me are still rounded. Is this a body a man would want to inhabit? Would a man want to be—I mean walk, sleep, move—in this frame?

When I started to read the *Little House on the Prairie* books to my son, I was prepared. While I loved the characters, and identified with them fully—the sisters whose hands were cut from twisting straw into makeshift logs for the fire, their bare faces browned by hot, summer

■ Another repetition: Here is the second time Purpura writes that she wants to be a man she sees. How does this episode differ from the first? How does Purpura ask us to think about how we look and the desire to be someone else? What gives rise to the desire?

■ Do you think that the paragraph beginning "When I started to read the *Little House on the Prairie*…" provides an answer to the two questions that end the paragraph before?

sun, their calico dresses, the rough crunch of batting and ticking at night as they slept—I was prepared for him not to like the books. I was ready for him to say "this is for girls." But he didn't. Not once. I believe he felt that slightest membrane between bodies, that he saw how easily one form can inhabit another. There, on the prairie, in the dug-out, the lean-to, he tasted their water, cool from a dipper. He slapped down the bread and basted by lamplight. He sang with the family. He blew out a candle. He slept with a quilt.

He wanted to be one of them.

As he very much did not want to be small, and displayed at a fair in the heat of August.

■ Why do you think Purpura ends the essay with these observations about her son, and how he does want to be part of the *Little House on the Prairie* family but does not want to be The Smallest Woman in the World? (And how might Purpura's descriptions echo here of how she has at various times wanted to be different men?)

TO ANALYZE: "THE SMALLEST WOMAN IN THE WORLD"

■ **Write and discuss:** Write in a sentence or two what you think Purpura's purpose(s) might be in this essay.

Compare your sense of the purpose with that of others. As you compare, find passages in the essay that support your sense of purpose, and modify what you have written to account for the passages other people use to support their interpretations.

■ **Chart and discuss:** Purpura never explicitly states that she is writing about how seeing, age, and gender entwine. But given how often she repeats episodes in which men (and boys) look at and respond to women, and how she contrasts her ways of seeing at her different ages, we think she must be making some argument about the connections among those aspects of our lives.

With a colored pen or pencil, and with a partner, circle or underline every instance of seeing in the essay. Then, in a second color, indicate every instance of age; in a third color indicate every instance of gender.

Are there enough colored markings to suggest that Purpura is making some sort of argument about seeing, age, and gender? Might there be some other term or concept that should be included in this discussion?

When you look at the colored markings, does any pattern emerge? Does gender always come first, for example, or are gender and age always together, or...? Do any patterns emerge over the whole essay?

Describe the relation among the terms the first times they appear together, and then describe the relations for the last time. What has changed? What does this suggest about what Purpura might be arguing here?

■ **Discuss:** "How to Look at the Periodic Table" focuses reader's attention on *seeing objects*. "The Smallest Woman in the World" focuses on the writer's personal experiences around the matter of *seeing people as objects*.

Based on your reading, what perspectives does Purpura offer readers for how we think of people as objects for sight? Does she think it's always bad, or...?

"In How to Look at the Periodic Table," Elkins wants us to look at different versions of the same object in order to help us understand how differing ways of seeing shift how we think about the world. Why might Purpura—given the evidence of her essay—not make a similar argument about how we might look at different people as objects in order to expand our understanding of how the world works?

Do you think we should look at objects and people in different ways?

447

"THE PLAINTIFF SPEAKS"

"The Plaintiff Speaks" appeared in *Picturing Us: African American Identity in Photography*, a collection of essays by multiple authors.

We aren't going to tell you here about the author of the essay, Clarissa Sligh, because this essay is about her and her experiences and so depends completely on how she constructs her ethos through her words. We would like for you to attend carefully to how Sligh constructs the relation she does with her readers.

In addition, as you read, attend to the same author choices we have emphasized for the earlier essays:

- **titles**

- **beginnings**

- **endings**

- **repetitions**

- **breaks between sections**

■ As a reader, you probably look at these photographs before you read anything of the essay. What do you take from these photographs? How do they shape how you read? How might others—people who are not of your ethnicity—respond to this page, or does that matter?

Newspaper Clipping, 1956
(COURTESY CLARISSA SLIGH AND THE WASHINGTON POST)

THE PLAINTIFF SPEAKS

Clarissa T. Sligh

I WAS A TEENAGER WHEN I FIRST SAW THIS GROUP OF PHOTOGRAPHS and the article that they appeared with, on June 1, 1956, in the *Washington Post and Times Herald*, the major daily newspaper in the Washington, D.C., area. Since I was one of the people in the pictures, I knew that they were to be published and had been looking forward to seeing them with great anticipation for several months. Now, as I recall the time when I first saw the photographs and read the words, I remember how I felt very disappointed and let down. I felt that I had been used, although back then, I had no one to whom I could try to articulate why I felt that I had been "wronged."

The difference between right and wrong had been etched in my mind, in large measure at the neighborhood baptist church that we attended. At the Mt. Salvation Baptist Church, you were either on one side of the line or the other; there was never any "maybe" about it. The article appeared during the development of my second great period of cynicism. The first began at the early age of four years old, when it dawned on me that my oldest brother, Clarence Junior, controlled our household. No amount of telling my momma the mean things he did to me could protect me from his wrath.

I did not trust anyone except my brother Stephen, who was three years younger than me. But now that I had begun menstruating, more and more things in my life seemed too complicated and shameful to talk with him about.

I did not know anyone else who would understand me, who would not respond with blank looks or harsh disapproving words. The thoughts that ran through my mind were something like, "Be grateful! What do you expect? You are lucky to get any photograph in the *Washington Post* at all!" It was a newspaper for which we blacks were usually invisible, except as criminals or welfare recipients.

The mingled voices in my head were of my grandma, momma, daddy, the black preacher, and teachers all trying to teach me how to live in the world with a broken heart. As a young black female growing

- How would you characterize the tone of voice Sligh chooses to use in this writing? Does it sound to you as though this piece were written, or does it sound as though she is speaking out loud?

- How do you, as a reader, respond to the last two sentences of Sligh's first paragraph?

- What sense of Sligh do you develop from her choice of talking almost immediately about the sense of right and wrong she learned in church?

- Why might Sligh write about the coming of puberty and how it made her life feel complicated and shameful? How might different readers respond?

up in the American South of the 1940s and '50s, I was taught, in words and by example, how to stand on my own two feet and not expect too much from anybody, no matter how sincere they appeared.

They were trying to teach me how to survive. My grandmother's father and my mother's grandmother had been slaves in this country. They were afraid that if I didn't "get it," I would end up in a madhouse or get myself killed. My father, however, didn't want me to become *too* independent. He would say that nobody would want to marry me.

I loved the out-of-doors, and I learned to do everything my brothers could do and relished the look on their faces when they saw me do it better. But my father's attitude was that doing women's work made a man a "sissy," and he would have no part of it. So I wondered, "Then why should *I* want to do it?" When he sent my brothers out to do chores in the yard, he would look at me and say, "Go help your mother." These words never failed to bring anger and disappointment to my heart. But I thought he would slap me down if I dared to talk back to him. Yet he never put a hand on me, except at my mother's urging, when she felt I was more than she could handle.

My father's only goal for me was to get a husband. He made it pretty clear to me that if I did not remain a virgin, or, worse, if I got pregnant, no man would ever want to touch me. He made it sound like I would spend the rest of my life wandering through hell. Yet I was aware at the same time that he felt that my failing to remain a virgin would be more a matter of another male getting over on him than it being a weakness on my part.

I knew my mother resented the isolated, tedious drudgery of raising babies and doing housework all the time. As the oldest girl, I was the only one who heard her complaints. Neither of us liked her life, and I knew she wanted more for me. So Momma and I were pretty excited when we found out that my picture was to be taken as part of a story about efforts to desegregate schools in Arlington. But Daddy did not want any part of it.

Two years earlier, in 1954, when the Supreme Court ruled that racially segregated schools were unconstitutional, it was like an invisible bomb dropping on our neighborhood. We lived in one of four black communities in the county that was totally surrounded by whites. Since the time when I was about eight my mother had been taking me to state and national NAACP meetings where people gave reports on civil rights

---

■ Why might Sligh emphasize her "education" as a woman here?

■ What sense do you develop of Sligh's parents from how she writes about them? What sense of her do you develop through how she talks about her parents?

■ What choices do you see Sligh making in how she talks about white people?

work that was going on throughout the South and discussed future strategies and ways to raise money for the legal work.

I did not believe that things would ever change. Momma, however, would quietly sit and listen. She was not one of those people who asked questions or spoke out in public, but I could tell she was intensely interested, because when she wasn't, she would be sound asleep, even while sitting upright in her chair.

Many times, she could not go because no one was available to stay with my three baby sisters, Gloria, Lillian, and Jean. My father refused to do any baby-related tasks. So, on those occasions, she would send me to the meetings with a neighbor or someone from our church. I was supposed to listen and come back and tell her everything that was said, a job I took very seriously.

Prior to the Supreme Court decision, I was "bussed" to the black high school on the south side of the county when I entered the seventh grade. One night while lying awake in bed, I heard my parents talk about how I was not getting much of an education. My bed was against the wall. I could also hear that they were not considering any plans to send me someplace else. I figured that it must have been because I was a girl. My two older brothers, Clarence Junior and Carroll, had been enrolled in the "better" schools of Washington, D.C.

Both of my parents had completed high school. At that time, it was considered the minimum requirement for getting a "decent" job. My mother had come to the D.C. area from Hickory, North Carolina, in order to find work. She had had a dream of going to Howard University, but she had no money to do it. My father grew up in D.C.. He had studied Latin and had read all the classics, but it did not seem to help him get any further than his job as a shipping-room clerk at the Bureau of Engraving. He griped about the stupid white men who were the bosses over his all-black group of workers. He was very bitter about it.

My mother had become a full-time domestic worker, shuttling to different white women's houses every day. She worked for the minimum wage until she was too old to do it anymore. Whenever she wanted to pull me up short, she would scream that if I didn't do well in school I would "end up working in some white woman's kitchen." To her that was as low as you could go. They struggled to make ends meet, and they knew that life would be very hard for us kids if we did not have at least

■ Here is more information about Sligh's parents and their attitudes toward Sligh's being a girl. How is the way Sligh is telling these details of her life shaping your sense of her parents, her world, and her ethos?

a high school education. Without that diploma, the most widely available job opportunities for blacks, where we lived, were domestic work for women and ditch digging for men. I saw that my parents were shut out of jobs available to whites with far fewer qualifications. Of course, employment want ads in the *Washington Post* generally began "Whites Only," and that was one qualification they would never have, no matter how much education they got.

My high school was being remodeled, but when I started there two years earlier, the school barely met the state of Virginia's minimum requirements for black students. There had been no gymnasium, cafeteria, science lab, or rooms to take home economics and shop classes in. When it rained, we put buckets around the room in our physical education class to catch the water that poured in. We did not have a library and all our textbooks were used books sent over to us from the local white schools. I remember opening up the books and seeing the names of the white kids who had used them before they were handed down to us. When we complained about it Mrs. Mackley, our math teacher, would say, "Count your blessings. You are lucky to get anything at all."

My mother had thought that the Supreme Court decision would mean that I would begin tenth grade at the white high school that was located near us. I had been pushed by my teachers and I got good grades. However, I felt a little nervous about going, and, I wondered how I would fare. After all, everybody knew that our black school was "not as good." Also, I did not think I was very smart. There were a lot of kids in my neighborhood who I felt were smarter than me but who got lower grades. School was boring; there was no doubt about that. They essentially refused to read or discuss the totally racist materials we were given. It made us feel bad about who we were. They did not believe that it was going to make their lives any different or better. I did not believe it would either, but I was hoping that it might. And I knew, that in going to the white school, we would be expected to prove that we were just as good, which meant doing more work for the same or a lower grade.

Some schools in nearby D.C. and Maryland were desegregated the following fall. In Arlington, however, we were sent back to our segregated schools. In one southern Virginia county, all the schools were shut down in response to the Court's order. I was completely stunned that something like that could happen.

CHAPTER 13: Analyzing essays

452

■ How much emotion does Sligh show as she writes about her schooling? Why might she choose to use emotion as she does, and how does her use of emotion shape your sense of the world in which she lived?

■ What would someone have to believe beforehand if she were then "stunned" by a state government's decision to close schools rather than desegregate?

This, however, did not deter my momma, who wanted more for her children than she had had for herself. I still recall the determination with which she went to meetings with people from the local NAACP and other black parents from our neighborhood to see what they could do about it. This was after being on her feet all day as a domestic worker. All of us kids had to help make dinner, but she saw that we sat down to eat. The following spring, when I was completing tenth grade, she asked me if I was willing to be part of a school integration court case with other kids from the neighborhood, and I agreed to do it. I figured it wouldn't be too bad if we all went together.

This, however, was the summer of 1955, when Emmett Till, a fourteen-year-old black boy, was lynched in Mississippi for "speaking to a white woman." It was in all the papers, but the local black newspaper, and *Ebony* and *Jet* magazines, which we followed carefully for the latest developments on school desegregation, wrote about it in great detail.

Two white men took him from his folk's house in the middle of the night, beat him and lynched him, tied weights to his body, and dropped him in the river. The black publications were the only ones we saw that showed photographs of Emmett Till's body after it came out of the river. Even after the undertaker "fixed up his body," it did not look like the face of a person who had ever been on the earth. I had grown up hearing about whites lynching black men, but because he was so near me in age, the horror of this truly seeped into my bones.

To whom could I turn to express my rage and indignation at the injustices being done? How could the adults around me accept that the white men who killed him would never be punished? Why didn't the major newspapers treat it like the horrible crime it was? I did not know what to do. I felt like a caged animal in a burning house. What was going to happen to me in a white school? How was I going to be able to sit in a classroom without showing how I felt? Whenever I blurted out what was on my mind, my mother would punish me for not behaving myself. At that time I had no idea the price I was paying.

During the fall of 1955, as I returned for eleventh grade to my old school on the south side, the Virginia Legislature passed something called the "massive resistance laws," which gave the governor the power to close down any school system that attempted to desegregate. I tried to talk with my momma about it, but she would say nothing to me

■ Has Sligh called her mother "momma" before this? Why might she make this word choice here?

■ Why tell about Emmett Till here?

■ Has Sligh sounded full of rage or indignant?

Read this whole page aloud: You ought to hear the rhythms change in this paragraph with this list of questions and short declarative statements. What emotions does Sligh evoke through this use of rhythm? Why might she be doing this here?

■ What price has Sligh paid? Does she describe the price explicitly? Why, do you think?

about it. Still, she continued going to the NAACP meetings with the other parents from the neighborhood.

Meanwhile, miles away in Montgomery, Alabama, Rosa Parks was being arrested for not moving to the back of a city bus. The bus boycott that followed was exciting news to us. Everybody talked about it. Blacks were fighting back. We saw news photographs of elderly black people walking many miles to work. It inspired us to see that our people, who were further south than us, and in a more hostile environment, were determined not to take it anymore.

At first there was a lot in our local newspapers about it. I read every word of every article I saw. And when the local newspapers stopped reporting what was going on, I went with my mother to some of the meetings where people who had just come from Montgomery told about what was going on, and asked for donations to help out. I would hold my breath as I listened to the accounts of how the city council and the courts were trying to break up the bus boycott by harassing people in so many ways. I could not imagine that they would be able to keep going with the people in power using all their resources against them. After these meetings, I would go home and pray very hard that God would help them hold out. Finally, we heard Dr. Martin Luther King speak on television. Daddy was really impressed. And Daddy was a man who rarely gave anybody any credit at all.

The month after the bus boycott began in Montgomery, whites rioted on the campus of the University of Alabama for three days after Autherine Lucy, a black woman, enrolled there. Because I too was going to be a desegregation plaintiff, I wanted to know everything that was going on. After all, I might find myself in her shoes.

I read every word of every article about it that I saw. She was barred from attending classes. After the rioting ended, she was eventually suspended. I was looking for clues about what I could expect when my time came to enter our local white high school.

A few months later, my mother asked me if I would be willing to be the lead plaintiff in the Arlington school desegregation case. She explained to me that some of the students who had been selected previously were about to graduate and that another student withdrew because her father was going to be fired from his job if she stayed in. I never expected that the court case would take over a year to be put

---

■ From the beginning, when she described how she learned about right and wrong, Sligh has been comparing her expectations of the world with what actually happens. For example, here she says that "I could not imagine that they would be able to keep going with the people in power using all their resources against them." How might readers respond to these ways in which Sligh juxtaposes her sense of right and wrong and human ability with what happens?

together. And I had definitely never expected to be singled out from what was originally a group of over twenty-five black students. I could only imagine that my life would be in a shambles.

I remember thinking, "Here I am already finishing the eleventh grade. Why would I want to go to a white school for my senior year?"

Although Momma said I didn't have to do it if I didn't want to, I could tell she wanted me to agree. Terrible images flashed through my adolescent mind: of Emmett Till being killed for saying something to a white woman; of Rosa Parks going to jail rather than give up her seat to a white man; of all those elderly black folks walking miles to their jobs in Montgomery; of Autherine Lucy at the University of Alabama. I swallowed hard and told her that I would. Since the age of eight, I had been "in it"; I knew that I was expected to do my part.

On May 17, 1956, the NAACP attorneys filed our lawsuit: *Clarissa Thompson et al. v. the Arlington County School Board et al.* I had no idea what sort of changes it would make in my life. What was happening did not really sink in until the newspaper let us know that they wanted to come out to take our pictures for an article about the case.

The photographs were taken by a newspaper photographer who accompanied the reporter to the home of Mrs. Barbara Marx, a white woman who was vice-president of the local NAACP chapter. Momma could not drive, and Daddy refused to be involved in what was going on. I rode with her in someone else's car to the neighborhood where Mrs. Marx lived. The group had asked my mother beforehand to have me prepare a statement.

During the interview, I was very nervous. I tried to act cool, but the underarms of my blouse were soaking wet. Cold sweat ran down the inside of my clothes. I sat and listened as the newspaper reporter interviewed the adults who were present; they included Edwin Brown, an attorney for the NAACP, and James Browne, the local NAACP chapter president. They talked about the history and background of the court action and about what they wanted to accomplish. When the reporter asked me why I wanted to go to a white school, I remember saying something about wanting equality and an end to being a second-class citizen.

Afterward, the reporter directed the staff photographer to take pictures of us. Then, the reporter, looking at eight-year-old Ann, said,

■ Do you see Sligh using any strategies to encourage you to empathize with her, to imagine yourself at the age she is describing, going through the experiences she is?

■ We've known from the opening paragraph of this essay that it was to be about the set of photographs shown opposite the title page—and yet it is only here, seven pages in, that Sligh starts speaking about the photographs. What has she done in the preceding paragraphs to prepare readers for her understanding of the photographs and what their accompanying article does?

CHAPTER 13: Analyzing essays

455

"Isn't she included in the case too? Let's include her in the photographs!"

The photographer began by taking pictures of Mrs. Marx and her daughter, Ann. He asked her to hold up a piece of paper as though she was reading something. I remember her fumbling around in a drawer until she found an envelope, took out a letter and held it up. It is only now, in looking back, that I realize how nervous she too must have been.

Next, the photographer decided to take photographs of Ann and me outdoors. I felt very stiff; I recall that I was very surprised that Ann and I would be photographed together. As I listened to the adults talk, it was the first time that I heard that her mother had included her and her sister, Claire, who was about to graduate from high school, in the suit. She was one of three white students in the class-action suit of twenty-two students. I was one of nineteen black students. It hardly seemed equal to me.

The photographer shot a number of pictures of Ann and me together. By now she seemed to be enjoying the attention and was very relaxed. I, on the other hand, was freaking out. Here I was, a sixteen-year-old, very self-conscious black female, with these white folks up in this white neighborhood, and I'm supposed to be relaxed? They killed Emmet Till. In addition to trying to keep myself together, I felt very awkward towering above this little girl, in height, as the photographer took shots of us standing together. I was sixteen years old and she was eight, not twelve as stated in the newspaper photo caption. Somehow, it seemed insulting to me to be photographed with an eight-year-old. At the same time, I felt bad that the other black students in the suit were not there. Despite the feelings I had, I tried hard to look agreeable and pleasant. I was hoping that the photographs would come out well, so that people would think I was an "all right" person. After taking several shots, he asked us to walk toward him. Then he asked us to carry a book in our hands as we walked toward him. Finally, he said "Okay, that's it." I was glad when it was over.

When the photographs were published, a picture of Barbara and Ann Marx appeared at the top of the page, just above the headline, which read: SUIT CHARGES BIAS AGAINST WHITE PUPILS. The photograph, which was taken at fairly close range, was shot at just about eye level. Ann is standing next to her mother, who is seated at what appears to be

■ How has Sligh prepared you to understand why she "freaks out"? Why might she choose "freaking out" instead of "confused" or "upset"?

a desk or a table. This makes Ann's head a little higher than her mother's. The edges around both of their heads appear to have been painted in order to make them stand out against the background. The shape of the shadows cast by their heads suggest circular forms, giving the effect of halos behind their heads similar to those in the Christian religious art of the Middle Ages.

The mother and daughter are holding a piece of paper, supposedly a page from the papers filed in the suit; they are both smiling, as if they are happy and satisfied with what they have done. If I am a viewer who is at all sympathetic toward them, I look at this image without thinking how wonderfully honorable and courageous they must be. If I am a viewer who is angered by what they have done, I will be aware that any action I take against them is going to make me look like a "bad guy," so I am not going to express my feelings very publicly.

The second photograph, a closely cropped head shot of me, was placed to the upper right of the picture described above. It was shot from below my eye level, so that I appear to be looking down at the camera. You can tell by the shadow areas under my eyes, nose, and face, that the light source comes from the upper left hand side. This cropped head shot reminds me of the way photographs of "monsters" are lighted and shot. The angle of the lens, pointing up into my nostrils, also suggests to me certain European paintings of horses being ridden into battle. Moreover, the placement of the picture seems to suggest that the mother and daughter are placing themselves at risk by taking the moral action and putting themselves into this position, and that I am their "white man's burden." The caption read: "Clarissa Thompson...asks for equality." The small amount of white background does not give the viewer any clues as to where the picture was taken.

My head was printed larger than that of Barbara or Ann Marx, and the placement of the top of the photograph just above the top of their picture makes it pop off the page more than the other image. Even though the photograph of me is about one third the size of the photograph of Barbara and Ann Marx, the angle of the shot of my dark-skinned face puts my blackness in opposition to their whiteness. The relative placement of the photographs seems to suggest that people who are white are human and nice and that people who are black are threatening to those nice white people.

■ Sligh now gives readers her interpretation of how the photographs advocate an attitude toward the white people shown in them and toward her. Look at the number of details to which she attends: How does the range of details affect your understanding of the photographs you first saw many pages ago?

■ If you are not a black person, what authority does Sligh have to interpret these photographs that you do not? What authority does she have as the subject of the photographs for speaking about them?

458

■ How do you think Sligh is hoping to shift readers' understanding of the photographs—and the article they illustrate—by giving readers knowledge about the context of the photographs and about who was at the meetings?

This meant that whites would only be able to see that generic black face they carried in their minds. They would not have to wonder about the life, the aspirations, the universal humanity hidden behind my dark skin. They would not be forced to examine, in a personal way, the injustice of the life I was forced to live.

The third photograph was printed on a different page. It is a picture of me and Ann walking toward the photographer, and he was crouching down when he shot it. It is close to evening. The photographer has his back to the sun. In the picture, I am on the left, Ann is on the right. We are both smiling and we each carry a book. The image is cropped to show our full bodies, but my right arm is nevertheless cut off. It looks as though I am walking out of the frame. It may even suggest that I am less than a whole person. Portions of the areas around our heads and shoulders have been painted to make us stand out from the background.

This photograph of me and Ann reminds me of similar images of young whites pictured with older, usually adult, blacks. Three references that immediately come to mind are Huckleberry Finn with the slave Jim, various movies of Shirley Temple in which she shows benevolence to an older, black, white-haired male servant/slave, and, of course, images from *Uncle Tom's Cabin*.

The article itself was written about the few whites who worked with us on the school desegregation case. None of the adults from my neighborhood, who had worked on the case for over a year, and who were the parents of the twenty-five black students, were even mentioned. In photographs and words, Barbara Marx and her daughter, a white mother and child, were thus highlighted and elevated to a position of significance over all the black people involved in the case.

If I had not been there on the two occasions when the reporter interviewed us, I would never have known that black adults participated in those meetings. I remember how seriously and carefully they made sure that what they said to the reporter was accurate and correct; how they helped each other find the words to describe exactly what they meant; how they sometimes told jokes to break the tension. Why was none of what they said included?

Except for me, none of the other black students was named in the article. The next to the last sentence in the article states, "The case will be known as Clarissa Thompson et al. vs. the Arlington County School

Board et al. because the 11th grade Negro girl leads the list of plaintiffs." It was made clear that my photograph was there only because my name was at the top of a list. Simply by looking at the photographs, both whites and blacks would think that the suit was initiated and organized by whites.

Today, I can still remember the safety I felt being surrounded by the black adults from my community during the interview. I remember all their faces but only a few of their names. By leaving them out of the article and photographs, the newspaper made them invisible. If one reads the article today, it looks like they never existed. Their being left out also made me feel unprotected and more vulnerable than ever as time went by. Their courage had been devalued. Their lack of power, of control over the situation, was magnified before my eyes. Even then, it was clear to me that readers of the newspaper would get the message that it was whites, not blacks, who were leading the interracial group to fight racial segregation in Virginia. It reinforced the stereotype that we had to be led by whites.

Today, I ask myself how those meetings with the reporter and photographer might have been different. Why were the interviews held at Barbara Marx's rather than the NAACP president James Browne's house? Both their homes were equally convenient from the highway. If the group had not made the decision beforehand to include Barbara Marx's daughter in the photo session, why didn't they object when the reporter suggested it? Were the black adults afraid to give the appearance of "slighting" a little white girl? Had they in some way gone along with their exclusion from the decision-making process? Had we blacks been excluded from participating in the so-called democratic decision-making process for so long and in so many ways, that any ordinary white person took our exclusion for granted—and so, perhaps, did we?

Today, I also ask myself about the motivations of the reporter. I remember her as being a white woman; yet the reporter's name, as published, appears to be masculine. Was it a pseudonym? As a southern white, would she have been capable of writing a news article that included a black person's point of view? Was she able or willing to hear any of the things we blacks were saying? Did she come there intending to write a story about white people? Certainly a story about the civil rights movement that included whites got more attention than one

■ Notice how in the first sentences of this paragraph Sligh calls to our minds how the adults of her community made her feel safe—and how she calls their faces to our minds. Only then does she state that the newspaper article and photographs made them invisible. Why might she order her sentences in this way?

about blacks alone. It later became a tactic which the black leaders in the movement themselves took advantage of. They saw that photographs of whites being beaten up while exercising their civil rights got much more attention; here was something unbelieving American whites could identify with, much more so than with photographs of black protestors being beaten by whites.

When the article was printed I felt betrayed. I had thought that it was really going to be a piece of investigative reporting about our work to win our civil rights under the Supreme Court ruling in *Brown v. Board of Education*. I wanted terribly to believe that I could have rights under the Fourteenth Amendment to the Constitution, which guarantees equal protection under the law. I wanted to believe in the Pledge of Allegiance, the National Anthem, the Bible, and all that other shit I had to regurgitate in school, even though I knew it clearly did not apply to me. I wanted the article to show that black people from my neighborhood were part of the struggle against legalized racial segregation too.

My mother did not say much to me about the article after it appeared. She did mention in passing, that some of the people from the community who had met with the reporter were not happy with the way the article turned out. Still, she seemed happy and satisfied that her daughter's picture was in the *Washington Post*. It was a big thing that would elevate her status in the neighborhood and beyond. She did not seem to fear that she would lose any of her domestic work; on the contrary, she seemed to be looking forward to the reaction of her employers.

The publication of those photographs, however, placed me in a new relationship to both the white and the black worlds. It wrenched me from what I considered to be the safety and security of my anonymous family into the spotlight of the hostile public's scrutiny. People began to notice me. I could no longer be just another black girl, or just myself. I had to mind my p's and q's. My behavior, my grades and test scores, my interests and accomplishments became public information.

I began to be expected to address groups of liberal white people, whose support was being solicited for our case. As a young black person, my personal contact with whites had been minimal before this. In fact, I had heard mostly bad things about them, so I was always scared to be with them. In Arlington, we were barred from the movies, restaurants, white churches, and most other public places. I could check out a

■ Why "shit"?

Why this indication of such anger here?

■ Why might Sligh write, "I began to be expected to address...," rather than just, "I began to address..."?

book from the public library, but I could not sit down to read it. On my way home from the District of Columbia I often sat alone on the bus, even when it was crowded, because none of the whites would sit beside me. I used to get upset about it, but then tried to act like I didn't see them.

Before I had been invisible. Now I was being scrutinized, not only by whites, but also by the black adults who took me into these new situations. I went along with it, but I tried really hard to hide what I really thought and who I really was.

I felt lucky to have met my boyfriend, Albert, before the photographs were published, because afterward I could not just hang out with my classmates or even slip into some of the places that were considered off-limits for "good girls." Nicknamed "Professor" by some of my classmates, I was never among the more popular girls at a party anyway. Now I could tell I was being seen in an even more distant light.

My teachers did not like my boyfriend, Albert. Considered a street guy, he was not heavy into the books. "Before the photographs," I regularly got good grades and that seemed to be enough; but now they expected me to be outstanding in every way. And even though my teachers were anxious about the future of their jobs if school desegregation were to occur, now I was a representative of their work and they wanted me to look good. They wanted me to succeed. Only one of them came out and said it, but the message from all of them came down to this: Don't you mess up everything by getting pregnant or getting into some other kind of trouble.

To people outside my neighborhood, I was considered a representative not only for black girls but for all young black people. I began to get some understanding of what it must be like to be a Joe Louis or a Jackie Robinson. When they knocked out a white man or hit a home run, it was not just for themselves but for all black people. For whites who did not believe we could do it or who were against us, taking a jab at me was like striking a blow at all blacks. Who I really was and how I really felt was not important. The group was more important. I was a good choice for the role. Because I was a good girl, I tried really hard to be better in every way I could.

This state of tension was the beginning of my learning to live a divided and alienated life. Even as a young person, I knew I had made the decision to allow myself to be used in a way that was unpleasant

■ Sligh again talks of visibility and invisibility here, about how we do and do not see, and about being made visible or invisible to others through actions and events out of our control—or about making decisions to see or not.

What actions or events does Sligh describe that have these effects or encourage such decisions? Why does this matter to her, and how is she trying to make it matter to her readers?

■ Why might Sligh describe the effects of the photographs and article on her own life and the way she felt about herself and her place in the world?

461

and uncomfortable to me. It is true that I had been trained for it, but I could have opted out. I was hoping that it would lead to opportunities that would give me more economic independence and make my life better than my mother's. I learned how to hide myself and my thoughts by keeping my mouth shut, by covering my terror with a smile, and by acting as if everything was going to be all right. In order to get through it, I searched for support, for meaning to my life in the Mt. Salvation Baptist Church. Whenever tough times came, rather than argue or fight, I turned inward and prayed very hard. Later, when the church disappointed me, as it surely had to, I began to smoke and drink. Fortunately for me, stronger drugs were not as available to young people as they are now.

Since those days the nonobjective reporting of newspaper journalism has always been of interest to me. To the average person, news photographs represent reality, but I ask "Whose reality?" and "Why?" As I travel from city to city and from country to country, I see how newspapers vary tremendously in their points of view. I see how photographs are used to reinforce the credibility of stories; and how the same picture is often used to reinforce stories written from opposing points of view. Placing one photograph beside another changes the way the viewer reads it. Adding words to a photograph can make it say almost anything.

It is hard for photographers not to base the photographs they make on pictures they already have in their minds. Even so, their specific intent can easily be altered by an editor's intent, which may be controlled, in turn, by the newspaper's publishers. And then, of course, advertisers often influence what publishers "feel comfortable" including in their pages.

I became a photographer partly in response to the continuous omission and misrepresentation of me and my point of view as a black working-class female who grew up poor. I know I can make a photograph say a lot of different things. However, I hope that the way I make images helps the viewer become better aware of how photographs are really abstracted constructions.

■ At the end of the essay, Sligh explicitly states how the photographs and article affected her, even shaping her career. What do you think she is hoping her readers will learn from her experiences? How has she prepared readers for this learning?

TO ANALYZE: "THE PLAINTIFF SPEAKS"

■ **Write with others:** List adjectives that describe for you the ethos Sligh constructs in her essay. What strategies does she use to construct that ethos?

■ **Discuss and write with others:** How emotional is this essay? Does Sligh write as though she is angry and barely controlled, or does she write in a more distanced manner? Try modifying the paragraphs where she names her emotional states so that the paragraphs make no mention of emotion. How does this change how you understand what is going on?

■ **Discuss with others:** What do you take to be Sligh's purpose in writing this essay? How important is her ethos in persuading you toward her arguments? How does Sligh's use of pathos help her make her arguments?

■ **Discuss with others, and then write:** The earlier essay "Higher Education" is written by a white man writing about a (dead) black man; it considers the effects of racism on that man's life and on white people. In "The Plaintiff Speaks," Sligh uses her own experiences as a ground for arguing about some effects of being represented by others, as Perry Reese Jr. was represented by Smith.

Given Sligh's arguments and given that it is a particularly awkward situation in our time and place for a white man to claim to understand how racism shapes the lives of black men, what strategies do you see Smith (the author of "Higher Education") using to try to persuade us that he is worth heeding? Is Smith worth heeding? How does your reading of Sligh shape how you look back on Smith's essay? How might Sligh speak about that earlier essay?

Write a short paper in which you address these questions.

■ **Write:** After reading Sligh's essay, what considerations will you now have in mind as you look at newspaper (or Facebook) photographs? What considerations will you have in mind as you take photographs of others or write about them?

Based on your reading of Sligh's essay, write a set of recommendations for anyone writing about or taking photographs of others. With your recommendations, help others understand how their photographs might affect those being photographed.

■ **Write:** Sligh's essay and Purpura's essay are both about how we look at others and how, in turn, it feels to be looked at. Purpura brings up matters of gender and age; Sligh attends to ethnicity and gender.

Imagine a conversation between Purpura and Sligh over these matters. Where might they agree? Where might they disagree? With what do *you* agree and disagree—and why?

Write a short paper in which you discuss your understandings of the recommendations that Purpura and Sligh make to us about how we look at others—and how we think about being looked at—and explain your perspectives on these matters. As you write, draw on your experiences as someone who looks and as someone who is looked at.

PREPARING TO READ THE ESSAY "WHAT DOES IT MEAN TO BE COOL?"

About the essay's author

Born in West Germany, Thorsten Botz-Bornstein was educated in Germany, France, and England, where he earned a PhD in philosophy. Following his PhD, he continued his research in Finland, Japan, and China and has taught at colleges in the United States and Kuwait.

Botz-Bornstein has written widely on philosophic aspects of contemporary life, saying—of his concerns—that he believes that "play, style, and dreams have something in common and that any cultural phenomenon should be examined within a triangle formed by these three notions." He has published or edited books with the following titles: *The Philosophy of Viagra: Bioethical Responses to the Viagrification of the Modern World*; *The Cool-Kawaii: Afro-Japanese Aesthetics and New World Modernity*; *Films and Dreams*; and *Virtual Reality: The Last Human Narrative?* His articles include "Liquid Grammar, Liquid Style: On the East Asian Way of Speaking English or Reflections on the Linguistic Air-Guitar," "The New Mini and Japanese Pottery: Of Pasts and Pastes," and "In Praise of Blandness: Some Thoughts on Japanese Television."

What stands out as you read?

"What Does It Mean to Be Cool?" differs from the earlier essays: It is not about an object, a person, or a community. Instead, it is an essay about how we define human behavior and why the behavior matters; it is an essay about ideas and how we shape and are shaped by ideas.

Because the essay concerns ideas, it might seem at times to you to be abstract and intellectual—but we included this essay because we thought you might be interested in this author's take on an attitude with which you are probably familiar. And even though there might be times in this essay when Botz-Bornstein uses terms that might be unfamiliar to you, we think that his argument is still accessible—and intriguing for what it implies about an attitude that many of us seek.

Before you read

What's your understanding of "cool"? Take a minute or two to jot down your understanding of the term, so that—as you read—you can compare your understanding to Botz-Bornstein's.

In addition, if any of the following words are new to you, take the time to look them up: *aesthetics, anomie, idealist, paradox*, and *alienation*. Also, when you come to the expression "linear structures," think of this as a description of just being able to do things in a straightforward, direct manner.

Finally, note that the author has a European background—and so some of his spellings (such as "behavioural") are correct in the contexts where he mostly lives.

- Is the title preparing this essay's audience to read an essay on the definition of "cool," or is it preparing them for more—or something different?

- Botz-Bornstein immediately defines how he thinks most people understand "cool"—but then immediately calls that definition into question. Do you think most readers will agree with this move?

- How does acting "cool" hide "any level of serious intent"?

- How is "cool" paradoxical? Do you think most readers will agree that being cool is a "classic case of resistance to authority"?

- The link goes to the U.S. Department of State website from which the quotation comes.

- What attitude do you think Botz-Bornstein wants readers to take toward this "world-wide" phenomenon of being "cool"?

- How does this paragraph prepare readers for the next section?

- Earlier Botz-Bornstein said that cool people are mysterious, and in "What Is Cool," he says they can be unpredictable. How do those characterizations square with the opening claim that cool developed as a way to avoid being offensive or seeming dangerous?

Philosophy *Now*
a magazine of ideas

The Human Condition

What Does It Mean To Be Cool?

Thorsten Botz-Bornstein links Stoicism and Hip Hop.

🖨 Print

✉ Email

🗩 Discuss

Share
f t 🖼 🖼 🖼

In principle, to be cool means to remain calm even under stress. But this doesn't explain why there is now a global culture of cool. What is cool, and why is it so cool to be cool?

The aesthetics of cool developed mainly as a behavioral attitude practiced by black men in the United States at the time of slavery. Slavery made necessary the cultivation of special defense mechanisms which employed emotional detachment and irony. A cool attitude helped slaves and former slaves to cope with exploitation or simply made it possible to walk the streets at night. During slavery, and long afterwards, overt aggression by blacks was punishable by death. Provocation had to remain relatively inoffensive, and any level of serious intent had to be disguised or suppressed. So cool represents a paradoxical fusion of submission and subversion. It's a classic case of resistance to authority through creativity and innovation.

Modern Cool

Today the aesthetics of cool represents the most important phenomenon in youth culture. The aesthetic is spread by Hip Hop culture for example, which has become "the center of a mega music and fashion industry around the world" (*montevideo.usembassy.gov*). Black aesthetics, whose stylistic, cognitive, and behavioural tropes are largely based on cool-mindedness, has arguably become "the only distinctive American artistic creation" (White & Cones, *Black Man Emerging: Facing the Past and Seizing the Future*, 1999, p.60). The African American philosopher Cornel West sees the "black-based Hip Hop culture of youth around the world" as a grand example of the "shattering of male, WASP cultural homogeneity" (*Keeping Faith: Philosophy and Race in America*, 1993, p.15). While several recent studies have shown that American brand names have dramatically slipped in their cool quotients worldwide, symbols of black coolness such as Hip Hop remain exportable.

However, 'cool' does not only refer to a respected aspect of masculine display, it's also a symptom of *anomie*, confusion, anxiety, self-gratification and escapism, since being cool can push individuals towards passivity more than towards an active fulfillment of life's potential. Often "it is more important to be 'cool and down' with the peer group than to demonstrate academic achievement," write White & Cones (p.87). On the one hand, the message produced by a cool pose fascinates the world because of its inherent mysteriousness. The stylized way of offering resistance that insists more on appearance than on substance can turn cool people into untouchable objects of desire. On the other hand, to be cool can be seen as a decadent attitude leading to individual passivity and social decay. The ambiguity residing in this constellation lends the cool scheme its dynamics, but it also makes its evaluation very difficult.

What is Cool?

In spite of the ambiguity, it seems that we remain capable of distinguishing cool attitudes from uncool ones. So what is cool? Let me say that *cool resists linear structures*. Thus a straightforward, linear search for power is not cool. Constant loss of power is not cool either. Winning is cool; but being ready to do anything to win is not. Both moralists and totally immoral people are uncool, while people who maintain moral standards in straightforwardly immoral environments are most likely to be cool. A CEO is not cool, unless he is a reasonable risk-taker and refrains from pursuing success in a predictable fashion. Coolness is a nonconformist balance that manages to square circles and to personify paradoxes. This has been well known since at least the time of cool jazz. This paradoxical nature has much to do with cool's origins being the fusion of submission and subversion.

More articles from this issue

465

A president is uncool if he clings to absolute power, but becomes cooler as soon as he voluntarily concedes power in order to maintain democratic values. This does not mean that the cool person needs to be an idealist. On the contrary, very few of the coolest rappers are idealists. Idealism can be extremely uncool, as shown by the self-righteous examples of both neoDarwinists and creationists. Cool is a balance created by the cool person's style, not through straightforward rules or imposed standards. Coolness implies the power of abstraction without becoming overly abstract. Similarly, the cool person stays close to real life without getting absorbed by it. Going with the masses is as uncool as being overly eccentric. It is not cool to take everything, nor is it cool to give everything away: it seems rather that the master of cool handles the give and take of life as if it were a game. The notion of 'play' is important to cool, because in games power gets fractured and becomes less serious, which enables the player to develop a certain detached style while playing. For the cool, this detached style matters more than the pursuit of money, power and ideals.

Classic Greek Cool

In ancient Greece, the Stoic philosophers supported a vision of coolness in a turbulent world. The Stoic indifference to fate can be interpreted as the supreme principle of coolness, and has even been been viewed as such in the context of African American culture. The style of the jazz musician Lester Young, for example, was credible mostly because Young was neither proud nor ashamed. This is a Stoic attitude. Also, in 'Rap as Art and Philosophy' (in Lott & Pittman (eds), *A Companion to African American Philosophy*), Richard Shusterman likens Hip Hop culture to a philosophical spirit which is also implicit in Stoicism.

Epictetus the Stoic posited a strict difference between those things that depend on us and those things that do not depend on us, and advocated developing an attitude of regarding the things we can't influence as unimportant. What depends upon us are our impulses, passions, attitudes, opinions, desires, beliefs and judgments. These things we must improve. Everything that cannot be controlled by us – death, the actions of others, or the past, for examples – should leave us indifferent. Through this insight that all the things upon which we have no influence are best neglected, a 'cool' attitude is nurtured.

Stoics have been criticized for being deterministic and fatalistic. As a matter of fact, we find in this materialist and rationalist philosophy the same spectrum of problems that are linked with coolness, because the Stoic, just like the Cool, has to continually decide what is up to him and what is not. In as far as his indifference extends to areas of life that are within his power because he wrongly believes them to be outside his power, the result will be fatalism, decadence and alienation. Yet should he decide to care about things he believes to be within his power although they are not he loses his coolness. Once again, coolness is a matter of balance; or more precisely, of negotiating a way to survive in a paradoxical condition. It's about maintaining control while never looking as though you might have lost control. All this is why losing and still keeping a straight face is probably the coolest behavior one can imagine.

Living With the Paradox of Cool

Coolness is control; but the dictator who controls everything is not cool because he does not balance a paradox. The self-control of cool black behavior in and before the 1960s, on the other hand, is immediately linked to the African American inability to control political and cultural oppression. This paradox of the need for self-control in the face of a lack of control nurtured a cool attitude. Thus, instead of revelling in either total control or total detachment, the aesthetics and ethics of cool fractures and alienates in order to bring forward unusual constellations of ideas and actions. In a phrase: the cool person lives in a constant state of alienation.

© Dr Thorsten Botz-BorNstein 2010

Thorsten Botz-Bornstein is staying cool as assistant professor of philosophy at the Gulf University for Science and Technology, Kuwait.

- How would you summarize all that Botz-Bornstein has to say here about the relations between power and being cool?

- Earlier Botz-Bornstein said that acting cool was developed by blacks as a defense mechanism during the times of slavery. Why might he want to connect this idea to the Stoics, ancient Greek philosophers from several thousand years ago?

- What does the discussion of "what is or is not beyond our control" add to what Botz-Bornstein has said about cool already? Is this a new idea in the essay?

- Here we return to the idea of cool being paradoxical, of being a tension between a need for one kind of control—"self-control"—when one has no political or cultural control. Does Botz-Bornstein's argument about cool—and the history he argues for it—seem reasonable to you?

- If we define "alienation" (thinking of its roots in "alien") as "being isolated from a group to which one should belong or from an activity in which one should be participating," has Botz-Bornstein persuaded you that "the cool person lives in a constant state of alienation"?

TO ANALYZE: "WHAT DOES IT MEAN TO BE COOL?"

■ **Write, and then discuss with others:**
Restate Botz-Bornstein's definition of "cool" in your own words. How is this definition different from your usual understanding of "cool"? What do you find strange or unexpected about Botz-Bornstein's understanding of "cool"? What do you take to be Botz-Bornstein's purpose in defining "cool" as he does—and in writing this essay? What makes "cool" problematic for Botz-Bornstein?

Compare what you have written with others. How do you account for these differing understandings of "cool": your understanding, the understanding of your peers, and Botz-Bornstein's understanding?

What does your understanding of "cool" help you explain? What does Botz-Bornstein's understanding of "cool" help you explain?

■ **Discuss with others:** As we have mentioned in earlier questions about this chapter's essays, many of the essays address looking and representation. In "Higher Education," Smith, a white author, represents the experiences of a black coach in a white community; in "The Smallest Woman in the World," Purpura asks us to consider how our age and gender affect how we look and how it feels to be looked at; in "The Plaintiff Speaks," Sligh describes her experiences of being represented by others.

"What Does It Mean to Be Cool" argues that "cool" is an attitude of self-representation. People who have no cultural or political power nonetheless have the personal power to shape how others see them: They make themselves be cool.

Does Sligh make herself cool through her analysis of how she was represented in the newspaper, how is she seeking another attitude, or how to claim power for herself? What kind of power might she be seeking?

Does Purpura make herself cool through her analysis of looking and being looked at, or is she seeking another attitude or to claim power for herself? What kind of power might she be seeking?

■ **Discuss with others:** Botz-Bornstein proposes "cool" as a solution to a social problem: How do people represent themselves—and show themselves worthy of respect—in situations where they cannot get what they need through direct, straightforward means?

List other social attitudes of which you can think—hipness, snottiness or arrogance, sassiness, smoothness—and consider how they offer solutions to social problems: Under what circumstances does one take on those attitudes, and why?

Think of times when you have taken on an attitude in order to solve or get out of a problem. How did you represent yourself, and why?

THINKING THROUGH PRODUCTION

- Douglas Hesse, a writer and teacher, has written that, "Form in an essay is not dictated by conventions of deductive logic or formal convention but rather by the author's attempt to create a satisfying and finished verbal artifact out of the materials at hand." Use this criterion of "a satisfying and finished verbal artifact" to write a comparison and evaluation of two of the essays in this chapter. You will have to define what "satisfying" and "finished" mean for you in an essay.

- In a magazine or online, find an essay on a topic of concern or interest to you. Prepare it for others to read as we have prepared this chapter's essays for you: Write a page to introduce people to the author and the essay's strategies; develop margin questions to help others see what you think matters in the essay, and then write analysis questions to help others think in more detail about the essay. (Doing this work is fine preparation for you to write your own rhetorical analysis of the essay you choose.)

- Use any of the essays in this chapter as inspiration and support for writing your own essay on a matter of concern to you. From chapters 1–3, use the steps for rhetorical composition to help you develop a statement of purpose and then a design plan—and then produce the essay.

  As you design your essay, consider—in addition to all other strategies you might use—how the essay should look on the page (or screen) and whether you need to include photographs.

- Using any of the rubrics we have presented in earlier chapters for testing compositions, develop a rubric for testing an essay that you write for a class (such as the essay we suggest).

analyzing comics

Some researchers say comics started in the 19th century with "Penny Dreadfuls," teaching tools (that look like present-day Sunday comics) for working class people. Others see the origins of comics in Egyptian painting or Mayan folding books.

The comics with which we are most familiar—those in the Sunday papers, comic books, or graphic novels—depend on particular technologies and audiences. Prior to computers, comics were drawn by hand. Like posters, print comics couldn't exist without technologies for mass-producing hand-drawn illustrations. Also like posters, comics require a large enough literate audience willing to buy them that others will pay for them to be produced.

Because comics are sequences of pictures with captions, they have been considered less serious than books without pictures. As we noted in the first paragraph, however, some people believe them to have been first produced for the working class. In the United States in the 1950s, Congress heard from experts on child behavior about how the experts believed comic books were corrupting youth. In the 1960s, comics underwent a renaissance; in the time's social and political upheaval, cultural assumptions were questioned, and comic books were seen as one way for those who were—or considered themselves to be—outside the mainstream to express or question what couldn't be expressed or questioned in "traditional" formats. As a result, comic books can now be art form as well as children's entertainment and can be a structure for serious thinking in combined words and drawings.

HOW COMICS WORK

"The angry tangle of confusion and remembered pain [was] hanging in a comic-book bubble over his head. Mine was similarly dark and matted."

Joan L. Richards, Angles of Reflection

Comics have become such a part of our lives that we can use their conventions in other kinds of communication, as Joan L. Richards does in the passage above: She writes about how her son looked after a long and difficult time he spent in hospitals because of leg problems. How does her use of "comic book bubble" encourage you to see the situation she describes? (And how might you apply similar descriptive strategies in your own writing?)

How we understand comics because we have bodies

Until the digital age, print comics were almost always reproductions of drawings made by hand. Our bodies link us in two ways to such comics.

First, because almost all of us know what it is to draw, we know something of the bodily gestures of producing the drawings in comics. When we look at such drawings, we therefore have a sense of physical closeness to the drawings that we do not have with photographs (for example) because photographs are not produced directly by hand.

Second, the other bodily link we have to comics (and now we can discuss comics that are made from photographs or digital reproduction as well as those that are drawn) is to the objects and bodies in the comics. When we look at comics—just as when we look at posters and photographs—it is in no small part because we have bodies that move in the world that we understand characters' gestures, postures, and emotions.

How we understand comics because we live in particular times and places

The 1895 cartoon reproduced on the facing page—"Merry Xmas Morning in Hogan's Alley"—comes from a series that helped start the practice of newspaper cartoons in the United States. Published originally in the *New York World*, "Hogan's Alley," by R. F. Outcault, depicted the impoverished people living in that (made-up) alley. Notice the little boy blowing a horn, behind the girl at front left who is begging; this character went on to become the "Yellow Kid":

Here is how Outcault described the "Yellow Kid":

The Yellow Kid was not an individual but a type. When I used to go about the slums on newspaper assignments I would encounter him often, wandering out of doorways or sitting down on dirty doorsteps. I always loved the Kid. He had a sweet character and a sunny disposition, and was generous to a fault. Malice, envy or selfishness were not traits of his, and he never lost his temper.

The Yellow Kid was such a success that his picture was soon on buttons, cracker tins, cigarette packs, and ladies' fans; eventually he was a character in a Broadway play. The success of "The Kid" led other newspapers to develop similar strips, to the Sunday comics sections, and—eventually—to bound editions of these comics. This led to comic books, which could stand on their own as continuing stories about children, animals, families, spies, detectives and crooks, ghosts, and superheroes.

Like all other comics that followed, the Hogan's Alley comic used conventions that we've had to learn. The lines coming out of the Kid's trumpet are supposed to mean that he's making noise, and the way the dog's ears bend back are supposed to mean the sound is loud and making the ears bend. The Kid doesn't look like anyone you'd encounter on the street, but because of comic conventions, we probably don't look at him twice. (Think of all the various cartoon and comic characters you've seen in your life and how many of them look like people only in the sketchiest ways—and yet you accept that they talk and behave like people.)

We've used just one panel of a comic here to get started, but think about the conventions of multipanel comics. You've learned how to read comics so that you make connections

MERRY XMAS MORNING IN HOGAN'S ALLEY.

among the panels of a page, understanding how (for example) the passage of time or a shift in location is shown by changes between panels.

Finally, we couldn't understand any of these drawn elements without having grown up in a culture where it's perfectly normal to think flat drawn pictures somehow have movement, sound, and life in them.

Mix into all of this how many conventions we have for using words (and think about how many years you had to spend learning to read and write) and you have a sense of how complex comics are.

Strategies we emphasize in this chapter

Comics bring words and pictures together and so can use any of the rhetorical strategies we discussed in section 3. But there are also strategies particular to comics—and so, in this chapter, we focus on the following ones:

- **How composers shape the relations of words and pictures in comics to support their purposes.**

- **How composers take advantage of the shape and size of comic panels to support their purposes.**

A COMIC'S PANELS

The comic strip here, "Little Sammy Sneeze," was written and drawn by Winsor McCay, an American cartoonist and animator. (McCay is probably best known for his 1914 animated cartoon, "Gertie the Dinosaur," and his newspaper comic, "Little Nemo in Slumberland,"which ran from 1905–1914.) As Jim Vadeboncoeur, Jr. (a long-time collector of comic art and a biographer of comic book artists) describes about Little Sammy,

> Little Sammy sneezed every Sunday from July 24, 1904 to December 9, 1906. Since everyone knew what was going to happen in each strip, it was the build-up that mattered. Each strip was exactly six panels with the last reserved for Sammy's comeuppance, so pacing was everything. And it worked for 2½ years.

What conventions about comics do you have to know to make sense of the Little Sammy strip? What conventions from outside the world of comics help you understand?

With comics, we have to understand that—from panel to panel—time is passing. The space between each panel represents the little bit of time between the steps of Sammy's building sneeze (and how have we learned not to think that there's a new person in each panel?). We also have to understand both that the word bubbles are the sounds Sammy makes and that the size of the words corresponds to sound volume.

In this strip, McCay plays with the conventions of the panel. In most comics, we tend to overlook the panel because we've learned to overlook it—and we've learned to overlook it because most comic book artists use it only to help us see the separate actions that make up a comic strip. But look at how McCay draws the panel as though it were really part of Sammy's world, capable of being broken, and that this playing with convention is what makes us laugh.

As you read the two comics on the following pages, attend to how each composer uses her panels rhetorically.

Word–picture relations

On pages 266–267 we provide an initial discussion of word–picture relations, the aspect of comics that, in addition to panels, differentiates them from other media. The questions we ask of the two comics in this chapter will also help you learn more about word-picture relations.

"COMMON SCENTS"

Lynda Barry, who produced this strip, is primarily known as a cartoonist: Her work has been syndicated in more than 100 alternative papers and published in many books. Barry also paints, writes essays, welds, and provides commentary on National Public Radio.

It will help you in reading this comic, which presents itself as autobiographical, if you know that Barry is one-quarter Filipino and grew up in a working class Seattle neighborhood. (She now lives in the Midwest.)

Look for Barry's subtle strategies as you read. She uses self-deprecation and indirection to bring up and consider an issue we don't talk about too much: smell.

52

- "Common Scents" is the fourth story in the book *One! Hundred! Demons!* In the earlier stories, we learn that Barry represents her younger self in her drawings by the speckled, red-haired girl. What is the effect on her ethos of her visually representing herself in this less-than-flattering way?

- The captions represent Barry's thinking in the present. What ethos does she develop through the words (including how the words are drawn)?

BUT THERE WERE BAD MYS-TERIES TOO, LIKE THE MYSTERY OF THE BLEACH PEOPLE WHOSE HOUSE GAVE OFF FUMES YOU COULD SMELL FROM THE STREET. WE KEPT WAITING FOR THAT HOUSE TO EXPLODE. THE BUGS DIDN'T EVEN GO IN THEIR YARD.

ALSO GIVING OFF BLEACH FUMES

HEYA, JANINA.

HEYA.

'N I ASK YOU A PERSONAL THING?

POSSIBLY.

HOW COME YOUR HOUSE SMELLS LIKE THAT?

SMELLS LIKE WHAT?

SOME SMELLS WERE MYS-TERIOUSLY WONDERFUL LIKE AT THE PALINKI'S WHERE IT WAS A COMBINATION OF MINT, TAN-GERINES, AND LIBRARY BOOKS. BUT HOW? I NEVER SAW ANY OF THOSE THINGS THERE.

WHAT'S YOUR KIND OF AIR FRESHENER, BECAUSE THAT'S THE KIND I WANT MY MOM TO GET.

I DON'T USE AIR FRESHENER, DEAR.

WELL, THAT'S WEIRD BECAUSE YOUR HOUSE SMELLS PERFECT.

53

■ As you read, compare the written words in the captions to the drawings and what the characters say in the drawings. What do you learn from the captions that you don't learn from the drawings and word balloons—and vice versa?

54

■ What attitude does Barry encourage you to take toward her family and her family home? What strategies does she use to shape this attitude?

■ This panel shows the third time someone hasn't noticed the smells of their own homes. Why do you think Barry doesn't just simply write, "People don't notice their own smells"? Why might she leave it up to her audience to notice the repetition and the argument it is making?

> THE TRUTH WAS WE DID SAVE OUR GREASE IN A HILLS BROTHERS COFFEE CAN AND YES, MY GRANDMA DID COOK THINGS LIKE PIG'S BLOOD STEW. BOILING AND FRYING WENT ON IN THE HOUSE EVERY DAY.

> THAT'S WHY I'M NOT SPOSTA COME OVER, 'CAUSE THE SMELL GETS ON MY CLOTHES, MAKES MY MOM SICK.

> THE GIRL WHO SHOCKED ME WITH THE NEWS ABOUT THE SMELL OF MY HOUSE WAS THE ONE WHOSE HOUSE SMELLED LIKE THE FRESH BUS BATHROOM. HER MOTHER WAS THE MOST DISINFECTING, AIR FRESHENER SPRAYING PERSON THAT EVER LIVED.

55

- The colors here are bright and saturated. Notice how there is very little black—except for the outlines—and no gray. This means that in many cases we would describe the colors Barry uses as cheerful. If you were to read only the words in the captions, would they have you picturing the colors Barry uses? Why?

- What conventions of drawing do you have to know to understand what is going on in this panel? How did you learn those conventions?

SHE HAD THOSE CAR FRESHENER CHRISTMAS TREE THINGS HANGING EVERYWHERE. EVEN THE MARSHMALLOW TREATS SHE MADE HAD A FRESH PINE-SPRAY FLAVOR. SHE WAS FREE WITH HER OBSERVATIONS ABOUT THE SMELL OF OTHERS.

YOUR ORIENTALS HAVE AN ARRAY, WITH YOUR CHINESE SMELLING STRONGER THAN YOUR JAPANESE AND YOUR KOREANS FALLING SOMEWHERES IN THE MIDDLE AND DON'T GET ME STARTED ON YOUR FILIPINOS.

SHE DETAILED THE SMELLS OF BLACKS, MEXICANS, ITALIANS, SOME PEOPLE I NEVER HEARD OF CALLED "BO-HUNKS" AND THE DIFFERENCE IT MADE IF THEY WERE WET OR DRY, FAT OR SKINNY. NATURALLY I BROUGHT THIS INFORMATION HOME.

AIE N'AKO! WHITE LADIES SMELL BAD TOO, NAMAN! SHE NEVER WASH HER POOKIE! HER KILI-KILI ALWAYS SWEAT-SWEATING! THE OLD ONES SMELL LIKE E-HEE! THAT LADY IS TUNG-AH!

56

■ This is Barry's grandmother with the black hair, using words from a language most of us probably don't know—although you might feel you can make a good guess about what the words are. Why do you think Barry chooses to use the non-English words?

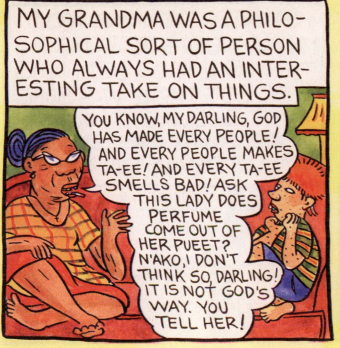

57

■ What emotions do you think Barry is working to shape for her audience? What attitudes to their pasts and to others is she trying to shape? What strategies has she chosen for evoking these emotions and attitudes?

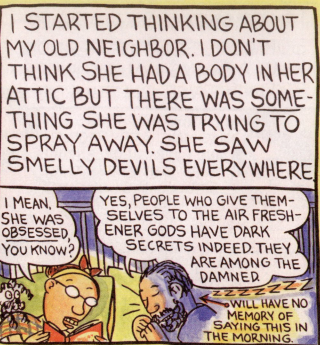

58

■ Why might Barry choose to bring us into the

present on this page?

I'VE NEVER HEARD A SINGLE PERSON EVER SAY THEY LOVED THE SMELL OF AIR FRESHENER AND YET THERE ARE SO MANY PEOPLE WHO FILL THEIR HOMES WITH IT.

PLUG-INS

POP UPS

LIGHT BULB SCENT RINGS

POTPOURRI MIXES

AIR WICKS

DANGLERS

STICK ONS

SPRAYS

SCENTED CANDLE NIGHTMARE

CAT PEE INCENSE

WHEN COMBINED WITH NATURAL BUT POWER-FILLED SMELLS, THE RESULTS CAN BE TRAUMATIC.

CHERRY POP-UP FRIED LIVER

TROPICAL PASSION AROMA THERAPY CAT BOX

VANILLA-SPICE DIAPER PAIL

STRAWBERRY-DREAMSCAPE PLUG-IN FRIED FLOUNDER

PINEY WOODS PIG'S BLOOD STEW BREAKDOWN

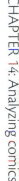

59

60

■ Why do you think Barry ends with this note of nostalgia, saying that she'd like a can of this improbably smelling air freshener? How are smells connected with memory and with our relations to those closest to us?

TO ANALYZE: "COMMON SCENTS"

■ **Discuss with others:** If you were to see only the pictures in Barry's comic, what would you think it was about? How seriously would you take it?

How different would the comic be if the words were in a more serious typeface?

If you were to see only the words of Barry's comic in a more serious typeface, how might you respond?

■ **Write:** In this textbook, we've focused on sight and hearing: These are the senses addressed by writing, drawings, photographs, and oral communication. Barry asks us to consider smell.

Because smells are tied to bodies and personal spaces, Barry shows how they work both to hold us together and to set us apart. If people smell different from us—or have smells at all (Barry argues that we don't notice our home smells, only those of others)—then we can judge them as different and therefore bad. Those who smell like us (or who don't seem to have smells because they smell like us) we recognize as close, as our family or our culture.

Smells are thus very much tied to emotion, but Barry seems to believe that if we can see how smells both bind and separate us, then we can make more thoughtful and generous decisions about our lives with others.

In two to three pages of writing, discuss how persuasive you find Barry's arguments. What strategies does she use to pull you into the experiences of smell, families, and neighborhoods so that you will consider smell as she presents it? If you are not persuaded, what more or different would Barry have needed to do to convince *you*?

■ **Discuss with others:** Like us and like Barry, you probably have had experiences in which others (or their cooking) smelled very strange, if not offensive. Smells can have surprising intensity in shaping how we think about others.

And so Barry's argument about the intensity and complexity of relations among different people is very serious, yet her ways of drawing and writing letters is cartoonish. Her ways of drawing and writing her letters can suggest a childish approach to interpreting the past and our relations with others. Why might she choose such visual approaches to considering relations among people, both adults and children?

How do you think adult audiences—made up of people like you—will respond to such a "childish" approach? Is this a way to "sneak up" on audiences, to present them something serious by leading them to think it's not? Or do you think that this is a way to use emotion in ways that are hard to do with writing so that Barry can more easily make us feel what is at stake in how we use smells?

PREPARING TO READ "LITTLE HOUSE IN THE BIG CITY"

About the comic's author

Sabrina Jones has been a comic artist for over 20 years, after earning a master's degree in fine arts (MFA) from the School of Visual Arts in New York City.

Many of her shorter comics, such as "Female Complaints" and "Life during Wartime," have appeared in *World War 3 Illustrated*, a "semi-annual political comix magazine" that has been published since 1980. In the 1990s, Jones cofounded *Girltalk*, an anthology of women's autobiographical comics published by Fantagraphics. She has developed shorter historical comics (see her piece in *Wobblies! A Graphic History of the Industrial Workers of the World*) as well as the book-length comic *Isadora Duncan, A Graphic Biography*. In addition to her comic work, Jones is also a member of United Scenic Artists Local 829, painting scenery for film, theater, and television.

See more of Jones's work at http://www.sabrinaland.com.

What stands out as you read?

Because comics are extended considerations of different topics, just like essays, ask of this comic the same questions we recommended for essays, concerning:

- **titles**
- **beginnings**
- **endings**
- **repetitions**
- **breaks between sections**

But also ask questions of the following:

- **Word–picture relations.** See pages 266–267 to remind you of some possible relations between words and pictures.

- **Panels**. Compare the panels of the four examples in this chapter, "Hogan's Alley," "Sammy's Sneeze," "Common Scents," and "Little House in the Big City." The panels are all drawn differently; what are the rhetorical effects of the different approaches?

■ Why might Jones reference *Little House on the Prairie* in her title?

■ Jones starts with describing her own experiences with New York City (of which the East Village is part). What sense do you develop of her ethos from how she describes herself and her actions? Why might she start with the personal?

485

■ What adjectives describe Jones's drawing style for you? Why? What sense of Jones—what sense of her ethos—do you take from her drawing style?

- Has what precedes this panel prepared you for Jones's shift in attentions from her life in New York City to the notions of slums and urban renewal?

WHOLE NEIGHBORHOODS WERE DEMOLISHED.

IN THEIR PLACE ROSE THE NEW SUPERBLOCKS.

UNIFORM TOWERS →

UNUSED OPEN SPACE

← MULTI-LANE EXPRESSWAYS →

WHAT WERE THE PLANNERS THINKING? AND HOW WAS THIS SYSTEMATIC ASSAULT ON URBAN LIVING TURNED AROUND?

IN THE 1920s, SWISS ARCHITECT LE CORBUSIER LOOKED AT A STREET CHOKED WITH TRAFFIC.

IT'S TOO BAD. CHILDREN CAN'T PLAY HERE ANYMORE.

HIS SOLUTION:

WE CAN NEVER GO BACK, SO...

...WE MUST EMBRACE THE CAR!

What attitudes do you think Jones wants readers to have toward the events she describes on this page? What strategies does she use to suggest attitude?

■ Each page is broken into three horizontal sections with some variation in their size. How many different ways does Jones draw the panels within the sections, and what effects do the differences create, both individually and together?

■ Could this comic make the same argument(s) through its words alone? What do the pictures add to the words?

IN THE 1950'S, JANE JACOBS RODE HER BIKE FROM HER HOME AT 555 HUDSON STREET IN THE FUNKY, SCRUFFY, ARTY WEST VILLAGE

UPTOWN TO HER JOB AT ROCKEFELLER CENTER.

SHE WAS A WRITER AND EDITOR FOR ARCHITECTURAL FORUM MAGAZINE.

SHE LOVED TO EXPLORE THE CITY AND WRITE ABOUT ITS VARIOUS DISTRICTS— THE DIAMOND DISTRICT, THE FUR DISTRICT, AND THE FLOWER DISTRICT.

SHE WENT TO PHILADELPHIA TO COVER A HIGHLY PRAISED RENEWAL PROJECT.

FIRST, CITY PLANNER ED BACON SHOWED HER THE OFFENDING SLUM THAT WAS BEING REPLACED.

THEY'RE OBVIOUSLY POOR, BUT THEY'RE ENJOYING THEMSELVES AND EACH OTHER.

THEN THE BRAND-NEW PROJECT

BUT WHERE ARE THE PEOPLE?

THEY DON'T APPRECIATE THESE THINGS.

■ What strategies has Jones used to prepare readers for this transition to a discussion of Jane Jacobs?

■ What might be the effect for a reader of turning the page from the previous panels to this close-up panel of Jacobs thinking?

■ Imagine different drawing styles for the bottom three panels on this page—and imagine the panels drawn with borders. How might different styles and panel borders change the effect of these panels?

JACOBS' IDEAS LED HER TO CLASH WITH NEW YORK'S POWERFUL PARKS COMMISSIONER, ROBERT MOSES. HE WANTED TO RUN A HIGHWAY THROUGH WASHINGTON SQUARE PARK, AS PART OF A VILLAGE RENEWAL PROJECT.

JACOBS JOINED THE EMERGENCY COMMITTEE TO CLOSE WASHINGTON SQUARE PARK TO ALL BUT EMERGENCY TRAFFIC.

SAVE OUR PARK

SOP

NO

URBAN RENEWAL SCHEMES TENDED TO TARGET COMMUNITIES OF COLOR. EARLIER PROJECTS IN EAST HARLEM AND THE BRONX HAD BEEN PUSHED THROUGH OVER THE PROTESTS OF RESIDENTS.

WHAT ABOUT MY STORE?

THEIR PLEAS WERE IGNORED. DISPLACED BUSINESSES RECEIVED NO COMPENSATION.

MOSES WAS USED TO GETTING HIS WAY. AT A PUBLIC MEETING:

THERE IS NOBODY AGAINST THIS... NOBODY BUT A BUNCH OF MOTHERS!

"A BUNCH OF MOTHERS" COLLECTED SIGNATURES, ALERTED THE MEDIA, LOBBIED POLITICIANS, PACKED MEETINGS, AND WON.

ELEANOR ROOSEVELT, RESIDENT, 29 WASHINGTON SQUARE WEST

■ What might be the effect of these panels being more "perfect" and less hand drawn?

■ Has Jones constructed sufficient authority to make the claims she does in this panel? Why or why not? How in a comic might she build more authority?

■ How does Jones construct a sense of continuity between panels, even though there are large jumps between the spaces and sometimes the time in which the panel actions occurred?

JACOBS' TWO SONS WERE REACHING DRAFT AGE AT THE HEIGHT OF THE VIETNAM WAR.

HELL NO WE WON'T GO

WE DIDN'T RAISE THESE BOYS TO FIGHT A WAR THAT WE'RE AGAINST!

HER HUSBAND ROBERT AGREED.

IN 1968 THE CHAMPION OF NEW YORK'S NEIGHBORHOODS MOVED WITH HER WHOLE FAMILY TO TORONTO.

SHE BECAME A CANADIAN CITIZEN AND STAYED THERE UNTIL HER DEATH IN 2006.

SHE ARRIVED JUST IN TIME TO BLOCK THE SPADINA EXPRESSWAY, WHICH WOULD HAVE PLOWED THROUGH HER NEW NEIGHBORHOOD.

"DEATH AND LIFE" VALIDATED AND INSPIRED POPULAR RESISTANCE TO URBAN RENEWAL.

NOW THIS FORMER BOMBSHELL IS REQUIRED READING FOR PLANNERS AND POLICY MAKERS. IT HAS NEVER BEEN OUT OF PRINT SINCE 1961.

Jacobs

The Death and Life of Great American Cities

ITS VISION OF THE HEALTHY BLOCK AS CHILD-FRIENDLY IS ECHOED IN THE 1969 LAUNCH OF

SESAME STREET

■ Why might Jones have decided to add these particular aspects of Jacobs's personal life to the comic?

■ To what audiences will the *Sesame Street* reference appeal?

■ How has Jones prepared readers for the transition back to describing her personal life? What part does the little picture of Jones's face play in the transition?

■ Why might Jones have decided to end this comic with a return to her personal experiences?

■ Why might Jones have decided that the last picture would be Jacobs's old house with its price tag?

TO ANALYZE: "LITTLE HOUSE IN THE BIG CITY"

■ **Write and discuss:** Write a one- or two-sentence summary of Jones's comic. Then write several paragraphs in which you use examples of her words and illustrations to support your summary. Compare your summary and supporting examples with those of two or three other people in your class to see how differently you use Jones's words and illustrations to support your summaries.

■ **Write:** Draw up what you think might have been Jones's design plan.

■ **Discuss:** Why might Jones have decided to tell about Jacobs's life through a comic instead of through some other medium? How might this work about Jacobs be different had it been an essay or a podcast?

■ **Write:** Compare how Barry and Jones use captions in their comics. Drawing on your comparison and on any comics you know, list how comic producers can use captions as strategies. As you make your list, consider how the captions interact with—support, or add information to, or work together with or against—the drawings.

■ **Discuss:** How would Barry's comic be different if it were drawn in Jones's style—and vice versa?

THINKING THROUGH PRODUCTION

■ Choose a text you've already produced, such as a paper for a class, a brochure, or an informational website. Using the technologies available to you, reproduce the text as a paper or online comic book. (Use the various strategies you see in this chapter or in examples you know from elsewhere to make choices about your arrangements, media, and other strategies.) Test the original text and the comic with similar audiences: How do audience responses differ? How do you account for the differences?

Write a short paper (or make another comic) in which you analyze the differences between the original text and the comic. What different kinds of relationships can you develop with your audience in your different texts? What differing kinds of ethos, pathos, and logos can you develop in the different texts?

■ The examples of this chapter suggest to us that there is a tremendous amount of untapped potential in comics for making arguments we've not seen in comics.

Choose a topic that you haven't seen addressed in comics, and use the rhetorical design process from chapters 1–3 to plan, produce, and test a comic on that topic.

■ As we produced this chapter about comics, we realized that at least two of our examples show how emotions are complexly woven within our lives. Both Barry and Jones use what some people might characterize as childish or exuberant drawings to engage us in considering the strong and rich emotional lives we have and how those lives are shaped by what goes on around us.

Choose a complex emotional event from your experiences, and develop it as a comic. Use the rhetorical design process from chapters 1–3 to plan, produce, and test your comic. (Use the various strategies you see in this chapter or in examples you know from elsewhere to make choices about your arrangements, media, and other strategies.)

CREDITS

PHOTO CREDITS

TEXT CREDITS

Page 130: "I'll Have Large Fries, a Hamburger, a Diet Coke, and an MBA." Hold the Pickles, *Homo Consumericus*, Gad Saad. Reprinted with permission.

Page 130: "Are Students Customers of Their Universities?" Stephany Schings, *Society for Industrial and Organizational Psychology*, 2011. Reprinted with permission.

Pages 202-205: Reprinted by permission of Waveland Press, Inc. from Sonja K. Foss and Karen A. Foss, *Inviting Transformation: Presentational Speaking for a Changing World*. (Long Grove, IL: Waveland Press, Inc., 2003). All rights reserved.

Pages 291-296: Reprinted with the permission of Simon & Schuster, Inc., from *The Partly Cloudy Patriot* by Sarah Vowell. Copyright 2002 by Sarah Vowell. All rights reserved.

Pages 299-302: Copyright © 2011 Chris Hedges. Reprinted by permission of Nation Books, a member of the Perseus Books Group.

Pages 311, 382: Reprinted with permission of AlestleLive.

Page 318: Reprinted with permission of Love146.com.

Page 320: © Habitat for Humanity International.

Pages 386, 388: "Separating fact from fiction in video game debate," Christopher Ferguson, Tampa Bay Online, November 15th, 2010.

Pages 392-393: Reprinted Courtesy of Daily Freeman, Kingston, NY.

Pages 394-395: From *The New York Times*, July 2, 2011 © 2011 *The New York Times*. All rights reserved. Used by permission and protected by the Copyright Laws of the United States. The printing, copying, redistribution, or retransmission of this Content without express written permission is prohibited."

Pages 396-397: "Violence, video games, and what we're not playing," Chris Plante, *Game Pro* July 15, 2011. Reprinted with permission.

Pages 400-401: "Editorial - Court majority was right. But parents still need to monitor video game violence." *The Register Guard*, Thursday, June 30, 2011, page A6. Reprinted with permission.

Pages 406-413: Copyright (2000) From *How to Use Your Eyes* by James Elkins, reproduced by permission of Taylor and Francis Group, LLC, Inc, a division of Informa plc.

Pages 422-435: "Higher Education," Gary Smith, *Sports Illustrated*, March 5, 2001. Reprinted with permission.

Page 439: From *The Best American Nonrequired Reading*, Edited by Dave Eggers. Reprinted by permission of Houghton Mifflin Harcourt Publishing Company. All rights reserved.

Pages 441-446: Lia Purpura, "The Smallest Woman in the World" from *On Looking: Essays*. Copyright © 2006 by Lia Purpura. Reprinted with the permission of The Permissions Company, Inc., on behalf of Sarabande Books, www .sarabande-books.org.

Pages 448-462: "The Plaintiff Speaks" by Clarissa Sligh, from *Picturing Us: African American Identity in Photography* edited by Deborah Willis, published by The New Press. Reprinted by permission of the author.

Pages 465-466: Thorsten Botz-Bornstein teaches philosophy at the Gulf University for Science and Technology in Kuwait

INDEX